THE KENNEDYS
A NEW YORK TIMES PROFILE

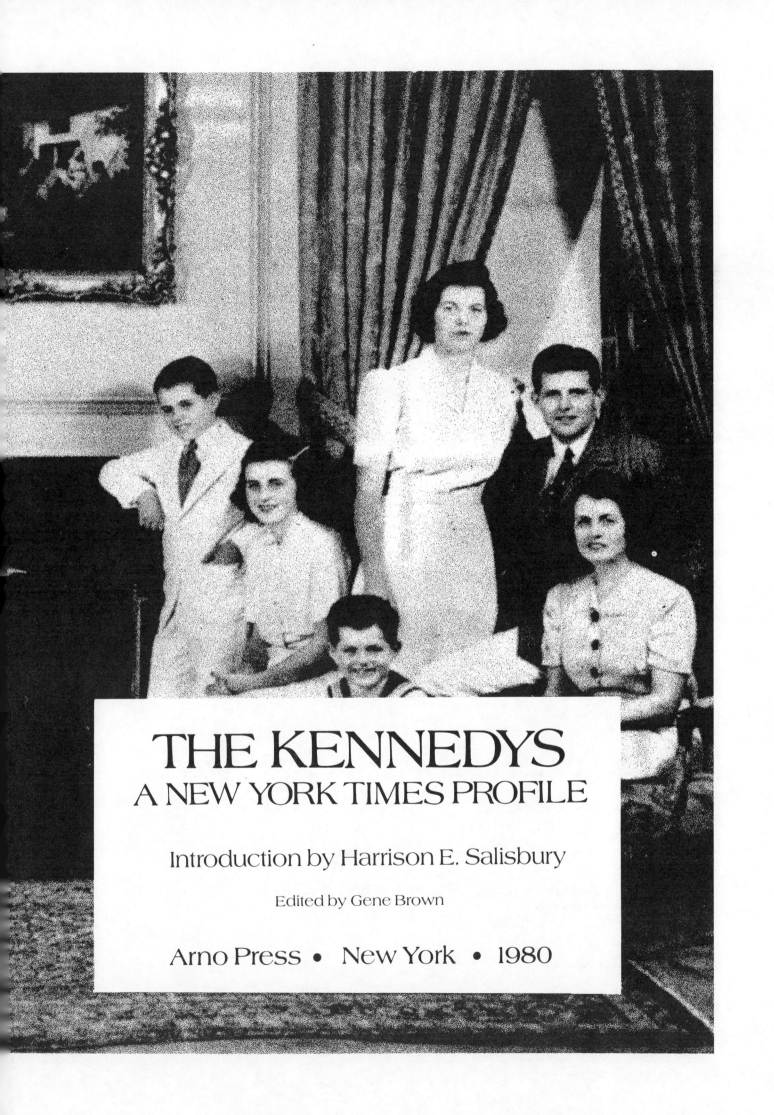

THE KENNEDYS
A NEW YORK TIMES PROFILE

Introduction by Harrison E. Salisbury

Edited by Gene Brown

Arno Press • New York • 1980

Copyright © 1928, 1934, 1935, 1936, 1938, 1939, 1940, 1941, 1943, 1944, 1945, 1946, 1947, 1948, 1949, 1952, 1953, 1954, 1955, 1956, 1957, 1958, 1959, 1960, 1961, 1962, 1963, 1964, 1965, 1967, 1968, 1969, 1970, 1971, 1972, 1973, 1974, 1975, 1976 1977, 1978, 1979, by The New York Times Company.

Library of Congress Cataloging in Publication Data

Main entry under title:

The Kennedys.

    Includes index.
    1. Kennedy family—Addresses, essays, lectures.
I. Brown, Gene. II. New York times.
E843.K494   973.9'092'2
ISBN 0-405-12937-8

Manufactured in the United States of America.

Book design by Lynn Yost.

Contents

Introduction

American politics has known three great political dynasties—those of the Adams, the Roosevelts, and the Kennedys. They do not fit Tolstoy's famous aphorism that all happy families resemble each other. In fact, the differences among the three clans are extraordinary except in one respect: into each family was bred a tradition of service to the country—one of national leadership. In none was this dedication to be more intense than in the Kennedy family.

A tradition of leadership emerged naturally within the Adams family. John Adams was a signer of the Declaration of Independence, a stalwart of the American Revolution. His heirs, through the 19th Century, followed in his footsteps. The Roosevelt tradition was born in family, fortune, and patrician heritage. Theodore Roosevelt entered the political arena and was followed by his cousin Franklin D. Roosevelt. To FDR's wife, Eleanor, (a cousin of both TR and FDR) and successive generations of Roosevelt children, nothing seemed more natural than the family's place in politics.

The Kennedy dynasty was different. The Kennedys came to America as part of a tide of immigration which famine in Ireland had set in motion in the 1840s. It was as if they had been waiting in the Irish countryside to take up their roles in the bumptious politics of Boston, milieu of the "Last Hurrah."

If the Kennedy brothers—John, Robert and Edward—came to epitomize American political life in the last half of the 20th Century, it was a calling which had been nurtured for two generations. Their political antecedents went back to two locally famous Boston political practitioners, Patrick Joseph Kennedy, a quiet, no-nonsense ward boss and saloon keeper, and John Francis (Honey Fitz) Fitzgerald. Patrick Joseph Kennedy served in the Massachusetts State Senate in the 1890s. So did Honey Fitz but he went on to tread a broader stage —entering the Boston City Council, being elected to Congress and to the mayorship of Boston. The fortunes of the Kennedys and the Fitzgeralds became entwined when in 1914 Kennedy's oldest son, Joseph P. Kennedy, married Rose, the oldest of Fitzgerald's six children. Honey Fitz unsuccessfully opposed the union and the young people were married by Cardinal O'Connell in October 1914.

Joseph Kennedy was a man of driving ambition and high goals. From the beginning he made clear to his family the nature of the role in which he cast his aspirations: first he would make money. He succeeded in this extraordinarily and swiftly. Within a dozen years he had made himself a millionaire and moved his family out of Boston to the New York suburb of Riverdale—but never broke his ties with Boston. To Joseph Kennedy, New York was a good place to make money, and money to Kennedy was a means to an end. He was clever— unscrupulous his enemies said—at making it. But he valued money only for what could be done with it. Business for the sake of business held no appeal. "All businessmen are sons of bitches," Jack Kennedy was later to say. "My father told me that."

Joseph Kennedy raised his children for something else. They were trained and dedicated to public service and when he spoke of service, he meant it at the highest level. A Kennedy child—one of *his* children—was to be President. And perhaps more than one. This was the thrust of his iron will.

There were nine Kennedy children; Joseph Jr., John, Rosemary, Kathleen, Eunice, Pat, Robert, Jean and Edward. Their father's code for them was simple: to be the best at everything. As far as Joseph Kennedy was concerned, there was no second place. "We don't want any losers around here," the children recall him saying—not without some bitterness.

Boston and the hierarchical and ethnic structure of its society played a role in forging Joseph Kennedy's ambition for his family. In the late 19th Century the emigrant Irish began to challenge Boston's traditional political leaders, the Cabots and Lodges. They had started to make their way upward, economically and financially. But socially, the dictum still stood: "Irish need not apply." In national politics the notion of an Irish Catholic President was still unthinkable.

But nothing would deter Joseph Kennedy. He himself entered national politics, forming an early friendship with Franklin D. Roosevelt and vigorously supporting his candidacy in 1932. Kennedy was rewarded with the chairmanship of the newly-created Securities and Exchange Commission. After a brilliant career as founding SEC chairman and a stint running the U.S. Maritime Commission he became Roosevelt's Ambassador to the Court of St. James in 1938.

Looking back it would be plain that at every step Kennedy was involving his children: furthering their intellectual and political interests; forming alliances and making friendships which he felt would be useful in taking a Kennedy to the very top.

The Kennedy selected for this role was, not unnaturally, his first son, Joe. But what later was to become known as the "Kennedy fate" intervened.

Joseph Kennedy, Sr. emerged from his ambassadorship in England a foe of intervention, an "America firster." But even before the bombing of Pearl Harbor his oldest sons, Joe Jr. and John, had enlisted. On August 12, 1944, young Joe died in the explosion of his Navy plane over England. John already had been sent home an invalid after a Japanese destroyer rammed his PT boat in 1943 in the South Pacific. Tragedy was to stalk glory in the Kennedy epic.

It was the death of Joseph Jr. in World War II which launched John Kennedy into politics. As he once conceded: "It was my father. He did it." To the senior Kennedy politics was not a career for one son or one office —it was for the whole family.

As soon as the war was over Jack Kennedy, at age 29, was off and running for Congress. He won the election and in 1946 launched the career which was to take him to the White House 14 years later. Robert, 21 and just out of the Navy, assisted his brother in the Congressional race, then returned to Harvard.

John Kennedy won his first Senate seat in 1952 over Republican incumbent, Henry Cabot Lodge in spite of a landslide vote for President Dwight D. Eisenhower. In this race, Robert was campaign manager also. Then at his father's bidding Robert worked for six months for Senator Joseph McCarthy's Senate subcommittee investigating communism in government. Robert then became counsel for the Democratic minority on the McCarthy committee and later majority counsel sparkplug of the investigation of Jimmy Hoffa and corruption in the Teamster's Union.

After eight years in the Senate John sought the presidency. Robert was again his campaign manager. John Kennedy went to the White House on January 20, 1961. Robert followed him into the administration as Attorney General, chief confidant and right-hand man. Teddy Kennedy, in the family tradition, won election to the Senate from Massachusetts in 1962.

The ambitions of Joseph Kennedy seemed fulfilled: his oldest surviving son was President, his next son was Attorney General, his youngest son was a Senator. The way seemed clear for eight years of John's presidency, possibly followed by Robert and—who could say—even Teddy. It was the culmination of Joseph's ambition and a family achievement unparalleled in American politics.

But this was not to last. John was struck down by an assassin's bullet on November 22, 1963. Robert continued as Attorney General under President Johnson, despite their open antagonism. In 1964 Robert ran for the Senate from the State of New York and won. In 1968 the glimmer of the lost vision of Camelot showed again with Robert's Democratic primary race for the presidency—a vision cut short by a second assassin.

Now Teddy was left to fulfill the political aspirations of his father. Shocked by the family's tragedy, he seemed to retreat. And then his own tragedy, Chappaquiddick, threatened to put the seal of misfortune on his political career. Ten years passed before he stepped into the political limelight to put his name on the presidential candidate lists in 1979. Once again a Kennedy moved onto the national scene.

As to the nature of the Kennedy image, there will be debate amongst historians far into the future. Some believed that Teddy's candidacy would recall the bright young hopes of the nation as epitomized by John F. Kennedy's inaugural address of January 20, 1961 — "Ask not what your country can do for you, but ask what you can do for your country"—an emblazonment of idealism, of the faith in American virtue and the democratic way of government.

There are also critics who interpret the Kennedy image differently; who contend that behind the façade of the "Kennedy legend" there lies an involvement in the ways of the elder Kennedy. There are those who blame John

Kennedy for the escalation of the war in Vietnam on which President Johnson based his fateful commitments and the agony of our involvement in Southeast Asia. There are those who saw in Robert Kennedy's association with Joseph McCarthy the dark stain of Joseph Kennedy's reactionary philosophy. These same critics questioned Robert's zeal in pursuing his brother's aims, regardless of legal niceties. And there are those who do not find in Ted Kennedy's spotless Senate record of liberalism and dedicated public service, sufficient retribution to pay for the tragedy of Chappaquiddick.

All this considered, there are few historians who do not acknowledge the Kennedy dynasty as constituting a unique page in the American political legacy: Joseph Kennedy's contribution to a new era in American financial and economic morality as marked by his vigorous chairmanship of the SEC; John Kennedy's achievement in lifting the morale of a dispirited nation; Robert Kennedy's tragedy-haunted maturity when he finally ran for the presidency in the footsteps of his martyred brother; Ted Kennedy's dogged determination to show himself worthy of the best in the family tradition.

There has been nothing like it in past American political dynasties. There is a togetherness in the Kennedy family and a unity in its philosophy which could not have been achieved by the quarrelsome Adams tribe or the politically divided Roosevelts. And there is every indication that the Kennedy tradition is too firmly etched in the family psychology and family mores to end with the generation of the three brothers, Jack, Bobby and Teddy. Behind them stands a tribe of new Kennedys, the third generation after the elder Joseph, the fourth generation after Honey Fitz, almost all of them trained, eager and oriented in the family roles carved out by their grandfather, certain and confident that the only real career for a Kennedy is service—service to their country.

—*Harrison E. Salisbury*

The Family Emerges

MOVIE CHIEF'S RAPID RISE

J. P. Kennedy Began Career on a Sight-seeing Bus

Joseph P. Kennedy

SIXTEEN years ago a young man just graduated from Harvard began his business career as a lecturer on board the sight-seeing bus in which he had invested his entire capital of $300. A few days ago that man took up his duties as Chairman of the board of a corporation in which millions of dollars are represented. His name is Joseph P.

Kennedy and he is not yet 40. The business with which he is newly identified is that of the Keith-Albee-Orpheum vaudeville circuit, operating thirty theatres in New York City and others in all parts of the country.

Between the megaphone of the sight-seeing bus and the gavel of the new chairmanship were a variety of activities, including banking, the steel industry, the making of motion pictures and an association of interests which are to be called upon jointly to help bring the spoken word to the aid of the pictures screen. Besides being Chairman of the K. A. O. Circuit, Mr. Kennedy is President of the FBO Pictures Corporation, in which the Radio Corporation of America, the General Electric Company and the Westinghouse Electric and Manufacturing Company have a substantial interest. He is also business adviser to the Pathé Company.

Plans of Development.

Mr. Kennedy, asked for details of a program of expansion for the K. A. O. theatres which he is said to be organizing, replied that the chief problem confronting vaudeville and moving picture theatres alike is the building up of a larger audience, and he expressed the hope that the photophone, or talking movie, would prove to be attractive. Within sixty days, he said, the necessary apparatus is to be installed in a number of the circuit's New York theatres for the complete presentation of speaking pictures, and the equipment of others will follow as rapidly as possible.

Plans for producing "talking movies" are going forward at Hollywood and the public is soon to have the opportunity of making its response. While the circuit of which Mr. Kennedy is President is not engaged in the making of pictures, as one of the large exhibitors it is very much interested in their production and, therefore, an influence in shaping their character.

Mr. Kennedy feels that the business of making photoplays is in a peculiar state. Nobody is satisfied with it. The discontent starts with the "extra" and touches every one, including the picture-going public. The actor does not like his part; the producer is not satisfied with his actors; the exhibitor does not like the price, and the audience, though it continues to lay its money down at the box office, is not increasing fast enough.

While gross receipts are growing, "the net is bad," said Mr. Kennedy. "We're going to have to change our merchandizing methods. We are going to have to scratch and find new ways to entertain the public."

The public enters more intimately into the picture business than it does into any other, Mr. Kennedy believes, because everybody considers himself an expert in the art of the films.

"When you make a steel rail," said Mr. Kennedy, who used to work for Charles M. Schwab, "you make something that is so long and so heavy and of such and such a quality. But when you make a foot of film, it is subject to the judgment of millions of people, each with his own standards of measurement. As Douglas Fairbanks once told me, everybody has two businesses—his own and the moving picture. That is what makes our work difficult."

Mr. Kennedy expressed his respect for the pioneers of the picture business who, during a period of less than a generation, have seen it develop into fourth or fifth in size among the industries of this country. But it had not been his intention to enter the business. After his bus venture in Boston had shown a profit over a period of three years and he had managed to save $5,000, he decided to become a banker. With that end in view, he entered the Harvard business school, after he had married Miss Rose Fitzgerald, daughter of the Mayor of Boston.

After leaving business school Mr. Kennedy was State Inspector of Banks in Massachusetts. For three years he and a growing family were limited to an income of $125 a month. At the end of that time the Board of Directors of the Columbia Trust Company of Boston sent for him and told him they were looking for a President. Thus at 28 he became one of the youngest bank Presidents in the country.

There followed soon an appointment by the city to be a director in the Collateral Loan Company. There he conducted his own investigation into the affairs of that semi-public savings institution, and made a report which attracted considerable attention. Three years later he was asked to become general manager of the Hayden-Stone Company, one of the large private banks of New England.

Wartime Steel Work.

Mr. Kennedy's experience in the steel business was during the period of the war. Charles M. Schwab, who had contracts with the American and allied Governments for the building and repair of warships at the Fore River yards, called him in to take charge of 50,000 workmen. At the close of the war Mr. Kennedy went back to the Hayden-Stone Company and there remained until three years ago, when he decided to go into business for himself. He did not think of the picture business at the time, but when, a little later, he observed that an English company had invested $7,000,000 in an American film corporation without conspicuous success, he made a trip to London and offered them a million dollars for their holdings. Later the offer was accepted and Mr. Kennedy found himself at the head of the Film Booking Offices, which in two years has expanded largely.

Mr. Kennedy's entrance into the K.A.O circuit followed the announcement that the Radio Corporation of America, the General Electric Company and the Westinghouse Electric and Manufacturing Company had acquired substantial interest in the FBO. Mr. Kennedy himself conducted the negotiations with David Sarnoff, Vice President of the Radio Corporation of America. He has thus brought together the two industries—film and radio—which would necessarily be concerned in the production and exhibition of talking pictures. The devices and developments of the Radio Corporation and the two electrical companies do not, however, become available exclusively to FBO Pictures.

June 3, 1928

THE KENNEDYS: A NEW YORK TIMES PROFILE

WASHINGTON, June 30.—As his last act tonight in cleaning up essential business before sailing from Annapolis for a month's holiday today, President Roosevelt named the personnel of the Securities and Exchange Commission.

He did not designate a chairman, there being some doubt as to his authority to do so, but it was understood in well-informed quarters that responsibility for the commission's work under the sweeping Stock Exchange Control Act would fall upon Joseph P. Kennedy, New York financier, who was designated to serve for five years. Four other commissioners were named for periods varying from one to four years.

The personnel of the commission follows:

JOSEPH P. KENNEDY of New York, five-year term.

GEORGE C. MATHEWS of Wisconsin, four-year term.

JAMES M. LANDIS of Massachusetts, three-year term.

ROBERT E. HEALY of Vermont, two-year term.

FERDINAND PECORA of New York, one-year term.

Messrs. Mathews and Landis are members of the Federal Trade Commission. Mr. Pecora was counsel for the Senate Banking and Currency Committee during the period in which it aired publicly for the first time in twenty years the manifold operations of securities exchanges and investment banking houses. As committee counsel he played a large part in shaping the law under which the commission will operate.

The naming of the Securities and Exchange Commission came after President Roosevelt, in a day of intensive work, had also named the Communications Commission and a commission to plan coordination of aircraft development, and has issued statements announcing the signing of the Frazier–Lemke Farm Mortgage Bill and the Railroad Pensions Bill.

Kennedy Close to Farley.

The membership of the Securities and Exchange Commission had been pretty generally forecast, but even so its composition was full of surprises, particularly the obvious placing in line for the chairmanship of Mr. Kennedy.

This is the first emergence of the New Yorker from what seemed to be political eclipse since the campaign of 1932, when he was distinguished both as a heavy contributor and important raiser of campaign funds, and because of his close association with President Roosevelt on the campaign train and elsewhere.

He was known then as being quite close both to Mr. Roosevelt and to Postmaster General Farley, chairman of the Democratic National Committee.

Then, after the election, Mr. Kennedy dropped out of political affairs, although he maintained close relations with the Roosevelt family and entertained James Roosevelt, the President's eldest son, at Palm Beach last Winter.

Mr. Kennedy apparently will receive the honored place on the commission which most observers here had thought would go to Mr. Landis, also a co-author of the Exchange Control Act. However, Mr. Landis was thought to have been apprised in advance of the announcement of the personnel of the commission that he would not be its chairman, as he was received at the White House late today.

July 1, 1934

EXCHANGE, LABOR BOARDS NAMED;

KENNEDY IN 'CHANGE POST

The Others Are Mathews, Landis, Healy, Pecora for Varying Terms.

HYDE PARK, N. Y., Sept. 20. The resignation of Joseph P. Kennedy as chairman of the Securities and Exchange Commission, submitted two weeks ago, was accepted by President Roosevelt today. Mr. Kennedy will relinquish his post on Monday and sail for Europe with his family on the following day.

The resignation was marked by an exchange of correspondence that attested the strong personal ties between the President and Mr. Kennedy, who, although occupying a non-political post, has been considered by White House intimates not only as one of the closest friends of the President but also as probably his most outspoken critic in the private conferences that have preceded the making of important decisions.

The SEC chairman seldom went to the President's office in Washington, but he was a frequent after-dinner guest at the White House. His greatest value to the President during the past year probably has consisted of his faculty for expressing opinions in short and easily understood words not hampered by the fact that he was addressing the President of the United States.

No Indication of Successor.

President Roosevelt did not indicate even remotely who might succeed Mr. Kennedy. Neither did he give any idea whether the new chairman would be one who would work aggressively for the immediate regulation of holding companies or one of conservative tendencies who would give them a breathing spell in which to comply voluntarily with the new Utilities Act.

The act provides for eventual dissolution of all but primary and secondary holding companies except in unusual cases, and there have been two sharply divided schools of thought whether the SEC, using the broad authority granted in the law, should take the initiative in the right to "reform" holding companies or give them an opportunity to work out their own solution.

Necessarily the policy to be followed will be reflected, if not determined to a large extent, by Mr. Kennedy's successor.

KENNEDY RESIGNS AS SEC CHAIRMAN

Roosevelt Praises His Leadership in Winning Confidence of Investors and Financiers.

UTILITY ACT IS NEW TASK

Retiring Head Says It Needs 'Continuity' in His Post—Successor to Guide Its Policy.

Reasons for Resignation.

Mr. Kennedy's resignation was based primarily on the fact that he could not spend a longer time in public office, a fact that was made clear at the time of his appointment, in 1934, when he qualified his acceptance with the statement that he could not remain more than one year.

He also stated in his letter, dated Sept. 6, that since the SEC had the new responsibility of administering the Utilities Holding Company Act it should have the benefit of "a continuity of administration."

He expressed "genuine regret" that his private affairs forced his severance of official connection with the administration, to which he pledged his continued support.

Mr. Roosevelt, in his letter accepting the resignation, commended Mr. Kennedy for his leadership of the SEC, which he said had administered the Securities Act and the Stock Exchange Act "so effectively as to win the confidence of the general investing public and the financial community, for the protection of both of which these statutes were designed."

LETTER OF RESIGNATION.

Mr. Kennedy's letter to the President tendering his resignation was as follows:

Dear Mr. President:

At the time of my appointment to the Securities and Exchange Commission in 1934, for which signal honor I shall always be grateful, I indicated to you the probability that I could not remain in office much longer than a year. For personal reasons it is now necessary for me to ask you to relieve me by Sept. 23, 1935.

My decision to ask to go at this time is made easier by the realization that the commission is now strongly established as a going concern and that the lines of policy for the administration of these two great measures, the Securities Act and the Securities Exchange Act, have been firmly laid.

There remain a few major problems in this first phase of the work of the commission, but as to these also general principles have been agreed upon and the commission is working toward an early announcement of conclusions, with which I am in agreement.

The Public Utility Act of 1935 (which you have just signed) places additional large responsibilities upon the commission. For quite some time the energies of the commission in this field will be devoted largely to studies of the various holding company systems. Many of the most vital problems arising out of this legislation will not be imminent for a year and beyond.

It seems most important that, in working out the policies of the new act, there should be a continuity of administration. Therefore the private exigencies which compel me to ask you to relieve me coincide with the commission's requirements for administrative direction of long duration.

Personal Tribute to President.

To discontinue my official relations with you is not an easy task. Rather is it one involving genuine regret assuaged only by the privilege of your friendship. As a chief you have been unfailingly considerate and stimulating. In the pioneer work of the commission my colleagues and I have had your whole-hearted and enthusiastic support. Without your backing our accomplishments for the protection of the investors would not have been possible.

You know how deeply devoted I am to you personally and to the success of your administration. Because of this devotion, after retiring from the post of chairman of the Securities and Exchange Commission, I shall still deem myself a part of your administration.

I suggest this particular date of Sept. 23 because, as you know, Mrs. Kennedy and I plan to go abroad with the children the latter part of the month, and it seems wiser for me to terminate my official relations prior to leaving.

Faithfully yours,
JOSEPH P. KENNEDY.
Sept. 6, 1935.
The President, White House, Washington, D. C.

THE PRESIDENT'S REPLY.

In reply to Mr. Kennedy the President wrote the following letter:

Hyde Park, N. Y., Sept. 20.
Dear Joe:

Of course I am very sorry to let you go, but you rightly remind me that you accepted the chairmanship of the Securities Commission with the distinct understanding that your private affairs would not permit you to stay beyond a year. You have done better than that and I cannot, in fairness, now ask you to remain after Sept. 23.

You undertook a pioneer piece of administration, the successful achievement of which was as difficult as it was important for the country.

Under your leadership the Securities and Exchange Commission took two of the most important regulatory measures ever passed by the Congress—the Securities Act and the Stock Exchange Act—and administered them so effectively as to win the confidence of the general investing public and of the financial community, for the protection of both of which these statutes were designed.

Praise for Leadership.

You have indeed every right to feel that the Securities and Exchange Commission is now a going concern and that the major lines of policy for the administration of the Securities Act and the Stock Exchange Act have been firmly laid.

Such a result never just happens. It comes to pass only through skill, resourcefulness, good sense, and devotion to the public interest.

All your colleagues, I know, have contributed in full measure to the fine results that the commission has accomplished. But every group, no matter how able, requires leadership. In you, your colleagues have had an able leader.

And so I am extremely sorry that your personal circumstances compel you to retire from the chairmanship of the Securities and Exchange Commission. But you are wholly right in assuming that in retiring from your administrative post you do not cease to be a member of my administration. Quite the contrary. In the

future, as in the past, I shall freely turn to you for support and counsel.

I hope that you will have a delightful trip and a good vacation. Be sure to come in to see me and tell me about it when you get back.

My best wishes to you,
Always sincerely,
FRANKLIN D. ROOSEVELT.
Hon. Joseph P. Kennedy,
Securities and Exchange Commission, Washington, D. C.

The President and Mr. Kennedy have been close friends for more than fifteen years, since a time in the World War when both as young men held high responsibilities. Mr. Roosevelt, as Assistant Secretary of the Navy, was charged with procurement of naval supplies.

Tangency of Two Careers.

Mr. Kennedy, who had been out of Harvard only a few years, was a governmental adviser on procurement. His short business experience had then comprised work as a bank examiner in Massachusetts, presidency of a Boston bank at the age of 28 and service as director of 50,000 men on warship construction in the Fore River shipyards.

After the war Mr. Roosevelt and Mr. Kennedy separated and the latter went on to further business success, for a time with the Hayden-Stone Company and later on his own as an investment banker, until ill health forced his retirement in 1929.

The friendly contact between Mr. Roosevelt and Mr. Kennedy again ripened into close association when the former, then Governor of New York, began to loom as Presidential material. Mr. Kennedy not only worked actively in his behalf, accompanying Mr. Roosevelt on many of his speaking tours, but also contributed money to the campaign.

But Mr. Kennedy disappeared from the circle of the President's inmates soon after the inauguration, a circumstance that was never explained but which was credited in some circles to the large influence wielded by the "brain trust" during Mr. Roosevelt's first year in office.

If the absence of Mr. Kennedy from the administration scene represented a break, however, the reuniting that followed when he accepted the chairmanship of the SEC was complete.

September 1, 1935

KENNEDY AT SON'S BEDSIDE

Former SEC Head Flies to Boy Hurt in Harvard Football.

BOSTON, Sept. 30 (AP).—Joseph P. Kennedy, former head of the Federal Securities and Exchange Commission, today tended his son, Joseph P. Jr., a patient in Massachusetts General Hospital. Mr. Kennedy flew here yesterday to be with his boy, who was a leading contender for an end position on the Harvard varsity until injuries put him out of competition.

The youth suffered a leg injury some months ago. In a recent scrimmage he broke several ribs and fractured a knee.

Dr. Thomas K. Richards operated to remove part of the knee bone and to strap the boy's ribs.

Mr. Kennedy's other son, John, also bears bruises from football practice. He limped into the hospital to greet his father last night while the latter was predicting that the older boy's football career was ended.

October 1, 1936

Cardinal Visits Kennedys

On his return here yesterday afternoon from his luncheon visit with President Roosevelt, Cardinal Pacelli stopped at the home of Joseph P. Kennedy, at 294 Pondfield Road, Bronxville, N. Y., where Mr. and Mrs. Kennedy entertained the Papal Secretary of State, his secretary, Enrico Galleazzi, and Bishop Francis J. Spellman of Boston, at tea.

November 6, 1936

THE KENNEDYS: A NEW YORK TIMES PROFILE

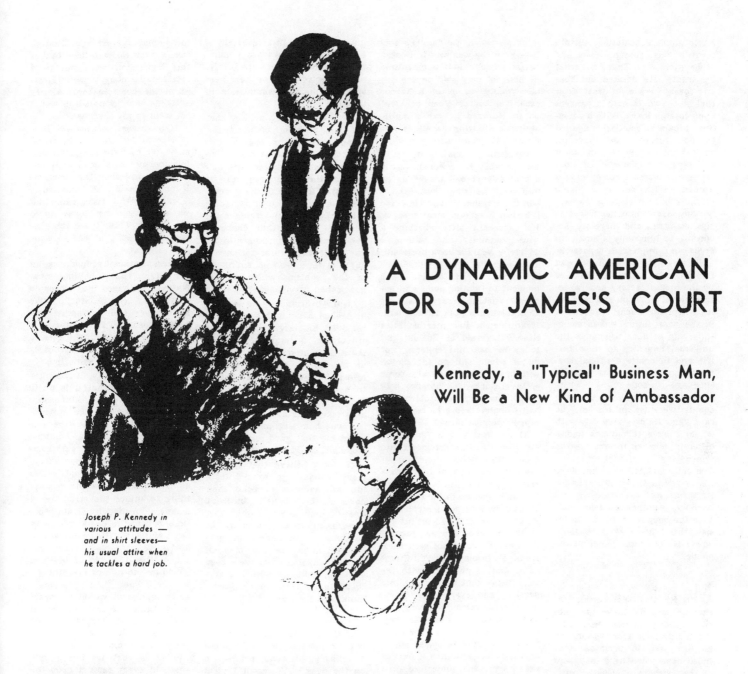

A DYNAMIC AMERICAN
FOR ST. JAMES'S COURT

Kennedy, a "Typical" Business Man, Will Be a New Kind of Ambassador

Joseph P. Kennedy in various attitudes — and in shirt sleeves— his usual attire when he tackles a hard job.

A FORMER newsboy will soon take up his residence in London as American Ambassador to the Court of St. James. Poets, historians, publishers, statesmen and editors heretofore have been named to head our most important diplomatic mission, and family lineage often has played a part in their selection. Joseph P. Kennedy is very different from all his predecessors and perhaps his appointment means a new type of diplomacy.

His career stretches from the wharves of Boston to the Klieg lights of Hollywood, from the caverns of Wall Street to the Ionic-columned buildings of Washington. He has brushed off the sands of Palm Beach to fly to New York when a gigantic business deal awaited completion. In the film capital he has ditched productions in which he had invested close to a million dollars and merged movie companies with immense profits to himself. He is a man of multiple interests.

His political career has been brief but important. When, as he put it, no one with more than $12 in the bank favored the nomination of Franklin Roosevelt he came out for the Governor of New York and predicted that his election would be a "pushover." Mr. Kennedy, with a reputation as a stock-market operator, was named to head the Securities and Exchange Commission set up under the New Deal and in 431 days effected reforms in Exchanges throughout the country. When he had completed his task he returned to private life, but the President drafted him less than a year ago to organize the newly created Maritime Commission; he was the head of that body when he was named as our envoy to Great Britain.

B IG, tall and red-headed, Mr. Kennedy habitually works in his shirt sleeves, carries on a great deal of his business over the telephone, makes up his mind with no hesitation and will not take a train if he can fly. When he talked to me in his office recently he sat with his coat off, his feet at times were on his desk, and he interspersed his trenchant remarks concerning the state of the country with picturesque slang.

In many ways Mr. Kennedy stands for the Britishers' conception of the typical American. His "pep" is inexhaustible; he is a go-getter. Foolish conventions mean little to him, red tape bothers him, formalities bore him. Although he is a college graduate, he lives far from the shades of academe and when occasion demands he can speak the language of the street as well as a stevedore. He did a few weeks ago when he flew to Seattle. He made a forceful address, in conventional English, before the Chamber of Commerce there. But his first speech in that city was to the striking longshoremen, and he used their own tongue.

"I don't know where the hell we are going to finish,. if we keep up the way we're going," he said. "Everybody knows the shipping business is lousy. This sort of thing isn't going to make things any better for you. You want to work and the shipowners want you to. * * * The American Merchant Marine is a mess today--it's either got to get in more capital or be turned over to government ownership. As things are now, private capital is scared. Everybody would be a lot happier if we could get together."

The strike was settled before Mr. Kennedy left the city. Shipowners and strikers were satisfied.

The new Ambassador will say little about his job in London. "I don't know anything about it, yet," he explained "so I am not going to talk. I've heard too many people blab about things they were ignorant of and make fools of themselves. I have to go over there and size things up before I express any opinion."

B UT behind his reticence, one feels, is the conviction in Mr. Kennedy that diplomacy in Whitehall is not going to be any different from diplomacy in Wall Street or Washington; that human beings are alike despite superficial differences and that the struggle which democracy is making for its existence in this world--a struggle in the outcome of which this country and Great Britain are both vitally concerned—requires straight speaking as well as straight thinking.

"One of the penalties that we have to pay for the privilege of living in a democracy," he said, "is that we don't know exactly what we want and another is that we cannot agree on procedure. But I think that, even at that, democracy is worth the price we have to pay for it."

He did, speak, however, about business. "A lot of business men hold up the 1929 conditions as the goal toward which we should strive," he said. "To me that was a false prosperity based upon speculation, installment buying, foreign loans and other stimulants. That's not what we want." He pointed out that our foreign trade, at least after the war, was largely dependent upon foreign loans. With a cessation of loans as retaliation against the poor record of debt-payment he does not see how we can expect any expansion in our exports except as we increase our purchases abroad. With our own plants working only part time we cannot buy large quantities from foreign countries and therefore, according to him, only a small increase in foreign trade is possible.

He views the whole question of foreign relation as complicated by the unsatisfactory general international situation and sees but little hope for much improvement in the near future unless something can be done to change the universal tendency to raise tariffs and to create artificial barriers against the international exchange of goods.

"I've been going around the country recently quite a lot," he said, "and almost everybody with whom I have talked has had a different idea as to what is the remedy for our present condition One chap will tell you that were we to repeal the Wagner Labor Relations Act everything would be okay. Another one says, 'Balance the budget.' A third will insist that the real purchasing power is not in the hands of the public."

Mr. KENNEDY acknowledged that he does not know the solution, although he has been studying the problem from the inside; he has been in business since those days when he sold papers on the streets of East Boston more than forty years ago.

He was born there in 1888, the son of an Irish-American who was a State Senator at 32. In addition to playing a part in politics the father was in turn a neighborhood banker, a coal merchant, a wholesale liquor dealer and a partner in two saloons. Eventually he became Election Commissioner and Fire Commissioner of Boston

The future Ambassador first attended a parochial school, but later on, when the family's fortune grew, he was sent to Boston Latin School. In the meantime he had not only sold papers but also peddled candy on a harbor excursion boat. When he went on to Harvard he ran a sightseeing bus during vacations and cleared $5,000 in three years.

Upon his graduation it was a toss-up whether he would become a professional ball player or go into the banking business in which his father by this time had achieved a certain local success. He chose the latter, became a bank examiner and within a couple of years a bank president. That was the real beginning of his career. From floating loans he went to floating ships and became assistant general manager of Bethlehem's Fore River Plant. Meantime, he had married Miss Rose Fitzgerald of Boston, and today he has nine children, not all of whom will go to London with him. What to do with some of them during his absence was one of the personal problems he had to solve before he could accept his appointment.

At the next step in his career Mr. Kennedy talked himself into a job with Hayden, Stone and became the manager of that firm's stock department in Boston. Soon he was immersed in the financing of new moving-picture concerns At the same time he kept his eye on the blackboard which records the ups and downs of securities. He began to play the Wall Street game and he played it with the same nerve that he had put into baseball and every other game he has undertaken. He combined movie, radio and vaudeville projects; he saved a taxi company from ruin; he was concerned in hundreds of activities, some of which were the subject of criticism when President Roosevelt appointed him chairman of the Securities and Exchange Commission.

WHEN he returned to Washington to head the Maritime Commission seventy-three days remained before operating subsidies had to be awarded to steamship companies in the place of the mail subsidies. He settled claims of $73,000,000 against the government for three-quarters of a million. He awarded a number of subsidy contracts involving commitments for new vessels and put the commission in working order.

Mr. Kennedy is convinced that the big problem of American shipping is to reconcile the difference between what private industry can do and what the welfare of the nation requires; he feels that it is up to the government to do the job of replacing the majority of our aging ships and he believes that changing conditions require changes in the government's attitude not only in our maritime problem but in all of the problems which we are now called upon to meet.

"Our government," he said, as he leaned back in his chair and removed his large horn-rimmed spectacles, "is frequently accused these days of meddling. This is an old story. No governmental reform has ever been born except to a chorus of charges on that score. Now, as one who has had experience both as a meddler and one who has been meddled with, I can say that good results come from meddling.

"I don't believe that government officials go around looking for excuses to poke their noses into people's business. There is generally a condition that screams for treatment before the cumbersome machinery of government is brought into play. Of course, mistakes have been made; I don't agree with everything that's been done I don't think any one does."

THIS business man about to enter diplomacy leaned forward and clasped his hands before him on the desk. "A recent typical example of what I have been talking about and one with which I am intimately familiar," he said, "was the legislation creating the Securities and Exchange Commission. This was opposed by one of the most formidable campaigns ever launched.

"But the legislation, instead of ruining the market as had been predicted, was really the savior of the investment business. It has smoothed the path of legitimate investment and protected the public against the flood of fake securities. I believe that if this legislation were put to a vote today among those interested in the business the majority of those who opposed it would not want to see it repealed.

"Government policies are freely blamed for the current recession. We hear the complaint that our money is no good, that our securities are shot, that business is on the skids, that insurance is wabbly. While recognizing that we are not by any means out of the woods, I can't see that the picture is nearly as bad as some paint it.

"Sure, national economy is out of kilter. That's nothing new. National economy has never in our history been satisfactory. We have never had a planned economic existence. Our history has been a series of adjustments to social change. It will probably continue along the same line.

"I am primarily a business man and I feel that it is up to business to accord a full measure of cooperation in the government's problem to restore our ailing economy. The administration is not out to get' business. No one with any conception of the economic intricacies of modern society would do anything to injure the structure of business. Although certain practices, believed to be harmful, may be assailed with considerable heat, nevertheless every one knows that the ruin of business would be the ruin of everything.

"The collaboration of business and government would be greatly facilitated if the commercial interests of the country would only get together on what they want. As I told you before, the trouble is that no two people agree in every respect upon the faults of our economic system and the steps that should be taken to set it right. It does seem possible to me, however, that the business interests might be able to agree on some of the things which they now discuss with many voices. If they could only decide just what they want and then come to government in a cooperative spirit I think there would be a good chance that we might get somewhere."

February 13, 1938

Kennedy Gets Hole-in-One On New British Course

LONDON, March 5. — Playing his first round on a British golf course today, United States Ambassador Joseph P. Kennedy did a hole-in-one. The Ambassador entered golf's exclusive circle on the Stoke Poges new course in Buckinghamshire to which he had motored after experiencing his first London fog.

He struck a fine tee shot at the second hole, measuring 128 yards, and the ball trickled into the cup.

For a moment after making the shot the Ambassador did not realize what had happened.

"Just fancy I had to come all the way over here to do my first hole-in-one," Mr. Kennedy said.

March 6, 1938

THE KENNEDYS: A NEW YORK TIMES PROFILE

LONDON, March 8.—Three British state carriages with coachmen, footmen and outriders in top hats and long scarlet cloaks carried Ambassador Joseph P. Kennedy and his staff to Buckingham Palace this morning, where he presented his credentials to the King.

Following the traditional United States procedure, Ambassador Kennedy and members of the staff of the embassy wore tailcoats, white ties and long trousers for the occasion.

Mr. Kennedy had half an hour with the King, who was in the uniform of an Admiral of the Fleet, and it was reported later that the King showed interest in the new Ambassador's nine children and expressed a wish to see them when they all arrive.

The presentation of credentials was the last formal step in Mr. Kennedy's finally becoming Ambassador. Technically he did not represent his country until he had been received by the King.

March 9, 1938

Harvard Class Honors Kennedy

CAMBRIDGE, Mass., March 17.—Joseph P. Kennedy Jr. of Bronxville, N. Y., son of the Ambassador to England, has been elected chairman of the class day committee of the Harvard senior class. Kennedy received 395 votes to 287 for George F. Lowman of New Canaan, Conn.

He is a member of the football squad and the student council. There were nineteen candidates for the seven places on the committee. The one receiving the most votes automatically becomes chairman.

March 18, 1938

PRECAUTION BY KENNEDY

Ambassador's Children Sent to Ireland in Case of Bombing

BOSTON, Mass., Sept. 19.—The younger children of Ambassador and Mrs. Joseph P. Kennedy have been sent from the London Embassy to Southern Ireland "in order to be away from any possible bombings in England in the event of sudden declaration of war," the children's grandfather, former Mayor John F. Fitzgerald of this city, revealed today.

Mr. Fitzgerald learned of the step during the course of a transatlantic telephone conversation with his daughter, Mrs. Rose Fitzgerald Kennedy, yesterday when she called to congratulate her parents on the occasion of their forty-ninth wedding anniversary.

Mr. Fitzgerald quoted his daughter as saying that she and her husband were optimistic about the outcome of the present European situation, but they had sent the children out of England as a precautionary measure.

The conversation also revealed a postponement of the plans of Joseph P. Kennedy Jr. to enter Harvard Law School this Fall. It was said that he had taken a position at the United States Embassy at Paris.

September 20, 1938

KENNEDY FOR AMITY WITH FASCIST BLOC

Urges That Democracies and Dictatorships Forget Their Differences in Outlook

CALLS FOR DISARMAMENT

At Same Time He Asks British to Recognize Our Need for an Auxiliary Merchant Navy

LONDON, Oct. 19.—Democracies and dictatorships should cooperate for the common good rather than emphasize "self-apparent differences," United States Ambassador Joseph P. Kennedy declared at the annual Trafalgar Day dinner of the Navy League tonight.

"It is true that democratic and dictator countries have important fundamental divergencies in outlook which in certain matters go deeper than politics," said the Ambassador. "But there is simply no sense, common or otherwise, in letting these differences grow into unrelenting antagonisms. After all, we have to live together in the same world, whether we like it or not."

This passage, which was carefully labeled "a theory of mine," is an excellent summary of the attitude repeatedly stated here by Prime Minister Neville Chamberlain and his Cabinet colleagues. Inevitably it will cause speculation here, in view of the attitude of the United States Government, as expressed in President Roosevelt's "quarantine" speech at Chicago and his subsequent speech at Kingston, Ontario, last Summer.

In the circumstances there is bound to be speculation whether Mr. Kennedy's speech, vaguely as it was phrased, indicated that President Roosevelt is swinging away from his policy of contrasting peaceful democracies and regimented aggressive dictatorships.

In the same speech Mr. Kennedy, despite the fact that the United States is arming at the fastest peace-time pace in its history, pleaded in the name of the American people for international action to end the armaments race, which, he said, "threatens sooner or later to engulf us all in a major disaster."

Acknowledging the necessity of strength in the modern world and the impossibility of one nation's stopping the "vicious circle," Mr. Kennedy nevertheless said the world must get together if the standard of living was to be maintained at its present level. Further rearming, he asserted, would bring economic difficulties as surely as war, and those difficulties would fall mainly on the world's workers.

"For this reason," he declared, "the American people look forward to the day when the nations of the world will realize that they must agree on limitation and reduction of armaments."

Cites Need of Auxiliary

But a few minutes later Mr. Kennedy reminded his hearers that the United States was spending a billion dollars on its fleet this year and asked them to understand the necessity of building up a merchant fleet primarily as an auxiliary to this increased naval strength.

Granting that it would be economic sense for Americans to abandon the attempt to maintain their own merchant marine and let the British do it for them, he expressed regret that the world "is not organized on a purely economic basis."

"We try to understand your need for a great merchant fleet," he added. "We hope you will try to understand our need for a small one."

This part of the Ambassador's speech was made as a plea for dismissal of British fears of competition from the United States' merchant fleet, which is being built largely as a result of Mr. Kennedy's work on the Maritime Commission. It followed a reminder that the United States and Great Britain had reached a complete understanding on naval policy after a century of rivalry.

Carefully stressing the statement that there is no naval alliance, not even a negative one, Mr. Kennedy said the present relationship of the two countries in this respect represented "probably the first time two nations not bound by an alliance have actually welcomed every ship launched by the other."

Lord Lloyd, president of the league, introduced Mr. Kennedy with the remark that he was the first foreigner ever to speak at the dinner of the league.

"'Foreigner' does not fit very well either you or Mrs. Kennedy," said Lord Lloyd, "especially in naval affairs."

Admiral Sir Roger Backhouse, First Sea Lord of the Admiralty, endorsed "every word" Mr. Kennedy said about the friendliness between the two navies, adding that it was a pleasure for officers and men of the British fleet to meet and cooperate with the United States Navy whenever mutual interests made it advisable.

Lord Lloyd, who, although a Conservative, has been a severe critic of Mr. Chamberlain's foreign policy, especially of the Munich agreement, commented that the speed with which the British navy mobilized—"as tardy as some of us think the order was"—was the only event in the recent crisis "from which Britons could derive pride and satisfaction."

"It was the only effective argument," he asserted, "in the conversations that took place on the other side of the Channel."

With a scathing reference to former Prime Minister Earl Baldwin's "policy of disarmament," Lord Lloyd expressed pleasure at the state of the British fleet, but warned that the merchant marine was in a highly unsatisfactory condition. Admiral Backhouse echoed this warning.

October 20, 1938

JOHN KENNEDY GETS JOB

Ambassador's Son Will Be Office Boy in London and Paris

LONDON, Feb. 12.—John F. Kennedy, 21-year-old son of the American Ambassador, will have a six-month tryout as "office boy" at the Embassies in London and Paris to see whether or not he wants a career in the diplomatic service. He will come to England in two weeks, while his father will land from the Queen Mary on Wednesday.

Mrs. Kennedy, speaking from Paris, told The Daily Sketch tonight that it was Mr. Kennedy who thought of John's making the experiment.

"It is not going to be a holiday for John," said Mrs. Kennedy, "although he has only just left Harvard. A definite plan of work has been arranged for him."

February 13, 1939

Son of Kennedy Visits Besieged Madrid; 'Just Looking Around,' Says Ambassador

MADRID, Feb. 16 (AP).—Joseph P. Kennedy Jr., 23-year-old son of the United States Ambassador to London, arrived here tonight just as Insurgent gunners ended a shelling of this Spanish Government capital.

Arrangements were made to put him up at the United States Embassy building, where he could learn for himself what it was like to live in a besieged city on a diet of sardines and rice.

LONDON, Feb. 16 (AP).—Joseph P. Kennedy Jr., son of the United States Ambassador here, jolted along to Madrid from Valencia this afternoon in a special bus placed at his disposal by Spanish Government authorities.

His father received the following cablegram tonight from his son:

"Sorry I missed you Stop Arrived safely Valencia Stop Going Madrid tonight Regards Joe."

"And that," remarked the Ambassador, who arrived back in England only yesterday from the United States, "is the reception I get after being away for two months."

He laughingly explained that his son "is just looking around."

Joseph Jr. wrote his thesis for Harvard University on the Spanish Non-Intervention Committee and decided he wanted to see what Spain looked like. He left London last Saturday and, his father said, "he will be back when we see him."

The Ambassador said young Joe's adventures were nothing new.

"During the (September) crisis I started counting noses and Joe was missing," he said. "It turned out he was in Czecho-Slovakia."

[The Kennedys have four sons and five daughters.]

He added that Joe had been "prowling around Russia, too."

Joseph Jr. recently was reported engaged to Megan Taylor, world figure skating champion—but the Ambassador denied that one.

"He is not engaged to anybody," he said. "He is going back to Cambridge to the Harvard Law School in the Fall."

February 17, 1939

POPE'S 'ADMIRATION' WON BY ROOSEVELT

President Praised by Pontiff In Course of Audience Accorded to Kennedy

PIUS REPEATS PEACE PLEA

Response to Congratulations of the Cardinals Dedicates His Pontificate Anew

VATICAN CITY, March 13 (AP).—Pope Pius XII was quoted today by Joseph P. Kennedy, United States Ambassador to London, as expressing "great admiration for President Roosevelt because he always admired his stand for religion."

The Pope received Mr. Kennedy, who was President Roosevelt's personal representative at yesterday's coronation ceremony, Mrs. Kennedy and eight of the nine Kennedy children in a private audience. The only one absent was Joseph P. Jr., who had telegraphed the family that he was unable to arrive in time for the coronation from Madrid, where he was visiting.

"The Pope expressed gratitude to President Roosevelt for having sent a representative," Mr. Kennedy stated.

The Ambassador said that the Pontiff, who usually remains seated during audiences, rose to greet him, and when the children came in the Pope went to a table to get them rosaries, his gift to the family.

Visit to United States Recalled

The Pope recalled his visit to the Kennedy home in Bronxville, N. Y., in 1936, the Ambassador said. He added that the Pope remembered taking young Teddy Kennedy on his lap and recalled how the boy asked about the cross that hung from his neck.

The Pontiff was described as having spoken of the pleasure he had in meeting the President's family and his private secretary, Marguerite Le Hand, when he visited Hyde Park on his American trip.

Before concluding the audience, the Pope blessed the Ambassador, his family and aides who accompanied him. He also sent his blessing to all American people.

The Ambassador was received first. Afterward audiences were granted to Mrs. Kennedy, the children and their governess, the Ambassador's secretary, Edward Moore, and Franklin C. Gowen of the United States consular staff in London.

Those presented to the Pontiff included also Mrs. Moore, Miss Elizabeth Dunn of Boston, the Kennedy children's nurse, and Miss Luella Hennessy of Boston, their governess.

The Kennedys then called on Lugi Cardinal Maglione, Papal Secretary of State, and visited the Sistine Chapel.

While the Ambassador was talking with Cardinal Maglione, the Secretary expressed great interest on learning that the Kennedys had nine children. Because he was the ninth child in his own family, Cardinal Maglione asked to see the ninth young Kennedy. Teddy, the youngest, was brought in to see the Cardinal, who shook him by both hands and wished him good luck, in Italian.

Papal attendants carried a silver tray of rosaries and medallions to the waiting Kennedy car.

Teddy, who is 7 years old, said afterward that he wasn't "frightened at all" at meeting Pope Pius XII.

In a brief interview after the Pontiff had received the Kennedy family the Ambassador's youngest son described his sensations during the minutes he spent with the Pope.

"I told my sister Patricia I wasn't frightened at all," he said. "He (the Pope) patted my hand and told me I was a smart little fellow. He gave me the first rosary beads from the table before he gave my sister any."

Busy Day for Kennedys

Ambassador and Mrs. Kennedy were among the guests at the tea at Castel Gandolfo and topped off a busy day by meeting Count Galeazzo Ciano, the Italian Foreign Minister, and the Countess, a daughter of Premier Benito Mussolini, at a dinner for the Count at the American Embassy residence.

Ambassador William Phillips invited forty guests from among the diplomatic corps and Rome society for tonight's embassy dinner. The coronation of the Pope provided another distinguested guest in John McCormick, Irish tenor, who sang after dinner. Mr. McCormick had attended the coronation ceremonies as a Papal Count.

Among the diplomatic guests were the German Ambassador, Hans-Georg Vikton von Mackensen, and the Countess of Perth, whose husband, the British Ambassador, is recovering from an attack of influenza.

Mr. Kennedy and his family plan to spend the rest of the week in Italy sightseeing.

Pope Pius received eight foreign missions today. Besides that to Mr. Kennedy, he granted audiences to the envoys of England, Peru, China, Hungary, Yugoslavia, Bulgaria and Luxembourg.

Meanwhile, William Cardinal O'Connell of Boston left for Naples to sail for the United States on the Vulcania next Sunday. Denis Cardinal Dougherty of Philadelphia is expected to sail on the Rex next Thursday. George Cardinal Mundelein of Chicago plans to leave for home late this week via Paris.

March 14, 1939

THE KENNEDYS: A NEW YORK TIMES PROFILE

IF ever the call goes out to join the Kennedys and see the world, there should be plenty of volunteers, for to the Ambassador's nine children doors swing open which few Americans have ever entered. The young Kennedys are seeing Britain and the rest of Europe as it never has been seen before. So widely do they travel that often the marble-halled official residence of the American Ambassador to the Court of St. James is almost deserted, with only four or five young Kennedys on hand.

Being Kennedys, the youngsters would probably be going places and seeing things under any circumstances, but the opportunities here are almost endless and the youngsters are making the most of them. Their father, of course, is something of a traveler himself. He has been all around Britain and Ireland to make speeches and receive honorary degrees, has gone to Rome to represent President Roosevelt at the coronation of Pope Pius XII, to Cannes for a vacation, and has made two quick voyages back to America. But compared with his children he has been a virtual stay-at-home.

They have been all over the British Isles, to France, Germany, the Netherlands, Switzerland and Italy. Their film collection of personal travelogues already takes a couple of hours to show. Mathematicians quail at the thought of adding up their total mileage. And they have met almost everybody. They are swamped with attentions that seem to come as much from their own charm as from their father's position. They are so well known that other youngsters ask them for their autographs.

MR. AND MRS. KENNEDY are doing their best to keep the youngsters unspoiled. They went to Rome in a special Pullman car, but ordinarily it is against the rules for any young Kennedy to travel first class. Usually they travel by bus. One reason is that on buses they get a chance to talk to many people. And they like to talk to everybody. Like all good travelers, they try to learn the daily life of the people.

There are five girls and four boys in the Kennedy family. Oldest of the group is Joseph Jr., aged 23, who is also the most traveled of the nine. Then comes John better known as Jack, who is 21. Rosemary is 20 and Kathleen is 19. Kathleen came here with her father, ahead of the rest of the family, and served as his official hostess for several weeks before her mother arrived. Next is Eunice, 17 years old, who rounds out the older group. There are four younger children Patricia, who is 14; Robert 13, Jean 11, and Edward, or Teddy, the baby of the family, who is 7.

The five in the older group knew Europe before their father became an Ambassador. Joseph Jr. studied at the London School of Economics five years ago, went to Geneva to watch the workings of the League of Nations, then made a wide tour of the Continent, which included five weeks in Russia. Kathleen studied in France, went to Russia with her mother and spent the Summer of 1937 in Ireland.

Rosemary and Eunice were in Europe in 1936. Jack came here in 1937 on a motor tour with college friends, ran short of funds, bought gasoline instead of food and finally had to call home for help.

The younger four had never been in Europe until they arrived with their mother last Spring. But they have wasted no time. While the furniture was still being moved into their new home they were on their way, and three and a half weeks later they came back with a pretty good idea of what France, Switzerland and the Netherlands had to offer for future excursions

But the Kennedys didn't really get going until last Summer, after Joseph Jr., or Joe, as he is generally known, was graduated from Harvard and Jack had finished his sophomore year there. The family was assembled in London and moved on to Cannes for a mass vacation. They spent two and a half months there. Then they were off, individually and in groups.

JOE went to Paris to work for a while at the United States Embassy. He was there until after the September crisis, but as soon as the Munich agreement was signed he headed for Czecho-Slovakia to see what was happening. The frontier was closed, but Joe was carrying dispatches to the legation in Prague; he got through when everybody else was being turned back.

He saw the final agonies of the Benes regime, then moved on to Warsaw, Leningrad, Helsingfors, Stockholm, Copenhagen and Berlin before returning to Paris. He seems to have a knack of being where things are happening.

The European situation having quieted down, he came back to London and studied the operations of the great financial houses in the City from the inside. For a Christmas vacation he went with the family to St. Moritz, where he made a reputation as one of the most daring riders on the Cresta bobsled run. Then he headed for Spain.

He says he was "lucky." In any case, he was in Barcelona the day it fell to General Franco's troops. From there he made a dash to Majorca, caught a ride on a British destroyer and returned to what was left of the Loyalist Spanish territory. For seven weeks he was at the American Embassy in Madrid, watching the death-throes of the Republican Government. He saw the fall of the Negrin regime, the brief rule of the Casado military junta and the final occupation by the Nationalists. And he sent letters to his father that were so filled with factual observation that Prime Minister Chamberlain asked to see them. Thus he had the distinction of serving as unofficial observer, supplying reports for the head of the British Government

Joe says he is going back to Harvard next Fall to study law, but meantime he is working in an American newspaper office here in London. All London lies before him, of course. As he said recently "So far I've only met Chamberlain and Halifax and the Labor leaders and some people in the City no, not Montagu Norman. But, then, I've only been in London six weeks in all."

AFTER the vacation in Cannes last Summer, Jack and Kathleen took a midget car and went for a tour through old Austria. Then Jack had to return to Harvard. But he plowed through his junior year's work there before Christmas and came back to London. He had already been presented to the King and Queen, and now he went with the rest of the family to Rome for the coronation of the Pope. After that he went to Paris and took a job in the American Embassy. He is still there, but, thinking of brother Joe's travels, he is planning to go to Poland, or anywhere else that seems to promise eventful times between now and next Fall, when he will return to finish at Harvard.

Kathleen and Rosemary were presented at court last year and enjoyed to the full the glitter of a London "season." Both of them are continuing their studies and making vacation trips to the Continent. Late last Summer Eunice, Patricia, Bobby and Jean made a tour of Ireland and Scotland. They were joined in Scotland by Rosemary, who had already toured Ireland. Then the younger group came back to London for school.

Meantime Teddy had to content himself with the Cannes trip and the vacation in St. Moritz. But he had his big moment when the whole family except Joe went to Rome for the coronation.

The Kennedys had seats of honor at the ceremony and a

There are nine of them and all are eager to go places and do things

By T. J. HAMILTON

The Kennedy family, minus Rose and John, sight-seeing in London.

private audience afterward with His Holiness. But even that was as nothing compared with Teddy's distinction. When Cardinal Pacelli was in New York a few years ago he visited at the Kennedy home and Teddy sat on his knee and twisted the chain around the Cardinal's neck. Now, as Pope, the former Cardinal remembered, and he arranged that Teddy should take his first communion from the Pope himself in the private chapel in the Vatican. Vatican authorities could not recall that any other little boy had ever attained this distinction. Asked about it later, Teddy said, "I wasn't afraid. He was very nice to me and he patted me on the head."

THAT seems to be the spirit of the whole Kennedy family. They aren't afraid; they're out to see the world, and to enjoy it. If they meet interesting people on their bus travels, they talk; and if they meet shy people, they overcome their shyness with gifts of chewing gum. They are natural "mixers."

Naturally, it took them a little

time to adjust themselves to Europe and European ways. The English rain was too much for them for a while, and they still prefer American food; in fact, when they are all home from school for week-ends it is worth the cook's life to serve such English standbys as mutton or cabbage.

The children are used to abundant but simple food at home—not the elaborate course dinners, including soup and fish, joint, sweet and savory, that the older English children get. Teddy is accustomed to having his meals with his father and mother and the rest of the family, and it is known that he speaks a disapproving piece about the English custom of banishing his contemporaries to the nursery, where they have tea and toast at 6, before being put to bed. He takes his tea at 4:30, and wants his supper, too, with the rest of the family.

The younger children have carefully recorded their impressions of Europe in the diaries all the family are keeping. Of all the pictures they have seen, Rem-

brandt's "The Anatomy Lesson" they consider the most remarkable.

THE younger children are day pupils in convent schools where there are virtually no Americans. As a result, they have made English friends. But they still think the Oxford accent is funny. The first time they heard the word "topping," however, they decided they needed it and added it to their vocabulary. Certain ambassadorial objections put a stop to its use, for the Kennedys are American and intend to remain so. But now Bobby and Teddy have taken up "jolly" in its stead. And they've undertaken cricket along with American football, both of which are played in the embassy's formal garden any week-end when the Kennedy clan is more or less united.

They've met royalty and deported themselves well. Bobby recalls that at the garden party where he met Princess Elizabeth things were a little formal until he began discussing St. Moritz and skiing technique with her. After that "everything was all

right."

THE greatest family triumph, of course, was the dinner for the King and Queen just before they left for Canada and the United States. The younger boys were in navy blue suits like those they wear at home, and the younger girls were in white, and all nine of the young Kennedys stood in line to welcome Their Majesties. Passing down the line, the King and Queen greeted them all personally. And, for perhaps the first time at an ambassadorial dinner party, the children of the Ambassador made their appropriate reverence, the boys bowing stiffly, the girls dropping curtseys. Then, as the company went in to dinner, the four younger children dropped out, and the other five went to a special table.

It's only a guess, of course, but that was probably a time when young Teddy spoke his piece about English custom. For Teddy likes his dinner with the rest of the family, royalty or no royalty. Teddy is a Kennedy to the core, one of the nine stout American Kennedy kids.

June 4, 1939

'KEEP OUT OF WAR', KENNEDY ADVISES

PEACE 'ANYBODY'S GUESS'

All Want End of Strife, Envoy Declares in Boston, but Differ on Basis

BOSTON, Dec. 10—In his first speech since the start of the European war, Joseph P. Kennedy, Ambassador to Great Britain, strongly urged tonight that the United States "keep out" of the conflict.

"As you love America, don't let anything that comes out of any country in the world make you believe you can make a situation one whit better by getting into the war," he said.

"There is no place in this fight for us. It's going to be bad enough as it is."

He spoke etxemporaneously at a reunion of parishioners of Our Lady of Assumption Church, where he served as an altar boy.

Smiling, but admittedly "not optimistic" concerning the world

situation, he later declared in an interview:

"There is no reason—economic, financial or social—to justify the United States entering the war."

One of the chief influences that might bring such an involvement, he said, was the American people's "sporting spirit" in "not wanting to see an unfair or immoral thing done," but he reiterated that "this is not our fight."

Asked whether there was any possibility of peace in the near future, he replied that it was "anybody's guess."

"All want peace but all have their own ideas as to what peace should be," he asserted. "Under such circumstances, who can say

when there will be peace."

Emphasizing his feeling that the United States should "stay out," he declared:

"If anybody advocates our entering the war, the American public should demand a specific answer to the question: 'Why?'"

In the same vein, he said that, speaking as an individual, he believed that candidates for public office should be faced with a demand for an answer as to "how" they would do the things they advocate.

"They don't have to tell us what ought to be done," he added. "We know. Let them tell us just how they would do it."

December 11, 1939

WASHINGTON, Feb. 13—Joseph P. Kennedy, Ambassador to Great Britain, declared tonight that he was not a candidate for the Democratic nomination for President. His action was the result of the movement started in Massachusetts to seek delegates for him.

"My attention has been called to newspaper reports that my name may be submitted in Massachusetts and other States for the election of delegates pledged to me for President in the forthcoming Democratic national convention," Mr. Kennedy said in a statement.

"Appreciating as I must the great honor implied in this step, nevertheless I must with positiveness state that I am not a candidate. Even though consideration for such an honor is most flattering, I cannot forget that I now occupy a most important government post which at this particular time involves matters so precious to the American people that no private consideration should permit my energies or interests to be diverted."

Ambassador Kennedy, who came out early for the renomination of the President, and still favors him, it is said, was not influenced to take himself out of the race by the Roosevelt sentiment stirred up in the Bay State after Farley petitions had been filed for the March 5 primaries.

Talks Long With the President

Following a long conference with President Roosevelt the Ambassador denied that he intended resigning his London post in the near future. He said he planned to sail for London by way of Genoa on the George Washington Feb. 24.

"I'm certainly not going over there for the ride," said Mr. Kennedy when told of reports that he might return to this country in a few weeks. "The fact that I am going back to my post should be sufficient answer to all resignation rumors."

Mr. Kennedy told reporters that the President and he discussed plans whereby foreign holdings of American securities might be liquidated in an orderly fashion. Mr. Kennedy said he would discuss the plan further with officials before leaving for Boston Thursday.

Mr. Kennedy had "no comment" on the situation in Europe, but did say he had discussed with the President a proposal to find new uses for American ships tied up by the Neutrality Act. He remarked: "There is a serious question of finding jobs for the American seamen formerly on vessels whose registry has been changed."

Mr. Kennedy said he expected to discuss with Mr. Roosevelt a plan for putting some idle American ships on British runs outside the combat areas.

The Ambassador hopes also to work out an arrangement for increased sale of American pine and fir lumber, which Great Britain needs but for which shipping facilities are lacking.

He disclosed this idea as he was leaving a forty-five-minute conference with Secretary Hull.

February 14, 1940

NOT A CANDIDATE, KENNEDY ASSERTS

Won't Permit Filing of Name for President in Primary in Massachusetts, He Says

ENVOY SEES ROOSEVELT

Plans for Orderly Selling of Foreign-Held Securities Among Topics Discussed

Kennedy Jr. on Farley Slate
BOSTON, Feb. 15 (AP)—William H. Burke Jr., chairman of the Massachusetts Democratic Committee, announced today that Joseph P. Kennedy Jr., son of the Ambassador to Great Britain, has agreed to run as a delegate to the national convention pledged to Postmaster General Farley. The younger Kennedy is a student at Harvard.

February 16, 1940

Kennedys Excel at Sailing
HYANNISPORT, Mass., Sept. 3 (UP)—Seven of the nine children of Joseph P. Kennedy, United States Ambassador to Great Britain, won most of the annual prize awards last night at the Hyannisport and Wianno Yacht Club. Jack, Rosemary, Eunice, Pat, Jean, Bobby and Teddy, received a total of twelve prizes, including at least one in each class. The awards included silver cups, silver trays, book sets, clocks and desk sets. The prizes were for sailing victories in contests in three classes of yachting.

September 4, 1940

Kennedy's Son John Is Called
While Ambassador Joseph P. Kennedy was telling a radio audience last night that he and Mrs. Kennedy had given "nine hostages to fortune," a dispatch revealed that John Kennedy, one of the nine, had become No. 18 on Palo Alto, Calif., draft board rolls. Mr. Kennedy, whose serial number was 2,748, is a graduate student at Stanford University.

October 30, 1940

KENNEDY DISAVOWS INTERVIEW ON WAR

Envoy Says He Talked 'Off the Record' in Boston—Story Gave Wrong Impression

INACCURACY IS CHARGED

Was Quoted as Saying That 'Democracy Is Finished' in Great Britain

Joseph P. Kennedy, United States Ambassador to England, issued a formal statement yesterday repudiating a story of an interview with him written by Louis M. Lyons of The Boston Globe and syndicated by the North American Newspaper Alliance. Mr. Kennedy said the story was based on an off-the-record conversation undertaken with the understanding that he would make no statements that would be printed at this time and declared that as published it contained many "inaccurate" statements.

In The Globe's report, Mr. Kennedy was represented as believing that "democracy is finished in England" and that "it may be here," that the loss of our foreign trade will threaten to change our form of government, that the appointment of labor leaders to the British Cabinet meant that national socialism was going to emerge from the war effort, that it was "the bunk" that England was fighting for democracy, and as expressing himself on other controversial questions.

Text of Kennedy Statement

References to the story appeared in other newspapers. Mr. Kennedy's statement follows:

"I have read the interview that I am supposed to have given to Mr. Louis M. Lyons of The Boston Globe.

"When Mr. Lyons came to see me in Boston I made it clear to him, in the presence of Mr. Coglan and Mr. Edmondson of The St. Louis Post-Dispatch, that I should be very happy to give them my thoughts off the record, but I would make no statements that should be printed at this time.

"In the week that I have been home, I have turned down all the many other newspapers and leading magazines which have sought interviews and articles. It was on this basis that our conversation proceeded.

"Mr. Lyons made no notes during the visit. Whatever he wrote was entirely from memory. Many statements in the article show this to be true because they create a different impression entirely than I would want to set forth. Many of them were inaccurate.

"He admits I said to him, 'Well, I am afraid you didn't get much of a story.' Of course, the reason I said that was that I assumed the entire conversation had been conducted on the basis of my original statement—that it was an off-the-record discussion.

"I consider this interview, regardless of the handling of the material, as the first serious violation of the newspaper code on an off-the-record interview that I have ever experienced. I may be guilty of errors of judgment, but I hope never guilty of errors of good taste.

"If I ever give out material touching such important questions I would certainly insist on checking it so that mistakes and inaccuracies might not be made."

The Ambassador, who returned recently by clipper from London, was quoted in the Lyons interview as asserting that the United States would enter the war "over my dead body."

"What would we get out of it?" he was quoted as asking. "Lindbergh isn't crazy either, you know."

November 12, 1940

KENNEDY RESIGNS AS LONDON ENVOY TO COMBAT WAR

Reveals Action of Nov. 6 After Talk With President — Will Await Naming of Successor

WON'T RETURN TO BRITAIN

Ambassador Says He Will Now Help Roosevelt 'Keep the United States Out of War'

WASHINGTON, Dec. 1—Joseph P. Kennedy announced tonight that he had submitted his resignation as United States Ambassador to Great Britain so that he might devote his time to "the greatest cause in the world today, to help the President keep the United States out of war."

He said he submitted his resignation to President Roosevelt on Nov. 6 but that he had acceded to Mr. Roosevelt's wish that he continue to serve until his successor was chosen. Mr. Kennedy added, however, that he would not return to London as Ambassador.

As the President is expected to be away from Washington on a defense inspection trip, it was assumed that he would defer any decision on Mr. Kennedy's successor until his return about Dec. 16.

Mr. Kennedy announced his resignation after an unscheduled conference with the Chief Executive this morning.

Statement by Mr. Kennedy

In a prepared statement he said:

"On Nov. 6 I tendered to the President my resignation as his Ambassador to the Court of St. James.

"Today the President was good enough to express regret over my decision, but to say that, not yet being prepared to appoint my successor, he wishes me to retain my designation as Ambassador until he is. But I shall not return to London in that capacity.

"My plan is, after a short holiday, to devote my efforts to what seems to me the greatest cause in the world today, and means, if successful, the preservation of the American form of democracy. That cause is to help the President keep the United States out of war."

Mr. Kennedy's resignation had been anticipated generally. He flew back from London six weeks ago amid widespread rumors that he would resign immediately because he disagreed with the Administration on foreign policy. He met these reports, however, with a nationally broadcast speech urging Mr. Roosevelt's re-election.

To Work as Private Citizen

Mr. Kennedy flew into Washington unexpectedly today, and went directly to the White House for a long and leisurely discussion with Mr. Roosevelt on the whole problem of British-United States relations and this country's representation at the Court of St. James.

Mr. Kennedy, it was learned, told Mr. Roosevelt that he felt he could render his country greater service by remaining here and working with the President to keep the United States out of war. This work would be carried on as a private individual. It would indicate that Mr. Kennedy would not retain any government capacity after relinquishing his Ambassadorship.

A source close to both Mr. Roosevelt and Mr. Kennedy said that their conference today was most amicable and that the President and his Ambassador found themselves in general agreement on most questions affecting British-United States relations.

William C. Bullitt, who resigned as Ambassador to France early last month, has been prominently mentioned for the London post.

J. Anthony Drexel Biddle, Ambassador to Poland, who returned to the United States when that country was invaded by Germany, also has been mentioned along with John G. Winant, head of the International Labor Office, as a possible successor to Mr. Kennedy.

Mr. Winant, former Governor of New Hampshire and one-time chairman of the Social Security Board, conferred with Mr. Roosevelt last week, leading many observers to believe that he was in line for a diplomatic post.

December 2, 1940

KENNEDY JR. FOR BARTER

Calls Such Dealing With Nazis Better Than 'Total War'

BOSTON, Jan. 6 (UP)—Joseph P. Kennedy Jr., oldest son of the man who recently resigned as Ambassador to Great Britain, believes that the United States would be better off under a barter system with a Nazi-conquered Europe than engaging in a total war on the side of Great Britain.

"All our trade would not be cut off if Britain lost," young Kennedy told a Ford Hall Folks meeting yesterday.

He said that the policy of giving aid to Britain would demand in time that "we send an air force to Britain with pilots and battleships to convoy supplies and we shall be in the war, a total war which may last six or seven years."

The American economy, he asserted, would not stand the strain of a total war.

January 7, 1941

A UNITED STATES TORPEDO BOAT BASE, New Georgia, Aug. 8 (Delayed)—Out of the darkness, a Japanese destroyer appeared suddenly. It sliced diagonally in two the PT boat skippered by Lieut. (j.g.) John F. Kennedy, son of the former American Ambassador in London, Joseph P. Kennedy.

Crews of two other PT boats, patrolling close by, saw flaming high octane gasoline spread over the water. They gave up "Skipper" Kennedy and all his crew as lost that morning of Aug. 2.

But Lieutenant Kennedy, 26, and ten of his men were rescued today from a small coral island deep inside Japanese-controlled Solomons Island territory and within range of enemy shore guns.

The PT boat making the rescue performed a daring and skillful bit of navigation through reef-choked waters off Ferguson Passage. [Ferguson Passage is between Gizo and Wanawawa Islands in the New Georgia group.]

Two men of Lieutenant Kennedy's crew were lost when the enemy destroyer rammed the boat at a speed estimated by the skipper at forty knots.

Those who were rescued with Lieutenant Kennedy were:

Ensign Leonard Thom of Sandusky, Ohio, executive officer and former Ohio State tackle; Ensign George Henry Robertson (Barney) Ross of Highland Park, Ill.; Machinist's Mate Patrick H. McMahon, 39, of Los Angeles; Machinist's Mate Gerald E. Zinzer of Belleville, Ill.; Gunner's Mate Charles Harris of Boston; Radioman John Maguire of Hastings-on-Hudson, N.Y.; Machinist's Mate William Johnston of Dorchester, Mass.; Ordnanceman Edmond Mowrer of St. Louis; Torpedoman Roy L. Starkey of Garden Grove, Calif., and Seaman First Class Raymond Albert of Cleveland.

McMahon's Stamina Praised

McMahon was burned badly on his face, hands and arms. Although the burns were infected by salt water and exposure, he did not once utter a word of complaint.

"McMahon's a terrific guy," Lieutenant Kennedy said. "It was something which really got you, seeing old Mac lie there."

"You could see he was suffering such pain that his lips twitched and his hands trembled," Ensign Thom added. "You'd watch him and think if you were in his place you'd probably be yelling, 'Why doesn't somebody do something?' But every time you asked Mac how he was doing, he'd wrinkle his face and give you a grin."

Zinser suffered burns on both arms. Johnston, a tough little fellow called "Jockey," was sickened by fumes he had inhaled. Ensign Ross was unhurt, but suffered an arm infection from coral cuts. All the others came through their experience without injury.

On three nights Lieutenant Kennedy, once a backstroke man on the Harvard swimming team, swam out into Ferguson Passage hoping to flag down PT boats going through on patrol. Ensign Ross did the same one other night.

But they made no contacts.

On the afternoon on the fourth day two natives found the survivors and carried to the PT boat base a message Lieutenant Kennedy crudely cut on a green coconut husk.

Chronologically, Lieutenant Kennedy, Ensign Thom and the crewmen told the story this way:

Four Japanese destroyers came down Blackett Strait around the south coast of Kolombangara Island about 2:30 A. M. on Aug. 2. In two phases of a confused engagement the PT's claimed three hits and three probable hits on one of the enemy ships.

It was while the destroyers were returning, probably after delivering supplies and reinforcements near Japan's base at Vila, on Kolombangara, that the enemy ship rammed the Kennedy boat. Ross and Kennedy saw the destroyer coming.

"At first I thought it was a PT," Kennedy said. "I think it was going at least forty knots. As soon as I decided it was a destroyer, I turned to make a torpedo run."

But Kennedy, nicknamed "Shafty" by his mates, quickly realized the range was too short for the torpedo to charge and explode.

"The destroyer then turned straight for us," he said.

"It all happened so fast there wasn't a chance to do a thing. The destroyer hit our starboard forward gun station and sliced right through. I was in the cockpit. I looked up and saw a red glow and streamlined stacks. Our tanks were ripped open and gas was flaming on the water about twenty yards away.

Kennedy went out to get McMahon, who had been at the engine station and was knocked into the water in the midst of flaming gasoline.

"McMahon and I were about an hour getting back to the boat," Kennedy said. Watertight bulkheads had kept the bow afloat, the skipper explained. "There was a very strong current."

After getting McMahon aboard, Kennedy swam out again to get Harris.

The skipper and his men shouted and called for the two missing men but could get no response.

"We seemed to be drifting toward Kolombangara," Kennedy said. "We figured the Japs would be sure to get us in the morning, but everybody was tired and we slept."

Just before dawn the current changed to carry the survivors away from the Japanese-held coast. About 2 P. M. Kennedy decided to abandon the bow section and try to reach a small island.

Kennedy swam to the island, towing McMahon. The others clung to a plank and swam in a group. It took about three hours to make it. The men stayed on this island until Wednesday, when all coconuts on the island's two trees had been eaten.

Late that afternoon they swam to a larger island, where there were plenty of coconuts.

At night, Kennedy put on a lifebelt and swam into Ferguson Passage to try to signal an expected PT boat.

The two natives found the survivor group Thursday afternoon. On Saturday morning a large can e loaded with natives brought food

Kennedy's Son Is Hero in Pacific As Destroyer Splits His PT Boat

Lieut. John F. Kennedy

and a small kerosene stove and gave the men a real feed and hot coffee. That night, a little after midnight, a PT rescue boat, guided by a native pilot, went in the twisting passages to make contact with Kennedy on an outer island.

Kennedy's Parents Overjoyed

HYANNIS. Mass., Aug. 19 (AP)— Former Ambassador and Mrs. Kennedy today shouted in joy when informed of the exploit of their son.

Mrs. Kennedy, first to hear the news by telephone at their summer home, expressed "deep sorrow" for the two crewmen who lost their lives.

"That's wonderful," Mrs. Kennedy said when told her son was safe.

The former Ambassador then exclaimed: "Phew, I think Mrs. Kennedy has said enough for both of us."

August 20, 1943

The Family Emerges

MISS KENNEDY WED TO DEVONSHIRE HEIR

Daughter of Ex-Envoy Bride of Marquess of Hartington in London Registry Office

---

HER BROTHER IS PRESENT

Reception Held at Home of Lady Hambleden—Couple First Met at Court in '38

LONDON, May 6—Miss Kathleen Kennedy second daughter of Joseph P. Kennedy, former Ambassador to Great Britain, and Mrs. Kennedy, was married here today in the Chelsea Register Office to the Marquess of Hartington, eldest son and heir of the Duke of Devonshire.

The wedding was a simple civil ceremony, but the bareness of the office was relieved by vases of pink carnations.

A distinguished group of guests attended, including the Duke and Duchess of Devonshire, the Duke's sister, Lady Elizabeth Cavendish, the Marchioness of Salisbury and Lady Astor.

The bridegroom whose age is 26, was first to arrive at the register office. He was accompanied by his sister, Lady Anne Cavendish. Lord Hartington is a captain in the Coldstream Guards and attending him as best man was a fellow-officer, the Duke of Rutland. The bride, who is 24 years old, arrived with her brother, Lieut. Joseph P. Kennedy Jr., USN.

Wears Pink Suede Crepe

The bride wore a frock of pink suede crepe beneath a short jacket of brown mink, and a small hat of blue and pink ostrich feathers. The bridegroom wore his Army uniform. The wedding ring is an heirloom in the Devonshire family.

Flower petals were tossed over the couple as they left the register office, and afterward there was a reception. About two hundred guests attended, including fellow-workers of the bride at the American Red Cross club and service men who frequent the club.

The wedding cake had no icing, in conformity with the war-time "austerity," but there was champagne.

The Marquess and Marchioness went by train afterward to Bournemouth and walked from the station a half mile to Compton Place, one of the Duke of Devonshire's several estates, where they will spend two or three weeks.

Plans for Religious Ceremony

Within the next day or so, it was learned tonight from acquaintances of the Marquess, a private religious ceremony will be held in the drawing room of Compton Place. The family has not yet confirmed this report.

The nature of ceremony could not be learned, but it was assumed that it would be Protestant. Although the bride was brought up in the Roman Catholic faith of her parents, the Devonshire family always has been strongly Protestant. The first Duke withdrew from the Privy Council of King Charles II in the seventeenth century in protest against Roman Catholic influence.

The heirs have traditionally held the West Derbyshire seat in the House of Commons before succeeding to the dukedom. The present Marquess, however, was defeated recently for the seat.

The couple first met in 1938 when the bride's father was Ambassador here. Their acquaintance was revived when she returned to London to do Red Cross work and the engagement was announced on Thursday.

Mother Leaves for "Rest"

Mrs. Joseph P. Kennedy arrived by airplane at La Guardia Field, Queens, early yesterday afternoon from Boston. Asked to comment on her daughter's marriage, she said, "I am not making any statements."

Earlier in the day Mrs. Kennedy's father, John F. FitzGerald, former Mayor of Boston, stated that she will go from New York to Hot Springs, Va., for a "much needed rest." Mrs. Kennedy yesterday left the New England Baptist Hospital in Boston, where she had been confined for two weeks for a routine physical check-up.

The bride, who is one of nine children, served as official hostess for her father for several weeks when he was Ambassador to Great Britain.

The former Miss Kennedy was graduated from the Convent of the Sacred Heart in Noroton, Conn., attended a convent near Paris and later studied art and decoration here. She was introduced to society on April 7, 1938, in London at a dinner and reception given by her parents.

LONDON, May 6 (Reuter)—The reception after the marriage of Lord Hartington and Miss Kennedy was held at the home of Lady Hambleden on Eaton Square, because the Duke of Devonshire's town house has been blitzed.

May 7, 1944

Lord Hartington and his bride, the former Kathleen Kennedy, after their marriage in London yesterday. In the background is the bride's brother, Lieut. Joseph Kennedy Jr.

THE KENNEDYS: A NEW YORK TIMES PROFILE

WASHINGTON, June 11 (U.P.)—The Navy and Marine Corps Medal has been awarded to Lieut. John F. Kennedy, son of Joseph P. Kennedy ,former United States Ambassador to Great Britain, for "extremely heroic conduct" when his PT boat was cut in two and sunk by a Japanese destroyer, the Navy said tonight.

Lieutenant Kennedy, 27, a native of Brookline, Mass., was a lieutenant (j. g.) at the time of the action for which he was cited.

He was skipper of a PT boat in the Solomon Islands area in August, 1943. A group of the motor torpedo boats were out on patrol on the night of Aug. 1 near Kolombangara Island, which the Japanese were trying desperately to supply.

It was a dark night. Lieutenant Kennedy looked up to see a dark shape looming up on his starboard bow about 250 yards away. He turned to fire a "fish" into the vessel and the ship bore down on the PT at about 40 knots. It was a Japanese destroyer which rammed the midget vessel about ten seconds after it was sighted. The small PT boat was cut in two, scattering its crew in the water. Then followed hours in the shark-infested seas when Lieutenant Kennedy swam about rescuing his crew members. They finally got to a tiny unoccupied island and from there to a slightly larger island and were discovered by natives a week later. Another PT boat from their base made a daring sortie to pick up the eleven surviving members of the thirteen-man crew.

The Kennedy citation reads as follows:

"For extremely heroic conduct as commanding officer of Motor Torpedo Boat 109 following the collision and sinking of that vessel in the Pacific war area on Aug. 1-2. Unmindful of personal danger, Lieutenant Kennedy unhesitatingly braved the difficulties and hazards of darkness to direct rescue operations, swimming many hours to secure aid and food after he had succeeded in getting his crew ashore. His outstanding courage, endurance and leadership contributed to the saving of several lives and were in keeping with the highest traditions of the United States Naval Service."

June 12, 1944

Lieut. Kennedy Cited as Hero by the Navy For Saving Men of PT Crew in Solomons

---

SON OF J. P. KENNEDY KILLED IN ACTION

WASHINGTON, Aug. 14—Lieut. Joseph Patrick Kennedy Jr., 29-year-old son of the former United States Ambassador to England, was lost last Saturday, the Navy said today, while piloting a Navy plane on a special mission in the European theatre.

After Mr. and Mrs. Kennedy had been notified at their Hyannisport, Mass., home that the oldest of their nine children had been killed, the Navy confirmed the news of the accident. The Kennedy family was informed that Lieutenant Kennedy had been killed, but the Navy's announcement stated merely that he was missing as the result of an explosion during an operational flight in the European theatre on Aug. 12. Navy regulations provide that unless there is actual proof of death, a victim

is listed as missing for twelve months before he is presumed dead.

Details Not Made Public

Details of the operation in which Lieutenant Kennedy and Lieut. Willford J. Willy, 35, of Newark, N. J., were lost, were not available for security reasons. It was learned, however, that Lieut. Kennedy had an opportunity to come to the United States some time ago when all of his crew were sent back, but he asked to be allowed to stay on in order to continue the type of work to which he was assigned.

Joseph P. Kennedy Jr. was born July 25, 1915, at Natasket Beach, Hull, Mass. He attended Choate School, then graduated cum laude from Harvard in 1938. He played football at Harvard.

In 1938 and 1939 he served as private secretary in the American Embassies at London and Paris,

then returned to the United States in 1939 and entered the Harvard Law School.

While young Kennedy along with a peace group of Harvard students did not approve of United States entry into the war, and said so in a public speech he made in Boston in January, 1941, he became a cadet in the Naval Aviation Reserve on Oct. 15, 1941. He had his flight training in Jacksonville, and was commissioned as an ensign in April, 1942. After eight months of duty with a transition training squadron, he joined a patrol squadron on Jan. 10, 1943. He was promoted to lieutenant (j. g.) on May 1, 1943; was transferred to a bombing squadron in July of 1943, and became a full lieutenant on July 1, 1944.

August 15, 1944

Kennedy's Son-in-Law Killed While Fighting With British in France

LONDON, Sept. 18 (AP)—The Marquess of Hartington, husband of the former Kathleen Kennedy, daughter of former United States Ambassador Joseph P. Kennedy, was killed in action in France Sept. 10.

They were married May 6.

The Marquess was heir to the Duchy of Devonshire and a captain of the Coldstream Guards. He was 26 years of age.

The War Office informed the

Duke today of his son's death, but no detail was available.

The Marchioness arrived in New York on Aug. 16, two days after Mr. and Mrs. Kennedy had been informed by the Navy Department of the death of their son, Lieut. Joseph P. Kennedy Jr., 27.

He had been listed as missing on Aug. 12 after an explosion during an operational flight in the European theatre.

Lieutenant Kennedy was one of

the witnesses at the marriage of his sister.

Mr. and Mrs. Kennedy have seven other children, including Lieut. John Kennedy, who returned to this country recently after winning decorations as the commander of a PT boat in the Pacific theatre. John was listed as missing for ten days before his parents received word he was alive and well.

September 19, 1944

LT. KENNEDY HONORED

Navy Cross Awarded to Dead Flier Posthumously in Boston

BOSTON, Mass., June 27—The Navy Cross, awarded posthumously to Lieut. Joseph Patrick Kennedy Jr., was presented today to his mother, Mrs. Rose Fitzgerald Kennedy of Hyannisport, Mass., by Rear Admiral Felix Gygax, commandant of the First Naval District.

The simple ceremony was witnessed by only immediate members of the family, including the aviator's father, Joseph P. Kennedy, former Ambassador to Great Britain, and four of the Kennedy children.

Lieutenant Kennedy was reported missing in the European theatre of operations on Aug. 12, 1944, while on a secret and hazardous flight for which he volunteered. The official citation accompanying the Navy's highest decoration stated he "willingly risked his life in the supreme measure of service" as pilot of a Liberator bomber.

A new destroyer now under construction at the Quincy, Mass., shipyard of the Bethlehem Steel Company, has been named for Lieutenant Kennedy.

June 28, 1945

YOUNG KENNEDY A SEAMAN

Ex-Envoy's Son Is on Destroyer Named for His Brother

BOSTON, April 11—Robert Kennedy, seaman, second class, volunteered for duty on the destroyer Joseph P. Kennedy Jr., it was revealed today as his father, the former Ambassador to Great Britain, visited the ship for the first time since it was launched last July.

Kennedy, the seaman, escorted his father on a tour of the 2,200-ton vessel, which was named in honor of his brother, a Navy flier who was killed in 1944 when a pilotless, radio-controlled plane exploded in mid-air during a special mission. Robert was a Navy V-12 student at Harvard.

April 12, 1946

SEEKS SEAT IN CONGRESS

J. E. Kennedy, Ex-Envoy's Son, Is Massachusetts Candidate

BOSTON, April 22—John E. Kennedy, former Navy officer and second son of former Ambassador Joseph P. Kennedy, formally announced tonight his candidacy for the Democratic nomination for United States Representative from the Eleventh Massachusetts District. The district is now represented by Maj. James M. Curley, who will not seek re-election.

Mr. Kennedy, who will be 29 next month, declared that "the temper of the times imposes an obligation upon every thinking citizen to work diligently in peace, as we served tirelessly in war."

He was graduated from Harvard with honors in 1940 and served as a PT boat commander in the South Pacific during the war. Unmarried, he lives with his grandfather, former Mayor John F. Fitzgerald, who represented the same district in Congress fifty years ago.

April 23, 1946

SEEKING TO REPLACE MAYOR CURLEY IN HOUSE

Kennedy Makes Political Bow

BOSTON, June 18—The Massachusetts primary produced few surprises today with a light vote and the favored candidates running about as expected.

Gov. Maurice J. Tobin won the Democratic nomination for Governor handily over Francis D. Harrigan, Boston lawyer. The Governor carried Boston by a 2-to-1 margin. He will oppose Lieut. Gov. Robert F. Bardford in the November election.

John F. Kennedy, son of Joseph P. Kennedy, former Ambassador to Great Britain, making his political debut, ran well ahead of nine rivals for the Democratic nomination in the Eleventh Congressional District, currently represented by Mayor James M. Curley. Nomination in the district is equivalent to election because the Republicans do not seriously contest the Democratic nominee.

Arthur W. Coolidge of Reading, State Senate president, won in the Republican primary for Lieutenant Governor and Paul A Dever of Cambridge was nominated as the Democratic candidate.

The top place on both tickets was occupied by Senator David I. Walsh, Democrat, and former Senator Henry Cabot Lodge Jr., Republican. Both were unopposed.

It appeared that only about 30 per cent of the registered voters participated in the first June primary held in the State. The weather was rainy today.

June 19, 1946

John F. Kennedy, war veteran and son of Joseph P. Kennedy, former Ambassador to England, voting in the Massachusetts primary elections, in which he is running as a Democratic candidate for Congress in the Eleventh District, the seat now held by Boston's chief executive. With him is his grandmother, Mrs. John F. Fitzgerald.

POST FOR EUNICE KENNEDY

Daughter of Ex-Envoy Will Aid Clark on Juveniles

WASHINGTON, Jan. 16—Miss Eunice Kennedy, daughter of former Ambassador Joseph P. Kennedy, has been appointed executive secretary for the Activities of the Department of Justice in the field of juvenile delinquency, Attorney General Tom C. Clark announced today.

He said that she would act as liaison officer to the National Conference on the Juvenile Problem, the interested Federal and State agencies and private organizations.

A graduate of Stamford University, Miss Kennedy was employed during the war in the Special War Problems Division of the State Department, which dealt with American prisoners of war in Germany.

January 17, 1947

Congressman J. F. Kennedy III

BOSTON, Oct. 17 (AP)—Representative John F. Kennedy, Democrat, of Massachusetts, was admitted to the New England Baptist Hospital last night for treatment of a malarial attack a few hours after he had debarked from the liner Queen Elizabeth in New York. The youthful Congressman was brought to Boston in a chartered plane. Mr. Kennedy was confined to the ship's hospital during the trip from England.

October 18, 1947

Air Crash Kills Lady Hartington

PARIS, Friday, May 14—French gendarmes said early today that Lady Kathleen Hartington had been killed in a plane crash near St. Bauzile in the Rhône River valley north of Marseille. She was the daughter of Joseph P. Kennedy, former United States Ambassador to Britain.

The gendarmerie at Privas, near St. Bauzile, said Lady Hartington, identified from her United States passport, was one of four persons whose bodies had been found in the wreckage.

The gendarmes said bad weather was hampering night searches and clearing weather later in the morning might bring the discovery of more bodies.

The plane was an unidentified British aircraft that had crashed in a storm last night.

Informed in Paris of the report of the death of his daughter, Mr. Kennedy declined any comment, pending definite confirmation. He said he was shocked.

Reached again a short time later, Mr. Kennedy said he intended to rush by air to Lyon, up the Rhone River from the scene of the crash, and then hurry to Privas as quickly as possible.

He said he would not give up hope until the last possible moment that there might be some mistake in the identification of the dead woman, even though gendarmes said his daughter's passport was found at the crash.

The gendarmerie at Privas said rescue parties would require considerable time to get back through the mountains.

Lady Hartington was 28 years old, the widow of the English Marquess of Hartington.

She met the Marquess in court circles in 1938 while her father was Ambassador to the Court of St. James. They were married at the Chelsea register office May 6, 1944. She was then 24 and he was 26.

The Marquess, heir of the Duke of Devonshire, shortly before had been defeated as a Government candidate for the House of Commons. A Conservative, he ran with the endorsement of former Prime Minister Churchill.

Lord Hartington, a captain of the Coldstream Guards in World War II, was killed in action in France Sept. 10, 1944.

Lady Hartington at the time of her marriage had been serving for several months as a resident helper at a Red Cross club.

The Marchioness' brother, Joseph P. Kennedy Jr., 27, was killed in an operational flight over Europe less than a month before her husband.

The Navy Department listed him as missing after an explosion Aug. 12 and notified his parents of his death two days later.

In October, 1946, London burglars robbed the Marchioness of $40,000 in jewelry. Subsequently she appealed to the burglars through the newspapers to return two mementoes—her husband's cufflinks and her brother's pilot wings.

French airport authorities at Orly said they believed the plane might be a private Skyways aircraft, registration mark G-Ajou, which had left Le Bourget Field, Paris, yesterday for Cannes on the French Riviera. They said they had no confirmation of this.

May 14, 1948

WARNING TO HITLER ON U. S. DISCLOSED

Notes by Washington Envoy Found in Captured Papers— London Advice Differed

By HAROLD B. HINTON

WASHINGTON, July 16—Adolf Hitler was receiving conflicting estimates, through the German Foreign Office, of opinion and reactions in the United States during the crucial months leading up to the invasion of Czechoslovakia in 1939, it was revealed in a publication of captured German state papers made public today by the State Department.

Dr. Hans Dieckhoff, his Ambassador in Washington, was sending long and frequent reports warning Hitler and the Foreign Ministry against overestimating isolationist sentiment in the United States. He was firm in his predictions that the United States would be on the side of Great Britain in the event German policy forced war in Europe.

As early as March 22, 1938, Ambassador Dieckhoff expressed the fear that "I am perhaps becoming a bore in Berlin," in a letter to Baron Ernst von Weizsaecker, then Under Secretary in the Foreign Office. The captured original bears a notation in the latter's handwriting, as follows: "Certainly not."

During this same epoch, however, Hitler's Ambassador in London, Dr. Herbert von Dirksen, was sending reports throwing doubt on the question of United States help for Great Britain in war, and indicating reservoirs of good-will for Germany within the United States. Some of these ideas he obtained, he wrote the Foreign Ministry, in interviews with Joseph P. Kennedy, then United States Ambassador in London.

The German papers published today are the result of joint Anglo-American enterprise, it was stated in the introduction to them. The French Government has participated since 1947.

Units of the United States First Army discovered 300 tons of the records in the Harz Mountains in April, 1945. Others were found in Thuringia.

"The archives of the German Foreign Ministry came into Anglo-American custody partly as a result of planning, partly by accident, but chiefly through the incomplete execution of orders to destroy the most important portions," it was said.

Ambassador Dieckhoff sent a series of messages during 1938 pointing out the harm being done to German-American relations by the activities of the German-American Bund, under the leadership of Fritz Kuhn. His warnings seem to have been largely instrumental in the ultimate complete disavowal of Kuhn and the bund by the German Government.

His messages paint Kuhn as a headstrong fanatic who could not, or would not, understand the futility and bad psychology of trying to impose on any considerable number of German-Americans the uniforms, ritual and discipline of the National Socialist party in Germany. He was contemptuous of the theory (not directly attributed to Kuhn) that as many as 20,000 determined Nazis could be recruited in the United States to serve as "assault troops" at the "crucial moment."

"With such conspiratorial child's play," he wrote to Berlin, "something may, perhaps, be accomplished now and then in the Balkans or in other parts of the world, but most certainly not in the United States. The membership roll of this assault troop would be in the hands of the American police shortly after it was founded; the investigation of the German Bund just terminated by the Department of Justice demonstrates how such things are done here by undercover men.

"Members of the troop would be immediately arrested at the crucial moment, and even if they could go into action here and there, it would all come to naught. I know that scarcely anyone sincerely believes in anything so nonsensical, but I repeat that such ideas are not merely childish, they are dangerous.

"They could only tend to arouse justifiable distrust throughout the American Government, from which they could, of course, not remain hidden."

Dr. Dieckhoff attributed the resignation of Jacob Gould Schurman, former United States Ambassador to Germany, as vice president of the Carl Schurz Memorial Foundation to the growing anti-German sentiment fanned by the antics of the bund.

Ambassador von Dirksen, on the other hand, seemed to be determined to draw all possible favorable inferences from his talks in London with Ambassador Kennedy. The first of these on which he reported took place early in June, just before Mr. Kennedy was to return to Washington for a visit.

He reported that Mr. Kennedy told him the United States would have to establish friendly relations with Germany, and that he was going to Washington to inform President Roosevelt on European conditions.

"Kennedy seemed to be strongly convinced of the strength of his position," the report continued. "He said that neither Secretary of State Hull nor any of the other Cabinet members or influential persons could jeopardize his position. The only one whom he had to recognize as superior was President Roosevelt."

He reported Mr. Kennedy as saying that President Roosevelt was not anti-German, but that no one coming from Europe ever reported to the President anything friendly "regarding present-day Germany." Mr. Kennedy is alleged to have said that most of Mr. Roosevelt's trusted informants were Jews "and did not dare say anything good about Germany."

"The report by the well-known flier, Colonel Lindbergh, who had spoken very favorably of Germany, made a strong impression upon Ambassador Kennedy, as I know from an earlier conversation with him," Ambassador von Dirksen continued. "Lindbergh and his wife spoke to me in the same manner regarding their impressions of Germany and of German aviation when I became acquainted with them recently at a court ball in Buckingham Palace."

After Mr. Kennedy returned to London, the German Ambassador had another talk with him, which he reported on July 20. He said that Mr. Kennedy had found many changes in the political climate at home.

"The average American blamed Germany for the general insecurity which prevailed in the world and which prevented economic recovery," he reported Mr. Kennedy as telling him. "Germany was accused of wanting to provoke war. People were not clear about the intentions of the German Government, and all this resulted in increased hostility toward Germany, which, of course, was also being fomented for a great many other reasons."

"From all the statements by the American Ambassador one fact became very obvious," he summed up. "The United States regards itself as the protector and helper of England, which, in turn, however, has to pay for this help with subservience and obedience."

The captured papers have been screened by a board of editors-in-chief, of which the United States members are Raymond James Sontag and E. Malcolm Carroll.

United States members of the board of editors of the volume issued today are James Stuart Beddie, Fritz Epstein, Paul Sweet, John Huizenga, Joachim Remak, Otto Pflanze and Jean Brownell Dulaney.

July 17, 1949

VATICAN TITLE GIVEN TO MRS. J. P. KENNEDY

The title of Papal Countess was conferred yesterday on Mrs. Joseph P. Kennedy, wife of the former Ambassador to the Court of St. James, in recognition of her "exemplary motherhood and many charitable works."

A scroll signed by the Secretary of State of the Vatican was presented to Mrs. Kennedy by Cardinal Spellman, on behalf of Pope Pius XII, in a brief ceremony at the Lieut. Joseph P. Kennedy Jr. Home for Children, 1770 Stillwell Avenue, the Bronx. The home was opened last year with a grant of $2,500,000 from the foundation named for the Kennedys' son.

Cardinal Spellman described the honor as an "extraordinarily high" one. He said that, to his knowledge, only two other American women hold the title.

"I am overwhelmed with emotion and happiness," Mrs. Kennedy said. "My first emotion is to feel that I am not worthy of something like this."

Mrs. Kennedy, who was accompanied by her husband and a daughter, Miss Patricia Kennedy, said that children are the chief interest of her husband and herself and "we feel that this particular group has been neglected." She is the mother of nine children, seven of whom are still living.

The Bronx home, set up to care for neglected and dependent children of all faiths between the ages of 6 and 18, is one of two named for Lieutenant Kennedy, who was killed in action as a Navy flyer over the English Channel in 1944. The other is located in Hanover, Mass.

The group inspected the home's nearly-completed St. Rose Chapel, named for Mrs. Kennedy's patron saint. Cardinal Spellman said he would dedicate it on his return from a Christmas visit to the troops in Korea. The home, caring for 300 children, is one of the forty-four child-caring institutions run by the New York Catholic Charities.

December 14, 1951

THE KENNEDYS: A NEW YORK TIMES PROFILE

BOSTON, Nov. 5—Republican jubilation over the sweep by Gen. Dwight D. Eisenhower of New England's forty electoral votes was tempered today by the confirmation of defeat for one of the men chiefly responsible for his nomination, Senator Henry Cabot Lodge Jr. of Massachusetts.

Mr. Lodge started the Eisenhower bandwagon rolling last March in New England, during the General's duty-enforced absence in Europe. He was scheduled finally to introduce General Eisenhower in person to a capacity audience of the region's voters on the eve of Election Day in Boston Garden. A prolonged ovation, cutting into television and radio time, prevented this.

At 7 A. M. today, Mr. Lodge conceded victory, by a plurality of 68,753, to Representative John F. Kennedy, 35 years old, of Boston, who has had three terms in Congress.

Associates of Mr. Lodge said he had been a "casualty" of the campaign. They acknowledged Mr. Kennedy was very popular but asserted that Mr. Lodge had been cut severely by disgruntled followers of Senator Robert A. Taft of Ohio, the unsuccessful candidate for the nomination for the Presidency.

Herter Tops Dever in Upset

General Eisenhower's plurality of 206,879 in Massachusetts, on the other hand, helped the Republicans to score an upset of their own, at the state level. This was the victory of Representative Christian A. Herter over Gov. Paul A. Dever, who had been the keynote speaker at the Democratic National Convention. Mr. Dever was seeking a third term.

Complete returns from the 1,967 precincts in Massachusetts were:

PRESIDENT

Eisenhower	1,293,800
Stevenson	1,086,921

UNITED STATES SENATOR

Kennedy	1,207,105
Lodge	1,138,352

November 6, 1952

LODGE A 'CASUALTY' IN MASSACHUSETTS

Associates Assert Opposition of Taft Backers Was Factor in Defeat by Kennedy

By JOHN H. FENTON

Representative John F. Kennedy, Democrat, as his victory over Senator Henry Cabot Lodge Jr. was assured in Massachusetts.

Senator Kennedy 'Much Better'

WASHINGTON, July 15 (AP)— Senator John F. Kennedy, Democrat of Massachusetts, was reported today to be recovering at George Washington University Hospital from malaria. A war-contracted malady recurred and he entered the hospital yesterday. Senator Kennedy's aides said he was "much better" today and expected to go to his Cape Cod home over the week-end. They said he would return to his office early next week.

July 16, 1953

AIDE TO M'CARTHY RESIGNS

Kennedy, Brother of Senator, to Enter Private Law Practice

WASHINGTON, July 31 (UP)— Robert F. Kennedy, brother of Senator John F. Kennedy, Democrat of Massachusetts, resigned tonight as assistant counsel of Senator Joseph R. McCarthy's Senate Permanent Subcommittee on Investigations.

Mr. Kennedy said he was leaving to "enter the private practice of law at an early date." Senator McCarthy accepted in a letter expressing "very much regret."

He wrote the 27-year-old attorney, a son of the former Ambassador to England, Joseph P. Kennedy, that the subcommittee's members all felt Mr. Kennedy was "a great credit to the committee and did a tremendous job."

The Kennedy resignation was the latest of several shifts in the staffs of Senator McCarthy's subcommittee and also the Government Operations Committee, which the Wisconsin Republican also heads.

August 1, 1953

Notables Attend Senator's Wedding

NEWPORT, R. I., Sept. 12— A crowd of 3,000 persons broke through police lines and nearly crushed the bride, Miss Jacqueline Lee Bouvier, when she arrived for her marriage here this morning to United States Senator John Fitzgerald Kennedy of Massachusetts. The throng had milled around St. Mary's Roman Catholic Church for more than an hour before the guests began to arrive. The ceremony far surpassed the Astor-French wedding of 1934 in public interest. The crowd pressed forward again as the couple left the church and posed briefly for photographers, Senator Kennedy with a grin on his face and the bride appearing a little startled. The church was filled with some 800 guests, including most of the Newport summer colony, and many political notables. Gov. Dennis E. Roberts of Rhode Island received a big hand from the crowd as he arrived shortly after United States Senator Leverett Saltonstall of Massachusetts, who was not recognized. The bridegroom's parents also received an ovation as they walked from their car to the church.

Other United States Senators present were Theodore Francis Green of Rhode Island, Frederick G. Payne of Maine and William A. Purtell of Connecticut. Also attending were many Representatives from near-by states, including Eugene J. Keogh of New York.

The bride is the daughter of Mrs. Hugh D. Auchincloss of Hammersmith Farm, Newport, and Merrywood, McLean Va., and John V. Bouvier 3d of New York. Senator Kennedy is the son of Joseph P. Kennedy, former Ambassador to the Court of St. James, and Mrs. Kennedy of Hyannisport, Mass., and Palm Beach, Fla.

The Most Rev. Richard J. Cushing, Archbishop of the Archdiocese of Boston, performed the ceremony and was the celebrant of the nuptial mass. He also read a special blessing from the Pope.

In the Sanctuary were also Bishop Christopher J. Weldon of Springfield, Mass.; the Very Rev. John J. Cavanaugh, former president of the University of Notre Dame, and the Rev. James Keller of New York, head of the Christophers.

Assisting Archbishop Cushing at the mass were the Msgr. Francis S. Rossiter, Boston Archdiocesan master of ceremonies; the Rev. Walter Leo Flynn, the pastor; the Rev. Edmund P. Boland and the Rev. Stephen K. Callaghan of St. Mary's.

Luigi Vena of Boston was tenor soloist and sang "Ave Maria," "Panis Angelicus" and "Jesu Amor Mi" during the ceremony.

More than 1,200 persons attended the reception at Hammersmith Farms, the 300-acre estate of the bride's mother and stepfather overlooking Narragansett Bay.

So great was the traffic that cars were backed up nearly half a mile and it took almost two hours for the guests to pass through the reception line to greet the couple. Then they passed to the terrace where tables had been set up both under a huge canopy and under parasols on the lawns.

Escorted at the ceremony by Mr. Auchincloss because of the illness of her father, the bride wore a gown of ivory silk taffeta, made with a fitted bodice embellished with interwoven bands of tucking, finished with a portrait neckline, and a bouffant skirt. She wore an heirloom veil of rosepoint lace that had been worn by her grandmother. The veil was draped from a tiara of lace and orange blossoms and extended in a long train. She carried a bouquet of pink and white spray orchids and gardenias.

The bride was preceded up the aisle by her matron of honor, her sister, Mrs. Michael T. Canfield of New York, and maid of honor, Miss Nina G. Auchincloss of Newport and McLean, and the other bridal attendants. They were Mrs. Robert F. Kennedy of Hyannisport,

Senator John F. Kennedy and his bride at reception after their marriage at Newport

THE KENNEDYS: A NEW YORK TIMES PROFILE

Mrs. Charles L. Bartlett and Mrs. Josiah Spaulding of Washington, Mrs. Bowdoin Travers of Oyster Bay, L. I., and the Misses Nancy L. Tuckerman of New York, Jean Kennedy of Palm Beach, Sylvia Whitehouse of Newport and Shirley Oakes of London.

All of the bridal attendants were attired alike in gowns of pink taffeta, made with fitted bodices, cap sleeves and long bouffant skirts. The gowns of the matron and maid of honor were embellished with cummerbunds of pink silk faille terminating in long streamers, and they wore also Tudor caps of matching faille. The gowns of the other bridal attendants had similar cummerbunds of red silk faille and they wore also matching Tudor caps.

Also in the bridal procession were a flower girl, Janet Jennings Auchincloss, who wore a miniature replica of the gowns worn by the other bridal attendants, embellished with a sash of red silk faille; and a page, James Lee Auchincloss, who was attired in short black velvet trousers and a white silk shirt embellished with a lace jabot and cuffs.

Robert F. Kennedy was best man for his brother. The ushers, who led the party up the aisle, were United States Senator George A. Smathers of Florida, Charles L. Bartlett of Washington, Hugh D. Auchincloss Jr. and Thomas G. Auchincloss of Newport, K. Lemoyne Billings of Baltimore, Torbert MacDonald of Malden, Mass.; Paul B. Fay Jr. of San Francisco, R. Sargent Shriver Jr. of Chicago, James Reed of Longmeadow, Mass.; Benjamin Smith 2d of Gloucester, Mass.; Joseph Gargan of Lowell, Mass.; Edward Kennedy of Hyannisport, Charles F. Spalding of Greenwich, Conn., and Mr. Canfield of New York.

The bride, who was graduated from Miss Porter's School in Farmington, Conn., attended Vassar College and the Sorbonne in Paris. She was graduated in 1951 from George Washington University. Until recently, she did the Inquiring Photographer column for The Washington Times-Herald.

Mrs. Kennedy is a granddaughter of James T. Lee of New York, the late Mrs. Lee, and the late Mr. and Mrs. John Vernou Bouvier Jr. of New York.

Senator Kennedy was graduated in 1940 from Harvard College, where he was a member of Hasty Pudding-Institute of 1770 and the Spee Club. During World War II, he commanded a PT boat in the South Pacific.

He was elected to the House of Representatives in 1946 and reelected to the Eighty-first and Eighty-second Congresses. In 1952, he was elected to the Senate on the Democratic ticket, defeating Henry Cabot Lodge Jr., now United States delegate to the United Nations.

The bridegroom is a grandson of the late John F. Fitzgerald, former Mayor of Boston; the late Mrs. Fitzgerald, the late Patrick J. Kennedy, who was a former Massachusetts State Senator, and the late Mrs. Kennedy.

Among the invited guests were the Peruvian Ambassador and Señora de Berckemeyer, Mr. and Mrs. Bernard F. Gimbel, Mr. and Mrs. George B. St. George, Mr. and Mrs. Arthur Krock and Mr. and Mrs. Alfred G. Vanderbilt.

September 13, 1953

The marriage of Miss Patricia Kennedy to Peter Lawford of Los Angeles, British-born film actor, took place yesterday afternoon in the Roman Catholic Church of St. Thomas More.

The bride is a daughter of Joseph P. Kennedy, former United States Ambassador to the Court of St. James, and Mrs. Kennedy of Hyannisport, Mass., and Palm Beach, Fla. The bridegroom is the son of Lady Lawford of London and the late Lieut. Gen. Sir Sydney Lawford.

Several notables from the film world attended the ceremony. A crowd of 3,000 persons, mostly women, gathered behind police barricades in Eighty-ninth Street between Park and Madison Avenues to watch the wedding party arrive and depart. The throng broke through the police lines as the couple emerged from the church and delayed the departure of their car.

The ceremony was performed by the Rev. John J. Cavanaugh, former president of the University of Notre Dame. A reception was given in the Terrace Room of the Plaza for members of the immediate families and a few close friends.

Escorted by her father, the bride wore a gown of white satin made with a fitted bodice finished with a portrait neckline, three-quarter-length sleeves and a draped skirt terminating in a train. Her veil of tulle was attached to a cap of woven bands of satin, and she carried a bouquet of white orchids.

Miss Jean Kennedy, sister of the bride, was the only bridal attendant. She wore a bouffant gown of pink and blue hydrangea printed silk taffeta, a picture hat of hyacinth blue Milan trimmed

with matching velvet ribbon, and carried a Victorian bouquet of pink, blue and lavender blossoms.

J. Robert Neal Jr. of Houston, Tex., was best man. The ushers were United States Senator John F. Kennedy and Robert F. Kennedy of Washington and Edward M. Kennedy of Boston, brothers of the bride; Peter Sabiston of Los Angeles, and Lemoyne Billings of Baltimore.

After a wedding trip to Hawaii, the couple will make their home in California.

The bride attended the Convent of the Sacred Heart in Roehampton, England, and the Convent of the Sacred Heart, Maplehurst, this city. She was graduated from Rosemont (Pa.) College.

She is a granddaughter of the late John F. Fitzgerald, onetime Mayor of Boston and United States Representative from Massachusetts, and of the late Patrick Kennedy, who was a Massachusetts State Senator.

Mrs. Lawford is a sister also of Miss Rosemary Kennedy, Mrs. Sargent Shriver and the late Kathleen Lady Hartington. Another brother, Lieut. Joseph P. Kennedy Jr., was killed during World War II while serving with the Navy, and received posthumously the Navy Cross.

The bridegroom, who first appeared on the English stage at the age of 7, has starred in many motion pictures.

April 25, 1954

PATRICIA KENNEDY MARRIED TO ACTOR

Daughter of Former Envoy Is Bride of Peter Lawford in St. Thomas More's

Mr. and Mrs. Peter Lawford, whose marriage took place in the Roman Catholic Church of St. Thomas More yesterday.

KENNEDY SAYS U. S. LAGS

Senator Finds No Affirmative, Long-Range Policies

PRINCETON, N. J., May 11—United States prestige and control of world events have fallen to "a dangerous low," Senator John F. Kennedy, Democrat of Massachusetts, charged tonight in a speech at Princeton University.

"The initiative has fallen from our grasp in our failure to develop affirmative, long-range policies," he declared.

"An essential element in Western policy must be the granting of independence to all areas which are prepared for self-government and which are now held under Western colonial domination.

"By announcing a decrease in the strength of our conventional forces for resistance in so-called brush fire wars while threatening atomic retaliation only against very substantial overt acts which threaten our freedom, we in effect invited, rather than deterred, expansion by the Communists in areas such as Indo-China."

May 12, 1954

COHN THREATENS TO 'GET' SENATOR FOR GIBE AT SCHINE

Assails Jackson in Exchange With Kennedy, Whom He Challenges to Fight

By W. H. LAWRENCE

WASHINGTON, June 11—Roy M. Cohn angrily threatened tonight to "get" a Democratic Senator because of his sharp cross-examination of Senator Joseph R. McCarthy in the Army-McCarthy hearings.

Mr. Cohn, the chief counsel for the Permanent Subcommittee on Investigations, made his threat against Senator Henry M. Jackson of Washington in a bitter post-adjournment exchange with Robert F. Kennedy, counsel for the three Democratic members of the subcommittee.

Mr. Kennedy told reporters that Mr. Cohn had threatened to bring out evidence that Senator Jackson had "written something favorably inclined toward Communists."

Senator Jackson served formal public notice that he would not be intimidated by any threats of "retaliatory action" but would "continue to do everything in my power to get all the facts in order to reach a fair and honest decision as to the merits in this controversy."

Says It Is Not First Threat

The Washington Democrat said it was not the first threat Mr. Cohn had made against Senators since the hearings began. The main charges at issue are that Mr. Cohn and Senator McCarthy used improper means to seek special treatment for Pvt. G. David Schine, who was an unpaid subcommittee consultant until he was drafted; they countercharged that the private was an Army "hostage."

[Mr. Cohn denied in New York Friday night that he had threatened to "get" Senator Jackson. He declared that Mr. Kennedy "is indulging in a long-standing personal hatred for me."]

The Cohn-Kennedy row did not occur until today's hearings had adjourned for the week-end, but it overshadowed in importance the day-long cross examination of Senator McCarthy, who branded as "false" testimony by Army witnesses that he repeatedly had sought a New York assignment for Private Schine.

While it was understood no final decision had been reached, it was said that the McCarthy camp was considering the possibility of introducing in evidence Monday a letter. It allegedly links Senator Jackson to the Federal job application in 1945 of a person who later figured in a Communist investigation conducted by the Senate Internal Security subcommittee. The letter, purportedly by Senator Jackson, recommended the unidentified individual for employment.

The letter evidently was the basis for Mr. Cohn's threat to Mr. Kennedy, as the young Boston lawyer repeated it to newsmen.

Mr. Cohn would not concede that he had directly linked his threat to "get" Senator Jackson to anything dealing with communism. He did not deny, however, that he had quarreled with Mr. Kennedy. Some of the angry words had been overheard behind the big committee table at the close of the day's session.

"Don't you make any warnings to us about Democratic Senators," Mr. Kennedy said.

"I'll make any warnings to you that I want to—any time, anywhere," replied Mr. Cohn. "Do you want to fight right here?"

The display came after Senator Jackson, in cross-examining Senator McCarthy had ridiculed and poked fun at a Schine plan to sell democracy on a global basis by formation of a "Deminform."

Mr. Schine's plan for psychological warfare had been turned down by the State Department before he joined the McCarthy subcommittee primarily to direct a major investigation of the "Voice of America" and other governmental information programs.

The feud between Mr. Cohn and Mr. Kennedy is of long standing. But the young Democratic counsel, a son of Joseph P. Kennedy, former Ambassador to Great Britain, and a brother of Senator John F. Kennedy of Massachusetts, has remained on very friendly terms with Senator McCarthy himself. It is Mr. Kennedy's job in this inquiry to type out pertinent questions for the Democratic Senators, and it was his role in this connection that served to spark the explosion today.

Mr. Cohn agreed that he had protested to Mr. Kennedy that it was unfair for him to serve in the inquiry because of his "hatred for one of the principals," an apparent reference to himself.

Mr. Kennedy said that he had replied that if he had "a dislike" for anyone in the case, "I was certain that it was justified."

He also said he told Mr. Cohn to carry his own threats to Senator Jackson in person, and added that it was "a great state of affairs when a Senate committee employe could start threatening the Senators."

June 12, 1954

Senator Kennedy Has Surgery

Senator John F. Kennedy, Democrat of Massachusetts, underwent a spinal operations yesterday at the Hospital for Special Surgery, 321 East Forty-second Street, where his condition was reported as "good."

October 22, 1954

KENNEDY HAS SURGERY

Senator Returns to Hospital for Removal of Metal Plate

Senator John F. Kennedy, Democrat of Massachusetts, was "progressing normally" yesterday at the Hospital for Special Surgery.

He was admitted Feb. 10 for the removal of a metal plate that was slowing recovery from an operation last October resulting from a World War II injury to his spine.

It was expected that Senator Kennedy would be able to leave the hospital within a week and take up his duties in Washington before the end of March.

February 17, 1955

$1,178,000 TO CHURCH

Foundation Makes New Grant to Boston Archdiocese

BOSTON, Feb. 9—A grant of $1,178,000 by the Joseph P. Kennedy Jr. Foundation to the Roman Catholic Archdiocese of Boston was announced today by Archbishop Richard J. Cushing.

This brings to $2,609,000 the total given to the Archdiocese by the foundation in memory of a naval flyer killed in World War II. He was the son of the former United States Ambassador to Great Britain and a brother of Senator John F. Kennedy, Democrat of Massachusetts.

Senator Kennedy and two brothers, Edward and Robert, visited the residence of the Archbishop to make the presentation.

Archbishop Cushing said part of the grant would go to the Kennedy Memorial Hospital at Brighton. The project will be named, at the wish of the foundation, the Archbishop Cushing Research Department and will be engaged in a "research program related to mental retardation and physical defects due to brain injuries."

February 10, 1956

Miss Jean Ann Kennedy Married

Wed in Lady Chapel of St. Patrick's to Edward Smith

Miss Jean Ann Kennedy was married to Stephen Edward Smith yesterday morning in the Lady Chapel of St. Patrick's Cathedral.

The bride is a daughter of Joseph P. Kennedy, former United States Ambassador to the Court of St. James, and Mrs. Kennedy of Hyannisport, Mass., and Palm Beach, Fla. Mr. Smith is a son of Mrs. John J. Smith of New York and the late Mr. Smith.

The ceremony was performed by Francis Cardinal Spellman, who also celebrated the nuptial mass and read the papal blessing. A reception for members of the families and a few close friends was held in the Baroque Suite and Crystal Room of the Plaza.

The bride, escorted by her father, wore a gown of champagne-colored slipper satin cut along princess lines, and made with a fitted bodice, a short matching Empire jacket and a full skirt terminating in a train. She wore also a veil of tulle attached to a coronet of orange blossoms, and carried a cascade bouquet of white orchids and stephanotis.

Mrs. R. Sargent Shriver of Chicago, a sister of the bride, was matron of honor and the only attendant. She was attired in a bouffant gown of white organza, a headdress to match, and carried a bouquet of pink roses.

Philip Smith of Manhasset, L. I., was best man for his brother. The ushers were John Smith of New York, another brother of the bridegroom; United States Senator John F. Kennedy of Massachusetts, Robert Kennedy, chief counsel of the Senate Permanent Subcommittee on Investigations, and Edward M. Kennedy of Boston, brothers of the bride; Theodore Donahue of Stamford, Conn., and Lemoyne Billings of Baltimore.

Mr. Smith and his bride will go to Europe for their wedding trip.

The bride attended Sacred Heart convents in this country and in Roehampton, England, while her father was Ambassador there. She was graduated from Manhattanville College of the Sacred Heart. For the last two years, she has been with the Christopher movement.

Mrs. Smith's other sisters are Mrs. Peter Lawford, Miss Rosemary Kennedy and the late Lady Hartington. Another brother, Lieut. Joseph P. Kennedy Jr., U. S. N. R., was killed during World War II.

Mrs. Smith is a granddaughter of the late John F. Fitzgerald, who was Mayor of Boston and a United States Representative from Massachusetts, and of the late Patrick Kennedy, who served as a Massachusetts State Senator.

The bridegroom was graduated in 1944 from the Polytechnic Preparatory Country Day School in Brooklyn, and in 1948 from Georgetown University. He served as a first lieutenant in the Air Force. Mr. Smith is with the transportation firm of Cleary Brothers, Inc., founded in 1870 by his grandfather, the late William E. Cleary.

May 20, 1956

Mr. and Mrs. Stephen Edward Smith, who were married here yesterday in the Lady Chapel of St. Patrick's Cathedral.

Kennedy Nominates Stevenson

Massachusetts Senator Says His Candidate Is 'Man Equal to Our Times'

By DOUGLAS DALES

CHICAGO, Aug. 16 — Today was the day for the "man who" oratory of the Democratic National Convention.

To youthful Senator John F. Kennedy went the honor of placing before the convention the name of the man the delegates later chose for the Presidential nomination—Adlai E. Stevenson. In all, ten persons were nominated.

Mr. Stevenson announced this morning that he had requested the junior Senator from Massachusetts to put his name in nomination. The choice of Senator Kennedy, who has been waging a strong campaign for second place on the ticket, would help assuage the disappointment of his followers if he failed in his bid.

A surprise in the nominating oratory was a speech by Harry S. Truman seconding the nomination of Governor Harriman, whose name was placed before the convention by Gov. Raymond Gary of Oklahoma.

It was the second appearance before the convention of the former President, who threw his support to the New York Governor Saturday. Mr. Truman, not a delegate, addressed an appeal to the convention last night for a stronger civil rights plank.

Mr. Truman, the fourth and last seconder of the Harriman candidacy, told the delegates he had come to Chicago to "express my preference for the man I believe best qualified." And he added:

"I've had a little experience in that line. But I'm also here to tell you that I am a Democrat with a big D."

Truman Expects Unity

Predicting that the delegates would go home united behind the party nominee, he declared:

"If there was ever a time when it was necessary for the Democrats to win an election it is now."

Mr. Stevenson's was the second name to be placed in nomination and Mr. Harriman's the fifth.

The first name to be placed before the convention was that of Senator Warren G. Magnuson of Washington. He is facing a hard fight for re-election against Gov. Arthur B. Langlie, the keynoter at the Republican National Convention in San Francisco next week.

Mr. Magnuson's nomination was made by Senator Henry M. Jackson, the junior Senator from Washington, and sparked the first demonstration of the day.

The Senator withdrew immediately after a seconding speech by Representative Don Magnuson, who is no relation to the nominee. Senator Magnuson said the country needed him as a Democratic Senator "to protect the country's heritage" more than it needed him for President.

A compound of boos and cheers greeted Gov. Marvin Griffin of Georgia as he espoused the doctrine of "constitutional government and states' rights" in a speech nominating Representative James C. Davis of Georgia's Fifth Congressional District.

Called 'The Only Man'

Senator Kennedy described Mr. Stevenson as "the one man and the only man" fully to be entrusted to guard the country against the mounting threats from abroad and to handle what the Senator called the domestic problems of big business concentration, low farm income, inadequate schools and the country's health.

The nominee of the convention must be something more than just a good candidate, a good politician, a good conservative or a good liberal, since he may guide the destinies of not only the country but the free world, the Senator said.

He told the delegates that the Democratic slate would be up against "two tough candidates, one who takes the high road and one who takes the low road." Mr. Stevenson, he contended, is the "man who can best carry our case to the people."

August 17, 1956

Kefauver Nominated for Vice President Defeating Kennedy on the Second Ballot

By W. H. LAWRENCE

CHICAGO, Aug. 17 — Senator Estes Kefauver seized the Democratic Vice-Presidential nomination by an eyelash today.

The Tennessean edged out Senator John F. Kennedy of Massachusetts on the second ballot in an open floor fight to become the running mate of Adlai E. Stevenson of Illinois. Mr. Stevenson was renominated for the Presidency last night.

The Democrats picked two men who fought each other bitterly in the primaries to oppose the Republican slate in November. President Eisenhower and Vice President Richard M. Nixon are expected to be renominated at San Francisco next week.

The Stevenson-Kefauver team shared the spotlight at the final session tonight of the Democratic National Convention with former President Harry S. Truman, who had opposed the selection of both.

Tonight they came to accept their nominations. Mr. Truman came to bid for party unity and to take back some of the harsh things he had said against Mr. Stevenson this week. Besides saying that Mr. Stevenson was "too defeatist to win," Mr. Truman in his private conversations has mispronounced the Tennessean's name as if it were spelled "Cowfever." Tonight he pronounced it correctly.

States Switch Votes

After Mr. Stevenson's speech and the singing of "The Lord's Prayer" the thirty-second convention ended at 10:52 P. M., Central daylight time [11:52 P. M. Eastern daylight time].

The final ballot was as dramatic as any Democratic convention has witnessed.

Senator Kefauver's nomination was made by acclamation upon the motion of Senator Kennedy. When the second roll-call was completed, but before the result had been announced, Senator Kennedy had 648 votes, 38½ votes short of the required majority. He was far ahead of the Tennessee Senator.

Then the states began to wave their standards to switch their votes. The lead seesawed. At that point, Senator Albert Gore of Tennessee, who was running third, withdrew in favor of his colleague and released the delegates pledged to him.

That started a stampede to the 53-year-old Mr. Kefauver. The Senator went over the top on the basis of new votes that Missouri had cast for Senator Hubert H. Humphrey of Minnesota.

The final official tabulation as reported by The Associated Press gave Senator Kefauver 755½ votes and Senator Kennedy 589. This Convention had 1,372 delegates, with 686½ votes comprising a majority.

Earlier figures on the final tally were confusing because of the sudden switches on the Convention floor.

Senator Kefauver's victory was one for the rank-and-file delegates, achieved over the last-ditch opposition of most of the party's old-time professionals. Such party stalwarts as Senator Lyndon B. Johnson of Texas, the Senate majority leader, and Speaker Sam Rayburn of the House of Representatives, also of Texas, had argued in vain against Mr. Stevenson's sudden decision to leave the choice of a running mate to the convention.

The professionals had argued that Mr. Stevenson should follow precedent and indicate at least a preference among candidates available for the No. 2 spot. The professionals argued that failure to do this would lead inevitably to Senator Kefauver's nomination. But Mr. Stevenson, however, wished to contrast the Democrats' procedure with that expected at the Republican convention next week. There, the party leadership has scheduled quick renomination of Vice President Nixon as well as President Eisenhower.

Obviously, Senator Kefauver was the choice of a majority of the convention delegates. Many estimated that his free-wheeling campaigning would strengthen the ticket both in the farm belt and in major industrial areas.

But Southerners, except Florida, were restive. Gov. James P. Coleman of Mississippi said, "This leaves the situation in Mississippi in grave doubt."

Senator Kefauver is a strong advocate of civil rights.

Mr. Stevenson, who lost to Senator Kefauver in Minnesota but defeated him later in Alaska, the District of Columbia, Florida and California, welcomed his old rival to the ticket.

"I think what has occurred this afternoon is clear evidence of the great vitality and virility of the Democratic party," Mr. Stevenson said.

"I am happy that Senator Estes Kefauver is to be my running mate. I know how formidable a candidate he will be, because I ran against him in several primaries. He is an old friend and an able leader. I welcome him on the ticket."

Fears Borne Out

Mr. Stevenson had insisted on a free, democratic choice. And it was certainly democratic, often disorderly. The balloting verged on a mob scene in the final minutes of the vote switching that made Senator Kefauver the victor. Friends of the Tennessean had been working actively for second place for him since he withdrew as a Presidential candidate shortly before the convention and pledged his backing to Mr. Stevenson.

There was no doubt about his popularity with rank-and-file Democrats. Many of them had been favorable to Mr. Stevenson's renomination. What happened this afternoon was precisely what the party professionals had feared.

Just after 1 P. M. the roll-call of states for nominations began. The field was entered in this order:

Senator Gore.
Senator Kefauver.
Senator Kennedy.
Gov. Leroy Collins of Florida.
Senator Humphrey.
Mayor Wagner of New York.
Gov. Luther Hodges of North Carolina.

On the first ballot, Senator Kefauver received 483½ votes, 203 less than the majority required for nomination.

This was the rest of the line-up:

Senator Kennedy........304
Senator Gore 178
Mayor Wagner 162½
Senator Humphrey 134½
Governor Hodges 40
Pitt Tyson Maner of Ala.. 33
Senator Clinton P.
Anderson of N. M....... 16
Gov. Frank G. Clement of
Tenn. 13½
Governor Collins 1½
Edmund G. Brown Attorney General of Calif. ... 1
Senator Stuart Symington
of Missouri 1
Senator Johnson .... ½

Three votes were not recorded. Messrs. Maner, Anderson, Brown, Symington and Johnson had not been placed in nomination, but got votes from the floor anyway. There was a burst of laughter as the Kentucky delegation, labeling itself "unpredictable," cast 30 votes for Mr. Maner in appreciation for his having

served as campaign manager for Gov. A. B. (Happy) Chandler's own favorite son campaign for the Presidency.

Coalition's Hopes Rose

It looked then as if Senator Kefauver might be stopped, and that the coalition opposed to him could swing a majority behind Senators Kennedy or Gore. Illinois, home state of Mr. Stevenson, was giving most of its votes to Senator Kennedy.

On the second ballot, Arkansas and New York tried to lead the result in that direction. Arkansas moved from Senator Gore, New York from Mayor Wagner.

Most of the Southern states had lined up behind Senator Kennedy. Those that held out on the first ballot, except Florida, moved to the Massachusetts candidate on the second. There was strong sentiment in the Florida delegation that Senator Kefauver could help them regain the state, which voted Republican four years ago.

The Kefauver strength was widely distributed. If Mr. Stevenson's Illinois was giving a majority of its votes to Senator Kennedy, this was counterbalanced in Pennsylvania, home state of Mr. Stevenson's campaign manager, James A. Finnegan.

When all the state and territorial delegations had answered the second roll-call, Senator Kennedy was leading. Senator Gore huddled with Governor Clement to carry out the instruction of the Tennessee Democratic Convention that its votes should go to any Tennessean with a serious prospect of winning the nomination. Governor Clement waved the Tennessee banner to ask recognition from Speaker Rayburn.

The votes for Senator Anderson later were switched to Mr. Maner.

On the second ballot, Pennsylvania gave 64 of its 74 votes to Senator Kefauver. The Tennessean had big votes in such other industrial states as Ohio and Michigan, and across the farm belt.

An interesting feature was that Senator Kefauver had no support at all from the Tennessee delegates. Under the unit rule, they had been committed first to Governor Clement and later to Senator Gore.

And when Tennessee originally stood pat for Senator Gore on the second ballot, there were boos in the hall. But in the final analysis it was Senator Gore's withdrawal that gave Senator Kefauver's bandwagon the last needed shove.

The convention floor scene was one of continuously feverish activity. Scores of important strategy sessions proceeded simultaneously. The delegates had to caucus in their seats, since there were only two minutes between the end of the first roll-call and the start of the second.

The Kentucky spokesman drew laughs when he said—inaccurately as it turned out—that his state was moving to the majority side after having been with the minority on all other convention decisions.

Then Senator Gore dropped in favor of Senator Kefauver. Oklahoma promptly switched its 28 votes from Senator Gore to the eventual winner.

Senators Kennedy and Kefauver dueled toward the finish, until Missouri switched 33 votes that had been cast earlier for Senator Humphrey. There the majority was reached. Senator Kefauver was in.

When all the switches were in, the results of the second roll-call were announced as follows:

Senator Kefauver..........755½
Senator Kennedy.........589
Senator Gore 13½
Mayor Wagner........... 6
Senator Humphrey....... 2
Governor Clement........ ½
Absent 5½

Because of confusion in the International Amphitheatre, the tellers had difficulty in hearing the announcement. There was some confusion over the exact figures.

The switches were stopped when Speaker Rayburn recognized the youthful Senator Kennedy, who got a big hand from all sides as stepped to the rostrum.

He thanked the convention for its generosity and kindness. He added that today's action had demonstrated the party's strength and unity and the "good judgment" of Mr. Stevenson in bringing the Vice-Presidential issue to the floor instead of hand-picking his successor, as has been the custom.

He said Senator Kefauver was a tireless campaigner and would make an admirable running mate for Mr. Stevenson.

"I move we suspend the rules and make this nomination by acclamation," said Senator Kennedy.

Speaker Rayburn called for the "ayes" and the crowd roared its approval.

"No 'noes,'" the speaker said, without asking for negative reactions.

The Speaker wielded a firm gavel to get the Democrats through the Vice-Presidential selection expeditiously. He announced in advance unanimous consent agreements to limit nominating speeches to five minutes, seconding speeches to two of not more than three minutes, and a ban on any floor demonstrations. To the surprise o. everyone, including Speaker Rayburn, the delegates did not demonstrate when their favorite: were placed in nomination. Placards and other equipment fo: marches were in place.

The nominating process brough: two of the defeated aspirant: for the Presidency to the convention platform. Governor Harriman of New York, who wa Mr. Truman's choice against Mr. Stevenson, got a standing reception from delegates in every section of the hall as he placed in nomination Mayor Wagner of New York. There was a big hand, too, for Senator Symington, when he nominated Senator Humphrey.

Senator Kefauver was placed in nomination by Michael V. DiSalle, former Toledo Mayor who now is the Democratic nominee for Governor of Ohio.

August 18, 1956

KENNEDY AIDS NEGROES

Senator Presents $500 Pulitzer Check to College Fund

BOSTON, May 11—Senator John F. Kennedy of Massachusetts presented today to the United Negro College Fund the $500 check he received as a Pulitzer award.

The Democratic Senator won the Pulitzer biography prize for his volume, "Profiles in Courage."

The United Negro College Fund supports scholarships in thirty-one Southern colleges and universities. It is now conducting a $2,000,000 fund campaign.

May 12, 1957

Mrs. Kennedy Loses Her Baby

NEWPORT, R. I., Aug. 23—Mrs. Jacqueline Kennedy, wife of Senator John F. Kennedy of Massachusetts, who was expecting her first child in October, lost the baby this evening in an emergency operation at Newport Hospital. She has been staying here with her stepfather and mother, Mr. and Mrs. Hugh D. Auchincloss. At the hospital her condition was reported as good.

August 24, 1956

Child to the John Kennedys

A daughter, their first child, was born to United States Senator John F. Kennedy and Mrs. Kennedy at Lying-In Hospital here yesterday. Mrs. Kennedy is the former Miss Jacqueline Lee Bouvier, daughter of the late Mr. and Mrs. John Vernou Bouvier of New York. The child is a granddaughter also of Joseph P. Kennedy, former United States Ambassador to the Court of St. James's and Mrs. Kennedy.

November 28, 1957

Kennedy's Brother Is Fined

CHARLOTTESVILLE, Va., June 4 (UPI)—Edward M. Kennedy, brother of Senator John F. Kennedy, Democrat of Massachusetts, was found guilty today of speeding sixty-five miles an hour in a fifty-five-mile zone. He was fined $15 and court costs. Edward Kennedy is a second-year law student at the University of Virginia.

June 5, 1958

KENNEDY, FURCOLO IN VAN OF SWEEP

Lead Democrats to Their Biggest Victory in Years in Massachusetts

BOSTON, Nov. 4 — Senator John F. Kennedy buttressed his position as a leading Presidential prospect today by rolling up a massive majoirty at the head of a Massachusetts Democratic sweep.

Gov. Foster Furcolo also scored an impressive victory in the most thorough party triumph in years.

Mr. Kennedy headed for a possible new plurality record in the state in defeating his Republican opponent, Vincent J. Celeste, 34-year-old Boston lawyer.

The Governor went so far ahead of his opponent, Charles Gibbons, that The Boston Herald, independent Republican newspaper, conceded his re-election at 8:50 P. M.

Returns from 1,110 districts out of 1,970 gave:

SENATOR
Kennedy (D) 678,866
Celeste (R) 232,111
GOVERNOR
Furcolo (D) 547,765
Gibbons (R) 396,380

November 5, 1958

Like Son, Unlike Father

Joseph P. Kennedy, the former Ambassador to Britain who set up a trust fund for each of his nine children at birth that made them independently wealthy, savors the family joke that his son Robert, chief counsel of the Senate Rackets Committee, is frugal.

Visiting Washington last week, the elder Kennedy used his son's guest privileges at the Metropolitan Club and invited a friend to lunch.

Signing Robert's name to the lunch order, as the rules provide, he thereupon scrutinized the menu to find the most expensive dishes and consumed them with great relish, his friend assisting.

"I usually don't eat much for lunch and look for the bargains," the Ambassador explained. "But this is rare opportunity that must not be wasted."

September 15, 1958

BRONXVILLE, N. Y., Nov. 29 —In St. Joseph's Roman Catholic Church here this morning Miss Joan Bennett, daughter of Mr. and Mrs. Harry Wiggin Bennett, became the bride of Edward Moore Kennedy. He is the son of Joseph P. Kennedy, former United States Ambassador to the Court of St. James's, and Mrs. Kennedy of Boston, Hyannisport, Mass., and Palm Beach, Fla.

Cardinal Spellman performed the ceremony and celebrated the nuptial mass. There was a reception in the Siwanoy Country Club.

Mr. Bennett escorted his daughter, who wore a gown of ivory satin, adorned at its sweetheart neckline with rosepoint lace, and fashioned with a fitted bodice, long sleeves and a full skirt. With it she wore a family veil of rosepoint lace and carried a cascade bouquet of cream-colored white roses, carnations, stephanotis and stock.

Her sister, Miss Candace Bennett, was maid of honor. The other attendants were Mrs. Stephen E. Smith Jr., a sister of the bridegroom; Miss Margot Murray and Miss Danné Brokaw.

United States Senator John F. Kennedy of Massachusetts was best man for his brother, whose ushers were Robert F. Kennedy, another brother; Webster E. Janssen Jr., a cousin of the bride; Kirk Le Moyne Billings, Richard Clasby, Joseph Gargan, Claude E. Hooton Jr., Garret Schenck and Varick Tunney.

Mrs. Kennedy, a June graduate of Manhattanville College, was presented at the 1954 Gotham Ball and at the Debutante Cotillion and Christmas Ball, both in New York.

She is a granddaughter of Mrs. William Albert Stead of New York, the late Mr. Stead and the late Mr. and Mrs. Harry Wiggin Bennett of New York, Alstead Center, N. H., and Tung Acres, Gainesville, Fla.

Her husband prepared at the Milton Academy for Harvard, where he received a degree in 1954 and belonged to the Owl Club and Hasty-Pudding Institute of 1770. He is in his final year at the University of Virginia Law School, where he is president of the Student Legal Forum. Mr. Kennedy also attended the International School of Law at the Peace Palace at The Hague, the Netherlands, and served with the infantry in France and Germany.

The bridegroom is a grandson of Mrs. John F. Fitzgerald of Boston, the late Mr. Fitzgerald, onetime Mayor of Boston and United States Representative; the late Patrick J. Kennedy, who was a Massachusetts State Senator and the late Mrs. Kennedy.

After a wedding trip, the couple will live in Charlottesville, Va.

November 30, 1958

Edward Kennedy Weds Joan Bennett

Brother of Senator and Manhattanville Alumna Married

Mr. and Mrs. Edward Moore Kennedy after marriage yesterday in Bronxville. Bride is former Joan Bennett.

WASHINGTON, Jan. 20 — Senator John F. Kennedy offered Congress today a labor-management reform bill that he said would either reform or drive out racketeers. In addressing the Senate, Mr. Kennedy, a Massachusetts Democrat, specifically named James R. Hoffa, president of the International Brotherhood of Teamsters, "and his ilk."

If enacted, he said, the bill would "virtually put Mr. Hoffa and his associates out of business."

Mr. Hoffa said he had no comment on Senator Kennedy's statement.

The bill would impose criminal penalties for false reports of union financial affairs; punish the misuse of union funds; require secret ballot election of officers at regular intervals;

Kennedy Offers Labor Bill Aimed at Hoffa 'and His Ilk'

By JOSEPH A. LOFTUS

The Family Emerges

prohibit "shakedown" picketing and prohibit solicitation or payment of extortionate fees for unloading cargo from interstate carriers.

Some Taft-Hartley Changes

It would also require public reports of certain types of middleman operations in labor-management relations and make a few changes in the Taft-Hartley Law, most of them sought by unions.

Hearings will start next Tuesday and run not more than nine days, Mr. Kennedy hopes. Senate action in February is possible, informed sources said.

In the House of Representatives, Stewart L. Udall, Democrat of Arizona, said he would introduce a similar, if not identical, bill.

Senator Kennedy's bill is the 1959 version of the Kennedy-Ives bill, which the Senate approved last June by an 88-to-1 vote. The House killed it.

Senator Kennedy called the bill "bipartisan" but acknowledged that there was no Republican sponsor. Former Senator Irving M. Ives, Republican of New York, wrote to Mr. Kennedy wishing him success with the bill. It was reported that Senator John Sherman Cooper, Republican of Kentucky, had considered sponsoring the bill with Mr. Kennedy but withdrew.

Democratic co-sponsors of the bill were Senators Sam J. Ervin Jr. of North Carolina, Lister Hill of Alabama, James E. Murray of Montana, Wayne Morse of Oregon, Joseph S. Clark of Pennsylvania, Harrison A. Williams Jr. of New Jersey, Frank Church of Idaho and John J. Sparkman of Alabama.

The new version of the reform bill contains some substantive changes from the Kenedy-Ives bill, which Mr. Kennedy hoped would meet the objections of employers. A quick check showed that the bill was still unsatisfactory to them.

One of these provisions deals with public reports by employers on their spending for labor

relations. Senator Kennedy rewrote that section to protect legitimate employer - employe communications. A lawyer for an employers' association commented: "It's not drafted right." But he said it was better than last year's version.

Chamber to Discuss Bill

The Chamber of Commerce of the United States said its labor relations committee would meet next week to take a position on the bill.

Senator Kennedy stressed that this was an anti-racketeering bill, not a labor-management relations bill. He announced appointment of a nine-man nongovernment committee to review the Labor Management Relations (Taft-Hartley) Act of 1947. He said the committee would report in April.

Members of the advisory panel are:

PUBLIC — Archibald Cox, Professor of Law at Harvard University; David L. Cole of Paterson, N. J., former director of the Federal Mediation and Conciliation Service; Charles O. Gregory, Professor of Law at the University of Virginia; Russell Smith, Professor of Law at the University of Michigan, and W. Willard Wirtz of Chicago who headed wage stabilization boards in two periods of emergency controls.

MANAGEMENT — Gerard Reilly and Guy Farmer of Washington, who have served on the National Labor Relations Board.

LABOR—Arthur J. Goldberg of Washington, special counsel for the American Federation of Labor and Congress of Industrial Organizations, and Louis Sherman, general counsel for the International Brotherhood of Electrical Workers.

The new Kennedy anti-racketeering bill contained a few amendments to the Taft-Hartley Act. He called these "relatively noncontroversial." The word "relatively" in this case is in itself controversial.

One management lawyer said he did not know why these amendments were "mixed in" the bill if there was going to be a study of Taft-Hartley later.

Senator Barry Goldwater of Arizona, ranking Republican on the Senate Labor Committee, made a Senate speech questioning the Kennedy bill and the Senator's statements. He will sponsor the Administration's labor program.

He said Senator Kennedy's remarks "would seem to indicate that no revision of Taft-Hartley is contemplated in this bill." However, Senator Goldwater said Senator Kennedy had admitted that he included some Taft-Hartley amendments because they had been part of a "package" requested last year by ranking Republicans.

Challenges Kennedy Bill

"If the Senator is genuinely desirous of cooperating with the Administration in his expressed objective of enacting a bipartisan labor reform bill," Senator Goldwater asked, "why does he fail in his bill to include any provisions imposing necessary limitations on secondary boycotts and certain completely unjustified types of minority picketing?"

Senator Goldwater said both these provisions were in the Administration bill last year and would be in it this year.

It is doubtful that the union leaders would support the reform bill if Senator Kennedy's changes in the Taft-Hartley Act were excluded. There is little confidence anywhere that Congress will pass a separate, comprehensive Taft-Hartley revision bill to the labor leaders' satisfaction.

The Taft-Hartley changes in the bill, among other things, would permit strikers, though replaced by their employer, to vote in a representation election. They would allow building trades unions to make agreements with contractors even before employes have been hired. They would also permit compulsory unionism to take effect in these cases seven days after hiring, instead of after thirty days.

Senator John L. McClellan, Democrat of Arkansas and chairman of the Select Committee on Improper Activities in the Labor or Management Field, will introduce his own bill on racketeering control.

Racket hearings scheduled to resume tomorrow have been postponed until next Tuesday. The announced reason was the Republicans' delay in filling the place formerly held by Mr. Ives.

January 21, 1959

R. F. Kennedy Cites Influence Proposals

By RICHARD J. H. JOHNSTON

MILWAUKEE, Wis., March 6—Robert F. Kennedy said here today that a company and a labor union involved in the Senate rackets inquiry had approached him in the last year with political proposals.

Each organization, he said at a news conference, offered to help the political career of Mr. Kennedy's brother, Senator John F. Kennedy of Massachusetts, if a Senate investigation into its affairs could be softened or diverted.

Robert Kennedy is chief counsel of the Senate Select Committee on Improper Activities in the Labor or Management Field. Senator Kennedy is regarded as a leading contender for the Democratic Presidential nomination in 1960.

Robert Kennedy said he had "brushed off" the proposals. He did not say whether he had discussed them with his brother, nor would he identify those who had approached him.

The committee counsel is in Milwaukee to participate in a labor panel discussion at the two-day Midwest Democratic Conference here. Party leaders from thirteen Midwestern states are attending the sessions.

Mr. Kennedy's disclosure of the two proposals came in response to a reporter's question whether any bribes had ever been offered to him in connection with the committee's work.

He said the two organizations had been under the scrutiny of the committee during the last year.

Mr. Kennedy said he had not reported the offers to the committee chairman, Senator John L. McClellan, Democrat of Arkansas.

When asked if his failure to report these approaches might not constitute an illegal act, Mr. Kennedy said he had not thought of it to that extent. He repeated that when the offers were made he had "brushed them off."

Mr. Kennedy responded to a series of questions concerning his revelation with the deliberateness of a witness before his committee.

He would not say when the proposals had been made. Nor would he give the details of what form the offers of assistance to his brother would take.

Mr. Kennedy said, however, that the offers had been of a "specific" nature and that he thought they had been made seriously.

As reporters sought to draw him out further on the subject, Mr. Kennedy said abruptly:

"I've discussed it enough."

Mr. Kennedy said he had never received outright offers of money in return for a relaxation of the committee's efforts. He declared that on only "one occasion" had he received a threat to his safety. He said he had not regarded this as serious.

McClellan Unaware

WASHINGTON, March 6— Senator McClellan disclaimed today any knowledge of the proposals reported by Mr. Kennedy.

March 7, 1959

WASHINGTON, July 26 — James R. Hoffa and Robert F. Kennedy squared away again today on consecutive television programs.

Mr. Hoffa, general president of the International Brotherhood of Teamsters, accused Mr. Kennedy and the Senate's Select Committee on Improper Activities in the Labor or Management Field of attacking him to gain publicity and political advantage.

Mr. Kennedy, chief counsel of the committee, which has been exposing Mr. Hoffa's activities for the last two years, denounced the union leader and challenged him to sue him for libel.

Hoffa appeared on the Columbia Broadcasting System program, "Face the Nation." Mr. Kennedy appeared immediately after on National Broadcasting Company's "Meet the Press."

Repeats Statements

The panel of reporters questioning Hoffa confined their inquiries principally to what he thought of labor reform legislation now pending in Congress. Mr. Kennedy said he understood the reporters had "made some agreement" with the union leader not to ask him about his personal activities that the Senate committee had investigated.

Mr. Kennedy repeated previous statements that Mr. Hoffa had "entered into collusive deals with employers," "betrayed union members," "sold out union members," "put criminals in high position in the union" and "misused union funds."

He said Hoffa should sue him for libel at once—which Hoffa has threatened to do—and let the courts decide who was right.

"If he loses," Mr. Kennedy said, "he should resign as president of the teamsters, because if he is guilty of any one of those charges he is not worthy to be president."

Hoffa said the Senate committee's investigation had been held "for headlines and for some individuals on the committee desiring the Presidency of the United States." That was a reference to Mr. Kennedy's brother, Senator John F. Kennedy, Democrat of Massachusetts.

Hoffa repeated the statement he has made to the committee that at the conclusion of its investigation he would call in accused teamster officials and hold his own investigation of their conduct.

Mr. Kennedy urged the public to write to members of Congress in support of the labor reform legislation now before Congress. A bill authored by his brother recently passed the Senate; a watered-down version was recently sent to the House floor by the House Labor Committee and awaits action by the House.

July 27, 1959

HOFFA IS BERATED BY R. F. KENNEDY

Senate Aide Defies Teamster to Sue—Union Chief Says Inquiry Seeks Headlines

---

WASHINGTON, Sept. 10 — Robert F. Kennedy resigned today as chief counsel of the Senate Select Committee on Improper Activities in the Labor or Management Field.

The decision was announced in a letter to the chairman, Senator John L. McClellan, Democrat of Arkansas.

The Senate committee tentatively ended yesterday its three-year inquiry into labor and management corruption.

Mr. Kennedy praised and thanked the Senator and said the purpose of the committee "has been fruitfully realized."

"In many areas," he wrote, "we look to marked improvements in the labor-management picture. The labor movement itself has taken forceful action where it has had the opportunity to rid itself of racketeers and crooks.

"It is regretful that this action by organized labor has not been matched by either organized business groups or bar associations."

Mr. Kennedy said that the enactment of the labor reform bill would "help in many areas," but that a great responsibility would still fall on local law enforcement officials.

This local enforcement, he went on, "has failed to meet its responsibilities" in many areas in the past.

"Only in the Teamsters Union," he continued, "did there seem to be a reluctance to clean up."

Mr. Kennedy also resigned as chief counsel of the Senate Permanent Subcommittee on Investigations, which actually started the investigation that was taken over by the select committee. Senator McClellan also headed the subcommittee.

Mr. Kennedy has contracted with Harper and Brothers to write a book on Congressional investigations in general, and the select committee's in particular. It is expected that the book will be published early next year.

Friends expect that he will join the political staff of his brother, Senator John F. Kennedy, Democrat of Massachusetts, an unannounced candidate for the nomination for President.

September 11, 1959

Kennedy Quits as Inquiry Aide; Confident of Reform in Unions

At Home in the White House

Kennedy Enters Presidential Race and Bars Second Spot Under 'Any Condition'

CHALLENGES FOES TO PRIMARY TESTS

Insists All Aspirants Should Contend for Nomination in State Balloting

By RUSSELL BAKER

WASHINGTON, Jan. 2—Senator John F. Kennedy made it official today.

He told a news conference that he was a candidate for the Democratic Presidential nomination and was convinced that he could win both the nomination and the election.

At the same time Democratic leaders who believe that his following can be consolidated behind the Democratic ticket if Mr. Kennedy is given the Vice-Presidential nomination were given a sober warning.

If he is rejected for top place on the ticket, the Senator said, he will refuse to accept the Vice-Presidential nomination "under any condition."

'Not Subject to Change'

This decision, he added, "will not be subject to change under any condition."

The 42-year-old Massachusetts Democrat, first serious Roman Catholic contender for the Presidency since Alfred E. Smith ran in 1928, delivered his long-expected announcement to a crowded news conference in the Senate Caucus Room.

Of the many Democratic contenders, Senator Hubert H. Humphrey of Minnesota is the only other who has announced his candidacy for the Presidential nomination.

Regarding religion, Mr. Kennedy said:

"I would think that there is really only one issue involved in the whole question of a candidate's religion—that is, does a candidate believe in the Constitution, does he believe in the First Amendment, does he believe in the separation of church and state. When the candidate gives his views on that question, and I think I have given my views fully, I think the subject is exhausted."

Audience Applauds

An audience of about 300 supporters and friends applauded various answers to the reporters, giving the session the flavor of of a political rally. Mrs. Kennedy also attended the conference.

Mr. Kennedy has been openly campaigning for the Democratic nomination for months. thus today's ceremonial announcement came as no surprise.

At present the Senator is the acknowledged front-runner in the crowded field of Democratic contenders. But the large number of serious candidates and favorite sons threatens to prevent him from building a strong lead.

Part of the Kennedy strategy is to break out of his political containing wall by showing strength in the Presidential primaries.

As expected, he announced that he would enter the New Hampshire primary on March 8. He will announce his intentions about other primaries—in Wisconsin, Oregon, Nebraska, Indiana, Maryland, Ohio, Florida and California—within the next six weeks, he said.

He also issued a challenge to Senator Stuart Symington, who is playing a waiting game, to contest with him in the primaries.

Seeks Competition

Asked whether he was challenging the Missouri Democrat "to come in and get his feet wet" in the primaries, Senator Kennedy replied that any man who expected to be considered a serious candidate at the convention "should enter some representative primaries."

Mr. Humphrey formally entered the race Wednesday. The Minnesotan, forecasting "an uphill fight" to realize his own ambitions, plans to enter primaries in Wisconsin April 5, the District of Columbia May 3, Oregon May 20 and South Dakota June 7.

THE KENNEDYS: A NEW YORK TIMES PROFILE

Senator Kennedy is unlikely to have opposition in the New Hampshire primary, where he is considered unbeatable. Thus the first showdowns will presumably come between him and Senator Humphrey in Wisconsin and Oregon.

There is wide speculation within the party that no candidate will be able to win a clear majority of delegates before the July convention in Los Angeles and that, after a deadlock develops, the delegates will turn to a compromise nominee.

Kennedy Doubts Theory

Those most frequently mentioned as compromise choices are Senator Symington, Senator Lyndon B. Johnson of Texas and Adlai E. Stevenson, twice the standard bearer against General Eisenhower.

Senator Kennedy today took issue with this theory.

"My opinion is that by April or May we will have a pretty good idea of who is going to get nominated in July," he said. "I think when the primaries are through we are going to have a pretty clear idea as to who is going to be the nominee.

"I don't believe there is going to be a deadlocked convention. I don't agree with that concept at all. I would think that even before the convention the pattern will be quite clear."

In his formal statement, the Senator said that the President during the next four years would have to make "the most crucial decisions of this century."

Issues Listed

These, he listed as follows:

¶"How to end or alter the burdensome arms race."

¶"How to maintain freedom and order in the newly emerging nations."

¶"How to rebuild the stature of American science and education."

¶"How to prevent the collapse of our farm economy and the decay of our cities."

SHE KNEW IT ALL THE TIME: Mrs. John F. Kennedy with her husband yesterday after Massachusetts Democrat announced he was candidate for Presidential nomination.

¶"How to achieve without further inflation or unemployment expanded economic growth."

¶"How to give direction to our traditional moral purpose, awakening every American to the dangers and opportunities that confront us."

Praises Humphrey

Senator Kennedy declined to rate the comparative strength of his opponents for the nomination. There were no "substantive differences" between himself and Senator Humphrey, he said. Their voting records are "quite comparable" and both are "Liberal Democrats," he added.

"I think Senator Humphrey would be a good nominee and I would support him wholeheartedly."

Questioned about Governor Rockefeller's withdrawal from contention for the Republican nomination, Mr. Kennedy said that he had been surprised. "In some ways I think it makes Mr. Nixon's problem more difficult," he said.

He did not elaborate although many Democrats are trying to use the Rockefeller withdrawal to depict Vice President Nixon as the candidate of the Republican bosses.

What attracted the most attention here today, however, was the firmness with which Mr. Kennedy rejected the pos-

sibility of the Vice-Presidential nomination. Statements of this type are a standard feature of every announcement of candidacy, but Mr. Kennedy's categorical notice that he would not be available was considered unusual.

"I am a candidate for the Presidency," he said, "and if I fail to achieve that nomination, then I shall return to the Senate." The duties of the Vice-Presidency are limited, he noted, to presiding over the Senate, to voting in case of ties in Senatorial roll-calls "and to watching the health of the President."

January 3, 1960

Kennedy's Unruly Hair Gets Political Training

WASHINGTON, Jan. 11 (AP)—Has Senator John F. Kennedy finally tamed that unruly shock of hair, in the hope of improving his candidacy for the Presidency?

Newsmen who have been covering some of Senator Kennedy's recent appearances have noticed that the Massachusetts Democrat's barber has apparently figured out a way to tame the boyish-looking forelock that has supplied

cartoonists with a handy means of caricature.

Some of Mr. Kennedy's friends say he hopes to make himself appear more mature. Aides in his Senate office refused to discuss the matter. At his campaign headquarters here Pierre Salinger, press assistant, told a reporter:

"I think you're wrong. I haven't noticed any change in his hair-do at all."

The Senator himself is out of the city, winding up a week-end trip to West Palm Beach, Fla.

January 12, 1960

At Home In The White House

KENNEDY'S WIFE CHARMS VOTERS

Takes Stump in Wisconsin
While Senator Is Away—
Shows Relaxed Style

By DONALD JANSON

STEVENS POINT, Wis., March 10—Mrs. John F. Kennedy took over the hustings today, filling speaking engagements for her husband in his campaign to win the Wisconsin Presidential primary April 5.

Senator Kennedy left his auto caravan in La Crosse last night to return to Washington to vote to limit debate on civil rights legislation. He will return tomorrow.

His wife Jacqueline, a 30-year-old brunette, and his youngest brother, Edward H. Kennedy, filled in for the Massachusetts contender.

Clusters of people at pre-arranged meeting places in small towns from La Crosse to Stevens Point were charmed with Mrs. Kennedy.

"Isn't she lovely?" and "she's gorgeous" were frequent comments by women.

A typical male reaction after one of Mrs. Kennedy's brief, extemporaneous talks was:

"She handled herself well for an amateur at this political business."

First Time for Her

Mrs. Kennedy travels regularly with her husband, but he has not asked her to speak before. Mrs. Hubert H. Humphrey speaks frequently for her husband, the Minnesotan, who is Mr. Kennedy's opponent in the crucial Democratic primary. Wisconsin's thirty-one-delegate votes at the national convention in Los Angeles July 11 are at stake.

Mrs. Kennedy, who said she was nervous but seemed relaxed, told seventy-five persons at a luncheon in the Charles Hotel in Marshfield:

"We've been working so hard in Wisconsin, and I know that if you do see fit to support my husband you will find you haven't misplaced your trust."

At a Neillsville radio station she said:

"He has served his country fourteen years in the Navy and in Congress. He cares deeply about the welfare of his country, and as President could make the greatest contribution to its future."

She did not discuss issues but hit a sympathetic chord with parents, talking about their children and her daughter, Caroline, 2, home in Washington.

In a school gymnasium in Fairchild she pointed to kindergartners and said they made her feel lonesome.

March 11, 1960

THE KENNEDY BOYS RETURN TO STUMP

Robert and Teddy Campaign
for John in West Virginia
but Women Stay Out

CHARLESTON, W. Va., April 30—Senator John F. Kennedy's brothers are back on the campaign trail, in West Virginia, but his mother and sisters are not.

The Kennedy women were impressive in the Wisconsin primary campaign, organizing women's activities, including coffee hours, receptions and an occasional television appearance. On at least one occasion Mrs. Joseph P. Kennedy, mother of the Senator, argued with a Protestant minister about the qualifications of her son, as a Roman Catholic, to serve as President.

They did a good job, were well received and harvested a lot of publicity for the Democratic Presidential aspirations of the Massachusetts Senator.

In fact, Senator Hubert H. Humphrey of Minnesota, a rival in the primaries here and in Wisconsin, complained frequently that the Kennedy women got more notice in the Wisconsin newspapers than did his wife Muriel and his sister, Mrs. Frances Howard of Baltimore, who were campaigning at the same time.

Jacqueline Appears

The Humphrey women are back on the stump here, but there are no plans to bring back Mrs. Kennedy or her daughters, Mrs. Eunice Shriver of Chicago, Mrs. Jean Smith of New York and Mrs. Patricia Lawford of Hollywood.

Senator Kennedy's wife Jacqueline has been here part-time, but she prefers to remain in the background as much as possible.

There are no official explanations of the benching of the Kennedy women. But in political circles, the opinion is that they were judged too attractive, too well dressed and too rich to parade before the people of this economically depressed state, with its thousands of unemployed coal miners.

There also is less organized social activity here than in Wisconsin and the Kennedy campaign is less dependent on coffee hours and similar functions.

Brothers Working Hard

But the Kennedy brothers— Robert and Edward, or Bobby and Teddy, as they are known —are working just as hard in this state as they did up North.

Robert, the former chief counsel of the Senate Select Committee on Improper Activities in the Labor or Management Field, is both a campaign headquarters organizer and an active speaker in various parts of the state.

Teddy specializes in personal contact with voters, showing up at dance halls, community parties, and not infrequently descending deep into a coal mine. He is friendly and willing to buy a beer and talk politics.

May 1, 1960

KENNEDY WINNER OVER HUMPHREY IN WEST VIRGINIA

By W. H. LAWRENCE

CHARLESTON, W. Va., Wednesday, May 11—Senator John F. Kennedy of Massachusetts won a smashing upset victory in yesterday's West Virginia's Presidential preferential primary.

The Senator promptly forecast that he would be nominated at the Democratic National Convention, which starts July 11.

His "significant and clearcut" victory was conceded at 1 A.M. Eastern standard time (2 A.M. New York time) by Senator Hubert H. Humphrey of Minnesota.

Senator Humphrey also announced that he would withdraw from the race for the Democratic Presidential nomination. For Senator Kennedy, a Roman Catholic it was a surprising victory in a state where it had appeared that anti-Catholic sentiment had made Senator Humphrey the pre-primary favorite.

Turnout Is Heavy

The Associated Press, reporting on returns from 1,168 of 2,750 precincts, gave:

Kennedy 93,341
Humphrey 60,889

Observers estimated that 400,-000 of the 670,000 registered Democrats had turned out to vote on a raw, chilly day.

[In the Nebraska primary, Mr. Kennedy and Vice President Nixon received impressive popular support. Mr. Kennedy was the only Presidential candidate entered. Mr. Nixon was backed by write-in votes.]

Senator Kennedy flew here from Washington after the vote trend had established him as the probable winner. He told a television audience that the West Virginia vote had demonstrated that his religion was not a major issue with the nation's voters.

He said the results here should go far toward "quieting" the concern he said some Democratic leaders had felt about nominating a Catholic for the Presidency. The vote here, Senator Kennedy said, demonstrated that religion would not be a dominant issue if he were picked by the Democrats to run against Vice President Nixon, the expected Republican Presidential nominee.

Senator Kennedy said the West Virginia primary was "the key" to all the primaries" and should be "extremely helpful on the road to Los Angeles."

"After our victory here, I think we are going to be nominated," Senator Kennedy told a television audience.

The Kennedy victory was built in every section of the state but especially in the Southern coal fields where a combination of factors, including religion, had made Senator Humphrey appear the stronger candidate in advance of yesterday's balloting.

The Massachusetts Senator smashed the "stop-Kennedy" drive led by Senator Robert C. Byrd of West Virginia. He had urged all those who wanted any other Democratic nominee to vote for Senator Humphrey or they would lose their "last chance" to prevent Senator Kennedy's nomination.

Senator Byrd openly supported Lyndon B. Johnson of Texas, but his appeal for Humphrey votes also was aimed at those who preferred the nomination of Senator Stuart Symington of Missouri or Adlai E. Stevenson of Illinois, the twice-defeated Democratic nominee of 1952 and 1956.

This was a hard-fought, and often harsh, campaign between Senators Kennedy and Humphrey. Senator Kennedy abandoned the bland impersonal campaign he had followed to victory in Wisconsin over Senator Humphrey. Instead he struck directly at the Minnesotan as a front man for other candidates who had no hope of nomination himself.

Party Unity

But the work of restoring party unity and healing the wounds began as soon as the election here was decided.

Robert F. Kennedy, brother of the Senator, paid a quick call on Senator Humphrey at his hotel headquarters as soon as he had conceded defeat. Together they walked to the Humphrey campaign headquarters for a news conference.

In withdrawing from the Presidential race, Senator Humphrey said he would be a candidate for re-election to the Senate from Minnesota this year but would continue at the national level to seek nomination by the Democrats of "liberal candidates and a liberal platform." In conceding, he also congratulated Senator Kennedy and referred to him as his "friend and Senate colleague."

At Home In The White House

There were early reports of vote-buying and other election irregularities in the state and local races. But none of it was connected directly with campaign efforts for Senator Kennedy, who is wealthy, or Senator Humphrey, who has complained that he is in debt from his Presidential campaign efforts.

"There is a hell of a lot of vote-buying here," said Charles Hylton, managing editor of The Logan Banner. "It's the worst I've ever seen. But it is among the local, not Presidential candidates."

"One of my reporters said that the price fluctuated quite a bit right here in Logan," he said. "Some were selling their votes for $2 and a drink of whisky, while others were getting $6 and two pints of whisky."

Both candidates campaigned briefly in the Charleston area early yesterday and then flew to Washington to attend a luncheon honoring Mrs. Franklin D. Roosevelt.

Senator Humphrey returned to the state. Senator Kennedy is expected in Maryland later today to begin a last-minute drive in his contest there with Senator Wayne Morse of Oregon. That contest will be decided next Tuesday.

Senator Kennedy considered himself the underdog in West Virginia as the campaign ended, whereas he had appeared almost overconfident when he opened his campaign headquarters here in mid-March. On that March day, Senator Kennedy had spent about five hours in Charleston and reporters traveling with him had sampled local expert opinion on the probable outcome of this contest.

'Not Worried' at All

As they flew off that evening in the Kennedy Convair campaign plane for Wisconsin, the Senator asked the reporters their opinions of the West Virginia race. All said that the local experts had agreed it would be a hard fight for him to win.

"I'm not worried about West Virginia at all," Senator Kennedy had said.

Reaching into his brief case, Senator Kennedy tossed on the table a thick gray-colored volume—a West Virginia poll completed for him in early January by Louis Harris & Associates, who have done his public opinion sampling in many states.

"This shows me winning 70-30 over Senator Humphrey," Senator Kennedy said.

Reporters were allowed to read the Harris poll. In the first sampling of sentiment of about 1,000 West Virginians the results in percentages were: Stevenson 30, Kennedy 27, Johnson 15, Humphrey 9, Gov. G. Mennen Williams of Michigan 2, and undecided 17.

It was clear even by then that only Senators Kennedy and Humphrey were likely to enter the West Virginia race, so Mr. Harris then asked voters to choose only between these two candidates. The result in this poll was Kennedy 54, Humphrey

23 and undecided 23. With the undecideds thrown out, Mr. Harris arrived at his 70-30 percentage in favor of Senator Kennedy.

But that obviously did not take into account an organized effort, led by Senator Byrd and his organization, to persuade voters who favored anybody but Senator Kennedy to vote for Senator Humphrey in this race.

The argument was openly made to voters that Senator Humphrey was not likely to profit greatly from a victory here but that a Kennedy victory would perhaps eliminate any chance of other men being considered for the Presidency.

The Kennedy-Humphrey fight was entirely a popularity contest, without bearing on the choice of West Virginia's bloc of fifty delegates with twenty-five votes to the Democratic convention.

There were 108 candidates for these delegate posts, but most were uncommitted in advance. Of the few willing to state a preference, Messrs. Stevenson and Kennedy had twelve each and Senator Humphrey had two.

Democrats also had a heated, scandal-marred three-man primary fight for Governor. Attorney General W. W. Barron was charged with having offered one of his rivals, State Treasurer Orval J. Skeen, $65,000 to drop out of the race. Mr. Barron retaliated with a $300,000 slander suit against Mr. Skeen. The third candidate, Hulett C. Smith, hopes to profit from the dispute.

The Republican primary was little noticed. The state's twenty-two Republican convention votes were solid for Vice President Nixon. There was a gubernatorial primary fight between former Senator Chapman Revercomb and Harold Neeley, who had the backing of the present Republican Governor, Cecil Underwood.

Senator Jennings Randolph was unopposed for re-election in the Democratic primary. Governor Underwood, seeking a Senate seat, had no Republican opponent in the primary.

May 11, 1960

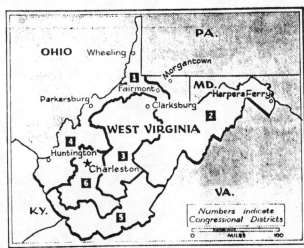

The New York Times   May 11, 1960

VOTE SCENE: West Virginia's six Congressional districts

Random Notes in Washington: Little Girl's Geography Lesson

WASHINGTON, May 22 -- Caroline Kennedy is 2 years old. Her father is a United States Senator. Her mother reports that her first three words were "plane," "good-by" and "New Hampshire" and that she has learned more recently to say "Wisconsin" and "West Virginia." She is expected to say "Maryland" and "Oregon" very soon.

May 23, 1960

Caroline and her parents in Hyannis Port, Mass.

'FATHER OF YEAR' NAMED

Robert Kennedy, 34, Youngest to Be Given the Honor

Robert F. Kennedy, former chief counsel of the Senate's Select Committee on Labor and Management Practices, was named "father of the year" yesterday.

He received the honor from the National Fathers' Day Committee at its annual meeting in the Waldorf-Astoria Hotel. At the age of 34, he is the youngest man to be chosen for the award.

Mr. Kennedy, a son of Joseph P. Kennedy, former Ambassador to Great Britain, and brother of Senator John F. Kennedy of Massachusetts, has seven children ranging in age from 8 years to 6 months. He is married to the former Ethel Skakel of Greenwich, Conn.

May 27, 1960

Kennedy Clan United on Coast As Senator Faces the Outsiders

By NAN ROBERTSON

LOS ANGELES, July 9-- John Fitzgerald Kennedy, the tousle-headed Senator from Massachusetts, flew in here today to the sound of trumpets.

Before him this week came his blood kin, his kissing kin, his kin by wedlock. Last night Mrs. Joseph P. Kennedy, the Senator's mother, arrived by jet airliner. This makes at least twenty children and adults in Jack Kennedy's immediate family or married into it who have descended on Los Angeles.

The Kennedys' interlocking relationships are difficult to sort.

Here is the tally of the Senator's tribe. Other, more distant relatives are probably here but as yet unidentified.

Robert Kennedy, brother, 34 years old; his wife, Ethel, and four of their six children—Kathleen, Joe, Bobby and David. Robert, better known as Bobby, will be his brother's floor manager in the convention.

Edward (Ted) Kennedy, brother, 28, and his wife, Virginia.

Eunice Kennedy, sister, who is 40 years old today; her husband, R. Sargent Shriver, and son Bob.

Jean Kennedy, sister, 32, and husband, Stephen Smith.

Patricia Kennedy, sister, 36; her husband, Peter Lawford, the actor, and three children--

Christopher, Sidney and Victoria.

Seem to Be Everywhere

Even the in-laws in this phalanx have youth, health, good teeth and the bone-crushing grip of Japanese wrestlers. They seem to be everywhere--at the Biltmore Hotel's convention headquarters, on television, on the street, at the airport greeting other relatives.

Teddy, the youngest of the family, is the legman and general factotum. At the moment, he is busy lining up delegates from the Rocky Mountain states.

The sisters and sisters-in-law will all appear tomorrow at a giant Kennedy reception for delegates. The Senator's mother will be hostess.

The twentieth member of the clan remains silent and invisible in Los Angeles. He is Joseph Patrick Kennedy, the 71-year-old patriarch, who has shaped the seven of his children who remain alive and through them, their progeny. The eldest daughter, Rosemary, is in a nursing home in Wisconsin.

He has given the others, including his son Jack, toughness, family unity, wealth and the will to win.

Joseph Kennedy, the former ambassador to Britain who opposed United States intervention on that country's behalf during World War II, arrived quietly with his niece early this

week. He has rented a Spanish colonial villa in Beverly Hills.

Shielded From Public View

The mansion is perched on a hill, shielded from the street by a twelve-foot wall, tall trees and luxuriant semi-tropical vegetation. The long, winding drive up to it is aflame with bougain-villaea blossoms and in the courtyard, a fountain splashes into a tiled pool. The butler who opened the great mahogany door yesterday said the ambassador was resting and could see no one.

Last night when his wife flew in, she was met by her son-in-law, Mr. Lawford. Joseph Kennedy was not there, nor is he due to be at tomorrow's reception.

When Mr. Lawford was asked why other members of the family were not at the airport, he replied:

"They're all too busy working downtown [at convention headquarters]."

Senator Kennedy's wife, Jacqueline, is notably absent while the family rallies arounnd. She is staying at the family's summer house in Hyannis Port, Mass., with her 2-year-old daughter Caroline. Mrs. Kennedy is expecting another child later this year.

She will watch the convention on televison but plans to fly to the West Coast if her husband wins the nomination.

July 10, 1960

LOS ANGELES, Thursday, July 14—Senator John F. Kennedy smashed his way to a first-ballot Presidential nomination at the Democratic National Convention last night and won the right to oppose Vice President Nixon in November.

The 43-year-old Massachusetts Senator overwhelmed his opposition, piling up 806 votes to 409 ballots for his nearest rival, Senator Lyndon B. Johnson of Texas, the Senate majority leader. Senator Kennedy's victory came just before 11 o'clock last night [2 A. M. Thursday, New York time].

Then the convention made it unanimous on motion of Gov. James T. Blair Jr. of Missouri, who had placed Senator Stuart Symington of Missouri in nomination.

'We Shall Win'

Senator Kennedy, appearing before the shouting convention early today, pledged he would carry the fight to the country in the fall "and we shall win."

He thanked his defeated rivals for their generosity and appealed to all of their backers to keep the party strong and united in a tremendously important election. He spoke directly of Senators Johnson and Symington and the favorite sons, but made no reference to Adlai E. Stevenson.

The third session of the national convention adjourned after his speech. The next session will convene at 5 P. M. today.

Little Wyoming, well down the roll-call, provided the decisive fifteen votes that gave victory to Senator Kennedy. Two favorite-son states, Minnesota and New Jersey, waited in vain to give the on-rushing Kennedy bandwagon the final shove.

When Wyoming came in with its vote, the Kennedy total had mounted to 765 votes, or four more than the 761 votes required for nomination.

It was a tremendous victory for Senator Kennedy. Mr. Johnson, the Senate majority leader, had fought desperately to reverse a Kennedy tide that had been running for months. But Senator Johnson quickly telephoned his congratulations to Senator Kennedy and forecast his election in November.

Senator Kennedy, who chose the tough preferential primary road to victory, had demonstrated to the party's big state leaders that he could win votes.

He reasoned that only through the primaries could he, as a Roman Catholic, remove the lingering fear of party leaders that he was destined for the same kind of defeat suffered by former Gov. Alfred E. Smith of New York, a Catholic, in 1928.

At Home In The White House

The convention will assemble today to ratify Senator Kennedy's choice of a Vice-Presidential running mate. Key names under consideration are those of Senator Symington, Gov. Orville L. Freeman of Minnesota and Senator Henry M. Jackson of Washington.

The Kennedy bandwagon could not be stopped despite the pressure of the combined Congressional leadership, including Speaker Sam Rayburn of Texas, and of former President Harry S. Truman. Mr. Truman had boycotted this meeting on a charge that the convention had been rigged for Senator Kennedy's nomination.

Efforts to breathe life in a "draft" movement for Mr. Stevenson, the 1952 and 1956 nominee, failed, despite a noisy, rowdy demonstration mostly by non-delegates who had infiltrated the hall by various devices.

At the end of the roll-call, Mr. Stevenson had only 79½ votes, slightly fewer than the 86 cast for Senator Symington.

Gov. Robert B. Meyner of New Jersey did not get a chance to shift his 41 favorite-son votes. Minnesota, with 31 votes cast for Senator Hubert H. Humphrey even after he had authorized their release from first-ballot obligations, also failed to put them over. The Kansas delegation, which had declined to let its Gov. George Docking join the Kennedy parade still was in caucus when the Kennedy vote passed the 761 vote total.

Nine Put in Nomination

Senator Kennedy's victory was national in scope with the exception of the solid South, which gave nearly all its votes to Senator Johnson. Of the fifty-four delegations, including the District of Columbia, the Canal Zone, Puerto Rico and the Virgin Islands, Senator Kennedy ran ahead in thirty-two of them.

All but one of the big states—New York, Pennsylvania, Michigan, Illinois and Massachusetts—gave Senator Kennedy tremendous margins. California was the exception, where he narrowly topped Mr. Stevenson by a two and one-half vote plurality, picking up 33½, or well under a majority of the state's 81-vote total.

Nine candidates had been placed in nomination, but two favorite sons—Governor Docking of Kansas and Gov. Herschel C. Loveless of Iowa—withdrew before the balloting began.

As the balloting progressed alphabetically, Senator Kennedy was well over the 100 mark after Illinois, over the 200-vote mark with Iowa, over 300 with his own State of Massachusetts, just short of 500 after New York gave him 104½ votes, and over the 650 mark after Pennsylvania.

When West Virginia brought him to the 750 mark, the stage was set for Wyoming to move into the national limelight.

It was an orderly, swift roll-call without a challenge to any state and the resulting poll of

the delegation to confirm the accuracy of the announced vote.

It had taken about six and a half hours to place the nine candidates in nomination and to allow their supporters to shout and parade around the hall in wild, but well-organized demonstrations. Only the Stevenson camp violated the convention rules limiting outside demonstrators to a maximum of 125 persons, including bands, for each candidate.

Charges Repeated

The Stevenson group passed entry badges back and forth until nearly 500 outsiders had come in, and than tried to crash through without any kind of passes, forcing a call for two-score more policemen to guard the gates.

Mr. Stevenson started out with the idea that he would not seek the nomination. But cheered by the enthusiasm of Southern Californians, he entered into the political in-fighting of the last few days.

He contributed to the faltering "stop-Kennedy" movement, which before his arrival had shown visible signs of pronounced political fatigue.

Even at the end, Senator Kennedy hoped that Mr. Stevenson would not seek a third nomination and would consent to place Senator Kennedy's name in nomination before the convention.

But finally Mr. Stevenson said that he could not reciprocate the favor Senator Kennedy had performed in 1956 when he placed Mr. Stevenson in nomination at Chicago.

There has been speculation for months that Mr. Stevenson would be Secretary of State in any new Democratic administration.

Gov. LeRoy Collins of Florida, the convention permanent chairman, gaveled the session to order at 3:16 P. M., yesterday.

The political in-fighting and maneuvering continued to the wire, with all the candidates, including Mr. Stevenson, working tirelessly to convince wavering or uncommitted delegates.

Senator Johnson slashed harshly at Senator Kennedy in what many delegates interpreted as desperation maneuvers, aimed at undermining the majority indicated for his young rival. He hit at the Senator's father, Joseph P. Kennedy, wartime Ambassador to Britain, as a friend of Prime Minister Neville Chamberlain and one who opposed American entry into the war against Hitler.

The Senate majority leader also attacked Senator Kennedy's failure to vote for censure of Senator Joseph R. McCarthy—at a time when Senator Kennedy was critically ill in Florida.

The Johnson forces contended that a "revolt" of delegates "hogtied" to Kennedy already was under way and there was no doubt that the Texan would eventually win.

However, the Kennedy camp remained cool and confident, but watchful of any developing

KENNEDY NOMINATED

LONG DRIVE WINS

By W. H. LAWRENCE

signs of weakness in the delegations.

As the serious business of nominating a candidate began, Governor Collins angrily demanded that the milling delegates take their seats and listen with more attentiveness than they had demonstrated at the first two sessions.

Alphabetical Switches

At the outset, Mr. Collins said he would permit orderly withdrawal of non serious favorite-son candidates. He said the convention would proceed, in alphabetical order, to allow states to change their votes between the completion of the first roll-call of states and before tabulation of the final tally on any ballot. Opponents of Senator Kennedy at one stage had announced an effort to change the rules to prevent such vote switching, but this plan was abandoned.

Alabama, first on the list of states, yielded to Texas and the honor of being first placed in nomination went to Senator Johnson.

Speaker Rayburn in his nominating speech said it was the duty of Democrats to "choose the very best leader that we have," and that Senator Johnton had demonstrated "that he knows how to lead."

"This man is a winner," Speaker Rayburn declared. "He can bring together people of all walks of life, of every faith and persuasion. We must not be divided; we must be united. This man can unite us. He will lead us to reason and to work together, for over many years he has proven that he posseses the magic gift of being able to lead men in a common cause. There is no abler man in our party.

"This man belonge to no class, no section, no faction. This is a man for all Americans—a leader matured by long experience, a soldier seasoned in many battles, a tall, sun-crowned man who stands ready now to lead America and lovers of freedom everywhere through our most fateful hours."

Pour Into the Aisles

Hoisting their placards and other paraphenelia of the traditional political demonstration high, Southern supporters of Senator Johnson poured into the aisles as Speaker Rayburn concluded his nominating speech.

With a ten-minute limit for all demonstrations, Mr. Collins allowed this one to run for thirteen minutes before he began banging his gavel and eleven minutes later, it was over.

While seconding speeches were being made for Senator Johnson, the big eighty-one-vote California delegation was polled on the convention floor. Senator Kennedy took the lead from Mr. Stevenson with a one-vote margin. Mr. Stevenson had a one-vote edge yesterday.

Alaska yielded to Minnesota, and Senator Kennedy was the second candidate placed in nomination. The principal nominating speech was by Governor Freeman, who said his candi-

date was a "proven liberal" and a demonstrated leader who could win in November.

An original backer of Senator Humphrey before his withdrawal, Governor Freeman said he had chosen Senator Kennedy as his candidate oniy after "soul searching" and long study.

Arkansas yielded to Florida, and this put favorite-son Senator George Smathers in nomination as the third candidate, coming in ahead of Senator Symington and Mr. Stevenson.

His nominating speech was made by his senior colleague. Senator Spessard Holland.

While the climactic act of the convention brought more spectators than the earlier sessions, even this was not enough to fill all of the 12,000 spectator seats in the new, gleaming Los Angeles Memorial Sports Arena. There still were hundreds of empty seats against the top of the bowl-like structure.

Govenor Blair praised Senator Symington's experience in business and government in urging the nomination of a Midwesterner who could win in November.

A new and unexpected favorite son developed during the long nominating process. He was Gov. Ross Barnett of Mississippi who chose Judge Tom Brady, author of "Black Monday," a book highly critical of the Supreme Courts' decision on racial segregation, to nominate him.

Mississippi leaders said the idea was to give Governor Barnett twenty-three complimentary votes on the first ballot then swing into line with the rest of the South behind Senator Johnson.

Wires for Stevenson

After Senator Symington, Iowa presented its favorite son, Governor Loveless who had already delivered a seconding speech in behalf of Senator Kennedy. As the Democratic nominee for the Senate, Governor Loveless had his name presented to take advantage of the wide exposure nation-wide television would give him.

Delegates reported an attempted telegraphic blitz for Mr. Stevenson, with thousands of telegrams urging his selection arriving while the nominating festivities were in progress. The clear signs also were that Stevenson fans had packed the galleries. He is perhaps stronger in Southern California than in any other place in the nation.

Governor Loveless withdrew as a candidate after the demonstration in his favor, pointing out he already had seconded the nomination of Senator Kennedy.

"I am not running against John Kennedy, so I ask the chair to remove my name from nomination," Governor Loveless said.

This set off a demonstration by Kennedy supporters, as Governor Collins announced that no further consideration would be given to the Iowan's candidacy.

Next to be placed in nomination was Gov. George Docking of Kansas, who was kept in

the race against his will by the action of a delegation majority created by a combination of Symington and Johnson supporters. Governor Docking wanted to back Senator Kennedy at once.

Mrs. Franklin D. Roosevelt touched off another wild demonstration as she enterd the hall to take a balcony spectator's seat, interrupting the nominating speech for Governor Docking being made by Frank Theis, the Kansas Democratic chairman.

She was framed in a spotlight as she walked to her seat, and Governor Collins noted that the demonstration was in her honor.

"We hope you will come again, again and again," Governor Collins said.

The pro-Stevenson galleries roared with approval at Senator Eugene J. McCarthy's introduction of Mr. Stevenson.

The Minnesotan asked delegates to reconsider decisions taken earlier before "all the candidates" were in the race, and before the issues were clear.

"I say to all you candidates and spokesmen for candidates who say you are confident of your strength, let this go to a second ballot," Senator McCarthy said.

"Let it go to a second ballot when all of the delegates will be free of instructions," he added.

The cheers that went up were from the galleries and from the Stevenson demonstrators already lined up. The bulk of the delegates sat silent, or occasionally, booed.

All-out Attack

The McCarthy speech was an all-out attack upon Senator Kennedy, using against him his own phrase about "a time for greatness."

"Power," the Minnesotan said, "is best exercised by those who are sought after.

"Do not reject this man who made us proud to be called Democrats."

"Do not reject this man who is not the favorite son of one state, but is the favorite son of fifty states and of every country on earth," Senator McCarthy said.

The big Stevenson demonstration that followed was dominated by outsiders who had infiltrated the convention hall. The great majority of delegates did not join the parading groups. It was the first major attempt of a gallery to blitz a convention since Wendell L. Willkie triumphed over other Republican hopefuls at Philadelphia in 1940.

Paul M. Butler, Democratic National Chairman, said the taking over of the convention floor by Stevenson backers was "the best answer to charges of rigging [of the convention] for Jack Kennedy."

Aided Movement

These charges have been thrown at Mr. Butler repeatedly by Senator Kennedy's opponents, including Mr. Truman.

Mr. Butler said that the Stevenson group, like all other candidates, had been granted a total of 125 "demonstrator" badges to provide bands and placard carriers for the floor shows.

But once in the hall, Mr. Butler said, the Stevenson group sent the badges back out to others, until the police had counted as many as 450 outside demonstrators.

When the ten-minute time limit had expired, Governor Collins rapped repeatedly for order, and, in his anger, told the Stevenson demonstrators to keep on with their show "if you want the name of this convention associated with hoodlumism."

"We must stop this demonstration," Governor Collins exclaimed. "I am sure that if Governor Stevenson were here he would join me in telling you to end this demonstration."

Senator Harrison A. Williams Jr. of New Jersey placed Governor Meyner in nomination, but the Governor had already ended his long hold-out and was ready to join the pro-Kennedy forces.

July 14, 1960

MRS. KENNEDY EXCITED'

But She Says Doctor Won't Let Her Go to Coast

HYANNIS PORT, Mass., July 14 (UPI)—Mrs. John F. Kennedy said here early today she would not be able to join her husband in Los Angeles.

Mrs. Kennedy met briefly with newsmen waiting outside the family's summer home. She said that her physician had ruled out the trip. She is expecting a second child before the November election.

Mrs. Kennedy accepted congratulations on her husband's nomination with smiles and repeated several times, "I'm so excited."

July 14, 1960

Narrow Escape for Kennedy

LOS ANGELES, July 13 (UPI)—Senator John F. Kennedy narrowly escaped a possible mishap on an hotel escalator today. Senator Kennedy and his party had just stepped off the descending escalator at the Statler Hilton Hotel when it suddenly doubled its normal speed, catapulting newsmen and photographers off the bottom stair.

July 14, 1960

HYANNIS PORT, Mass., July 14 (UPI)—Mrs. John F. Kennedy described her husband today as "strict—but very affectionate."

Jacqueline Bouvier Kennedy, 30 years old, acknowledged that she was not much interested in politics before she married Senator Kennedy, the Democratic Presidential nominee, in 1953.

"But I am interested now. And you get it all by osmosis," she told newsmen gathered in the living room of the Kennedy summer home in this Cape Cod town.

Mrs. Kennedy said she expected her husband to fly home Sunday. She said they would "cut off" the telephone and relax on Cape Cod for two or three weeks.

Mrs. Kennedy, who expects her second child about the time of the November election, said that "running a house around a man as busy as my husband is a full-time job."

She said she was "so happy" that her husband had won the nomination. "He worked so hard," she declared.

She was not sure of what role she would play in the election campaign.

Mrs. Kennedy, trim and chestnut-haired, was poised and charming in a gray suit. She wore a string of gray acorn-size beads. She firmly shook the hand of each newsman.

At the news conference today, Mrs. Kennedy appeared with her stepfather and mother, Mr. and Mrs. Hugh D. Auchincloss of Newport, R. I., and Arlington, Va., and her stepsister and stepbrother, Janet Auchincloss, 15, and James Auchincloss, 13.

Someone asked her how she thought it would feel to live in the White House. She laughed and said:

"I don't know. You tell me."

As to being the First Lady, she said, "everyone is different and the important thing is to help your husband."

Mrs. Kennedy watched the nomination of her husband on television last night with "great suspense." She said he and her physician had advised her not to go to the Democratic convention at Los Angeles.

"Jack said there's too much pandemonium out there," she said. She talked to him by telephone last night after he was nominated but before he entered the convention hall to address the delegates.

She was asked if she had any preference as to her husband's running mate. "I like everyone," she replied.

To another question, about what kind of a disciplinarian the Senator is, she said:

"He is strict—but very affectionate, like I try to be."

Their 2-year-old daughter, Caroline, she said, is "excited but doesn't know why. She's too little to know what it is all about."

July 15, 1960

Mrs. Kennedy Learned Politics by 'Osmosis'

Nominee's Wife Is Expecting Husband Sunday for Brief Vacation on Cape Cod

---

At Home In The White House

KENNEDY CALLS FOR SACRIFICES IN U.S. TO HELP THE WORLD MEET CHALLENGES OF 'NEW FRONTIER'

NIXON IS ASSAILED

Johnson Joins Attack —Acceptance Talks Close Convention

By W. H. LAWRENCE

'I ACCEPT THE NOMINATION,' Senator John F. Kennedy of Massachusetts tells a cheering crowd at the Los Angeles Coliseum. The 43-year-old Democratic Presidential nominee stressed the need for party and national unity.

LOS ANGELES, July 15—Senator John F. Kennedy formally opened his Democratic Presidential campaign tonight with a warning that the national road to a "New Frontier" called for more sacrifices, not more luxuries.

He slashed at his probable Republican Presidential rival, Vice President Nixon, as he joined with his surprise Vice-Presidential running mate, Senator Lyndon B. Johnson of Texas, in formally accepting nomination at the final session of the Democratic National Convention.

The 43-year-old Massachusetts Senator said that world and domestic challenges required new, positive answers to the unknown problems ahead. It is essential, he said, for Democrats to move beyond the New Deal and Fair Deal concepts.

'Challenges, Not Promises'

"Woodrow Wilson's New Freedom promised our nation a new political and economic framework," Senator Kennedy said. "Franklin Roosevelt's New Deal promised security and suc-

cor to those in need. But the New Frontier of which I speak is not a set of promises—it is a set of challenges.

"It sums up not what I intend to offer to the American people, but what I intend to ask of them. It appeals to their pride, it appeals to our pride, not our security—it holds out the promise of more sacrifice instead of more security."

"The New Frontier is here, whether we seek it or not.

"It would be easier to shrink from that frontier, to look to the safe mediocrity of the past, to be lulled with good intentions and high rhetoric—and those who prefer that course should not vote for me or the Democratic party."

Senator Kennedy was interrupted by applause thirty-six times during his speech.

In accepting nomination, Senator Kennedy frankly raised the question of his Roman Catholic faith. He said that he recognized that many regarded this as a "new and hazardous risk" that Democrats had not taken since they last chose a Catholic, Alfred E. Smith, to head

a ticket that lost in 1928. But Mr. Kennedy denied that this was a risk. Then he said:

"But I look at it this way: The Democratic party has once again placed its confidence in the American people, and in their ability to render a free, fair judgment, and you have, at the same time, placed your confidence in me, and in my ability to render a free, fair judgment —to uphold the Constitution and my oath of office—and to reject any kind of religious pressure or obligation that might directly or indirectly interfere with my conduct of the Presidency in the national interest. My record of fourteen years supporting public education— supporting complete separation of church and state—and resisting pressure from any source on any issue should be clear by now to everyone.

"I hope that no American, considering the really critical issues facing this country, will waste his franchise by voting either for me or against me solely on account of my religious affiliation."

Together, Senators Kennedy and Johnson proclaimed the need for party and national unity, and their own rapprochement from their fierce battle of this convention as a symbol of what they could do for the nation.

At 8:34 P. M., Pacific daylight time (11:34 New York time), the convention was gaveled to its close by the Permanent Chairman, Gov. LeRoy Collins of Florida.

The only remaining business is the selection of Senator Henry M. Jackson of Washington as Democratic National Chairman at tomorrow's meeting of the new National Committee.

Vice President Nixon took the full brunt of the Democratic oratory.

Senator Kennedy said that the Nixon career was the direct antithesis of that of Abraham Lincoln in that Mr. Nixon often "seemed to show charity toward none and malice for all."

Senator Kennedy said that the millions of Americans who had voted for President Eisenhower well might conclude that Mr. Nixon "did not measure to the footsteps of Dwight D. Eisenhower."

As a young Senator, the Democratic nominee insisted that the times called for young, new and vigorous leadership by men "who can cast off the old slogans and delusions and suspicions."

Likened to McKinley

"The Republican nominee-to-be, of course, is also a young man," he continued. "But his approach is as old as McKinley. His speeches are generalities from Poor Richard's Almanac."

But the Kennedy acceptance speech was much more than a partisan attack upon the Vice President and his Republican allies.

It was also a statement of the problems the Senator saw the nation and the world facing, a statement compressed by him into a description of the New Frontier.

It was a far sterner message than most of the political acceptance speeches of the past, which were designed largely to reflect partisan political appeals that would cheer the party's followers.

Senator Johnson, who had been Senator Kennedy's bitter foe for the Presidential nomination, emphasized the party-unifying implications of his nomination for second place. He said that this action boded well for "a new day of hope and harmony for all Americans—regardless of religion, race or regions."

As the Senate majority leader,

he claimed credit for his party for having made divided Government work while a Republican occupied the White House. But he said that this division must end.

Senator Johnson provoked a roar of approval from the crowd of 50,000 when he moved that the nomination of Senator Kennedy be made unanimous. The crowd rose to its feet applauding.

Introduced by Stevenson

The Democrats' final big show was a calculated effort to demonstrate renewed unity in the party. The unsuccessful contenders for the Presidency, including Senator Stuart Symington of Missouri and the favorite sons, spoke first. Adlai E. Stevenson, the nominee of 1952 and 1956, for whom a draft effort failed this year, introduced Senator Kennedy.

One conspicuous Democrat was absent. He was former President Harry S. Truman, who had boycotted the convention that ignored his efforts to stop Senator Kennedy and nominate almost any other leading Democrat.

However, Mr. Truman sent a telegram to convention officials, urging the party to close ranks

for the campaign.

Senator Hubert H. Humphrey of Minnesota was the first of the original aspirants for renomination to speak to the crowd.

He said the "sunshine of victory" was beating down on the Coliseum crowd.

Mrs. Franklin D. Roosevelt, who battled for the nomination of Mr. Stevenson, left before the convention ended, but her son, Representative James Roosevelt of California, a Kennedy backer, spoke her sentiments for party unity.

He said she had always known the courage and ability of Senator Kennedy, and her prayer was that with God's help he would make his place in history as "one of the greatest Presidents of the United States."

Senator Symington said Senator Kennedy had reached top place on the Democratic ticket because he had "just a little more courage, just a little more stamina, just a little more wisdom, and a little more character" than any of the "rest of us."

Mr. Symington then introduced Senator Johnson with high praise of his record as leader of the Senate.

July 16, 1960

AN ACTOR DETAILS VISIT BY KENNEDY

HOLLYWOOD, July 18 (AP) —Senator John F. Kennedy made a trip down a fire escape and over a back fence the night he was nominated.

The flight was witnessed by William Gargan, an actor, who at first said he did not know where Senator Kennedy had gone. However, he said later that Senator Kennedy had visited his mother. Newspapermen and television personnel were camped in front of the Democratic Presidential nominee's apartment on Rossmore Avenue.

The apartment was just above one rented by Mr. Gargan.

Last Wednesday night," Mr. Gargan said, "it was still day-

light. I was out in the backyard. All of a sudden I see Senator Kennedy coming down the back fire escape. As he climbed over the back fence, he said: 'Keep this quiet, will you?'

"I don't know where he went but he was back upstairs by the time the balloting started. We could hear him walking around. Just about the time the roll-call got to California, he came to our door.

" 'May I look at your television set?' he asked. 'Mine won't work.' "

"Just before the roll-call got to Wyoming, he jumped up and excused himself. 'I've got to get upstairs,' he said. 'Bobby [his brother] will be calling me. And I want to call my wife.' "

July 19, 1960

'The Woman Who'...Wins High Fashion's Vote Is Jacqueline Kennedy

By MARYLIN BENDER

REGARDLESS of what happens in November, Mrs. John F. Kennedy is a shoo-in for first lady of American fashion. If her husband is elected, she can qualify as one of the most glamorous White House hostesses in United States history.

The men and women who design fashion, manufacture it, sell it and promote it regard Jacqueline Kennedy as a pro. "Fantastically chic" is the phrase most often applied to her. They respect her style sense as a genuine talent that could have flourished even on a budget. She was a 1951 winner of Vogue's Prix de Paris contest but declined the prize, a year's job in the magazine's Paris office.

Mind Of Her Own

Mrs. Kennedy approaches the subject of clothes with the same qualities that gained political success for her husband—confidence, individuality, a mind of one's own and a knowledge of the issues.

A saleswoman in a New York specialty shop described her as "very fussy and demanding, but a woman who really knows." She is more interested in silhouette than in price or a designer's label.

Jacqueline Kennedy is a pace-setter who has worn sausage-skin pants, streaked hair, chemise dresses and sleeveless tunics long before these became popular currency. At 30, she has the kind of tall, slender and rather muscular figure that seems to inspire creative American designers and the younger crop of Parisian couturiers.

Mrs. Kennedy was educated in the United States and Paris, speaks fluent French and good Italian. Her wardrobe also is multilingual. She is a loyal customer of the Paris haute couture, whose members consider her the epitome of the best in American taste—the look of superbly tailored clothes, carefully accessorized and worn with restraint.

Givenchy and Balenciaga are her favorites. She has sometimes patronized Cardin. Givenchy has, on occasion, designed exclusively for her. This year she ordered by mail two black cocktail dresses, a pink evening gown and a red piqué coat from sketches. After these selections were made Givenchy chose the accessories and mailed photographs of them to her for approval.

Among the Americans represented in her closet are the forward-looking designers, Norell and Galanos, and Brigance, the bathing-suit maker. Hanging there, too, are the leg-clinging pants of designer Emilio Pucci and line-for-line, made-in-America copies of Paris couture originals. Her New York shopping tours take her on and off Fifth Avenue from Ohrbach's to Lord & Taylor and on to Bendel's.

Black . . . and Color

A disciple of the little black dress, Mrs. Kennedy also subscribes to unabashed color, particularly reds, pinks, yellows and greens. During the Wisconsin primary campaign, her red coat—a Givenchy copy—was reported by male political correspondents who ordinarily disdain the woman's angle of a story.

Jacqueline Kennedy gives the millinery industry no cause for rejoicing. She creates the impression of hatlessness. Part of this is owing to her bouffant coiffure, which gives her broad, wide-eyed face the look of a beautiful lion and which also discourages the wearing of a hat. Two of New York's hairdressers—Claude and Kenneth of Lilly Daché—claim her as a client.

Expectant motherhood probably will keep Mrs. Kennedy off the campaign trail. If she does make any public appearances, the maternity manufacturers and the anticipating segment of American womanhood will sit up and take notes.

July 15, 1960

Senator Kennedy was not the only one to make news in the recent Wisconsin primary. Several dispatches mentioned this bright red coat worn by Mrs. Kennedy in rare appearance wearing a hat. A copy of a Givenchy design, it reportedly was purchased at Ohrbach's.

THE KENNEDYS: A NEW YORK TIMES PROFILE

Mrs. Kennedy often has been described as "the perfect customer" by Paris couturier, Givenchy, who has been quoted as saying he "delights in designing for her."

Kennedy Takes a Deep Breath

WASHINGTON, Aug. 21 — The trials of a Presidential candidate are many and varied.

Senator John F. Kennedy, for instance, has disclosed to close friends that his occasional loss of voice results from the faulty speech habit of talking from his throat. So, when he can find a moment free from politicking, the Democratic candidate from Massachusetts is taking lessons on speaking from the diaphragm.

August 22, 1960

SCOTT SCORES USE OF KENNEDY FUNDS

Says 'Good Deal' of Family Fortune Has Already Been Spent for Buying Votes

By E. W. KENWORTHY

WASHINGTON, Aug. 21 — Senator Hugh Scott charged today that "a good deal" of the family fortune of Senator John F. Kennedy had been used in an attempt to buy votes in the Presidential race.

The Pennsylvania Republican said on the American Broadcasting Company's television program "College News Conference" that Republicans "are going to have an awful lot of questions of abuse of money in this campaign."

Mr. Scott was then asked by one of the panelists whether he meant "to say that the $400,-000,000 of the Kennedy family might be used to try to buy the American votes."

The Senator replied:

"Well, a good deal of it has already been used for that purpose. Estimates vary between $1,500,000 and $7,000,000 already used, and I am sure that millions more will be used if means can be found to evade the election laws."

Senator Scott was recently named a member of the "Republican Truth Squad" by Senator Thruston B. Morton of Kentucky, the party chairman.

[In Des Moines, Senator Kennedy called Senator Scott's charges untrue. He was cheered when he said the Pennsylvanian might have lost his membership on the "truth squad."]

In support of his charge today, Senator Scott cited the offer of $100,000 by the Joseph P. Kennedy Jr. Foundation to pay the transportation of 250 African students to the United States. The charitable foundation was established by Senator John F. Kennedy's father and named after a brother killed in World War II in a flight over Germany.

Senator Scott repeated a charge first made on the Senate floor last Wednesday night that the tax-exempt Kennedy Foundation, "for blatant political purposes," had "outbid" the State Department. The department agreed to finance the student transportation project after two intercessions by Vice President Nixon's office. But its offer was rejected.

The project—known as Airlift Africa—was sponsored by the African-American Students Foundation. The head of the organization is Frank Montero; one of the trustees is Jackie Robinson, former baseball star.

Early last July, the organization approached the State Department about financing Air Force transportation for the students. Vice President Nixon, on the urging of Mr. Robinson, supported the request. On July 7, the State Department, for various reasons, said it could not agree to the use of funds for the project.

The sponsors, again with the support of Mr. Nixon's office, asked for reconsideration. From here on the facts are in dispute.

Lincoln White, State Department press officer, said last Thursday that the department had reversed its earlier decision on Aug. 13, and that the news had been communicated to Mr. Nixon's office on Aug. 15—last Monday.

Senator Kennedy said last Thursday, in answer to Senator Scott's charges, that the foundation had agreed to pick up the $100,000 tab on Aug. 10, and that it did so in the belief that the State Department would not. He said also that the foundation had stipulated that its action not be made public.

Timing of the Offer

Senator Scott insisted today in the television interview that "the truth is that the Kennedy Foundation offered nothing until they had heard of the State Department offer" last Monday. Before that, Senator Scott said, Mr. Kennedy had himself offered only $5,000 for the project to Tom Mboya, Kenya nationalist leader.

Senator Scott called attention to the fact that R. Sargent Shriver, Mr. Kennedy's brother-in-law, is both a trustee of the foundation and the Senator's adviser on civil rights.

Mr. Scott said:

"If a foundation which belongs to a family and has a faucet which can be turned on by Mr. Kennedy or his brother-in-law, who is one of his campaign managers, to gain some advantage with any group of our people, they can do the same thing with the farmers.

"They can organize a farm study group and pay a lot of farmers with made-work money and get the farm vote. They can do the same with the parents and families of immigrants. They can organize a reception committee and pay the transportation of all the immigrants to this country and then they will help themselves with another group of people."

August 22, 1960

DES MOINES, Aug. 21—Senator Kennedy was cheered today when he declared that Senator Scott "may well have lost his membership" on the Republican "truth squad" for false charges about the use of Kennedy money in the political campaign.

The Massachusetts Democrat was asked at a news conference about Senator Scott's television comments. One of the Republican Senator's charges was that the Kennedy fortune made it possible for Senator Kennedy to "turn on the faucet and buy the farm vote."

"I don't share the view that the farm vote is for sale," Senator Kennedy said. "I believe the voters in November will deal with the truth squad, the strategy board and, I believe, the Vice President of the United States."

"Senator Scott," he said, "is a member of the Republican truth squad but he may well have lost his membership today."

The "truth squad" was named to follow former President Harry S. Truman in his campaign for the Democratic nominee.

August 22, 1960

KENNEDY ASSURES TEXAS MINISTERS OF INDEPENDENCE

Says He'd Quit Presidency if Unable to Withstand Any Church Pressure

By W. H. LAWRENCE

HOUSTON, Tex., Sept. 12—Senator John F. Kennedy told Protestant ministers here tonight that he would resign as President if he could not make every decision in the national interest "without regard to outside religious pressures or dictates."

Senator Kennedy's address, to the Greater Houston Ministerial Association, was televised throughout Texas.

It constituted an affirmation of his belief in the separation of church and state. It was also his answer to critics who have sought to mobilize anti-Catholic sentiment against him by contending he would not resist church pressure on major issues.

"I do not speak for my church on public matters," Senator Kennedy declared, "and the church does not speak for me.

Would Ignore 'Pressures'

"Whatever issue may come before me as President — on birth control, divorce, censorship, gambling, or any other subject—I will make my decision in accordance with what my conscience tells me to be the national interest, and without regard to outside religious pressures or dictates."

Public officials, the Senator said, should not request or accept instructions on public policy directly or indirectly from the Pope, from the National Council of Churches, or from any other ecclesiastical source seeking to impose its will on the general public.

Mr. Kennedy said, "No power or threat of punishment could cause me" to deviate from the national interest.

No Conflict Seen

"But if the time should ever come—I do not concede any conflict to be even remotely possible — when my office would require me to either violate my conscience or violate the national interest," Senator Kennedy said, "then I would resign the office; and I hope any conscientious public servant would do the same."

Mr. Kennedy also struck at the group of Protestant clergymen, led by the Rev. Dr. Norman Vincent Peale, that has questioned his ability to withstand Roman Catholic pressures if he were President. Dr. Peale is minister of the Marble Collegiate Church in New York.

Such groups, Mr. Kennedy said, are working to "subvert" the declaration, in Article VI of the Constitution, that there shall be no religious test of office. They should be out openly working for repeal of Article VI, he said, rather than trying to change it by indirection.

The speech represented a major effort by Senator Kennedy to meet the religious issue head on. In it, he also continued to try to draw back into the Democratic party a segment of its membership, particularly in the South and the Midwest, that has made known its unwillingness to vote for a Catholic.

Asks Judging of Record

Mr. Kennedy asked voters to judge him on his public record from fourteen years of Congress. This record, he said, included his "declared stands against an Ambassador to the Vatican, against unconstitutional aid to parochial schools, and against any boycott of the public schools." He pointed out he had gone to public schools himself.

He said he believed equally that no Catholic prelate should tell a President how to act and that no Protestant minister should tell his parishioners how to vote.

"This is the kind of America I believe in," he asserted, "and this is the kind of America I fought for in the South Pacific, and the kind my brother died for in Europe. No one suggested then that we might have a 'divided loyalty,' that we did 'not believe in liberty' or that we belonged to a disloyal group that threatened the 'freedoms for which our forefathers died.'"

The quotations Mr. Kennedy cited were from the manifesto of the Peale group, which calls itself the National Conference for Religious Freedom.

Controversy Recalled

One passage in Senator Kennedy's speech bore on a controversy with another clergyman, the Rev. Dr. Daniel Poling, a Baptist and former unsuccessful Republican candidate for Mayor of Philadelphia. The issue involved in the controversy has been widely used against the Democratic nominee.

It concerns his not participating in 1947 in the dedication of the Chapel of the Four Chaplains. The chapel is an interfaith memorial in the Temple Baptist Church in Philadelphia.

It honors four Protestant, Catholic and Jewish chaplains who perished together on a Navy ship during World War II, giving up their chances of survival in favor of others. One of the victims was Dr. Poling's son.

Dr. Polling has asserted that Mr. Kennedy was forced by pressure from the late Dennis Cardinal Dougherty to decline an invitation he originally had accepted.

Senator Kennedy explained before the National Press Club last January that he canceled his appearance when he learned that the chapel was in a Protestant church. Thus, he said, the Catholic altar could not be consecrated under the tenets of his church, which does not participate with other faiths in religious ceremonies.

Basis of Objection

Mr. Kennedy said that had he been invited as an individual or as a member of the House of Representatives, he would have gone and his church would have interposed no objections.

He was quoted by his campaign assistants last Thursday on the same incident.

"I was invited by the Rev. Dr. Poling," he said, "to attend the dinner in connection with the financial drive to build the Chapel of the Four Chaplains." I was happy to accept.

"A few days before the event, I learned, as the Rev. Dr. Poling describes in his book, that I was to be the spokesman for the Catholic faith. I was not being invited as a former member of Congress or as an individual, but as an official representative of a religious organization.

"I further learned that the memorial was to be located in the sanctuary of a church of a different faith. This is against the precepts of the Catholic Church."

The Senator alluded to this issue tonight when he said that the President of all the people should "attend any ceremony, service or dinner his office may, appropriately, require of him—and whose fulfillment of his Presidential oath is not limited or conditioned by any religious oath, ritual or obligation."

September 13, 1960

KENNEDY'S WIFE REPLIES ON 'CHIC'

Laughs at Report That She Spends $30,000 and Says Critics Are Very Unfair

By NAN ROBERTSON

Mrs. John F. Kennedy, stung by reports that women resent her because she is "too chic" and spends too much money on clothes, called her critics "dreadfully unfair" yesterday.

"I'm sure I spend less than Mrs. Nixon on clothes," the 31-year-old wife of the Democratic candidate said. "She gets hers at Elizabeth Arden, and nothing there costs less than $200 or $300."

Jacqueline Kennedy, who has been described in the fashion trade as "fantastically chic" and who was voted the most beautiful debutante of the year when she came out in Newport, R. I., and New York in 1948, expressed hurt and surprise at slurs on her avant-garde dressing habits.

"They're beginning to snipe at me about that as often as they attack Jack on Catholicism," she said. "I think it's dreadfully unfair."

Mrs. Nixon, who dresses smartly, has shopped at Elizabeth Arden and at less expensive New York shops. Her 1957 inaugural ballgown was designed by Count Ferdinando Sarmi, then employed by Miss Arden.

"My Arden ball gowns cost from about $500 to more than $1,000," Count Sarmi said yesterday. "But Miss Arden is very Republican. I have the impression she gave Mrs. Nixon the gown—which was in upper price range, at cost. She didn't have too much money to spend."

Mrs. Kennedy spoke her mind during a frantic morning at her thirty-seventh floor suite in the Waldorf Towers while awaiting her husband's arrival from St. Louis. Her voice is soft, high, and only a notch above a whisper.

She shuttled between her bedroom and living room to pose for photographers, talk with reporters and try on maternity dresses sent from a Fifth Avenue store. She is expecting her second child in mid-December.

"The baby is not coming on Election Day, as some people have said," Mrs. Kennedy said.

A woman reporter helped her to climb in and out of the maternity outfits, most of which buttoned awkwardly down the back from neck to hem. They cost $30 to $40 each. Mrs. Kennedy finally selected two.

"A newspaper reported Sunday that I spend $30,000 a year buying Paris clothes and that women hate me for it," Mrs. Kennedy said. "I couldn't spend that much unless I wore sable underwear."

She was referring to an article that said she "spends, together with her mother-in-law, Mrs. Joseph P. Kennedy, some $30,000 a year in the Paris salons (a distinct handicap)."

The original report, from a Paris correspondent of Women's Wear Daily, was published in that New York trade paper some weeks ago.

"I've lived in Paris and I have a younger sister, Lee, who lives abroad," Mrs. Kennedy said. "So I go there when I can. But I never buy more than one suit or coat from Balenciaga and Givenchy."

She said her mother-in-law, who purchased her wardrobe from Paris high-fashion houses every summer, "always brings back one outfit for each of the girls in our family."

Mrs. Kennedy said:

"I hate a full closet. I've gotten ruthless about what looks best on me. I don't have much chance to plod around the stores, but anybody in public life must be equipped with clothes in advance."

The hazel-eyed brunette said she did "a lot of shopping from magazines."

"Some clothes I have made by a little dressmaker in Washington," she said. "She's the only one who can fit into my crazy schedule."

She also buys from Norman Norell, a New York fashion designer considered the greatest in the country. Mr. Norell's designs cost $300 to more than $1,000 at retail.

On a coffee table in Mrs. Kennedy's hotel room was a book of Norell dress sketches sent with fabric swatches.

Mrs. Kennedy was also nettled yesterday by snide remarks about her bouffant hairdo. Some wrathful letter-writers have described it as a "floor-mop" and worse.

"I'm surprised at them," Mrs. Kennedy retorted. "I try to keep it neat and well groomed. Do you think it looks offensive?"

She then turned to other matters.

"I feel guilty I can't campaign with Jack," she said. "But I lost one child in 1954, a year after we married, and another in 1956, one week after I came home from the Democratic convention in Chicago. My doctors thinks the heat and crowds did it."

Her only child, Caroline, will be 3 years old on Nov. 27.

Mrs. Kennedy, who spent most of the afternoon and evening yesterday with her husband while he spoke at rallies, meetings, receptions, a lunch and two dinners, said she found public life "exhilarating."

"It was most difficult our first year of marriage. Being married to a Senator, you have to adjust to the fact that the only routine is no routine."

Friends, who described Mrs. Kennedy as basically introspective, say she was terrified at her Newport wedding in 1953, when a crowd of 3,000 broke through the police lines and nearly crushed the bride.

She now is calm, controlled and smiling when pressed by crowds.

Yesterday, as she wrestled with the buttons of a black maternity dress, Mrs. Kennedy was asked what she thought her husband's greatest contribution might be to the Presidency.

"I think Jack has a sense of history, and the past of his country," she said. "He cares about it. His brother was lost in World War II and Jack nearly died in the Pacific.

"A terrible, frightening decade is ahead. People are too complacent about this country's power. Someone has to talk to the Russians. If my country were in Jack's hands, to give the decade a start, I'd feel safe."

September 15, 1960

Mrs. Joseph P. Kennedy of Boston, formerly of the Bronx, returned to that borough yesterday to tell women why she thinks her son John would make a splendid President.

Se said events in Senator John F. Kennedy's youth and young manhood seemed to have molded him for so high a destiny at so vigorous a stage of his life.

Her son's political education, she said, began when he was only "knee high," when his father took him to Boston Common to show him where patriots had pelted British soldiers with snowballs.

She depicted the Democratic nominee as having been intimate with world affairs at an age "when most young men were spending their time in just the irresponsible outdoor sports."

Mrs. Kennedy, at no loss for ease among the cloth-coat set, spoke twice at political teas late on a drizzly afternoon.

Having been picked up at the family's residence at 277 Park Avenue by a hired limousine, she went first to the loft headquarters of the Siwanoy Democratic Club at 970 Morris Park Avenue in the Eleventh Assembly District.

There she greeted 250 women, of whom eight wore fur pieces, and fourteen men, of whom six were smoking cigars.

Later she was driven to a narrow three-story frame house with peeling yellow paint at 1447 Ferris Place, near Westchester Avenue, where she shook hands with 300 women. This was the Tenth Assembly District's Chippewa Democratic Club.

Mrs. Kennedy wore what a woman obligingly described as "a not quite American beauty, almost rose velvet toque hat." There was not a trace of white in her dark hair. A woman said she looked "fabulously young."

At both stops Mrs. Kennedy gave almost identical brief speeches. Each time she was introduced as "the mother of the next President of the United States."

She told how her son had met "Churchill and Eden and others who were making history before the Second World War." She told of his travels in Eu-

rope and the Soviet Union, of his war exploits as a PT boat commander in the Pacific, for which he was decorated, and his accession to Congress.

"So you see him, you find all of the vigor and idealism, health and enthusiasm of youth, but still with a wonderful background," she said.

She recalled that she had lost her eldest son, Joseph Jr., and a son-in-law in the war.

"Jack knows the sorrow, the grief, the tears and the heartbreaking grief and loneliness that comes to a family when a mother has lost her eldest son and a young bride has lost her

bridegroom," she said. "So I know that Jack will never get us into war."

Every seat in the long, narrow hall at the Chippewa Club was taken and nearly every inch of wall space was hung with red white and blue bunting. The scene resembled a miniature Democratic convention.

She said she had lived in Bronxville and Riverdale when Jack was a youngster.

Asked her age by a reporter, the 70-year-old grandmother of seventeen children said with sarcasm: "Oh, 75. I'm at least 75."

September 19, 1960

MRS. KENNEDY, 70, STUMPS IN BRONX

Tells Women Why She Feels Her Son Would Do Well in the White House

By McCANDLISH PHILLIPS

TEA-TIME CAMPAIGNER: Mrs. Joseph P. Kennedy, mother of Senator John F. Kennedy.

WASHINGTON, Sept. 19— Mrs. John F. Kennedy said today she would record some foreign language broadcasts for use in her husband's campaign for President.

The first will be for Italian-speaking voters. Mrs. Kennedy also speaks French and Spanish and hopes to record campaign appeals in those languages.

Starting this week, Mrs. Kennedy is also turning out a weekly newspaper column, "Campaign Wife," available on request from the Democratic National Committee.

"I feel so very sad not to participate in the major endeavor of his life," the dark-eyed young matron, who is expecting a second child early in December, explained of her own campaign efforts.

Mrs. Kennedy received reporters at the first of a series of teas at her home in Georgetown. She led her guests into the more informal of two adjoining parlors, a place of blond settees and easy chairs, books and prints, and seated herself on a bench in front of the fireplace.

"Jack gets seventy-five people into this little place," she said.

Asked if she felt up to the large-scale entertaining of the White House, she replied with spirit, "I have been married to one of the busiest men in the country for seven years. I ran three houses for him. I have entertained for large and small groups on long and short notice."

She said she would be willing to hold press conferences in the White House if her husband asked her to. As to writing a daily column there—"if Jack

BROADCASTS SET BY MRS. KENNEDY

Candidate's Wife to Record Appeal to Italian Voters —Plans Weekly Column

By BESS FURMAN

At Home In The White House

wanted me to, I'd be glad to."

Asked if she thought being the First Lady would change her, she said, "I wouldn't put on a mask and pretend to be anything that I wasn't."

Mrs. Kennedy said she thought that former President Truman had made the best comment on the "whose clothes cost more?" issue raised last week about Mrs. Kennedy and Mrs. Nixon, wife of the Republican candidate.

What Mr. Truman said was: "The wives of these candidates are both wonderful ladies and that's the way they ought to be treated."

Mrs. Kennedy said she received more than 250 letters a day and dictated answers. She said she felt it was one way she could stay close to the campaign.

If the baby is a boy, she said, she will name him for his father. She hasn't decided on a girl's name, but she would equally welcome a girl.

She said she had followed Dr. Benjamin Spock's advice not to tell her three-year-old daughter Caroline about the new baby too soon, as children that age get tired of waiting. But Caroline's little cousin now has a new baby brother, "so Caroline now wants a baby."

"Dr. Spock has just come out for my husband," said Mrs. Kennedy triumphantly, "and I'm for Dr. Spock."

Earlier, Mrs. Margaret Price, vice chairman of the Democratic National Committee, said she didn't think Mrs. Kennedy's clothes were a real campaign issue.

"I have been in thirteen states," Mrs. Price said as she came in from a West Coast-Texas-New Jersey swing with Senator Kennedy, "and I have not had one question on Mrs. Kennedy's wardrobe."

Mrs. Price said that she had found the women of more than fifty cities with whom she had chatted during her tour much more interested in other things.

The two issues upppermost in their minds, she said, were the need for vital, intelligent, strong economic leadership, and world peace.

September 20, 1960

Nixon and Kennedy Campaigns A Contrast of Methods and Men

Vice President Is Making Points With Reasoned Exposition While Senator, Paradoxically, Appeals to Emotions

By RUSSELL BAKER

CHICAGO, Sept. 24 — At Pomona Airport near Atlantic City last Monday several hundred moist-eyed women were mauling each other with bargain basement techniques to win positions against the wire retaining fence.

Breaking loose from New Jersey's cigar smokers, Senator John F. Kennedy walked over toward the crowd of women and a chorus of squeals reached out to greet him.

Silvery haired grandmothers, matrons in the clutch of middle age and young girls who should have been in school contended heatedly for his outstretched hand, or failing that, reached out to touch his shoulders, his sleeve.

Walks Along Fence

As he worked his way down the protective fence, he was followed by a ripple of giggles.

Two days earlier, at the Macalester College fieldhouse in Minneapolis, Vice President Nixon had addressed a big enthusiastic crowd, with a heavy preponderance of women.

As systematically and persuasively as a trial lawyer, he gave them his big campaign theme: the Republican Administration had "gotten this country out of one war, kept it out of other wars and maintained the peace without surrender of principle or territory."

This was still the most powerful nation on earth. Peace and greatness would continue, with ultimate victory in the "cold war," if the voters picked the man (Mr. Nixon) "best qualified to maintain the peace without surrender and extend freedom throughout the world."

The women filled the gymnasium with the shout of 5,000 happy furies.

Paradox Illustrated

These two tableaux from the last two weeks of campaigning illustrate a strange paradox in this contest for the Presidency.

Mr. Kennedy, whose campaign argument is pitched to the presumably worried thinking man, is profiting heavily from his appeal to the emotions.

Mr. Nixon, whose appeal is to the emotions—pride of country, fear of war, satisfaction with the status quo in the pocket book—is communicating by reasoned exposition of his case.

The trouble is that each candidate's peculiar personal assets are poorly suited to the campaign arguments they are making.

Mr. Nixon, a restless and aggressive politician, is arguing the case for relaxation. Mr. Kennedy, a politician whose presence is more exciting to the masses than his mesage, is telling the country it had better ease up on the pleasures and buckle down to work.

The campaign styles and techniques of the two men reflect the paradox. At times, Mr. Kennedy seems irritated by the force of his personal appeal and determined not to exploit it.

At Sioux City, Iowa, this week he arrived after midnight by the Eastern clock to find 2,000 people had been waiting two hours at the cold, windy airport. He rewarded them with a twenty-second greeting, then raced into town for an indoors rally.

Last week in Omaha, Mr. Nixon arrived even later after twenty hours of campaigning and found another big crowd on hand. He delivered an extemporaneous twenty-minute speech against the roar of airplane engines.

In their speaking styles, the contrast is also sharp. Mr. Kennedy, though his argument is sophisticated and easily misunderstood, rarely speaks longer than twenty minutes in his big appearances. Mr. Nixon usually takes that long just to warm up.

Biggest Ovation at Start

Mr. Kennedy's biggest ovation invariably comes when he first appears before his audiences and gets the shriek of recognition. The crowd responses, however, wane when he wades into his speech.

Partly this is so because of his unusual speech style and accent. He speaks with head tilted back and chin thrust forward, rattling off his lines at ferocious speed. He has been clocked at 240 words a minute, about 100 words a minute faster than normal speaking rate.

His voice has a high passionate ring, but the cadence becomes hypnotically sing-song, and as he speeds along it is difficult to follow the message for the rhythm.

When the crowds start to applaud, he is often carried by his own momentum through the first outburst, smothering the uproar.

Conveys Sense of Conviction

For all this, his platform style conveys a sense of passion and conviction that seems to reach the crowd, even when his reasoning is lost.

Mr. Nixon, by contrast, is a polished political orator of the classical school.

He has an instinctive feel for his audiences and knows how to bring them to the applauding point, where to stop for the big reaction and how to top it with the line that raises the roof.

His argument is rammed home line by line and point by point with the skill of a great courtroom lawyer delivering the summation. The applause and cheering build to ever higher peaks as he works to his peroration.

September 25, 1960

CHICAGO, Sept. 26—Vice President Nixon and Senator John F. Kennedy argued genteelly tonight in history's first nationally televised debate between Presidential candidates.

The two men, confronting each other in a Chicago television studio, centered their argument on which candidate and which party offered the nation the best means for spurring United States growth in an era of international peril.

The candidates, without ever generating any real heat in their exchanges, clashed on the following points:

◖Mr. Nixon's farm program, which Senator Kennedy said was merely another version of policies that had been tried and had failed under Ezra Taft Benson, Secretary of Agriculture.

◖The Republican and Democratic performance records on efforts to increase the minimum wage of $1 an hour and broaden its coverage, school construction legislation and medical-care for the aged. Mr. Kennedy charged that the Republican record on these measures showed the party gave only "lip service" to them.

◖The comparative records of the Truman and Eisenhower Administrations on fiscal security. Mr. Nixon asserted that in school and hospital construction the Republican years had seen an improvement over the previous seven Democratic years. Moreover, he said, wages had risen "five times as much" in the Eisenhower Administration as during the Truman Ad-

ministration, while the rise in prices has been only one-fifth of that in the Truman years.

In one of the sharper exchanges of the hour-long encounter, Mr. Nixon charged that the Democratic domestic program advanced by Senator Kennedy would cost the taxpayer from $13,200,000,000 to $18,000,000,000.

This meant, Mr. Nixon contended, that "either he will have to raise taxes or you have to unbalance the budget."

Unbalancing the budget, he went on, would mean another period of inflation and a consequent "blow" to the country's aged living on pension income.

"That," declared Senator Kennedy, in one of the evening's few shows if incipient heat, "is wholly wrong wholly in error." Mr. Nixon, he said, was attempting to create the impression that he was "in favor of unbalancing the budget."

In fact, Mr. Kennedy contended, many of his programs for such things as medical care for the aged, natural resources development, Federal assistance to school construction and teachers salaries could be financed without undue burden on the taxpayer if his policies for increasing the rate of economic growth were adopted.

"I don't believe in big government, but I believe in effective government," Mr. Kennedy said. "I think we can do a better job. I think we are going to have to do a better job."

Continuing his portrayal of the Eisenhower years as a period of stagnation, he asserted that the United States last year had the lowest rate of economic growth of any industrial state

in the world. Steel production, he noted, was only 50 per cent of capacity. The Soviet Union, he said, is "turning out twice as many engineers as we are."

At the present rate of hydro-electric-power construction, he went on, the Soviet Union would be "producing more power than we are" by 1975.

"I think it's time America started moving again," he declared.

Nixon Disagrees

Mr. Nixon replied that he had no quarrel with Mr. Kennedy's goal of increasing the rate of national growth. But, he said, Mr. Kennedy's statistics showing a slow growth rate last year were misleading because they were based on activity in a recession year. This year, by contrast, the rate is 6.9 per cent—"one of the highest rates in the world," he said.

In other areas of debate, these were the major points:

◖Mr. Nixon asserted that Senator Kennedy's failure to get any significant part of his program enacted at the August session of Congress was not due to President Eisenhower's threatened vetoes but to lack of national support for items in the program. It was "not because the President was against them," Mr. Nixon said. "It was because the people were against them. They were too extreme."

◖Mr. Kennedy answered Mr. Nixon's frequently repeated campaign assertion that he was too immature for the Presidency by asserting that Abraham Lincoln had come out of obscurity, as an inexperienced Congressman, to the White House. He and Mr. Nixon had "both come to Congress together" in the same year — 1946, Mr. Kennedy noted.

"Our experience in government is comparable." And, he contended, "there is no certain road to the Presidency. There

NIXON AND KENNEDY CLASH IN TV DEBATE ON SPENDING, FARMS AND SOCIAL ISSUES

EXCHANGE IS CALM

Sharp Retorts Are Few as Candidates Meet Face to Face

By RUSSELL BAKER

is no guarantee that if you take one road or the other you will be a successful President."

¶Mr. Nixon, using the only language heard all evening that bordered on the colorful, contrasted the Republican program for national growth with Mr. Kennedy's in these terms. Mr. Kennedy's, he said, "seem to be simply retreads of programs of the Truman Administration."

For the most part, the exchanges were distinguished by a suavity, earnestness and courtesy that suggested that the two men were more concerned about "image projection" to their huge television audience than about scoring debating points.

Senator Kennedy, using no television makeup, rarely smiled during the hour and maintained an expression of gravity suitable for a candidate for the highest office in the land.

Mr. Nixon, wearing pancake makeup to cover his dark beard, smiled more frequently as he made his points and dabbed frequently at the perspiration that beaded out on his chin.

The debate was carried simultaneously by all three major television networks, the American Broadcasting Company, the National Broadcasting Company and the Columbia Broadcasting System. It was also carried by the radio networks of all three and that of the Mutual Broadcasting System.

The first debate, produced by C. B. S., took place in a big studio at the C. B. S. Chicago outlet, Station WBBM-TV. Studio One, in which they met, was sealed off from the hundreds who swarmed through its corridors and sat in adjoining studios to watch the show on station monitors.

When the debate was over, the two candidates were spirited out of the studio through a freight driveway.

Nixon Noncommittal

At his hotel later, Mr. Nixon was noncommittal about how well he thought he had done. "A debater," he said, "never knows who wins. That will be decided by the people Nov. 8."

Mr. Kennedy was not available for comment, but his advisers said they were elated over his performance.

The only persons permitted in the studio besides television crewmen were two wire service reporters, three photographers and one aide to each candidate.

When the show ended, each man was asked how he felt about the outcome.

"A good exchange of views," said Mr. Nixon.

"We had an exchange of views," Mr. Kennedy agreed.

Under the rules agreed upon by the candidates, each man opened with an eight-minute exposition of his general position on domestic affairs.

This was followed by about thrity-five muntes of question-and-answer with the questions being put by four television newsmen selected by each of the four networks. This was followed by three minute closing statements by each candidate.

The television news representatives on the panel were Sander Vanocur of N. B. C., Robert Fleming of A. B. C., Charles Warren of Mutual and Stuart Novins of C. B. S. Howard K. Smith of the C. B. S. Washington staff acted as moderator, but except for introducing the two, had a quiet evening.

Nixon Arrives First

Mr. Nixon arrived first at the studio on Chicago's Near North Side near the lakefront. His car entered the building through a freight driveway and pulled up by a receiving line of network executives.

Mr. Nixon made small talk for a few moments, then entered the studio accompanied by his press secretary, Herbert G. Klein.

Senator Kennedy arrived eight minutes later, accompanied by several of his campaign aides.

After working the broadcasting executives reception line, he entered the studio where Mr. Nixon was waiting. The two men smiled and shook hands.

"Good to see you. I heard you had a big audience in Cleveland," Mr. Nixon told Mr. Kennedy. The Senator's reply was lost in the hubhub as the photographers worked.

Outside the building several hundred demonstrators with printed placards demonstrated at the curb for Mr. Kennedy. There was no evidence of any Nixon rooting section.

September 27, 1960

Squaring off—Senator Kennedy and Vice President Nixon before start of their debate last night in Chicago.

THE KENNEDYS: A NEW YORK TIMES PROFILE

PHILADELPHIA, Oct. 28 — Senator John F. Kennedy was acclaimed by more than 500,000 persons today on a 150-mile motorcade through economically depressed industrial and mining areas of northeast Pennsylvania.

Crowds cheered the Democratic nominee for mile after mile in an area that voted heavily for President Eisenhower in the last two elections.

The Senator shook or touched so many hands that his right hand was swollen and bleeding.

Gov. David L. Lawrence, with a background of fifty years in Pennsylvania politics, said the turnouts in the area exceeded those for Franklin D. Roosevelt and President Eisenhower.

Governor Makes Estimate

It was Governor Lawrence who provided the estimate in excess of 500,000. Most newsmen traveling with Senator Kennedy thought the estimate was not excessive.

"You must remember," the Governor said, "that this is one of the most depressed economic areas in the nation. And these people look to this fellow [Senator Kennedy] as a messiah who will lead them out."

From Bethlehem through the major centers of Allentown, Hazleton, Wilkes-Barre and Scranton, all the crowds were large.

The greatest concentration was an almost solid throng that lined the Senator's nineteen-mile route from Wilkes-Barre to Scranton. It took more than two and a half hours to make the trip.

During one ten-mile stretch, a bus driver for the press said he was able to shift from low gear to second gear only once, and then only briefly.

From Scranton, Mr. Kennedy flew to Philadelphia, where he has a heavy day of suburban campaigning tomorrow.

Highly pleased, Senator Kennedy said the crowd turnouts today and in New York were the greatest of his campaign.

Mr. Kennedy stressed "bread and butter" issues, charging that Republican inaction was responsible for declining business and rising unemployment. He promised swift action by a Democratic Administration to revive and expand the economy, and emergency measures to redevelop the hard-coal areas whose principal industry is virtually dead.

Governor Lawrence said he was confident the Massachusetts Senator would take the state's thirty-two electoral votes.

He discounted reports that Senator Kennedy, a Roman Catholic, would suffer heavily in rural Protestant areas where anti-Catholicism is said to be strong.

Senator Joseph S. Clark forecast a 300,000-vote margin for Senator Kennedy in this state, which has cast its electoral votes for Republican Presidential nominees in every election since 1944.

"It looks so good, I'm scared," Senator Clark said. "I wish the election were today."

Many of the areas that Senator Kennedy visited were heavily pro-Eisenhower in 1952 and 1956. But in towns visited by both Mr. Kennedy and Vice President Nixon, the crowds that turned out for the Senator today exceeded those drawn by the Vice President, according to local reporters and the police.

14,000 at Airport

A noisy crowd in excess of 14,000 turned out after midnight to welcome Senator Kennedy at the airport in Allentown.

His first stop this morning was at the duplex home in Bethlehem of John Duffy, an unemployed steel worker with three children. Mr. Duffy said his unemployment insurance came to $72 a month, in contrast to his regular weekly pay of $120. Mr. Kennedy and Mr. Duffy made a television short together.

At Moravian College, a Protestant institution, the main auditorium was filled with more than 6,500 persons. An equal number outside could not gain admission. Here Mr. Kennedy was introduced and praised by Representative Francis E. Walter of Pennsylvania, co-author of the McCarran-Walter Immigration Act that Senator Kennedy has criticized.

In Allentown, the police estimated the crowd at 8,000 to 14,000. Here Senator Kennedy drew a loud cheer, coupled with boos, as he declared that "if you want the philosophy of Harding and Coolidge, then Nixon is your man."

As the motorcade moved down the Pennsylvania Turnpike, Senator Kennedy stopped briefly at a two-room frame school. He wrote this message on the blackboard:

"Knowledge is power.
"Francis Bacon.
"John F. Kennedy, 1960."

One of those who met him at Pittsville was Mrs. Julia Oshinski of Shamokin, whose son, Robert J. Oshinski, is one of eleven fliers still unaccounted for after his aircraft was shot down over Soviet Armenia. She asked the Senator to press an investigation of her son's fate, and Mr. Kennedy told her he would do so.

Several thousand persons blocked the main streets of both Tamaqua and McAdoo, forcing brief unscheduled stops. At Hazleton policemen estimated the crowd at 15,000. They said it was the town's biggest turnout since 1938, when a Hazleton High School football team was welcomed back after it had captured the state championship.

Sitting on the platform at Hazleton was Thomas Kennedy, president of the United Mine Workers of America, who long since announced his personal support of Senator Kennedy. The union is uncommitted, partly because its president emeritus, John L. Lewis, is opposed to Senator Kennedy. The union president said most of its officers and members were backing the Democratic ticket.

Despite their depressed economic conditions, the Pennsylvania crowds were in a holiday mood. Frequently persons along the route tossed presents to Senator Kennedy as his car moved along.

The Kennedy motorcade encountered many school Halloween parties, and children pranced into the streets wearing masks and costumes.

Big crowds at Sugar Notch and Nanticoke crowded into the streets, forcing more unscheduled stops. At Sugar Notch, the Senator placed a blanket of flowers, presented to him earlier, at the base of a war memorial.

Downtown Wilkes-Barre was jammed, but much of the crowd moved off before the Senator started his speech.

Senator Kennedy's headquarters announced tonight the cancellation of his planned appearance tomorrow evening on the American Broadcasting Company television show "Campaign Roundup."

The broadcast was dropped it was said, "because Senator Kennedy simply had too much to do." It was scheduled for broadcast from the Philadelphia studios of WFIL-TV at 7 P. M.

October 29, 1960

KENNEDY CHEERED IN PENNSYLVANIA

500,000 Acclaim Senator as He Motors Through Area of High Unemployment

---

By W. H. LAWRENCE

14 Quick Votes for Kennedy
BOSTON, Nov. 2 (AP)—Senator John F. Kennedy has one big advantage, his mother, Mrs. Joseph P. Kennedy, said at a news conference today. There are fourteen votes for him in his immediate family, and many more among his relatives. And, Mrs. Kennedy said, they are all campaigning for him.

November 3, 1960

KENNEDY'S VICTORY WON BY CLOSE MARGIN

BALLOTING SHIFTS POWER BALANCE

Democrats Again in Control, Ending Division Between Capitol and President

RESULTS DELAYED

Popular Vote Almost Even—300-185 Is Electoral Tally

By JAMES RESTON

Senator John F. Kennedy of Massachusetts finally won the 1960 Presidential election from Vice President Nixon by the astonishing margin of less than two votes per voting precinct.

Senator Kennedy's electoral vote total stood yesterday at 300, just thirty-one more than the 269 needed for election. The Vice President's total was 185. Fifty-two additional electoral votes, including California's thirty-two, were still in doubt last night.

But the popular vote was a different story. The two candidates ran virtually even. Senator Kennedy's lead last night was little more than 300,000 in a total tabulated vote of about 66,000,000 cast in 165,826 precincts.

That was a plurality for the Senator of less than one-half of 1 per cent of the total vote—the smallest percentage difference between the popular vote of two Presidential candidates since 1880, when James A. Garfield outran Gen. Winfield Scott Hancock by 7,000 votes in a total of almost 9,000,000.

End Divided Government

Nevertheless, yesterday's voting radically altered the political balance of power in America in favor of the Democrats and put them in a commanding position in the Federal and state capitals unknown since the heyday of Franklin D. Roosevelt.

They regained control of the White House for the first time since 1952 and thus ended divided government in Washington. They retained control of the Senate and the House of Representatives, although with slightly reduced margins. And they increased their hold on the state governorships by one, bringing the Democratic margin to 34—16.

The President-elect is the first Roman Catholic ever to win the nation's highest office. The only other member of his church nominated for President was Alfred E. Smith, who was defeated by Herbert Hoover in 1928.

Faces Difficult Questions

Despite his personal triumph, President-elect Kennedy is confronted by a number of hard questions:

In the face of such a narrow victory how can he get through the Congress the liberal program he proposed during the campaign?

Can so close an election produce any impetus for loosening the conservative coalition of Republicans and Southern Democrats which has blocked most liberal legislation in the House?

Will the new President be able successfully to claim a mandate for legislation such as the $1.25 minimum wage, Federal school aid and a broader medical assistance to the aged which he advocated from the stump?

In the campaign Senator Kennedy promised a "first hundred days" equal to that great period of reform in the Administration of Franklin D. Roosevelt. But the result made it more than ever likely that he would have to reach an accommodation with the conservative South, which has opposed much of his program within the Democratic party.

Senator Lyndon B. Johnson of Texas, Senator Kennedy's Vice-Presidential running mate, contributed much to Mr. Kennedy's victory and more than justified the controversial last minute tactic of putting the Texan on the ticket over the loud protests of the Northern Democratic liberals.

Johnson's Contribution

Without much question, he was responsible for bringing Texas back to the Democratic fold for the first time since 1948, and for helping to hold North and South Carolina, which most of the experts gave to the Republicans a month ago. Meanwhile, there was nothing to suggest that he had hurt the Democrats, as predicted, in the liberal areas of the urban North.

Not since President Harry S. Truman's surprising victory over Gov. Thomas E. Dewey of New York in the election of 1948 — and perhaps not even since Woodrow Wilson's triumph in the photo-finish election of 1916—have there been so many dramatic swings and changes of political fortune as occurred all through the night Tuesday and even into yesterday afternoon.

It is worth recalling also that Mr. Truman's victory, dramatic as it was, came with a plurality of more than 2,000,000 votes—compared with Senator Kennedy's less than 400,000 so far.

Shortly before midnight Tuesday the signs had seemed to point to a substantial Kennedy victory.

Victory Projected Into West

The Senator's national plurality of the popular vote, which had been climbing steadily all evening, was about 2,000,000. The Chicago vote had given him a big lead in Illinois, and the analysts were projecting westward his smashing triumph in the Northeast.

But actually that was the peak of Senator Kennedy's momentum. Just about midnight a slow process of attrition set in that whittled away at his "sure" win until, in the dramatic hours of the early morning, it was clear that this was the closest election in generations.

The Kennedy popular-vote margin melted to 800,000 by 5 A. M. yesterday, and the trend was still downward. The Senator's Illinois lead dropped from almost 200,000 to around 50,000, and state Democratic leaders began to sound brave when they forecast a final victory margin of "at least" 28,000.

And it became increasingly evident that the magic worked by Senator Kennedy in the East was less effective on the other side of the Mississippi. As returns began coming in from the West, the race drew closer and closer.

The returns were so close in many Western states that it became impossible to get a clear picture. Leads of a few hundred or a few thousand votes changed hands again and again in Nevada, New Mexico, Montana, Washington, Hawaii and Alaska.

By 5 or 6 A. M. yesterday, the Kennedy margin seemed to be facing a real threat in Minnesota as well as Illinois.

Nixon Finally Concedes

It became clear that Senator Kennedy had to win one of the three big undecided states —Illinois, Minnesota or California—to get his needed 269 electoral votes.

At no time did Vice President Nixon have a chance to win 269 electoral votes on his own. Even if all three of the major doubtful states and every one of the smaller western states had fallen to him, he would have been four votes short.

But in such a situation Senator Kennedy would also have been denied a majority. The power to decide the winner would then have rested with fourteen unpledged electors from Alabama and Mississippi who bolted the regular Democratic ticket as a protest against Northern Democratic views.

Throughout yesterday morning the result hung in the balance. Senator Kennedy's margin fell slowly in Illinois and Minnesota, and indeed at one point Mr. Nixon pulled ahead in the former until a last batch of Chicago votes was produced for Mr. Kennedy.

Then at 12:33 o'clock Senator Kennedy clinched Minnesota and the election. Thirteen minutes later Mr. Nixon made his formal concession.

Strength Combined

Senators Kennedy and Johnson won by putting together their combined strength in the great cities of the North and the rural areas of the traditionally Democratic South; but they were remarkably weak elsewhere.

For example, they won eight of the nine so-called large decisive states, but in some of them their margins were tighter than a Pullman window: 6,000-6,500 in Illinois; 22,000 in New Jersey, 60,000 in Texas, 65,000 in Michigan, 131,-000 in Pennsylvania.

Only in New York and Kennedy's home state of Massachusetts did the Democrats win by truly large majorities—404,000 in New York and 498,000 in Massachussetts. Each of these margins was larger than Mr. Kennedy's margin of victory in the nation as a whole.

The anomalies in the results were sometimes startling.

Why should Mr. Kennedy win by 131,000 in Pennsylvania and lose in neighboring Ohio, with much the same mixture of union and Catholic voters, by 263,000?

Senator Kennedy campaigned on a liberal program but could not have won without the support of conservative Catholics in the North and conservative Protestants in the South.

Contrasts in Jersey

In most areas populated by Catholics, Mr. Kennedy did well, but in some, Hudson County, N. J., for example, his showing was a great disappointment to his managers, while he did remarkably well in the more Republican territory of Essex County, N. J.

While the Senator was heavily supported in the cities of the North, Southern industrial areas such as Charlotte and Winston-Salem, N. C., went Republican. He did well in the Southern "Black Belts," as indeed did Smith in 1928, but he did poorly in the farm belts of the North, where he expected his attacks on Secretary of Agriculture Ezra Taft Benson might even swing some of the Plains States into the Democratic column.

Also, while Mr. Kennedy was regaining some of the Democratic party's lost strength in the South, he managed at the same time to pick up additional strength among Negroes, who have been complaining about the Democratic party's political associations with the South.

Senator Thruston B. Morton, the genial and relaxed chairman of the Republican National Committee, said yesterday that the main reason why Vice President Nixon had lost the election was that he had failed to hold the Northern Negro vote, which had gone so heavily to President Eisenhower in the two previous Presidential elections.

Chairman Morton's estimate was that the Vice President had got only between 10 to 12 per cent of the Negro vote, while President Eisenhower got about 26 per cent in 1952 and 1956.

Ironically, Senator Kennedy, whose political reputation rested primarily on his arresting and attractive personality, ran about 7 per cent behind the Democratic local candidates on a national basis.

This was not true in the Northeast, where he was near his home base and where his sophisticated manner was quite popular, but it was definitely true in Illinois, Minnesota, Wisconsin, and Indiana, where he ran well behind the Democratic ticket.

Nevertheless, the most striking facts of all lay in the contrasts in the voting returns from the various regions of the country.

In New England, Senator Kennedy split the six states, three to three, but built up a plurality of 592,036 votes.

He swept all six Middle Atlantic States—Delaware, Maryland, New Jersey, New York, Pennsylvania and West Virginia with another huge plurality of 684,549. Then, as the voting moved westward, his power declined.

A Deficit in Midwest

He split the East Central States, winning Illinois by a whisker and Michigan, but lost Ohio and Indiana, and came out of the region with a deficit of 422,904.

He lost six of the eight West central states, Iowa, Kansas, Nebraska, North and South Dakota and Wisconsin and won only two, Minnesota and Missouri. Here again, Vice President Nixon piled up a plurality for the region of 526,235.

In the Mountain states, New Mexico swung to Kennedy last night, but Mr. Nixon took six of the others, and Senator Kennedy won only Nevada. The same trend prevailed here, with the Vice President getting a plurality of at least 160,000.

Even in the Pacific Coast states, Mr. Nixon's plurality was over 22,000, and while Mr. Kennedy had a plurality of 245,000 in the South, where he won everything except Florida, Oklahoma, Kentucky, Tennessee and Virginia, the Republicans piled up a comparatively large Southern vote, 5,300,000.

November 10, 1960

A PRANCING PRESIDENT-ELECT: Senator John F. Kennedy gives daughter, Caroline, a ride at Hayannis Port.

Exultant Family Joins Kennedy In Triumph It Helped to Forge

Senator's Father Appears with Him for First Time Since Start of Campaign —Wife Serene at Armory Talk

By NAN ROBERTSON

HYANNIS, Mass., Nov. 9—The Kennedy family, tired but exultant, stood in triumph today behind the man they had helped elect President as he accepted his defeated rival's congratulations.

The sisters, brothers-in-law and parents of John F. Kennedy — twelve in all — were massed with solemn faces on the bunting-draped stage of the National Guard Armory after a nerve-wracking night.

Beside the President-elect was his 31-year-old wife Jacqueline, serene and smiling, her eyes fixed on her husband as he spoke. She was hatless and wore a purple wool coat that did not mask the fact that she was expecting a child within three weeks.

Senator Kennedy referred to this when he said that they were preparing "for a new Administration and a new baby."

Father Appears With Son

For the first time since the Kennedy campaign began officially in the primaries early this year, the President-elect's father, Joseph P. Kennedy, appeared with his son.

The 71-year-old former Ambassador to Britain, dressed in a gray business suit, listened until the short speech was done. Then he turned smilingly to his wife Rose, seated beside him in the front row of wooden folding chairs.

Although the whole family had worked hard and long to lift Senator Kennedy to the Presidency, one member could be singled out as the relative who had done most to achieve his election.

Robert F. Kennedy, the Senator's 34-year-old brother and campaign manager, had slaved single-handedly and beyond the point of exhaustion to win the prize.

He stood tensely at first beside a United States Flag at the side of the stage, hands in his pockets, staring at his brother and the family. Then he sat down beside his father, arms folded across his chest.

Sister Not Present

The only adult member of

the President-elect's immediate family who was missing today was his sister Rosemary, who was in a Wisconsin nursing home. The rest, except for his father, have campaigned singly and together for months.

None of them looked haggard this afternoon on the armory platform, despite weeks without enough sleep.

Most of the family had gathered last night at Robert Kennedy's house, the "campaign post" next-door to Joseph Kennedy's "Big House," to receive returns.

The Senator spent most of the night at his own home, a hundred yards away, with his wife. He went to bed at 3:50 A. M. today after Vice President Nixon declined to concede the election. His wife retired shortly before this. The other members of the family called it a night about 4 A. M.

Play Touch Football

They were up bright and early today. With astonishing energy some played touch football on the father's lawn facing Nantucket Sound. Others walked on the beach.

Members of the family played a second football game, the Kennedys' favorite communal exercise, this afternoon.

Sometime before 6 A. M. eighteen Secret Service men had been detailed to guard the next President.

At 9:40 A. M., the President-elect appeared at a second-story window of his Cape Cod house, grinning and clad in pajamas.

About 9:30 A. M., the Senator's daughter Caroline left the house with the Senator's cousin, Ann Gargan, and her Welsh terrier Charlie. The little girl wore the same blue sweater and matching knitted cap she had worn yesterday while posing for photographers. Caroline, who is not quite 3, later went riding on her Irish pony with her paternal grandfather.

Carries Daughter

About 11 A. M., the President-elect walked to his father's house. Forty-five minutes later he strolled back home, hand-in-hand with Caroline and his youngest brother Edward, who is 28.

The Senator suggested a hike on the beach. Caroline lifted her arms and begged for a piggyback ride. With difficulty, her father swung the child on his back.

After a brisk walk, joined by Senator Kennedy's sisters Pat, Eunice and Jean and Theodore C. Sorensen, his chief policy adviser, the President-elect greeted neighbors at the gate to his father's house.

A number said: "Hi, Jack, we're awfully proud of you." A young man, trying out the phrase, said: "Mr. President. How do you like that, Jack?"

Mr. Kennedy replied, "Well, I don't know."

A woman neighbor broke in with: "Nice going, Jack. Let's give a cheer." None of the eighteen well-wishers at the gate took her up on it.

Drive to The Armory

After a few moments of chit-chat about mending fences and passing on best regards from others not present, Senator Kennedy returned to his father's house.

The fourteen Kennedys, including the President-elect and

wife, then got into four automobiles for the mile-and-a-half drive to the armory.

After the Senator's speech, a formal photographic session was held for all the family—with the usual crises. Joseph Kennedy grumpily objected to his wife's being placed in an enormous wing chair. "That's an awkward pose," he said. "There are plenty of chairs in the house." He dispatched someone for another chair.

At one point Jacqueline Kennedy, in a scarlet dress, stood next to her mother-in-law, who wore cerise. "Our dresses clash horribly for color photography," said Mrs. Joseph Kennedy. Her daughter-in law took another position.

The family then drove back to Joseph Kennedy's house.

R. Sargent Shriver, husband of Eunice Kennedy, tossed a football in the air several times as he went up the porch steps.

His wife was asked how she had felt last night while the family received election returns.

"It was," she said, "the longest night in history."

November 10, 1960

A Portrait of Mrs. Kennedy: Spirited, Shy and Chic

Asked if she felt up to the large-scale entertaining of the White House, she replied with spirit, "I have been married to one of the busiest men in the country for seven years. I ran three houses for him. I have entertained for large and small groups on long and short notice."

BESS FURMAN,
N. Y. Times.
Sept. 20, 1960.

•

Of all the Kennedy women, the Senator's wife Jacqueline cottons least to campaigning. She is ill at ease among strangers, and her luminous beauty shines at its best when she entertains small groups of friends at home. Critics chide her reluctance to pump hands, make speeches and pose for the press.

LOOK MAGAZINE.
Oct. 11, 1960.

•

She comes close to being a certifiable egghead, who speaks French, Italian, and Spanish fluently, read voraciously in history, biography, and current affairs, helps her husband with his highly literate speeches, and paints with flair. Yet her favorite expression in everyday conversation is "Oh yeah?" —not a cynical phrase, as she uses it, but one of guileless wonderment and approbation.

NEWSWEEK.
Feb. 22, 1960.

•

When Jacqueline Kennedy, then five days the wife of a

Presidential candidate, stepped aboard the family yacht in Hyannis Port, Mass., wearing an orange pull-over sweater, shocking pink Capri pants and a bouffant hairdo that gamboled merrily in the breeze, even those newsmen present who could not tell shocking pink from Windsor Rose knew they were witnessing something of possibly vast political consequences."

MARTHA WEINMAN,
N. Y. Times Magazine.
Sept. 11, 1960.

•

Jackie is definitely no mixed-up kid, but she comes from a mixed family. She has a full sister, a stepsister, a half sister, two stepbrothers and a half brother. Divorce did it. * * *

I told her I recalled honeymoon pictures of her posed nautically in a sailboat and said she must be a great sailing enthusiast. "My husband is," she said, "They just shoved me into that boat long enough to take the picture."

GEORGE DIXON,
The Daily Mirror.
April 2, 1956.

•

She has a lovely shyness, and a piquant, delightful voice.

WILHELA CUSHMAN,
• Ladies' Home Journal.
November, 1960.

•

She, herself, wonders aloud to her friends about her political life. "This summer was something," she said a few days ago. "I was always coming

down to breakfast in my wrapper with Caroline, and there would be a couple of strange Governors or labor leaders I'd never seen before, smoking cigars and eating scrambled eggs."

NEWSWEEK.
Oct. 17, 1960.

•

While hardly immodest, she does not underestimate her contribution to her husband's life. Young Jack Kennedy—still boyish at 39—has long had a reputation as a genially absent-minded type, with great irreverance for the formalities of existence. He would forget suits in hotel rooms, emerge in the street without a dime in his pockets, keep his dinner guests waiting an unconscionable time before he got home from the office. (The thing to do was not to wait for the host.) Today all that has changed.

IRWIN ROSS, The N. Y. Post.
March 25, 1957.

•

She is not a simple girl and probably couldn't be one if she tried. * * *

Mrs. Kennedy, however, may be extra sensitive on the subject of her hair. The Senator has received a score of letters complaining about her hair style and urging that it be changed. (presumably to fit the Main Street, apple-pie image).

DAVID WISE,
N. Y. Herald Tribune.
Oct. 2, 1960.

•

She was a student at George Washington University in Washington, D. C., when she met her future husband, a millionaire bachelor and member of the U. S. House of Representatives, in 1952. * * * "It was a very spasmodic courtship," she has related. * * * "He'd call me from some oyster bar up there, with a great clinking of coins," she recalls, "to ask me out to the movies the following Wednesday in Washington."

U. S. NEWS & WORLD REPORT. July 25, 1960.

•

"I don't think she's mad about politics," remarked Mrs. Jean Smith. * * * Another good friend of the family, broker Charles Spalding, commented, "It requires a more rugged, less feminine girl than Jackie to be vitally involved in politics."

REDBOOK. March, 1960.

November 10, 1960

WASHINGTON, Nov. 22—Sweeping changes in the White House were forecast today by its incoming social secretary, Miss Lettia Baldridge.

An important change, she said, will be that the White House will become "a showcase of American art and history."

Miss Baldrige, a Republican, held her first news conference today at the Women's National Democratic Club. She sat down at a table set with microphones and said: "I'm very happy, very delighted, and very scared."

Then she plunged right into what she and Mrs. Kennedy had been planning. The first question was whether regular press conferences had been included in the plans.

"Mrs. Kennedy will have so much news to impart," she answered briskly, "that regular press conferences probably will be the best way to do it."

Miss Baldrige said that Mrs. Kennedy would be displaying in the White House fine paintings, sculpture, music and all other forms of American art.

"She will seek out the very finest names," she added.

Miss Baldrige also indicated the "entire entertainment program system" would be revamped.

She indicated that this would be done after the manner in which she had operated as social secretary in the United States Embassies in Paris and in Rome.

"It would be experimental," she said. "You can't tell what would appeal. You can only try out and see what goes."

For example, she noted that Mrs. Clare Boothe Luce, as Ambassador in Rome, had found that people preferred to come for an hour to a reception, greet her, and go on, rather than to stay for two hours.

This would provide a chance for a greater number of guests, Miss Baldrige said, giving more people a chance to see the President and giving him more of a chance to get political opinion.

November 23, 1960

ACTIVE ROLE SET BY MRS. KENNEDY

Her Social Secretary Tells of Plans to Change the Entertainment System

By BESS FURMAN

WASHINGTON, Friday, Nov. 25—Mrs. John F. Kennedy, wife of the President-elect, gave birth to a boy early this morning.

Her husband had left Washington only a few hours earlier to fly back to Palm Beach, Fla., where he has been vacationing since the election. He turned around immediately, and was scheduled to arrive here shortly before dawn.

Mrs. Kennedy was rushed by ambulance to Georgetown University Hospital, a few blocks from her home, at 10:55 o'clock last night. The baby was born at 12:22 o'clock this morning by Caesarean section.

A press representative for Mrs. Kennedy reported that the baby weighed 6 pounds and 2 ounces.

At 2 A. M. Dr. John W. Walsh, Mrs. Kennedy's personal physician, said:

"The mother is resting comfortably and is in excellent condition." Mrs. Kennedy was then still in the recovery room.

Dr. Walsh made no reference to the child, but Mrs. Kennedy's press spokesman said he was well.

Mrs. Kennedy, during the election campaign, said that if her baby was a boy, she would name him for his father, John Fitzgerald.

The Kennedys had expected the baby, their second, in mid-December. Their first child, Caroline, will have her third birthday Sunday. Senator Kennedy flew to Washington from Palm Beach Wednesday for a Thanksgiving-birthday celebration with the family.

Dr. Walsh sent Mrs. Kennedy to the hospital in an ambulance. She was accompanied by a Secret Service agent.

Her parents, Mr. and Mrs. Hugh D. Auchincloss, arrived at the hospital from their suburban Virginia estate a few minutes before the baby was born. A Roman Catholic priest was on the hospital floor.

The priest, who rode in the elevator with Mrs. Kennedy to the delivery room, was Father George Wilson of Auriesville, N. Y., assistant chaplain at the hospital.

Like the new baby, Caroline was born by Caesarean section. Mrs. Kennedy had two miscarriages. As a result, her activity during the campaign was limited by her physician.

Dr. Edward B. Broocks, Caroline Kennedy's pediatrician, was present at the delivery.

"Everything went well," he said. He added that the baby's condition was "good," and that he had "a big mop of hair."

The driver of the ambulance, Willard Baucom, arrived at the Kennedy home before Dr. Walsh and was directed upstairs to her bedroom. He said she was lying in bed in a nightgown and overcoat.

"She was smiling and looked like a baby doll," he said.

The driver and an assistant carried her down in a stretcher.

Senator Kennedy received word that his wife had gone to the hospital when he landed at 12:15 A. M. in Palm Beach. He hurried to the airport administration building and telephoned the hospital.

Aides said he spoke to a nurse, who informed him that Mrs. Kennedy was in the operating room for a Caesarean section.

The President-elect immediately decided to fly back to Washington. Instead of using the twin-engine plane that had brought him to Palm Beach, he chose a faster four-engine airliner.

The plane was airborne at 12:52 A. M. Senator Kennedy was receiving details about the baby by radio from a newspaper reporter in the control tower at the Palm Beach airport.

A crowd of 200 had greeted Mr. Kennedy at the Palm Beach airport. He quickly shouldered his way through to the administration building.

The Kennedys had spent a quiet day in their three-story brick town house here. They stayed inside all day, while the curious trickled by on foot and in cars. The Senator stepped outside once, to greet his only dinner guest, William Walton.

Mr. Walton, an artist, is a former newsman and was coordinator of the Kennedy campaign in New York State.

Mr. Kennedy assured the few newsmen who had been standing all morning on the sidewalk that he would not be out again until flight time.

"Look, he said, "I don't want to spoil your Thanksgiving."

Pierre Salinger, his press secretary, said that the two ducks Mr. Kennedy brought from Palm Beach as a gift for Caroline were at home in the bathtub.

He added that the Kennedys had planned to spend Christmas at Palm Beach.

November 25, 1960

Mrs. Kennedy Has a Boy After a Dash to Hospital

President-Elect Returns From South on Getting News at Airport

By RICHARD E. MOONEY

KENNEDY BRINGS CAROLINE NEWS

Tells Daughter About Baby, but His Wife Had Given Child Orientation

By BESS FURMAN

WASHINGTON, Nov. 25— President-elect John F. Kennedy has been puzzled about how to tell his 2-year-old daughter Caroline about her baby brother, but his wife has been building up to it for a long time.

"It's going to take some orientation," the President-elect told newsmen on watch at the Kennedys' Georgetown home.

Returning from a noon visit to the Georgetown University Hospital, Mr. Kennedy strolled hatless around the block with Caroline, who was airing her doll in a red buggy. He talked to her in a quiet voice, and from time to time helped her steer the doll carriage over the rough brick sidewalk and around tree trunks.

The tall Senator wore a blue-gray suit and dark overcoat, the little girl a red jacket and red ankle-length slacks. Where the going was smooth, she held to his hand.

Secret Service Discreet

At his request, only one Secret Service man followed— and at a discreet distance. A Secret Service radio car also trailed around the block.

Back at the house, Mr. Kennedy still hadn't made up his mind as to when to tell Caroline. But a half hour later his press secretary, Pierre E. Salinger, came out and informed reporters that Mr. Kennedy was telling Caroline.

"He was building himself up to it as I left," he said.

Mrs. Kennedy had been conducting her build-up since September. She said that she held with the theory that children should not be told too soon, as the long wait becomes wearisome.

Instead, she said, she was pointing out to Caroline how nice it would be to have a little baby brother or sister by using the infant son of her sister-in-law, Mrs. Stephen A. Smith, as a symbol.

Mrs. Smith, one of Mr. Kennedy's sisters, gave birth to her child after the nominating convention, and before the campaign was in full swing.

"Caroline went often to play with her little cousin Stevie so that she could see how nice it was to have a baby in the family," Mrs. Kennedy said recently.

Mrs. Kennedy also confessed that she had mixed feelings about wanting a son to be President of the United States.

"Being President is one thing —you could not help being proud of that," she said. "But running for office is another— an ordeal you would wish to spare sons and husbands."

Later, on another visit to the hospital, Senator Kennedy said he finally had told his daughter of the new baby.

"I told her her mother was getting a brother for her," Senator Kennedy said.

The early arrival of John F. Kennedy Jr. at twenty-two minutes after midnight created wide stirrings.

The Census Bureau calculated that his birth increased the nation's population to 182,006,267. The bureau has a clock in the Commerce Department, geared to statistics of births, deaths and migrations, that helps it to estimate such things.

By coincidence, and a twenty-two minute margin, the Kennedy baby was born on the birthday of the Pope. Pope John, who was born Nov. 25, 1881, celebrated his seventy-ninth birthday today.

'New Frontier' Noted

In Paris Vice President-elect Lyndon B. Johnson said:

"Since Kennedy already had his daughter Caroline and I've had two girls, this son represents a new frontier for the Administration." "New Frontier" was Senator Kennedy's campaign theme.

Congratulations poured into Georgetown University Hospital and the Kennedy home, including President Eisenhower's felicitations, which were delivered by hand.

Queen Elizabeth II and Prince Philip sent their congratulations through the British Ambassador here.

In Rome, the Vatican City newspaper L'Osservatore Romano, carried the front page headline "Happy Event in the Kennedy House." However, protocol does not call for cabled congratulations from the Pope as Mr. Kennedy is not yet President.

In West Berlin "A Son for Kennedy" was the banner headline for the newspaper Nacht Despesche.

Senator Kennedy arrived from Florida at about 4:20 A. M. Mrs. Gladys Uhl had served as press liaison for Mrs. Kennedy until the arrival of the Senator with his press secretary, who held a news conference at 4:30 A. M.

Mr. Uhl, who was present when the baby was lifted from its incubator to be shown to its grandmother, Mrs. Auchincloss, gave a description. She said:

"He's just wonderful. His eyes were closed. I think he had a tiny bit of dark hair. He was sort of wiggling a little bit."

November 26, 1960

The President and his daughter out for a stroll in Georgetown. The President was trying to figure out a way to tell Caroline of the birth of her new baby brother, John, Jr.

WASHINGTON, Nov. 29—In addition to the problems of taking over the Government, the new Democratic leaders face trouble on the male fashion front.

An omen appeared today in a rebuke by Representative Thomas M. Pelly, Republican of Washington, to Vice President-elect Lyndon B. Johnson for having ordered five suits at $147 each from a London tailor.

President-elect John F. Kennedy has irritated Washington tailoring circles by his predilection for Savile Row suits.

Mr. Pelly's objection to Mr. Johnson's London shopping was based on economic ground.

"At a time when it's important to the stability of the American dollar to hold down purchases from abroad, Senator Johnson sets a bad example for the American people by buying his suits from a London tailor," he said.

Mr. Kennedy, he suggested, could also "relieve the pressure on the dollar" and help end the gold drain by buying American.

Mr. Kennedy's London tailoring also drew a protest of hurt pride last week from Robert E. Stein, a Washington custom tailor. In a letter to The Washington Post, Mr. Stein complained that he saw no need for Mr. Kennedy to buy in London, since "the finest clothes in the world" were made "in the good old U. S. A."

According to reports from London, Savile Row was disturbed by Mr. Johnson, but only on the ground of taste. He insisted on suit jackets with two vents. In the best-dressed British circles, this style is suitable only for sports wear.

Pierre Salinger, press secretary, said Mr. Kennedy bought most of his clothes from H. Harris & Co., New York tailor.

The new Administration has still not decided how to deal with another fashion issue. The question is whether Mr. Kennedy, who normally goes bare leaded, will wear the traditional high silk hat for his Inauguration.

President Eisenhower scandalized traditionalists in 1953 by abandoning the topper for a Homburg. Asked today whether he would ride to the Capitol with a top hat, Mr. Kennedy replied, "I don't know."

November 30, 1960

Kennedy and Johnson Assailed For Purchasing British Clothes

President-elect John F. Kennedy though he prefers to go bareheaded, will wear a black silk topper for his Inauguration.

This will return the event to the formality that prevailed for decades, until President Eisenhower chose the Homburg in 1953.

Samuel Harris, who has been Mr. Kennedy's tailor for twelve years, said yesterday the Senator had asked his advice on the matter. He told Mr. Kennedy, he said, that he should wear a cutaway suit and a black topper, and the Senator replied: "O. K. I'll wear a topper."

Mr. Kennedy was hatless most of the campaign. He has worn hats infrequently, usually only when the occasion required it. According to a White House report, he is still sheepish about being photographed in a hat.

Recent Washington dispatches said the hatmakers of Connecticut had sent word to Mr. Kennedy through Gov. Abraham A. Ribicoff that it would be nice for him to wear a hat. The next day the President-elect emerged from his Georgetown home wearing a gray felt.

On Tuesday night when he attended the theatre here, he was barebeaded. Backstage at "Best Man," he told Lee Tracy, the actor:

"A friend told me I had better wear a hat. It might help the people in Danbury."

Mr. Harris said he went to the Kennedy suite in the Carlyle Hotel yesterday and fitted the President-elect for a cutaway suit—Oxford gray coat, light pearl gray waistcoat and worsted gray striped trousers.

Mr. Harris does not handle hats. He said he presumed Mr. Kennedy would get a topper in Washington.

December 9, 1960

Kennedy Decides: It'll Be a Topper

A KENNEDY IN LONDON

Edward on Way to Africa— Doubts He'll Take U.S. Post

LONDON, Dec. 3 (UPI)—Edward M. Kennedy, the President-elect's brother, arrived today on the way to Africa as an unofficial observer for the incoming United States Government, but with no idea of taking a job in his brother's administration.

"I haven't been offered one," said the 28-year-old lawyer, who played a major role in his brother's Presidential campaign.

"And I doubt very much if I would take one. My plans are at the moment to carry on with my practice."

Edward was scheduled to take off tomorrow for Salisbury, Southern Rhodesia, on a three-week study tour at his brother's request.

"I am going to see as much as I possibly can in the coming three weeks on all aspects of African life," he said.

He was greeted at London Airport by American embassy officials.

December 4, 1960

At Home In The White House

Dillon Appointed Secretary of Treasury; Kennedy's Brother Is Attorney General

Second Republican Gets Post in New Cabinet— President Approves

By W. H. LAWRENCE

WASHINGTON, Dec. 16 — President-elect John F. Kennedy designated a Republican, Douglas Dillon, as his Secretary of the Treasury today and named his brother, Robert F. Kennedy, as Attorney General.

Mr. Dillon, now serving the Eisenhower Administration as Under Secretary of State, disclosed that he had sought the assent of President Eisenhower this morning and of Vice President Nixon earlier.

"Neither of them had any objection if I felt that this was something that would be in the national security interest of the country, and if we were to work toward a sound fiscal policy as is the case," Mr. Dillon said.

Both appointments long had been forecast. But the choice of Robert Kennedy, 35 years old, is expected to provoke a political storm. Senator Kennedy set a precedent by naming his brother to the Cabinet.

Senator Kennedy said he would complete his Cabinet tomorrow by naming his Postmaster General from the family home at Palm Beach, Fla., where he is planning a prolonged holiday through Christmas and New Year's Day.

He left little doubt that his choice would be J. Edward Day, a California insurance executive, who flew in by jet from Los Angeles during the night and then flew South with the President-elect this afternoon.

The President-elect left Washington aboard his private twin-engine Convair. Caroline, at 4 P. M. Also aboard the airplane for the flight to Palm Beach were his brother, Robert, and two of Robert's children, Bobby and Joseph.

In two news conferences from the front stoop of his Georgetown home just after noon, Senator Kennedy announced first the choice of Mr. Dillon and then of his brother, Robert.

At the same time, he said Byron R. White, Denver attorney and former All-America football star at the University of Colorado, would be Deputy Attorney General. Harry J. Anslinger, Commissioner of Narcotics in the Treasury Department, has agreed to stay in that position, Senator Kennedy said.

Appointments Forecast

Highly placed Democrats forecast the following other major appointments by Senator Kennedy shortly:

¶Mrs. Elizabeth Smith, California's Democratic national committeewoman, as Treasurer of the United States, replacing Mrs. Ivy Baker Priest.

¶Fred Dutton of California

as secretary of the Kennedy Cabinet. He is a former executive secretary to Gov. Edmund G. Brown of California.

Mr. Dillon, 51 years old becomes the Cabinet's second Republican. He will serve with Robert S. McNamara, 44-year-old president of the Ford Motor Company, who has been chosen for Secretary of Defense.

While the new Treasury Secretary was a heavy contributor to the Nixon campaign this year, Senator Kennedy said he had sought in the three top Cabinet positions — State, Defense and Treasury—"the best people available in the United States regardless of their party."

His aim, he said, had been to find "men who are united by a common determination to see the United States move forward in the Sixties, to see our strength increased, to see us continue to be the great defender of freedom, to see us maintain our, in this case, fiscal stability, in the same sense as in the Defense Department we want to maintain our defense position and in State to maintain a vigorous foreign policy."

Mr. Dillon and his wife have contributed a total of $20,500 to Republican campaigns since 1958, according to the Congressional Quarterly. Of this amount $12,000 was contributed this year.

Their joint contribution in 1960 was $6,000 on May 18 to the Republican Congressional Committee. Mr. Dillon gave $5,000 to the Volunteers for Nixon-Lodge organization on Aug. 15 and Mrs. Dillon contributed $3,000 to the Republican Senatorial Committee on Aug. 19.

In 1958 Mr. Dillon gave $2,500 to the National Citizens for Ike Committee. In 1959 Mr. and Mrs. Dillon jointly contributed $5,000 to the Republican National Committee. The same year Mr. Dillon gave $550 for a dinner with the committee.

Congressional sources predicted prompt Senate confirmation of Robert Kennedy's appointment despite questions raised by some over the advisability of the choice.

Criticism Expected

Aware that the choice of his brother would bring him under criticism, Senator Kennedy said that all his Cabinet selections had been made with the desire to obtain "the most qualified men, men of ability, determination and a desire to serve their country."

"I have applied that same test in this case," he declared. "In looking for an Attorney General who must lead the fight for law enforcement, who must administer our laws without favor, and with matchless integrity, I have turned to a man in whom I have found these qualities," he said. "I have every confidence that he will bring to his new position this same ability, this same energy, this same courage, the same independence of judgment

and this same integrity."

The President-elect conceded that his brother had "had some reservations about accepting the responsibility," but he insisted that acceptance was "most important."

"I felt that he could do the job, that I wanted him to take it, and he finally agreed to accept it, with some reluctance," he added.

When Robert Kennedy was asked what his "reservations" had been, he replied that "those are matters between the President and myself, and they will remain as such."

"You can only surmise," Senator Kennedy observed with a smile.

When the President-elect was asked if there were any historic parallels for designation of his brother in the Cabinet, he responded:

"No. We are going to start one."

Later, he recalled that Dr. Milton Eisenhower had served his brother as President "in a number of important positions" and that the Eisenhower Administration had included two brothers—the late John Foster Dulles as Secretary of State and Allen W. Dulles as director of the Central Intelligence Agency. Both Messrs. Dulles, he said, have been "valuable public servants," and Allen Dulles has agreed to remain in the new Administration.

It was known that Robert Kennedy, who made a national reputation for himself as counsel for Senate investigating committees, had been reluctant to accept the Attorney General's post as recently as Wednesday night. He is said to have agreed only during a long conference with his brother yesterday morning.

Senator James O. Eastland of Mississippi, chairman of the Senate Judiciary Committee, which will pass on the appointment, said he would vote for confirmation. He said Robert Kennedy was "well-qualified for the job."

"I think he would make a good Attorney General," he declared.

Senator John A. Carroll of Colorado, a Democratic member of the committee said he questioned the "wisdom" of the appointment but did not oppose it.

He said Mr. Kennedy was well-qualified for the post and doubtless would be confirmed promptly. Senator Clifford Case, Republican of New Jersey, also called him professionally qualified for the post.

Robert, or Bobby as he is known in Washington, will be the second youngest chief of the Justice Department since it was created in 1870. The present Attorney General, William P. Rogers, has been the second youngest head of the department. He was 44 when he was named in 1957.

The youngest Attorney General was Richard Rush. He was 33 when he took office in 1814 in the Administration of President James Madison.

Announcing that Mr. White would serve as Deputy Attorney General, Senator Kennedy said that he had been anxious to have the Denver lawyer "serve in almost any area of Government because I have the highest possible opinion of his ability, and I know that he is the kind of valuable public servant that this country needs."

Early Kennedy Backer

Mr. White, an early Kennedy-for-President backer in the Rocky Mountain states, served during the campaign as national chairman of Citizens for Kennedy-Johnson.

The President-elect also conferred at his home with Gov. Foster Furcolo of Massachusetts, who may have the responsibility soon of appointing a successor to Senator Kennedy to serve until the November, 1962, elections. Another caller was Representative Clarence Cannon of Missouri, chairman of the House Appropriations Committee.

Governor Furcolo said he still considered himself in the running for the Senator's seat. He said he expected Senator Kennedy to resign Dec. 19 after the Electoral College meets that day to elect him formally to the Presidency.

A group of railway labor leaders also met with the President-elect for fifteen minutes. They declined to disclose the nature of their talk.

The group included H. C. Crotty of Detroit, president of the Brotherhood Maintenance of Ways Employes; G. E. Leighty of St. Louis, president of the Order of Railroad Telegraphers; C. T. Anderson, secretary of the Railway Political League; Michael Fox of Chicago, president of the Railway Employes Department, and Edward J. Hickey Jr., a Washington lawyer.

December 17, 1960

PALM BEACH, Fla., Dec. 29 —President-elect John F. Kennedy announced tonight that he plans to appoint a roving ambassador to represent him and the Secretary of State on vital diplomatic missions.

Well-informed quarters said his choice would be W. Averell Harriman, former Governor of New York and former Ambassador to Moscow and London.

Mr. Kennedy also announced the appointment of Robert V. Roosa of New York as Under Secretary of the Treasury for Monetary Affairs. Mr. Roosa is vice president for research of the New York Federal Reserve Bank.

In still another announcement the President-elect said that James M. Landis would join the White House staff on a temporary basis. His assignment will be to draw up proposals for reforming the Federal regulatory agencies, which he has just completed studying.

Mr. Kennedy announced his plan for the roving ambassador at a joint news conference with Senator J. W. Fulbright of Arkansas, chairman of the Senate Foreign Relations Committee. It came after a long day of conferences broken by a late afternoon round of golf.

The President-elect and the Arkansas Senator also made known their agreement that the bulk of foreign economic aid ought to be put on a long-term basis to make it more efficient and economical. They indicated Congress would be asked to approve such a program early in the new Administration.

Mr. Kennedy made it clear that a main purpose of appointing an ambassador-at-large would be to cut down where possible the foreign travel time both of the President and of his Secretary of State, who will be Dean Rusk.

He cited the growing number of new nations in Africa, whose leaders wanted and needed a more intimate contact with the President of the United States than could be provided by regular Ambassadors.

In response to questions, Mr. Kennedy made it clear that the kind of roving envoy he was planning to appoint would not have the extraordinary power that President Roosevelt had given to Col. Edwin House or President Roosevelt had given to Harry L. Hopkins.

Instead, the President-elect said, his ambassador-at-large would work directly under the Secretary of State. The role, as he saw it, would be more comparable to that of Philip C. Jessup in the Truman Administration and of Norman H. Davis in the early days of the Roosevelt Administration.

The Kennedy-Fulbright news conference was unusual in more ways than one. Darkness had descended on the patio of the Kennedy winter home by the time the two men had returned from their round of golf, and overcast skies kept the moonlight to a glimmer. The only illumination came from the bright lights of television motion picture cameras recording the scene for later broadcasting.

Three-year-old Caroline Kennedy broke into the news conference as her father was making a carefully expressed statement concerning the roving ambassador. Wearing a blue robe over pink pajamas, and carrying a pair of her mother's shoes, Caroline wandered into the patio, shouting "Daddy."

The President-elect blushed through his heavy tan. Then, while he grasped Caroline by one hand to lead her away, the girl slipped on her mother's shoes and awkwardly walked away, complaining:

"I want to see my Daddy."

In the official transcript of the news conference, Caroline's appearance drew this description: "[Slight delay]."

December 30, 1960

Kennedy Plans to Appoint Harriman a Roving Envoy

Roosa, New York Banker, to Manage U. S. Debt— Landis Is Given Job

By W. H. LAWRENCE

'I WANT TO SEE MY DADDY,' three-year-old Caroline Kennedy said, as she walked through the Kennedys' Palm Beach home in her mother's high-heel shoes. The President-elect's news conference with Senator J. W. Fulbright survived the interruption.

At Home In The White House

Joseph Kennedy Is Back on Scene After Seclusion in the Campaign

By IRA HENRY FREEMAN

Immediately after Vice President Nixon conceded the election of Senator John F. Kennedy on Nov. 9, the President-elect posed with his immediate relatives for newspaper pictures at the family estate at Hyannis Port, Mass.

In the large group, standing close behind his most famous son, was Joseph Patrick Kennedy, patriarch of the clan. It was the first time the father had permitted himself any public association, visible or oral, with the candidate since the start of the Kennedy campaign one year before.

Since Election Day, however, the father has not been shy about being seen with his son. On Nov. 29 he was pictured visiting him and his wife at Georgetown after the birth of the young couple's son. On Dec. 22, the grandfather was shown hugging President-elect Kennedy's daughter Caroline upon his arrival at Palm Beach to spend Christmas.

On Christmas Day he was photographed going to mass with the President-elect. During the candidate's post-election rest in Florida, his father was a frequent golf partner. When the President-elect arrived in New York last Wednesday for political conferences, his father met him at the airport and rode with him and Mayor Wagner in a limousine to Manhattan.

Change of Public Face

With his usual candor, Joseph Kennedy said last Friday that his change of public face was no accident—"there are no accidents in politics." He did think it discreet to absent himself from his son's campaign, but since "there is no contest any more, I can appear with him any time I want to now."

Why had he secluded himself

at an estate eleven miles from the Los Angeles convention that nominated his son for President and stayed at Hyannis Port and at his villa on the French Riviera during the campaign?

"Well, I'm 72 and I've had my day," he said. "It's the young folks' turn now."

However, it is no secret that the Kennedy campaigners regarded his father as a political embarrassment. Liberals disliked the elder Mr. Kennedy, who had been a friend and supporter of Senator Joseph R. McCarthy.

While the son was campaigning as an internatonalist, his father had been an isolationist during the early years of World War II. While ambassador to Britain from 1937 to 1940, Joseph Kennedy was said to have advised Washington not to aid Britain because Germany would win the war.

Although the President-elect had a majority of the Jewish vote, his father was accused of anti-Semitism. Reports by the German ambassador to London during World War II had indicated that Ambassador Kennedy "understood" the Nazi position on Jews.

The elder Kennedy protested that this was a lie. He pointed out he was the only gentile member of a Jewish golf club in Pam Beach. But the charge hurt.

John Kennedy was wooing the New Dealers within the Democratic party, but they remembered his father's breaking with Franklin Delano Roosevelt (whom he had supported in 1932 and 1936) over New Deal policies.

While John sought the support or organized labor, labor leaders recalled that his father allegedly tried to break the maritime unions while chair-

man of the United States Maritime Commission in 1938.

Finally, Joseph Kennedy was unpopular simply because he was one of the richest men in America (his fortune has been estimated at $250,000,000 to $400,000,000). As far back as February, 1959, Mrs. Franklin D. Roosevelt charged him with making excessive donations to his son's primary campaign expenses.

Money Charge Brought

Jaren Jones, Republican national committeeman from Utah, asserted last July that "Father Joe's money" had bought and rigged the Democratic convention for John.

There is no doubt that the Kennedy campaigns were expensive and that the Kennedy family contributed heavily. But no one knows how much the father put in.

Joseph Kennedy said in 1957:

"I was the one who got Jack into politics. I told him it was his responsibility to run for Congress; he didn't want to do it."

President-elect Kennedy said that entering politics was his own decision after his older brother, Joseph P. Kennedy Jr., who had such ambitions, was killed during World War II.

In any case, the father is not seen as a tyrannical old man running the nation through an obedient son-President. As Joseph Patrick Kennedy grew more conservative through the years, John Fitzgerald Kennedy grew more liberal, until now, as the son has said, "our disagreement is total."

But the two remain good friends. The Kennedy family solidarity has always been indestructible.

January 8, 1961

Kennedy Prefers 'J.F.K.' To 'Jack' for Headlines

PALM BEACH, Fla., Jan. 4 (AP)—President-elect John F. Kennedy wishes newspapers would stop referring to him as "Jack" in headlines.

But he has no objection to use of his initials, J. F. K.

The matter was brought up by a reporter who asked the President-elect's press secretary, Pierre Salinger, about

headline usage.

"He feels," Mr. Salinger said, "that if he had a choice he would prefer just 'Kennedy,' or that the initials 'J. F. K.' are all right, too. If he had a choice he would be against the use of 'Jack.'

"But he also feels that the choice is up to the newspapers."

Many newspapers refer to President Eisenhower as "Ike" in headlines.

January 5, 1961

Advertising: Kennedy School of Marketing

By ROBERT ALDEN

President-elect Kennedy is making one kind of news. His wife and family are quite involuntarily making news of another kind.

This news involves the Kennedys and the marketing picture.

Ever since man first recorded history, there is evidence that he liked to dress like and look like persons who were in the public eye. Even now, 2,000 years after her death, Cleopatra's name is still used to sell perfume, soaps and other appointments used by women to enhance their beauty.

The lady in the public eye at the moment is Jacqueline Kennedy. But not only Mrs. Kennedy is involved. The whole Kennedy family has a place on the marketing scene. The fact there are so many Kennedys makes it all the better as far as the marketing man is concerned.

Many women have already had the experience of going into a Fifth Avenue store or beauty salon and of being told: "Why, Mrs. Kennedy comes here regularly," or "Mrs. Kennedy has been coming here for

years. She even bought her clothes here just before Teddy was born."

Many Mrs. Kennedys

To unscramble things a little, it must be remembered that there are confusions of Mrs. Kennedys.

There is the President-elect's mother. (The lady obviously referred to as having "bought her clothes here just before Teddy was born." Teddy is the President-elect's younger brother.)

There are also the first lady, herself, and the wives of the two brothers of the President-elect. Three Kennedy sisters are also active Fifth Avenue shoppers.

So it is quite natural for clerks in the stores to spread the word around among shoppers that this Mrs. Kennedy or that Mrs. Kennedy or the President-elect's sisters are patrons of the store.

It is a matter of general interest and a good business technique as well.

In addition to the matter of marketing, President-elect Kennedy's wife is also having a distinct effect on advertising. Models who look like her or who

use the same style of bouffant hair-do are in demand.

In fact advertisers are getting quite bold in the use of illustrations closely resembling the first lady-to-be. Both Elizabeth Arden and Bonwit Teller have used sketches in their advertising that could be taken for Mrs. Kennedy. On Sunday of this week, Jay Thorpe used an illustration in a newspaper ad that had a resemblance to the first lady-to-be that was unmistakable.

The illustration accompanied an advertisement for a new line of hats: "We launch the look that is '61 American . . . young, vibrant, unmistakable."

A spokesman for the department store said that the store wished to make no comment on the illustration. He said that the store just wanted everyone to forget it.

The chances are that the particular Jay Thorpe illustration will be forgotten. But there will be others. A young President, with such a large and handsome family, is too good a marketing tool to overlook.

January 10, 1961

At Home In The White House

KENNEDY SWORN IN

NATION EXHORTED

Inaugural Says U. S. Will 'Pay Any Price' to Keep Freedom

By W. H. LAWRENCE

WASHINGTON, Jan. 20—John Fitzgerald Kennedy assumed the Presidency today with a call for "a grand and global alliance" to combat tyranny, poverty, disease and war.

In his Inaugural Address, he served notice on the world that the United States was ready to "pay any price, bear any burden, meet any hardship, support any friend, oppose any foe to assure the survival and the success of liberty."

But the nation is also ready, he said, to resume negotiations with the Soviet Union to ease and, if possible, remove world tensions.

"Let us begin anew," Mr. Kennedy declared. "Let us never negotiate out of fear. But let us never fear to negotiate."

Asks Aid of Countrymen

He called on his fellow-citizens to join his Administration's endeavor:

"Ask not what your country can do for you—ask what you can do for your country."

At 12:51 P. M., he was sworn by Chief Justice Earl Warren as the nation's thirty-fifth President, the first Roman Catholic to hold the office.

Ten minutes earlier, Lyndon Baines Johnson of Texas took the oath as Vice President. It was administered by Sam Rayburn, Speaker of the House of Representatives.

At 43 years of age, the youngest man ever elected to the Presidency, Mr. Kennedy took over the power vested for eight years in Dwight D. Eisenhower, who, at 70, was the oldest White House occupant.

President Eisenhower escorts his successor to the platform on the East Front of the Capitol.

President Kennedy alluded to this change of generation in his Inaugural.

'Torch Has Passed'

He said:

"Let the word go forth from this time and place, to friend and foe alike, that the torch has been passed to a new generation of Americans—born in this century, tempered by war, disciplined by a hard and bitter peace, proud of our ancient heritage—and unwilling to witness or per...it the slow undoing of those human rights to which this nation has always been committed, and to which we are committed today at home and around the world."

A blanket of 7.7 inches of newly fallen snow, bitter winds and a sub-freezing temperature of 22 degrees held down the crowds that watched the ceremonies in front of the newly renovated East Front of the Capitol.

But the crowds swelled under a cheering, if not warming, sun from a cloudless sky as the new President and his wife Jacqueline led the Inaugural parade from the Capitol back to the White House shortly after 2 P.M. The police estimated that the crowds might have totaled 1,000,000, but this seemed excessive.

A crowd estimated at 20,000 persons saw the new President assume office.

From snow-mantled Capitol Hill, he led the big parade, with peaceful themes as well as displays of military might, down broad Constitution and Pennsylvania Avenues to the White House. With his wife he rode in the familiar "bubbletop" Presidential limousine.

Reviews Parade

At the White House, he mounted the canopied reviewing stand, where he stayed for the entire three-and-a-half hour parade. Most of the time he was bareheaded and and occasionally he sipped soup and coffee.

The retiring Republican leaders—Mr. Eisenhower and Richard M. Nixon—joined in the applause as the new President outlined in sober terms and a deliberate manner the general course of his Administration.

Mr. Nixon, defeated for the Presidency by Mr. Kennedy last Nov. 8 in the closest election of modern times, was the first after Chief Justice Warren to shake hands with President Kennedy after the oath-taking.

The Kennedy Inaugural, which was both firm and conciliatory in its approach to the Soviet-led Communist bloc, was well received by both Republicans and Democrats on Capitol Hill.

President Kennedy called on the Soviet Union for a new beginning. He asked a renewed effort to negotiate problems that he said threatened destruction of the world, but, if settled, could afford hope that all forms of human poverty might be abolished.

Warning that civility should not be mistaken for weakness and that sincerity was always subject to proof, Mr. Kennedy asked "both sides" to explore what problems "unite us instead of belaboring those problems which divide us."

"Let both sides, for the first time, formulate serious and precise proposals for the inspection and control of arms—and bring the absolute power to destroy other nations under the absolute control of all nations," he continued.

"Let both sides seek of invoke the wonders of science instead of its terrors," he went on. "Together let us explore the stars, conquer the deserts, eradicate disease, tap the ocean depths and encourage the arts and commerce."

'New World of Law'

If a beachhead of cooperation could "push back the jungles of suspicion," Mr. Kennedy said, both sides could then join in a new endeavor, not simply for a new balance of power, but rather "a new world of law, where the strong are just and the weak secure and the peace preserved."

With Mr. Eisenhower sitting about a yard away, President Kennedy emphasized some of the stands he will take on foreign policy.

He told the newly emerging nations of Africa he would not "always expect fo find them supporting our view."

"But we shall always hope to find them strongly supporting their own freedom," he declared, "and to remember that, in the past, those who foolishly sought power riding the back of the tiger inevitably ended up inside."

He emphasized that he favored a stronger North Atlantic Treaty Organization, unqualified support of the United Nations, and helping the underdeveloped nations "break the bonds of mass misery."

"If a free society cannot help the many who are poor, it cannot save the few who are rich," he asserted.

In an apparent allusion to the regime of Premier Fidel Castro of Cuba, with which the Eisenhower Administration broke diplomatic relations earlier this month, the new President sounded a warning to the Russians not to interfere in the Western Hemisphere.

"Let all our neighbors know that we shall join with them to oppose aggression or subversion anywhere in the Americas," he said. "And let every other power know that this hemisphere intends to remain the master of its own house."

To the Latin-American nations generally, he offered "a special pledge" that good words would be converted "into good deeds" in an effort "to assist free men and free governments in casting off the chains of poverty."

Uses Family Bible

During his induction, President Kennedy's hand rested on a family Bible—a Douay version, the English translation made for Roman Catholics in the sixteenth century. He chose not to have it open to any particular passage, as has been the custom in some past inaugurations.

He took office with the prayers of four major faiths to bolster him in his pledges. The invocation was delivered by Richard Cardinal Cushing of Boston, a close friend of the Kennedy family.

The Protestant denomination to which Vice President Johnson belongs, Disciples of Christ, was represented by the Rev. Dr. John Barclay, pastor of the Central Christian Church of Austin, Tex. Archbishop Iakovos of New York, head of the Greek Orthodox Archdiocese of North and South America, also said prayers. Rabbi Nelson Glueck, president of the Hebrew Union College of Cincinnati, gave the benediction.

The ceremonies were presided over by Senator John J. Sparkman, Democrat of Alabama, chairman of the Joint Congressional Committee on Inaugural Arrangements.

They opened with "The Star-Spangled Banner," sung by Marian Anderson, the contralto.

Robert Frost, the New England poet, read his poem, "The Gift Outright," which President Kennedy had especially requested in inviting Mr. Frost to the Inaugural. He also sought to preface it with a verse he had written for the occasion to praise Mr. Kennedy for "summoning artists to participate." But the bright sun and wind combined to defeat him. He did not need to read "The Gift Outright."

Has 4 Hours of Sleep

In his day of triumph, President Kennedy seemed unaffected and unfrightened as he approached the responsibilities of leadership.

With barely four hours' sleep after last night's Inaugural concert and gala and a victory celebration thereafter, he was up at 8 A.M. He attended a mass in Holy Trinity Roman Catholic Church at 9 A.M.

Outside his Georgetown home at 3307 N. Street, N. W., he joked with reporters.

Recalling that President Eisenhower had broken with tradition eight years ago by decreeing black homburgs instead of tall silk top hats for inaugural wear, Mr. Kennedy was mockingly severe when he spotted a newsman in a homburg today.

"Didn't you get the word?" he asked. "Top hats are the rule this year."

Mr. Kennedy, who is usually hatless, seemed self-consciously uncomfortable in his topper. He wore it as briefly as possible in the trips back and forth from the White House to Capitol Hill. He also shed his coat frequently in the long day outdoors.

Bronzed by the Florida sun during his pre-inauguration holiday, with his brown hair neatly brushed, he looked the picture of health as he tackled the White House job.

He lost no time in getting to work. Minutes after he took the oath, he repaired to a Senate office to sign the official nominating papers for his ten Cabinet members and Adlai E. Stevenson as representative to the United Nations, a post with Cabinet status.

He also sent word to the White House staff to be on duty by 8:45 A. M. tomorrow, although tonight was a long night of celebration at five Inaugural balls at the National Guard Armory and four Washington hotels.

He told the Inaugural crowd it could expect no swift miracles to solve the nation's problems or end the "cold war."

His Administration's aims, he said, could not be finished in "the first 100 days," the period for which the first Franklin D. Roosevelt Administration is remembered because of the speed with which Congress and the new Administration moved.

Indeed, Mr. Kennedy went on, the problems of this world would not be solved in the first 1,000 days, "nor even perhaps in our lifetime on this planet."

January 21, 1961

WASHINGTON, Jan. 20—The first day for the new Democratic Administration was cold and blustery, but Jacqueline Bouvier Kennedy greeted it, and went through it to the end, with a warm smile.

If the wife of President Kennedy had any secret misgivings about the official life now closing in about her, she did not betray them today.

From the moment she arrived at the portico of the White House at 11:04 A. M. to be greeted by President Eisenhower until she finally retired from the parade-reviewing stand many hours later, she seemed to enjoy genuinely the ceremonies crowning her husband's long struggle for what is considered to be the world's toughest and loneliest job.

Although she is still recuperating from the Caesarean delivery of her son, John Jr., only eight weeks ago, she appeared in glowing health.

Mrs. Kennedy has a reputation for wearing smart clothes smartly, and it was easy to see why today. She was dressed in a simple, fitted beige coat with a circlet fur collar. A matching pillbox was poised on her dark hair. She carried a small mink muff.

On the platform before the Capitol, Mrs. Kennedy sat between Mr. Eisenhower on her left and Lady Bird Johnson, wife of the Vice President, on her right. Mrs. Johnson wore an olive green suit, a matching pillbox hat and a mink coat.

From time to time Mrs. Kennedy chatted animatedly with Mr. Eisenhower and Mrs. Johnson. She also leaned across to talk to Mrs. Richard M. Nixon, wife of the outgoing Vice President.

Follows Closely

Mrs. Kennedy followed the proceedings with close attention. When Richard Cardinal Cushing, who had performed her wedding ceremony, began the invocation, she made the sign of the cross. During the long prayer a wisp of a smile passed across her face.

She followed the Inauguration Address raptly, as though it were entirely new to her. After it was over, the President turned to smile at his 31-year-old wife, and she gave him a "you-did-all-right" smile in return.

As she sat beside her husband on the ride from the Capitol to the White House, she smiled, sometimes almost gaily, at the crowds along Constitution and Pennsylvania Avenues. Occasionally she gave a small diffident wave as if she were quite unpracticed in the public arts of a politician's wife.

Once, however, she nudged her husband's arm and waved vigorously. That was when their car passed the Treasury Building, where, gathered at a window in a special room, were fourteen grandchildren of Mr. and Mrs. Joseph P. Kennedy, the President's parents.

The large Kennedy family, minus the grandchildren, had seats of honor on the Inaugural platform behind the President, his wife and retiring President Eisenhower.

The Family Group

In the Kennedy family group, besides the President's father and mother, were his brother Edward and his wife, the wife of his brother Robert, and three sisters—Eunice, Pat and Jean—and their husbands, R. Sargent Shriver, Peter Lawford and Stephen Smith. Robert, who will be Attorney General, sat with the new Cabinet.

After the Inaugural ceremony, while the President and Mrs. Kennedy were dining at the Capitol, Joseph Kennedy had the family, including the grandchildren, for a buffet luncheon at the Mayflower Hotel. Kerry, one-year-old son of Robert, had a bottle of milk. Also at the luncheon were Mr. and Mrs. Hugh D. Auchincloss, mother and stepfather of Jacqueline.

the President's father said he was "proud and happy." His mother said she felt "wonderful."

At 3:27 P. M., Jacqueline Kennedy left the reviewing stand and retired to her new home at 1600 Pennsylvania Avenue to rest for the five Inaugural Balls.

Mrs. Franklin D. Roosevelt, who went through a similar day twenty-eight years ago, said, "I know she'll manage very well."

January 21, 1963

It Was a Long, but Proud Day For Wife of the New President

Following the ceremony, the President and Mrs. Kennedy leave the platform.

Kennedy Getting 4 Hours' Sleep As Festivities Keep Him Up Late

President Looks In on 5 Inaugural Balls Although His Wife Drops Out After 3— Spends First Night in White House

By ANTHONY LEWIS

WASHINGTON, Jan. 21— President Kennedy began his second day in the office, like his first, on only four hours of sleep.

On the eve of his inauguration he got home at 3:48 A. M. On inauguration night, it was 3:30. That was when he reached the White House this morning, after an exhausting evening that must have had more duty than pleasure in it for the new President.

Most of the night was spent going from one of the five inaugural balls to another. The Presidential caravan raced through the dark streets, Secret Service cars strung out behind the limousine.

When Mr. and Mrs. Kennedy arrived, Secret Service men would hold back the crowds while the couple took seats. Then they would sit and be stared at by crowds crushed up as close as safety permitted. They never danced.

Vice President and Mrs. Johnson went to all five balls. The new Cabinet members and their wives, transported in a large bus, made it most of the way before they began dropping out.

Mrs. Kennedy Goes Home

Mrs. Kennedy lasted through the first three balls visited—at the Mayflower and Statler Ho-

tels and the National Guard Armory. When the caravan reached the Sheraton Park Hotel, shortly before 1 A. M., she did not get out but was driven back to the White House.

Alone, the President was somewhat less reserved. He seemed more relaxed, and his manner became more informal. For the first time he reached out and shook hands with some in the crowd. And for the first time he said a few words.

"I think this is an ideal way to spend an evening," he said to the jammed Sheraton Park crowd, which laughed.

"I hope we can all meet here again tomorrow at 1 and do it all over again."

At the next stop, the Shoreham Hotel, he put it this way:

"I don't know a better way to spend an evening—you looking at us and we looking back at you."

Then the caravan moved on to the Statler, for a second visit there. The Kennedys had never actually gone into the ballroom the first time, because of a scheduling hitch.

Wants to See Dancers

"The Johnsons and I have been to five balls tonight," President Kennedy said.

"We still have one unfulfilled

ambition—and that is to see somebody dance."

There was dancing at the balls, but not while the President was present. The crowds just rushed toward him, stood and stared. Presidents and their wives haven't danced at inaugural balls for years, primarily because of the security problems involved in such jammed ballrooms.

A few minutes before 2 A. M. the Secret Service men thought their day was over. They were wrong.

The Presidential caravan, now without accompanying motorcycle police, wound quietly through the narrow streets of Georgetown, even stopping at traffic lights. It pulled up at 2720 Dumbarton Avenue, N. W., the home of Joseph Alsop, the newspaper columnist. Mr. Alsop is an old friend of the President's.

The President walked up the steps alone, knocked at the door and waited more than a minute before someone let him in. Mr. Alsop lowered the venetian blinds.

At 3:22 Mr. Kennedy emerged and went back to his new home.

On the previous night, Mr. Kennedy stayed late at a party given by his father, Joseph P. Kennedy.

January 22, 1961

PRESIDENT TAKES WALK TO CHURCH

Picks Up Papers at Home in Georgetown and Calls on Neighbors There

WASHINGTON, Jan. 22 (UPI) — President Kennedy walked part of the way to church today after picking up newspapers at his home in the Georgetown section of Washington and dropping in on a neighbor.

The President rode out of the White House in a black limousine. He was driven to his Georgetown home, where he got out with his youngest brother, Edward M. Kennedy.

He picked up some newspapers from the stoop and then dropped in on Benjamin C. Bradlee, a Newsweek magazine correspondent who lives two doors away.

"Anyone at home?" he called out as he walked into Mr. Bradlee's home and looked up the stairway. His brother followed.

Mr. Bradlee, taken by surprise, ran down the steps and said, "Sure, why don't you come up for a few minutes?"

Pats Boy on Head

Mr. Bradlee's son Dino, who is about 2 years old, came out

with his father. The President patted the boy's head and then went in to say hello to Mrs. Bradlee, who was wearing orange Capri pants, a gold blouse and a cocoa sweater.

A few minutes later, the Bradlees saw President Kennedy to the door. The President asked Mr. Bradlee whether he had enjoyed the inauguration. Mr. Bradlee, who had sat with his wife in the Presidential box at one of the inaugural balls, said: "Yes, but I was cold up to my eyeballs."

Mrs. Bradlee told the President to have "Jackie," Mrs. Kennedy, call her.

"She will," the President said as he went down the steps.

The President then started walking down the street. Bareheaded and wearing a gray suit with a black topcoat, he trudged through the snow without galoshes and seemed to enjoy the brisk walk to Holy Trinity Catholic Church, where he has worshiped for years.

Along the way, some pedestrians spotted him and called, "Hi, Mr. President."

Applauded at Church

About 300 persons, most of them young people, stood across the street from the church and waited for the President to arrive. They applauded him as he went into a side entrance and walked to a front pew. The church was filled.

The President rode back to the White House in his limousine.

President Kennedy had his first long sleep in several days last night. He returned to the White House from a social affair at 11:15 P. M. and was up at 8:45 A. M.

His first caller today was Robert Frost, the poet, who had read a special poem at the inauguration. The President showed Mr. Frost around the White House and posed for photographs with him on the front porch.

The President wound up his day when he and his wife entertained Mr. and Mrs. Franklin D. Roosevelt Jr. at a White House dinner. There has been speculation that Mr. Roosevelt might get an appointment in the Administration.

January 23, 1961

Ted Kennedy Expected to Go Into First Public Post Monday

BOSTON, Feb. 3—The youngest of the Kennedy brothers, Edward M. (Ted) Kennedy, is expected to launch his own political career Monday as an assistant district attorney here.

But everyone concerned, including the 28-year-old Ted, as he is best known, is keeping official silence. He has said that he would reveal his plans next

week. He was not available today and his Boston telephone was reported "disconnected."

The possibility of Mr. Kennedy's becoming an aide in the office of District Attorney Garrett H. Byrne of Suffolk County, which is composed mostly of Boston, has been discussed for some time. It is considered that he could have such a post for

the asking.

The District Attorney's office commented today that "there is nothing to be said." Assistant District Attorney Ralph S. Bernard, with whom Mr. Kennedy purportedly would work, said that "it is news to me."

Edward Kennedy was campaign coordinator for his brother's Presidential campaign in

THE KENNEDYS: A NEW YORK TIMES PROFILE

eleven Western states plus Alaska and Hawaii. Soon after the election he rented an apartment at 9 Louisburg Square, a fashionable address on Beacon Hill here.

In the Kennedy tradition he was graduated from Harvard College. He took his law degree at the University of Virginia. He was admitted to the Massachusetts bar in November 1959.

Mr. Kennedy has been mentioned as possibly becoming active in three political areas. One view has been that he might run for a seat in the national House of Representatives. President Kennedy started his political career as Representative from the Eleventh Massachusetts District, which takes in the Beacon Hill section of Boston.

Another view has been that the younger Mr. Kennedy might run in 1962 for the Senate seat vacated by his brother after his election as President. The seat is held by appointment for two years by former Mayor Benjamin A. Smith 2d of Gloucester.

The third possibility mentioned has been that Edward Kennedy might be active in the

leadership of the Democratic party in Massachusetts. President Kennedy, since he moved up to the national post, has held an absentee landlord title on the organization. Recently he asked John M. (Pat) Lynch, the state chairman, to stay on. Mr. Lynch agreed, although he could have been appointed Collector of the Port of Boston.

February 4, 1961

WASHINGTON, Feb. 23—The White House has called for and received pledges of secrecy from its household staff.

It disclosed today that members of the staff were being asked to sign written pledges that they would not "commercialize" their White House relationships by discussing them or writing about them, even after retirement.

The aim is to prevent a flow of intimate White House memoirs written after retirement by cooks, maids, ushers and similar employes. In the past such accounts have often been critical of their employers and the way they ran the Presidential residence.

Pierre Salinger, White House press secretary, disclosed the pledges while being questioned anew about job inquiries made by the White House to a famous Vietnamese chef, Bui Van Han, employed by the French Ambassador to London. Mr. Bui Van Han has decided to stay with the French Ambassador.

Mr. Salinger had two busy sessions over the pledges. He finally issued a statement reading as follows:

"In response to further inquiries we have looked into the matter of the White House household staff.

"When the President and Mrs. Kennedy moved into the White House on Jan. 2, Mr. [J. Bernard] West, the chief usher [who has been on the White

House staff for many years] who is responsible for the operation of the White House, suggested that the members of the household staff be asked not to commercialize their relationship with the White House.

"Mr. West then requested the members of the household—to which they agreed—not to engage in publicity which might adversely reflect on the White House as a national monument. It was hoped in this way that the dignity of the White House would be preserved."

Mr. Salinger said the move had also been taken to insure privacy for the Kennedys.

The pledges were an innovation at the White House. At least a dozen books have been published so far this century containing the memoirs of butlers, ushers, housekeepers, doorkeepers and mail room attendants. One more, reportedly highly critical of Mrs. Eisenhower, is due for publication next Monday by a retired maid, Lillian Rogers Parks, entitled "My Thirty Years Backstairs at the White House."

Portions of Mrs. Parks' book appeared in the January issue of Good Housekeeping, but Mr. Salinger would not say whether her book had anything to do with the new order.

Mrs. Parks, daughter of a deceased White House maid of fifty years service, said that White House employes always spoke of "the rule of the hills,"

meaning they could disclose nothing while working at the White House but were free to write their memoirs the instant they retired. She said her mother had died before she could complete her memoirs.

Mr. Salinger would not provide the text of the agreement the employes had signed. Nor would he ascertain with any accuracy the number of employes that had signed. He said sixty-seven employes listed on the domestic and gardening staff were the maximum covered by the agreement.

The writing ban does not apply to him or other members of the Presidential staff, Mr. Salinger said.

But he did say Mrs. Kennedy's three secretaries, Letitia Baldrige, Pamela Turnure and Ann Lincoln, had been asked to sign the agreement and "were considering it." It is doubtful that the pledge would be legally enforced.

Permanent White House staff employes generally remain for many years although not recruited under civil service. They are paid by the National Capital Parks.

The new White House pledge appears similar to one adopted by the British Government for royal household staff members after the publication in 1950 of a book called "The Little Princesses," written by a governess, Miss Marion Crawford.

February 24, 1961

Domestic Staff at White House Pledges Secrecy on Life There

Publicity Barred

By W. H. LAWRENCE

Teacher Called To White House

WASHINGTON, March 1—Mrs. John F. Kennedy has asked a teacher at an experimental school in near-by Bethesda, Md., to set up and teach a nursery class at the White House for 3-year-old Caroline Kennedy and her friends.

The teacher, Mrs. Robert

Waldrop, is one of two at the experimental school, which is operated by the Bio-Social Growth Center, National Institutes of Health, in Bethesda. Mrs. Waldrop is now considering the teaching job in the White House.

Miss Pamela Turnure, press secretary to Mrs. Kennedy, said that the White House had "nothing to announce" on the nursery school.

Miss Turnure said, however, that Mrs. Kennedy had inspected the experimental school

some two weeks ago, but insisted the visit was a "courtesy call" made because the First Lady was interested in the school's operation.

The Government-run experimental school in Bethesda has six students—all 2-year-old girls, each of whom has one sister. The two teachers use modern equipment, including closed-circuit television, and the process is observed by three experts.

March 3, 1961

Attorney General Finds Football Is Useful in Tackling Problems

WASHINGTON, March 2 (AP) —Now we know why the Attorney General keeps a football in his office. He keeps it there to have a football to throw around the office.

The word that Robert F. Kennedy mixes the forward pass with antitrust suits came out at the Justice Department today.

Visitors had been curious about the football sitting on the fireplace mantel of Mr. Kennedy's fifth-floor office in the Justice Building.

He and Deputy Attorney General Byron R. White, it develops, toss the pigskin to and fro while deliberating matters of law.

For many years the Attorney General has been one of the mainstays in a family that is fond of touch football games. He also qualifies with experience as a varsity end at Harvard.

Mr. White possesses more distinguished credentials. Known as "Whizzer" White, he was an All-America halfback at the University of Colorado in 1937 and later starred as a professional at Pittsburgh and Detroit.

The story has gone around that a Justice Department employe was startled one evening shortly after Jan. 20 when he saw two persons moving about the building.

"Anything I can do for you?" he asked suspiciously.

"Yes," replied the younger of the two strangers. "I'm Bob Kennedy and this is Mr. White. We're looking for the gym."

The employe escorted them to their exercise.

The Attorney General's brother, President Kennedy, has played only one abbreviated round of golf since Inauguration Day, but he also is enthusiastic about physical fitness. The President played football in prep school, swam at Harvard and still goes in for golf, tennis, swimming and sailing.

March 3, 1961

Dedicated to Peace
Robert Sargent Shriver

THE train of events that led Robert Sargent Shriver to Washington and a high place in the Kennedy Administration started the night he met his future wife. Mr. Shriver, who announced his plans yesterday as head of the Peace Corps, met Eunice M. Kennedy, sister of the President, at a dinner party here in 1945. But Mr. Shriver, who had displayed some degree of versatility in his career, might have got to Washington, anyway. He has been president of the Chicago Board of Education; was mentioned as a possible Democratic candidate for Governor of Illinois; headed the Yale alumni one year, and has been prominent in lay Roman Catholic affairs.

Man in the News

At the time he met President Kennedy's sister, he was an assistant to the editor of Newsweek magazine. He had obtained the job on his return from Navy service in World War II, during which he had risen to the rank of lieutenant commander.

Before the war, Mr. Shriver studied law at Yale and served a brief apprenticeship in a New York law firm. He had been active on The Yale Daily News, and could not seem to wash off the printers' ink.

Joseph P. Kennedy, Eunice's father, was looking for someone to edit the letters of his son, Joseph Jr., who had been killed on a wartime air mission over the English Channel.

Did Chicago Survey

He was impressed with Mr. Shriver and eventually took him into his business organization.

Mr. Shriver was sent to Chicago to do a survey of the Merchandise Mart, the world's largest commercial building, which Mr. Kennedy had just purchased. He became assistant manager of the mart and has made Chicago his home since 1946.

He married the girl, too. But it took eight years of courting and commuting between Chicago, New York, Palm Beach and Hyannis Port, Mass. They were wed in St. Patrick's Cathedral here in 1953.

Mr. Shriver, 45 years old, stands 5 feet 11 inches and carries his 175 pounds like an athlete. An easy-going man, his customary approach to a newcomer is an outstretched hand and this greeting: "Hi, I'm Sarg Shriver, Jack Kennedy's brother-in-law."

Informality marks most of his contacts, his friends say. But behind it is a cool, analytical mind, a dedication to public service and intellectualism.

Mr. Shriver is a defender of intellectuals. America needs business and professional men, he has said, but it also needs "sages, saints, scholars and statesmen—master minds and master spirits."

Unlike the Kennedys, Mr. Shriver is not a touch-football enthusiast. "He plays tennis while the rest of us run around on the field," his wife explains.

He also shoots a good game of golf and is an expert skin diver. He is a modest collector of modern paintings.

He was born in Westminster, Md. His late father, who bore the same name, was a vice president of the Baltimore Trust Company and a director of two New York investment houses, J. C. Wilson & Co., and Young & Ottley. His mother lives in New York.

Mr. Shriver is descended from Colonial families. One ancestor was David Shriver, a signer of the Bill of Rights. Another, Robert Owings, held an original land grant from Cecil Calvert, Lord Baltimore.

Mr. Shriver attended Canterbury School at New Milford, Conn., and was graduated cum laude from Yale in 1938. He was a campus politician, a colleague recalls, and a founder of the America First organization there.

The Shrivers have two sons, Robert Sargent, 6, and Bern, 2, and a daughter, Maria Owings, 5. They live in an eleven-room duplex apartment overlooking Lincoln Park and Lake Michigan in Chicago. They entertain a great deal.

March 7, 1961

Defender of the intellectuals.

WASHINGTON, March 11 (AP) — The 3-year-old girl who says "hi, daddy" to the President of the United States is getting a lot of fun out of life in the White House.

Caroline Kennedy has obviously made the Presidential mansion her playground. She's full of surprises, packing a toy pistol, blithely helping her father play host to world leaders.

For instance, reporters at the White House were surprised today when they saw Caroline in earnest conversation with one of her favorite persons, Vice President Johnson.

Caroline was thought to have been with her mother at Glen Ora, the Kennedys' country estate at Middleburg, Va. Mrs. Kennedy went there last night with her sister and brother-in-law, Princess Lee Radziwill and Prince Stanislaus Radziwill.

She Wanted Apple

The White House had announced that Caroline would go along, too.

But reporters saw her after she had met the Vice President in a White House corridor—on her way to the press office to see if somebody had an apple.

Mr. Kennedy will take Caroline with him to Glen Ora, aides said, when he joins Mrs. Kennedy and her guests there tomorrow.

Caroline and Mr. Johnson engaged in animated conversation on some topic reporters were not told about.

Although Mrs. Kennedy says she would like Caroline kept out of the public spotlight, the President seems willing enough to have his blonde daughter share public appearances with him.

Caroline is as full of spirit and questions as any 3-year-old. Right now, she seems to observers to be unspoiled by the unusual life into which she has been thrust. She has obviously taken to it with delight.

Although she is in the charge of a British nurse, Caroline manges to get off on her own for unexpected appearances.

Clattering in her mother's high-heeled shoes, she broke up an important news conference her father was conducting in Palm Beach, Fla. In a flash, she turned the television cameras from the then President-elect to make her own TV debut in pink pajamas.

Caroline isn't adverse to giving out secrets, either. She wandered into the White House communications room one Sunday and, when asked what her daddy was doing, replied:

"He's not doing anything. He's just sitting up there with his shoes and socks off, doing nothing."

Caroline is meeting some of the world's most famous people.

Mrs. Franklin D. Roosevelt reports that the President's daughter is the type that likes to "tag along."

Caroline goes on tours of the private family quarters with her father and his friends. She takes the interest of a grown-up hostess, too.

"Isn't it sad mommy isn't here," she told Mrs. Roosevelt, referring to Mrs. Kennedy's absence on a Palm Beach, Fla., visit.

And, then, when Mr. Kennedy turned to two men in the group and asked whether they wanted a drink, Caroline piped up:

"They've already had a drink, daddy. There's their glasses."

The President shares the amusement in Caroline's antics and, like many a parent, he puts her up to a few cute tricks himself.

When former President Harry S. Truman came to call this week, Mr. Kennedy introduced him to Caroline, then reminded her:

"What did I tell you to tell him?"

"Oh, yes," Caroline obliged, "you used to live in our house."

In contrast to her husband's obvious delight in showing off his daughter, Mrs. Kennedy has taken steps to assure Caroline of some privacy.

Much of the girl's time will probably be spent now at Glen Ora, where Mrs. Kennedy can keep Caroline in more normal surroundings and let her play with friends her own age.

Caroline has a bevy of small Kennedy cousins, too, with whom she can frolic away from the White House.

The Kennedys apparently believe in letting Caroline be one of the Presidential family at home and taking part in what's going on in their mansion home, including riding the elevators.

March 12, 1961

Caroline Finds the White House To Be Just One Big Playground

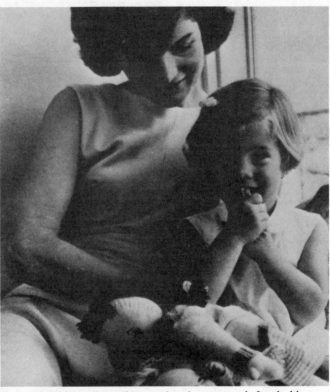

Three-year-old Caroline and her mother share a story before bedtime.

WASHINGTON, March 13—President Kennedy set forth tonight a ten-point, ten-year economic and social development program for Latin America to meet the challenge of "a future full of peril, but bright with hope."

The President outlined his program in an unusual White House ceremony that combined a diplomatic reception with a major speech.

Mr. Kennedy told 250 persons, including diplomats from Latin America and leaders of Congress and their wives, that the United States was prepared to give financial aid "if the countries of Latin America are ready to do their part." His plan sought to help "all."

He spoke in the East Room after he and Mrs. Kennedy received their guests in the Red, Blue and Green Rooms.

Although the President does not speak Spanish, his twenty-minute speech contained several Spanish phrases. He spoke for twenty minutes while his audience sat on gilt chairs arranged in semicircles on both sides of the rostrum. Mr. Kennedy declared:

"Our motto is what it has always been—"Progress, yes! Tyranny, no!"—"Progreso, si! Tirania, no!"

He Lists Ten Points

The President reiterated his campaign pledge to put new life and vigor into the "good neighbor" policy of Franklin D. Roosevelt as he proposed this ten-point effort:

1. A ten-year plan to raise the living standards of all Americans, provide basic education, end hunger and place each nation on a basis of self-sustaining growth.

2. An early ministerial meeting of the Inter-American Economic and Social Council at which each nation will be expected to put forward long-range programs.

3. A request to Congress for the $500,000,000 in American aid promised in the Act of Bogotá.

4. Support for all "economic integration which is a genuine step toward larger markets and greater competitive opportunity."

5. Cooperation by the United States in "serious, case-by-case examinations of commodity market problems."

6. A step-up now in the Food

PRESIDENT GIVES 10-YEAR AID PLAN TO LATIN AMERICA

By W. H. LAWRENCE

for Peace emergency program.

7. An invitation to Latin-American scientists to work with the United States.

8. Rapid expansion of training programs.

9. Reaffirmation of the United States pledge to go to the defense of an American nation whose independence is endangered.

10. An invitation to contribute to the enrichment of life and culture in the United States by providing teachers here and welcoming United States students to Latin-American universities.

The President warned that the economic development program he advocated looked toward modification of "social patterns so that all, and not just a priviliged few, share the fruits of growth."

Friendship to Cuban People

President Kennedy included in his talk an expression of "special friendship to the people of Cuba and the Dominican Republic—and the hope that they will soon rejoin the society of free men, uniting with us in our common effort."

The broad program he outlined today, to be explained in a special message to Congress tomorrow, bore no price tag other than the $500,000,000 commitment that was made by the Eisenhower Administration last year.

But Mr. Kennedy compared his plan with the Marshall Plan, which rebuilt the war-damaged economies of Western Europe. He said the United States should provide "resources of a scope and magnitude sufficient to make this bold development program a success."

The President noted Communist encroachment in Cuba. He warned of the perils faced by the Western Hemisphere and said the dream of progress, freedom and glory never had been in "greater danger" from the forces that "have imperiled America throughout its history —the alien forces which once again seek to impose the despotisms of the Old World on the people of the New.

Mr. Kennedy said that the revolution of freedom that began at Philadelphia in 1776, and at Caracas, Venezuela in 1811, was not finished and that the hemisphere's mission was not yet complete.

"For our unfulfilled task is to demonstrate to the entire world that man's unsatisfied aspiration for economic progress and social justice can best be achieved by free men working within a framework of democratic institutions," he declared.

The President's words were transmitted at   ce by the Voice of Amer   1 English, Spanish, Portugu and French to the nations of t..e South. It was not broadcast live here, but was recorded and videotaped.

March 14, 1961

Kennedy Uses a Rocking Chair to Relax on the Job

WASHINGTON, March 21 (AP)—A rocking chair in President Kennedy's office is one of his most treasured possessions, and has been for more than five years.

Dr. Janet Travell, the White House physician, is glad he likes it so much. She is convinced that rocking in a good high-backed chair is a fine way to relax.

"Such a chair," said the physician, "provides gentle, constant exercise and helps prevent muscular fatigue."

A reporter went to Dr. Travell after noticing Mr. Kennedy using the rocker during a recent conference with Vice President Johnson and Secretary of Defense Robert S. McNamara. The chair is in front of the fireplace in Mr. Kennedy's office—across the room from his big desk.

The reporter asked whether the rocker was something Dr. Travell had prescribed because of the trouble the President has had with his back— an ailment she first treated in 1955.

Dr. Travell replied that she had not prescribed the rocker, but that Mr. Kennedy had it because he saw one just like it in her New York office when he first came to her in 1955.

As a Senator, Mr. Kennedy used the chair a good deal. He had it brought to the White House when he became President.

The high-backed wooden rocker originally had a light finish, but it was stained a mahogany shade a few weeks ago to match the other furniture in Mr. Kennedy's office. The seat cushions and the arm and back pads had been reupholstered in a beige tone to harmonize with a pair of sofas.

March 22, 1961

President Kennedy, in his favorite high-back rocker

Kennedy Golf Ball Hits Secret Service Agent

WASHINGTON, April 5— A golf ball hit by President Kennedy struck the head of a Secret Service agent at Palm Beach, Fla., Monday but did not injure him.

The incident was confirmed by the White House today. Pierre Salinger, White House press secretary, said the ball bounced once before striking the agent.

The agent insisted that he was not hurt, but the President directed that he be taken to a hospital for a check. The agent returned before the Presidential party had proceeded more than three holes, and he walked the rest of the way around the course, Mr. Salinger said.

The Secret Service declined to give the name of the agent.

April 6, 1961

No! No! Not Lay-ahs; It's Laos, as in House

WASHINGTON, March 23 (UPI)—Throughout his news conference President Kennedy kept referring to Laos as Lay'-ahs. Reporters asking the questions called it "Louse," one syllable.

A call to the embassy to find out which is right, brought this comment from the Chargé d'Affaires:

"No! No! No! Not Lay'-ahs. Laos, as in house."

March 24, 1961

KENNEDY SAYS U.S. WON'T ALLOW COMMUNISM TO TAKE OVER CUBA; DOES NOT BAR UNILATERAL MOVE

Address to Editors Asserts Nonintervention Has Limit —He Talks With Rebels

By W. H. LAWRENCE

WASHINGTON, April 20 — President Kennedy said today that United States restraint was "not inexhaustible" and that it did not intend to abandon Cuba to communism.

In a speech before the American Society of Newspaper Editors that was broadcast by television and radio, he said that he would not permit the traditional inter-American policy of nonintervention to conceal or excuse a policy of inaction.

If United States intervention becomes necessary in Cuba, Mr. Kennedy said, the nation will strive for complete victory, neither expecting nor accepting the same outcome that the "small band of gallant Cuban refugees must have known they were chancing" in landing on the island.

The President spoke after the rebel beachhead had been wiped out and after he had talked secretly at the White House with Dr. José Miro Cardona, president of the Cuban Revolutionary Council, and five other council members.

Secret Trip to Washington

Late today, Pierre Salinger, White House press secretary, said the main reason the Cubans had visited the White House was to ask President Kennedy to use his influence with the Organization of American States.

He requested that it try to insure that Cubans who have been captured will not be executed and that those who have been wounded will receive adequate medical care.

The President gave assurance that he would exert his influence with the O. A. S. in the matter, Mr. Salinger said.

Dr. Miro Cardona and his associates were flown secretly to Washington yesterday from Miami, where they had been directing rebel efforts. They entered the White House by a back door. The others present were Dr. Antonio Verona, Dr. Justo Carrillo, Dr. Antonio Maceo, Manuel Ray and Carlos Hevia.

Qualified Administration sources said the aim of Mr. Kennedy's speech today was to warn the Government of Premier Fidel Castro and its Communist supporters abroad that the United States would tolerate neither a large Communist arms build-up in Cuba nor summary executions of United States citizens by the Cuban regime.

Unlike earlier pronouncements, Mr. Kennedy did not rule out the possibility that the United States—alone, if need be —would undertake armed intervention if convinced that its security interests were being endangered.

"But let the record show that our restraint is not inexhaustible," he said. "Should it ever appear that the inter-American doctrine of noninterference merely conceals or excuses a policy of non-action; if the nations of this hemisphere should fail to meet their commitments against outside Communist penetration, then I want it clearly understood that this Government will not hesitate in meeting its primary obligations, which are the security of our nation."

Time Made Indefinite

Mr. Kennedy did not imply that the time for possible unilateral action was at hand. He referred instead to the future with the phrase, "should that time ever come." A highly placed official said there was no intention at present to ask a quick judgment by the Organization of American States against the Castro regime.

The President, addressing 1,000 editors and their guests in the Statler-Hilton Hotel for barely fifteen minutes, spoke from a text completed less than an hour before.

In his remarks the President acknowledged that the news from Cuba in the last twenty-four hours had "grown worse instead of better." It was understood Dr. Miro Cardona had requested the White House conference when it became clear that the rebels' small beachhead could not hold out against the Communist-equipped Cuban forces.

Informed sources said the beachhead, established Monday, had grown to perhaps 1,200 men. Of these, a considerable number were said to have escaped with supplies and equipment to the Escambray Mountains to join guerrilla forces there.

No one could say with authority how many anti-Castro Cubans had fallen in the fighting. However, it was emphasized that the force committed never approached the figure of 5,000 originally reported by some Cuban sources.

In his speech before the editors to whom he was introduced by Turner Catledge, president of their society and managing editor of The New York Times, Mr. Kennedy said Communist tactics in Cuba were the same as in Laos and around the world. Behind the shield of Communist armies and nuclear weapons, he explained, the forces of expanding communism use subversion, infiltration and a host of other tactics to pick off vulnerable areas one by one in situations that do not permit armed intervention by anti-Communist forces.

The President's main plea was to those Latin-American nations that have not been so concerned about the growth of communism in Cuba as has the United States.

"It is clear that this nation, in concert with all the free nations of this hemisphere, must take an ever closer and more realistic look at the menace of external Communist intervention and domination in Cuba," he said.

"The American people are not complacent about Iron Curtain tanks and planes less than ninety miles from their shore, but a nation of Cuba's size is less a threat to our survival than it is a base for subverting the survival of other free nations throughout the hemisphere. It is not our interest or our security but theirs which is now today in greater peril."

The hour is late, he added, and "we and our Latin friends will have to face the fact that we cannot postpone any longer the real issue of survival." On that issue, he declared, there can be "no middle ground."

The greatest task facing the nation and the Administration is to cope with the problems of Communist expansion not alone

by arms but by subversion that could endanger the United States security without the firing of a shot, the President said.

"We intend to profit from this lesson," he declared. "We intend to re-examine and re-orient our forces of all kinds, our tactics, and our institutions here in this community. We intend to intensify our efforts for a struggle in many ways more difficult than war, where disappointment often will accompany us."

"Should that time ever come," he said, "we do not intend to be lectured on 'intervention' by those whose character was stamped for all time on the bloody streets of Budapest."

That shot at the Kremlin brought a burst of applause.

On Capitol Hill the dominant reaction continued to be bipartisan support of the firm Kennedy policy. But there also

were criticisms in the light of the failure of the rebel effort.

One critic was Senator Barry Goldwater of Arizona, leader of Right-wing Republicans, who said every American should be filled with "apprehension and shame" because of the abortive attempt. He blamed United States failures on "inepititude" in the State Department in recent years.

Dr. Miro Cardona and his associates talked with several Administration leaders during their brief visit. The White House would not say where they had gone from here nor how they traveled.

The Cuban situation was discussed this morning at a Cabinet meeting in the White House. Te session had been scheduled for two weeks and officials said it dealt mainly with the budget.

April 21, 1961

KENNEDY ASKS 1.8 BILLION THIS YEAR TO ACCELERATE SPACE EXPLORATION, ADD FOREIGN AID, BOLSTER DEFENSE

MOON TRIP URGED

Kennedy Tells Congressmen Nation Is Ready to Make Necessary Sacrifices

---

By W. H. LAWRENCE

WASHINGTON, May 72 — President Kennedy proposed to Congress today bold and expensive new measures to rocket a man to the moon, to expand non-nuclear military strength and to increase foreign aid spending.

These actions, he said, are needed to promote a "freedom doctrine" around the globe.

For the first year, the cost of the new programs exceeded $1,800,000,000 in appropriations, including $679,000,000 for space projects. But the President made it clear that the new space program alone would cost $7,000,000,000 to $9,000,000,000 over the next five years, and that the costs of other projects would also increase sharply.

To emphasize the urgency of his proposals, Mr. Kennedy appeared personally before a joint session of Congress. His speech was televised and broadcast nationally by all networks.

Applauded 18 Times

The President called his forty-seven-minute talk a second State of the Union Message, departing from the tradition that such messages are usually delivered by Presidents once a year, in January.

Legislators, diplomats, Cabinet members and the packed public galleries interrupted the President eighteen times with applause.

The loudest and most sustained hand-clapping greeted his promise that he would make it clear to Premier Khrushchev at their meeting in Vienna next month that "America's enduring concern is for both peace and freedom."

Major Increases Listed

The major categories of gov-

ernmental activity for which increased funds were asked for the fiscal year beginning next July 1 included the following:

¶For accelerated space exploration, including the manned moon shot, nuclear rocket development and communications and weather satellites — $679,000,000.

¶For increased foreign economic and military aid — $535,000,000.

¶For strengthening the Army and Marine Corps—$160,000,000.

¶For the Small Business Administration—$130,000,000.

¶For expanded retraining of unemployed workers — $75,000,000.

¶For the United States Information Agency, largely for new radio and television broadcasts to Latin America and Southeast Asia—$2,400,000.

The President also announced an Administration decision for Federal participation in the construction of civilian fall-out shelters to ward off nuclear attack. This program, he said, would "more than triple" current budget requests of $104,000,000 for civil defense.

He exercised his authority for governmental reorganization to shift civil defense activities from the Office of Civil and Defense Moblization to the Secretary of Defense. He said new, increased budget estimates for civil defense would be submitted later.

David E. Bell, director of the Budget Bureau, estimated that actual spending in the next fiscal year under the new programs, excluding civil defense, would total about $724,000,000.

This would mean a total Federal budget of $84,893,000,000 and an unexpected deficit of at least $3,500,000,000. The final budget submitted by President

Eisenhower as he left office was $80,865,000,000, with an expected surplus of $1,500,000,000

Calls for Sacrifices

Although he did not ask new or increased taxes now to finance the new programs, Mr. Kennedy said sacrifices would be required of the American people in the battle for freedom.

The nation's greatest asset, he said, is the willingness of its people to pay the price for these programs, to accept a long struggle and to share their resources with less fortunate people. He expressed confidence that the nation would also exercise self-restraint against increasing wages or prices or over-producing certain crops.

He answered in some detail a question often asked of him since his Inaugural posed the challenge to Americans to "ask not what your country can do for you—ask what you can do for your country."

Self-restraint, he said, would also stop people from "spreading military secrets, or urging unessential expenditures or improper monopolies or harmful work stoppages."

This spirit, he continued, would lead them to serve in the Peace Corps, or the armed forces, or Congress and to strive for excellence in their schools, their cities and their physical fitness. It would also cause them to take part in civil defense, to pay higher postal rates, higher payroll taxes and higher teachers' salaries, he declared.

The President said the problems of survival for some of the nation's allies were complicatd where conditions of social injustice and economic chaos were allowed to fester and to invite Communist subversion. It would be the nation's aim, he said, to help them solve such economic problems as well as to provide them with military assistance.

Of his forthcoming trip abroad, Mr. Kennedy told Congress he welcomed the opportunity to see President de Gaulle, whom he described as "the great captain of the Western world."

He conceded policy differences with General de Gaulle, saying the serious conversations they would have "do not require a pale unanimity—they are rather the instruments of trust and understanding over a long road."

As for the Soviet Union, the President expressed renewed hopes that an effective treaty banning nuclear weapons tests could be negotiated. Despite disappointing response from the Russians until now, he said, "we intend to go the last mile in patience."

He said, amid applause, that the problem of general disarmament remained high on the Administration's agenda of hopes, and that he would soon ask Congress to establish a strengthened and enlarged disarmament agency.

The President's major emphasis was on the necessity of sending a man to the moon, and of getting him there first if possible. He told Congress a firm national decision was essential now on whether this nation would go all the way on a big space program that "will last for many years and carry very heavy costs."

"If we were to go only half way, or reduce our sights in the face of difficulty, it would be better not to go at all," he said.

Wants 'Leading' Space Role

The President conceded that Congress might not hold the same views he did. But "I believe we should go to the moon," he declared. It was time, he said, for the United States "to take a clearly leading role in space achievement," which may "hold the key to our future on earth."

May 26, 1961

PARIS, June 2—"I do not think it altogether inappropriate to introduce myself to this audience. I am the man who accompanied Jacqueline Kennedy to Paris, and I have enjoyed it."

This was how President Kennedy presented himself today to 400 journalists at a press luncheon. The remark was humorous and appreciated as such but it reflected the extraordinary impression that the President's wife has made on Paris.

Not since Queen Elizabeth II of Britain was here in 1957 have Paris newspapers packed their pages with so many bouquets.

One of these bouquets was a cartoon in the newspaper Liberation. Mrs. Kennedy was so delighted with it that she asked for and received the original drawing.

The cartoon, drawn by an artist named Escaro, who harbors no warm feelings for President de Gaulle, depicts a great canopied double bed.

In the bed is General de Gaulle, the covers pulled up to his nose and his eyes tightly closed. Over his head is a cartoonist's balloon, which frames a photograph of Mrs. Kennedy.

Mme de Gaulle is shown sitting bolt upright next to her husbnd with her mouth open and her eyes fixed on the dream.

The caption under the drawing simply says, "Charles!"

Today, after two days of almost uninterrupted state functions, Mrs. Kennedy was able to do a few things more in keeping with her interests than standing in reception lines and rushing from one official function to another.

Quick Trip to Museum

This morning, after it was hurriedly arranged yesterday, she visited the Jeu de Paume Museum, which houses France's finest collection of impressionist paintings. She was escorted through the museum by André Malraux, the French Minister of Culture.

Mrs. Kennedy was driven to the museum in a plastic-roofed car that has provided Parisians with opportunities to see America's First Lady, if only in passing.

She was wearing a tailored gray suit. her jewelry was pearls and a half-bow gold diamond shoulder pin. He also wore a back-of-the-head beret in a glazed white straw fabric with a black border, and half-length white gloves.

A small crowd watched her arrival, including some tourists who were told that the museum was closed for the morning because of Mrs. Kennedy's visit.

Only the official party was allowed to accompany the First Lady as she spent fifty-five minutes admiring the works of

Just an Escort, Kennedy Jokes As Wife's Charm Enchants Paris

First Lady Wins Bouquets From Press —She Also Has Brief Chance to Visit Museum and Admire Manet

By W. GRANGER BLAIR

Jacqueline Kennedy, followed by the usual troop of photographers, on a tour of some of the museums of Paris.

such impressionists as Degas, Manet, Renoir, Seurat and Monet.

When she emerged from the museum, which is in the Tuileries Gardens on the Place de la Concorde side, she brushed past the police cordon to pose for the tourists with cameras and to chat for a moment with journalists. She said that she had been most impressed by Manet's "Olympia," a painting of a nude reclining on a couch.

Then, with a smile and a fare-well wave, she climbed back into her car to drive to Malmaison and the second stop of what the newspaper referred to as her "day of culture." Malmaison, ten miles west of Paris, was the residence of Josephine Bonaparte and is now a national monument and museum.

On her tour of Malmaison, Mrs. Kennedy was escorted by M. Malraux, Pierre Schoomer, conservator of the chateau, and Mme. Maurice Couve de Murville, wife of the French Foreign Minister.

Mrs. Kennedy Amused

M. Malraux was said to have described Josephine as a "real camel" and to have expressed wonder that Napoleon had cared so deeply for her. This description of the Empress was reported to have amused Mrs. Kennedy a great deal.

M. Schoomer told the First Lady that Josephine had been "extremely jealous" of Napoleon."

"She was quite right and I don't blame her," Mrs. Kennedy replied in French with a laugh.

This evening, after saying their official farewells to President and Mme de Gaulle late in the afternoon, President and Mrs. Kennedy dined quietly at the United States Embassy residence. Originally scheduled to spend the night at the residence, they returned to their suite at the French Foreign Ministry for their final night in Paris.

June 3, 1961

FIRST LADY WINS KHRUSHCHEV, TOO

Premier, at Dinner, Says He'd Like to Shake Her Hand Before Kennedy's

VIENNA, June 3—Premier Khrushchev met Mrs. John F. Kennedy in the splendor of Schoenbrunn Palace tonight and a twinkle lit up his eyes.

"Mr. Khrushchev," a photographer asked, "won't you shake hands with Mr. Kennedy for us?"

With a grin, Premier Khrushchev nodded toward the President's wife, Jacqueline, stately and beautiful in a long white gown, and replied.

"I'd like to shake her hand first."

The occasion was the state dinner given by Austria in the country residence of the former Habsburg emperors.

6,000 at Palace Gates

More than 6,000 Viennese crowded around the floodlit gates of the 267-year-old palace to watch the leaders of East and West enter.

Premier Khrushchev, dressed in a plain dark suit and a checked gray tie, arrived first. He was accompanied by his wife, Mme. Nina Petrovna Khrushchev, who wore a dark silk dress laced with a faint golden thread

President and Mrs. Kennedy arrived ten minutes later—and five minutes late.

"The American princess," exclaimed a woman in the crowd, referring to Mrs. Kennedy.

President Kennedy went to Premier Khrushchev as soon as he saw him and apologized for having been late. The Soviet leader graciously accepted.

Despite six hours together earlier in the day, Mr. Khrushchev, who is 67 years old, and President Kennedy, 44, looked remarkably fresh.

Waiters in knee breeches and gold braid moved through the corridors and across the spacious rooms bearing silver trays laden with drinks.

The heavy scent of spring flowers, lavishly banked through the old palace, floated into every room.

President Adolf Schaerf of Austria welcomed the Khrushchevs and the Kennedys and members of their delegations.

President Kennedy made a striking figure beside his blue-eyed wife and the shorter Khrushchevs. The President found much to talk about with Mme. Khrushchev.

Mr. Khrushchev barged with good nature from group to group. Laughing and gesticulating with both hands, he shouldered his way to talk to Mrs. Kennedy again.

When the guests took their seats for the musical entertainment after dinner, Premier Khrushchev sat beside Mrs. Kennedy. There was about a foot between their chairs. Mr. Khrushchev shifted his chair closer.

The Soviet Premier regaled the American President's wife with anecdotes. At one point, she put her gloved hand over her mouth and feigned amazement as he developed one story.

When he came to the punchline, she threw back her head and laughed heartily.

President Kennedy interrupted once and suggested that the Soviet Premier should tell Mrs. Kennedy a story Mr. Khrushchev had told the President previously.

The dinner was lavishly served on the imperial dishes of the Habsburgs. Spring soup was first, followed by asparagus tips, fish in wine sauce, and beefsteak with mushrooms. This was topped off by pastries and creams, for which Vienna is famous.

During the meal an orchestra played Viennese waltzes. There were no toasts.

After dinner, held in the palace's great gallery, the hosts and their 600 guests retired to the ceremonial room for coffee and cognac. The gallery later was cleared for an evening of ballet and opera.

June 4, 1961

Premier Nikita Khrushchev chatting with Mrs. Kennedy.

WASHINGTON, June 8—The White House disclosed today that President Kennedy strained his back on May 16 and had since been in "constant discomfort." The injury occurred at a tree-planting ceremony in Canada. The President's physician, Dr. Janet Travell, said there was "no serious concern" about the ailment and expressed confidence that Mr. Kennedy would recover rapidly. Everyone emphasized that the strain had no connection with his previous serious back troubles. Pierre Salinger, White House press secretary, gave the news at a hurriedly called briefing this morning. He began by saying, "The President will appear today using crutches."

The back strain was a secret kept even from the President's staff, and apparently the reason for the announcement was that Mr. Kennedy had planned to appear in public on crutches. But in the middle of the briefing that idea was dropped.

The President telephoned Mr. Salinger during the briefing. He said he had talked again with Dr. Travell and decided, in Mr. Salinger's words, "to try another day without the crutches."

The purpose of the crutches, according to Mr. Salinger, was to rest the strained muscle. He has used them once since the injury occurred—in the privacy of the family home in Hyannis Port, Mass., the week-end before last.

Mr. Kennedy flew to Palm Beach, Fla., this afternoon for a three-day rest. Dr. Travell went with him.

Limped Slightly

Reporters who watched him walk to his jet at Andrews Air Force base thought he limped slightly and carried himself a bit awkwardly. In public appearances earlier in the day he walked somewhat gingerly.

The back strain occurred at a ceremonial tree-planting in Ottawa during the President's Canadian visit. Mr. Kennedy lifted a silver-plated shovel three times digging a hole for a red oak tree outside Government House.

Mr. Salinger said the President felt "immediate pain" during the ceremonial shoveling. He did nothing about it for several days in the hope that it would go away.

Then, two weeks ago, Mr. Salinger said, the President's back "began to bother him seriously." Dr. Travell went to Hyannis Port to treat him.

The press secretary quoted Dr. Travell as having said that the pain from the injury was "a kind of constant discomfort, something like a steady toothache."

A Common Injury

Dr. Travell called the injury a lumbosacral strain. This is a common low-back muscle strain. It can come from any sudden or unusual movement, even picking up a pencil.

Mr. Salinger said the point of the strain was between the lowest lumbar vertebrae, or section of the spine, and the sacrum. The sacrum is a fixed bone that is part of the pelvis. Muscles surrounding the juncture of the lumbar region and the sacrum are quite frequently subject to strain.

The treatment being used by Dr. Travell consists of injections of novcain, a pain-relieving drug, and application of hot pads. She has also recommended swimming in a warm pool.

"The President plans to do extensive swimming at Palm Beach," Mr. Salinger said. The estate of Mr. and Mrs. Charles B. Wrightsman, where he will be staying, has a heated swimming pool.

Mr. Salinger said X-rays showed that the injury was definitely not a slipped or ruptured disk of the spine.

Mr. Salinger told the reporters that he had known nothing about the President's injury until today. He said the President had kept it from everyone on his staff except Dr. Travell.

Mr. Kennedy's back problems began with a football injury at Harvard. He suffered what was apparently a ruptured disk in the lower back.

A severe recurrence of this trouble came when his PT boat was cut in half by a Japanese destroyer in 1943.

Gelatinous material escaped from the ruptured disk and pressed on the nerve in Mr. Kennedy's back. Severe pain was relieved by an operation in 1944 to remove some of the extraneous material from the nerve roots.

But some muscle spasm remained in Mr. Kennedy's back, and in the next few years this gradually worsened. One reason, discovered later, was that one of his legs was a trifle longer than the other.

The pain grew worse in 1952, when Mr. Kennedy went through a hard campaign for the Senate, and continued to get worse. In 1954 he was using crutches.

In October, 1954, Mr. Kennedy underwent surgery—insertion of a small metal plate to fuse the lower vertebrae. But the operation was unsuccessful. He developed an infection and, according to members of his family, was near death. He received the last rites of the Roman Catholic Church.

After weeks of rest in Florida, he underwent another operation. This time the metal plate was removed, and the infection was healed. He walked out of the hospital in February, 1955, and went to Florida for a long convalescence.

Later the same year he was referred to Dr. Travell, who tried the novocain treatment and succeeded in stopping the pain.

Since that time Mr. Kennedy has worn a small lift in all his shoes—even sandals. And he wears a surgical corset to give his back support. Until this new injury, he had been without back trouble for years.

June 9, 1961

President's Back Strain at Tree Planting Is Disclosed

By ANTHONY LEWIS

WASHINGTON, July 25—President Kennedy asked tonight for an over-all increase in the nation's military preparedness to meet a Soviet threat he described as "world-wide."

The President proposed adding 217,000 men to the armed forces and increasing expenditures by $3,457,000,000, including $297,000,000 for civil defense.

Mr. Kennedy said that $1,800,000,000 of the total would be earmarked for non-nuclear weapons, and ammunition and equipment.

The President spoke from his desk in the White House. His address, carried by all radio and television networks at 10 P.M., was firm in tone.

Offers to Negotiate

He held out an offer to negotiate on Berlin, however, and declared that if the Russians "seek genuine understanding—not concessions of our rights—we shall meet with them."

Mr. Kennedy said that the preparedness measures he was requesting would bring the expected budget deficit for this year to more than $5,000,000,000. Nonetheless, he said, he is requesting no new taxes at this time.

The President indicated, however, that new taxes might become necessary later.

"I intend to submit to the Congress in January a budget for the next fiscal year which will be strictly in balance," he said. "Never-

theless, should an incrase in taxes be needed to achieve that balance in view of these or subsequent defense rises, those increased taxes will be requested."

Support of People Asked

There was no suggestion in the speech that Mr. Kennedy would declare a national emergency. In a personal note added at the end of his prepared text, however, Mr. Kennedy left no doubt how gravely he regarded the situation.

"We must look to long days ahead," he said. "In these coming months, I need your goodwill and your support—and above all, your prayers."

Kennedy Asks Increase in Defenses

207 Million Is Sought for Civil Defense in Speech on Berlin

By TOM WICKER

At Home In The White House

73

The President said that the "first steps" he was asking "will require sacrifice on the part of many citizens." He said further sacrifices might be needed in the future. "Courage and perseverance for many years to come," Mr. Kennedy said, will be required of all Americans, if the Communist challenge is to be met.

In addition to the money he said was needed, the President said he would ask for an increase in the Army's strength from 875,000 to 1,000,000 men, and increases of 29,000 and 63,000 men respectively for the Navy and the Air Force.

These manpower needs, Mr. Kennedy said, would be met by doubling and tripling draft calls in the coming months. In addition, he said he would ask Congress for authority to order active duty for some ready reserve units and individual reservists, and extended duty for others.

"'We do not want to fight," he asserted, "but we have fought before."

With the increases sought by the President the total requested defense budget will become $47,500,000,000, or about $6,000,000,000 more than was sought in the budget submitted last January by former President Eisenhower.

Mr. Kennedy put heavy stress on the role of our allies in helping to maintain the West's position in Berlin and strengthen the West's hand elsewhere.

"A first need is to hasten progress toward the military goals which the North Atlantic allies have set for themselves," the President said. "We will put even greater resources into fulfilling those goals, and look to our allies to do the same."

Despite the military moves he outlined, the President said "our response to the Berlin crisis will not be merely military or negative."

"It will be more than merely standing firm," he said, "for we do not intend to leave it to others to choose and monopolize the forum and framework of discussion. We do not intend to abandon our duty to manking to seek a peaceful solution."

Mr. Kennedy also insisted that Berlin did not present a black and white choice between "resistance and retreat, between atomic holocaust and surrender."

"We intend," he declared, "to have a wider choice than humiliation or all-out nuclear action."

The President made two proposals concerning the West's presence in Berlin.

One was a "free vote in Berlin, and if possible among all the German people" on the question whether the presence of the West is desired by the people of West Berlin, "compared to East German feelings about their regime."

The other proposal was the adjudication of the West's legal right to be in Berlin, if anyone doubted it. Mr. Kennedy did not say to what court or forum the issue would be submitted.

There was a hint, too, that Mr. Kennedy might be planning to carry the Berlin issue directly to Mr. Khrushchev.

The Soviet Premier, he said, "may find that his invitation to other nations to jon in a meaningless treaty may lead to their inviting him to join in the community of peaceful men, in abandoning the use of force, and in respecting the sanctity of agreements."

This was viewed as a possible indication that the President was thinking of submitting the

Berlin issue to the United Nations or perhaps to a multination conference, at which the issue of self-determination might be raised against the puppet East German regime.

The President made it clear, however, that he was not reacting solely to Soviet prodding in Berlin.

"That isolated outpost is not an isolated problem," he said. "The threat is world-wide. Our effort must be equally wide and strong, and not be obsessed by a single manufactured crisis."

He cited the Communist challenge in Southeast Asia, and another "in our own hemisphere" —an apparent reference to the Castro regime in Cuba.

This world-wide view was reflected in another specific request. Mr. Kennedy said he would order to active duty a number of air transport squadrons and Air National Guard tactical squadrons "to give us the airlift capacity and protection we may need."

The President plans to present details of all his requests to Congress in a series of messages, the first of which will be sent tomorrow. It is expected to detail his civil defense requests.

He made this pledge to his audience of millions:

"Everything essential to the security of freedom will be done; and if that should require more men, taxes, controls or other new powers, I shall not hesitate to request them."

The President laid down this doctrine for the crucial months to come:

"While we will not let panic shape our policy, neither will we permit timidity to direct our program."

He cautioned others against assuming that the West was too soft and selfish to defend its freedoms.

He repeated, however, that

"we are willing to consider any arrangement for a treaty in Germany consistent with the maintenance of peace and freedom and with the legitimate security interests of all nations."

"We have previously indicated our readiness to remove any actual irritants in West Berlin," Mr. Kennedy said, "but the freedom of that city is not negotiable."

Recovery Is Seen

He said that the nation was recovering from last winter's recession, increasing its output but maintaining both wholesale and retail price stability. The nation's gold position is improving, he said, "and the dollar is more respected."

All this, Mr. Kennedy argued, would mean improved revenues and would make possible the balanced budget he envisioned for fiscal year 1963.

Mr. Kennedy closed his address with an appeal to the Russian people and a tribute to their bravery in World War II.

As for the people of the United States, the President vowed, "we seek peace but we shall not surrender."

Then Mr. Kennedy made an extemporaneous personal appeal. No one could realize, he said, the seriousness of the Communist challenge until he bore "the burdens of this office."

"I must tell you that there is no quick and easy solution," Mr. Kennedy warned. As he did so often in his campaign for the Presidency, he then asked for the help and advice of his hearers.

"All of us love our country, and we shall do our best to serve it," he concluded.

July 26, 1961

President Is Host to 18 Children

HYANNIS PORT, Mass., Sept. 1 — President Kennedy loaded eighteen youngsters aboard his big white golf cart tonight for a twilight visit to the neighborhood candy store. He wound up the trip with a weeping youngster in his lap. As Mr. Kennedy started the cart for the block and a half trip back to his summer home, three youngsters toppled off the rear. One sat down hard. The boy started crying, and a policeman picked him up and carried him to the President. Mr. Kennedy soothed the little

boy, and drove home with the youngster in his lap. The boy was one of the seven children of Attorney General Robert F. Kennedy, the President's brother. Mr. Kennedy pulled the cart around the corner and the children made a beeline for the shop with the President's daughter, Caroline, among the front-runners. The children got candy bars, and the bill was about $1.50. The President will spend the week-end here.

September 2, 1961

WASHINGTON, Oct. 24 (AP) —Mrs. Robert F. Kennedy, the wife of the United States Attorney General, didn't place, but she made a game try at the Washington International Horse Show tonight.

In full hunting attire, 32-year-old Ethel Kennedy, the mother of seven children, rode Sky's Pride, a chestnut mare, over the ten fences.

She toppled a brush-and-rail obstacle and lost her black bowler hat, but Mrs. Kennedy got a big hand for her effort from the opening-night crowd.

"I thought she did very well," said her husband, who watched with five of their children from a ringside box.

Cold Climate Frost

The judges, though, gave the DeFranceaux Challenge Trophy to Cold Climate, a chestnut gelding owned by Mrs. J. Deane Rucker of Grosse Pointe, Mich.

Mrs. Kennedy, whose mount is owned by Claude W. Owen of Potomac, Md., was the last rider in the conformation-hunter-in-appointments class. With ring turf still on her hat, Mrs. Kennedy indicated she would also compete later in the week-long show.

The Robert Kennedys donated the Joseph P. Kennedy Jr. Memorial Trophy for the international jumping event in memory of the Attorney General's brother, a pilot killed in World War II.

Mrs. Kennedy changed from her black hunting coat with the orange collar—denoting membership in the Fairfield (Conn.)

Westchester Hunt—fawn-colored breeches and black boots into a sleek black velvet evening gown to present the trophy later.

2,500 at Show

The show drew about 2,500 persons to the National Guard Armory.

The Kennedys occupied the Presidential box, where Mrs. John F. Kennedy, the President's wife, will sit Friday night when she presents a new perpetual challenge cup for open jumpers.

Ethel Kennedy bundled her children off home after she had made her appearance. Two of the oldest, Kathleen, 10, and Joseph, 9, will compete in a pony class on Sunday.

October 25, 1961

FANS CHEER RIDE BY ETHEL KENNEDY

Attorney General Sees Wife Compete in Horse Show

Ethel Kennedy's moment in the spotlight is over; she is once again, Mother.

An Errant Call Finds Kennedy on the Line

WASHINGTON, Aug. 2 (AP)—Even President Kennedy's emergency telephone in his bedroom is not immune to wrong number calls. He answered one last week from an insistent caller asking for an animal hospital.

The incident was confirmed today by White House press secretary Pierre Salinger.

Mr. Salinger said he did not know what time the President's emergency-use phone rang, but Mr. Kennedy still was awake. The President picked up the phone and heard a strange voice ask:

"Is this the animal hospital?"

Mr. Kennedy said no.

"Is this South 5-6855?" the insistent caller inquired.

"No, this is the White House," the President replied.

"Is Mr. Stevenson there?" the caller asked.

"No, this is the President," the President insisted.

At this point, the caller hung up.

There was no explanation as to how the animal hospital's number buzzed the President's private phone.

August 3, 1961

EDWARD KENNEDY WINS

President's Brother Victor in First Case as Prosecutor

BOSTON, Nov. 21 (UPI)— Edward M. Kennedy won his first major case as an assistant district attorney yesterday when he obtained a conviction against a man for the armed robbery of a liquor store.

The youngest brother of President Kennedy successfully prosecuted James J. McCarthy, 34 years old, of Charlestown, despite testimony by an alleged confederate that McCarthy did not participate in the hold-up.

McCarthy was sentenced to five to seven years in prison after being convicted by a Superior Court jury. Mr. Kennedy is an assistant district attorney of Suffolk County.

November 22, 1961

Weekly Lectures Held At R. F. Kennedy Home

WASHINGTON, Dec. 8 (AP)—The Evening Star says selected members of the Kennedy Administration, including several Cabinet officers, have been attending weekly lectures on abstruse subjects.

The gatherings are held at the home in McLean, Va. of Attorney General Robert F. Kennedy. The Attorney General and his wife, it was said today, developed their enthusiasm for seminars on a skiing vacation at Aspen, Colo. They were said to have seen the device in operation at the Institute for Humanistic Studies.

According to the article, the opening lecture on Nov. 27 was delivered by Arthur M. Schlesinger Jr., special assistant to President Kennedy and Pulitzer Prize-winning biographer and former Harvard historian. He spoke on the broad sweep of history.

Last Wednesday, the article went on, Walt W. Rostow, a former Professor of International Economics at Massachusetts Institute of Technology, spoke on the subject of the relation between economic development and democratic institutions.

December 9, 1961

Courtesy at Car Leaves Kennedy Out in Cold

Mayor Wagner and Adlai E. Stevenson, chief United States delegate to the United Nations, encountered a confusing point of courtesy yesterday that apparently was not covered in the rigid plans for the President's visit.

Who, they found themselves asking, would sit next to Mr. Kennedy on the ride from La Guardia Airport to Manhattan? For several moments, they demurred to one another over who would get into the car first while the coatless President stood in the cold wind and looked on.

Mr. Stevenson finally solved the issue, by entering the car first—but he took a folding seat behind the driver and left the seat at the President's left to the Mayor.

January 20, 1962

Joseph Kennedy Has Serious Stroke; President Flies to Bedside in Florida

By JOSEPH A. LOFTUS

WEST PALM BEACH, Fla., Dec. 19—Joseph P. Kennedy, 73-year-old father of the President, suffered a stroke at his home in Palm Beach today.

President Kennedy flew here from Washington and went immediately to St. Mary's Hospital, where the elder Mr. Kennedy, the former Ambassador to Britain, was undergoing emergency treatment for a condition described tonight as "serious."

Medical sources said there had been some paralysis but that they would not know how serious the condition of the President's father was until diagnostic tests were completed. However, last rites of the Roman Catholic Church were administered by the Rev. Eugene Seraphin, chaplain of St. Mary's Hospital, as soon as Mr. Kennedy was admitted.

He fell ill this morning after playing six holes of golf and returned home to rest. About 1 P. M. he complained of feeling no better, and an ambulance was summoned to take him to the hospital.

Not long after, President Kennedy was informed in Washington that his father had suffered the attack. The President met with the National Security Council at 4 P. M., and when the meeting ended fifty-five minutes later, left his office to hurry here.

He entered a limousine with his brother, Attorney General Robert F. Kennedy, and their sister, Mrs. Stephen E. Smith, and rode behind a police escort to Andrews Air Force base in about twenty-eight minutes.

Fog blanketed the field and a light drizzle was falling, but the President strode bareheaded from the car to the plane. He was unsmiling and did not wave to a small group of onlookers.

The President left the base in Maryland at 5:42 P. M. and arrived in Florida two hours later. He went immediately to the hospital, arriving at 8:07. He spoke briefly with a nun, then proceeded to his father's suite on the third floor, in a wing of the hospital donated by the Kennedy family.

Others at Hospital

Also at the hospital at different intervals during the afternoon and evening were the President's mother, Mrs. Rose Kennedy, his wife, Jacqueline and his brother, Edward M. Kennedy.

The President did not get to see his father when he arrived at the hospital, but was escorted to a sitting room across the hall, where he conferred with physicians and with members of the Kennedy family.

After leaving the area of his father's room, the President went with his wife and brother Robert to the hospital chapel in a separate building just off the main entranec of the Catholic institution. They were in the chapel for a few minutes, then walked to their car.

Returns to Hospital

The President and Mrs. Kennedy left the hospital at 9:49 P. M. for the home of C. M. Paul, where they had arranged to stay for the Christmas holidays. Less than an hour later the President paid a second call to the hospital.

Ninety minutes after the elder Mr. Kennedy was taken to the hospital, Physicians said in a bulletin that his ocndition was "satisfactory." Early this evening, however, his condition was described as "serious."

Pierre Salinger, the White House press secretary, said at 8:35 P. M. that tests conducted by three physicians had caused a plan for an operation to be dropped.

He said the doctors had described the test as a carotid arteriogram, to locate the thrombosis. A thrombosis is an obstruction to the flow of blood.

The test was performed by injecting a dye into the big artery of the neck and then watching its progress by X-ray. Mr. Salinger said that if the thrombosis had been found to be outside the cranial area, an operation would have been performed. In the former Ambassador's case, he said, the thrombosis was found to be inside the head, and no operation was possible.

After the test, the doctors succeeded with some difficulty in getting the former Ambassador to sleep. They said no prognosis would be possible for twenty-four to forty-eight hours.

It was because the physicians had had trouble in getting the President's father to sleep that the President did not speak to him. The three physicians who performed the tests on the President's father were Dr. Walter R. Newbern, a brain surgeon, Dr. Marco Johannsen, an internist, and Dr. James Cooley, a neurosurgeon, all of Palm Beach.

A vascular specialist, Dr. William T. Foley of New York, arrived here on the Air Force plane that brought the President's brother Edward, and they were taken immediately to the elder Mr. Kennedy's floor at the hospital. They joined the President, his wife and the At-torney General, who were still on the third floor.

The President, his wife, and brother Robert were able to spend about fifteen minutes with the elder Mr. Kennedy, who was conscious and recognized them but was unable to speak. Later Mr. Salinger said that "there is some paralysis" and added that it was because of the stroke, and not medica-tion, that the elder Mr. Kennedy could not speak.

President Kennedy, his wife, and the Attorney General left the hospital at midnight. Presi-dent Kennedy told reporters that his father's condition was "about the same." Dr. Foley ex-amined the elder Mr. Kennedy and informed the President that his father was still in serious condition. Physicians at the hospital expressed hope that the patient would be able to sleep through the night.

Edward Kennedy and Miss Ann Gargan, the elder Mr. Ken-nedy's niece, planned to remain at the hospital overnight.

There was apparently a see-saw pattern in the reaction of the elder Mr. Kennedy to the stroke. At 7:30 P. M. Dr. Johan-nsen reported that the former Ambassador was "somewhat improved." An hour later Mr. Kennedy's condition was re-ported as "serious."

Asked whether surgery was indicated, Dr. Johannsen said "surgery will not be necessary." To an inquiry on whether Mr. Kennedy's stroke could be de-scribed as a "massive" one, Dr. Johannsen said: "No, I wouldn't say that."

Only this morning, the elder Mr. Kennedy had seen his son off here as the President board-ed a plane for Washington.

Among those who saw the elder Mr. Kennedy in the hospi-tal were the Most Rev. Coleman F. Carroll, Bishop of the Dio-cese of Miami, who flew from Miami, and Msgr. Jeremiah O'Mahoney, pastor of St. Ed-ward's Church, in Palm Beach.

December 20, 1962

AFTER the first twelve months of having the Ken-nedy family in residence at the White House, the average American has a much clear-er idea of what it must be like to have everything. The Kennedys and their numerous clan have opened wide a win-dow on the life of the un-idle rich. These are the people who have youth and vigor, wealth and wit and an aspiration to be wise.

The influence of the Ken-nedys at home and abroad, in matters domestic, social and familial, may be said to in-clude an awareness of rock-ing chairs, of classic French cuisine, of serious music and art, and of Vassar and Har-vard. The forward-looking homemaker no longer feels that she has to live with mod-ern furniture. And in rearing children, it appears that some little girls can be seen—and also heard.

Mrs Kennedy entered the fishbowl existence of a First Lady somewhat shyly and hesitantly, but, by the spring of last year, the President of the United States was telling the French, "I am the man who accompanied Jacqueline Kennedy to Paris."

Undoubtedly, she has made the world safe for brunettes by subtly usurping the au-thority of the pretty, empty-headed blonde. It is now quite all right for a woman to be a bit brainy or cultured as long as she tempers her intelli-gence with a "t'rific" girlish rhetoric. And hardly anyone considers it affected these days to be able to hold a con-versation in a couple of lan-guages.

When Mrs. Kennedy crossed the threshold of the White House, the sound of her alligator pumps rever-berated through the fashion world. Her administration got off to a controversial start with the designation of a personal dress designer. Her back-tilted hats and her bouffant hairdo became na-tional fads. A New York rid-ing emporium reported a boom in its tailoring business caused by eager equestrians who feared being caught in frayed breeches should Mrs. Kennedy put in an appear-ance at a hunt or horse show.

Mrs. Kennedy made the masses class-conscious. Her unadorned, sleeveless dresses, her skinny golfing and sailing pants and her preference for cloth coats instead of mink by the yard were upper-crust habits that were suddenly adopted by the common woman.

If her hopes for her per-sonal project are realized, then the lasting, nonpolitical achievement of the Kennedy stay on Pennsylvania Avenue will be the feeling on the part of the American people that the newly redecorated White House is a home that truly belongs to them.

January 20, 1962

The Kennedys, in White House a Year, Bring New Look to Domestic Scene

At the dinner given for winners of the Nobel Prize for literature, President and Mrs. Kennedy chat with Pearl S. Buck and Robert Frost.

Culture Makes a Hit At the White House

The flurry of cultural activities there reflects its occupants' interest in the arts.

By ARTHUR and BARBARA GELB

THE palpable love affair between the White House and a jade called Culture shows signs of reaching an impassioned peak this year. With Robert Frost's participation in the inaugural ceremony heralding the romance, and three command performances at the Executive Mansion cementing it in recent months, the extraordinary liaison between politics and art has been attracting comment abroad and speculation at home—particularly in the cultural wasteland of Washington itself. It is a notorious fact that the performing arts have few or inadequate facilities in the capital and have had, until very lately, even fewer friends. As a correspondent for The Sunday Times of London observed in hailing the new White House interest in culture, "Because Washington society prefers talk to listening, the performing arts suffer."

Unlike the great capitals of London, Paris and Moscow, Washington has little to offer artistically to native visitors from outlying communities or to diplomats from abroad; aside from its art galleries and chamber music concerts (admittedly among the finest) it has consistently lagged behind. It has only one experimental theatre—the Arena Stage—and one commercial playhouse—the National—where pre-Broadway tryouts and road companies stop over; its National Symphony Orchestra is not in the first rank, its Opera Society, while enterprising, is limited in resources, and its home-grown ballet company performs only sporadically.

Indeed, among many politicians, the arts are considered a laughing matter, if they are considered at all—as witness the recent comment by a Congressman from Virginia, who observed that poker playing was "an artful occupation" and that it was as logical to subsidize poker players as artists.

IN the face of such well-established anti-estheticism in Washington, it now appears that President and Mrs. Kennedy are systematically planning to turn Washingtonians into better listeners and to expand their artistic "patronage" in the tradition of European heads of state. Not since Thomas Jefferson occupied what was then known as the President's Palace has culture had such good friends in the White House.

The flow of guests from the fields of the arts to the Executive Mansion has been unprecedented since Mr. Kennedy took office. Not only have Metropolitan Opera stars, a troupe of Shakespearean actors and Pablo Casals been issued formal invitations to perform in the East Room at state dinners, but the list of private and official guests invited to the White House over the past months forms a Who's Who of culture —everyone from Carl Sandburg, Gian Carlo Menotti and Leonard Bernstein to Igor Stravinsky, George Balanchine, Elia Kazan and Ralph Richardson have been welcomed there.

The President and his wife have attended the opening performances of both the Opera Society and the National Symphony Orchestra, and Mrs. Kennedy has attended the Washington Ballet and a performance at the Library of Congress of "The Importance of Being Oscar," Micheal MacLiammoir's one-man reading from the works of Oscar Wilde.

In addition, Mr. Kennedy has taken a public stand in favor of culture giving his support to the proposed National Cultural Center in Washington—a multi-million dollar project comparable in scope to New York City's Lincoln Center for the Performing Arts.

HE has also gone out of his way to commend various groups for their artistic achievements, including the Theatre Guild American Repertory Company, which toured Europe, the Near East and Latin America under the auspices of the State Department; and he took the trouble to write personally to Jack Landau, who staged the command program of Shakespeare at the White House, congratulating him on "a very exciting performance" and expressing his and Mrs. Kennedy's pride in "our American theatre."

Perhaps none of these cultural pats on the back (as some snipers aver) add up to the start of a cultural renaissance in Washington. But those close to the President point out that command performances have set the machinery in motion. This is borne out by the facts that, for the first time in White House history, a permanent stage has been built that can be stored and put into place at almost a moment's notice; that future flirtations with all the lively arts — ballet, contemporary theatre, classical music and even jazz—are being planned on a bimonthly basis at the White House; and that poetry seminars, sponsored by the Cabinet under the aegis of Mrs. Kennedy, are to be regularly scheduled events in the capital (Robert Frost has already presided over one and Carl Sandburg over another). Moreover, Presidential patronage of the arts in the form of annual contests, prizes and an official cultural coordinator is promised.

THE question being asked by some keepers of the flame of status quo is: will the arty atmosphere of the White House damage the President politically? They maintain that the majority of the voting

Robert Frost, reading one of his poems at the Kennedy Inaugural ceremony.

THE KENNEDYS: A NEW YORK TIMES PROFILE

public looks askance at the egghead and that things were much cozier with the Eisenhowers, who invited mainly popular television performers to entertain their guests. The Kennedys have endeared themselves to the country's intellectuals, say these lowbrows, but how many intellectuals are there among the registered voters, compared with the ranks of solid, stolid citizens to whom culture is a dirty word?

All this cultural frenzy, they add, is having no elevating effect on the average citizen, who will continue to relegate culture to the realm of the effete and will vote the chi-chi Kennedys out of office, come 1964.

EVEN the highbrows are questioning certain aspects of the vaunted romance with the arts. How much of it, they ask, is an effort to create a new public image in intellectual circles of the President as a patron of the arts; and is it likely that once the publicity value wears off, the White House passion for culture will cool?

While no one denies that the President is aware of and pleased with the publicity value of his nod to culture, it is apparent that there is much more behind it, and the results have already proved a justification of his program. At any rate, he appears to discount the Neanderthal position and to take heart from the fact that there is considerable support, both at home and abroad, for his theory that a great nation may profit as much from the artistic achievement it fosters as from the wisdom of its political leadership.

The President's Cabinet is firmly behind Mr. Kennedy in this point of view and Labor Secretary Arthur Goldberg is even one step ahead. Last month Mr. Goldberg came out publicly in support of subsidizing the arts. He and other Government officials are known to attend cultural events, admit to being avid readers of the classics, and enjoy discussing various aspects of the arts at White House functions, both informal and official.

THIS is all highly unorthodox behavior — and highly gratifying to this country's artists. Elia Kazan, the director, is among those who are impressed with the thoroughness of the Kennedy cultural approach.

"I think," said Mr. Kazan, shortly after a visit to the White House, "that Mr. Kennedy's conception of the Presidency is that it should have the broadest possible scope. It's had a great effect on all

of us in the theatre."

Ralph Bellamy, president of Actors Equity Association, recently told Mr. Kennedy apropos the Casals command performance: "You have lent stature to my own field of endeavor. Even the least of my craft gains a measure of dignity from your reception of this great artist."

The remarkable thing about the White House espousal of culture is that no one can justifiably bring a charge of bookwormism or arty insulation against a President who is as vigorous and physical-health-conscious as Mr. Kennedy, or his golfing, horseback-riding, water-skiing First Lady. Indeed, the public image of this handsome young couple, cheerfully endorsing the arts as part of a rich, full life, cannot fail to have an impact on the country in general, whatever the snipers may say.

"When Kennedy endorses ballet, painting and theatre, the average man is bound to change his mind about such things being effete," Dore Schary recently remarked.

"Even the old-line politician gets the notion that he ought to take an interest in the arts — especially if he hopes or expects to be invited to a cultural evening at the White House. It's a way of ingratiating himself with the boss — as in the case of a corporation employe who knows his boss is keen on golf; the employe takes up golf in the hope of someday being invited by his boss to make up a foursome."

THERE is also a growing cultural respect for the Presidency in foreign capitals, as no one recognizes more clearly than Philip H. Coombs, who fills the new position of Assistant Secretary of State for Educational and Cultural Affairs.

Mr. Coombs, who is working on a "cultural manifesto" that will attempt to clarify this country's attitude toward the arts, said that the reaction in the foreign embassies to the artistic evenings at the White House has been highly enthusiastic.

Both Mr. and Mrs. Kennedy of course, had more than a nodding acquaintance with the arts long before they moved into the White House. Their current program of patronage is a legitimate and natural extension of their accustomed way of life.

In the President's case, the extension may be a bit more strained than in Mrs. Kennedy's. He is, like most of us, not as well-rounded culturally as he might wish— and his participation in cultural events is necessarily restricted by the pressures of more vital matters.

His tastes in classical music and painting range from middlebrow to noncommittal. He will sit happily through the portion of a concert that includes a well-known Tchaikovsky symphony, but after that he is apt to fidget. He admires the Cézannes his wife has hung in the Green Room of the White House, and will point them out proudly to visitors, but his admiration seems directed primarily toward his wife's expertise in this field.

HIS tastes in pure literature (he is, of course, an omnivorous reader of history and political biography) are not committed to record — though one friend says he enjoyed the Norman Mailer novel, "The Deer Park," and another states that "Dr. Zhivago" and "The Leopard" were recent novels of which he expressed approval. His bedtime reading, it is said, runs to detective fiction.

In the theatre, his preference is for musicals and light comedy. Since his election, he has attended Broadway performances of "Do Re Mi" and "The Best Man." One of his favorite characterizations was Sam Levene's Nathan Detroit in "Guys and Dolls" and he can knowledgeably hold a discussion of Method acting with the actress, Shelley Winters — an ardent pre-election campaigner.

The President enjoys satirical comics, particularly Bob Newhart, Joey Bishop and Mort Sahl. (During the campaign, he borrowed at least one joke from Mr. Sahl; replying to the charge of a Protestant minister that, if elected, he would "build a tunnel to Rome," the candidate delivered this Sahlism: "I am against public works projects of any kind.")

Mr. Kennedy is decidedly a movie fan — particularly of

red-blooded films like "La Dolce Vita" and "Spartacus," which he watched at a theatre near the White House that has a wide screen. Private screenings are frequently given at the White House and when a film bores Mr. Kennedy, he either leaves his guests, or orders the final reel run so he can see how it turns out— as was the case with "L'Avventura," which he found slow-paced.

AGAIN, all this does not add up to Culture; and the President is the first to admit that modern man, however willing to be culturally saturated, is confronted with certain difficulties. One of his close friends (and an occasional week-end guest at the White House, the playwright Gore Vidal has pointed out that the President is both aware of and regretful about the lack of comprehensive cultural training of modern man.

"We recently got onto the subject of the American Revolution," Mr. Vidal said, "and the President pointed out that while the eighteenth century produced, out of a little country of only 3,000,000 people, two all-around geniuses— Franklin and Jefferson—as well as an extraordinary number of slightly less gifted men, twentieth-century America had produced no equivalents. Where was today's equivalent for a man like Adams, he said, who could write and think and design a building and box a compass?

"The President observed rather wistfully that few Americans today even had a second language, or knew the classics intimately, and though we study, there are vast areas that were comprehended by our predecessors which are unfamiliar to us. We don't have long, leisurely winters at Monticello, the sort of atmosphere

POET—Carl Sandburg talks with President Kennedy at the White House.

MUSIC—The President congratulates Pablo Casals after the distinguished 'cellist's White House concert. Mrs. Kennedy and Governor Luis Muñoz Marín of Puerto Rico look on.

where you are forced onto your own mental resources."

Recognizing this lack, the President takes pains to express his support of highbrow art such as chamber music and ballet ("I think it is tremendously important that we regard music not just as part of our arsenal in the cold war, but as an integral part of a free society," he recently said) and he happily endorses Shakespeare.

Furthermore, he is pleased to follow the tastes of his wife, who happens to be well qualified for the role of unofficial Minister of Culture.

CULTURE has been an integral part of Jacqueline Kennedy's life since childhood, and

COMPOSER—Mrs. Kennedy welcomes Igor Stravinsky—a recent guest for dinner — at the White House.

she has been guiding her husband's participation in (if not always spontaneous enjoyment of) the esthetic since their marriage.

Her stepfather, Hugh Auchincloss, is a noted collector of eighteenth-century books and art, which greatly influenced her early life. Her preferences in music, literature, painting and the performing arts, unlike the President's, are categorically on record; they are the tastes of a well-born young woman with polite and gracious standards, and they are, by comparison with her husband's, decidedly highbrow.

Mrs. Kennedy, an amateur painter herself, collects eighteenth and nineteenth century drawings, has several Renoirs on loan in her private rooms at the White House and owns a Boudin seascape and works by such contemporary painters as Goodenough, Walt Kuhn and William Walton. She is knowledgeable about antiques (her redecoration of the White House and restoration of historical objects d'art are well known by now).

She is a balletomane and a fond concertgoer, having a preference for the romantic music of the nineteenth century. She reads philosophy, one of her favorite playwrights is Oscar Wilde, and she regards among her best-liked authors Henry James, Henry Adams, Nathaniel Hawthorne, Ernest Hemingway, F. Scott Fitzgerald (whose daughter,

Frances Lanahan, is a friend) and Edgar Allan Poe. She is partial to biographies of eighteenth-century figures.

Mrs. Kennedy's chief advisers on cultural matters (aside from her Fine Arts Committee for the White House) are the President's press secretary, Pierre Salinger, Presidential assistant Arthur Schlesinger Jr., and her social secretary, Letitia Baldridge.

MR. SALINGER grew up in the world of music, for his mother was a music and art critic in San Francisco. Soon after the inauguration, he and Mr. Schlesinger met with Mrs. Kennedy and among them they agreed that "it was important to demonstrate that the White House could be an influence in encouraging public acceptance of the arts." It was Mr. Salinger who engineered the Pablo Casals command performance in November.

Mr. Salinger's advice is being sought by Mrs. Kennedy with regard to what he describes as a "two-faceted program" to be inaugurated later this year. A committee will be named to give prizes for the best composition and the best instrumental performance in a national competition, and the winners will participate in a week's musical activities in Washington, finally giving a televised concert at the White House with the National Symphony Orchestra.

IN addition, Presidential medals will be awarded annually for the best contributions in other spheres of the arts. Committees appointed by the White House will pick the winners. Money to underwrite this program will be privately raised and, according to Mr. Salinger, $100,000 already has been pledged.

Mr. Schlesinger puts his broad knowledge of the theatre at Mrs. Kennedy's disposal. A movie buff, he also has a hand in the selection of films screened at the White House.

"Jackie's tastes are intuitive on artistic choices," he said recently. "Both she and the President enjoy being with creative people, and feel that artists are very central figures in the health of a country. The President is aware of practically everything that is going on, which includes the field of the arts. He has the most unexpected areas of information. He reads everything."

Miss Baldridge is perhaps the most indispensable member of Mrs. Kennedy's cultural cabinet. She is in touch with key people in the theatre world and in her job of sifting the numerous offers and suggestions of groups clamoring to perform at the White House, she has the help of a network that seems almost as comprehensive as the C. I. A.

On a recent afternoon, her sunny White House office was cluttered with mail from amateur and professional groups all over the country. On her desk, among numerous manuscripts, were three new one-act plays by Thornton Wilder (which recently opened in New York.)

Miss Baldridge had not yet had time to read the plays; they had, in fact, only reached her a day or two earlier, having been submitted with a summary of their contents by Mrs. Lanahan. Miss Baldridge was weighing their suitability for White House presentation.

MISS BALDRIDGE said the next state dinner, not yet scheduled, would feature excerpts from Jerome Robbins' "Ballets U. S. A." and his dances for "West Side Story." On Feb. 7 Mrs. Kennedy will give a musicale in the East Room for the children of Washington's diplomatic corps; the junior company of the Metropolitan Opera will perform an English version of "Così fan tutte." Also planned for the future is an appearance by a ballet company under Agnes de Mille's direction and a concert by a prominent jazz musician—possibly Benny Goodman or Louis Armstrong.

"This is only the beginning," Miss Baldridge said.

January 28, 1962

THE KENNEDYS: A NEW YORK TIMES PROFILE

By ANTHONY LEWIS

·WASHINGTON, Feb. 1— Attorney General Robert F. Kennedy took off today on a goodwill trip around the world. He is scheduled to be gone about a month, returning at the end of February. He will spend a week each in Japan and Indonesia and make shorter visits to Hong Kong, Iran, Italy, West Germany, the Netherlands and probably some other countries. It will be a relatively informal tour, with the emphasis on meeting young people. Mr. Kennedy's wife, Ethel, will be with him. Also in the party are Mrs. Donald Wilson, wife of the deputy director of the United States Information Agency, a family friend; John Seigenthaler, the Attorney General's administrative assistant; Brandon Grove, a State Department guide, and four reporters and a photographer.

According to diplomatic reports, the host countries regard this visit as the most important and they could receive from any American other than the President. Mr. Kennedy had to decline strongly pressed invitations for other stops because his trip had already grown to a most unusual length.

The trip symbolized the extraordinary role played by Robert Kennedy in this Administration.

"The second most powerful man in Government." That is the estimate of the Attorney General given by insiders with reason to know.

Far more than any previous Attorney General, he is involved in affairs outside the problems of law enforcement— foreign policy, intelligence, even the farm program. No Cabinet officer is unfamiliar with the sound of his voice on the telephone.

Entertained Adzhubeis

No one thought it unnatural when he and Mrs. Kennedy entertained Premier Khrushchev's son-in-law, Aleksei I. Adzhubei, at lunch yesterday. It will be no great surprise if the now-disavowed approach made to him to visit the Soviet Union leads eventually to such a visit.

The reasons for his unusual position are evident.

He is the President's brother. He is a trusted confidant, a position that does not automatically follow from his relationship to a President who confides in few men. He is the political expert who helped make his brother President.

The exact nature of his activities and influence is less easy to pin down. So much depends on his intimate relationship with the President that an aide says:

"Probably no one but the two men really knows what Robert's role is."

But there are clues.

Trujillo Incident Recalled

When Generalissimo Rafael Leonidas Trujillo Molina, the dictator of the Dominican Republic, was assassinated last May, the President was in Paris. Members of a special task force that met at the State Department that night found the Attorney General there, participating actively and sitting in, as one member put it, for his brother.

During the preparation of the new farm program, a regional expert on one crop was telephoned by the Attorney General and asked to come to Washington for a talk. Mr. Kennedy explained:

"You know my brother is very busy with international problems. We try to help all we can on the domestic side."

The President turned to his brother publicly in a most difficult hour—to head an inquiry into the Central Intelligence Agency after the abortive Cuban invasion last April. The President seeks his brother's counsel privately on numberless problems.

"Call Bobby, get together with him and come back with an idea on this." A White House aide says that is a familiar order from the President.

Advises on Appointments

Robert Kennedy plays an important part in advising on appointments, some believe with more influence in that area than on policy. He was influential, for example, in the choice of John A. McCone to head the Central Intelligence Agency. There are unconfirmed reports that he played a part in the dropping of Gen. C. P. Cabell as the C. I. A.'s deputy director.

He is useful in estimating political responses to ideas, notably on Capitol Hill. He maintains the relationships he built up with members of Congress in both parties while he was counsel to the Senate committee. When a Democratic Governor comes to Washington, he usually heads for the Attorney General's office.

From what is known about the Attorney General's activities, it is clear that he does not have operational responsibilities outside the Justice Department. He is no Sherman Adams—a general administrative arm of the President.

Rather, his importance lies in his influence on the President and in his usefulness as a stimulant to other men.

Absolute Candor

From the President's point of view, it is said, candor is probably the most important factor in the relationship. There is no one from whom he can get advice so frank and so free of inhibition or fear.

Robert Kennedy does not have to worry about pleasing the President when he puts forward an idea. Nor does the President have to be delicate in saying no. An observer comments:

"Robert doesn't lose any face — or any sleep—if his ideas are rejected."

Indeed, officials who have dealt with them say they see no evidence that the President gives his brother's opinion special weight just because they are brothers.

A notable example was a National Security Council meeting at which the question of aid to the Volta Dam project in Ghana was discussed. Robert Kennedy sat behind his brother.

The President went around the table, heard the comments and remarked that the consensus was in favor of advancing the aid. Then he added:

"The Attorney General has not spoken, but I can feel the hot breath of his disapproval on the back of my neck."

Robert Kennedy spoke against aiding the dam, emphasizing what he termed the bad influence of Ghana's President Kwame Nkrumah on the rest of Africa. The President then made the decision to aid the project.

In addition to candor, the Attorney General brings to the relationship with his brother a special ability to size up problems swiftly, even when he is not familiar with them, and to propose a concrete course of action.

Those who have dealt with the Attorney General on affairs outside his immediate area, such as foreign policy, remark on the same characteristics. They say that even when he has not been briefed and is not well informed he always knows the President's objective and quickly grasps the problem.

In this respect, for all their differences in personality, he may be something like Harry Hopkins, Franklin D. Roosevelt's assistant, whom Winston Churchill dubbed "Lord Root of the Matter." And he may be playing a similar sort of role for the President.

The freshness of his approach may stimulate those over-educated on a problem. He played a large part in the reappraisal of policy toward Cuba after the invasion fiasco, and one official remarks on the way he then "questioned assumptions."

Informality is, of course, a trademark of Robert Kennedy. A typical photograph shows him grilling hamburgers on the office fireplace for a group of children. The same informal air characterizes his dealings with Secretary of State Dean Rusk, or any Government official.

For example, he is in the habit of picking up the telephone when he has an idea instead of waiting to draft a memorandum. Once those on the receiving end get used to the technique, they seem to enjoy its artlessness and enthusiasm.

The Attorney General may see something in the morning paper about a fellow Cabinet member's political problem. He is likely to telephone and say something like "stick it out," or "go ahead, you can pull it off."

This telephone habit may create an impression that he spends more time on matters outside the Justice Department than he really does, an aide of his pointed out.

The aide estimates that the Attorney General spends 80 per cent of his working hours on Justice Department business, 5 per cent on meetings with members of the press (an extremely large proportion), 5 per cent on political activities and meeting visitors and, finally, 10 per cent on foreign policy and other government affairs outside the Justice Department.

There is much less resentment of the Attorney General's special role than might be expected among other Government officials. One hears grumbling about "Little Brother" at lower levels but virtually none higher up or among men who have actually dealt with him.

Among the reasons may be the very informality with which he plays the part, plus the realization that he has no Svengali-like control over the President's views.

But officials emphasize another reason for the lack of resentment. This is the apparently unanimous feeling that personal ambition plays no part in his activities—that he is motivated instead by an overwhelming desire to help his brother and to make the Kennedy Administration a success.

"That is one of the most engaging things about him," one official remarks. "He is really quite a selfless guy."

"I'm not saying he will go to the pasture after his brother has served eight year.," the official says. "But ambition is not what's motivating him now. He is serving the President."

Inevitably, questions have arisen about Robert Kennedy's future. Will he want to move officially into some foreign affairs role? Will he run for President himself some day? The answer from those who know him best is that the questions are simply premature — he is not thinking about them now.

Recently the President read somewhere that his brother had been called "the second most important man in the Western world." He told the Attorney General wryly:

"You have nowhere to go but down."

February 2, 1962

Mrs. Kennedy TV Hostess to the Nation

Tells of Restoration of Interior of the White House

By JACK GOULD

Millions of television viewers went through the White House last night with Mrs. John F. Kennedy leading the way.

With verve and pleasure, the President's wife undertook to explain the restoration she has made in the interior of the Executive Mansion. She was to prove a virtuoso among guides.

In the hour-long program, recorded on tape last month, Mrs. Kennedy was a historian savoring the small facts and human story behind the evolution of White House décor. She was an art critic of subtlety and standard. She was an antiquarian relishing pursuit of the elusive treasure. She was a poised TV narrator.

Mrs. Kennedy, wearing a wool suit of simple line and three strings of pearls, animatedly strolled through rooms on the ground, first and second floors in what was described as the most extensive public view of the White House ever shown.

The hour was rich in detail and diversity. The viewer saw the magnificence of the State Dining Room, a battered old Lincoln chair plucked from a warehouse, many of the antiques and paintings recently donated to the White House in response to Mrs. Kennedy's pleas, the rich warmth of the Red Room and the unfinished Monroe Room that is to shield the President's visitors from the perils of a passing baby carriage.

But the First Lady's vivacious scholarship was fully as vital as the visual pageantry. With her soft and measured voice, she ranged in comment from warm appreciation of past First Ladies and Presidents to delicate but telling dismissal of the second-rate in the arts. Her effortless familiarity with dates and names attested to homework done for the occasion.

Carried on Two Networks

Mrs. Kennedy's companion on the tour was Charles Collingwood, a reporter for the Columbia Broadcasting System's news department, which conceived and produced the program. C. B. S. also made the presentation available to the National Broadcasting Company. Both networks carried the program simultaneously on a sustaining basis from 10 to 11 o'clock.

C. B. S. will repeat the program March 25.

After Mrs. Kennedy completed the tour, the President appeared briefly to second his wife's efforts to impart a sense of living history to the White House.

An awareness of history can be a source of strength in meeting the problems of the future, he said.

The President reported that more than 1,300,000 persons passed through the White House last year. Mrs. Kennedy's audience last night was expected to exceed that number by many-fold, but estimates of the program's rating were not expected to be available until today.

Competes With 'Naked City'

Mrs. Kennedy's competition in the ratings last night came from "Naked City," a police adventure series presented by the American Broadcasting Company. A. B. C. said that it could not afford to share in the total production cost of Mrs. Kennedy's program, estimated at more than $100,000, because of unforeseen expense in covering the delayed orbital flight of Lieut. Col. John H. Glenn Jr.

Mrs. Kennedy and her associates and a special C. B. S. staff, headed by Perry Wolff, the program's producer, and Franklin Schaffner, director, made careful preparations for the first televised tour of the White House since President Harry S. Truman inaugurated the format May 4, 1952.

Agreement on a final outline enabled Mrs. Kennedy to go through most of the program in a single day, Jan. 15, without retakes. Close-up shots of specific antiques were taken initially and were subsequently integrated into Mrs. Kennedy's running commentary, an editing procedure designed to spare the President's wife unnecessary delay. The President chose to record his part of the program a second time.

The program started with Mrs. Kennedy's own off-screen narration of the history of the White House. Then she and Mr. Collingwood met in the curator's office on the ground floor.

Visits Original Kitchen

Next was the Diplomatic Reception Room, and then came the original White House kitchen, later used by Franklin D. Roosevelt as a broadcast room. The kitchen is now Mrs. Kennedy's upholstery repair shop.

Mrs. Kennedy went up to the first floor and in succession through the East Room, the the State Dining Room, where the table was fully set; the Red Room, Blue Room and Green Room. Then the First Lady went up the second floor, rarely visited by the public, and viewers were taken into the Lincoln and Monroe Rooms.

Mrs. Kennedy, whose restoration efforts have drawn Washington's bipartisan approval, had special praise for the past contributions of Theodore Roosevelt and James Monroe. Similarly, in admiring Gilbert Stuart's portrait of Washington, she deplored the fact that so many pictures of later Presidents had been done by inferior artists.

With delightful understatement, she recalled that Grant's renovaton of the East Room had been called a unique mixture of two styles: ancient Greek and "Mississippi River Boat."

In terms of television viewing, "A Tour of the White House with Mrs. John F. Kennedy" will undoubtedly stand as a distinctive contribution of the electronic era: an unusual feminine personality imparting her own kind of excitement to national history and national taste.

Richard S. Salant, president of C.B.S. News, said last night that arrangements for the program had not included any conditions for a contribution to the Fine Arts Commission, which is assisting Mrs. Kennedy's restoration effeorts.

"There is absolutely no truth to such a report," Mr. Salant said. "There was no suggestion from the White House for a quid pro quo. There has been no discussion of it."

May Make Contribution

C. B. S. might wish to make a contribution on its own initiative at a later date, Mr. Salant said.

If it were decided to aid the White House restoration efforts, he said, it has been suggested that any other network carrying Mrs. Kennedy's program might wish to join in. A. B. C., which did not carry the program, disapproved of the proposal, Mr. Salant said.

In Washington, however, it was understood that the White House had misgivings over the idea over any network contributions to aid Mrs. Kennedy's project.

Through the Federal Communications Commission, the Government exercises a degree of regulation over chain broadcasting and also licenses individual stations owned by the networks.

February 15, 1962

WASHINGTON, Feb. 14 — Responding to criticism, President Kennedy said today he was being as frank as possible about United States involvement in the war in Vietnam. He asked that such sensitive matters be left to "responsible leaders" of both parties.

The President countered charges of excessive secrecy with a statement that no American combat troops "in the generally understood sense of the word" had been sent into Vietnam. Yet he conceded, without giving statistics, that military support had been increased to match increased Communist activity.

That support, Mr. Kennedy said at his news conference, is consistent with a ten-year policy of trying to keep South Vietnam out of Communist hands. He disagreed with complaints that Congress had not been properly briefed on the situation and he expressed hope that he could maintain the present "very strong bipartisan consensus."

Uses Notes in Replying

The President came prepared with notes to answer criticism in the press and from the Republican National Committee that he was withholding information about the growing involvement of American troops in the developing warfare in South Vietnam.

Mr. Kennedy did not comment on the progress of that war—which the Administration expects to continue for years—but he displayed a new uneasiness about the situation in neighboring Laos.

The cease-fire between royal Laotian and Leftist rebel forces was "becoming increasingly frayed," the President said. He noted that renewed fighting at Nam Tha was close to the border of Communist China—it is about fifteen miles away—and by implication expressed concern about Chinese intervention.

If the cease-fire breaks down, the President added, "we would be faced with the most serious decision."

Soviet Held to Promise

It was to avoid the painful choice between surrender of Laos to the Communists and intervention by United States troops that Mr. Kennedy has tried to keep the Soviet leaders to their promise of turning Laos into a neutral and independent buffer state.

Thus far the President feels the Russians have kept their word, but he has been unable to persuade the royalist Rightwing forces in Laos to surrender power to the nominated neutralist leader, Prince Souvanna Phouma.

Progress in the negotiations among the three rival Laotian princes has been very slow over the last month, Mr. Kennedy said, noting that the dangers increased with every passing day.

Editorial questioning of the President's handling of both Laos and Vietnam has been seized upon recently by a number of Republicans and developed into major criticism.

The Republican National Committee's bulletin, Battle Line, summarized some of the charges yesterday. It said the Administration was "forcing the legitimate Government of Laos into a perilous coalition with the Reds" and promoting "the pretense that the United States is merely acting as military adviser to South Vietnam."

The people should not have to wait until the casualty lists arrive to learn of the country's commitments, Battle Line asserted. It asked whether the country was "moving toward another Korea which might embroil the entire Far East."

When asked to comment, the President was ready with a list of previous commitments to Vietnam by the Administrations of Presidents Truman and Eisenhower. As the war increased over the last two years, the United States increased its support in South Vietnam for the Government of President Ngo Dinh Diem, especially so in recent months, Mr. Kennedy said.

Repeating earlier statements on the extent of the United States build-up, the President said:

"We are supplying logistic assistance, transportation assistance, training, and we have a number of Americans who are taking part in that effort."

Recent reports from Saigon have said that as many as 4,000 United States troops were now serving with the South Vietnam forces, but the President did not go beyond "some."

No Americans are combat troops, Mr. Kennedy explained, "although the training missions that we have there have been instructed that if they are fired upon they are, of course, to fire back, to protect themselves."

Casualty List Supplied

A list of American casualties in South Vietnam in recent months, supplied later by the Pentagon, showed no fatalities in any such exchange of fire. The Defense Department listed thirteen deaths and one missing.

Two members of the Air Force were killed in the crash of a C-123 plane on a practice run Feb. 2. Six airmen and two members of the Army were killed in the crash of a C-47 last Sunday. An Army driver was killed when his truck struck a mine and two soldiers were killed by a grenade hurled into their barracks.

The President said he had fully briefed Congressional leaders on the Vietnam situation at a White House review of foreign affairs in early January. Further information had been given Congressional committees by Secretary of State Dean Rusk and Robert S. McNamara, Secretary of Defense.

February 15, 1962

Kennedy Denies Secrecy On Vietnam Is Excessive

Calls Situation Sensitive
By MAX FRANKEL

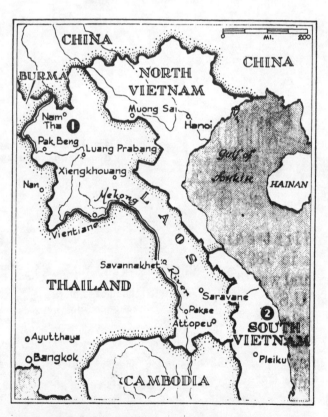

TROUBLE SPOTS: President Kennedy voiced concern over renewed fighting at Nam Tha (1) in Laos and cited action against Communist activity in South Vietnam (2), where American planes have halted propaganda flights.

Mrs. Kennedy Takes Children for a Sleigh Ride

WASHINGTON, Feb. 13—Mrs. John F. Kennedy took her daughter Caroline and several of Caroline's playmates for a sleigh ride over the lawn of the White House today. A brown and white pony named Macaroni drew the black cutter around the huge back lawn three times while the First Lady, at the reins, was surrounded by her young passengers. Four-year-old Caroline was accompanied by her friends from the nursery school class that meets at the White House. After they had finished their ride, Mrs. Kennedy had the pony unhitched and walked it up to the veranda outside the President's office, where he could see it through French windows. Then she put their 4-month-old son, John, Jr. on the pony and held him while trying at the same time to lead the animal so that the baby could have a ride.

She had a bit of trouble getting the pony to comply. Macaroni showed more interest in some grass showing through the snow.

A groom then led the pony while Mrs. Kennedy held John, Jr., in place for a circular trip of several minutes outside the mansion's back door.

Mrs. Kennedy wore a white sweater and beige riding trousers. The children were snuggled in woolens against the cold weather.

The pony, which belongs to Caroline, had been hauled to the White House in a trailer from Glen Ora, the estate the Kennedys have leased near Middleburg, Va.

Mrs. Kennedy took both of her children for a sleigh ride at Glen Ora during the weekend.

February 14, 1962

Mrs. John F. Kennedy takes daughter Caroline and playmates for sleigh ride on White House lawn. In background is Executive Office Building, formerly the State Department.

CRANK LETTERS RISE

Kennedy Receiving 52% More Than Eisenhower Did

WASHINGTON, Feb. 27 (UPI)—The Secret Service has reported that the number of "threatening, obscene, abusive" communications sent to the White House increased 52 per cent during President Kennedy's first year in office.

A House Appropriations subcommittee was told that 870 such cases were investigated last year, compared with 573 in 1960, former President Dwight D. Eisenhower's last year in office.

James J. Rowley, chief of the Secret Service said in testimony released today that the number of cranks appearing at the White House gates also increased, from 435 in 1960 to 643 last year.

He asked for fifty-eight additional special agents to cope with the increased workload.

Mr. Rowley said the greater manpower was made necessary by Mr. Kennedy's many trips and activities.

February 28, 1962

BOSTON, March 14—Edward M. Kennedy officially began today his campaign for the Senate seat once held by his brother, the President.

The youngest of the three Kennedy brothers said he had made his decision to run "in full knowledge of the obstacle I will face, the charges that will be made."

Mr. Kennedy's announcement started a campaign that will first pit him against Edward J. McCormack Jr., Massachusetts Attorney General, who is a nephew of House Speaker John W. McCormack.

Mr. McCormack, also a Democrat, announced his candidacy March 5. He said then he was prepared "to go all the way" to win. But he retreated from a firm commitment to enter the primary in September if he failed to be endorsed at a pre-primary party convention in June.

He said that he did not expect to "lose" at the convention, and that the question of entering the primary would be considered later.

However, Mr. Kennedy said he believed there was no alternative but to go through both tests, if necessary.

Mr. Kennedy served as a campaign manager for his brother in the 1960 Presidential race. He is now an assistant district attorney for Suffolk County (Boston) at a $1-a-year salary.

In Springfield Mr. McCormack commented, "Competition is healthy." He said he would be nominated on his record, experience and ability. He has served five years on the Boston City Council and four as Attorney General.

He declared he would hammer on the theme of "experience."

If the President and Attorney General Robert F. Kennedy campaign for their brother, he said, "it might lend credence to what some people say—that the family relationship is his only qualification for office."

Carried Out Missions

Mr. Kennedy reached the age of 30, the minimum for a Senator, last month. Mr. McCormack is 38.

The new candidate has traveled considerably on fact-finding missions for the President and on his own.

The campaign is expected to be bitter. Several years ago, in a test of strength for control of the Democratic State Committee, President Kennedy, then a Senator, defeated Representative McCormack, then majority leader of the national House.

If Edward Kennedy is successful in the primary tests, his Republican challenger in November may be George Cabot Lodge, whose father and grandfather also were Senators from Massachusetts.

In 1952 George Cabot Lodge's father, Senator Henry Cabot Lodge, was unseated by President Kennedy, then Representative from the Eleventh Massachusetts District.

Also seeking the Republican nomination for Senate is Representative Laurence Curtis, whose Tenth District seat is to be erased by reapportionment.

Mr. Kennedy's home is in Mr. Curtis' district. It is part of Ward 5, long known as a Republican "silk-stocking" territory.

Mr. Kennedy announced his candidacy at his home. His wife Joan stood smilingly at his side. Reporters and photographers jammed the room.

After having canvassed the Commonwealth, he said, he is convinced that the Senate is where he can "best serve the people of my home state."

He said Massachusetts needed "a new vitality, a new image and a new vigor." In referring to charges he said he would face, he explained that he meant those arising from the fact that his eldest brother was President and his elder brother Attorney General.

He repeatedly said "the people of Massachusetts will make the determination."

He does not expect his brothers to campaign here for him, Mr. Kennedy declared, but his sisters "may be visiting in the state, and we certainly won't keept them in a closet."

Senator Benjamin A. Smith 2d, who holds the seat vacated by President Kennedy, a week ago made known his decision not to seek election.

March 15, 1962

EDWARD KENNEDY IS IN SENATE RACE

Massachusetts Seat Sought by President's Brother, 30

By JOHN H. FENTON

BOSTON, March 30—Edward M. Kennedy, a candidate for a Democratic Senate nomination, admitted today that he had withdrawn from Harvard College as a freshman in 1951 at the college's request.

In a statement, Mr. Kennedy said that the reason was that he had "arranged" to have a classmate take an examination in his stead in a foreign language course. He did not specify the language, but it was learned that it was Spanish.

Rumors that the President's brother had been asked to leave Harvard under a cloud had been gathering since before the formal announcement of his political plans on March 14.

His statement was issued after he was asked about the incident by a Washington correspondent from Boston who is a long-time friend of the Kennedy family.

In his statement, Mr. Kennedy gave this version of the incident:

"During the second semester of my freshman year I made a mistake. I was having difficulty in one course, a foreign language. I became so apprehensive about it that I arranged with a fellow freshman of mine to take the examination for me in that course.

"The dean learned of this and my friend and I were asked to withdraw, with the understanding that we might reapply for admission after a period of absence, provided that during that time we could demonstrate a record of constructive and responsible citizenship.

"What I did was wrong. I have regretted it ever since. The unhappiness I caused my family and my friends, even though eleven years ago, has been a bitter experience for me, but it also has been a very valuable lesson. That is the story."

Mr. Kennedy's office here refused to amplify his statement, rejecting questions as to whether Mr. Kennedy's friend had actually taken the examination for him and also declining to identify the friend.

Spokesmen at Harvard, across the Charles River in Cambridge, also refused to discuss the incident. The college office indicated that the incident was Mr. Kennedy's private affair.

After his withdrawal, which occurred when he was 18 years old, Mr. Kennedy enlisted in the Army and spent two years in the infantry in Europe. On his return his application to re-enter Harvard was accepted, as was that of his friend.

Mr. Kennedy said that he had played football, "worked hard and passed all my courses, some with honors, and was graduated in good standing in 1956."

When Mr. Kennedy later enrolled in the law course at the University of Virginia, officials were told of the Harvard incident, his statement said.

Speculation on the impact of Mr. Kennedy's disclosure on his political career was varied today.

Political leaders of both parties shied away from commenting publicly on the situation. Privately they were as divided as the casual voter.

There were three major viewpoints on the subject. One viewpoint was, "who hasn't done something foolish in his youth?" This seemed to be a popular opinion among older persons. Another was that the incident would soon be forgotten. This was the attitude of younger persons. The third was that the story was not too widely known and that it should have been ignored. This was the position of some old-time politicians.

Edward Kennedy Admits Ouster By Harvard; Had an Exam Proxy

He Acknowledges Incident as a Freshman of 18—College Later Readmitted Him

By JOHN H. FENTON

In his quest for the nomination Mr. Kennedy faces opposition from Edward J. McCormack Jr., the State's Attorney General. Mr. McCormack is a nephew of House Speaker John W. McCormack. The first test will be at a party endorsing convention June 7, 8 and 9 at Springfield. Each has indicated he will take the fight to the state primary Sept. 18 if necessary. Both Mr. McCormack and

Mr. Kennedy utilized recent trips abroad to campaign for the nomination.

The Republican nominee in November is expected to be either George Cabot Lodge, son of Henry Cabot Lodge, former United Nations representative, or Representative Laurence Curtis, whose Tenth Congressional District has been eliminated by reapportionment.

However, it was noted that

Mr. Kennedy had been admitted to the Massachusetts bar in 1959. This entailed a character examination as well as written tests.

Today's disclosure recalled one involving the late James M. Curley, a Boston politician of a generation ago. Mr. Curley, serving as a Boston Alderman in 1904, was sent to jail for two months for taking a Civil Service examination "for a destitute

friend with several children."

Subsequently Mr. Curley not only won re-election as an Alderman but he also went on to be Mayor of Boston four times, a member of the House of Representatives four times, and Governor of Massachusetts for one term. He also served a second jail term, for mail fraud, during his last tenure as Mayor in 1947.

March 31, 1962

Steel: 72-Hour Drama With An All-Star Cast

PRICE RISES SET STAGE ON APRIL 10

Kennedy's Quick and Angry Reaction to News Touched Off Fast-Paced Play

By WALLACE CARROLL

WASHINGTON, April 22—It was peaceful at the White House on the afternoon of Tuesday, April 10—so peaceful that the President of the United States thought he might have time for a nap or a little relaxed reading.

Just to be sure, he called his personal secretary, Mrs. Evelyn Lincoln, and asked what the rest of the day would bring.

"You have Mr. Blough at a quarter to six," said Mrs. Lincoln.

"Mr. Blough?" exclaimed the President.

"Yes," said Mrs. Lincoln.

There must be a mistake, thought the President. The steel negotiations had been wound up the previous week.

"Get me Kenny O'Donnell," he said.

But there had been no mistake—at least not on the part of Kenneth P. O'Donnell, the President's appointment secretary.

Whether Mr. Blough—Roger M. Blough, chairman of the board of United States Steel Corporation—had made a mistake was a different question.

For when he walked into the President's office two hours later with the news that his company had raised the price of steel, he set off seventy-two hours of activity such as he and his colleagues could not have expected.

Period of Excitement

During those seventy-two hours, four antitrust investigations of the steel industry were conceived, a bill to roll back the price increases was seriously considered, legislation to impose price and wage controls on the steel industry was discussed, agents of the Federal Bureau of Investigation questioned newspaper men by the dawn's early light, and the Defense Department—biggest buyer in the nation—began to divert purchases away from United States Steel.

Also in those seventy-two hours—and this was far more significant—the Administration maintained its right to look over the shoulders of capital and labor when they came to the bargaining table and its in-

sistence that any agreement they reached would have to respect the national interest.

And in those seventy-two hours, new content and meaning were poured into that magnificent abstraction, "the Presidency," for the historically minded to argue about as long as men remained interested in the affairs of this republic.

A full and entirely accurate account of those seventy-two hours may never be written. The characters were many. They moved so fast that no one will be able to retrace all of what they did.

Understandably, industry participants—facing official investigation now—would not talk much. Nor were Government participants willing to tell all.

Nevertheless, a team of New York Times reporters undertook to piece the tale together while memories were fresh.

Here is what they learned:

Early on that afternoon of April 10, Roger Blough had met with his colleagues of United States Steel's executive committee in the board room on the twentieth floor at 71 Broadway, New York. Three of the twelve members were absent, but Leslie B. Worthington, president of the company, and Robert C. Tyson, chairman of the finance committee, were there.

Hints of Rise Given

For several months these men had been giving out hints, largely overlooked in Washington, that the company would have to raise prices to meet increasing costs.

The Kennedy Administration had striven last fall to prevent a steel price increase, and there had been no increase. It had pressed again for a modest wage contract this year, and a modest contract had been signed a few days earlier. The Administration expected no price increase now.

The company's executive committee reviewed the situation. The sales department had concurred in a recommendation to increase prices by 3½ per cent —about $6 on top of the going average of $170 a ton.

Mr. Blough had taken soundings within the company on the

public relations aspects. Everyone realized that the move would not win any popularity prize, but the committee voted unanimously to go ahead.

With the decision made, Mr. Blough took a plane to Washington. Word was telephoned to the White House that he wanted to see the President and had something "important" to say about steel.

A few minutes after 5:45 the President received him in his oval office, motioned him to a seat on a sofa to his right and made himself comfortable in his rocking chair.

With little preliminary, Mr. Blough handed the President a four-page mimeographed press release that was about to be sent to newspaper offices in Pittsburgh and New York.

The President read:

"Pittsburgh, Pa., April 10— For the first time in nearly four years, United States Steel today announced an increase in the general level of its steel prices."

Mr. Kennedy raced through the announcement. Then he summoned Arthur J. Goldberg, the Secretary of Labor. Minutes later Mr. Goldberg reached the President's office four blocks away.

Grimly, the President gave the paper to Mr. Goldberg and said it had been distributed to the press. Mr. Goldberg skimmed over it and asked Mr. Blough what was the point of the meeting, since the price decision had been made.

Mr. Blough replied that he thought he should personally inform the President as a matter of courtesy. Mr. Goldberg retorted it was hardly a courtesy to announce a decision and confront the President with an accomplished fact.

In the half-hour discussion that followed President Kennedy seems to have kept his temper. But Mr. Goldberg lectured Mr. Blough with some heat. The price increase, the Secretary said, would jeopardize the Government's entire economic policy. It would damage the interests of United States Steel itself. It would undercut responsible collective bargaining. Finally he said, the decision could be viewed only as a double-cross of the President because the company had given no hint of its intentions while the Administration was urging the United Steelworkers of America to moderate its wage demands.

Mr. Blough, a high school teacher turned lawyer and company executive, defended himself and the company in a quiet voice.

When he had gone President Kennedy called for the three members of his Council of Economic Advisers. Dr. Walter W. Heller, the chairman, a lean and scholarly looking man, came running from his office across the street. Dr. Kermit Gordon followed in three minutes. James Tobin, the third member hurried back to his office later in the evening.

Into the President's office came Theodore C. Sorensen, the White House special counsel, Mr. O'Donnell and Andrew T. Hatcher, acting press secretary in the absence of Pierre Salinger, who was on vacation.

Now the President, who usually keeps his temper under rein, let go. He felt he had been double-crossed — deliberately. The office of the President had been affronted. The national interest had been flouted.

Bitterly, he recalled that: "My father always told me that all business men were sons-of-bitches but I never believed it till now!"

It was clear that the Administration would fight. No one knew exactly what could be done, but from that moment the awesome power of the Federal Government began to move.

How It Developed

To understand the massive reaction of the Kennedy Administration, a word of background is necessary.

Nothing in the range of domestic economic policy had brought forth a greater effort by the Administration than the restraint it sought to impose on steel prices and wages.

Starting last May the Administration worked on the industry, publicly and privately, not to raise its prices when wages went up in the fall. And when the price line held, the Administration turned its efforts to getting an early and "noninflationary" wage contract this year.

Above all, the Administration constantly tried to impress on both sides that the national interest was riding on their decisions. A price increase or an inflationary wage settlement, it argued, would set off a new wage-price spiral that would stunt economic growth, keep unemployment high, cut into export sales, weaken the dollar and further aggravate the outflow of gold.

On Friday and Saturday, April 6 and 7, the major steel companies had signed the new contract. President Kennedy had hailed it as "noninflationary." Privately, some steel leaders agreed with him.

Thus, the President confidently expected that the companies would not increase prices. And the standard had been set, he hoped, for other industries and unions.

This was the background against which the group in the President's office went to work.

By about 8 P. M. some decisions had been reached.

President Kennedy would deliver the first counter-attack at his news conference scheduled for 3:30 the following afternoon.

Messrs. Goldberg, Heller and Sorensen would gather material for the President's statement. Other material of a statistical nature would be prepared in a longer-range effort to prove the price increase was unjustified.

While the discussion was going on, the President called his brother, Robert F. Kennedy, the Attorney General; Secretary of Defense Robert S. McNamara, and the Secretary of the Treasury, Douglas Dillon, who had just arrived in Hobe Sound, Fla., for a short vacation.

At his home on Hillbrook Lane, Senator Estes Kefauver of Tennessee, chairman of the Senate Antitrust Subcommittee, was getting ready to go out for the evening. The phone rang. It was the President. Would Senator Kefauver publicly register "dismay" at the price increase and consider an investigation?

The Senator certainly would. He promised an investigation. So did the Justice Department.

In the President's office, meanwhile, there had been some talk of what could be done to keep other steel companies from raising prices. Most of the discussion centered on the economic rebuttal of the case made by United States Steel.

Mr. Goldberg and Dr. Heller decided to pool resources. Mr. Goldberg called Hyman L. Lewis, chief of the Office of Labor Economics of the Bureau of Labor Statistics, and asked him to assemble a crew.

Mr. Lewis reached three members of the bureau—Peter Henle, special assistant to the Commissioner of Labor Statistics; Arnold E. Chase, chief of the Division of Prices and Cost of Living, and Leon Greenberg, chief of the Productivity Division.

He told them what was wanted and asked them to go to Dr. Heller's office in the old State Department Building.

Dr. Heller who had been working on the problem in his office, hurried off after a few minutes to the German Ambassador's residence on Foxhall Road.

The Ambassador was giving a dinner, a black tie affair, in honor of Prof. Walter Hallstein, president of the European Common Market. The guests were well into the meal when Dr. Heller arrived, looking, as one of the guests remarked, like Banquo's ghost in a tuxedo.

White House Reception

Back at the White House the President had also changed to black tie. The members of Congress and their wives were coming to his annual reception at 9:45. Ruefully, the President recalled that the news of the Cuban disaster had arrived during his reception in 1961.

"I'll never hold another Congressional reception," he remarked.

But as he and Mrs. Kennedy received the leaders of Congress and their wives, he easily relaxed into small talk.

What did the men think, he asked, of the break with tradition by making this a black tie, instead of a white tie, affair? Republicans and Democrats

unanimously favored the change. Many of the younger members of Congress, they pointed out, did not have a white tie and all that went with it.

With the party spread through three rooms, no one could tell how many times Mr. Kennedy slipped out to talk about steel. He stayed until 12:08 A. M. Then he retired.

By that time, the White House staff, the Council of Economic Advisers and the Departments of Labor, Justice, Defense, Commerce and The Treasury were all at work on the counter-attack.

WEDNESDAY

Midnight had struck when Walter Heller, still in black tie, returned to his office from the German Embassy. With him, also in black tie, came another dinner guest, George W. Ball, Under Secretary of State.

Dr. Heller's two colleagues in the Council of Economic Advisers, Dr. Gordon and Dr. Tobin, were already there.

At about 2:45 A. M. the four men from the Bureau of Labor Statistics left the session. Their assignment from then on was to bring up to date a fact book on steel put out by the Eisenhower Administration two years ago.

The idea was to turn it into a kind of "white paper" that would show that the price increase was unjustified.

Toward 4 o'clock Dr. Heller and Dr. Tobin went home for two or three hours' sleep. Dr. Gordon lay down on the couch in his office for a couple of hours.

As the normal working day began, President Kennedy held a breakfast meeting at the White House with Vice President Johnson; Secretary of State Dean Rusk (who played no part in the steel crisis); Secretary Goldberg; Mr. Sorensen; Myer Feldman, Mr. Sorensen's deputy; Dr. Heller and Andrew Hatcher.

The meeting lasted an hour and forty-five minutes. Mr. Goldberg and Dr. Heller reported on the night's work. Mr. Sorensen was assigned to draft the President's statement on steel for the news conference. Mr. Goldberg gave him a two-page report from the Bureau of Labor Statistics headed:

"Change in Unit Employment Costs in the Steel Industry 1958 to 1961."

It said in part:

"While employment costs per hour of all wage and salaried employes in the basic iron and steel industry rose from 1958 to 1961, there was an equivalent increase in output per man-hour.

"As a result, employment costs per unit of steel output in 1961 was essentially the same as in 1958."

The latter sentence was quoted that afternoon in the President's statement.

During the morning the President had called Secretary Dillon in Florida and discussed with him the Treasury's work on tax write-offs that would encourage investment in more modern plant and machinery. The two decided that the course would not be altered.

The President also telephoned Secretary of Commerce Luther H. Hodges, who was about to testify before a House Maritime subcommittee. After giving his testimony Secretary Hodges spent most of the day on the phone to business men around the country.

In Wall Street that morning United States Steel shares opened at 70¾, up 2¾ from the day before. But on Capitol Hill the company's stock was down.

Senator Mike Mansfield, the majority leader, called the price increase "unjustified." Speaker John W. McCormack said the company's action was "shocking," "arrogant," "irresponsible." Senator Hubert H. Humphrey, the Democratic whip, spoke of "an affront to the President."

Curb by Law Suggested

Senator Albert Gore of Tennessee suggested a law that would empower the courts to prohibit price increases in basic industries such as steel until there had been a "cooling-off period."

Representative Emanuel Celler of Brooklyn, chairman of the House Antitrust subcommittee, scheduled a broad investigation of the steel industry. So did Senator Kefauver.

The pressures on United States Steel were beginning to mount. But now some of the other titans of the industry began to fall in line behind Big Steel.

As the President came out of the White House shortly before noon to go to the airport where he was to welcome the Shah of Iran, he was shown a news bulletin. Bethlehem Steel, second in size only to United States Steel, had announced a price increase.

Others followed in short order —Republic, Jones and Laughlin, Youngstown and Wheeling. And Inland, Kaiser and Colorado Fuel & Iron said they were "studying" the situation.

When he faced the newsmen and television cameras at 3:30, President Kennedy spoke with cold fury. The price increase, he said, was a "wholly unjustifiable and irresponsible defiance of the public interest." The steel men had shown "utter contempt" for their fellow citizens.

He spoke approvingly of the proposed investigations. But what did he hope to accomplish that might still save the Administration's broad economic program?

In his conference statement the President had seemed to hold out no hope that the price increases could be rolled back. If the increases held, what imminent comfort could there be in possible antitrust decrees that would take three years to come from the courts?

Actually, the possibility of making United States Steel retract the increase had been considered early in the consultation.

Drs. Heller and Gordon, and possibly some of the other economists, had argued that the principal thrust of the Administration's effort should be to convince one or two significant producers to hold out. In a market such as steel, they said, the high-priced sellers would have to come down if the others did not go up.

This suggested a line of strategy that probably proved decisive.

Hold-outs Emerge

As one member of the Big Twelve after another raised prices, only Armco, Inland, Kaiser, C F & I and McLouth were holding the line. These five hold-outs represented 14 per cent of total industry capacity, or 17 per cent of the capacity of the Big Twelve.

Everything pointed to Inland as the key to the situation.

Inland Steel Corporation with headquarters in Chicago is a highly efficient producer. It could make a profit at lower prices than those of some of the bigger companies. And any company that sold in the Midwest, such as United States Steel, would feel Inland's price competition.

Moreover, there was a tradition of public service at Inland. Clarence B. Randall, a former chairman of the board, had served both the Eisenhower and Kennedy Administrations. (But he played no part in this crisis.)

Joseph Leopold Block, Inland's present chairman, who was in Japan at the moment, had been a member of President Kennedy's Labor-Management Advisory Committee.

At 7:45 that Wednesday morning, Philip D. Block Jr., vice chairman of Inland, was called to the telephone in his apartment at 1540 North Lake Shore Drive in Chicago.

"Hello, P. D.," said Edward Gudeman, Under Secretary of Commerce, a former schoolmate and friend of Mr. Block's, calling from Washington.

"What do you think of this price increase of United States Steel's?"

Mr. Block said he had been surprised.

"I didn't ask P. D. what Inland might do," said Mr. Gudeman several days later. "I didn't want them to feel that the Administration was putting them on the spot. I just wanted him to know how we felt and to ask his consideration."

Agree to Consider It

Inland officials said they had not been coaxed or threatened by any of the officials who called them.

The approach, which seems to have developed rather spontaneously in many of the calls that were made to business men, was to ask their opinion, state the Government's viewpoint, and leave it at that.

But there also were calls with a more pointed aim — to steel users, asking them to call their steel friends and perhaps even issue public statements.

Another call to Inland was made by Henry H. Fowler, Under Secretary of the Treasury and Acting Secretary in Mr. Dillon's absence.

After Mr. Kennedy's afternoon news conference Mr. Fowler called John F. Smith Jr., Inland's president. Like other Treasury officials who telephoned other business men, Mr.

Fowler talked about the effect of a steel price increase on imports and exports and the further pressure it would place on the balance of payments.

A third call went to Inland that day. It was from Secretary Goldberg to Leigh B. Block, vice president for purchasing.

Both Inland and Government officials insist that there was no call from the White House or from any Government office to Joseph Block in Japan.

Though no concrete assurance was asked or volunteered in these conversations, the Administration gathered assurance that Inland would hold the line for at least another day or two.

Next came Armco, sixth largest in the nation. Walter Heller had a line into that company. So did others. Calls were made. And through these channels the Administration learned that Armco was holding off for the time being, but there would be no public announcement one way or the other.

Meanwhile, Mr. Gudeman had called a friend in the upper reaches of the Kaiser Company. Secretary McNamara had called a number of friends, one of them at Allegheny-Ludlum, a large manufacturer of stainless.

How many calls were made by President Kennedy himself cannot be told. But some time during all the activity he talked to Edgar Kaiser, chairman of Kaiser Steel, in California.

According to one official who was deeply involved in all this effort, the over-all objective was to line up companies representing 18 per cent of the nation's capacity. If this could be done, according to friendly sources in the steel industry, these companies with their lower prices soon would be doing 25 per cent of the business. Then Big Steel would have to yield.

Antitrust Line Pushed

Parallel with this "divide-and-conquer" maneuver, the effort moved forward on the antitrust line.

During the morning, someone had spotted in the newspapers a statement attributed to Edmund F. Martin, president of Bethlehem Steel. Speaking to reporters on Tuesday after a stockholders' meeting in Wilmington, Del., Mr. Martin was quoted as having said:

"There shouldn't be any price rise. We shouldn't do anything to increase our costs if we are to survive. We have more competition both domestically and from foreign firms."

If Mr. Martin had opposed a price rise on Tuesday, before United States Steel announced its increase, and if Bethlehem raised its prices on Wednesday after that announcement, his statement might prove useful in antitrust proceedings. It could be used to support a Government argument that United States Steel, because of its bigness, exercised an undue influence over other steel producers.

F. B. I. Told to Check

At about 6 o'clock Wednesday evening, according to of-

ficials of the Justice Department, Attorney General Kennedy ordered the Federal Bureau of Investigation to find out exactly what Mr. Martin had said.

At about this same time, Paul Rand Dixon, chairman of the Federal Trade Commission, told reporters that his agency had begun an informal investigation to determine whether the steel companies had violated a consent decree of June 15, 1951.

That decree bound the industry to refrain from collusive price fixing or maintaining identical delivered prices. It provided penalties running up to $5,000 a day.

Meanwhile, more calls were going out from Washington.

The Democratic National Committee called many of the Democratic Governors and asked them to do two things:

First, to make statements supporting the President and, second, to ask steel producers in their states to hold the price line.

Among those called were David L. Lawrence of Pennsylvania, Richard J. Hughes of New Jersey and Edmund G. Brown of California. But the National Committee said nothing in its own name. The smell of "politics" was not to be allowed to contaminate the Administration's efforts.

A Morgan Man Called

Another call was made by Robert V. Roosa, an Under Secretary of the Treasury, to Henry Alexander, chairman of Morgan Guaranty Trust Company in New York. Morgan is represented on United States Steel's board of directors and is widely considered one of the most powerful influences within the company.

Thus by nightfall on Wednesday—twenty-four hours after Mr. Blough's call on the President—the Administration was pressing forward on four lines of action:

First, the rallying of public opinion behind the President and against the companies.

Second, divide-and-conquer operation within the steel industry.

Third, antitrust pressure from the Justice Department, the Federal Trade Commission, the Senate and the House.

Fourth, the mobilization of friendly forces within the business world to put additional pressure on the companies.

That night at the White House the Kennedys gave a state dinner for the visiting Shah and his Empress.

In a toast to his guests, President Kennedy, a man seemingly without a care in the world, observed that he and the Shah shared a common "burden." Each of them had made a visit to Paris and each of them might as well have stayed at home, for the Parisians had eyes only for their wives.

When the guests had gone, the President put in a call to Tucson, Ariz. It came through at 12:15 A. M.

THURSDAY

Archibald Cox, the Solicitor

General, had left by plane on Wednesday afternoon for Tucson, where he was to make two speeches to the Arizona Bar.

On arriving at his hotel that night, he received a message to call the President. When he called he was asked what suggestions did he have for rolling back steel prices?

Mr. Cox had been chairman of the Wage Stabilization Board during the Korean War and had worked with young Senator Kennedy on statements about steel prices and strikes of the past.

After the call, Mr. Cox stayed up all night, thinking and making notes, mostly about legislation. From past experience Mr. Cox had concluded that the antitrust laws could not cope with the steel problem and that special legislation would be necessary.

Mr. Cox made his two speeches, flew back to Washington and stayed up most of that night working on the legislative draft.

But Mr. Cox was not the only one at work on the steel problem in the early hours of Thursday.

Awakened By F. B. I.

At 3 A. M. Lee Linder, a reporter in the Philadelphia bureau of the Associated Press, was awakened by a phone call. It was the F. B. I. At first Mr. Linder thought he was being fooled. Then he determined that the call was genuine. The agents asked him a question or two and then told him:

'We are coming right out to see you."

Mr. Linder had been at the stockholders' meeting of Bethlehem Steel in Wilmington on Tuesday and had quoted Mr. Martin about the undesirability of a price increase. Bethlehem Steel later called the quotation incorrect.

The agents were checking on that quotation. Mr. Linder said later that he had given them the same report he had written for The Associated Press.

At 6:30 A. M. James L. Parks Jr. of The Wilmington Evening Journal arrived at his office. Two F. B. I. agents were waiting for him. He had talked to Mr. Martin after the meeting, together with Mr. Linder and John Lawrence of The Wall Street Journal. Later in the day the Federal agents interviewed Mr. Lawrence.

This descent of the F. B. I. on the newsmen was the most criticized incident in the seventy-two frenzied hours.

Republicans, who had kept an embarrassed silence up to this point, pounced on this F.B.I. episode. Representative William E. Miller of upstate New York, chairman of the Republican National Committee, compared it to the "knock on the door" techniques of Hitler's Gestapo.

In Chicago, as the day progressed, Philip Block and two other high officials of Inland reached a decision: prices would not be raised. They called Joseph Block in Kyoto. He concurred and they agreed to call a directors' meeting to ratify their decision the next morning.

No announcement was to be made until the morning and no one in Washington was told.

Back in Washington, the President was holding an early meeting in the Cabinet Room at the White House. Present were: Attorney General Kennedy; Secretaries McNamara, Goldberg, Hodges; Under Secretary of the Treasury Fowler; Mr. Dixon, chairman of the Federal Trade Commission; Dr. Heller and Mr. Sorensen.

Quick Rebuttal Planned

Roger Blough was scheduled to hold a televised news conference in New York at 3:30 that afternoon. The White House meeting decided that the Administration should put in a speedy rebuttal to his case for United States Steel.

Secretary Hodges had long-scheduled engagements that day in Philadelphia and New York. It was decided that he would hold a news conference in New York at 5 P. M. and try to rebut Mr. Blough point by point.

Meanwhile two of the most secret initiatives of the entire seventy-two hours had been set in motion.

Helps Friends to Meet

The first involved a newspaperman—Charles L. Bartlett, the Washington correspondent of The Chattanooga Times. All Mr. Bartlett would say later was:

"I helped two friends get in touch with each other again."

One friend was President Kennedy— Mr. Bartlett and his wife are members of the Kennedy social set. The other friend was an officer of United States Steel. His identity has not been definitely established, but Mr. Bartlett knows Mr. Blough.

What came of this effort to reopen "diplomatic relations" is not known, although at least one Cabinet member thought it was useful. What came of the second secret initiative, however, can be reported.

At noon or earlier on Thursday President Kennedy phoned Clark Clifford, a Washington lawyer who had first come to national prominence as counsel for President Truman.

Secretary Goldberg, said the President, knew the officers of United States Steel very well and could, of course, talk to them on behalf of the Administration. But Mr. Goldberg, he went on, was known to the steel men mainly as an adversary.

For years he had been the counsel for the steel workers' union and one of their chief strategists in negotiations with the company. In view of this would Mr. Clifford, familiar as he was with the outlook of corporation executives through his law work, join Mr. Goldberg in speaking to United States Steel?

Supports President

Mr. Clifford agreed, flew to New York and met Mr. Blough. He presented himself as a friend of the disputants, but he made clear that he was in 100 per cent agreement with the President. His purpose, he said, was to see if a tragic mistake could be rectified. The mistake, he left no doubt, was on the

company's side.

For fourteen months, he continued, President Kennedy and Mr. Goldberg had worked for healthy conditions in the steel industry. They had tried to create an atmosphere of co-operation in the hope of protecting the national interest. Now all this was gone.

The President, he went on, believed there had been a dozen or more occasions when the company's leaders could easily have told him that despite all he had done they might have to raise prices. But they never had told him. The President, to put it bluntly, felt double-crossed.

What Mr. Blough said in reply could not be learned. But he indicated at the end that he would welcome further talks and he hoped Mr. Clifford would participate in them. Mr. Clifford returned to Washington the same day.

Secretary Hodges, meanwhile, arrived at the University Club in New York at about 3:40, ten minutes after Mr. Blough had begun his news conference.

While Mr. Hodges shaved and changed his shirt, his assistant, William M. Ruder, tried to take notes on Mr. Blough's broadcast, but the static he heard sounded like the Grand Central shuttle.

The Blough news conference was held in the ground floor auditorium at 71 Broadway.

"Let me say respectfully," Mr. Blough began, "that we have no wish to add acrimony or misunderstanding."

On several occasions, he said, he had made it clear that United States Steel was in a cost-price torque that could not be tolerated forever, that a company without profits is a company that cannot modernize, and that the price increase would add "almost negligibly" to the cost of other products — $10.64 for the steel in a standard automobile, 3 cents for a toaster.

One question and answer in the fifty - eight - minute session caught the ears of people in Washington: Could United States Steel hold its new price if Armco and Inland stood pat?

"It would definitely affect us," conceded Mr. Blough. "I don't know how long we could maintain our position."

A half-hour after Mr. Blough finished, Secretary Hodges held his news conference in the Empire State Building.

But the words that probably hit Big Steel the hardest came that day from two Pennsylvania Republicans — Representatives William W. Scranton, the party's candidate for Governor, and James E. Van Zandt, the candidate for Senator.

"The increase at this time," they wired Mr. Blough, "is wrong — wrong for Pennsylvania, wrong for America, wrong for the free world. The increase surely will set off another round of inflation. It will hurt people most who can least afford to be hurt."

U.S. Serves Subpoenas

Meanwhile, Justice Department agents appeared at the headquarters of United States Steel, Bethlehem, Jones & Laughlin and other companies

and served subpoenas for documents bearing on the price increase and other matters.

And at 7 P.M. Attorney General Kennedy announced that the Justice Department had ordered a grand jury investigation of the increase.

By that time, President and Mrs. Kennedy were getting ready for another state dinner with the Shah and Empress — this time at the Iranian Embassy.

FRIDAY

The first big news of the day came from Kyoto, Japan. Joseph Block, Inland's chairman, had told a reporter for the Chicago Daily News:

"We do not feel that an advance in steel prices at this time would be in the national interest."

That news heartened the Administration but it did not stop planning or operations. Nor did Inland's official announcement from Chicago at 10:08 A. M., Washington time, that it would hold the price line.

At 10:15 Solicitor General Cox met in Mr. Sorensen's office with representatives of the Treasury, Commerce and Labor Departments, Budget Bureau and Council of Economic Advisers.

The discussion was on emergency wage-price legislation of three broad kinds:

First, ad hoc legislation limited to the current steel situation; second, permanent legislation imposing some mechanism on wages and prices in the steel industry alone, and third, permanent legislation for steel and other basic industries, setting up "fact-finding" procedures.

Defense Orders Shifted

At 11:45 Secretary McNamara said at his news conference that the Defense Department had ordered defense contractors to shift steel purchases to companies that had not raised prices. Later in the day the department awarded to the Lukens Steel Company, which had not raised prices, a contract for more than $5,000,-000 worth of a special armor plate for Polaris-missile submarines.

At 12:15 President Kennedy and most of the Thursday group met again in the Cabinet Room. It was estimated at that time that the price line was being held on 16 per cent of the nation's steel capacity.

Inland had announced. Armco had decided to hold but not announce. Kaiser's announcement came in while the meeting was on. This might be enough to force the bigger companies down again, but the sentiment of the meeting was that the retreat would not come soon.

Accordingly, preparations continued for a long struggle. Lists of directors of the companies that were holding the line were distributed, and each man present was asked to call men he knew.

Notably absent from this meeting was Secretary Goldberg. He was on his way to New York with Mr. Clifford in a Military Air Transport plane.

A secret rendezvous had been arranged with Mr. Blough and some of the other leaders of United States Steel at the Carlyle Hotel.

At this meeting, as in Mr. Clifford's talk with Mr. Blough on the previous day, no demands or threats or promises came from the Government side.

Finds Outlook 'Abysmal'

The discussion seems to have been a general one about what lay ahead. The outlook, said Mr. Clifford, was "abysmal."

United States Steel, he contended, had failed to weigh the consequences of its action. If it held this position, its interest and those of the industry would inevitably be damaged, and the nation as a whole would suffer.

While the talk was going on, Mr. Blough was called to the phone. Then Mr. Goldberg was called. Each received the same message. Bethlehem Steel had rescinded the price increase— the news had come through at 3:20 P. M.

President Kennedy heard the news while flying to Norfolk for a week-end with the fleet. It was unexpected.

The Administration had made no special effort with Bethlehem. To this day, officials here are uncertain what did it.

Among other things, Bethlehem's officials were struck by the Inland and Kaiser announcement that morning. Inland posed direct competition to Bethlehem's sales in the Midwest—the largest steel market —and Kaiser posed it on the West Coast.

Further, special questions were raised by the Pentagon's order to defense industries to shift their steel buying to mills that did not raise prices. What did this mean for Bethlehem's vast operations as a ship builder?

Whatever the compelling factors were, Bethlehem's decision brought the end of the battle clearly in sight. The competitive situation was such that United States Steel's executive committee was not called into session to reverse its action of the previous Tuesday. The company's officers acted on their own.

The big capitulation came at 5:28. Mrs. Barbara Gamarekian, a secretary in the White House press office, was checking the Associated Press news ticker. And there was the announcement—United States Steel had pulled back the price increase.

Mrs. Gamarekian tore it off and ran into the office of Mr. Sorensen, who was on the phone to the acting press secretary, Mr. Hatcher, in Norfolk.

"Well," Mr. Sorensen was saying, "I guess there isn't anything new."

Mrs. Gamarekian put the news bulletin under his eye.

"Wait a minute!" shouted Mr. Sorensen.

Mr. Hatcher gave the news to the President as he came off the nuclear submarine, Thomas A. Edison, in Norfolk.

It was just seventy-two hours since Roger Blough had dropped in on Mr. Kennedy.

April 23, 1962

PRESIDENT CALLS FOR COOPERATION OF BUSINESS MEN

Speech at Yale Asks Help in
Making Economy Work
at Its Fullest Capacity

HE DENOUNCES 'MYTHS'

Government Size and Fiscal
Policy Cited as Examples
of Outmoded Thinking

By PETER KIHSS

NEW HAVEN, June 11 — President Kennedy appealed to business today to cooperate in finding solutions to the problem of how to "make our free economy work at full capacity." He warned against misleading economic "stereotypes" and "myths."

Addressing 12,000 persons at the 261st annual commencement of Yale University, the President said that it was false to ascribe "any and all unfavorable turns of the speculative wheel" to lack of confidence in his Administration.

In what was taken as an allusion to the recent spectacular price declines on the New York Stock Exchange, he asserted that such gyrations might be temporary and "plainly speculative in character."

Predictions of inflation based on the Federal budget deficit during the current fiscal year ending June 30, he said, had "helped push the market up." He asserted that "the recent reality of non-inflation helped bring it down."

Appeal to Alumni

Mr. Kennedy made a direct appeal to his new brother Yale alumni—he received a doctorate of laws at the ceremony — to "smoke the clay pipe of friendship." Among these he specified Roger M. Blough, chairman of the United States Steel Corporation, whom he had forced this spring to back down on a proposed price increase.

Just after the pageantry and oratory, a White House spokesman announced that the President would meet Mr. Blough in Washington tonight in the latter's capacity as chairman of the Business Council to discuss the gold problem and the balance of payments. White House sources held this to be a significant example of the kind of get-together for which Mr. Kennedy appealed this morning.

A hot sun blazed brilliantly on the throng of graduates and guests on Yale's elm-studded Old Campus as Mr. Kennedy stood up under a canopy of dark Yale blue to become an honorary alumnus. In his own days as a Harvard collegian, class of '40, he had represented Yale's traditional rival in Crimson efforts to defeat the Blues in swimming and golf.

Today Mr. Kennedy drew appreciative laughter when he announced that "it might be said now that I have the best of both worlds, a Harvard education and a Yale degree."

Fifteen times in the first few minutes of a thirty-two-minute address he elicited laughter and applause by sallies about his new affiliation.

Many of his troubles, he said, came from Yale men. He listed a disagreement with Mr. Blough, complaints from Henry Ford 2d, the automobile maker; a difference with John Hay Whitney, publisher of The New York Herald Tribune; Henry R. Luce, editor in chief of Time magazine, and William F. Buckley Jr.

The name of Mr. Buckley, publisher of the conservative National Review magazine and a controversial figure here for his book "God and Man at Yale," evoked especial delight.

Mr. Kennedy even suggested that former President William Howard Taft had found that a White House term was "preparation far becoming a member of this faculty."

But then he turned serious to warn against letting economic myths or stereotypes prevent what he called "a new, difficult but essential confrontation with reality." He listed three.

First, he said, is a myth that government is "steadily getting bigger and worse." For fifteen years, he asserted, the Federal Government has "grown less rapidly than the economy as a whole." Size can bring benefits, he said, reporting that three-fourths of all university research in science and medicine in 1961 were paid by the Federal Government.

Calls Budget Misleading

Next, he said, myths about fiscal policy are legion. He called the conventional administrative budget a misleading measure of Federal fiscal integrity because it omitted trust funds and changes in assets and failed to distinguish loans from straight expenditures or operating expenditures from long-term investments.

Deficits may be dangerous, he said, but in recent years they have not upset basic price stability. Surpluses after the war, on the other hand, "did not prevent inflation," he said.

The national debt, he said, has actually increased only 8 per cent since World War II, while private debt has increased 305 per cent and debts of state and local governments 378 per cent.

Lastly, he asserted, business confidence is actually economic confidence in the nation's ability to invest, produce and consume. It is not simply political confidence, he contended, for recessions occurred in 1929, 1954, 1958 and 1960 during business-approved Administrations.

He ended with a bid for "sober, dispassionate" business and government discussions of technical answers to these problems: How to budget without slowing growth? How to set interest rates without weakening the dollar abroad? How to promote markets without unfairness to the consumer? How to automate and yet give jobs to 500,000 unskilled youngsters dropping out of school each year?

"If there is any current trend toward meeting present problems with old cliches, this is the moment to stop it, before it lands us all in a bog of sterile acrimony," Mr. Kennedy said.

More than usual, the President stuck to his prepared text. However, he dropped one portion of it that would have made an even stronger pledge of goodwill to business.

The omitted section had said: "This Administration is not going to give way to general hostility to business merely because there has been a single temporary disagreement with an industry, nor will the future belong to those who ignore the realities of our economic life in a neurotic search for unending reassurance."

At least some alumni questioned his economic views and his use of the occasion, the first time Yale has had an orator at its actual commencement ceremony since 1903. "He had a captive audience," one father of a graduate said. "He made a partisan speech."

On the other hand, the historic event had brought an exceptional demand for tickets, the only means for admission. Many graduating students were frankly delighted by the President's appearance as added cause for celebration.

Mayor Richard C. Lee of New Haven and a company of the Governor's Foot Guards, in red eighteenth-century uniforms, greeted President Kennedy on his arrival from New York. He reached Tweed-New Haven Municipal Airport in his Air Force DC 6-B plane at 9:47 A.M.

After a private luncheon with university dignitaries, Mr. Kennedy departed for Washington at 2:23 P. M.

June 12, 1962

WHITE HOUSE REVISES ITS NEWSPAPER LIST

WASHINGTON, May 30 (UPI)—The White House said today that President Kennedy had dropped one New York newspaper and added a Midwest daily to his subscription list.

Pierre Salinger, White House press secretary, said:

"It is true that the White House no longer receives The New York Herald Tribune."

Twenty-two copies of the morning newspaper formerly were delivered daily to the White House. Beginning tomorrow, the President has subscribed to twenty-two daily copies of The St. Louis Post-Dispatch.

White House officials attributed dropping of The Herald Tribune to diversification of reading. They said the President had decided it would be to his advantage and to the advantage of his staff to receive newspapers from other parts of the country.

The White House currently subscribes to four New York newspapers—The Times, The Post, The Daily News and The Journal-American. The President also receives daily the three Washington newspapers —The Daily News, The Post and The Evening Star. Other dailies subscribed to for the President are The Wall Street Journal, The Chicago Tribune, The Baltimore Sun, The Philadelphia Inquirer, The Los Angeles Times and The Nashville Tennessean.

This morning, The Washington Post said, "The President and Mrs. Kennedy are known to have been annoyed more than once by sharp criticism and stories they believed were unfair in the Republican Herald Tribune."

In a front page editorial this morning, The Herald Tribune says it hopes the President will renew the White House subscriptions, and asserts he "will miss a lot if he misses the Herald Tribune." It expresses hope that the subscription has not been canceled because of "hard reporting by our greatly respected staff" or editorial criticisms of the Administration.

May 31, 1962

MRS. R. F. KENNEDY PLUNGES INTO POOL

WASHINGTON, June 20 (UPI)—Mrs. Robert F. Kennedy, wife of the Attorney General, fell into the family pool during an outdoor dinner dance Saturday night, it was learned today.

So did Arthur Schlesinger Jr., special Presidential adviser, and Mrs. Spencer Davis, a friend of Mrs. Kennedy, who were guests.

A source close to the family said Mrs. Kennedy, in evening attire, plunged into the water after a leg of a chair slipped off a plank placed across the pool's edges. The same thing happened later to Mr. Schlesinger and Mrs. Davis. All three changed clothes and returned to the party.

But another guest, Lieut. Col. John H. Glenn Jr., kept his chair upright although its legs were but three inches from the edge of the plank.

June 21, 1962

Caroline Kennedy Gets A Diplomatic Passport

WASHINGTON, July 19 (AP)—Four-year-old Caroline Kennedy has a diplomatic passport.

It alerts the countries of the world that the bearer is one who should get all the proper courtesies and pass without delay or hindrance because she is "a dependent of the President of the United States."

A small picture identifies Caroline, who will make her first trip abroad early in August on a vacation in Italy with her mother.

Since Caroline is a minor, the law requires that someone swear to the truth of the statements on her passport and take the oath of allegiance for her.

President Kennedy did that with a flourish of his pen at the White House Monday.

July 20, 1962

Kennedy, at 22, Posed for Angel In Wood Panel Given to Vatican

WASHINGTON, June 22 (AP)—A sculptured likeness of President Kennedy as a winged angel, for which he posed twenty-three years ago—is part of an altar panel in the Vatican,

United Press International Telephoto

Part of a Vatican altar panel by Irena Wiley, sculptress. She said President Kennedy posed for the angel in 1939.

The Washington Post and Times-Herald related today.

The Post, in an article by Winzola McLendon, quoted a Washington sculptress, Irena Wiley. It said Mr. Kennedy, a Roman Catholic, had posed for the figure in a wood sculptured panel in an altar that Mrs. Wiley had carved and given to the Vatican.

He was the "most charming and patient model," recalls Mrs. Wiley, wife of John Cooper Wiley, a Foreign Service officer.

The incident is contained in a book Mrs. Wiley has written, "Around the Globe in Twenty Years," which will be published in August by the David McKay Company.

According to Mrs. Wiley, she sculptured the panel in 1939, just before World War II, when her husband was serving as a diplomat in Latvia and Estonia and President Kennedy's father was Ambassador to the Court of St. James.

Mr. Kennedy, now 45 years old, was 22 then.

Mr. Kennedy, who she said was "trying to learn as much as he could about Europe," came to spend a week or so of his summer vacation with the Wileys.

"I was doing an altar of St. Theresa of Lisieux, my favorite saint," Mrs. Wiley said, "and I needed a model for the angel in one of the panels. Jack with his curly hair and his youthful serenity of expression was literally God-sent."

The altar is a life-size statue-in-the-round of St. Therese and is surrounded by twelve panels, each depicting a chapter in the saint's life.

The panel for which Mrs. Wiley says Mr. Kennedy posed shows an angel hovering over St. Therese who is kneeling before an open book.

June 23, 1962

FIRST LADY FINDS LACK OF PRIVACY

WASHINGTON, July 21 —As they say of marriage, Mrs. John F. Kennedy says of the White House—the first year is the hardest.

Turning 33 years of age, and finishing eighteen months as First Lady, she is over that trying period now. But she still faces the constant glare of the limelight, public curiosity and increasing state functions and official appearances.

She finds her biggest problem is maintaining privacy for her two children, Caroline, 4½, and John, Jr., 20 months.

She carefully schedules her time to be with her children as much as possible.

These are some of the comments from Mrs. Kennedy, who answered a reporter's questions about her views on the White House and her role there.

She finds her life in the White House difficult but not disagreeable.

Her greatest source of pride is her husband.

And she feels that any woman, including a First Lady, is entitled to change her mind.

Mrs. Kennedy, the nation's third-youngest First Lady, observes her thirty-third birthday on Saturday, July 28. About ten days later she will leave for Italy on a two-week August holiday visit, taking Caroline along.

Foreign trips, both official and unofficial, her children and refurbishing the White House have been among Mrs. Kennedy's primary concerns in the year and a half she has been First Lady.

In response to a few personal questions, Mrs. Kennedy gave her reactions. The White House said the comments represented the First Lady's own views, though she preferred not to be quoted directly except in a few instances.

Sees Role Differently

Mrs. Kennedy believes that her view of the role as First Lady is undoubtedly different from that of other First Ladies in recent history because she has young children.

"I think the more official life takes me away from my young children, the more I should make it up to them," Mrs. Kennedy said.

Therefore, she decided early in her husband's term of office that she could best serve her family and fulfill her duties as wife of the President by undertaking only those projects to which she could truly contribute.

Chief among these she lists her Fine Arts Committee project to refurnish the White House with historic antiques and paintings, and the starting of a series of youth concerts, performed by youngsters at the White House before an audience of boys and girls.

While undertaking such projects, Mrs. Kennedy carefully limited her other engagements to certain traditional functions such as national charitable projects and Congressional gatherings. She does not go out during the day to luncheons or teas, and in this way, she says, she has the time that she should devote to her young family.

Difficulties Were Expected

She was asked if the White House role was more or less difficult than she had expected.

Mrs. Kennedy said that she had expected it to be difficult, for she knew it would be a complete change from the more or less private and anonymous life she had in the past.

Mrs. Kennedy was quoted as making this comment at her husband's inauguration:

"I felt as though I had just turned into a piece of public property. It's frightening to lose your anonymity at 31."

The first year in the White House was the hardest part, Mrs. Kennedy reports now, with moving her family in, trying to create a home for them in rooms that had not yet been furnished, making a plan of her own routine, organizing her staff and her committees' projects. All this was topped by the fact that it took her a long time to recover from the birth of her son and to get the strength to answer the many demands of the early months.

But, when in good health, she enjoys a challenge and, while things may have been difficult at times, they have never been disagreeable, she says.

Husband a Source of Pride

She was asked what aspects of her White House life she enjoyed most.

Mrs. Kennedy believes that her husband has been a good President, and that has been her greatest source of pride—watching him work and adapt to events.

Her greatest satisfaction, she adds, has been arranging their private life to provide him with maximum absence of stress, so that he finds relaxation once he leaves his office, and his energies are renewed for his job.

She also appreciates having the chance to meet leaders of other countries, both here and on trips abroad, as well as the broadening experience of the trips she has taken in the last year and a half to both familiar and unfamiliar countries.

Mrs. Kennedy has visited a total of eleven countries. Most of her journeys were with President Kennedy on state visits. She went on her own last March to India and Pakistan on a semi-official visit, made a vacation call on Greece last summer and plans to vacation sometime next month in Italy with her sister, Princess Lee Radziwill, taking Caroline along for the trip. Officials rate Mrs. Kennedy very highly in her diplomatic role—supporting President Kennedy in his foreign policy missions.

She Changes Her Mind

When Mrs. Kennedy returned from India and Pakistan, her homecoming comments indicated that she would not want to make another such ceremonial, semi-official foray abroad again without her husband.

Asked about this, the First Lady invoked the woman's prerogative to change her mind.

She made it clear that she had meant what she said at the time, for she had missed her family and also would have liked to have shared the trip with her husband. However, she said that she never made irrevocable decisions on such matters. She prefers to ride with events, and if her husband wanted her to go again, she would.

Mrs. Kennedy also has found gratifying the "warm reception" that her Fine Arts Committee's work has received. Her television tour of the refurbished state rooms was widely praised.

And Mrs. Kennedy said that she had enjoyed "working on the White House guidebook for a year and having it at last a reality." The 132-page pamphlet is the first official guide to the 162-year-old White House. It went on sale to the public July 4 at one dollar a copy. The profits will go to the project of finding historic and significant furnishings for the President's house.

Privacy a Big Problem

She was asked what unexpected problems she and her family had encountered?

Privacy for the children has been the greatest problem, Mrs. Kennedy reports.

While this problem was not unexpected, she did not realize it would be so difficult.

She believes that the children should be able to play out o doors with their friends, as other children do. But they cannot help being aware of photographers at the fence when they are on the South Lawn of the White House, where a playground has been installed.

Mrs. Kennedy feels that her youngsters should be able to go on planned excursions with their mother, to see circuses and amusement parks, or just to go on shopping expeditions. But the public attention involved is confusing and distracting to the children.

Mrs. Kennedy has often made her complaint about photographing of Caroline at play, going to dancing school or atop her pet horse Macaroni.

Out recently with her father, Caroline herself admonished cameramen: "No photographs."

Has Some Excursions

But, the public's interest in the Kennedys and their children is insatiable both at home and abroad.

Despite the complications, Mrs. Kennedy has made every effort to give Caroline some of the little excursions other youngsters take for granted. They have been able to eat hamburgers undisturbed in a Palm Beach, Fla., snack shop, and to sneak off together to take a look at a freight train chugging down a Washington railroad track.

Caroline has been to the local amusement park and a children's theatre. But, at these spots, Secret Service agents, a maid or friends have gone along, while Mrs. Kennedy stayed away lest her presence focus attention on the child. Mostly, these jaunts have been accomplished successfully without photographing.

But President Kennedy's week-end excursions to the candy store with Caroline and her cousins at Hyannis Port, Mass., last summer became well photographed missions, despite objections from the President himself.

Amid her comments, Mrs. Kennedy gave this sample of the psychology that is her guidepost:

"It isn't fair to children in the limelight to leave them to the care of others and then to expect that they will turn out all right. They need their mother's affection and guidance and long periods of time alone with her. That is what gives them security in an often confusing new world."

July 22, 1962

WASHINGTON, July 24 (UPI) —President Kennedy's mother, who resents wisecracks about political dynasties, said today she would campaign to help her youngest son, Edward M., win a Senate seat in Massachusetts.

Mrs. Joseph P. Kennedy disclosed this intention in an interview at the White House, where she is acting as official hostess while the President's wife is on vacation.

She discussed her views on political clans, Edward's chances, the changes in the White House, the "wonderful" job the First Lady is doing and her "unspoiled" granddaughter Caroline.

"Oh, certainly," Mrs. Kennedy said when asked if she thought Edward would win a Senate seat. She said Edward had invited her to campaign for him and "I expect I will."

Mrs. Kennedy said she wanted to help him become her third son to hold national office "even though I'm past retirement age." Mrs. Kennedy is 72 years old. She said her husband, former Ambassador Joseph P. Kennedy, had urged Edward to seek political office.

Edward Kennedy has been endorsed for the Senate by the Massachusetts Democratic convention. He will be opposed in

At Home In The White House

President's Mother to Help Son in Senate Race

a primary Sept. 18 by State Attorney General Edward J. McCormack Jr. Mrs. Kennedy indicated she would start helping her son in the primary campaign.

The subject of political dynasties came up at yesterday's White House luncheon for President Carlos Julio Arosemena Monroy of Ecuador, Mrs. Kennedy said. President Arosemena's father also had been President of his country.

Señora Arosemena confided to her hostess that her 10-year-old son, Carlos Julio Jr., who also made the state visit to Washington, had made up his mind to be a soldier. She said he did not want to be President because he had heard "so many cracks about a family dynasty."

Mrs. Kennedy, who has heard the same sort of gibes at her family's political aspirations, spoke out wtih some feeling—and with some exasperation:

"I think it's wonderful if people want to serve their country. I think it's a great thing."

She cited her admiration for the Adams family for their contribution to American history. "They were wonderful," she said, "something to be proud of.

"I don't understand why people don't approve of it," she went on. "I think boys should be encouraged to go into public service. I think it's a thing to be praised."

Mrs. Kennedy made these comments on other subjects:

President Kennedy—"I think he's wonderful. He looks very well. He seems to enjoy it and responds to all the challenges. It is a terrific responsibility. So much depends on his judgment."

The First Lady—"I think she's doing a wonderful job. Everyone all over the world admires her. So many people say so. I know she enjoys it."

Rearing children—"I wanted my family to go to public and parochial schools so they would get to know all groups of children and they would see that a chauffeur's or a mechanic's son is sometimes smarter than they are."

White House restoration—"I like the changes very much."

Her husband, who suffered a stroke last December—"He's better now, but he gets impatient. He's very interested in the Massachusetts campaign."

Her 4-year-old granddaughter, Caroline—"I don't think she's spoiled. She's too young to realize—all these luxuries. She probably thinks it's natural for children to go off in their own planes. If she was older, she would be more spoiled. But she is with her cousins, and some of them dance and swim better than she. They do not allow her to take special precedence. Little children accept things."

July 25, 1962

Festive Clan on Cape

HYANNIS PORT, Mass., July 29—Clan Kennedy gathered at nearly full strength in the family's summer enclave here this week-end to celebrate the thirty-third birthday of the dark-haired Bouvier girl who married brother Jack. Counting the President's parents, brothers Bobby and Teddy, sisters-in-law Ethel and Joan, sisters Jean, Eunice and Pat, brothers-in-law Steve Smith, Sargent Shriver (Peter Lawford was absent) and all the kids, there were thirty-three to feed. That's a lot of lobster.

Talk of Hyannis Port

When the family set sail yesterday across Lewis Bay for the swimming and water - skiing off Great Island, it looked like a convoy. A white Coast Guard vessel, the family cruisers Marlin and Patrick J., a black launch operated by Barnstable County's harbor police, and two small water - jet speedboats manned by the Secret Service made up the fleet.

The natives and summer visitors pay the President and his wife little mind, except when they go to church. Then a crowd of about 600 vacationers gathers in the parking lot of St. Xavier's Church to watch the first family enter and leave by a side door.

Two weeks ago Bishop Regan, a Bostonian and Maryknoll priest who had been imprisoned by the Chinese Communists, preached the sermon. A special collection was taken for his diocese in Mindanao in the Philippines. The parishioners of St. Xavier's call such collections "Daly doubles" after their priest, Monsignor Daly.

Incidentally, a member of the congregation reports that the President is a "sermon-twitcher." He continually pushes a hand through his hair, adjusts his tie and counts his fingers, as if he had his mind on the unregenerate in the Ways and Means Committee, rather than the 100,000 pagans Bishop Regan has reported in his spiritual pasture.

July 30, 1962

Justice Department Has a Shaggy Dog: Robert Kennedy's

WASHINGTON, Aug. 3 (UPI)—A frequent visitor at the Justice Department these days is a big, shambling, sad-countenanced animal answering to the name of Brumus. He goes walking with pretty girls.

He is a Labrador dog, and one of the many pets Attorney General Robert F. Kennedy has collected for his seven children.

Lately Brumus has been accompanying his master to work. And this raises the question of whether this practice violates a Government building regulation that says:

"Dogs and other animals, except for Seeing Eye dogs, shall not be brought upon [government] property for other than official purposes."

The maximum penalty for violation is a $50 fine and thirty days in jail.

The Attorney General, explaining Brumus' presence to visitors recently, said:

"He usually stays at home with the children. But the children are away on vacation and he gets very lonely. So I bring him down here and get pretty girls to take him for walks."

At the age of 14 months, Brumus is almost as big, and not nearly as graceful, as a pony. He is considered well-behaved, most of the time, but has something of the ham in him.

Some of the Attorney General's aides have jokingly suggested that Brumus might qualify as a watchdog and thus gain "official" status.

But the rules would seem to bar any other member of the Attorney General's menagerie, which includes two other dogs, ponies, horses, geese, a burro, a sea lion, Hungarian pigeons, twenty goldfish, rabbits, turtles and a salamander.

August 4, 1962

WASHINGTON, Sept. 17—The Washington Post published today the widely circulated rumor — and a denial — that President Kennedy was once secretly married.

It printed an article on the subject from Newsweek magazine, which it owns. The article, in this week's issue of the magazine, describes the rumor as groundless, and the newspaper concurs.

The newspaper said it had found the report to be false as long ago as August, 1961, but that the "recent revival of the rumor has brought it to public attention and made notice of it seem advisable."

Both The Post and Newsweek are published by companies headed by Philip L. Graham. Mr. Graham is a close friend of President Kennedy.

White House Silent

In Newport, R. I., where the President and Mrs. Kennedy are spending a long week-end, Pierre Salinger, the White House press secretary, refused to discuss the matter today.

Earlier, however, the White House had repeatedly denied the story with the statement: "The President has been married only once—to his wife Jacqueline Kennedy."

The rumor has been in circulation for more than a year. It is to the effect that the President was married early in 1947 to Durie Malcolm and that, soon afterward, the marriage was dissolved by divorce or annulment. Durie Malcolm had been twice married and twice divorced by early 1947.

The President's marriage to Jacqueline Bouvier took place on Sept. 12, 1953.

The rumor was intensively investigated by news media representatives. They were unable to find any supporting evidence for the allegation, and no major publication gave it circulation until Sept. 2.

Denial in Parade

At that time, Parade, a nationally distributed supplement in Sunday newspapers, printed a letter from a reader asking if the story were true. Parade's reply to the reader was that there never had been such a marriage.

The British Sunday press simultaneously gave full reports on the Parade publication. Today the rumor was the subject of a column by Walter Winchell. Mr. Winchell said he could find "no proof" of the story.

Until today the rumor had been disseminated mostly by several extreme right-wing and racist publications and organizations. Prominent among them is The Thunderbolt, organ of the National States Rights party, which is published in Birmingham, Ala.

In the May, 1962, issue The Thunderbolt accused the press of suppressing the story.

The White House had long considered a public denial and refutation of these reports but decided against it in the belief that such a statement might propagate a story that other-

wise would die down. For the same reason Durie Malcolm, now Mrs. Thomas Shevlin, has refused all comment. Efforts to reach Mrs. Shevlin today were unavailing. Her Palm Beach telephone was said to be temporarily disconnected. She was reported to be in Newport. R. I., but this could not be confirmed.

Started in Genealogy

The story of the alleged marriage had its origin in an entry in the Blauvelt Family Genealogy, published in 1957 by the late Louis L. Blauvelt of East Orange, N. J. The genealogy purports to be a "comprehensive compilation of the descendants of Gerrt Hendrickson (Blauvelt) (1620-1687) who came to America in 1638."

The entry, on page 884, under the eleventh generation, reads as follows:

"(12,427) DURIE (Kerr) Malcom [sic]. (Isabel O. Cooper, 11,304). We have no birth date. She was born Kerr, but took the name of her stepfather. She first married Firmin [sic] Desloge, IV. They were divorced. Durie then married F. John Bersbach. They were divorced, and she married, third, John F. Kennedy, son of Joseph P. Kennedy, one time Ambassador to England. There were no children of the second or third marriages.

"The only child of Firmin [sic] V. Desloge and Durie, (Kerr), Malcom [sic] (12,427), was:

"12,642 Durie, born ——, ——, ——."

Commenting on this entry, a White House spokesman has said:

"It has three mistakes.

"First, it has the order of her [Miss Malcolm's] first two marriages reversed.

"Second, despite the fact that the book was written in 1956, it makes no mention that Miss Malcolm married Thomas Shevlin of Palm Beach, Fla., in 1947 and has been married to him since.

"Third, Miss Malcolm was never married to John F. Kennedy."

Names Misspelled

Other errors in the entry are two misspellings—"Malcom" instead of "Malcolm," and "Firmin" instead of "Firman."

The White House has received hundreds of letters about the entry and has always denied its accuracy in the words quoted above.

Durie Malcolm's family had a house in Palm Beach across the street from that of Joseph P. Kennedy. All the Kennedy family knew her, her mother, Isabel Malcolm, and her stepfather, George H. Malcolm. Friends of President Kennedy have quoted him as saying he had known her; that she now lived near his father's home in Palm Beach; that he had dated her a few times in 1947; but that they had not been married.

Durie Malcolm was born Dec. 30, 1916. On a passport application in 1961, she gave her place of birth as Chicago. In a marriage application at Fort

Lee, N. J., on July 5, 1947, she said her birthplace was New York.

There are records of three marriages.

On April 3, 1937, she married F. John Bersbach at Lake Forest, Ill. They were divorced July 15, 1938.

On Jan. 2, 1939, she married Firman Desloge 4th at Palm Beach. They were divorced Jan. 24, 1947.

On July 11, 1947, she married Thomas Shevlin Jr. at Fort Lee. They are still married and live in Palm Beach.

There is no record of any marriage to John F. Kennedy that reporters have been able to find.

What basis did Louis L. Blauvelt, who died in 1958 at the age of 79, have for his statement? Some members of the Blauvelt family have said Howard Ira Durie, a title searcher of Woodcliff Lake, N. J., supplied the item.

However, Mr. Durie has denied this.

James N. Blauvelt of Chevy Chase, Md., who is president of the Association of Blauvelt Descendants, said:

"I am sure that Louis Blauvelt could not have put it in his book unless he were sure of his facts. Where he got his information I would not know."

'No Proof at All'

Miss Elsie Gilbert, a school teacher of South Orange, N. J., who has been designated by the family to carry on Louis Blauvelt's work, said of the item:

"We have nothing to substantiate it, no proof at all. I don't know anything about it."

She supported Mr. Durie's contention that he was not the source of the item.

Mrs. Edward L. Harner of East Orange, one of the editorial assistants on the book, told one investigator:

"A letter has been written to the White House saying that there was nothing to verify the entry. This was done at the White House's request. We are at a loss to know how he [Louis Blauvelt] made such a mistake."

The daughter of the author, Mrs. William Keys Smith, a teacher at Newark Academy, said to a reporter:

"It can be considered an error." That is all I have to say. I would like to have it considered an error."

An aide of the President has checked the original files of material on which Mr. Blauvelt based his genealogy and has stated that the envelope on Durie Malcolm contains only one item mentioning John F. Kennedy—a newspaper clipping that they had been "seen" together on a date.

The White House has a statement from Mr. Blauvelt's son-in-law, William Keys Smith, who is the custodian of the historian's records, saying that this clipping is the only basis for the erroneous entry about a "marriage."

Mr. Smith, who lives in East Orange, reiterated today that "we haven't been able to find any other documentary evidence

At Home In The White House

for the entry."

He said this was "surprising" because Mr. Blauvelt was "a careful and thorough genealogist." He acknowledged that some errors had been found in the work but he asserted that most were of a "minor" nature.

Although the genealogy was not published until 1957, the Kennedy entry was made in 1947, according to Mr. Smith.

On the theory that Miss Malcolm, having wed Mr. Shevlin in Fort Lee in 1947, might possibly have wed Mr. Kennedy there also, reporters have combed the newspaper files and official records in Bergen County between the dates of Jan. 24, 1947, and July 11, 1947— the dates bracketing her divorce from Mr. Desloge and her marriage to Mr. Shevlin. They have discovered no record of a marriage.

It is not known with certainty what started the story

in circulation. According to one account from a high Administration source, it began in May, 1961, after somebody browsing through the library of the Daughters of the American Revolution here noticed the entry.

In March, 1962, a New York publication entitled The Realist, which characterizes itself as a magazine devoted to "free-thought criticism and satire," published the text of the entry.

About this time, the Christian Educational Association of Union, N. J., obtained a copy of the Blauvelt Genealogy. This association is headed by Conde McGinley, who put out a publication entitled Common Sense.

Mr. McGinley sent the copy to the National States Rights party.

In May The Thunderbolt, which describes itself on its masthead as "the official white

racial organ of the National States Rights party," ran the text of the Kennedy entry under the headline, "Kennedy's Divorce Exposed! Is Present Marriage Valid? Excommunication Possible."

The articles about the "marriage" have also been carried by The Gordon Winrod Letter, in June and July, 1962.

The Valley Paper Company of Holyoke, Mass., is mailing the "marriage" story to a selected list of "patriots."

The first known publication hinting at the information in the Blauvelt genealogy record is believed to have been in Roll Call, a publication for capital employes, in 1961. It said:

"Who is the former Senator, now in high public office, who is concealing his former marriage?"

September 18, 1962

A KENNEDY WRITES OF RETARDED SISTER

Mrs. Eunice Kennedy Shriver has publicly discussed the heart-break her family underwent with a retarded older sister, who is in an institution.

"It fills me with sadness to think this change might not have been necessary if we knew then what we know today," writes Mrs. Shriver in the issue of The Saturday Evening Post for Sept. 22. She is the wife of Sargent Shriver, Peace Corps director.

The girl, Rosemary Kennedy, now 43 years old, is the sister of President Kennedy. Mrs. Shriver, also a sister of the

President, writes:

"For a long time my family believed that all of us working together could provide my sister with a happy life in our midst."

After the Kennedys returned in 1941 from London, where Joseph P. Kennedy, father of the family, had served as U. S. Ambassador, Mrs. Shriver writes:

"Rosemary was not making progress but seemed instead to be going backward. At 22 she was becoming increasingly irritable and difficult. Her memory and concentration and her

judgment were declining.

"My mother took Rosemary to psychologists and to dozens of doctors. All of them said her condition would not get better and that she would be far happier in an institution, where competition was far less and where our numerous activities would not endanger her health.

"My mother found an excellent Catholic institution that specialized in the care of retarded children and adults. Rosemary is there now, living with others of her capacity."

September 18, 1962

EDWARD KENNEDY WON 69% OF VOTE

Margin in Senate Primary Stuns Massachusetts — National Impact Certain

---

By TOM WICKER

BOSTON, Sept. 19—Edward M. Kennedy's thundering victory in yesterday's Democratic Senatorial primary dominated Massachusetts politics today and made his candidacy a certain issue in the national campaign.

The 30-year-old brother of the President shocked almost everyone, including some of his campaign workers, by the dimensions of his victory over Edward J. McCormack Jr., the nephew of the Speaker of the House.

Complete unofficial returns gave Mr. Kennedy 559,251 votes, Mr. McCormack 247,366. Mr. Kennedy thus won by a margin of 311,885, collecting about 69 per cent of the 806,617 ballots cast by Democrats.

Wins in Boston

He carried all 22 of Boston's wards and 269 of its 275 precincts, although the city had been regarded as the stronghold of the McCormacks.

The landslide made Mr. Ken-

nedy an immediate favorite over George Cabot Lodge, 35, who won the Republican Senatorial nomination in a much closer race with Representative Laurence Curtis, and over H. Stuart Hughes, a Harvard professor, who will be on the November ballot as an independent.

Mr. Lodge received 245,210 votes to Mr. Curtis's 197,660. He won by a margin of 47,550, polling about 55 per cent of the 442,870 votes cast in the Republican primary.

Mr. Kennedy's landslide victory brought immediate reaction from national spokesmen of both parties, while President Kennedy maintained an official silence about his brother's triumph.

Satisfaction Expressed

Informed sources here believed the President would feel free to campaign in Massachusetts for his brother now that he is the official nominee for Senator.

In Washington, John M.

Bailey, the Democratic National Chairman, noted with satisfaction that the combined vote for the two Democratic Senatorial candidates, both of whom voiced support for the Kennedy Administration, was more than 360,000 votes higher than that received by the two Republican candidates, who were critical of the Administration.

Mr. Bailey called the Kennedy victory a portent for November. "The vote in Massachusetts," he said, "points clearly to a Democratic victory in the general election and also is an important indication of the national strength the Democratic party will display in November."

Representative William E. Miller of upstate New York, the Republican National Chairman, saw it another way. Mr. Kennedy's triumph, he said, was "a vivid demonstration of the power of money coupled with merciless political leverage."

'A Mocking Insult'

Mr. Miller declared, "The thinly veiled fiction that the winner was not aided in full measure in his campaign by his powerful brothers in Washington is a mocking insult which many Massachusetts Democrats properly resent.'"

There was little doubt that Republicans everywhere would pick up the so-called dynasty issue and the theme of "too many Kennedys."

They were expected to point out that Edward Kennedy was seeking the President's former seat in the Senate and that he would be the third of the Kennedy brothers to hold high public office at once. They were expected to argue that in view of his youth and lack of experience in any elected office, his candidacy was an arrogant grab for power by an arrogant family.

Could Hurt Nationally

Because this argument can be raised, some analysts believe that Edward Kennedy, although ranked a heavy favorite here on the basis of yesterday's showing, could become a national liability to the Democrats by giving Republicans generally an easy target to shoot at.

The size of his victory over Mr. McCormack was expected to add to the force of the Republicans' attack by enabling them to talk of a "steamroller" directed from the White House.

Mr. Lodge indicated today

that he, too, would attack Mr. Kennedy on these grounds, although he probably will do so somewhat more gingerly than most Republicans. As the son and great-grandson of two former Massachusetts Senators, and as one who has never held elective office himself, he was made the target of much the same type of attack by Mr. Curtis in the primary campaign.

Mr. Hughes, the independent candidate, who seems to delight in kicking sacred political cows, also set to work this morning to woo the dejected supporters of Edward McCormack.

He said he did not expect large numbers of McCormack men to back him in November, because many of them are Irish Catholics and he is an admitted agnostic. He said he did hope that some of the public figures who supported Mr. McCormack would now back him and thus influence the sizable Massachusetts independent vote.

There are about 1,200,000 registered independents in this state, compared with 900,000 Democrats and 600,000 Republicans.

Mr. Lodge and Mr. Hughes both challenged Mr. Kennedy today to televised debates. Each had in mind a three-way discussion, with all three men on the same program.

Mr. Kennedy agreed at once to debate Mr. Lodge, and said

he would be "delighted" to discuss issues with Mr. Hughes. He did not actually accept the idea of a three-way debate, however.

Observers here thought a three-way debate would inevitably find both Mr. Lodge and Mr. Hughes pressing a more or less concerted attack on Mr. Kennedy, the front-runner.

Today's developments were secondary to Boston's dazed contemplation of the smashing Kennedy majority and the huge total turnout in yesterday's primaries.

The total vote in the two senatorial contests was 1,249,-487. The previous record primary turnout in Massachusetts was 994,306.

Sources close to the Kennedy campaign offered the following analysis of their candidate's huge majority.

For one thing, they said, Edward Kennedy, for all his youth and inexperience, proved to be a hard-working and effective campaigner who saw and spoke to more voters in more places than any other candidate.

Mr. Kennedy also benefited, his aides believe, from the slashing attacks of Mr. McCormack, particularly in their first televised debate. These attacks may have backfired, particularly among women voters.

September 20, 1962

WASHINGTON, Sept. 30— President Kennedy appealed to the students and the people of Mississippi tonight to comply peacefully with Federal law and bring the desegregation crisis to an end. "The eyes of the nation and all the world are upon you and upon all of us," he said, "and the honor of your university and state are in the balance."

The President spoke to the nation on television less than an hour after Gov. Ross R. Barnett of Mississippi pulled back from his all-out defiance of Federal authority. The Governor indicated he would no longer attempt to block the enrollment of James H. Meredith, a Negro, at the University of Mississippi.

Mr. Kennedy expressed cautious hope that the great Federal-state conflict, the gravest since the Civil War, was coming to a peaceful end. He said Federal Court orders "are beginning to be carried out."

But he qualified his optimism most carefully, and indeed made clear that the Government was waiting anxiously to see how Mississippi officials and citizens behaved. There was still much concern here tonight about violence at the university in Oxford.

There were no recriminations in the President's talk, nor even a reference to Governor Barnett. It was addressed primarily to the students who will play so large a part in determining how the Meredith case turns out.

"Our nation is founded on the principle that observance of the law is the eternal safeguard of liberty," he said, "and defiance of the law is the surest road to tyranny.

"If this country should ever reach the point where any man or group of men by force or threat of force could long defy the commands of our court and our Constitution, then no law would stand free from doubt, no judge would be sure of his writ and no citizen would be safe from his neighbors."

Addresses Students

At the end of his talk, Mr. Kennedy spoke directly to the University of Mississippi students, those "who are most concerned."

"You have a new opportunity," he said, "to show that you are men of patriotism and integrity. For the most effective means of upholding the law is not the state policemen or the marshals or the national guard. It is you.

"It lies in your courage to accept those laws with which you disagree as well as those with which you agree.

"There is in short no reason

why the books on this case cannot now be quickly and quietly closed in the manner directed by the court.

"Let us preserve both the law and the peace; and then, healing those wounds that are within, we can turn to the greater crises that are without and stand united as one people in our pledge to man's freedom."

There was nothing in the President's speech to indicate that any kind of formal agreement had been reached with Governor Barnett after a series of telephone talks between the Governor, the President and his brother, Attorney General Robert F. Kennedy.

What optimism there was in the speech, and in the news from Oxford, reflected state withdrawal in the face of gathering Federal power.

That power was represented by the large force of marshals on the campus tonight, by the troops waiting for action if needed and by the threat of a heavy fine and jail for contempt hanging over Governor Barnett.

The Federal Government applied these sanctions slowly, and with manifest reluctance, in the hope that at some point the Governor would give way.

That hope seemed to be at least partly justified tonight, with Governor Barnett's bitter but capitulating words. But there was still the greater question of Mr. Meredith's safety from mob violence.

President Asks Mississippi To Comply With U.S. Laws

Voices Hope Racial Dispute Is Over at State U., but Optimism Is Guarded

By ANTHONY LEWIS

Meredith on Campus

President Kennedy noted that Mr. Meredith had reached the campus and taken up residence without the use of the National Guardsmen he federalized last night or the Army combat forces ready just outside Mississippi.

"It is to be hoped," the President added, again with a note of caution, 'that the law enforcement officers of the state of Mississippi and the Federal marshals will continue to be sufficient in the future."

The President, looking beyond the immediate events in Mississippi, made an effort to calm the emotions aroused throughout the South by the crisis. He praised the South as a whole for its adjustment to racial integration.

He went on to "express the thanks of the nation" to the Southerners who had helped bring about the "entrance of students regardless of race" into state - supported universities of eight Southern states—all but Mississippi, South Carolina and Alabama—and the border state of Kentucky.

Mr. Kennedy said he "deeply regretted" that any Federal action was necessary in the Meredith case, but that "all other avenues and alternatives, including persuasion and conciliation, had been tried and exhausted."

Has Typewritten Text

He wore a navy blue suit before the cameras, a white shirt and a blue tie that was knotted slightly off center of his collar. He spoke from a typewritten text in which he had penciled a few changes just before the cameras picked him up.

Immediately after the broadcast he joined his brother, the Attorney General, in the Cabinet room. There also were the assistant attorney general for civil rights, Burke Marshall, and three White House aides, Special Counsel Theodore C. Sorensen and Special Assistants Lawrence F. O'Brien and Kenneth O'Donnell.

The long day and evening before the speech were devoted to intricate maneuvers in the legal and political struggle with Mississippi.

The mobilizing of armed strength set in motion by the President at midnight last night went ahead. The Mississippi National Guard began to report for Federal service and regular Army troops were flown to nearby Memphis, Tenn.

There were 5,500 troops on the move in connection with the crisis.

This afternoon the Justice Department gave the order to send a force of Federal officers onto the university campus in Oxford, Miss. But, in line with the aim of avoiding the ultimate power as long as possible, no combat troops were used.

The Federal force was composed of 350 marshals and other civilian Federal officers. Military personnel were used only to transport the Federal officers.

In charge of the marshals were five Justice Department officials sent down from Washington today. The chief of the group was the Deputy Attorney General, Nicholas deB. Katzenbach.

With Mr. Katzenbach were the Assistant Attorney General in charge of the office of legal counsel, Norbert A. Schlei, and his first assistant, Harold F. Reis; the department's director of public information, Edwin O. Guthman; an assistant to the Attorney General, Dean Markham, and William A. Geoghegan, assistant to Mr. Katzenbach.

Reluctance to Press

There has never been any desire in the Administration to push the conflict with Mississippi to the last steps — armed clashes and the arrest of the Governor. Indeed, the President and the Attorney General have held back again and again in the hope of avoiding such showdowns.

The President's troop order and his accompanying proclamation commanding Mississippi and its officials to cease their defiance were delayed yesterday in just such an attempt at a peaceful settlement.

For a time, it was understood, the Administration felt it had an understanding with the Governor yesterday. But then, in one of the series of telephone talks with the President and the Attorney General he seemed to draw back.

The White House disclosed today that at 5:45 P.M. yesterday the President sent a telegram to Governor Barnett requesting guarantees of safety and compliance with court orders.

All day today members of the Mississippi Congressional delegation, all Democrats, did what they could to persuade the President against the actual dispatch of combat troops into the state.

Five members of a six-man delegation met in the office of Senator James O. Eastland. This statement was issued:

"The Mississippi delegation carried their plea to avoid the use of Federal armed forces in the Mississippi contest over registering Meredith directly to President Kennedy himself today.

"Members of the delegation strongly urged that all orders Federalizing and mobilizing the Mississippi National Guard be set aside. Both the Senators and five members of the House delegation stressed the terrible situation which could result. They renewed their previous request that force of arms not be used.

"Spokesmen for the group reported that they were assured only that efforts to resolve the issue would continue. The group has been closeted since early morning exploring possible avenues and attempting to arrive at an effective and adequate solution to the problem."

The one Mississippi Congressman absent from the group was Frank E. Smith, a relative moderate on racial matters. He has lost his seat and will soon become a member of the Tennessee Valley Authority.

October 1, 1962

KENNEDY READY FOR SOVIET SHOWDOWN ON MISSILE SITES

Says in Radio-TV Address That Soviet Broke Its Promises on Bases

By ANTHONY LEWIS

WASHINGTON, Oct. 22 — President Kennedy imposed a naval and air "quarantine" tonight on the shipment of offensive military equipment to Cuba.

In a speech of extraordinary gravity, he told the American people that the Soviet Union, contrary to promises, was building offensive missile and bomber bases in Cuba. He said the bases could handle missiles carrying nuclear warheads up to 2,000 miles.

Thus a critical moment in the cold war was at hand tonight. The President had decided on a direct confrontation with — and challenge to — the power of the Soviet Union.

Direct Thrust at Soviet

Two aspects of the speech were notable. One was its direct thrust at the Soviet Union as the party responsible for the crisis. Mr. Kennedy treated Cuba and the Government of Premier Fidel Castro as a mere pawn in Moscow's hands and drew the issue as one with the Soviet Government.

The President, in language of unusual bluntness, accused the Soviet leaders of deliberately "false statements about their intentions in Cuba."

The other aspect of the speech particularly noted by observers here was its flat commitment by the United States to act alone against the missile threat in Cuba.

Nation Ready to Act

The President made it clear that this country would not stop short of military action to end what he called a "clandestine, reckless and provocative threat to world peace."

Mr. Kennedy said the United States was asking for an emergency meeting of the United Nations Security Council to consider a resolution for "dismantling and withdrawal of all offensive weapons in Cuba."

He said the launching of a nuclear missile from Cuba against any nation in the Western Hemisphere would be regarded as an attack by the Soviet Union against the United States. It would be met, he said, by retaliation against the Soviet Union.

He called on Premier Khrushchev to withdraw the missiles from Cuba and so "move the world back from the abyss of destruction."

All this the President recited in an 18-minute radio and television address of a grimness unparalleled in recent times. He read the words rapidly, with little emotion, until he came to the peroration—a warning to Americans of the dangers ahead.

"Let no one doubt that this is a difficult and dangerous effort on which we have set out," the President said. "No one can foresee precisely what course it will take or what costs or casualties will be incurred."

"The path we have chosen for the present is full of hazards, as all paths are—but it is the one most consistent with our character and courage as a nation and our commitments around the world," he added.

"The cost of freedom is always high—but Americans have always paid it. And one path we shall never choose is the path of surrender or submission.

"Our goal is not the victory of

might but the vindication of right—not peace at the expense of freedom, but both peace and freedom, here in this hemisphere and, we hope, around the world. God willing, that goal will be achieved."

The President's speech did not actually start the naval blockade tonight. To meet the requirements of international law, the State Department will issue a formal proclamation late tomorrow, and that may delay the effectiveness of the action as long as another 24 hours.

Crisis Before Public

The speech laid before the American people a crisis that had gripped the highest officials here since last Tuesday, but had only begun to leak out to the public over the weekend. The President said it was at 9 A.M. Tuesday that he got the first firm intelligence report about the missile sites on Cuba.

Last month, he said, the Soviet Government publicly stated that its military equipment for Cuba was "exclusively for defensive purposes" and that the Soviet did not need retaliatory missile bases outside its own territory.

"That statement was false," Mr. Kennedy said.

Just last Thursday, he continued, the Soviet foreign minister, Andrei A. Gromyko, told him in a call at the White House that the Soviet Union "would never become involved" in building any offensive military capacity in Cuba.

"That statement was also false," the President said.

Appeal to Khrushchev

He made a direct appeal to Premier Khrushchev to abandon the Communist "course of world domination." An hour before the President spoke, a personal letter from him to Mr. Khrushchev was delivered to the Soviet government in Moscow.

Mr. Kennedy disclosed that he was calling for an immediate meeting of the Organ of Consultation of the Organization of American States to consider the crisis.

The O.A.S. promptly scheduled an emergency session for 9 A.M. tomorrow. State Department officials said they were confident of receiving the necessary 14 votes out of the 20 nations represented.

The President said the United States was prepared also to discuss the situation "in any other meeting that could be useful." This was taken as an allusion to a possible summit conference with Mr. Khrushchev.

But the President emphasized that discussion in any of these forums would be undertaken "without limiting our freedom of action." This meant that the United States was determined on this course no matter what any international organization —or even the United States' allies—might say.

Support From Congress

Congressional leaders of both parties, who were summoned to Washington today to be advised

Kennedy makes a televised report to the nation on the Cuban missile crisis from the Oval Office.

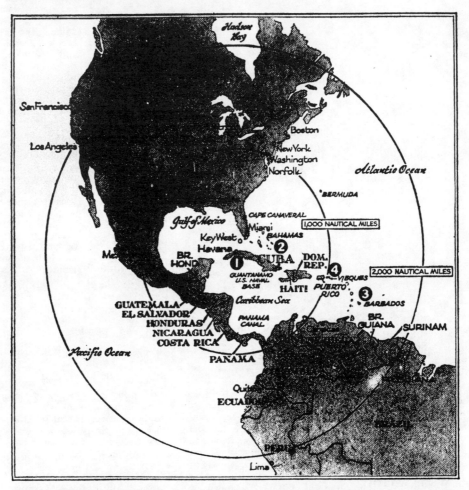

CUBAN EMERGENCY: Major points in the blockade of Cuba will be the harbor at Havana (1), the sea lanes that run through the Bahamas (2) and an arc extending from the Bahamas to Barbados (3). A landing at Vieques (4), which was to have been the climax of a United States training exercise, has been canceled. The inner circle, centered on Havana, indicates the range of medium-range ballistic missiles and the outer circle shows the range for intermediate range ballistic missiles. President Kennedy declared in his speech to the nation that sites for both types of missiles were being built in Cuba.

by the President of the crisis and his decision, gave him unanimous backing.

Mr. Kennedy went into considerable detail in his speech in outlining the nature of the military threat in Cuba, and this country's response.

He said "confirmed" intelligence indicates that the Cuban missile sites are of two types.

One kind, which his words implied were already or nearly completed, would be capable of handling medium-range ballistic missiles. The President said such missiles could carry nuclear weapons more than 1,000 nautical miles — to Washington, the Panama Canal, Cape Canaveral or Mexico City.

The second category of sites would be for intermediate range ballistics missiles, with a range of more than 2,000 miles. The President said they could hit "most of the major cities in the Western hemisphere" from Lima, Peru, to Hudson's Bay in Canada.

Mr. Kennedy declared:
"This urgent transformation of Cuba into an important strategic base by the presence of these large, long-range and clearly offensive weapons of sudden mass destruction constitutes an explicit threat to the peace and security of all the Americas."

He said the Soviet Union's action was "in flagrant and deliberate defiance" of the Rio (Inter-American) Pact of 1947, the United Nations Charter, Congressional resolution and his own public warnings to the Soviet Union.

October 23, 1962

Vessel Has Close Ties To the Kennedy Family

WASHINGTON, Oct. 26 (UPI)—The destroyer Joseph P. Kennedy Jr., which intercepted the Lebanese freighter Maruela today in the Cuban blockade ordered by President Kennedy, has more ties to the Kennedy family than just its name.

But first of all, there is the name. The President's older brother, Joseph, was a war hero and a navy flier. He was killed over Europe in 1944 while engaged in a deadly volunteer mission to fly a "drone" plane loaded with explosives that was to crash on a German V-2 rocket base.

The Navy decided to name a destroyer Joseph P. Kennedy Jr.

Robert F. Kennedy, now the Attorney General, volunteered for duty aboard. He got it— at Guantanamo Bay, Cuba, where the Joseph P. Kennedy Jr. had sailed on Feb. 4, 1946, for shakedown training.

The President has a model of the destroyer on display in the Fish Room of the White House.

October 27, 1962

U.S. AND SOVIET REACH ACCORD ON CUBA

By E. W. KENWORTHY

WASHINGTON, Oct. 28— President Kennedy and Premier Khrushchev reached apparent agreement today on a formula to end the crisis over Cuba and to begin talks on easing tensions in other areas.

Premier Khrushchev pledged the Soviet Union to stop work on its missile sites in Cuba, to dismantle the weapons and to crate them and take them home. All this would be done under verification of United Nations representatives.

President Kennedy, for his part, pledged the lifting of the Cuban arms blockade when the United Nations had taken the "necessary measures," and that the United States would not invade Cuba.

U. S. Conditions Met

Essentially this formula meets the conditions that President Kennedy set for the beginning of talks. If it is carried out, it would achieve the objective of the President in establishing the blockade last week: the removal of the Soviet missile bases in Cuba.

While officials were gratified at the agreement reached on United States terms, there was no sense either of triumph or jubilation. The agreement, they realized, was only the beginning. The terms of it were not nailed down and Soviet negotiators were expected to arrive at the United Nations with a "bag full of fine print."

Although Mr. Khrushchev mentioned verification of the dismantling by United Nations observers in today's note, sources here do not consider it unlikely that the Russians may suggest that the observers be under the procedures of the Security Council.

This would make their findings subject to a veto by the Soviet Union as one of the 11 members of the Council.

No Big Gains Envisioned

United States officials did not expect a Cuban settlement, if it materialized, to lead to any great breakthroughs on such problems as inspection for a nuclear test ban and disarmament.

On the other hand, it was thought possible that a Cuban settlement might set a precedent for limited reciprocal concessions in some areas.

The break in the crisis came dramatically early this morning after a night of steadily mounting fears that events were running ahead of diplomatic efforts to control them.

The break came with the arrival of a letter from Premier Khrushchev in which the Soviet leader again changed his course.

Friday night Mr. Khrushchev had sent a lengthy private letter to the President. Deep in it was the suggestion that the Soviet Union would remove its missiles from Cuba under supervision and not replace them if the United States would lift the blockade and give assurances that United States and other Western Hemisphere nations would not invade Cuba.

The President found this proposal generally acceptable and yesterday morning his aides were preparing a private reply. Then the Moscow radio broadcast the text of another letter that was on its way.

The second letter proposed that the Soviet Union remove its missiles from Cuba in return for the dismantling of United States missiles in Turkey. This was advanced as an equitable exchange.

Fearing that it would be viewed in this light by many neutral nations, the White House immediately postponed a reply to the first letter and issued a statement on the second.

The White House said that the "first imperative" was the removal of the threat of Soviet missiles. The United States would not consider "any proposals" until work was stopped on the Cuban bases, the weapons were "rendered inoperable," and further shipments of them were halted.

Then White House aides turned back to drafting a reply to the first letter. They hoped to persuade Mr. Khrushchev to stand by his first offer.

The President accepted the

first Khrushchev proposal as the basis for beginning talks. But he planted in it two warnings which, the White House hoped, would not be lost upon Mr. Khrushchev

Threat of Action Noted

First, he said the arrangement for putting into effect the Khrushchev plan could be completed in a "a couple of days" —a warning that the United States could take action to halt the work on the missile bases if Mr. Khrushchev did not order it stopped.

Second, the President said that if the work continued or if Mr. Khrushchev linked Cuba with broader questions of European security, the Cuban crisis would be intensified.

Just before 9 o'clock this morning, the Moscow radio said there would be an important announcement on the hour. It turned out to be a reply to Mr. Kennedy's letter of the night before.

Mr. Khrushchev said that in order to "complete with greater speed the liquidation of the conflict dangerous to the cause of peace," the Soviet Government had ordered work stopped on the bases in Cuba, and the dismantling, crating and return of the missiles.

Mr. Khrushchev said he trusted that, in return, "no attack will be made on Cuba — that no invasion will take place —not only by the United States, but also by other countries of the Western Hemisphere."

Kuznetzov to Negotiate

Mr. Khrushchev said that he was sending Vassily V. Kuznetzov, a First Deputy Foreign Minister to the United Nations to conduct negotiations for the Soviet Union. He arrived in New York tonight.

Without waiting for the formal delivery of the letter, the President issued a statement at noon, saying he welcomed Chairman Khrushchev's statesmanlike decision" an an "important and constructive contribution to peace."

Shortly before the statement was issued, the President flew by helicopter to Glen Ora, his country home in Middleburg, Va., to have lunch and he spent most of the afternoon with his wife and children.

All the communications this week between the two leaders — and there have been several more than have been made public — have been sent by the usual diplomatic route. First, they have been delivered to the Embassies, there translated, and send to the State Department or the Soviet Foreign office for delivery to Mr. Kennedy or Mr. Khrushchev.

Process Too Slow

This is a time-consuming process, and late this afternoon, the last section of Mr. Khrushchev's letter had not yet arrived at the White House when it was decided to make the President's reply public and speed it on its way.

The President said that he welcomed Mr. Khrushchev's

message because "developments were approaching a point where events could have become unmanageable."

Mr. Kennedy said:

"I think that you and I, with our heavy responsibilities for the maintenance of peace, were aware that developments were approaching a point where events could have become unmanageable. So I welcome this message and consider it an important contribution to peace."

He also stated that he regarded his letter of the night before and the Premier's reply as "firm undertakings" which both governments should carry out "promptly."

The President hoped that the "necessary measures" could be taken "at once" through the United Nations so that the quarantine could be removed on shipping.

All these matters, the President said, would be reported to members oft he Organization of American States, who "share a deep interest in a genuine peace in the Caribbean area."

And the President echoed Mr. Khrushchev's hope that the two nations could now turn their attention to disarmament "as it relates to the whole world and also to critical areas."

The President by tonight had not named the negotiator for the United States, but it was reported by authoritative sources that Adlai E. Stevenson, the head of the United States delegation at the United Nations, would get the assignment. The talks are expected to begin soon, probably tomorrow.

A spokesman at the State Department said in reply to questions:

"The quarantine remains in efefct but we don't anticipate any problems of interception since there are no ships moving into the quarantine area that appear to be carrying cargoes on the contraband list."

Fears About Castro

There was also some concern that Premier Fidel Castro, out of chagrin, might cause incidents over the United States surveillance flights.

Officials here believed that Dr. Castro was making a major effort to bring in extraneous issues, such as the evacuation of the United States base at Guantanamo Bay, to salvage his prestige.

However, the United States was not prepared to deal over the base, and the feeling here was that no other matters except the President's guarantee not to invade could be discussed until the dismantling of the missiles had been verified.

Officials emphasized today, as they reflected on the events of the week, that at all times the White House was trying to keep things on the track. At no time, they insisted, was any ultimatum delivered to Mr. Khrushchev, although he was made to understand that the missiles would be destroyed unless they were removed in a short time.

October 29, 1962

President and His Brother Give Salaries to Charity

By MARJORIE HUNTER

WASHINGTON, Nov. 14 — President Kennedy and his brother, Attorney General Robert F. Kennedy both donate their Government salaries to charity, sources close to the two men said today.

The President is paid $100,000 a year. The Attorney General is paid $25,000.

President Kennedy and other members of his family are independently wealthy. The President's wealth has been estimated in the millions of dollars, perhaps as much as $10,000,000.

Identical trust funds for all the Kennedy children were set up in 1926, 1936 and 1949 by their father, Joseph P. Kennedy.

White House sources said today that President Kennedy had donated his Government salary to charity ever since entering Congress in 1947. He served in the House six years and in the Senate eight years.

This was confirmation of an article today in The Minneapolis Tribune and The Des Moines Register.

Justice Department spokesmen said later that the Attorney General also gave his salary to charity.

It is considered likely that another brother, Edward M. Kennedy, recently elected Senator from Massachusetts, will turn his $22,500-a-year salary over to charity.

The President's salary is subject to withholding tax, as is that of all Government employes. However, White House sources said that the President donated the full $100,000 to charity, not just the amount after taxes.

In addition to salary, the President receives $50,000 a year to defray expenses resulting from official duties. This sum is taxable. He also receives up to $40,000 a year, nontaxable, for travel and official entertainment.

Another wealthy President, Herbert Hoover, donated his salary to charity and to supplementing the salaries of underpaid help.

President Kennedy's pay during his first year in the White House was actually slightly less than $100,000 because he did not take office until Jan. 20, 1961. He is paid monthly.

At the time of the inauguration White House aides said the President had an annual income of about $100,000, after taxes, from trust funds established by his father.

Two of major trust funds provide that parts of the principal go to President Kennedy and his six brothers and sisters when they reach certain ages.

The President received a fourth of his one-seventh interest in the 1926 and 1936 trust funds when he reached 40 years of age. Another fourth of his share went to him last May 29, when he reached the age of 45.

White House aides said at the time President Kennedy took office that he had converted into Federal, state and municipal bonds all the capital over which he had control.

The charities to which the President donates his funds were not identified by White House sources.

Sargent Shriver, a brother-in-law of the President, is on the Government payroll, too, in his capacity as director of the Peace Corps. However, he receives just a dollar a year.

November 15, 1962

'JACKIE' STORIES RAISE PROTESTS

White House Mail Decries Articles on Mrs. Kennedy in Movie Magazines

'COVER GIRL' QUESTION

As a 'Public Property' She Is Without Control Over Spate of Publicity

By MARJORIE HUNTER

WASHINGTON, Dec. 2—Mrs. John F. Kennedy has become the favorite "cover girl" of magazines that friends say she would never dream of reading.

With newsstands across the country plastered with movie magazines featuring pictures and stories about Mrs. Kennedy, the White House is busy answering letters of protest.

Why, the writers ask, does Mrs. Kennedy allow such stories?

The answer, White House aides say, is that nothing can be done about it. Mrs. Kennedy is in the public domain. On the day her husband was inaugurated as President, she said:

"I felt as though I had just turned into a piece of public property. It's frightening to lose your anonymity at 31."

A story about Mrs. Kennedy some months ago was prophetic. The cover of Photoplay carried her picture and blazing headlines: "Jacqueline Kennedy — America's newest star. What you should know about her fears."

More of the Same

Other movie magazines took up the cry.

Modern Screen: "Jackie turns her back on Hollywood." Screen Stories: "The story about Jackie Kennedy's movie." Movie, TV Secrets: "Another baby for Jackie. The wonderful news all America is waiting for!"

Photoplay, again: "Minister attacks Jackie."

As more and more of these stories appeared—rivaled only by the play given to Elizabeth Taylor and the late Marilyn Monroe—the White House mail grew heavier.

A girl from Fairfield, Pa., wrote:

"I am 14 years old and I admire Mrs. Kennedy very much.

I would greatly appreciate it if you could give me the answer to a question that puzzles me very much. Why does Mrs. Kennedy allow stories about 'How I fell in love' and similar stories to be printed in movie and 'confession' magazines? It is rather difficult to think of the First Lady in the same class as movie stars."

'Romance' Magazine Cited

A man in Inglewood, Calif., wrote:

"I was unpleasantly surprised to find our First Lady's picture on the cover of a popular movie magazine . . . The real blow, however, came when Mrs. Kennedy's picture appeared on one of those contemptible, cheap, trashy 'romance' magazines.

A woman in Paterson, N. J., declared that she was "shocked" and "angered" to find Mrs. Kennedy's picture on the cover of a movie magazine. She added, "I call your attention to this because I feel you are in a position to do something about this."

To these letters, and others, White House aides send replies stating:

"As Mrs. Kennedy is a public figure, articles can be published about her without her prior approval. Furthermore, there are numerous photographs of her which are in the public domain and which require no clearance from the White House to be published.

"I can only say that none of the magazines in question have, even as a courtesy, informed the White House of their intended articles on the First Lady, but had the White House been informed in advance about some of these stories, I doubt very much that the White House would have approved them."

The December issue of Mod-

ern Screen, proclaiming "Jackie turns her back on Hollywood," features a cover picture of Mrs. Kennedy, dressed in slacks and a striped jersey with her long hair hanging limply.

The story states that Mrs. Kennedy did not accompany her husband on trips to Hollywood. The magazine concludes that she wants to avoid glaring Hollywood publicity.

Another picture of Mrs. Kennedy, with a pink scarf tied around her head, appears on the cover of the December issue of Screen Stories. Inside is a story about the filming of her India and Pakistan trip.

The December issue of Photoplay carries a cover picture of Elizabeth Taylor. But it also carries headlines:

"Minister attacks Jackie. Has she gone too far—or has he? Vote today!".

The Movie-TV Secrets' "exclusive" on "Another baby for Jackie" merely recounts the birth of John F. Kennedy Jr. two years ago and speculates on the growth of the Kennedy family.

"The fondest dream of the American people," the magazine concludes, is that Jack and Jackie will be able to have the large family they want and the health and good luck they so richly deserve."

And there are other stories, in Teen Tempo, TV Guide, Movie World and others.

A new purse-size magazine— The Jacqueline Touch—is devoted entirely to Mrs. Kennedy. It carries her picture on the cover and announces:

"The First Lady's charm, beauty and fashions: How you can adapt 'The Jacqueline Touch' to your life."

Illustrations inside show how to roll up hair, apply make-up and greet visiting dignitaries.

Caroline Kennedy, too, has become a cover girl. The December issue of Motion Picture, carrying a picture of Caroline, has a headline:

"How long can they hide the truth from Caroline Kennedy?"

The story inside, illustrated with many pictures of the entire Kennedy family, asks:

"How long can they, her parents, hide the truth from Caroline Kennedy—that she is a celebrity, a star in her own right, and that father and mother aren't just like the family next door or the folks down the street?"

December 3, 1962

President Says Record 'Sounded Like Teddy'

WASHINGTON, Dec. 12—President Kennedy brought down the house at his press conference with the comment on "The First Family," the hit record parodying his voice.

"I thought it sounded more like Teddy than it did me."

Teddy is, of course, the President's younger brother, Edward, the new Democratic Senator from Massachusetts.

The question put at the conference whether the President had read the various publications poking fun at him and his family, or had heard the record.

December 13, 1962

'Jacqueline' Is Catching On As New Name for Babies

WASHINGTON, Dec. 20 (AP)—Representative Peter Frelinghuysen Jr., Republican of New Jersey, said that he had sent five Government infant-care books this month to parents in his heavily Republican Congressional District who had named their daughters Jacqueline That name was rarely mentioned in birth announcements from the district before President Kennedy, whose wife's name is Jacqueline, took office, an aide said.

December 21, 1962

WASHINGTON, June 11—President Kennedy told the nation tonight that it faced a "moral crisis" as a result of the rising tide of Negro discontent.

"This is a problem which faces us all in every city of the North as well as the South," Mr. Kennedy said in a brief address televised by all three national networks.

It is a time to act, the President said. He promised to send to Congress next week sweeping legislation to speed school desegregation and open public facilities to every American, regardless of color.

Problem 'Must Be Solved'

Above all, Mr. Kennedy solemnly told the millions of citizens watching him speak from the White House, the problem of the Negro's place in American life "must be solved in the homes of every American across the country."

The objective of every citizen, the President said, must be "for every American to enjoy the privilege of being American without regard to his race or color"—to be treated "as one would wish his children to be treated."

This is, he said, "a matter which concerns this country and what it stands for, and in meeting it I ask the support of all our citizens."

He asked it, the President said, because "this nation for all its hopes and all its boasts will not be fully free until its citizens are free."

Makes Broad Appeal

Mr. Kennedy's address, arranged late today, was made in part as the result of the successful desegregation of the University of Alabama. But the President seized the occasion to make a broad appeal that Negroes and liberals of both parties had been urging upon him for weeks.

The Administration had laid plans well in advance for meeting the Alabama crisis. An executive order federalizing the Alabama National Guard was ready for Mr. Kennedy's signature when the White House received word of Gov. George C. Wallace's defiance of court orders not to interfere with desegregation of the university.

Mr. Kennedy's address was one of the most emotional speeches yet delivered by a President who has often been criticized as being too "cool" and intellectual. Near the end of his talk, Mr. Kennedy appeared to be speaking without a text, and there was a fervor in his voice when he talked of the plight of some Americans.

Education Is Cited

"Today there are Negroes unemployed—two or three times as many compared to whites," he said. "Inadequate education, moving into the large cities, unable to find work, young people particularly out of work, without hope, denied equal

PRESIDENT SEES A 'MORAL CRISIS'

Asks Help of Citizens to Assure Equality of Rights to All

By TOM WICKER

rights, denied the opportunity to eat at a restaurant or a lunch counter, or go to a movie theater, denied the right to a decent education, denied—almost today—the right to attend a state university even though qualified."

Mr. Kennedy devoted only a few opening sentences of his 15-minute speech to the Alabama events.

"This afternoon," he began, "following a series of threats and defiant statements, the presence of Alabama National Guardsmen was required" to carry out court orders admitting to the university at Tuscaloosa "two clearly qualified young Alabama residents who happened to have been born Negro."

The President congratulated other Alabama students on their peaceful behavior and said:

"I hope that every American regardless of where he lives will stop and examine his conscience about this and other related incidents."

This is necessary, the President said, because of the position of the Negro in American life, which Mr. Kennedy described as follows:

"The Negro baby born in America today . . . has about one-half as much chance of completing high school as a white baby, born in the same place, on the same day; one-third as much chance of completing college; one-third as much chance of becoming a professional man; twice as much chance of becoming unemployed; about one-seventh as much chance of earning $10,000 a year; a life expectancy which is seven years shorter and the prospects of earning only half as much."

To white Americans, Mr. Kennedy addressed these questions:

"Who among us would then be content with the counsels of patience and delay?"

"Who among us would be content to have the color of his skin changed and stand in his place?"

The Negro's plight is not entirely a sectional situation, Mr. Kennedy emphasized repeatedly.

"The fires of frustration and discontent are burning in every city, North and South, where legal remedies are not at hand," he said.

"Difficulties over segregation and discrimination exist in every city, in every state of the Union, producing in many cities a rising tide of discontent that threatens the public safety."

Not a Partisan Matter

Nor is it a matter of partisan politics, Mr. Kennedy said, in what appeared to be a bid for bipartisan support of the measures he said he would send to Congress next week.

"This is not even a legal or legislative issue alone," the President said. "It is better to settle these matters in the courts than on the streets, and new laws are needed at every level.

"But law alone cannot make men see right. We are confronted primarily with a moral issue. It is as old as the Scriptures and is as clear as the American Constitution."

Mr. Kennedy prodded Congress as the only one of the three constitutional branches of Government that, he said, had not fully committed itself to "the proposition that race has no place in American life or law."

Necessary legislative measures to establish legal remedies for the wrongs of Negro citizens "must be provided at this session" of Congress, Mr. Kennedy insisted.

For, he said, "unless the Congress acts, their only remedy is the street."

Asks Accommodation Law

A public accommodations law is needed, the President said, because denial of the "elementary right" to be treated equally in hotels, restaurants and other establishments "is an arbitrary indignity that no American in 1963 should have to endure, but many do."

The law should be nationwide, he said, because some communities fear to move alone. But he noted that at least 75 cities had taken steps in the last two weeks to desegregate public facilities.

The President said he also would ask Congress to empower the Federal Government to "participate more fully in lawsuits" to end school segregation.

He pointed out that the desegregation of the University of Alabama put a Negro in a state-supported institution in every one of the 50 states.

"But the pace is very slow," the President said. And he noted that many Negroes did not have the financial resources or were too subject to harassment to initiate desegregation suits on their own.

Again and again, the President returned to the theme of the moral necessity for white Americans to treat Negro Americans as equals. In that respect, his was the broadest appeal on civil rights ever addressed to the nation by a President.

"We face," he said, "a moral crisis as a country and a people. It cannot be met by repressive police action. It cannot be left to increased demonstrations in the streets. It cannot be quieted by token moves or talk.

"It is a time to act in the Congress, in your state, and local legislative body, and above all, in all of our daily lives."

This was the President's prescription for such action:

"It is not enough to pin the blame on others, to say this is a problem of one section of the country or another, or deplore the facts that we face.

"A great change is at hand, and our task, our obligation is to make that revolution, that change, peaceful and constructive for all."

June 12, 1963

Random Notes From All Over: 'This IS the Attorney General'

WASHINGTON, June 23—Attorney General Robert E. Kennedy, a do-it-yourself man, recently picked up the telephone and called a businessman to ask him to come to the White House for a meeting to discuss lowering racial barriers.

"Yes, this IS the Attorney General," Mr. Kennedy said. "Yes, yes, I tell you I AM the Attorney General."

After a pause, the Attorney General said, "Very well," and hung up.

"That guy thinks I'm Vaughn Meader," he said. "He's going to call me back just to make sure."

Mr. Meader is the comedian who specializes in imitating the Kennedy brothers.

Practicing What They Preach

Speaking of the Attorney General, he and his wife have withdrawn applications for three of their boys at a Washington private school because the school, Landon, has admitted no Negro pupils.

The boys, Joesph, 10 years old, Robert Jr., 9, and David, 8, are in Our Lady of Victory, a Washington parochial school that is integrated. The Attorney General and Mrs. Kennedy hope to move them because the school is so crowded. There are about 50 children in a classroom.

The Kennedys had been told that Landon did not exclude Negroes. However, it appeared on further inquiry that while Landon has no official policy against Negroes, some have been turned down for admission and none accepted.

June 24, 1963

BERLIN, June 26—President Kennedy, inspired by a tumultuous welcome from more than a million of the inhabitants of this isolated and divided city, declared today he was proud to be "a Berliner."

He said his claim to being a Berliner was based on the fact that "all free men, wherever they may live, are citizens of Berlin."

In a rousing speech to 150,-000 West Berliners crowded before the City Hall, the President said anyone who thought "we can work with the Communists" should come to Berlin.

However, three hours later, in a less emotional setting, he reaffirmed his belief that the great powers must work together "to preserve the human race."

Warning on Communism

His earlier rejection of dealing with the Communists was a warning against trying to "ride the tiger" of popular fronts that unite democratic and Communist forces, Mr. Kennedy explained in an interpolation in a prepared speech.

The President's City Hall speech was the emotional high point of a spectacular welcome accorded the President by West Berlin. He saluted the city as the front line and shining example of humanity's struggle for freedom.

Those who profess not to understand the great issues between the free world and the Communist world or who think Communism is the wave of the future should come to Berlin, he said.

In his later speech, at the Free University of Berlin, President Kennedy returned firmly to the theme of his address at American University in Washington June 10 in which he called for an attempt to end the cold war.

'Wounds to Heal'

"When the possibilities of reconciliation appear, we in the West will make it clear that we are not hostile to any people or system, provided that they choose their own destiny without interfering with the free choice of others," he said.

"There will be wounds to heal and suspicions to be eased on both sides," he added. "The difference in living standards will have to be reduced—by leveling up, not down. Fair and effective agreements to end the arms race must be reached."

The changes might not come tomorrow, but "our efforts for a real settlement must continue," he said.

Then the President introduced an extemporaneous paragraph into his prepared text.

"As I said this morning, I am not impressed by the opportunities open to popular fronts throughout the world," he said. "I do not believe that any democrat can successfully ride that tiger. But I do believe in the necessity of great powers working together to preserve the human race."

Nuances of policy, however, were not the center of attention today in this city of at least 2,200,000 alert people. For them the only matter of importance was to give a heartfelt and spectacular welcome to the United States President and to see a youthful-looking smiling man obviously respond to their warmth.

Pierre Salinger, the President's press secretary, said the reception here was "the greatest he has had anywhere."

Along the route from Tegel airport to the United States mission headquarters in the southwest corner of Berlin, waving, cheering crowds lined every foot of the way.

Banners Hung at Gate

The crowds must have nearly equaled the population of the city, but many persons waved once and then sped ahead to greet Mr. Kennedy again.

Only once in a jammed eight hours, during which he was almost uninterruptedly on a television screen, did Mr. Kennedy fail to dominate the scene.

Shortly before noon he approached Brandenburg Gate where he caught his first view of the Communist-built wall that partitions Berlin.

The President had been scheduled to gaze over the wall through the gate onto Unter den Linden, once the main avenue of the German capital. However, the five arches of the gate were covered by huge red banners, blocking his view there of East Berlin.

The cloth barrier was put up by East Berlin officials last night.

Just across the wall from the podium where the President's party stood was a neatly-lettered yellow sign in English. It cited the Allied pledges at the 1945 Yalta conference to uproot Nazism and militarism from Germany and to see it would never again endanger world peace.

Asserting that the pledges had been fulfilled in East Germany, the sign called on President Kennedy to see that they were fulfilled in West Germany and West Berlin.

The President appeared not to read the words, busying himself with a map indicating key points along the wall.

Sees East Berliners

At Checkpoint Charlie, the United States-controlled crossing point to East Berlin on the Friedrichstrasse, Mr. Kennedy had an unobstructed view several hundred yards into the eastern sector.

About 300 yards away, well beyond the 100-yard forbidden zone decreed by the Communists last week, he glimpsed a small group of East Berliners attracted by his presence. Though he could not hear them, they cheered.

In West Berlin there was no Communist attempt to embarrass the President. The problem for West Berlin's 13,500-man police force and the President's Secret Service guards was to restrain excited crowds from rushing to the President to shake his hand or hand him gifts.

On his arrival this morning at Tegel airport protocol went wrong when Mr. Kennedy first grasped the hand of Chancellor Adenauer instead of that of Gen. Eduard Toulouse, the French commandant in West Berlin. The airport is in the French sector, and technically under French sovereignty.

Brandt Gives Reassurance

Mayor Willy Brandt, greeting the President, said West Berliners did not expect constantly renewed assertions of allied guarantees "because we trust our friends."

The President responded by saying: "The legendary morale and spirit of the people of West Berlin has lit a fire throughout the world. I am glad to come to this city. It reassures us."

At the first of six stops on the tour—the modernistic Congress Hall where the West German construction workers union was in convention, Mr. Kennedy told the union delegates a free trade union movement was a guarantee and proof of democracy. He urged West German unions to help newly independent countries establish a strong free union movement.

The Presidential motorcade arrived 15 minutes behind schedule at Schöneberger Rathaus, West Berlin's city hall.

Mr. Kennedy's speech was emotional and the West Berliners responded in like manner. Several times they chanted "Kennedy! Kennedy!"

The only break in the day of speech-making and waving to the crowds was a luncheon in the city hall given by Mayor Brandt.

From there the President drove to the Free University, endowed in 1948 by the Ford Foundation, where Mr. Kennedy was made an honorary citizen of the university. This is a traditional form of honor, dating from the days when European universities enjoyed autonomous political rights.

The motorcade went next to Clay Allee, named after Gen. Lucius D. Clay, defender of West Berlin during the blockade 15 years ago and who, as a member of the Kennedy party, won especial cheers today. There, the United States community of 15,000 soldiers and diplomats and members of their families greeted the President.

"No beleaguered garrison serves in comparable conditions under conditions so dangerous and with adversaries so numerous," the President told the soldiers.

"Your role is to commit the United States. But you are more than hostages. You are in a sense a real force, for you represent the will and perseverance of your fellow Americans."

This was the final stop and the motorcade then sped back to the airport, where, after a brief farewell, the President took off for Ireland.

June 27, 1963

Kennedy Prodded Anew On Hat He Doesn't Wear

LONDON, July 5 (AP)—A British fashion magazine today stepped up its campaign to persuade President Kennedy to wear a hat and pointedly asked him how a hatless man could properly greet a lady.

"How does the President acknowledge such an encounter?" asked Tailor and Cutter in an editorial, which the editor said he was sending to the White House.

"The deft touch of a raised hat, politely pinched between thumb and forefinger and held for a hesitant moment over the wearer's heart would bring a bright spark of gallantry to those modern diplomatic moves which seem to have lost so much of their old-world glamor in the current rush for time-saving practicalities," the magazine suggested.

HYANNIS PORT, Mass., July 5 (AP)—"What, again?" was the way one White House staff member reacted to a report of Tailor and Cutter's campaign.

Mr. Kennedy does carry a hat now and then, occasionally putting it on. Usually it's a gray felt.

Officially, the President's associates were silent.

July 6, 1963

KENNEDY AND KHRUSHCHEV CALL PACT A STEP TO PEACE BUT NOT A WAR PREVENTIVE

PRESIDENT ON TV

By TOM WICKER

WASHINGTON, July 26 — President Kennedy, speaking to the nation tonight in a "spirit of hope," described the treaty for a limited nuclear test ban as a "victory for mankind" in its pursuit of peace.

The treaty, initialed in Moscow yesterday by representatives of the United States, the Soviet Union and Britain, would ban nuclear tests in the atmosphere, in space and under water.

Describing the agreement as a "shaft of light cut into the darkness" of cold-war discords and tensions, Mr. Kennedy nonetheless warned that it was "not the millennium."

"It will not resolve all conflicts, or cause the Communists to forego their ambitions, or eliminate the dangers of war," he said. "It will not reduce the need for arms or allies or programs of assistance to others.

'A Step Away from War'

"But it is an important first step—a step toward peace—a step toward reason — a step away from war."

If "this short and simple treaty" could now be made a symbol of "the end of one era and the beginning of another," the President said, it could lead on to further reductions of tensions and broader areas of agreement.

Among them, he suggested, might be "controls on preparations for a surprise attack, or on numbers and types of armaments."

"There could be further limitations on the spread of nuclear weapons," he added.

The important point, Mr. Kennedy said, is that "the effort to seek new agreements will go forward."

The President appeared on all three national television networks and his words also were heard on four radio networks. He spoke from his office in the West Executive Wing of the White House.

Immediately after the speech, he departed for a weekend at Hyannis Port, Mass. There he will confer tomorrow with Under Secretary of State W. Averell Harriman, the United States representative to the suc-

cessful nuclear test ban talks, which began July 15 in Moscow.

Mr. Kennedy spoke with, unaccustomed slowness, as if to emphasize the gravity of the matters he discussed.

One by one, mostly from a prepared text but from notes at the conclusion of his speech, he made his points, the most important of which were as follows:

¶The treaty did not enganger the national security and the nation would continue both underground testing and its readiness to resume all testing if required.

¶But the treaty offered a promising opportunity to negotiate further relaxations of the cold war and to avoid the ultimate horror of nuclear war.

¶Therefore the Senate should ratify it and the American people should support it, even though it signified no more than a beginning of what remained a hard road to peace.

"There is an old Chinese proverb that says, "a journey of a thousand miles must begin with a first step,'" the President said in conclusion.

'First Step' Is Urged

Looking up from his notes and gazing directly into the cameras, Mr. Kennedy said slowly and distinctly:

"My fellow Americans—let us take the first step."

With an unusual ring of emotion in his voice, he also painted a grim picture of the possibilities of nuclear war.

"If only one thermonuclear bomb were to be dropped on any American, Russian or other city—whether it was launched by accident or design, by a madman or an enemy, by a large nation or a small, from any corner of the world—that one bomb could release more destructive force on the inhabitants of that one helpless city than all the bombs dropped during the Second World War," he said.

And in a full-scale nuclear exchange "lasting less than 60 minutes," the President added, more than 300,000,000 Americans, Europeans and Russians would perish.

Mr. Kennedy also quoted Premier Khrushchev's warning to the Chinese Communist that, in such an event, survivors in a devastated world "would envy the dead."

Reassurance Is Offered

Looking beyond American shores, the President also sought to reassure the nation's allies in two important respects.

First, he said, in any subsequent negotiations to meet the desire of the Soviet Union for a nonaggression pact or declaration, there would be "full consultation with our allies and full attention to their interests."

To President de Gaulle of France, which now possesses nuclear weapons, there was a special word. Mr. Kennedy linked France with the United States, the Soviet Union and Britain as "the four current nuclear powers."

These powers, he said, "have a great obligation to use whatever time remains to prevent the spread of nuclear weapons, to persuade other countries not to test, transfer, acquire, possess or produce such weapons."

France is not a party to the three-power test ban and has given no indication that she is ready to become one. Her accession to it would be regarded here as a long step toward prevention of the proliferation of nuclear weapons to still more countries.

"I ask you to stop and think for a moment what it would mean to have nuclear weapons in many hands—in the hands of countries large and small, stable and unstable, responsible and irresponsible, scattered throughout the world," Mr. Kennedy said, perhaps to General de Gaulle.

"There would be no rest for anyone then, no stability, no real security, and no chance of effective disarmament. There would only be increased chances of accidental war, and an increased necessity for the great powers to involve themselves in otherwise local conflicts."

A "small but significant" number of nations already had the capability to buy or produce nuclear weapons, the President said, but, o nthe other hand, "already we have heard from a number of countries who wish to join with us promptly."

Mr. Kennedy dwelt at length on the subject of national security. He conceded the possibility that secret tests might be conducted in outer space, but downgraded the risks inherent in such tests.

Tests Hard to Conceal

If necessary, he said, means of detecting such tests could be constructed. And, in any case, he added, "Tests which might be conducted so far out in space, which cannot be conducted more easily and efficiently and legally underground, would necessarily be of such magnitude that they would be extremely difficult to conceal."

But secret violation or sudden withdrawal from the treaty is possible, he said, and therefore "our own vigilance and strength must be maintained, as we remain ready to withdraw and to resume all forms of testing, if we must."

Underlying this statement was the fact that some United States testing will continue underground and that the remainder of the testing apparatus of the United States will be kept in readiness. Tests of peaceful applications of nuclear energy will continue, too, 'eading, it is believed here, to a number of gains in this field within five years.

It is also believed in Washington that Soviet underground testing capability lags behind that of the United States and cannot be brought to parity in less than six months to a year.

The strategic view here is that neither side will be able to make gains in weaponry under the treaty sufficient to alter the balance of power.

Risks Held Convincing

The President stated his belief that "the far greater risks" of unrestricted testing, the nuclear arms race, atmospheric pollution and nuclear war would convince all parties to the treaty that observing it would be "a matter of their own self-interest."

For the United States, he said, the treaty would be "safer by far" than an arms race.

The President also spoke with great feeling about the hazards of radioactive fallout to children yet unborn.

"The loss of even one human life, or the malformation of even one baby, who may be born long after we are gone, should be of concern to us all," Mr. Kennedy said.

"Our children and grandchildren are not merely statistics toward which we can be indifferent."

"And children," he added, "have no lobby here in Washington."

The President urged full discussion of all these matters in the Senate and among citizens.

"A document which may mark an historic and constructive opportunity for the world deserves an historic and constructive debate," he said.

July 27, 1963

KENNEDY INFANT DIES AT HOSPITAL

BOSTON, Friday, Aug. 9— The new baby boy of President and Mrs. Kennedy died early today, the White House announced at 4:26 A.M. The baby, born Wednesday, had been named Patrick Bouvier Kennedy.

The White House press secretary, Pierre Salinger, placed the time of death at 4:04 A.M.

"The struggle of the baby boy to keep breathing was too much for his heart," Mr. Salinger said.

The President, who spent the night at the Children's Hospital Medical Center, was awakened by doctors at 2:10 A.M.

From that time until the baby's death, Mr. Salinger said, its condition grew worse.

The President's brother, Robert F. Kennedy, the Attorney General, was notified two minutes later at his hotel. He left immediately for the hospital.

With the President when the baby died were Robert Kennedy and David F. Powers of Boston, a Presidential assistant.

Mr. Salinger said the President plans to fly to Otis Air Force Base leaving about 9:15 A. M., to see Mrs. Kennedy.

The baby was christened shortly after birth by Caesarean section early Wednesday afternoon. The baby, 5½ weeks premature, weighed 4 pounds, 10 ounces at birth.

Respiratory distress due to its lungs not being fully developed was apparent to physicians immediately.

In medical language, its ailment was diagnosed as idiopathic respiratory syndrome. In non-medical language, this is a respiratory problem which causes trouble in breathing. It is considered not uncommon in premature births.

It was the failure of the baby's heart, its struggle to keep breathing too much, that caused death, Mr. Salinger's statement indicated.

Shortly after his birth at the Otis Air Force Base hospital, the baby was brought to Children's Medical Center here by ambulance, because of the Boston hospital's extraordinarily fine equipment.

Rose Kennedy Tells of Her Retarded Daughter

Recalls How Little Aid Was Available 40 Years Ago

By EDITH EVANS ASBURY

The woman who is referring to the President of the United States when she says "My son, Jack," can speak today, a little less painfully than before of another of her nine children, Rosemary.

There were years when Mrs. Joseph P. Kennedy could not bear to speak to outsiders about her eldest daughter, who is 44 years old but who has failed to develop adult mentality. And she still finds it difficult.

Today her son will sign the first national legislation adopted to combat mental retardation. And Mrs. Rose Fitzgerald Kennedy hopes that from now on, there will be more public support and research to help other mothers and other Rosemarys.

The legislation, passed by the House last week, authorizes a $329 million program to deal with mental retardation through the construction of community health centers and through research and treatment.

Rosemary was the third of the nine Kennedy children, and Mrs. Kennedy recalled her daughter's childhood in an interview this week, in her New York apartment with the Columbia Broadcasting System and this reporter.

She mentioned the six later children "deliberately," Mrs. Kennedy said, explaining that she wanted mothers to know that having one retarded child does not mean that later ones will not be normal.

Sympathy Needed

Mrs. Kennedy, an energetic woman with blue eyes and black hair barely touched with gray, spoke of the need to extend sympathy to mothers of retarded children and to help them face the problem openly.

When it first became obvious that Rosemary was slower than her brothers in learning to crawl, walk, read and write, "there was very little help available, even for a family with our resources," Mrs. Kennedy said.

"I went first to the family physician," she recalled, "then to two psychologists at Harvard then to a Catholic priest who was a psychologist in Washington, and to every source they suggested. But at that time, nobody knew much about mental retardation, what steps could be taken."

As Rosemary grew, she wanted to go out in a boat alone, as her brothers and sisters did, although she was unable to steer. But the large family managed to include her in tennis and other games.

At dances, and parties, she was not as popular as her sisters and "that would upset her," Mrs. Kennedy said. "And as we all know, a mother gets more upset than the child."

In their determination to keep Rosemary as a member of the family circle, they presented her along with her sister Kathleen to the King and Queen of England while Mr. Kennedy was Ambassador to the Court of St. James's.

However, the fact that she could not lead a normal life had to be faced, and Rosemary was admitted to a special institution.

"People used to be ashamed of a mentally retarded child," Mrs. Kennedy said. "That's not true today. People don't think a child should be shunted away, and not mentioned."

Mrs. Kennedy told of the family foundation that has given more than $16.5 million since 1946 to hospitals, institutions, day-care centers and research projects in the field of mental retardation. The foundation now has 18 centers around the nation, she added.

She also talked exuberantly about her other children.

"There were so many" she said. "They were all so different." Of her other children, Robert is now the Attorney General; Edward, the junior Senator from Massachusetts; Pat, the wife of the actor Peter Lawford; Eunice, the wife of Sargent Shriver, head the Peace Corps; Jean, now Mrs. Stephen E. Smith and head of a fund-raising drive in New York for mental retardation.

"Jack, of course, was a prodigious reader," she added, when speaking of the President, and this "gave him a wonderful background of history and knowledge."

Since they all had "the same traditions, the same father and mother," Mrs. Kennedy said, she could not understand why they were all so different. And, she added, "they never fought or got jealous. They even like their in-laws."

'We Want to Know'

"In our family," she confided in a rush of words, "if you are not doing anything you are just left in a corner. We want to know where you have been and did you see Tito and what did he do and why did he do it."

Mrs. Kennedy, a slender figure in a simple black dress, a double strand of large, matched pearls and pearl and diamond earrings, clasped and unclasped her hands delightedly.

But in the midst of reminiscing about the family in England she called a halt to the interview, signaling the C.B.S.-TV cameramen who were filming this portion of it.

In England when her husband was Ambassador to the Court of St. James's, there were nine children. The oldest, Joseph P. Kennedy Jr., was killed during

World War II. Kathleen, Lady Hartington, died in a plane crash. The former Ambassador is incapacitated as a result of a stroke. Rosemary now lives in a Catholic institution in Wisconsin.

"That's all, that's all," Mrs. Kennedy said firmly. "I don't want to be interviewed about the family. I only want to talk about mental retardation.

"It's hard to talk about Rosemary," she said, sadly. "I could not do it years ago. But I want people to know it should be talked about. Not hidden. That there is hope, now."

October 31, 1963

WASHINGTON, Nov. 14—There is a vague feeling of doubt and disappointment in the country about President Kennedy's first term.

A reporter who asks about him in unfamiliar and varied communities comes away with a paradoxical impression. This is that he is not, as he is inclined to believe, in danger of defeat. The situation is more complex and disturbing than that. One has the distinct impression that the American people are going to reelect him, probably by a wide margin, but don't quite believe in him.

It is not easy to explain this paradox. Part of it is that the opposition is divided and weak. Part of it is that he is an attractive personality, dealing with problems beyond the wit of normal men. And part of it is that the more people feel that the big complex problems of government are beyond their comprehension the more they are inclined to go along with the man in the White House, no matter who he is and even if they don't understand what he's doing.

The Fatal Gap

A great many people respond to questions about the President with surprise and even astonishment, as if their opinions had nothing to do with Kennedy. And this is precisely the problem. The President in Washington seems a world apart. He talks about things like the balance of payments, and international "liquidity," and multilateral forces, and the "saturation" problem of antimissile missiles, and all this sounds important, but mysterious and remote.

He has touched the intellect of the country but not the heart. He has informed but not inspired the nation. He is undoubtedly the most popular political figure of the day, but he has been lucky in his competition. Or so it seems after an informal survey from Alabama to the Canadian border.

"I don't know what he's talking about most of the time, but I'm for him," an insurance salesman said in a suburb of New York. "All I know," said a carpenter in Cleveland, "is that we have work and peace."

The politicians from Birmingham to Cleveland and even north of the border in Ontario remark on this popular tendency to look at large political and economic problems in personal and even selfish terms.

Vietnam and Berlin are discussed as "Kennedy's problems," and one gets the impression that he can do almost anything with them he likes (provided he doesn't get into a big war), but new tax levies for schools are a matter of primary interest and concern, to be supported if you have kids in school and usually to be opposed if you don't.

The period since the war has been a time of exceptional change and more people now find themselves in a stranger environment than ever before. When they talk freely about it, and most of them are remarkably open and voluble even with strangers, they sound anxious about the atmosphere in which their children are growing up and even vaguely dissatisfied with the material possessions they have worked so hard to acquire.

This comes out occasionally in little spasms of criticism of the high society around the White House. It is not a general reaction, but there is clearly a feeling in the country, often expressed by middle-aged women, that the Kennedys are setting standards that are too fancy, too fast, and as one woman said in Philadelphia, "too European."

The popular questions that agitate Washington, however, do not seem to worry people out in the country to quite the same extent. For example, the case of Bobby Baker, with its overtones of corruption and undertones of sex, has apparently not made much of an impression on public opinion as yet, and if one mentions Secretary of the Navy Korth, who conducted his private business from his public office, few people seem to remember who he is.

Aside from the President himself, Senator Goldwater appears to be the only politician who inspires much emotion, pro or con, and most of those who talk enthusiastically about him spend most of their time damning "the Kennedys."

Not since the days of Franklin Roosevelt have there been so many men's-club stories in circulation against "that man in the White House."

Power of Publicity

In this atmosphere Kennedy dominates the field. He makes the news. He has the headlines. He is on the television screens more than all his opponents combined, and while there is clearly some opposition to his civil rights program in the North, particularly over the Negro's demands for equal housing and jobs, it would probably be wrong to talk about this as a "revolt" that might cost him the election.

Accordingly, his problem is probably not how to get elected but how to govern. He is admired, but he has not made the people feel as he feels, or lifted them beyond their private purposes to see the larger public purposes he has in mind.

He is simply better known than anybody else, and this will probably be enough to assure his re-election, but this is a far cry from the atmosphere he promised when he ran for the Presidency in 1960.

November 15, 1963

The Outlook for Kennedy: Victory With Tears

By JAMES RESTON

The End of an Era

KENNEDY IS KILLED BY SNIPER IN DALLAS; JOHNSON SWORN IN ON PLANE

Gov. Connally Shot; Mrs. Kennedy Safe

President Is Struck Down by a Rifle Shot From Building on Motorcade Route— Johnson, Riding Behind, Is Unhurt

---

By TOM WICKER

DALLAS, Nov. 22—President John Fitzgerald Kennedy was shot and killed by an assassin today.

He died of a wound in the brain caused by a rifle bullet that was fired at him as he was riding through downtown Dallas in a motorcade.

Vice President Lyndon Baines Johnson, who was riding in the third car behind Mr. Kennedy's, was sworn in as the 36th President of the United States 99 minutes after Mr. Kennedy's death.

Mr. Johnson is 55 years old; Mr. Kennedy was 46.

Shortly after the assassination, Lee H. Oswald, who once defected to the Soviet Union and who had been active in the Fair Play for Cuba Committee, was arrested by the Dallas police. Tonight he was accused of the killing.

Suspect Captured After Scuffle

Oswald, 24 years old, was also accused of slaying a policeman who had appraoched him in the street. Oswald was subdued after a suffle with a second policman in a nearby theater.

President Kennedy was shot at 12:30 P.M., Central standard time (1:30 P.M., New York time). He was pronounced dead at 1 P.M. and Mr. Johnson was sworn in at 2:39 P.M.

Mr. Johnson, who was uninjured in the shooting, took his oath in the Presidential jet plane as it stood on the runway at Love Field. The body of Mr. Kennedy was aboard. Immediately after the oath-taking, the plane took off for Washington.

Standing beside the new President as Mr. Johnson took the oath of office was Mrs. John F. Kennedy. Her stockings were spattered with her husband's blood.

Gov. John B. Connally Jr. of Texas, who was riding in the same car with Mr. Kennedy, was severely wounded in the chest, ribs and arm.

His condition was serious, but not critical.

The killer fired the rifle from a building just off the motorcade route. Mr. Kennedy, Governor Connally and Mr. Johnson had just received an enthusiastic welcome from a large crowd in downtown Dallas.

Mr. Kennedy apparently was hit by the first of what witnesses believed were three shots. He was driven at high speed to Dallas's Parkland Hospital. There, in an emergency operating room, with only physicians and nurses in attendance, he died without regaining consciousness.

Mrs. Kennedy, Mrs. Connally and a Secret Service agent were in the car with Mr. Kennedy and Governor Connally. Two Secret Service agents flanked the car. Other than Mr. Connally, none of this group was injured in the shooting. Mrs. Kennedy cried, "On no!" immediately after her husband was struck.

Mrs. Kennedy was in the hospital near her husband when he died, but not in the operating room. When the body was taken from the hospital in a bronze coffin about 2 P.M., Mrs. Kennedy walked beside it.

Her face was sorrowful. She looked steadily at the floor. She still wore the raspberry-colored suit in which she had greeted welcoming crowds in Fort Worth and Dallas. But she had taken off the matching pillbox hat she wore earlier in the day, and her dark hair was windblown and tangled. Her hand rested lightly on her husband's coffin as it was taken to a waiting hearse.

Mrs. Kennedy climbed in beside the coffin. Then the ambulance drove to Love Field, and Mr. Kennedy's body was placed aboard the Presidential jet. Mrs. Kennedy then attended the swearing-in ceremony for Mr. Johnson.

As Mr. Kennedy's body left Parkland Hospital, a few stunned persons stood outside. Nurses and doctors, whispering among themselves, looked from the window. A larger crowd that had gathered earlier, before it was known that the President was dead, had been dispersed by Secret Service men and policemen.

Priests Administer Last Rites

Two priests administered last rites to Mr. Kennedy, a Roman Catholic. They were the Very Rev. Oscar Huber, the pastor of the Holy Trinity Church in Dallas, and the Rev. James Thompson.

Mr. Johnson was sworn in as President by Federal Judge Sarah T. Hughes of the Northern District of Texas. She was appointed to the judgeship by Mr. Kennedy in October, 1961.

The ceremony, delayed about five minutes for Mrs. Kennedy's arrival, took place in the private Presidential cabin in the rear of the plane.

About 25 to 30 persons—members of the late President's staff, members of Congress who had been accompanying the President on a two-day tour of Texas cities and a few reporters—crowded into the little room.

No accurate listing of those present could be obtained. Mrs. Kennedy stood at the left of Mr. Johnson, her eyes and her face showing the signs of weeping that had apparently shaken her since she left the hospital not long before.

Mrs. Johnson, wearing a beige dress, stood at her husband's right.

As Judge Hughes read the brief oath of office, her eyes, too, were red from weeping. Mr. Johnson's hands rested on a black, leatherbound Bible as Judge Hugehes read and he repeated:

"I do solemnly swear that I will perform the duties of the President of the United States to the best of my ability and defend, protect and preserve the Constitution of the United States."

Those 34 words made Lyndon Baines Johnson, one-time farmboy and schoolteacher of Johnson City, the Presdient.

Johnson Embraces Mrs. Kennedy

Mr. Johnson made no statement. He embraced Mrs. Kennedy and she held his hand for a long moment. He also embraced Mrs. John-

John Fitzgerald Kennedy
1917-1963

son and Mrs. Evelyn Lincoln, Mr. Kennedy's private secretary.

"O.K.," Mr. Johnson said. "Let's get this plane back to Washingon."

At 2:46 P.M., seven minutes after he had become President, 106 minutes after Mr. Kennedy had become the fourth American president to succumb to an assassin's wounds, the white and red jet took off for Washington.

In the cabin when Mr. Johnson took the oath was Cecil Stoughton, an armed forces photographer assigned to the White House.

Mr. Kennedy's staff members appeared stunned and bewildered. Lawrence F. O'Brien, the Congressional liaison officer, and P. Kenneth O'Donnell, the appointment secretary, both long associates of Mr. Kennedy, showed evidences of weeping. None had anything to say.

Other staff members believed to be in the cabin for the swearing-in included David F. Powers, the White House receptionist; Miss Pamela Turnure, Mrs. Kennedy's press secretary, and Malcolm Kilduff, the assistant White House press secretary.

Mr. Kilduff announced the President's death, with choked voice and red-rimmed eyes, at about 1:36 P.M.

"President John F. Kennedy died at approximately 1 o'clock Central standard time today here in Dallas," Mr. Kilduff said at the hospital. "He died of a gunshot wound in the brain. I have no other details regarding the assassination of the President."

Mr. Kilduff also announced that Governor Connally had been hit by a bullet or bullets and that Mr. Johnson, who had not yet been sworn in, was safe in the protective custody of the Secret Service at an unannounced place, presumably the airplane at Love Field.

Mr. Kilduff indicated that the President had been shot once. Later medical reports raised the possibility that there had been two wounds. But the death was caused, as far as could be learned, by a massive wound in the brain.

Later in the afternoon, Dr. Malcolm Perry, an attending surgeon, and Dr. Kemp Clark, chief of neurosurgery at Parkland Hospital, gave more details.

Mr. Kennedy was hit by a bullet in the throat, just below the Adam's apple, they said. This wound had the appearance of a bullet's entry.

Mr. Kennedy also had a massive, gaping wound in the back and one on the right side of the head. However, the doctors said it was impossible to determine immediately whether the wounds had been caused by one bullet or two.

Resuscitation Attempted

Dr. Perry, the first physician to treat the President, said a number of resuscitative measures ahd been attempted, including oxygen, anesthesia, and indotracheal tube, a tracheotomy, blood and fluids. An electrocardiogram monitor was attached to measure Mr. Kennedy's heart beats.

Dr. Clark was summoned and arrived in a minute or two. By then, Dr. Perry said, Mr. Kennedy was "critically ill and moribund," or near death.

Dr. Clark said that on his first sight of the President, he had concluded immediately that Mr. Kennedy could not live.

"It was apparent that the President had sustained a lethal wound," he said. "A missile had gone in and out of the back of his head causing external lacerations and loss of brain tissue."

Shortly after he arrived, Dr. Clark said, "the President lost his heart action by the electrocardiogram." A closed-chest cardiograph massage was attempted, as were other emergency resuscitation measures.

Dr. Clark said these had produced "palpable pulses" for a short time, but all were "to no avail."

In Operating Room 40 Minutes

The President was on the emrgency table at the hospital for about 40 mintues, the doctors said. At the end, perhaps eight physicians were in Operating Room No. 1, where Mr. Kennedy remained until his death. Dr. Clark said it was difficult to determine the exact moment of death, but the doctors said officially that it occurred at 1 P.M.

Later, there were unofficial reports that Mr. Kennedy had been killed instantly. The source of these reports, Dr. Tom Shires, chief surgeon at the hospital and professor of surgery at the University of Texas Southwest Medical School, issued this statement tonight:

"Medically, it was apparent the President was not alive when he was brought in. There was no spontaneous respiration. He had dilated, fixed pupils. It was obvious he had a lethal head wound.

"Technically, however, by using vigorous resuscitation, intravenous tubes and all the usual supportive measures, we were able to raise a semblance of a heartbeat."

Dr. Shires said that he was "positive it was impossible" that President Kennedy could have spoken after being shot. "I am absolutely sure he never knew what hit him," Dr. Shires said.

Dr. Shires was not present when Mr. Kennedy was being treated at Parkland Hospital. He issued his statement, however, after lengthy conferences with the doctors who had attended the President.

Mr. Johnson remained in the hospital about 30 minutes after Mr. Kennedy died.

The details of what happened when shots first rang out, as the President's car moved along at about 25 miles an hour, were sketchy. Secret service agents, who might have given more details, were unavailable to the press at first, and then returned to Washington with President Johnson.

Kennedys Hailed at Breakfast

Mr. Kennedy had opened his day in Fort Worth, first with a speech in a parking lot and then at a Chamber of Commerce breakfast. The breakfast appearance was a particular triumph for Mrs. Kennedy, who entered late and was given an ovation.

Then the Presidential party, including Governor and Mrs. Connally, flew on to Dallas, an eight-minute flight. Mr. Johnson, as is customary, flew in a separate plane. The President and the Vice President do not travel together, out of fear of a double tragedy.

At Love Field, Mr. and Mrs. Kennedy linginered for 10 minutes, shaking hands with an enthusiastic group lining the fence. The group called itself "Grassroots Democrats."

Mr. Kennedy then entered his open Lincoln convertible at the head of the motorcade. He sat in the rear seat on the right-hand side. Mrs. Kennedy, who appeared to be enjoying one of the first political outings she had ever made with her husband, sat at his left.

In the "jump" seat, directly ahead of Mr. Kennedy, sat Governor Connally, with Mrs. Connally at his left in another "jump" seat. A Secret Service agent was driving and the two others ran alongside.

Behind the President's limousine was an open sedan carrying a number of Secret Service agents. Behind them, in an open convertible, rode Mr. and Mrs. Johnson and Texas's senior Senator, Ralph W. Yarborough, a Democrat.

The motorcade proceeded uneventfully along a 10-mile route through downtown Dallas, aiming for the Merchandise Mart. Mr. Kennedy was to address a group of the city's leading citizens at a luncheon in his honor.

In downtown Dallas, crowds were thick, enthusiastic and cheering. The turnout was somewhat unusual for this center of conservatism, where only a month ago Adlai E. Stevenson was attacked by a rightist crowd. It was also in Dallas, during the 1960 campaign, that Senator Lyndon B. Johnson and his wife were nearly mobbed in the lobby of the Baker Hotel.

As the motorcade neared its end and the President's car moved out of the thick crowds onto Stennonds Freeway near the Merchandise Mart, Mrs. Connally recalled later, "we were all very pleased with the reception in downtown Dallas."

Approaching 3-Street Underpass

Behind the three leading cars were a string of others carrying Texas and Dallas dignitaries, two buses of reporters, several open cars carrying photographers and other reporters, and a bus for White House staff members.

As Mrs. Connally recalled later, the President's car was almost ready to go underneath a "triple underpass" beneath three streets—Elm, Commerce and Main—when the first shot was fired.

The shot apprently struck Mr. Kennedy. Governor Connally turned in his seat at the sound and appeared immediately to be hit in the chest.

Mrs. Mary Norman of Dallas was standing at the curb and at that moment was aiming her camera at the President. She saw him slump forward, then slide down in the seat.

"My God," Mrs. Norman screamed, as she recalled it later, "he's shot!"

Mrs. Connally said that Mrs. Kennedy had reached and "grabbed" her husband. Mrs. Conanlly put her arms around the Governor. Mrs. Connally said that she and Mrs. Kennedy had then ducked low in the car as it sped off.

Mrs. Connally's recollections were reported by Julian Reade, an aide to the Governor.

Most reporters in the press buses were too far back to see the shootings, but they observed some quick scurrying by motor policemen accompanying the motorcade. It was noted that the President's car had picked up speed and raced away, but reporters were not aware that anything serious had occurred until they reached the Merchandise Mart two or three minutes later.

Rumors of the shooting already were spreading through the luncheon crowd of hundreds, which was having the first course. No White House officials or Secret Service agents were present, but the reporters were taken quickly to Parkland Hospital on the strength of the rumors.

There they encountered Senator Yarborough, white, shaken and horrified.

The shots, he said, seemed to have come from the right and the rear of the car in which he was riding, the third in the motorcade. Another eyewitness, Mel Crouch, a Dallas television reporter, reported that as the shots rang out he saw a rifle extended and then withdrawn from a window on the "fifth or sixth floor" of the Texas Public School Book Depository. This is a leased state buiding on Elm Street, to the right of the motorcade route.

Senator Yarborough said there had been a slight pause between the first two shots and a longer pause between the second and third. A Secret Service man riding in the Senator's car, the Senator said, immediately ordered Mr. and Mrs. Johnson to get down below the level of the doors. They did so, and Senator Yarborough also got down.

The leading cars of the motorcade then pulled away at high speed toward Parkland Hospital, which was not far away, by the fast highway.

"We knew by the speed that something was terribly wrong," Senator Yarborough reported. When he put his head up, he said, he saw a Secret Service man in the car ahead beating his fists aginst the trunk deck of the car in which he was riding, apparently in frustration and anguish.

Mrs. Kennedy's Reaction

Only White House staff members spoke with Mrs. Kennedy. A Dallas medical student, David Edwards, saw her in Parkland Hospital while she was waiting for news of her husband. He gave this desription:

"The look in her eyes was like an animal that has been trapped, like a little rabbit—brave, but fear was in the eyes."

Dr. Clark was reported to have informed Mrs. Kennedy of her husband's death.

No witness reported seeing or hearing any of the Secret Service agents or policemen fire back. One agent was seen to brandish a machine gun as the cars sped away. Mr. Crouch observed a policeman falling to the ground and pulling a weapon. But the events had occurred so quickly that there was apparently nothing for the men to shoot at.

Mr. Crouch said he saw two women, standing at a curb to watch the motorcade pass, fall to the ground when the shots rang out. He also saw a man snatch up his little girl and run along the road. Policemen, he said, immediately chased this man under the impression he had been involved in the shooting, but Mr. Crouch said he had been a fleeing spectator.

Mr. Kennedy's limousine—license No. GG300 under Ditsrict of Columbia registry—pulled up at the emergency entrance of Parkland Hospital. Senator Yarborough said the President had been inside on a stretcher.

By the time reporters arrived at the hospital, the police were guarding the Presidential car closely. They would allow no one to approach it. A bucket of water stood by the car, suggesting that the back seat had been scrubbed out.

Robert Clark of the American Broadcasting Company, who had been riding near the front of the motorcade, said Mr. Kennedy was motionless when he was carried inside. There was a great amount of blood on Mr. Kennedy's suit and shirtfront and the front of his body, Mr. Clark said.

Mrs. Kennedy was leaning over her husband when the car stopped, Mr. Clark said, and walked beside the wheeled stretcher into the hospital. Mr. Connally sat with his hands holding his stomach, his head bent over. He, too, was moved into the hospital in a stretcher, with Mrs. Connally at his side.

Robert McNeill of the National Broadcasting Comppany, who also was in the reporters' pool car, jumped out at the scene of the shooting. He said the police had taken two eyewitnesses into custody—an 8-year-old Negro boy and a white man—for informational purposes.

Many of these reports could not be verified immediately.

Eyewitness Describes Shooting

An unidentified Dallas man, interviewed on television here, said he had been waving at the President when the shots were fired. His belief was that Mr. Kennedy had been struck twice—once, as Mrs. Norman recalled, when he slumped in his seat; again when he slid down in it.

"It just seemed to knock him down," the man said.

Governor Connally's condition was reported as "satisfactory" tonight after four hours in surgery at Parkland Hospital.

Dr. Robert R. Shaw, a thoracic surgeon, operated on the Governor to repair damage to his left chest.

Later, Dr. Shaw said Governor Connally had been hit in the back just below the shoulder blade, and that the bullet had gone completely through the Governor's chest, taking out part of the fifth rib.

After leaving the body, he said, the bullet struck the Governor's right wrist, causing a compound fracture. It then lodged in the left thigh.

The thigh wound, Dr. Shaw said, was trivial. He said the compound fracture would heal.

Dr. Shaw said it would be unwise for Governor Connally to be moved in the next 10 to 14 days. Mrs. Connally was remaining at this side tonight.

Tour by Mrs. Kennedy Unusual

Mrs. Kennedy's presence near her husband's bedside at his death resulted from somewhat unusual circumstances. She had rarely accompanied him on his trips about the coutnry and had almost never made political trips with him.

The tour on which Mr. Kennedy was engaged yesterday and today was only quasi-political; the only open political activity was to have been a speech tonight to a fund-raising dinner at the state capitol in Austin.

In visiting Texas, Mr. Kennedy was seeking to improve his political fortunes in a pivotal state that he barely won in 1960. He was also hoping to patch a bitter internal dispute among Texas's Democrats.

At 8:45 A.M., when Mr. Kennedy left the Texas Hotel in Fort Worth, where he spent his last night, to address the parking lot crowd across the street, Mrs. Kennedy was not with him. There appeared to be some disappointment.

"Mrs. Kennedy is organizing herself," the President said good-naturedly. "It takes longer, but, of course, she looks better than we do when she does it."

Later, Mrs. Kennedy appeared late at the Chamber of Commerce breakfast in Fort Worth.

Again, Mr. Kennedy took note of her presence. "Two years ago," he said, "I introduced myself in Paris by saying that I was the man who had accompanied Mrs. Kennedy to Paris. I am getting somewhat the same sensation as I travel around Texas. Nobody wonders what Lyndon and I wear."

The speech Mr. Kennedy never delivered at the Merchandise Mart luncheon contained a passage commenting on a recent preoccupation of his, and a subject of much interest in this city, where right-wing conservatism is the rule rather than the exception.

Voices are being heard in the land, he said, "voices preaching doctrines wholly unrelated to reality, wholly unsuited to the sixties, doctrines which apparently assume that words will suffice without weapons, that vituperation is as good as victory and that peace is a sign of weakness."

The speech went on: "At a time when the national debt is steadily being reduced in terms of its burden on our economy, they see that debt as the greatest threat to our security. At a time when we are steadily reducing the number of Federal employees serving every thousand citizens, they fear those supposed hordes of civil servants far more than the actual hordes of opposing armies.

"We cannot expect that everyone, to use the phrase of a decade ago, will 'talk sense to the American people.' But we can hope that fewer people will listen to nonsense. And the notion that this nation is headed for defeat through deficit, or that strength is but a matter of slogans, is nothing but just plain nonsense."

November 23, 1963

THE FINAL HOURS OF KENNEDY'S LIFE

President Began Day With Talk in a Parking Lot

DALLAS, Nov. 22 (AP)—Following is a chronology of President Kennedy's final hours today:

At 8:45 A.M., Central standard time, 9:45 A.M. New York time, he walked through a misty rain into a parking lot across the street from the Hotel Texas in Fort Worth.

He spoke there to cheering Democrats who could not get tickets to see him at a breakfast appearance. He apologized because Mrs. Kennedy was not with him, explaining that she was "organizing herself—it takes longer."

At 9 A.M. the President and Mrs. Kennedy attended the breakfast in the Hotel Texas, sponsored by the Fort Worth Chamber of Commerce. Mrs. Kennedy's late entrance brought tremendous applause from the 2,500 guests.

Both Kennedys were given cowboy boots and the President got a cowboy hat. He declined to put it on, joking that he would wear it at the White House next Monday.

At 10:35 A.M. the President and Mrs. Kennedy left the hotel by automobile for Carswell Air Force Base and their short flight to Dallas.

The Presidential plane landed at Love Field in Dallas at 11:37 A.M. Mrs. Kennedy emerged from the plane and shook hands with airport greeters. She carried a bouquet of red roses. Young men in the crowd shouted, "Hey, Jackie," and squeezed forward for a closer look.

Several young girls were screaming over Mr. Kennedy as he made his way through the crowd. There was no sign of anti-Kennedy sentiment. The Kennedys left in a motorcade that was to take them over an 11-mile route, including downtown Dallas.

At 12:30 P.M. the motorcade approached a triple underpass that feeds into Stemmons Expressway. This is the five-lane route to the Dallas Trade Mart where Mr. Kennedy was to make a luncheon speech.

A series of rifle shots rang out. The President fell face down on the back seat of his car, a bullet in his head. Gov. John Connally slumped at his side, wounded in the back.

Mrs. Kennedy gasped, "Oh, no!" The motorcade raced to Parkland Hospital near the Trade Mart and Mr. Kennedy was taken to the emergency ward, where he received a blood transfusion and then extrme unction from Catholic priests.

He died at 1 P.M.

November 23, 1963

DALLAS, Saturday, Nov. 23 —Lee Harvey Oswald, a 24-year-old warehouse worker who once lived in the Soviet Union, was charged late last night with assassinating President Kennedy.

Oswald was arrested at 2:15 yesterday afternoon, nearly two hours after the assassination of the President, as the suspected killer of a policeman on the street in the Oak Cliff district, three miles from where the President was shot.

Chief of Police Jesse Curry announced that Oswald had been formally arraigned at 1:40 A.M., Central standard time, today on a charge of murder in the President's death. The arraignment was made before a justice of the peace in the homicide bureau at Police headquarters.

Capt. Will Fritz, head of the homicide bureau, identified Oswald as an adherent of the left-wing "Fair Play for Cuba Committee." But there were also reports that Oswald, apparently politcally erratic, had once tried to join anti-Castro forces.

Worked in Warehouse

Oswald was employed in the Texas School Book Depository, the warehouse from which the fatal shots were fired at the President's car.

The police said at least six witnesses placed Oswald in the building at the time of the assassination.

One was quoted as saying that Oswald had stayed behind on a upper floor when other employes went down to the street to see Mr. Kennedy pass by.

The defendant's only comment, shouted at reporters as he was being led handcuffed through a police building corridor to be questioned, was "I haven't shot anybody." "He has not confessed," Chief Curry said. "Physical evidence is the main thing we have."

He murmured seeming assent to a suggestion that such evidence included the assassination gun.

Fingerprint experts had been conspicuous in the procession of officers into and out of the homicide bureau during the afternoon and evening. They included agents of the Secret Service and the Federal Bureau of Investigation, who collaborated with city, county and state law enforcement officers in investigating the crime.

Three and a half hours before Chief Curry's announcement, Oswald had been arraigned on a charge of murder in the death of the policeman, J.D. Tippitt.

Dallas County District Attorney Henry Wade said there were "a few loose ends" in the case to be wrapped up, and he expected that he case would not go to the grand jury before next week.

Appears in Line-Up

Oswald faces a death sentence if convicted.

After the arraignment, the suspect, a slight, dark-haired man, was taken downstairs to appear in a line-up, presumably before witnesses of the Kennedy assassination.

The sequence of events leading to his arrest was as follows:

As a City-wide manhunt began during the hour following the assassination, an unidentified man notified police headquarters, over a police-car radio, that the car's officer had been shot and killed. The car was in the 400 block of East Jefferson Boulevard in the Oak Cliff section, on the edge of the downtown area.

The car's driver, Patrolman Tippitt, had not made any call that he was going to question anyone.

Eight other officers converged on the spot. They found Patrolman Tippitt lying on the sidewalk, dead from two .38-caliber bullet wounds.

They began a search of nearby buildings for the killer.

Then another call came to police headquarters from Julie Postal, cashier of the Texas Theatre at 231 West Jefferson Boulevard, six blocks from the scene of the policeman's slaying.

She said an usher had told her that a man who had just entered the theater was acting peculiarly.

The investigating police officers were dispatched to the theater. They began checking patrons, starting at the front of the house.

One of the officers, Sgt. Jerry Hill, said that when they came to Oswald, sitting in the rear four seats fromt he aisle, the suspect jumped up and exclaimed: "This is it!"

The Dallas Police Department appeared to be the nerve center of the overall investigation of the President's death, although the various lines this might be taking were not defined.

State Has Jurisdiction

The Justice of the Peace before whom Oswald was arraigned, David Johnston, said the assassination was a matter of state jurisdiction so far.

Little was known here about Oswald, except reports published locally in 1959 when he went to the Soviet Union after his discharge from the Marine Corps.

He was said to have tried to renounce his United States citizenship by turning in his passport to the United States Embassy in Moscow. The Embassy, it was reported then, advised him to hold on to it until he had some assurance of Soviet citizenship. He was reported to have worked in factories in the Soviet and to have married a Russian girl.

At the time of his quasi-defection, his mother and his brother, a milkman in nearby Fort Worth, sent messages vainly trying to dissuade him.

Shortly after he was escorted from his arraignment last night, a tall, slender woman with a little

girl about 2 years old and a baby in her arms left the homicide bureau. An officer said they were the suspect's wife and daughter.

A housekeeper at Oswald's rooming house said the young man entered his room shortly after the shooting of the President, got a coat, and went back out.

The housekeeper, Mrs. Earlene Roberts, said:

"He came in in a hurry in his shirt sleeves and I said, 'Oh, you're in a hurry,' and he didn't say anything. He went on in his room and got a coat and put it on. He went out to the bus stop and that's the last I saw of him."

Mrs. Roberts said Oswald rushed into the rooming house, at 1026 North Beckley Road in suburban Oak Cliff. This was shortly after Mrs. Roberts had learned, in a telephone call from a friend, that the President had been shot. She said she had not connected Oswald's appearance with the shooting.

She described Oswald, who had lived in the house since the end of October, as quiet.

Justice of the Peace Johnston said he was one of four from outlying communities, assembled for the Kennedy visit, who had been recruited to assist law enforcement officers with the inquiry.

Judge Johnston said Judge Theron Ward had been assigned to the President's death and Judge Joe B. Brown Jr. to the death of the policeman. Judge Johnston and Judge Lloyd Russell were assisting in such matters as the issuance of search warrants and handling the arraignment.

The arraignment involved no plea. Oswald was held without bail for grand jury action and was advised of his right to counsel.

Captain Fritz emerged from the homicide bureau after the arraignment and said: "We've charged this man with the killing of the officer."

Asked whether Oswald had been linked with the assassination, the officer replied: "He doesn't admit it—we have some more work to do on that case."

The revolver carried by Oswald in the theater was not suspected of having figured in President Kennedy's death.

Police ballistics experts were still studying with apparently no conclusive findings, the rifle found in the book warehouse.

Captain Fritz said it was of obscure foreign origin, possibly Italian, of about 1940 vintage, and of an unusual, undetermined caliber. He displayed a bullet he said fitted the gun. It was about .30 caliber and about two and one-half inches long, with a narrow tapered nose.

Sergeant Hill said Oswald had a .38-caliber revolver under his shirt, and that in a scuffle that ensued, it was fired once,

Leftist Charged With Murder in Assassination of Kennedy and Policeman's Death

He Is Subdued in Theater —Ex-Marine Defected to Soviet and Returned

By GLADWIN HILL

harmlessly. The time was 2:15 P.M. yersterday.

Oswald was subdued, handcuffed, rushed to downtown police headquarters and put in a fifth-floor cell.

At 6:35 P.M. he was taken down to the third-floor homicide bureau. He wore black slacks, black loafer shoes, a white undershirt and an olive plaid sport shirt, unbuttoned.

His left eye was slightly blackened, and there was a contusion on his right cheekbone.

November 23, 1963

Visitors to Family Were Advised To Be Ready for Football Game

The characteristics of the Kennedy clan probably were best summarized in a semi-humorous set of "Rules for Visiting the Kennedys," which were drafted by a close friend, Dave Hackett.

Here is what Mr. Hackett advised:

"Prepare yourself by reading The Congressional Record, U. S. News and World Report, Time, Newsweek, Fortune, The Nation, The Democratic Digest, The Ensign and the manual How to Play Sneaky Tennis. Memorize Page 2 of 'Jokes Guaranteed to Lay Them in the Aisles.' Anticipate that each Kennedy will ask you what you think of another Kennedy's (a) dress, (b) hairdo, (c) backhand, (d) latest achievement. You will find that "Terrific!" is a satisfactory answer. They won't listen to much detail.

"It's touch football but it's murder. The only way I know of to get out of playing is not to come at all, or to come with a broken leg. If you don't have a broken leg and if you come, you will play; that is, you will if you don't want to take your supper in the kitchen, or if you don't want to talk to anyone for the rest of the week-end.

"Make a lot of noise and make out that you never had a better time in your life. Things will go smoother if you do. Don't overdo this, though. Don't make out that you're having altogether too much fun. If you do, you'll be accused of not taking the game seriously enough.

"Look glum if your team doesn't score a touchdown and become gleeful when your team does. Don't sacrifice your teammates (it's a team game). And for goodness sake don't harp on any error of the enemy, because the enemy will be made up of Kennedys, too, and the Kennedy's don't like that sort of thing."

November 23, 1963

Sister Sees Dallas Telecast

JEFFERSON, Wis., Nov. 22 (UPI)—President Kennedy's younger sister, Rose, learned of his assassination today while watching a television broadcast from Dallas, Tex., where he was shot. "She knows he is dead," said a spokesman at St. Colleta's, a school for the retarded, where she has lived for the last 20 years. "She was watching on television."

November 23, 1963

Captain of Japanese Ship
That Sank PT-109 Mourns

FUKUSHIMA, Japan, Saturday, Nov. 23 (UPI) — The captain of the Japanese destroyer that rammed and sank PT-109, commanded by Lieut. (jg.) John F. Kennedy in World War II, expressed shock and sorrow today on learning of the President's death.

"I think his death is a great loss to Japan," said Kohei Hanai, 54-year-old former captain of the Japanese destroyer Amagiri. Mr. Hanai, now mayor of Shiyokawa, a town in northern Japan, said he was sorry that he had now lost the opportunity to meet Mr. Kennedy personally.

November 23, 1963

Children Learn Father Is Dead;
Mother Returns to White House

Caroline and John Jr. Receive the News —Mrs. Kennedy Stays Most of the Night at Bethesda Naval Hospital

By NAN ROBERTSON

WASHINGTON, Nov. 23— President Kennedy's two children were told last night that their father was dead. It was not known who had told them or what words had been used. Almost certainly it was not their mother.

Mrs. Kennedy stayed close to her husband from the moment he was shot by an assassin until his body was returned to the White House before dawn today. His body now lies in the East Room.

Mrs. Kennedy spent most of the night at Bethesda Naval Hospital, where the slain President was first taken from nearby Andrews Air Force Base.

She rode in the ambulance with the body and remained at the hospital from 7 o'clock last night until 4 A. M. today.

Her children were taken late yesterday afternoon from the White House to the home of Mrs. Hugh D. Auchincloss, their maternal grandmother, in Georgetown, an exclusive section of Washington. There they had dinner.

Then the children, Caroline and John, Jr., were taken back to the White House. They went to their private quarters upstairs about 7:30 P. M. with their nurse, Maud Shaw, who has been with the Kennedys since Caroline was 11 days old.

Funeral on Birthday

John Jr., nicknamed "John-John" by his father, will be 3 years old Monday, the day of his father's funeral. Caroline's sixth birthday will be Wednesday.

This morning the grief-stricken mother took both children to a private mass in the East Room. The closed bronze coffin reflected the flickering candles set about it.

The Roman Catholic mass, believed to be the first ever celebrated in the White House, was said by the Rev. John J. Cavanagh, former president of the University of Notre Dame, who is a close friend of the family.

About 75 friends and relatives attended the mass.

Princess Stanislas Radziwill flew in from France today to be with Mrs. Kennedy, her sister.

The President's mother, Mrs. Joseph P. Kennedy, will arrive from Hyannis Port tomorrow. Her husband, who suffered a stroke nearly three years ago, will remain in Hyannis Port.

There were reports yesterday that Caroline and John had been carefully protected from the news of their father's death and would not be told until their mother returned to the White House.

Mrs. Kennedy went directly from the airport to Bethesda, however. By the time she arrived at the White House at 4:25 this morning, the children had long been asleep.

Mr. Kennedy's press secretary, Pierre Salinger, said that by that time John Jr. and Caroline already knew their father was dead.

November 24, 1963

PRESIDENT'S ASSASSIN SHOT TO DEATH IN JAIL CORRIDOR BY A DALLAS CITIZEN

ONE BULLET FIRED

Night-Club Man Who Admired Kennedy Is Oswald's Slayer

By GLADWIN HILL

DALLAS, Nov. 24 — President Kennedy's assassin, Lee Harvey Oswald, was fatally shot by a Dallas night-club operator today as the police started to move him from the city jail to the county jail.

The shooting occurred in the basement of the municipal building at about 11:20 A.M. central standard time (12:20 P.M. New York time).

The assailant, Jack Rubenstein, known as Jack Ruby, lunged from a cluster of newsmen observing the transfer of Oswald from the jail to an armored truck.

Millions of viewers saw the shooting on television.

As the shot rang out, a police detective suddenly recognized Ruby and exclaimed: "Jack, you son of a bitch!"

A murder charge was filed against Ruby by Assistant District Attorney William F. Alexander. Justice of the Peace Pierce McBride ordered him held without bail.

Detectives Flank Him

Oswald was arrested Friday after Mr. Kennedy was shot dead while riding through Dallas in an open car. He was charged with murdering the President and a policeman who was shot a short time later while trying to question Oswald.

As the 24-year-old prisoner, flanked by two detectives, stepped onto a basement garage ramp, Ruby thrust a .38-caliber, snub-nose revolver into Oswald's left side and fired a single shot.

The 52-year-old night-club operator, an ardent admirer of President Kennedy and his family, was described as having been distraught.

[District Attorney Henry Wade said he understood that the police were looking into the possibility that Oswald had been slain to prevent him from talking. The Associated Press reported. Mr. Wade said that so far no connection between Oswald and Ruby had been established.]

Oswald slumped to the concrete paving, wordlessly clutching his side and writhing with pain.

Oswald apparently lost consciousness very quickly after the shooting. Whether he was at any point able to speak, if he wanted to, was not known.

The politically eccentric warehouse clerk was taken in a police ambulance to the Parkland Hospital, where President Kennedy died Friday. He died in surgery at 1:07 P.M., less than two hours after the shooting. The exact time Oswald was shot was not definitely estab-

lished.

Four plainclothes men, from a detail of about 50 police officers carrying out the transfer, pounced on Ruby as he fired the shot and overpowered him.

Ruby, who came to Dallas from Chicago 15 years ago, had a police record here listing six allegations of minor offenses. The disposition of five was not noted. A charge of liquor law violation was dismissed. Two of the entries, in July, 1953, and May, 1954, involved carrying concealed weapons.

The city police, working with the Secret Service and the Federal Bureau of Investigation, said last night that they had the case against Oswald "cinched."

After some 30 hours of intermittent interrogations and confrontations with scores of witnesses, Oswald was ordered transferred to the custody of the Dallas County sheriff.

This was preliminary to the planned presentation of the case, next Wednesday or the following Monday, to the county grand jury by District Attorney Wade.

The transfer involved a trip of about a mile from the uptown municipal building, where the Police Department and jail are. The route went down Main Street to the county jail, overlooking the spot where President Kennedy was killed and Gov. John B. Connally was wounded by shots from the book warehouse where Oswald worked.

A Change in Plans

The original plan had been for the sheriff to assume custody of Oswald at the city jail and handle the transfer. Late last night, for unspecified reasons, it was decided that the city police would move the prisoner.

Police Chief Jesse Curry declined to comment on suggestions that he had scheduled the transfer of Oswald at an unpropitious time because of pressure from news media.

Chief Curry announced about 9 o'clock last night that the investigation had reached a point where Oswald's presence was no longer needed. He said that Oswald would be turned over to the county sheriff today.

Asked when this would take place, the chief said: "If you fellows are here by 10 A.M., you'll be early enough."

When newsmen assembled at the police administrative offices at 10 o'clock, Chief Curry commented: "We could have done this earlier if I hadn't given you fellows that 10 o'clock time."

Armored Van Used

This was generally construed as meaning that preparations for the transfer had been in readiness for some hours, rather than implying a complaint from the chief that the press had had any part in setting the time.

Chief Curry disclosed this morning that to thwart an attempt against Oswald, the trip

was to be made in an armored van of the kind used to transfer money.

"We're not going to take any chances," he said. "Our squad cars are not bullet-proof. If somebody's going to try to do something, they wouldn't stop him."

A ramp dips through the basement garage of the municipal building, running from Main Street to Commerce Street. Patrol wagons drive down this ramp and discharge prisoners at a basement booking office. The garage ceiling was too low for the armored car, so the van was backed up in the Commerce Street portal of the ramp.

The plan was to lead Oswald out the doorway in the center of the basement and about 75 feet up the ramp to the back of the armored car.

Prisoner on Fourth Floor

At about 11 o'clock, Chief Curry left his third-floor office, followed by plainclothes detectives and newsmen, to go to the basement. Oswald was still in a fourth-floor jail cell.

As the group with the chief walked through a short corridor past the basement booking office and out the door onto the guarded ramp, uniformed policemen checked the reporters' credentials. But they passed familiar faces, such as those of policemen and collaborating Secret Service and F.B.I. agents.

Ruby's face was familiar to many policemen who had encountered him at his two night clubs and in his frequent visits to the municipal building.

Inconspicuous in Group

Neatly dressed in a dark suit and wearing a fedora, he was inconspicuous in a group of perhaps 50 men who for the next 20 minutes waited in a 12-foot-wide vestibule and adjacent portions of the ramp.

Television cameras, facing the vestibule, were set up against a metal railing separating the 15-foot-wide ramp from the rest of the garage. Some newsmen clustered along this railing.

Across Commerce Street, in front of a row of bail bondsmen's offices, a crowd of several hundred persons was held back by a police line.

Soon Oswald was taken in an elevator to the basement. He was led through the booking office to the open vestibule between two lines of detectives.

Walks Behind Captain

Captain Fritz, chief of the police homicide division, walked just ahead of him. Oswald was handcuffed, with a detective holding each arm and another following. On Oswald's right, in a light suit, was J. R. Leavelle and on his left, in a dark suit, L. C. Graves.

As they turned right from the vestibule to start up the ramp, Ruby jumped forward from against the railing. There was a sudden loud noise that sounded like the explosion of a photographer's flashbulb. It was

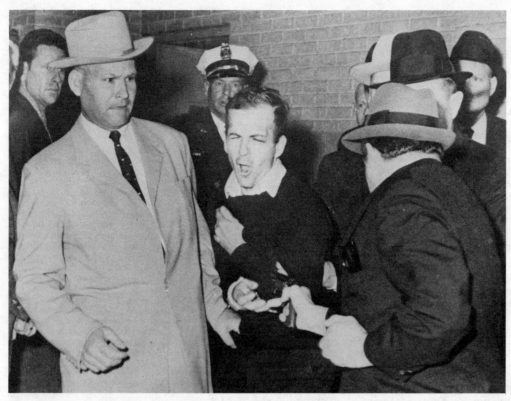

THE SUDDEN ATTACK: Jack Ruby closes in on Lee Harvey Oswald, in custody at jail in Dallas. Ruby put the muzzle of the pistol against the assassin, and then fired.

Ruby's revolver firing.

A momentary furor set in as Ruby was seized and hustled into the building. Policemen ran up the ramp in both directions to the street, followed by others with orders to seal off the building.

About five minutes elapsed before an ambulance could be rolled down the ramp to Oswald.

The ambulance, its siren sounding, was followed by police and press cars on the four-mile drive to the hospital.

The hospital's emergency department had been on the alert for possible injuries arising out of the projected transfer.

Oswald was moved almost immediately into an operating room, at the other end of the building from the one where President Kennedy was treated.

The bullet had entered Oswald's body just below his heart and had torn into most of the vital organs.

Dr. Tom Shires, the hospital's chief of surgery, who operated on Governor Connally Friday, took over the case. The gamut of emergency procedures—blood transfusion, fluid transfusion, breathing tube and chest drainage tube—was instituted immediately.

But Dr. Shires quickly reported through a hospital official that Oswald was in "extremely critical condition" and that surgery would take several hours.

Oswald's brother, George, a factory worker from Denton, Tex., got to the hospital before the assassin died.

The police took Oswald's mother, wife and two infant daughters into protective custody. They were escorted to the hospital to view the body, then were taken to an undisclosed lodging place in Dallas.

Governor Connally is still a patient at the Parkland Hospital. The excitement of the Oswald case swirled around the temporary office the Governor had set up there.

Back at the jail, Ruby was taken to the same fourth-floor cellblock where his victim had been the focus of attention the last two days.

Reports that filtered out about his preliminary remarks said that he had been impelled to kill President Kennedy's assassin by sympathy for Mrs. Kennedy. It was reported he did not want her to go through the ordeal of returning to Dallas for the trial of Oswald.

A half-dozen lawyers who have worked for Ruby converged on police headquarters in the next hour or two. They said they had been directed there by relatives and friends of Ruby and had not been called by Ruby himself.

One lawyer said that he had arranged for a hearing before a justice of the peace tomorrow morning to ask for Ruby's release on bail.

"He's a respectable citizen who's been here for years and certainly is entitled to bail," the lawyer said. "We'll make any amount of bail."

"He is a great admirer of President Kennedy," the lawyer said, "and police officers."

The last remark was an alusion to the fact that Oswald was accused of fatally shooting the Dallas patrolman after the President's assassination.

Ruby, the lawyer said, "is a very emotional man."

Chief Curry called the second formal news conference of the last three days in the police headquarters basement assembly room at 1:30 P.M.

His face drawn, he said in a husky voice:

"We have arrested the man. He will be charged with murder. The suspect is Jack Rubenstein. He also goes by the name of Jack Ruby. That's all I have to say."

Sheriff Bill Decker commented that the police "did everything humanly possible" to protect Oswald, as he said they had in the case of President Kennedy.

"I don't think it would have made a bit of difference if Oswald had been transferred at night," he said. "If someone is determined to commit murder, it's almost impossible to stop him."

Ironically, it appeared that Ruby might have had a number of far easier opportunities for killing Oswald than the method he finally used.

He was reported to have circulated repeatedly the last two days among the throng of people that was constantly in the third-floor corridor near the homicide bureau. Oswald was led along this corridor a number of times as he was taken down from the fourth-floor jail for interrogation.

November 25, 1963

KENNEDY LAID TO REST IN ARLINGTON; HUSHED NATION WATCHES AND GRIEVES; WORLD LEADERS PAY TRIBUTE AT GRAVE

A HERO'S BURIAL

Million in Capital See Cortege Roll On to Church and Grave

By TOM WICKER

WASHINGTON, Nov. 25—The body of John Fitzgerald Kennedy was returned today to the American earth.

The final resting place of the 35th President of the United States was on an open slope among the dead of the nation's wars in Arlington National Cemetery, within sight of the Lincoln Memorial.

Mr. Kennedy's body was carried from the Capitol to St. Matthew's Roman Catholic Cathedral for a requiem mass. From there, in a cortege, it was taken to the cemetery.

During the day, a million people stood in the streets to watch Mr. Kennedy's last passage.

Across the land, millions more—almost the entire population of the country at one time or another—saw the solemn ceremonies on television.

Cushing Says Mass

At the pontifical low mass said by Richard Cardinal Cushing of Boston, and following the caisson bearing Mr. Kennedy's body to his grave, were notable figures—among them President Johnson, President de Gaulle of France, Emperor Haile Selassie of Ethiopia, King Baudouin of the Belgians, Queen Frederika of the Hellenes, and Prince Philip, husband of Queen Elizabeth II of Britain.

As the caisson reached the graveside below the Custis-Lee Mansion that dominates the Arlington National Cemetery, a flight of 50 jet planes thundered overhead—one representing each state of the Union that Mr. Kennedy often called "the Great Republic." The jets were followed by Air Force 1, the President's personal plane.

Cardinal Cushing repeated the ancient words of the Roman Catholic graveside service, interpolating the phrase "this wonderful man, Jack Kennedy." Cannon boomed a 21-gun salute across the rows upon rows of white stones. A bugler sounded taps.

The eight body bearers who had placed Mr. Kennedy's coffin above his open grave folded the flag that had covered it for three days. It was presented to Mrs. Kennedy, who stood erect and still, her head covered by a long black veil.

Then she and Mr. Kennedy's brothers, Attorney General Robert F. Kennedy and Senator Edward M. Kennedy of Massachusetts, each touched a flaming wand to an "eternal flame" placed at the head of the grave.

That was all. For John F. Kennedy, 46 years of age, three years leader of his nation and the Western world, herald of a new generation of American purpose, the tumult and the shouting died. The captains and the kings departed.

This was a cold clear day in Washington—a day of hushed streets, empty buildings, silent throngs, standing in their massed thousands to watch the cortege pass, a day of brilliant sunshine falling like hope upon a people that mourned a felled leader but had to set their faces to the future.

Officially, the day began at 10:41 A.M. when Mrs. John F. Kennedy, with Robert and Edward Kennedy, entered the great, still Rotunda of the United States Capitol, where John Kennedy's body had lain in state since yesterday afternoon.

Hundreds of thousands of Americans had filed silently past the catafalque—the same upon which the murdered Lincoln lay 98 years ago—in a procession that continued through the night and until after 9 A.M. today.

Mrs. Kennedy, Robert and Edward Kennedy knelt by the coffin for a minute, then arose, backed away several steps, turned and went down the central steps of the Capitol to the East Plaza.

Between sentinels of all the armed services, posted in two long lines down the steps, the eight body bearers carried the flag-draped coffin and placed it upon the waiting caisson. Six matched gray horses pulled it away, carrying John Kennedy on this last journey to the White House.

The Kennedy family and others followed in a solemn line of cars along Pennsylvania Avenue. At the White House, the Kennedys left their car and went inside for a few minutes.

Across the street, in Lafayette Square, thousands stood to watch the procession to the church forming in the White House drive.

At 11:25, the foreign dignitaries who had come to pay their respects began lining up—President de Gaulle in the uniform and cap of the French Army, the diminutive Haile Selassie in gorgeous braid, Prince Philip in the blue of the British Navy, others in top hats, sashes, medals, or simple civilian clothes like those worn by Queen Frederika.

Altogether, State Department officials said, 220 persons representing 92 nations, five international agencies and the papacy came to Washington. Among them were eight heads of state, ten prime ministers, and most of the world's remaining royalty.

In the distance, as they waited, tolled the bells of St. John's Protestant Episcopal church on the other side of Lafayette Square. The flags of the 50 states, displayed along the White House drive, were dipped in the presence of the caisson.

Mrs. Kennedy Takes Place

At 11:35, Mrs. Kennedy came down the steps of the north portico, as a choir of midshipmen sang softly. She took her place behind the caisson, flanked by Robert Kennedy on the right.

Edward Kennedy on the left. Only once, as she waited, did she break her stillness to glance around at the world's great standing silently behind her.

Then, to a distant skirl of bagpipes from the Black Watch, flown to Washington to march in the funeral procession, the caisson and its followers moved down the drive, into Pennsylvania Avenue, past Blair House and onto 17th Street.

Five yards behind Mrs. Kennedy walked President Johnson and his wife, discreetly accompanied by numerous security agents.

Next, in a limousine, came Caroline and John Kennedy Jr., the dead President's children.

On foot behind them, in what soon became a straggling, confused mass, came the visiting delegations—a contrast to the precision of the military units and bands that marched ahead of the caisson.

Along 17th Street and Connecticut Avenue, on the eight-block route to St. Matthew's Cathedral, crowds had been gathering since early morning. They massed on the sidewalks and spilled over the curbs, clustered in the buildings that line one of Washington's smartest office and shopping areas, and backed up into the side streets.

Seldom had such personages gathered at once; certanly never had such a gathering been seen walking on foot along one of the busiest streets of the nation. De Valera, Mikoyan, Erhard, Douglas-Home, Ikeda, Thant—the parade of famous figures seemed endless.

Behind them came the Supreme Court Justices and the Cabinet; and after them, in a group of their own, some of Mr. Kennedy's closest associates. Another group of personal friends followed.

At the cathedral, those who were not marching in the procession had been gathering since before 11 A.M. Admission was by invitation only, and the capacity of the green-domed building limited those invited to somewhat more than 1,100.

These guests were varied: Harold Wilson, leader of the British Labor party; Mrs. Nelson Rockefeller and her busband, the Governor of New York; White House staff members; members of the Senate, among them Barry Goldwater of Arizona, and members of the House.

There was Gov. George Romney of Michigan and his wife; Gov. Bert Combs of Kentucky; David L. McDonald, president of the United Steelworkers of America; Mayor Richard J. Daley of Chicago and former Gov. Ernest Hollings of South Carolina; Gov. George C. Wallace of Alabama; Richard M. Nixon and Mrs. Nixon; Gov. and Mrs. William W. Scranton of Pennsylvania and Gov. Edmund G. Brown of California.

Seated near the front of the church were fomrmer President Harry S. Truman and his daughter, Mrs. E. C. Daniel of New York. Former President Dwight D. Eisenhower, with his wife on his arm, was seated near

Truman.

The diplomatic corps arrived in a body. Military ushers and several friends of Mr. Kennedy —among them two reporters, Hugh Sidey of Time magazine and Benjamin Bradlee of Newsweek—showed the great and the small to their seats.

The church was silent. Six massive candles, in tall gold holders, stood upon the white marble altar. From the ornate, domed ceiling — designed by Grant LaFarge — paintings, carvings, inscriptions looked down upon the rapidly filling cathedral.

Then came the sound of drums. The Black Watch bagpipes could be heard, faintly at first, rising as they passed the open doors, falling into silence. Shouted military commands sounded clearly through the door.

The choir in the loft above and to the left of the altar began to sing. Cardinal Cushing and a long line of prelates followed a crucifix held aloft by an acolyte as they marched slowly along the aisle to the open porch in front of the cathedral.

The caisson halted before the cathedral at 11:57 A.M. Mrs. Kennedy, walking with a sure and rapid stride, was just behind it with her husband's brothers. Cardinal Cushing in his lofty white mitre came down the steps.

Mrs. Kennedy's children, clad in identical blue and wearing red shoes, were brought to her and she took them by the hand. She bent to kiss the Cardinal's ring, then walked with Caroline and John Jr. into the cathedral.

Members of the Kennedy family and of Mrs. Kennedy's family followed. President and Mrs. Johnson came just behind them and were seated across the aisle.

As the mass of dignitaries and foreign visitors filed in, the coffin waited outside on its caisson. At 12:08, the body bearers lifted it, carried it across the street and to the cathedral porch. Cardinal Cushing sprinkled it with holy water, then bent to kiss it.

At 12:15, the acolyte carrying the crucifix moved slowly back up the aisle, flanked by two others carrying candles. The Cardinal, chanting in Latin, and the prelates followed.

Behind them, at funeral pace, stiffly erect as automatons, came the eight body bearers, wheeling the flag-draped coffin —three at each side, one at its head, another trailing.

The coffin was placed in the front and center of the church, a few feet from where the family sat. The bearers marched stiffly away. The doors of the church closed on the still, waiting crowds outside.

As Cardinal Cushing, in the familiar droning voice that had sounded the invocation at Mr. Kennedy's inauguration on Jan. 20, 1961, said the requiem mass Luigi Vena sang from the choir loft Gounod's "Ave Maria."

Mrs. Kennedy had requested that Mr. Vena do so. He had sung the same music at her marriage to John F. Kennedy in Newport, R. I., on Sept. 12, 1953—a ceremony at which Cardinal Cushing had also officiated.

The Cardinal—a tall and imposing figure in the massive church—said the mass entirely in the traditional Latin ("Dominus vobiscum. Et cum spiritu tuo.")

He moved steadily and without hesitation, sometimes in a sing-song voice that sounded more like a steady drone of sound than enunciated words— through the Introit, the Kyrie ("Kyrie eleison — Lord, have mercy. Christe eleison — Christ, have mercy"), the consecration, through all the other forms of the mass familiar to millions of Roman Catholics the world over, to the communion.

Mrs. Kennedy and Robert Kennedy were the first to receive communion. Edward Kennedy followed. Hundreds of others in the church also received communion and were given the peace of the Lord ("Pax Domini sit semper vobiscum").

When the celebration of the mass ended ("O God, who alone art ever merciful and sparing of punishment, humbly we pray Thee in behalf of the soul of Thy servant, John Fitzgerald Kennedy, whom Thou hast commanded to go forth today from this World . . ."), the Most Rev. Philip Hannan, Auxiliary Bishop of Washington, ascended to the pulpit and spoke for 11 minutes in English.

In a clear, almost uninflected voice, Bishop Hannan spoke of Biblical passages in Mr. Kennedy's speeches, including one from one of the last addresses he ever made, in Houston last Thursday night:
"Your old men shall dream dreams, your young men shall see visions, and where there is no vision the people shall perish."

He concluded with a reading of Mr. Kennedy's Inaugural Address with its famous passage, "Ask not what your country can do for you — ask what you can do for your country."

And once again, in the Bishop's unimpassioned voice — so different from that of the young President who spoke that snowy day in 1961 — there rang out a challenge that had stirred a nation:
"Now the trumpet summons again — not as a call to bear arms, though arms we need — not as a call to battle, though embattled we are — but a call to bear the burden of a long twilight struggle, year in and year out, 'rejoicing in hope, patient in tribulation' — a struggle against the common enemies of man: tyranny, poverty, disease and war itself."

The words did not seem less relevant — in the aftermath of Mr. Kennedy's murder they seemed if anything more challenging — than the day, on that crest of hope and belief, when he said them.

At 1:15 P.M., the church doors were opened, the cathedral service concluded. Once again, the procession of prelates followed the crucifix slowly up the aisle. The body bearers moved Mr. Kennedy's coffin behind them. From the street came the stirring sounds of "Hail to the Chief," to which Mr. Kennedy had stepped so often in his brisk stride.

Mrs. Kennedy, holding Caroline's hand — John had been taken from the church at the beginning of the mass — followed it. For a long moment, as the coffin was being taken down the steps and mounted for the third time upon the caisson, she had to stand in the aisle waiting.

She was weeping behind her veil. But as she stood unmoving and erect, she took control of herself with an obvious effort, and moved on out of the church. Robert Kennedy followed her with his mother, Mrs. Joseph P. Kennedy, on his arm. Then came the rest of the family mourners.

President Johnson and his family followed. In the jam of persons leaving the church, the foreign dignitaries stood for long moments in the aisle. President de Gaulle whispered something to King Baudouin.

Outside the church, Caroline and John Kennedy entered a limousine with their nurse, Mrs. Maude Shaw, and were driven to the White House.

Cardinal Cushing wiped tears from his eyes with a handkerchief as an Army band played a dirge. Attorney General Kennedy helped Mrs. Kennedy into a limousine. Both General Eisenhower and Mr. Truman leaned into her car and spoke to her briefly. They had been chatting on the cathedral porch as they waited for cars.

The body of the 35th President of the United States is borne on a caisson and followed by a riderless horse to Arlington National Cemetary, where Mr. Kennedy will be buried.

Later, the two former Presidents, none too friendly since the 1952 election, rode together in the procession to Arlington National Cemetery.

That procession formed up slowly in front of the cathedral in a jam of waiting limousines, and the dignitaries began to crowd to the curb. Angier Biddle Duke, the State Department chief of protocol, gave up the effort to escort each of them to a car, but all eventually found their places in the long, solemn parade.

Eight Secret Service men flanked the car in which President and Mrs. Johnson rode. Another large group of agents guarded the car of President de Gaulle.

So large was the Kennedy family group that President and Mrs. Johnson, whose car was immediately behind the group, were 10th in the long cortege.

Once again, on its final journey, the caisson rolled down Connecticut Avenue and Seventh Street, then turned right on Constitution Avenue. Behind it, Black Jack, the riderless gelding with the traditional reversed boots in the silver stirrups, pranced and pawed nervously at the pavement.

Untold thousands stood at the curbside—along the same route taken by masses of Negroes and whites last Aug. 28 in the March on Washington that Mr. Kennedy had encouraged.

Past the noble white marble of the Lincoln Memeorial, over the long stone reach of the Memorial Bridge across the serene Potomac toward the green slopes of Arlington and the pillared mansion where Robert E. Lee made his tragic choice to leave the Union with his state—onward to the grave rolled the cortege of the great grandson of an Irish immigrant.

Behind him, the leaders of the world—royalty and commoners, generals and revolu-

John-John bids a final farewell to his father.

tionaries—came on endlessly in their mourning-colored cars. The crowds wached silently, sorrowfully, respectfully. In the cold and the waning sunshine, they stood patiently, seeming almost not to move.

More than an hour after it had left the church, the caisson arrived at the graveside. On a nearby slope, masses of flowers were arranged. The metal coffin railings gleamed with polish. Beyond the river, the Lincoln and Jefferson Memorials, the soaring stone of the Washington Monument could be plainly seen.

Mrs. Kennedy, Robert and Edward Kennedy, the Kennedy sisters, Patricia, Eunice and Jean, and their mother, were seated in a single row at the front of the family group. As the limousines arrived one by one, the dignitaries took their palces—President de Gaulle and Haile Selåssie at the head of the grave.

For the graveside services, Cardinal Cushing spoke mostly in English. The words were familiar ("I am the Resurrection and the Life . . .")

Occasionally, he seemed to be hurrying, as if to end more quickly the anguish of Mrs. Kennedy and her family. But his harsh voice rang plainly across the hillside and the watching crowds and the thousands of graves as he intoned:

"O Lord, we implore Thee to grant this mercy to Thy dead servant, that he who held fast to Thy will by his intentions, may not receive punishment in return for his deeds; so that, as the true faith united him with the throng of the faithful on earth, Thy mercy may unite him with company of the holy angels in Heaven."

Three cannon, firing by turns,

boomed 21 times in the stillness. President de Gaulle and the other military men came to the salute. Then three riflemen fired three sharp volleys into the arching sky. Sgt. Keith Clark, an Army bugler, sounded the clear, melancholy lament of taps across the cemetery.

The flag was removed from the coffin, folded with whiplike precision by the body bearers, passed to Mrs. Kennedy. She and her husband's brother lit the eternal flame. Cardinal Cushing cast holy water upon the exposed coffin.

Stumbles and Recovers

Robert Kennedy led Mrs. Kennedy away. After a few steps, she stumbled on broken turf, quickly recovered her stride, and went steadily on.

The procession had been so long that many dignitaries, far back in the line of cars, were only arriving at the graveside. But if it had taken a long time for the men who followed John Kennedy to arrive at his last resting place, it seemed to take hardly any for the throng of uniforms and morning frock coats and veils and simple dark clothes to disperse and leave the dead for the living.

At 3:34 P.M., the coffin was lowered into the earth. The short life, the long day, was done forever. And none of the pomp and pagenatry, none of the ceremony and music, none of the words and grief, none of the faces at the curb, none of the still figures in the limousines, had seemed to say more than the brief prayer printed on the back of a photoraph of the dead President that had been distributed at the cathedral:

"Dear God—please take care of your servant—John Fitzgerald Kennedy."

November 26, 1963

WASHINGTON, Nov. 25 — Mrs. John F. Kennedy went bravely through her final hours of public grief today.

She walked the eight long blocks from the White House to St. Matthew's Roman Catholic Cathedral behind the caisson carrying the body of her husband to the funeral. It was a gesture that few who watched would ever forget.

She stood erect at his graveside, watching the powers of church and state bid him farewell.

She carried out a final duty as the President's wife, greeting at the White House the leaders of the nations who had come to pay tribute to Mr. Kennedy.

Through the long day of ceremony, she maintained the stoic dignity that she had displayed since an assassin's bullet killed her husband three days ago.

Only twice during the day did her tears appear. Once was in the cathedral, the second time after the burial service.

As the ceremony at the Arlington National Cemetery ended, she turned suddenly to Gen. Maxwell D. Taylor, chairman of the Joint Chiefs of Staff, who was a step or two away.

She embraced him and pressed her veiled cheek against his. Her dark eyes filled, and for an instant her face looked like that of a 34-year-old girl burdened with sorrow, instead of a President's wife.

Then Mrs. Kennedy turned away. She reached out and took the hand of her brother-in-law, Attorney General Robert F. Kennedy—a hand she held often during the day—and went back to the White House for the diplomatic reception.

Today happened to be the third birthday of her son, John, Jr., called 'John-John" by his father. John and his sister, Caroline, who will be 6 the day after tomorrow, were at the cathedral for the funeral service but were spared the ceremony at the cemetery.

As the children left the cathedral after the service John saw the honor guard of nine servicemen carry the flag-covered coffin of his father to the caisson that would bear it to Arlington.

He looked up at his mother. She whispered to him. Then he handed her a prayer book he was carrying, and his small right hand suddenly shot up a salute.

The children were taken back to the White House by their nurse, Miss Maud Shaw, and some Secret Service men.

The official business of the day began for Mrs. Kennedy at 10:25 o'clock this morning. She left the White House to travel by limousine to the Capitol, where thousands of persons had filed past the bier of the President.

Members of the White House staff lined the driveway. Across Pennsylvania Avenue, in Lafayette Park, the crowd was 20 to 30 persons deep. All was still.

The limousine soon reached the Capitol. Mrs. Kennedy walked up the steps with Robert Kennedy on her right and his brother, Edward M. Kennedy, on her left.

They walked together into the Rotunda and knelt for about half a minute at the foot of the coffin. Then they turned and went back out into the bright sun, with the body bearers carrying the coffin behind them.

When the procession reached the White House, Mrs. Kennedy got out of the car. She stood

Mrs. Kennedy Maintains a Stoic Dignity Throughout Final Hours of Public Grief

She Sheds Tears Only Twice —Returns to White House to Greet World Leaders

By ANTHONY LEWIS

The Kennedy Family leaves the Capitol rotunda. The President's body remained in the rotunda all day while thousands of people passed through, paying their respects.

The End of An Era

for a few moments behind the caisson in the driveway, her head high, her slight figure still. Once she glanced around at the dignitaries gathering behind her.

Then, to the strange sound of the bagpipes, she began the trip to the cathedral.

Past the silent crowds she walked, her two brothers-in-law on either side. Behind them came President Johnson and all the dignitaries. But the eyes of the people were on Mrs. Kennedy.

She was all in black. Her face and her brown hair could be seen only dimly from the distance, behind the black veil she flew against her face.

As the extraordinary walk began, she took Robert Kennedy's hand and held it. But then, resolutely, she dropped it and walked alone.

At the cathedral she waited for the children, who were driven over from the White House. She took them, one on each hand, and led them up the steps to meet Richard Cardinal Cushing. She dipped down in a genuflection and kissed his ring.

John seemed to be crying as they went into the cathedral, but his mother said a few words to him and he stopped. She could not so easily console Caroline, who wept after the service as they followed the coffin out of the church.

The procession formed again for the ride to Arlington. The horse-drawn caisson and the limousines crossed the Potomac. Probably few noticed the few fishermen with lines in the icy water.

The grave was at the base of the hill below the Custis-Lee Mansion, in an open space among the tall, bare elms. A single gnarled cedar still showed green.

The site, one of the most impressive in the 420-acre cemetery, had been selected by Robert Kennedy and Secretary of Defense Robert S. McNamara.

On the bank of the hill were wreaths of flowers, sent before Mrs. Kennedy could make known her wishes that flowers be withheld.

At 2:35 P.M., just before the procession arrived, two large bunches of white chrysanthemums and lilies were placed above the head of the grave. They were the gift of Mrs. Kennedy.

Units from each of the armed services filed in to stand beside the 100-foot-square of green carpet covering the earth.

It was noticeable that there were Negroes in each unit—a symbol of Mr. Kennedy's commitment against racial discrimination. One remembered the incident at his inauguration, when he remarked on the absence of Negro faces in a Coast Guard troop, an omission quickly remedied.

The caisson drew up at 2:43 P.M. At that moment leaves suddenly began floating down from what those waiting had thought was an empty sky.

The Marine Band played the national anthem. Then, slowly and eerily, Air Force bagpipers marched forward, three drums beating hollowly.

The coffin was carried up to the gravesite through two lines of Special Forces troops. Behind it, for the last time, went Mrs. Kennedy.

As they reached the gravesite, the bagpipes stopped. A moment later, 50 jet fighters flew overhead in formation with a reverberating roar. Then alone and much lower, came Air Force 1—the President's personal jet.

Robert Kennedy guided his sister-in-law to a chair. She sat at the left end of the row. To her right, in order, were Robert, Mrs. Rose Kennedy and the three Kennedy sisters — Mrs. Sargent Shriver, Mrs. Stephen E. Smith and Mrs. Peter Lawford.

Standing behind them were other members of the Kennedy family. Seven of the Attorney General's eight children were there, all but Christopher George, born last summer. Little blonde Mary Kerry, 4 years old, stood out on the side.

As the coffin was placed on the straps over the grave, Mrs. Kennedy and those beside her rose. The servicemen removed the flag that had covered it for three days and held it stretched tightly over the grave.

At Mrs. Kennedy's request, a troupe of Irish guards was on hand 26 young cadets in shiny brown boots from Ireland's West Point, the Army Cadet School. To commands shouted in Gaelic, they performed a brief drill, spinning their rifles slowly around.

Mrs. Kennedy held Robert's hand, then dropped it. Once or twice, as she stood to hear Cardinal Cushing's service, she leaned against Robert, as if for support.

When the wind came up, she put her hand to her hat. Her veil, falling almost to her waist behind her, moved in the breeze.

At 3:03 a gun on the hill began a 21-gun salute to the dead President. In the crowd, held behind ropes 100 yards away, a baby cried.

Mrs. Kennedy seemed to look at President de Gaulle of France, tall in the first row of spectators. Her friends thought his decision to come for the funeral meant something special to her as a lover of France and its civilization.

At 3:06 Robert Kennedy whispered to her, then led her forward to stand next to him at the head of the grave. Three rifle volleys were fired. A bugler sounded taps.

When the prayers were done, Mrs. Kennedy took a long-handled lighter and lit a flame at the head of the grave. The gas device had been installed there during the night, at her request, to burn as an eternal flame.

She handed the lighter to Robert Kennedy, who touched the flame again. Then Edward Kennedy, standing behind them with Cardinal Cushing, stepped forward and made the same gesture.

The eight men holding the flag folded it up and presented it, with a military salute, to the superintendent of the cemetery, John C. Metzler. He gave it to Mrs. Kennedy.

She and Robert shook the hands of Cardinal Cushing and the prelates with him. Suddenly, she embraced General Taylor. Then, after that moment of emotion, she resolutely took Robert Kennedy's hand and filed out through the line of soldiers.

The coffin, closed at the

Bethesda Naval Hospital early last Saturday morning with Mrs. Kennedy's wedding ring in her husband's hand, was still above ground. It was lowered into the earth at 3:34.

At the White House, after her return, Mrs. Kennedy met privately in the family quarters with three visiting heads of state—General de Gaulle, Emperor Haile Selassie of Ethiopia and President Eamon de Valera of Ireland.

Mrs. Kennedy saw the Emperor because of the circumstances of his visit to the United States last September. Mrs. Kennedy, then in mourning because of the death of her son Patrick Bouvier Kennedy the month before, interrupted her mourning and delayed a trip abroad for a day to meet the Emperor. He made it known this week that he was coming here for the funeral in respect for her as well as the President.

Then she went downstairs to meet the other foreign dignitaries in a formal receiving line. She shook hands with each as they filed into the Red Room of the White House from the State Dining Room.

With her in the receiving line were Robert Kennedy and his wife, Ethel; Edward Kennedy and his wife, Joan, and Mrs. Shriver and Mrs. Lawford.

There was no word tonight about Mrs. Kennedy's immediate plans—when she will leave the White House, where she and the children will spend Thanksgiving, where they will live.

An announcement is scheduled for tomorrow. The general belief is that Mrs. Kennedy will want to move out as soon as physically possible. And there is some feeling that she will stay in Washington.

Perhaps her choice of residence had something to do with the decision to bury Mr. Kennedy in the Arlington Cemetery rather than the family plot in Brookline, Mass. But Cardinal Cushing said that Arlington had been chosen to avoid prolonging the funeral period into tomorrow.

For Mrs. Kennedy, as for those who only watched, these three days of public anguish were as much as could be borne.

November 26, 1963

'Majesty of Mrs. Kennedy'

LONDON, Nov. 25 (AP)—"Jacqueline Kennedy has given the American people from this day on one thing they have always lacked—majesty."

This was the introduction of a dispatch from Washington in The

London Evening Standard today under the headline, 'Magic Majesty of Mrs. Kennedy.'

Accompanying this was a three-column portrait of Mrs. Kennedy, depicted as she looked upon her husband's coffin in the Capitol Rotunda.

November 26, 1963

MEADER IS DROPPING KENNEDY IMITATION

Vaughn Meader, who rose to popularity through a hit recording imitating President Kennedy and his family, will never do his comedy act again, he has announced through his manager.

His record, "The First Family," has sold more than 5 million copies since it was issued in November, 1962, a high for single-album sales in the United States. A second album made by Mr. Meader, "The Kennedy Family, Volume Two." sold fewer than 300,000.

A representative of the Booker-Doud organization, which wrote the albums and produced them through Cadence Records, said, "No new records of either album will be produced again under any circumstances."

Sam Goody, a leading retail record store, and Gimbels and Macy's record departments report that they have withdrawn the albums from sale. The Record Hunter, another large retail outlet, says that a few people have bought the album since the President's death.

Out of respect for the President, Mr. Meader has requested the postponement of two night-club commitments. The American Broadcasting Company has postponed Mr. Meader's appearance tonight on "Hootenanny." The Columbia Broadcasting System is putting off his five-day stint, starting Dec. 16, on the daily daytime television show, "To Tell the Truth."

November 30, 1963

HYANNIS PORT — She remembers how hot the sun was in Dallas, and the crowds— greater and wilder than the crowds in Mexico or in Vienna. The sun was blinding, streaming down, yet she could not put on sunglasses for she had to wave to the crowd.

And up ahead she remembers seeing a tunnel around a turn and thinking that there would be a moment of coolness under the tunnel. There was the sound of the motorcycles, as always in a parade, and the occasional backfire of a motorcycle. The sound of the shot came at that moment, like the sound of a backfire, and she remembers Connally saying, "No, no, no, no, no . . ."

She remembers the roses. Three times that day in Texas they had been greeted with the bouquets of yellow roses of Texas. Only, at Dallas they had given her red roses. She remembers thinking, how funny —red roses for me, and then the car was full of blood and red roses.

Much later, accompanying the body from the Dallas hospital to the airport, she was alone with Clint Hill —the first Secret Service man to come to their rescue—and with Dr. Burkley, the White House physician. Burkley gave her two roses that had slipped under the President's shirt when he fell, his head in her lap.

All through the night they tried to separate him from her, to sedate her, and take care of her—and she would not let them. She wanted to be with him. She remembered that Jack had said of his father, when his father suffered the stroke, that he could not live like that. Don't let that happen to me, he had said, when I have to go.

Now, in her hand she was holding a gold St. Christopher's medal.

She had given him a St.

Christopher's medal when they were married; but when Patrick died this summer, they had wanted to put something in the coffin with Patrick that was from them both, and so he had put in the St. Christopher's medal.

Then he had asked her to give him a new one to mark their 10th wedding anniversary, a month after Patrick's death.

He was carrying it when he died and she had found it. But it belonged to him—so she could not put that in the coffin with him. She wanted to give him something that was hers, something that she loved. So she had slipped off her wedding ring and put it on his finger. When she came out of the room in the hospital in Dallas, she asked: "Do you think it was right? Now I have nothing left." And Kenny O'Donnell said, "You leave it where it is."

That was at 1:30 P. M. in Texas.

But then, at Bethesda Hospital in Maryland at 1 A. M. the next morning, Kenny slipped into the chamber where the body lay and brought her back the ring, which, as she talked now, she twisted.

On her little finger was the other ring; a slim, gold circlet with green emerald chips—the one he had given her in memory of Patrick. There was a thought, too, that was always with her.

"When Jack quoted something, it was usually classical," she said, "but I'm so ashamed of myself—all I keep thinking of is this line from a musical comedy.

"At night, before we'd go to records; and the song he loved most came at the very end of this record. The lines he loved to hear were: Don't let it be forgot, that once there was a spot, for one brief shining moment that was known as Camelot."

She wanted to make sure that the point came clear and went

Mrs. Kennedy Likens the Capital Under Her Husband to 'Camelot'

She Recalls, in Life Interview, a 'Brief Shining Moment' and the President's 'Idealistic Hero Idea of History'

Theodore H. White, author of "The Making of the President, 1960," a close friend of President and Mrs. Kennedy, wrote "For President Kennedy an Epilogue" in the current issue of Life magazine.

Following is the full article, copyrighted by Time, Inc., publishers of Life, and made available to The Associated Press:

on: "There'll be great Presidents again—and the Johnsons are wonderful, they've been wonderful to me—but there'll never be another Camelot again.

"Once, the more I read of history the more bitter I got. For a while I thought history was something that bitter old men wrote. But then I realized history made Jack what he was. You must think of him as this little boy, sick so much of the time, reading in bed, reading history, reading the knights of the Round Table, reading Marlborough. For Jack, history was full of heroes. And if it made him this way—if it it made him see the heroes—maybe other little boys will see. Men are such a combination of good and bad. Jack had this hero idea of history, the idealistic view."

But she came back to the idea that transfixed her: "Don't let it be forgot, that once there was a spot, for one brief shining moment that was known as Camelot—and it will never be that way again."

The End of An Era

As for herself? She was horrified by stories that she might live abroad. "I'm never going to live in Europe. I'm not going to 'travel extensively abroad.'

"That's a desecration. I'm going to live in the places I lived with Jack. In Georgetown, and with the Kennedys at the Cape. They're my family. I'm going to bring up my children. I want John to grow up to be a good boy."

As for the President's memorial, at first she remembered that in every speech in their last days in Texas, he had spoken of how in December this nation would loft the largest rocket booster yet into the sky, making us first in space. So she had wanted something of his there when it went up—perhaps only his initials painted on a tiny corner of the great Saturn, where no one need even notice it. But now Americans will seek the moon from Cape Kennedy. The new name, born of her frail hope, came as a surprise.

The only thing she knew she must have for him was the eternal flame over his grave at Arlington.

"When ever you drive across the bridge from Washington into Virginia," she said, "you see the Lee mansion on the side of the hill in the distance. When Caroline was very little, the mansion was one of the first things she learned to recognize. Now, at night you can see his flame beneath the mansion for miles away."

She said it is time people paid attention to the new President and the new First Lady. But she does not want them to forget John F. Kennedy or read of him only in dusty or bitter histories:

For one brief shining moment there was Camelot.

December 5, 1963

Mrs. Kennedy Thanks 800,000 Who Expressed Their Sympathies

By NAN ROBERTSON

WASHINGTON, Jan. 14—Mrs. John F. Kennedy thanked the 800,000 persons from all over the world who have sent her and her two children messages of sympathy and grief. It was her first public statement in the 53 days since the assassination of her husband. She spoke before television cameras in the vaulted office of Attorney General Robert F. Kennedy, who has been a constant comfort to her from the day of his older brother's death. The Attorney General's younger brother, Senator Edward M. Kennedy, sat with him on a bright red sofa facing the former First Lady. She perched on the edge of a deep leather chair. Several times in her talk Mrs. Kennedy faltered slightly and held back tears. Her voice was barely audible to those standing a dozen feet away. She was dressed in a collarless black wool suit. The sole piece of jewelry she wore was her gold wedding band.

"The knowledge of the affection in which my husband was held by all of you has sustained me, and the warmth of these tributes is something I shall never forget," she said. "Whenever I can bear to, I read them."

"All his bright light gone from the world," she said, speaking more slowly.

"All of you who have written to me know how much we all loved him. . . ." Mrs. Kennedy hesitated, her eyes brimming, then went on, ". . . and that he returned that love in full measure."

Her voice grew stronger as she said: "It is my greatest wish that all of these letters be acknowledged. It will take a long time to do so, but I know you will understand."

Before the television cameras began to whirr, Mrs. Kennedy sat chatting and smiling with her brothers-in-law in front of a crackling log fire. She grew solemn when the time came for her message. Her hands were tightly clasped in her lap.

She told her audience that "each and every message is to be treasured" for her children and for future generations, and that all would be placed with President Kennedy's papers in the memorial library at Cambridge, Mass.

"I hope that you and your children will be able to visit the Kennedy library," she said.

When her 13-sentence statement was finished, she swallowed hard and looked at the Attorney General and his brother without speaking.

It was discovered afterward that there had been a technical breakdown. The American Broadcasting Company transmitted a picture of Mrs. Kennedy but no sound. The National Broadcasting Company had neither.

Mrs. John F. Kennedy with Senator Edward M. Kennedy and Attorney General Robert F. Kennedy before telecast

The Columbia Broadcasting System had both picture and sound and made its videotape available to the other networks.

A few minutes after making her statement, Mrs. Kennedy returned from an adjoining room to the Attorney General's office. He was at her side.

She walked toward a cluster of reporters she remembered from White House days. They scattered, thinking she wished to make her way through the crowd.

"Why are you all running away?" she said, and stretched out her hand, smiling. "I wanted to say hello."

Today Mrs. Kennedy made public a sampling of the hundreds of thousands of letters she had received from every section of this country and from such foreign cities as Addis Ababa, Saigon, Moscow, Paris and Ljubljana, Yugoslavia.

"I know this letter will probably never reach your hands" was a typical opening phrase.

A secretary at the University of Alabama whose husband is a graduate student there told how she heard the first news of the assassination:

"The Negro maid and I were in the kitchen of the building where I work when we heard the heart-shattering news of the shooting of your husband. We clung together, praying that he would live. Lolina, with tears running down her face, cried, 'He's the only one who has really tried to help us. Oh, please don't let him die.' "

January 15, 1964

WASHINGTON, Sept. 27— The assassination of President Kennedy was the work of one man, Lee Harvey Oswald. There was no conspiracy, foreign or domestic.

That was the central finding in the Warren Commission report, made public this evening. Chief Justice Earl Warren and the six other members of the President's Commission on the Assassination of President John F. Kennedy were unanimous on this and all questions.

The commission found that Jack Ruby was on his own in killing Oswald. It rejected all theories that the two men were in some way connected. It said that neither rightists nor Communists bore responsibility for the murder of the President in Dallas last Nov. 22.

Why did Oswald do it? To this most important and most mysterious question the commission had no certain answer. It suggested that Oswald had no rational purpose, no motive adequate if "judged by the standards of reasonable men."

A Product of His Life

Rather, the commission saw Oswald's terrible act as the product of his entire life—a life "characterized by isolation, frustration and failure." He was just 24 years old at the time of the assassination.

"Oswald was profoundly alienated from the world in which he lived," the report said. "He had very few, if any, close relationships with other people and he appeared to have had great difficulty in finding a meaningful place in the world.

"He was never satisfied with anything.

"When he was in the United States, he resented the capitalist system. When he was in the Soviet Union, he apparently resented the Communist party members, who were accorded special privileges and who he thought were betraying Communism, and he spoke well of the United States."

The commission found that Oswald shot at former Maj. Gen. Edwin A. Walker in Dallas on April 10, 1963, narrowly missing him. It cited this as evidence of his capacity for violence.

It listed as factors that might have led Oswald to the assassination "his deep-rooted resentment of all authority, which was expressed in a hostility toward every society in which he lived," his "urge to try to find a place in history" and his "avowed commitment to Marxism and Communism, as he understood the terms."

The report's findings on what happened in Dallas contained few surprises. The essential points had leaked out one way or another during the ten months since President Johnson appointed the commission last Nov. 29.

But the commission analyzed every issue in exhaustive, almost archeological detail. Experts traced the path of the bullets. Every critical event was re-enacted. Witnesses here and abroad testified to the most obscure points.

The question now is whether the report will satisfy those, especially abroad, who have insisted that there must have been a conspiracy in the assassination. The commission attempted to answer, specifically, every such theory and rumor.

The report did have surprises in its appraisal of the protection provided for the President by Federal agencies, and in its recommendations for improved methods of protection.

It was critical of the Secret Service for inadequate preventive measures, and of the Federal Bureau of Investigation for not giving the Secret Service the adverse information it had on Oswald. It called for higher-level Government attention to the problem of protecting the President, and possibly for reorganization.

The commission made public all the information it had bearing on the events in Dallas, whether agreeing with its findings or not. It withheld only a few names of sources, notably sources evidently within Communist embassies in Mexico, and each of these omissions was indicated.

All the testimony taken by the commission and its staff— from 552 witnesses—will be published separately. It will fill 15 supplementary volumes, and there will be eight or nine more large volumes of exhibits. They are to be made public soon.

The report itself ran 888 pages, with eight chapters and 18 appendices. The commission's thoroughness is indicated by the fact that it interviewed every known person who met Oswald during a brief trip he made to Mexico. Interviewing continued into this month.

Drafting of the report was done by the commission's legal staff under J. Lee Rankin, general counsel. But all seven members of the commission themselves went over, edited and substantially rewrote the entire work.

'A Group Product'

A staff lawyer remarked that this report was probably unlike any other in the history of commissions—"It really is a group product, the work of the commissioners."

The members, in addition to the chief justice, were Senators Richard B. Russell of Georgia and John Sherman Cooper of Kentucky, Representatives Hale Boggs of Louisiana and Gerald R. Ford of Michigan, Allen W. Dulles and John J. McCloy. All are Republicans save Mr. Russell and Mr. Boggs.

In a foreword, the commission says that it operated not as judge or jury—because Oswald could never have a trial— but as a dispassionate fact-finder. This is borne out by the report, which is neutral in tone and makes every effort to be fair in its discussions of Oswald.

Despite the group authorship and the legal approach, the report often achieves a genuine literary style. The very detail of the narrative is fascinating, and there are many moving passages.

Few who loved John Kennedy, or this country, will be able to read it without emotion.

Cheering Crowds

As the President's motorcade drove through Dallas on Nov. 22, large crowds cheered. Gov. John Conally's wife, who was in the car, said to Mr. Kennedy,

---

Warren Report Finds Oswald Guilty and Says He and Ruby Acted Alone

PANEL UNANIMOUS

Theory of Conspiracy by Left or Right Is Rejected

By ANTHONY LEWIS

"Mr. President, you can't say Dallas doesn't love you." He answered, "That is very obvious."

A moment later the shots were fired.

Mrs. Kennedy, according to the report, "saw the President's skull torn open" by the second bullet that hit him. She testified that she cried out, "Oh, my God! They've shot my husband. I love you, Jack."

A reader of the report is struck again and again by the series of events that had to fall into place to make the assassination possible. Over a period of years, so many men could have done so many things that would have changed history.

On Oct. 31, 1959, Oswald appeared at the United States Embassy in Moscow and stated that he wanted to renounce his citizenship. While he had a right to do so at once, consular officials did not want to let a young man take so final a step precipitously. They told him to come back the following week.

He never came back. If Oswald had been allowed to expatriate himself at once, he would have found it difficult or impossible to return to the United States when he tired of the Soviet Union.

Similarly, American officials helped Oswald and his Russian wife, Marina, when they wanted to come to the United States in 1962 because they thought it better for this country to bring a defector back. The report says "it is only from the vantage of the present that the tragic irony of their conclusion emerges."

When Oswald shot at General Walker, he told Marina. She warned him not to do a thing like that again—but she did not tell the police or anyone else. If she had, . . .

When he returned from Mexico, he applied for a job with a printing company in Dallas. He was not hired because a previous employer told the company he was a "troublemaker." On Oct. 15, 1963, he got a job with the Texas School Book Depository. A month later a Presidential route was chosen that went by that building.

The Federal Bureau of Investigation learned in early November, 1963, that Oswald—whom it knew as a defector and proclaimed friend of Castro—was in Dallas and worked at the depository. The agents neither interviewed Oswald nor reported the fact to the Secret Service when the President's motorcade route was published.

At the time of the assassination, Oswald had a room in Dallas while his wife stayed with friends in nearby Irving. The evening of Nov. 21 he asked her to move to Dallas with him. She was angry with him, and she refused.

In the depository the next day, Bonnie Ray Williams ate a lunch of chicken on the sixth floor and then went down to the fifth floor to watch the motorcade with friends. That left Oswald alone on the sixth.

It rained in Dallas that morning, but the rain stopped and

so officials took the plastic bubbletop off the President's car. That top was not bulletproof, but Oswald might not have known that and might in any event have had greater difficulty sighting through it.

Finally, there was the arrangement of the Presidential car.

Mr. and Mrs. Kennedy sat in the rear, Governor and Mrs. Connally on the jump seats. A Secret Service agent drove, and another sat next to him, but they were separated from the passenger compartment by the front seat and a metal bar 15 inches above it. And the President had asked that no agents ride on small running boards provided at the rear.

The second bullet that hit the President was the fatal one. The commission found that if a Secret Service man had been in a position to reach him quickly, "it is possible" that he could have protected the President from the second shot.

Confusion on Shots

The report clarified what had been considerable confusion about the bullets. Much of this stemmed from the necessarily hasty examination made by doctors at Parkland Memorial Hospital in Dallas in their desperate effort to save the President's life.

The commission found that in all probability three bullets were fired. Three empty cartridges were found inside the sixth floor window of the depository. Also recovered were one nearly whole bullet and fragments of one or two others.

One of the bullets missed, the report said. It was not certain whether this came before, between or after the two that hit.

The first of the two shots that did not miss hit the President in the lower back of the neck and emerged at the lower front. Mr. Kennedy grabbed at his throat and said "My God, I'm hit."

"President Kennedy could have survived the neck injury," the commission found. But between 4.8 and 5.6 seconds later —the time was calculated from an amateur movie film—the fatal bullet hit the back of the President's head.

Condition 'Hopeless'

The time was 12:30. When he arrived at the hospital five minutes later, the report said, Mr. Kennedy was alive "from a medical viewpoint"; there was a heart beat. But "his condition was hopeless." He was pronounced dead at 1 P.M.

Some uncertainty remains about how Governor Connally was hit. But the commission said the probability was that the first bullet that struck the President went on through the Governor's chest, then his wrist and finally lodged in his thigh.

All of these points were demonstrated by the commission with elaborate re-enactments, expert testimony and experiments on simulated skulls and bodies. The report contains many macabre pages of such detail.

"The cumulative evidence of eyewitnesses, firearms and ballistic experts and medical authorities," the report said, demonstrated that the shots were fired from the sixth floor of the depository building.

Experts said flatly that the nearly whole bullet and two large fragments recovered could only have been fired by the 6.5 millimeter Mannlicher-Carcano rifle found inside the depository window.

No Bullet From Front

One apparent conflict dismissed by the report was the talk that a mark on the Presidential car's windshield had been made by a bullet coming from in front of it. Experts testified that the glass had been hit by a fragment from behind. The commission found that no shots had come from the front.

In painstaking detail, the report connected Oswald with that rifle and that position at the window.

It traced his purchase of the gun. It showed that he had taken the gun to work in a homemade paper bag that morning.

His fingerprints were on the bag, and on some cartons on which the rifle apparently rested. A witness saw a man who looked like Oswald at the window with the gun.

And the commission found that he had the ability to hit the target easily at that distance, 177 to 266 feet, with a telescopic sight and the target moving off in a straight line from him.

It found that he killed a Dallas patrolman, J. D. Tippit, 45 minuthes later. Numerous eyewitnesses saw him during or after this shooting. And the bullets came from the revolver he carried when he was arrested shortly afterward.

In discussing Oswald's possible motives, the report portrayed a man of strange contradictions. He said he was "a Marxist but not a Leninist-Marxist." One of his favorite books was George Orwell's powerfully antitotalitarian "1984."

He wrote letters to American Communist party leaders volunteering his services. But some of these leaders testified that Oswald was never a member, and the commission so found.

The commission also rejected, after complete access to the files of the F.B.I. and the Central Intelligence Agency, the claim that Oswald may have been some kind of American undercover agent.

After his arrest, he told the police that "My wife and I like the President's family. They are interesting people."

He said: "I am not a malcontent; nothing irritated me about the President."

All the frustrations in Lee Harvey Oswald seemed to come to a climax in the last weeks of his life. The report paints a sad, sensitive picture.

His dream of glory in the Soviet Union had collapsed. He

had not been able to go to Cuba. He had a menial job, packing textbooks. His wife, the commission said, ridiculed his political views and complained about his sexual capacity.

Oswald ordinarily went from Dallas to the home of Mrs. Michael Paine, where his family was staying in Irving, Tex., for weekends. Marina asked him not to come the weekend of Nov. 16-17, 1963, because the Paines were having a birthday party.

Then Marina discovered that he was using an alias, O. H. Lee, at his rooming house in Dallas. When he telephoned on Nov. 18, she was angry with him. When he went to the house on Nov. 21, she at first refused to talk to him and then refused to move the family to Dallas.

"Oswald had an exaggerated sense of his own importance, but he had failed at almost everything he had ever tried to do," the commission concluded.

"It must have appeared to him that he was unable to command even the attention of his family. His family lived with Mrs. Paine, ostensibly because Oswald could not afford to keep an apartment in Dallas, but it was also, at least in part, because his wife did not want to live there with him."

The commission added that it did not believe that "the relations between Oswald and his wife caused him to assassinate the President. It is unlikely that the motivation was that simple.

Discussing the two days of Oswald's detention before his murder, the report rejected claims that he was not allowed counsel or was mistreated by the police. He saw his family and was offered a lawyer, it said.

But the commission was highly critical of the way the press and cameramen were allowed the free run of the Dallas police station, crowding around Oswald and very likely making possible Ruby's entry in the confusion of the final moments.

Police Criticized

During the "confusion and disorder" of those two days, the commission said, the police said much to much—some of it erroneous—about the case. They effectively convicted Oswald before he was tried, and the commission said a fair trial would have been difficult after all the publicity.

All conspiracy theories were flatly rejected in the report.

"The commission found no evidence that the Soviet Union or Cuba were involved in the assassination of President Kennedy," the report said. "Nor did the commission's investigation of Jack Ruby produce any grounds for believing that Ruby's killing of Oswald was part of a conspiracy."

The report added that these conclusions were also reached independently by Secretary of State Rusk, Secretary of Defense Robert S. McNamara, Secretary of the Treasury Douglas Dillon, the Central Intelligence Agency Director John A. McCone, the Secret Service Chief, James J. Rowley, the Federal Bureau of Investigation Director J. Edgar Hoover, and former Attorney General Robert F. Kennedy, the fallen President's brother.

It said that "because of the difficulty of proving negatives to a certainty, the possibility of others' being involved with either Oswald or Ruby cannot be established categorically, but if there is any such evidence it has been beyond the reach of all the investigative agencies and resources of the United States and has not come to the attention of this commission."

The commission reported that many steps had already been taken to tighten F.B.I. and Secret Service measures against potential assailants of the President. It called for further improvements.

On trips, the report said, the President's doctor should always be near him and much greater effort should be made to check buildings along motor routes.

A Cabinet-level committee should review and oversee the whole matter of protecting the President, the commission suggested. It said the question whether the job should remain with the Secret Service might be considered by such a committee.

Congress was urged to enact, at long last, legislation making assassination of the President a Federal crime. The report said such a law would end divided authority and possibly prevent disorder and confusion such as prevailed in Dallas after Nov. 22.

September 28, 1964

WARREN UNIT BACKED BY EDWARD KENNEDY

WASHINGTON, July 31 (UPI)—Senator Edward M. Kennedy said today that although he had not read the Warren Commission Report he was convinced Lee Harvey Oswald alone assassinated President Kennedy.

The 34-year-old Massachussetts Democratf said:

"I never read the Warren Commission Report. However, I am satisfied that it represents at least conclusively the results which I believe are accurate. I have not read it. And I do not intend to do so."

A recent book by Edward Jay Epstein, a Harvard University graduate student, said the Warren Report had been hastily prepared and was inaccurate and incomplete. Mr. Epstein concluded that the commission headed by Chief Justice Earl Warren had not proved its principal finding that Oswald had acted alone.

Richard N. Goodwin, a former speech writer and troubleshooter for the late President, suggested last week that an independent panel look into the charges and, if necessary, that Congress establish a new board to seek new evidence.

August 1, 1966

WASHINGTON, June 2 — The House Select Committee on Assassinations has gone substantially beyond the findings of the Warren Commission and has concluded that a conspiracy, perhaps involving organized crime figures, led to the assassination of President Kennedy.

After spending two and a half years and $5 million, the committee says in its final report, to be released soon, that the conspirators may have included organized crime figures, Cubans and James R. Hoffa, former president of the International Brotherhood of Teamsters. But a source close to the committee said the investigation did not produce "a smoking gun."

"There is no evidence of a meeting where the murder was planned, there is no account of the details of the plot," the source said. "There is a substantial body of evidence, a web of circumstantial evidence, to connect the death of the President to elements of organized crime. Not to a national crime syndicate, nor to one individual."

G. Robert Blakey, chief counsel and staff director of the committee, said from his home that he would not comment on the details of the committee report. Asked if he had a personal opinion of the committee's findings, Mr. Blakey, now a professor of law at Cornell University, said:

"I think the mob did it."

According to the committee source, the report establishes that "no longer are we able to accept the judgment of the Warren Commission that President Kennedy was killed by a loner who was a lone assassin."

The report also will urge the Department of Justice to renew its efforts to try to determine who worked with Lee Harvey Oswald, named by the Warren Commission as the sole assassin, to plot and carry out the murder of President Kennedy.

About six months ago, the committee

Assassination Panel's Final Report Backs Theory of Plot on Kennedy

By WENDELL RAWLS Jr.

presented acoustical evidence that it said showed that two gunmen had fired at the Presidential motorcade as it made its way through Dealy Plaza in Dallas on Nov. 22, 1963. But three members of the committee called the evidence into question and disagreed with its assertion that Oswald was not a lone gunman, as the Warren Commission insisted.

Additional Evidence

The New York Times learned today that the conclusion that the President was murdered as a result of a conspiracy rests on more than acoustical evidence.

According to sources familiar with the committee's investigation and final report, to be made public by the end of this month, extensive electronic surveillance material accumulated by the Federal Bureau of Investigation showed that major organized crime figures were deeply disturbed by prosecutions, investigations and other actions carried out against them by the Kennedy Justice Department and vowed revenge against both the President and his brother, Robert F. Kennedy, who was Attorney General.

The surveillance was conducted between 1959 and 1965, and thus covered years before and after the Kennedy Administration.

Although the authorities have long contended that the Government's surveillance covered all major rackets figures, the assassinations committee was surprised to find that it was not as comprehensive as generally thought.

Two major underworld figures, Carlos Marcello of New Orleans and Santos Trafficante of Tampa, were not covered by the electronic surveillance.

According to the committee source, extensive investigation of Marcello and Trafficante lieutenants disclosed that they were connected to the two principal figures in Dallas at the time of the shooting — Oswald and Jack Ruby, who shot Oswald to death as millions of Americans watched on live television.

The report will contend that Ruby had stalked his victim from the hours immediately after the assassination until he fired a bullet into Oswald's stomach two days later, and that he had had help gaining access to the assassin, perhaps unwittingly, from Dallas policemen.

The committee report maintains that Ruby also had extensive associations among organized crime figures and discloses that his telephone records indicate a small number of calls, possible relating to criminal activity, to a variety of people connected with the underworld, including Sam Giancana, who subsequently was murdered in his home in Chicago, and strong-arm men tied to Mr. Trafficante.

The committee discounts Ruby's statement before his own death that he had killed Oswald so that the President's widow would be spared a return to Dallas, where she might be forced to relive the shattering moments of the assassination as a witness at Oswald's trial.

That story was concocted by his lawyer, the committee asserts.

The final report, including some 30 volumes accumulated from public hearings, will also examine a variety of links between Oswald and the Soviet and Cuban Governments, anti-Castro Cuban groups and a small, amorphous left-wing group.

June 3, 1979

SENATOR KENNEDY HURT IN AIR CRASH; BAYH INJURED, TOO

Both Are in Fair Condition in Massachusetts Hospital —Pilot of Plane Killed

SOUTHAMPTON, Mass., Saturday, June 20—Senator Edward M. Kennedy, younger brother of President Kennedy, and Senator Birch Bayh were injured in the crash of a private plane last night while on the way to the Massachusetts Democratic Convention.

The pilot was killed and two other persons were injured. Mr. Kennedy was semiconscious.

Both Senators were reported in fair condition at Cooley Dickinson Hospital in nearby Northampton.

Also injured were Mrs. Bayh, reported in good condition, and Edward Moss of Andover, administrative aide to Mr. Kennedy, who was reported in critical condition.

The pilot was identified as Edwin J. Zimny, 48 years old, of Lawrence, a last-minute substitute for the regular Kennedy pilot.

Senator Kennedy, Democrat of Massachusetts, was treated in an emergency room for back and chest injuries. His wife, Joan, visited him after he was transferred to an intensive-care unit.

Senator Bayh, Democrat of Indiana, suffered a hip injury. Mrs. Bayh was reported suffering from shock.

Mr. Kennedy's parents, Mr. and Mrs. Joseph P. Kennedy, who were vacationing at their summer home in Hyannis Port, were not told of the plane crash.

Attorney General Robert F. Kennedy, brother of the Senator, boarded the family plane with an aide and was reported on the way to Boston.

Two Civil Aeronautics Board investigators were sent from New York to investigate the crash.

Robert Schauer of Southampton said he and two nephews talked with the Bayhs at the scene of the crash—an apple orchard near Hadley Airport.

Mr. Schauer said Mr. Kennedy was able to talk but did not want to be moved.

President Johnson telephoned the hospital to inquire about the conditions of the Senators.

The President was notified in San Francisco of the plane accident by White House communications as he rode in an automobile from the Fairmont Hotel to the Hilton Hotel to deliver a speech at a Democratic party fund-raising dinner.

Wife Goes to Hospital

Mrs. Kennedy, who was at the convention in Springfield, about 15 miles away, left for the hospital as soon as the crash was announced at the convention.

She was accompanied by Gov. Endicott Peabody of Massachusetts.

The convention chairman, former State Senate President

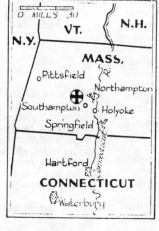

Air crash scene (cross)

John E. Powers, announced that Mr. Kennedy had survived the crash. A huge cheer went up from the convention.

Mr. Kennedy, who is 32 years old, was elected to the Senate in 1962, defeating George Cabot Lodge for the last two years of his brother's term. He is up for re-election to a full six-year term in the fall.

Born in the Boston suburb of Brookline, he is the youngest of the nine children of Joseph P. Kennedy, former Ambassador to Britain. His oldest brother, Joseph P. Kennedy Jr., was killed as a World War II fighter pilot.

Edward Kennedy's first plunge into politics came in 1958 when he served as campaign manager for John F. Kennedy. In 1960, he was Western states campaign coordinator in his brother's successful Presidential campaign.

Mr. Bayh, 36, also won his seat in the Senate in 1962. In a stunning upset, he defeated Republican Senator Homer Capehart, who was seeking his fourth term.

Mr. Kennedy had been scheduled to attend the convention's opening earlier in the day but was delayed in Washington by the vote on the civil rights bill. Mrs. Kennedy, however, was waiting for her husband in the convention hall.

At Page Aviation operations office at Washington National Airport, a registration card filed tonight by the pilot of the plane indicated that six persons had been scheduled to make the flight to New England.

The plane was a twin-engine Aero Commander that arrived at Washington National Airport at 5:20 P.M. today with two persons aboard and took off again at 8:35 P.M. after the pilot filed the registration card.

The plane was owned by Andover Aviation of Andover, Mass.

June 20, 1964

Weather Poor for Flight

SOUTHAMPTON, June 20 (UPI)—The Weather Bureau reported visibility was less than two and one-half miles because of fog at the time of the crash. Conditions were "marginal" even for landing a plane by instrument, it said.

Mr. Kennedy appeared to be lucid. He talked to nurses from his stretcher as he was taken from an ambulance.

Mr. Bayh appeared to be in pain, but asked that the others be treated first.

In Washington, Attorney General Kennedy's office said it understood the last rites of the Roman Catholic Church had been administered to Mr. Moss.

June 20, 1964

Mrs. John F. Kennedy, who celebrated her 35th birthday here yesterday, has agreed to buy a 15-room apartment on Fifth Avenue.

The apartment is on the top floor of a gray granite 15-story building at 1040 Fifth Avenue, at 85th Street. It has five bedrooms and overlooks a bridle path and the reservoir in Central Park.

Earlier this month, Mrs. Kennedy announced in Washington that she was giving up her Georgetown home and would move to New York in early fall.

The announcement indicated that the widow of the slain President wanted to leave the tragic memories of Washington, where her home had become a major tourist attraction.

Douglas L. Elliman, head of the real estate concern that is managing agent for the Fifth Avenue building, said last night that the apartment had been sold for about $200,000. Maintenance charges, he said, were about $14,000 annually.

The apartment has been owned by Mr. and Mrs. Lowell P. Weicker, who plan to move to a penthouse in the same building, Mr. Elliman said. Mr. Weicker is president of the Bigelow - Sanford Carpet Company.

Mr. Elliman said 30 other families lived in the building, which was built in the nineteen twenties and has two apartments on each floor. Mrs. Kennedy will occupy both apartments on the top floor.

The building is at the northeast corner of Fifth Avenue and 85th Street. Mrs. Kennedy's apartment has nine windows overlooking 85th Street and 14 windows on the Central Park side. There are no windows on the north side.

Many of the cooperative building's residents are in the Social Register. Mr. Elliman said that the Kennedy family would have to be approved by the building's board of directors, a procedure that may take as long as two months. Until then, the sale is not final.

Mrs. Kennedy has continued to live in Georgetown since last Feb. 1. Her home is only three blocks from a house she occupied with her husband when he was a Senator from Massachusetts.

Her new home will be only a few blocks from that of her sister, Princess Stanislaus Radziwill, who lives at 969 Fifth Avenue.

Mrs. Kennedy arrived in New York yesterday at La Guardia Airport from Hyannis Port, Mass., where she has been spending the summer with her children, Caroline, 6 years old, and John, Jr., 3.

Private Birthday Party

Last night, she attended a private birthday party with relatives and friends in a private dining room of the Four Seasons restaurant.

The guests at the party were Attorney General Robert F. Kennedy, Eugene Black, former president of the World Bank; McGeorge Bundy, President Johnson's assistant on national security affairs, Mr. Lawford and Stephen E. Smith. Mrs. Smith is another sister of President Kennedy.

Mrs. Kennedy, wearing a black-ribbed silk dress, was presented with a 15-inch cake decorated with sugar roses and one candle.

The party had apparently been called to discuss plans for the Kennedy Memorial Library in Cambridge, Mass., but it turned out instead to be a surprise party for Mrs. Kennedy.

Mrs. Kennedy is scheduled to leave today for Newport, R. I., where she will join her children at Annandale Farm, an estate adjoining Hammersmith, the home of her mother and stepfather, Mr. and Mrs. Hugh D. Auchincloss.

On Aug. 5, Mrs. Kennedy plans to begin a weeklong cruise off the coast of Yugoslavia on a yacht, The Radiant, owned by Mr. and Mrs. Charles Wrightsman of Palm Beach, Fla., and New York.

Among the residents of the building at 1040 Fifth Avenue are Kenneth C. Royall, former Secretary of the Army; Jack W. Schiffer, a broker; André Istel, former financial adviser to the French Government; Sheldon Whitehouse, former Minister to Guatemala and Colombia, and Mrs. Simon Guggenheim, president of the John Simon Guggenheim Foundation and the widow of Senator Simon Guggenheim of Colorado.

July 29, 1964

WASHINGTON, July 31 — Robert F. Kennedy was eliminated from consideration for the Democratic Vice-Presidential nomination because of the racial crisis and because President Johnson concluded that the Attorney General would hurt the ticket in crucial areas more than some other candidates.

The President's reasoning emerged from extensive polling, numerous conversations between himself and a wide range of political and business leaders and his own reading of the political situation.

That reading is as follows:

¶The vote of the Republican candidate, Senator Barry Goldwater, against the civil rights bill will have the effect of creating sharper racial conflict throughout the country while the Presidential campaign is in progress.

¶Since Senator Goldwater is expected to carry some of the Southern states, most likely Alabama, Mississippi, Virginia and Florida, the real campaign battleground will be in the border states and the big Midwestern states.

Racial Crisis a Factor

These views of the President can be set forth on the highest authority.

In Mr. Kennedy's case, the President came to the conclusion that it would be inadvisable to replace the Attorney General at a time of racial crisis exemplified by such events as the Rochester and Harlem riots and the disappearance of three civil rights workers in Mississippi.

In addition, Mr. Kennedy is so thoroughly identified with the civil rights issue that he would have created additional difficulties for the Democratic ticket in some Southern states that Mr. Johnson believes he can carry or in which he at least has a good chance to win.

But this was not the only weakness of the Attorney General, in the President's view. His polling and conversations also convinced him that Mr. Kennedy was bitterly opposed in crucial areas on grounds other than civil rights.

This opposition, much of it among businessmen, was centered on Mr. Kennedy's role in the steel-price rollback of 1962, particularly the use of the Federal Bureau of Investigation to gain information; on a reluctance to see a "Kennedy dynasty" created, and on a feeling that he was too young and ambitious.

A number of influential supporters, or potential supporters, of the Johnson candidacy, made it plain to the President that they could not back a ticket with Mr. Kennedy on it. A number of Democratic party leaders, aware of those sentiments, also opposed his nomination or were not active in support of it.

Mr. Johnson came to the conclusion that these factors outweighed Mr. Kennedy's strengths—the Kennedy name, his stature among Roman Catholics and ethnic groups, his organizational ability, his dedication to public service and his experience in national politics.

For instance, in one poll taken for the White House, the Attorney General emerged as the most popular of the several potential candidates among the general public. This was a nationwide poll, however, and did not reflect stiff opposition to him in crucial areas.

In another division of the same poll, Adlai E. Stevenson scored highest as the man the public believed most qualified to succeed to the Presidency, should something happen to Mr. Johnson.

Humphrey Was Second

Senator Hubert Humphrey of Minnesota placed second in

RIGHTS ROLE HURT KENNEDY CHANCES

Johnson Feared He Would Be Liability in Key Areas

By TOM WICKER

both divisions of the poll — on popularity and on qualifications for the Presidency. A separate poll showed that his Minnesota colleague, Senator Eugene McCarthy, would be the strongest candidate in the South and the border states.

Both Mr. Stevenson and Mr. Kennedy were eliminated from consideration by Mr. Johnson's statement yesterday that it would be inadvisable to recommend to the Democratic convention anyone in the Cabinet or meeting regularly with it.

Also eliminated yesterday — in the President's own listing — were Secretary of Defense Robert S. McNamara, Secretary of State Dean Rusk, Secretary of Agriculture Orville L. Freeman and R. Sargent Shriver, Director of the Peace Corps.

Mr. Johnson emphasized at the time of his announcement that he had made no decision on a running mate but speculation immediately centered on Senators Humphrey and McCarthy.

These men are not alone, however, in what Mr. Johnson considers to be the "A" group of potential candidates. He has mentioned no others, even to intimates, but a college president is among them.

Mr. Johnson wanted to head off speculation about his Cabinet and the Vice Presidency. In addition, he had informed some of those being talked abut that they would not be selected. Finally, he had been holding increasingly detailed conversations with political leaders about the Vice-Presidential choice, in which some of his views were becoming rather widely known.

Thus, to remove his Cabinet from the arena, and to head off the possibility of leaks about any of them and about his various conversations, Mr. Johnson took his sudden action yesterday.

To what extent it was motivated by a desire to settle the Robert Kennedy matter well before the convention on Aug. 24 is a matter of speculation. Mr. Kennedy was informed of the President's decision, by Mr. Johnson, on Wednesday.

Some of Mr. Johnson's considerations involving the others eliminated yesterday were as follows:

¶He believed that Mr. Shriver would be an able and attractive candidate but that his experience in Government was too limited to qualify him for the Presidency.

Clubs Were Taking Shape

¶Mr. McNamara was given strong consideration, but did not want the nomination and was opposed by Democratic party leaders because of his Republican background.

¶Mr. Stevenson's age, 64, was at least one factor in his elimination. In addition, Mr. Johnson believes Mr. Stevenson is better qualified than any other man to represent the United States in the United Nations, and there is no one as qualified to replace him.

In eliminating these and the others as and when he did, Mr. Johnson was also influenced by the fact that some public groups were being formed to support some of them — including Mr. Stevenson, Mr. Rusk and Mr. Kennedy. He felt it only fair to let those groups know in advance that their candidates had been eliminated from his list of potentials.

Several impressions have been made on Mr. Johnson by his numerous polls and his extensive conversations with Governors, Mayors, city and state Democratic leaders, and other political officials.

One of these is that Democrats, by and large, will nominate whomever he chooses, with little dissent. He found no widespread and powerful movement for any single candidate. In particular, he believes that reports of great party support for Mr. Kennedy were exaggerated.

From the polls he has studied, Mr. Johnson has drawn such conclusions as the following:

¶Among religious groups, more than 90 per cent of the Jews support him, and he has heavy support among Roman Catholics.

¶The so-called "white backlash" against the civil rights bill will have only a minor effect in the Northern states.

¶All the potential Vice-Presidential candidates in public speculation would hurt the ticket in some way. Mr. Johnson's polls show that he would be least hurt by a candidate who was accepted by the public as having excellent Presidential qualifications.

August 1, 1964

Success Spoils Kennedy Clan's Business Fling

Children's Sidewalk Stands at Hyannis Port Closed as Tourists Pour In

---

HYANNIS PORT, Mass., Aug. 7 (AP)—The sidewalk stores went out of business today. There were too many customers, and too many curious tourists.

The merchants were nieces and nephews of the late President Kennedy. They had set up shop on orange crates and were selling postcards with the President's picture, medallions and other things.

The object was to raise funds for the Kennedy Memorial Library to be built in Boston near Harvard University.

They had been doing pretty well, too, raising nearly $50 as of yesterday from sales to tourists who were flabbergasted — and willing — buyers when they discovered the identities of the storekeepers.

But the word got around today and Hyannis Port's narrow streets were jammed with cars and tourists.

The police were sent to help clear the jam, and, perhaps at their request, the orange crate sidewalk stores went out of business.

The storekeepers were the children of President Kennedy's brother Attorney General Robert F. Kennedy and of his sisters, Mrs. Sargent Shriver, Mrs.

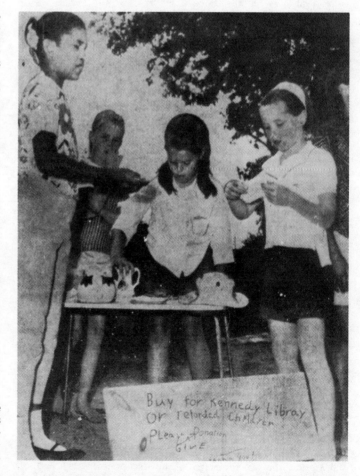

Maria Shriver, 8, daughter of Sargent Shriver, Peace Corps director, and Mrs. Shriver, arranges wares on table as Courtney Kennedy, 8, daughter of Attorney General Robert F. Kennedy and Mrs. Kennedy, prepares to sell postcard to a customer. Sign reads: "Buy for Kennedy Library or retarded children." Other Kennedy clan youngsters also became entrepreneurs yesterday at Hyannis Port, Mass., before police ended it—too many tourists.

Peter Lawford and Mrs. Stephen Smith.

One orange-crate stand was solely for the $10 million Kennedy Memorial Library.

Directly across the street, 8-year-old Maria Shriver had a stand bearing this hand-scrawled sign:

"Buy for Kennedy Libray or retarded children."

Hyannis Port residents said the children did a brisk business as tourists — looking for the late President's home — found out that they were nieces or nephews of John F. Kennedy. His children, Caroline, 6, and John Jr., 3, are at Newport,

R. I., for the summer.

Among the wares at the sidewalk stands were ash trays with the initials "JFK," medals bearing Mr. Kennedy's likeness and postcards with his picture.

August 8, 1964

Attorney General Robert F. Kennedy announced yesterday that he was a candidate for the Senate and said that President Johnson would come here to help in his campaign.

Mr. Kennedy, entering elective politics for the first time, is assured of the nomination at the Democratic State Convention on Sept. 1. His principal opponent in the November election will be Senator Kenneth B. Keating, a Republican.

With his wife, Ethel, on his left and Mayor Wagner on his right, Mr. Kennedy made his announcement on the lawn of Gracie Mansion, the Mayor's tree-shaded official residence facing the East River.

The Attorney General met squarely the charges of his opponents in the Democratic party that he is a "carpetbagger" who is interested in the Senate seat only because he needs a new political base.

"There may be some who believe that where a candidate voted in the past is more important than his capacity to serve the state," Mr. Kennedy said. "I cannot in fairness ask them to vote for me."

After recalling that his mother and father had maintained a New York apartment since 1926, Mr. Kennedy added: "I do not base my candidacy on these considerations.

"I base it on the belief that New York is not separate from the nation in the year 1964. I base it on the conviction that my experience and my record equip me to understand New York's problems and to do something about them."

The Attorney General's announcement was the climax of an intensive one-month campaign to capture the nomination. Stephen E. Smith, one of Mr. Kennedy's brothers-in-law, directed the campaign.

Representative Samuel S. Stratton of Amsterdam is the only other candidate for the nomination. He has promised to wage a floor fight at the convention.

Mr. Stratton's campaign manager, George V. Palmer of Schenectady, said yesterday that Mr. Kennedy's bid represented "callous and arrogant domination by big-city bosses."

"The nomination of a non-resident," Mr. Palmer said, "will be fought before the state committee, at the state convention, before the Secretary of State and in the courts."

Fred A. Young, the state Republican chairman, said he was glad Mr. Kennedy was running, and he predicted that "the nomination of this outsider" by the Democrats would contribute significantly to the re-election of Mr. Keating.

The Attorney General, dressed in a black, pin-striped suit with a black tie, walked down the steps of Gracie Mansion at 11:07 and mounted a small podium set up on the lawn. His hands trembled slightly as he read his statement in a somber voice to a circle of reporters.

Mr. Kennedy said in his prepared statement that he had decided to run here because he thought that the country was

facing "a fundamental political choice."

"All that President Kennedy stood for and all that President Johnson is trying to accomplish, all the progress that has been made, is threatened by a new and dangerous Republican assault," the Attorney General added.

"No one associated with President Kennedy and with President Johnson—no one committed to participating in public life—can sit on the sidelines with so much at stake."

Wife At His Side

After he had finished, Mr. Kennedy remained on the podium for 20 minutes answering questions. Mrs. Kennedy, who is expecting a ninth child in December, remained at his side.

During the question period, he said Mr. Johnson would cam-

KENNEDY ENTERS RACE FOR SENATE

Makes Formal Bid at Gracie Mansion—Says Johnson Will Help in Campaign

NEW FACE ON THE STATE SCENE: Attorney General Robert F. Kennedy announcing his candidacy for Senate seat from New York. Mr. Kennedy is flanked by Mayor Wagner and Mrs. Kennedy as he reads statement at Gracie Mansion, Mayor's residence.

The End of An Era

paign for him, indicated that he was tying his political future to New York, "win or lose," and said he did not think his move here would hurt Mayor Wagner's standing.

Asked if this was the first time he had ever run for public office, the Attorney General replied: "Yes, but I've had a couple of relatives who did."

Mrs. Kennedy later held an impromptu press conference on the porch of the mansion and said she would campaign for her husband. She wore a coat dress of navy blue twill, blue pumps and a triple strand of pearls.

At the same time, Mr. Kennedy was on a pre-campaign tour of the Gracie Mansion grounds, accompanied by two dogs he had brought with him— a retriever named Battle and a sheepdog named Panda.

Meets Housewives

At the fence that separates the mansion from Carl Schurz Park, the Attorney General stopped to shake hands with neighborhood housewives. He patted children on the head and signed autographs. One woman called him "Senator" and he smiled.

On East End Avenue, how-ever, seven pickets marched in a circle, holding placards that said "Go Home Bobby" and "New York for New Yorkers." Some of the pickets identified themselves as Republicans and some said they were Democrats.

Mr. Kennedy's announcement marked the end of one political career and the beginning of a new and very different one.

Short of running for office, the 38-year-old Attorney General has crammed into the dozen years since his graduation from law school political experience that many party leaders have taken a lifetime to accumulate.

At 26, he ran his brother's

campaign for the Senate. At 30, he almost won for him the Vice Presidential nomination. At 34, he ran the Presidential campaign and became Attorney General. He was the youngest man to fill that office since 1814.

During the two years and almost 11 months that his brother served in the White House, Robert Kennedy was his closest adviser. The question to be settled this fall is whether this wide experience can be converted into electoral appeal.

August 26, 1964

Alter Ego of Kennedys

Man in the News

WHEN ROBERT F. KENNEDY decided to move his new frontier to New York there was no necessity for him to rush up a scouting party to survey the state's political terrain. He already had a going political operation here in the person of Stephen Edward Smith, his 36-year-old brother-in-law and the eyes and ears of the Kennedy family in this state. Steve Smith is sometimes called "the Kennedy clansman nobody knows."

Slender and boyish-looking, he seems out of place among the wily pros who run the state Democratic party. A man with penchant for remaining in the background, he is polite, almost shy, in talking to strangers.

Yet he has directed the dazzling behind-the-scenes campaign that enabled the Attorney General to carry off the state's prized senatorial plum—a feat that stunned the old pros.

"Don't kid yourself about that boy," an old-line politician said after emerging from a session with Mr. Smith. "He's got that schoolboy manner about him, but he's sharp as a tack. You got to watch yourself at all times around him."

Between phone calls at his Pan Am Building office Saturday, Mr. Smith seemed surprised when asked why he shunned personal publicity.

"There's no advantage in talkng about myself," he replied,

his low-keyed, pleasant voice betraying a trace of huskiness from constant telephone conversations. "I'm not running for anything. I'm not contemplating running for anything."

But his 38-year-old brother-in-law is, and for weeks Steve Smith has been laying the groundwork for that campaign—cajoling county leaders and corraling state convention delegates, sounding out ethnic and religious groups, pouring over polls.

"For the last six years," a friend has remarked, "Steve has had only one goal—electing Kennedys to high office."

This is not quite accurate, but Mr. Smith does not quarrel with this assessment of his family role. Since 1961, when Joseph P. Kennedy suffered a crippling stroke, the young Mr. Smith has been in New York in the important job of managing the family's investment portfolio—which is estimated at more than $300 million.

Yet politics takes up most of his waking hours, as it does the rest of the family, and he directs both his business and political operations from the elder Kennedy's office suite in the pan Am Building.

Until eight years ago, when he married Jean, the youngest and least extroverted of the Kennedy sisters, Steve Smith had done nothing more political than to become elected president of his class at Georgetown University.

Since then, under the expert tutelage of the Kennedys, he has developed into such an astute political manager that one newsman, noting his slim, boyish appearance, referred to him as a "hard-boiled Freddie Bartholomew."

At the tender age of 30 he had his political baptism in 1958 as office manager for the Kennedy campaign headquarters. This was the year John F. Kennedy was re-elected overwhelmingly to the Senate from Massachusetts.

In the 1960 Presidential campaign, Mr. Smith worked with Matthew McCloskey, national Democratic treasurer, in raising millions of dollars for the

Stephen Edward Smith

Kennedy-Johnson ticket. Two years later he managed Edward M. Kennedy's campaign in which the younger Kennedy succeeded his brother John as Senator from Massachusetts.

So attuned was he to the President's way of thinking that Mr. Kennedy once said of him: "Anyone can talk to him and feel he's talking to the candidate himself."

A stickler for the most minute detail, Mr. Smith had decided on the number of campaign buttons and balloons needed for Robert Kennedy's campaign even before the Attorney General announced yesteredav that he was a candidate.

He feels that winning elections is grueling work and refuses to be optimistic about the Attorney General's chances of defeating the Republican Senator, Kenneth B. Keating, despite favorable polls. "It'll be rough," Mr. Smith says.

Though he keeps in superb physical condition and is regarded as the best athlete in the Kennedy family, he consistently loses weight during campaigns. In Teddy Kennedy's 1962 drive, he dropped 12 pounds off his 160-pound 5-foot 11-inch frame.

Steve Smith grew up in Brooklyn, the youngest of five boys of a well-to-do Irish Catholic family. The Smith family money came from Cleary Brothers, Inc., a water transportation company founded 100 years ago by grandfather William E. Cleary, who served seven years as a Democratic Representative from New York.

In prep school in Brooklyn, Steve played ice hockey, lacrosse and baseball. He is rated a good golfer and tennis player. He majored in social science at Georgetown, where he met Jean.

They have two children, Stephen Jr., now 7, and William Kennedy Smith, who is 3. They live in a five-bedroom cooperative apartment on Fifth Avenue at 76th Street, within walking distance of the new apartment home of Mrs. Jacqueline Kennedy.

August 26, 1964

Robert F. Kennedy's grueling three-day trek upstate last week has created an aftermath of extraordinary political excitement in that normally Republican area.

Whenever the Democratic candidate for the Senate showed his smiling face and called for "your help," the political climate changed almost overnight and is now more like late October than mid-September.

This became apparent during two days spent retracing much of the zigzagging route Mr. Kennedy took through Western Central and Northern New York. The survey was preceded by a trip with Mr. Kennedy.

Yesterday Mr. Kennedy was rousing Brooklyn and Staten Island to the same fevered demonstrations that stirred the upstate counties.

In the wake of his tumultuous receptions, sound trucks now roam the streets and political discussions sprout in restaurants, taverns, stores, shopping centers, factories, homes, airports and buses.

Thus, in a huge shopping center in Rochester, where, before Mr. Kennedy's visit, the women were concerned only with their purchases, the salespeople now hear so much talk of politics that they refrain from making observations about the candidates lest they offend customers.

In a Binghamton restaurant, where the pennant race seemed the most important topic among men a week ago, politics has become the major theme.

In a Rochester tavern, where until last week, there seemed little interest in politics, that subject is now so hot that the bartender urges customers to leave their politics outside.

This transformation is a tribute to the magic of Mr. Kennedy's rallies and to the personality, heritage and political style that have stamped a special brand on his campaign.

Though the trade mark of Kennedy rallies to date has been the near-hysteria of children—and many women—the subsurface aspects of these meetings are more important in the long run.

Large Numbers of Adults

Almost obscured, for instance, by the shrilling chants of "We Want Bobby!" and the screams for a touch of his hand, have been the large numbers of adults, who far outnumbered those at Republican meetings in the same communities.

These large numbers do not mean votes for Mr. Kennedy, necessarily. It is among these quieter grownups, in fact, that one hears strong reservations about him. Dozens of interviews among men and women at these rallies produced many quotes such as the following:

"Keating is very solid in this community . . . I came here to listen . . . Haven't made up my mind . . . They're both good men . . . Kennedy's a good man, but I think I'll be voting for Keating . . . A lot of us here are on the fence on Kennedy and Keating . . . We vote for people not for parties. . . ."

Not one of more than 100 persons who were interviewed in the attempt to retrace the candidate's path conceded that Mr. Kennedy's visit had change his or her vote. Nor, they all added, did they themselves know of anyone whose vote was altered by the Kennedy trip.

Most of those questioned were from the middle class or lower middle class, but they frequently said that Mr. Kennedy had undoubtedly picked up votes "among the masses."

Behavior of Women

Attention has repeatedly been called to the schoolgirlish behavior of women in Kennedy audiences. Very often they exclaim, almost in ecstasy, "I shook his hand!" Many women say little, but just wander through the crowd trying to find a good vantage point from which to see or photograph the tousled candidate.

But always, in these same crowds are women, like the one who said, after hearing Mr. Kennedy talk outside a shopping center:

"I don't think he persuaded me to change my vote." Her 10-year-old son broke in heatedly: "I'm for Kennedy." She replied with a touch of sadness: "Twelve years from now you may be voting for Kennedy."

Not all of the crowds that turn out to see Mr. Kennedy are made up of screaming women and youngsters. One of the most interesting rallies on the Kennedy tour was a lunch-hour meeting in the parking area at a large factory in the Buffalo-Niagara Falls area. No children were there and only a small percentage of the crowd was women. The candidate had gone to the rally stimulated by enormously enthusiastic meetings in Buffalo. The men at the plant belonged to a union that was known to be strongly Democratic.

Floundered in Speech

But it was at this meeting that Mr. Kennedy floundered in his speech. The applause, when it came, had to be started by strong Kennedy partisans and, even then, the rest of the audience was almost perfunctory in picking up the cues. Mr. Kennedy struggled to stir the audience. He repeated himself. He paused for effects. Nothing worked. He knew it.

Why did the Kennedy personality fail on this occasion? Was it because there were no children and the women in the audience were serious? Some listeners, particularly a group of engineers, made it clear, in interviews, that they felt they had learned little from the speech and that they had expected a more detailed discussion of issues.

Though most of those questioned said they still planned to vote for Mr. Kennedy, some of the engineers said this speech had left them uncertain.

Mr. Kennedy's speeches were almost ritualistic in their similarity. They contained an attack on Barry Goldwater and a gibe at Senator Keating for being unable to be for or against the Republican Presidential candidate.

Mr. Kennedy conceded that he would not be able to solve all problems, but said that at least he would face them. He said that it was silly for New York State to have two Republican Senators when the President and both houses would be Democratic. He indicated that he could do more to bring industry to the state than Senator Keating.

Mr. Kennedy does not have to have children in the audience to maintain enthusiasm. Although he certainly used them at the upstate rallies, to a large extent, the behavior of the children was genuine. But whenever they lagged, the candidate managed to rouse them.

Thus, on a few occasions, because the children were shy or their spirits had been wilted by the 90-degree heat, they hung back as he finished his speech and prepared to leave in his open car. On these occasions, he jumped from the car and walked over to one to shake hands. This was enough to touch off the usual screaming surge of children, with the gushing women not too far behind.

Jokes for Children

Mr. Kennedy often goes out of his way in his talks to address little jokes to the children. He will promise, if elected, to reduce the voting age to 6. He will ask them to remember that it was because of him that they had been let out of school that day. He promises to shorten the school term (cheers) and lengthen the school day (groans and a dazzling Kennedy smile).

The children serve another purpose that is not readily apparent. The former Attorney General concedes that many persons believe he has the cold, merciless quality sometimes attributed to the prosecuting attorney.

Children in the audience help him in his effort to destroy this impression. He shows a natural warmth in dealing with them and is sincere in his concern that they may be hurt in the crush around him. To help a child, he will, to the dismay of his aides, plunge from his car into a seething crowd. Adults, particularly women, cannot help notice how children take an immediate liking to him.

Since Mr. Kennedy, on this tour, did not strive to make "important" speeches, he had to rely on technique, as well as his name, to hold his gatherings.

The Democratic candidate approaches his platform work with the seriousness of a vaudevillian or night club performer. If a routine does not work, he drops it. If it has promise, he polishes and uses it many times thereafter, on the fairly safe assumption that his new audience does not know what he told the last one.

Thus, at one of several rallies at which some Goldwater signs were being waved, he called attention to them and criticized their slogans, but without embarrassing the young men who were holding them. It worked. The next time, he used such signs as the theme for his entire speech. It went very well.

Or there was the joke that he used in answering the "carpetbagger" criticism. He said that in a single day he had closed the population gap between New York and California by moving here with his pregnant wife and eight children. This seemed to get a chuckle. The rest of the trip he polished this joke with other audiences.

He is quick with off-the-cuff humor that delights the crowds. During a talk in one of many town squares, the bell in the town hall tower intoned loudly

just as he criticized Senator Goldwater. He paused, turned and looked up at the tolling bell. When it had sounded its fourth gong, he turned back to the audience and said: "Looks like my point was good enough to ring the bell."

Asks for Criticism

What Mr. Kennedy lacks in natural oratorical talent, he is determined to overcome by application. During his speeches he singles out faces in the audience to gauge reaction. He is

constantly asking those around him for criticism, wondering if the audience was sufficiently attentive.

By his own admission, Mr. Kennedy is not gregarious. When asked, during his upstate trip, if he ever envied those public figures who love to spout speeches from platforms, he replied, at once:

"No. When I hear them, I want to go home."

September 14, 1964

KENNEDY BEATS KEATING

KENNEDY EDGE 6-5

Keating's Defeat Is Termed a 'Tragedy' by Rockefeller

By R. W. APPLE Jr.

Robert F. Kennedy was elected to the United States Senate from New York yesterday in his first bid for elective office, overwhelming Republican Senator Kenneth B. Keating.

With more than 80 per cent of the vote counted, Mr. Kennedy held a 6-to-5 lead. Because most of the untallied vote was in heavily Democratic New York City, it appeared that the former Attorney General's plurality might reach 650,000.

Mr. Keating conceded defeat at 11:39 P.M. with the announcement at the Roosevelt Hotel that he had sent a congratulatory telegram to Mr. Kennedy.

Governor Rockefeller, standing beside the white-haired Rochester legislator, said Mr. Keating's defeat was "a tragedy for the state and nation."

Runs Behind Johnson

"Senator Keating, one of the great Senators in the history of New York, has been rolled under by a national landslide," the Governor added. "He waged a magnificent campaign."

Mr. Kennedy ran well behind President Johnson, who seemed to be headed for a record margin of 2.5 million votes or more in the state. The President won all of the state's 62 counties.

It thus appeared that about a million New York voters had split their ticket to cast votes for Mr. Johnson and Mr. Keating — but even this wasn't enough to make the Senate contest close.

A major surprise was the showing of the Liberal party, which had expected to deliver 600,000 votes for both Mr. Johnson and Mr. Kennedy. At 1 o'clock this morning, the Liberal total appeared unlikely to exceed 250,000 votes.

Mr. Kennedy appeared at a victory rally in the Statler Hilton Hotel about 1:30 A.M. He said he had won "an overwhelming mandate" to continue the policies of his older brother, John F. Kennedy.

Then, as he often did during the campaign, he offered a quo-

tation for his audience: "Come, my friends, 'tis not too late to build a better world."

"This," Mr. Kennedy added, "is what I dedicate myself to in the next six years for the State of New York."

Mr. Kennedy was getting 54.7 per cent of the vote. Mr. Keating 42.9 per cent, and Henry Paolucci, the Conservative nominee, 2.4 per cent.

Mr. Paolucci, nominated by the Conservatives to punish Mr. Keating for his refusal to endorse the Republican Presidential ticket, conceded defeat shortly after the polls closed.

The loss for Mr. Keating—a representative of the moderate wing of his party—was the first in an 18-year political career. The victory for Mr. Kennedy was almost certain to make him a Democratic contender for President in the future.

Mr. Kennedy ran strongly in New York City, although not so strongly as some Democratic candidates have in the past. He ran ahead of his Republican opponent in many of the traditional Republican counties upstate.

In Cattaraugus County, in the western part of the state, for example, the former Attorney General was ahead of Mr. Keating by a 4-to-3 margin. Cattaraugus, whose principal city is Olean, was on Mr. Kennedy's itinerary Sunday.

Onondaga County, a Republican stronghold since 1860, went to President Johnson, and Mr. Kennedy was ahead there by 20,000 votes late last night.

Mr. Kennedy carried Cayuga and Clinton counties, and shaved the Republican margin in Essex, Genesse, Schenectady and St. Lawrence to less than 1,000. But Mr. Keating was strong in Monroe County, his home area, and in Erie County, whose seat is Buffalo.

The Senator also swept the New York City suburbs, including Nassau, Suffolk and Westchester Counties. The race was close only in Suffolk.

The Negro and Puerto Rican vote went heavily to Mr. Kennedy, according to the C.B.S. analysis. The expected defection of Italian-American voters to Mr. Keating did not develop.

But Mr. Kennedy did run into trouble with Jewish voters. In election districts with heavy Jewish populations, Mr. Keating drew 39.8 per cent of the vote. Six years ago he got only 30.8 per cent in the same

districts.

The Democratic State Chairman, William H. McKeon, claimed victory for both Mr. Kennedy and President Johnson in New York State at 9:34 P.M.

Crucial Campaign

Mr. Kennedy's younger brother, Edward, was re-elected in Massachusetts. They will sit together in the Senate—the second such pair in American history. Theodore Foster of Rhode Island and Dwight Foster of Massachusetts, who served together on Capitol Hill from 1800 to 1803, were the first.

The former Attorney General's victory gave the Kennedy family another distinction. It is the first ever to send three brothers to the Senate—Robert, Edward and John, who served before being elected President in 1960.

Aside from the Presidential campaign, the Kennedy-Keating contest was perhaps the most crucial of the 1964 campaigns, and it involved many of the top names of American politics.

Mr. Keating, who arrived in Rochester Monday night, cast his ballot shortly after 8:30 A.M. at the Allen Creek School. He was applauded when he walked in, and some of the voters, obviously neighbors, said, "Good luck to you, Ken."

Asked whether he had voted for his party's Presidential nominee, Senator Barry Goldwater, the ruddy, white-haired candidate replied: "I said I'd leave it to my conscience, and this I've done." His voice was slightly gravelly.

Mr. Kennedy had pressed Mr. Keating throughout the campaign to state his choice for President. In a statement issued last week, the Senator implied that he would abstain.

After touring 18 polling places in Rochester—as he had always done on Election Day during his days as a Representative—Mr. Keating boarded a plane for the trip back to New York City.

The Senator made four stops with Senator Jacob K. Javits in a swing through Queens and Harlem. About 4 P.M., he returned to the Roosevelt Hotel, where he had stayed all during the nine-week campaign.

Neither Mr. Kennedy nor his wife, Ethel, voted yesterday.

They were ineligible to cast ballots in New York because they have lived in the state only since the first of October.

Nevertheless, the former Attorney General appeared at 4:50 A. M. at the Esquire Food Shop, 2359 Broadway, at 86th Street, for the annual breakfast of the West Side Democratic Club. He ate corn flakes with bananas and drank tea.

By 6:30 A.M., he was back in his suite at the Carlyle Hotel, having stopped at a breakfast on the East Side and at his two campaign headquarters.

Then, shortly after 11 A.M., Mr. Kennedy arrived, bareheaded and without a coat, at the Rainey Memorial Gate of the Bronx Zoo on Pelham Parkway. With him were Mrs. Kennedy and seven of their eight

children — all except the youngest.

With the help of Frank Leonard, the elephant keeper, the Kennedy family made friends with a 26-year-old African elephant named Pinky, and fed her some day-old loaves of white bread provided by Mr. Leonard.

November 4, 1964

WASHINGTON, Jan. 4 — Robert F. Kennedy took his seat in the Senate today—in the very back row.

In fact, a special new row of two seats, in a corner behind the four semicircular ranks of Senators' desks, was set up for the New York Democrat and Joseph D. Tydings of Maryland, who is even a notch lower in seniority.

President Kennedy, the Senator's brother, was also a back-bencher throughout his Senate career, sitting one desk off the center aisle in the fourth row. Last November's election, however, produced 68 Democratic Senators, and four rows would not hold them, so the New Yorker wound up in the corner.

In the nineteen thirties, during the last similar Senate emergency, the most junior Democrats were seated across the aisle, sharing the back row of the Republican side. This arrangement, called "the Cherokee Strip," was eliminated when Democratic strength dwindled again.

It got its name from a narrow strip of land once occupied by the Cherokee Indians, but ceded by them to the United States in 1866. It extended along the southern border of what is now Kansas.

Despite the relative obscurity of his seat, Mr. Kennedy's arrival in the Senate was something of an event.

Other Brothers Recalled

It was the first time, Congressional historians reported, that two brothers had taken the oath of office as Senators

together. The Senator from New York was sworn with Senator Edward M. Kennedy of Massachusetts at his side on the rostrum.

Brothers have served in the Senate before. They were Senators Theodore Foster of Rhode Island and Dwight Foster of Massachusetts, whose terms overlapped from 1800 to early 1803. They did not take the oath together.

It was Edward M. Kennedy's first appearance in the Capitol since he broke his back in an airplane crash last June. He seemed to favor his right side as he walked through the chamber, chatting with his colleagues, but his face did not betray any pain from the injuries that immobilized him for months.

In the Senate gallery for the ceremony were the two Senators' wives and three of their sisters—Mrs. Eunice Shriver, Mrs. Patricia Lawford and Mrs. Stephen Smith.

Sworn in Groups of 4

The 36 new and re-elected Senators were sworn in groups of four. Taking the oath with the Kennedys were Mike Mansfield of Montana and Eugene J. McCarthy of Minnesota.

As is traditional, the Kennedys were escorted to the rostrum by their colleagues from their home states: Robert by Senator Jacob K. Javits and Edward by Senator Leverett Saltonstall, both Republicans.

Asked later how he liked his seat in the back corner of the chamber, the New York Senator said with a grin, "Well, at least I got inside the building."

Mr. Kennedy is 98th of the 100 Senators on the seniority list. So far the Rules Committee has worked its way down to No. 45, Senator John Sherman Cooper of Kentucky, in reassigning office suites left vacant by defeat, retirement or other reasons.

At that rate it may be three or four weeks before the New Yorker's staff finds its permanent home. It is now staying in the former office of Senator Kenneth B. Keating, whom Mr. Kennedy defeated, but it will be dislodged soon by Senator Thomas H. Kuchel of California and have to move elsewhere.

Returns From Skiing

Senator Robert Kennedy had returned to his Virginia home from a skiing holiday in Colorado early this morning with several members of the family, including Mrs. John F. Kennedy. Senator Edward Kennedy arrived yesterday from Palm Beach.

After the swearing-in ceremony the New Yorker went to Senator Mansfield's office for a picture-taking session. There he told newsmen he was seeking assignment to the Labor, Commerce and District of Columbia Committees in the Senate.

He also said he favored liberalizing the Senate's anti-filibuster rule, but he offered no details. Then he returned to Hickory Hill, his home in McLean, Va., for lunch with members of the family, friends, staff members and workers in his campaign.

January 5, 1965

KENNEDY (D.-N.Y.) GETS A BACK SEAT

Sworn in Senate With His Massachusetts Brother

By WARREN WEAVER Jr.

MOUNT KENNEDY, Yukon Territory, March 24— Senator Robert F. Kennedy reached the top of Mount Kennedy today and became the first person to scale the 13,900-foot peak.

Until today it had been the highest unclimbed mountain in North America.

On reaching the summit, the Senator planted a black-bordered flag with the family crest—three silver helmets on a green background—in his brother's memory.

The Canadian Government named the mountain in the St. Elias Range last year in the memory of President

Kennedy, the Senator's brother.

The 39-year-old New York Senator was a member of one of three teams that made the ascent. It took five hours from Camp 2, which is 3,000 feet from the base.

Senator Kennedy was part of a three-man team that included Jim Whittaker, 36, of Seattle, who in 1963 became the first American to climb Mount Everest.

The third member of the team was Barry W. Prather, 26, of Tacoma, who was a member of that Mount Everest expedition.

The peak of Mount Ken-

nedy resembles an inverted ice cream cone. It juts up sharply about 500 feet from a smooth snow glacier plateau and the last part of the climb is believed to be the most difficult part of the expedition.

The Senator said that he had placed a copy of his brother's Inaugural Address at the summit along with several of the late President's PT-boat tie clasps that were used in the 1960 election campaign.

His climbing team also carried an American flag and two Canadian flags- one of the old Union Jack design, the other of the new Maple Leaf design— to plant on Mount Kennedy.

When the Senator's team ap-

Kennedy Puts Flag Atop Mt. Kennedy

By MARTIN ARNOLD

proached close to the summit, it is believed that his two fellow climbers allowed him to go ahead, making it possible for him to reach the summit first.

He reached the top at 1 P.M. (5 P.M. Eastern standard time).

Senator Kennedy had never climbed a mountain before.

He planted his flag in the ice that covers the granite peak. The day was bright with sunshine and the temperature at 5 degrees above zero, was said to be unusually warm for this time of year. The normal temperature for this period is 15 to 20 degrees below zero.

The second team to make the ascent was made up of William A. Allard, a photographer for the National Geographic Society, which with the Boston Museum of Science sponsored the Senator's expedition, and William N. Prater of Ellensburg, Wash.

On the third team were George R. Senner, a ranger from Mount Ranier; Dee Molenaar of Olympia, Wash., and Jim Craig, a lawyer from Vancouver.

Because of faulty radio equipment, there was no direct communication between expedition headquarters in Whitehorse and the climbers. The progress of the ascent was obtained by plane flight to the mountain.

The Senator and his party hiked from the base camp at 8,500 feet yesterday to Camp 2 where they joined an advance party.

On his six-hour climb yesterday, mostly in sunlight, Mr. Kennedy was bareheaded, wore sunglasses and snowshoes. A photographer from the Canadian National Film Board said that the Senator had made the ascent like a veteran as his group worked its way across snow and ice bridging crevasses.

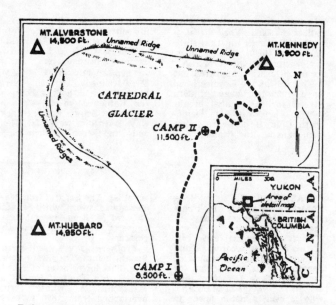

Robert Kennedy started climbing Mt. Kennedy from Base Camp I, stayed overnight at Camp II and reached the summit yesterday. Broken line indicates route. Map is based on a rough sketch by a reporter at the scene.

Senator Robert F. Kennedy after planting flag on top of Mount Kennedy

After reaching the summit, Senator Kennedy returned to Camp 2 to spend the night.

Senator Kennedy flew from New York to Seattle on Sunday and to Whitehorse, headquarters of the expedition, by way of Juneau, Alaska, the next day. At Whitehorse, he was advised to lay over for a day because of threatening weather. However, his answer was, "I want to get there."

At about 4:30 P.M., when the Senator's party had descended to the Camp, this reporter, Dr. Bradford Washburn, scientific leader of the expedition, and a photographer circled the area in a plane. Dr. Washburn dropped a note telling the climbers that if they wanted to be taken out early tomorrow morning, two members should lie down in the snow as a signal of assent.

When the note landed, two

men were seen reading the note and they immediately lay down side by side as instructed.

After Senator Kennedy leaves the mountain, probably sometime tomorrow, another team will scale the peak in order to place a survey target on it. This team will be made up of members of the National Geographic Society-Boston Museum of Science expedition.

The survey target consists of a 7-foot wooden 2-by-4 with an orange-colored two-foot-square plywood board attached to it.

The society and the museum will start the actual work of charting this area next month. The goal of the expedition and the one next month is to produce as precise as possible a map of an area 12-by-15 square miles surrounding Mount Kennedy.

March 25, 1965

Message From Brother

WASHINGTON, March 24 (UPI) Senator Edward M. Kennedy, Democrat of Massachusetts, congratulated his brother Robert today, for reaching the top of Mount Kennedy. But he could not resist the opportunity for a little teasing.

"I want to congratulate my brother and wish him well on the way down," the Massachusetts Senator said.

"At the same time I wish to point out for the record he is not the first Kennedy to climb a mountain. I climbed the Matterhorn in 1957, which is higher, and I didn't need the help of the Royal Canadian Mounted Police."

March 25, 1965

JOSEPH P. KENNEDY ENTERS A HOSPITAL

BOSTON, Aug. 31 (UPI)—Joseph P. Kennedy, 76 years old, the father of the late President, entered New England Baptist Hospital today after developing "congestion" in the throat and chest area.

Mr. Kennedy was admitted to the hospital as three of his grandchildren were on the mend from injuries suffered in accidents last weekend.

A doctor said the former Ambassador to Britain, who suffered a crippling stroke in December, 1961, would remain in the hospital for a "few days" for tests.

Dr. Russell S. Boles Jr., a gastro-intestinal specialist said after examining Mr. Kennedy for 45 minutes that the congestion was not the chief worry.

"He hasn't been doing as well as we would like him to," Dr. Boles said. "He hasn't been feeling as well as he should."

Meanwhile, two sons and a daughter of Senator Robert F. Kennedy, Democrat of New York, were recovering from injuries.

Kathleen Kennedy, 14, was hurt Sunday in a spill from her horse. The same day, her brother Joseph, 12, was hit in the chest by the boom of a sailboat. Robert Jr., 11, severely cut his leg in a fall Friday from a garage roof.

September 1, 1965

Kennedy Swam to Ship In High Seas on Sunday

HYANNIS PORT, Mass., Sept. 1—Senator Robert F. Kennedy put on a lifejacket and swam through stormy seas Sunday to reach a Coast Guard cutter that was trying to tell him that his 14-year-old daughter, Kathleen, had been injured, a Coast Guard officer said here tonight.

The Senator swam to the cutter because waves up to 20 feet high made it impossible for the ship to come alongside the schooner aboard which were the Senator, his wife and seven of their nine children.

The Coast Guard officer said the Senator swam a considerable distance, although he said he could not confirm a report that the ships were 50 yards apart. Senator Kennedy had no trouble reaching the cutter, the officer said. The cutter took the Senator to Woods Hole, Mass., and he went on to Cape Cod Hospital.

September 2, 1965

A portrait of John F. Kennedy as a parent is about to be added to the gallery of writings by former associates of the late President.

The December issue of The Ladies' Home Journal, which goes on sale Tuesday, will contain the first of three installments from a book by Miss Maud Shaw, former "nanny" to the late President's children, Caroline and John Jr.

The book, "My Life With Caroline and John-John," will be published in April by New American Library of World Literature.

The President's widow made "discreet inquiries" about the possibility of the book not being written, but Miss Shaw "was quite determined to go ahead, " Miss Pamela Turnure, press secretary to Mrs. Kennedy, said here yesterday. Miss Turnure said the book "violates Mrs. Kennedy's consistent effort to reserve the children's privacy."

She added:

"It is a disappointment that one so close would write about them, regardless of what is written. It is the principle of the thing."

Neither Miss Turnure nor Pete Wyden, executive editor of The Ladies' Home Journal, would comment on whether any changes had been made in the manuscript at Mrs. Kennedy's request.

Miss Shaw, who joined the Kennedys when Caroline was 11 days old, refers more often to the President than to Mrs. Kennedy in the first installment.

She tells of searching for John-John one Saturday afternoon and finding him with the President in the family helicopter. She tells how both were wearing helmets and were sitting at the controls, with the President "taking orders from John the flight captain, thoroughly absorbed in the make-believe."

Belief in Santa Claus

She also relates that Caroline was the first to address her father as "Mr. President," dashing into his bedroom early in the morning the day after the election to do so. The final results were not in, but Caroline had seen a Secret Service man on the lawn, and Miss Shaw had explained to her the probable reason for his presence.

Caroline believed in Santa Claus until she was 7 years old and was reluctant to abandon that belief then, Miss Shaw relates, because when she was younger the President had arranged for her to speak on the telephone with "Mrs. Santa Claus" from a White House telephone.

President Kennedy once asked her to cut John-John's hair, Miss Shaw relates.

"What could I say?" she writes. "I couldn't say that Mrs. Kennedy wanted it long, so I said it would be cut the next day. Well, I did trim it a bit, but not enough for the President.

"He came into the nursery, took a long look at his son, and turned to me.

"Miss Shaw, when are you going to cut John's hair?"

"But, sir,' I said. 'I have cut it, but Mrs. Kennedy...'

"I stopped before I said too much, but the President only grinned and said, in a kind of confidential way, 'I know, but let's have some of that fringe off. If anyone asks you, it was an order from the President,' and he winked."

November 19, 1965

KENNEDY 'NANNY' TELLS HER STORY

Late President's Wife Tried to Prevent the Book

By EDITH EVANS ASBURY

Crowds Swamp Mrs. Kennedy at Swiss Chalet

Tourists and Photographers Cause Ski-Lift Shutdown —Galbraith Annoyed

GSTAAD, Switzerland, Jan. 15 (AP)—Mrs. John F. Kennedy tried to go skiing today on the alpine slopes of Switzerland, but she was so badgered by curious tourists and by 25 carloads of reporters that she had to give up.

Friends reported that she was disgusted. John Kenneth Galbraith, Harvard professor and former Ambassador to India, who accompanied her, said, "There is no fun in what happened today."

Mrs. Kennedy arrived this morning with her son, John; her daughter, Caroline; a nurse and a United States Secret Service agent. She hoped for three weeks of privacy. The weather was icy, John's nose was running and tears ran down Caroline's cheeks.

The Kennedys moved into a rented chalet between a chalet belonging to Elizabeth Taylor and one belonging to Prince Rainier and Princess Grace of Monaco. After lunch, Mrs. Kennedy left the chalet with Mr. Galbraith, Mr. and Mrs. Melvin Urey of San Francisco and the Ureys' 12-year-old daughter, Elizabeth.

They drove to the village with a police car ahead of them and 25 press cars following.

Hundreds of Swiss jammed the narrow street as Mrs. Kennedy accompanied Mr. Galbraith into a sports shop to buy him ski pants. "There she is! That's her!" they shouted as Mrs. Kennedy fought her way back to the car.

The motorcade drove on to the terminal of the lift to the Eggli slope above Gstaad. The situation became tumultuous, and Mrs. Kennedy was separated from her friends and her escort. The police could do nothing as strangers forced their way into the same cable car of the lift with her. Women screamed. Cameras, skis and flashlights clattered to the floor.

Finally the lift manager shouted, "I'm sick of this!" and turned off the power while Mrs. Kennedy was being carried up the mountain. It took several minutes for matters to calm down so the lift could start moving again.

It was the same on the Eggli. Skiers recognized Mrs. Kennedy despite the huge goggles covering part of her face. She wore a dark blue nylon parka, a shiny red V-neck pullover on top of a black one, dark blue ski pants and a large woolen cap.

Each time she skied down, she had to go slowly and carefully, the slope was easy, but wherever she went a photographer was in the way. Amateurs soon joined the professionals, and there were more photographers than skiers on the slope.

Mrs. John F. Kennedy at Swiss ski resort.

November 19, 1965

PATRICIA LAWFORD DIVORCES ACTOR

Kennedy's Sister Is Granted Custody of 4 Children

GOODING, Idaho, Feb. 1— Mrs. Patricia Lawford, sister of President Kennedy and Senators Robert F. Kennedy of New York and Edward M. Kennedy of Massachusetts, was granted a divorce today from Peter Lawford, the actor, in a 12-minute court action that ended their 11-year marriage.

The decree was granted in the Fourth District Court in this small agricultural community 80 miles south of Sun Valley, where Mrs. Lawford completed her required six-week Idaho residency yesterday. The public and the press were barred from the hearing before Judge Charles Scoggin.

Mrs. Lawford spent eight minutes on the stand. She charged her husband with mental cruelty and was granted full custody of the couple's four children—Christopher, 10 years old; Sidney, 9; Victoria, 7, and Robin, 4. Mr. Lawford was granted visitation rights.

The couple earlier had entered into a separation agreement in New York City. This agreement is believed to have included a property settlement. The agreement was affirmed by the District Court here and then was withdrawn. It will not be made public.

Mrs. Lawford was accompanied to the court by her brother-in-law, Stephen E.

Patricia Kennedy Lawford

Peter Lawford

Smith, and her Idaho attorney, Everett E. Taylor of Sun Valley. Mr. Lawford was represented by Jack M. Murphy of Shoshone.

The divorce is the first obtained by the politically prominent and Roman Catholic Kennedy family.

Mrs. Lawford arrived at the Sun Valley resort Dec. 20 to begin her six weeks' residency. She was accompanied to the resort by Robert Kennedy and his family.

The Lawfords separated more than a year ago. She and her children moved into a New York City apartment and Mr. Lawford remained in California.

February 2, 1966

A new toy, an obsolete World War II observation plane, was deposited yesterday in the backyard of Mrs. John F. Kennedy's home in Hyannis Port, Mass.

The two-seat plane, whose engine has been deactivated so it cannot be flown, was a gift from former Ambassador Joseph P. Kennedy to his 24 grandchildren.

"My father wanted to surprise them," said Senator Robert F. Kennedy, the father of nine of the children.

"The children are fascinated by planes, just as all children," said Miss Ann Gargan, Mrs. Joseph P. Kennedy's niece, in a telephone interview.

About an hour after its arrival the wings had been attached to the craft and it had joined a doll house and a jungle gym in Mrs. Kennedy's backyard in this Cape Cod community.

Miss Gargan said the elder Mr. Kennedy had not discussed the gift with other members of the Kennedy family because he wanted the plane to be a "complete surprise."

"It's something for them to play around with," said Miss Gargan, who has cared for the 77-year-old Mr. Kennedy since he was disabled by a stroke in 1961.

Miss Gargan said that the 1940 vintage plane had been put in Mrs. Kennedy's backyard because the yard, which is about half the size of a football field, was "probably the largest single open space in Hyannis Port."

The project had been kept under wraps for three months. In February Mr. Kennedy approached the Page Airways in Rochester for a plane. Page in turn contacted Donald L. Metsger, owner of Bay Shore Airmotive, Inc., in Atlantic Highlands, N. J., who specializes in rebuilding old airplanes.

Mr. Metsger learned from Gordon Donald, president of Shore Air Services, Inc., which operated the Asbury Park airport, that two private fliers wanted to sell their 26-year-old Aeronca 65-TL, which met with Mr. Kennedy's specifications.

Mr. Metsger bought the plane and Kurt Wagner, chief mechanic of Shore Air, reconditioned and repainted it olive drab, with "the latest Air Force insignia," according to Mr. Metsger.

Mr. Metsger said he received his check from Mr. Kennedy Thursday but would not disclose the cost of the plane. He said such planes now sell for $600 to $800.

Miss Gargan said: "The Ambassador is always doing things like this for the children."

May 28, 1966

JOHN KENNEDY JR. BURNED BY COALS

HONOLULU, July 1—John F. Kennedy Jr., the 5-year-old son of the late President, was treated here this afternoon for first- and second-degree burns suffered when he fell into the coals of a dying cookout fire earlier today on Hawaii Island.

The boy was burned on the right hand and forearm and buttocks. He was given emergency treatment by Dr. K. E. Nesting of Kamuela, a town on the island about 180 miles southeast of here.

This afternoon he was carried onto a Hawaiian Airlines plane by his mother and flown to Honolulu, where he received further treatment.

Dr. Nesting said, "The injury is significant enough to be concerned about but I prefer you don't use the word 'serious.' It is not life-threatening."

John was carried off the plane by his mother, who took him directly to the Henry J. Kaiser Picnic House, about 18 miles from downtown Honolulu. He was treated there by Dr. Eldon R. Dykes, a plastic surgeon with the Straub Clinic. Dr. Dykes said that no surgery or hospitalization would be required.

The boy was reported resting comfortably tonight.

Mrs. Kennedy and John; her daughter, Caroline, 9, and young Sidney Lawford, the children's cousin, are living at the luxury Picnic House, a commercial guest house on the Kaiser estate. They had been visiting Hawaii Island and were guests there on the Laurance S. Rockefeller ranch house on Parker Ranch.

A member of the group with the Kennedy family said John was pulling at a sleeping bag when he tripped and fell backwards into the still-hot coals of the fire, which had been built for a hot dog roast last night.

Don Horio, press secretary to Gov. John A. Burns of Hawaii, said he knew of no plans for a change in the Kennedys' island vacation.

When Mrs. Kennedy and her party came here early this month they had intended to leave July 5. Recently, however, Mrs. Kennedy told friends they were enjoying the vacation so much they would prolong it at least two weeks.

Mr. Horio, acting as press liaison man for the Kennedy party, said, "Dr. Dykes has reported to me that these mild burns were treated and they do not require any surgery or hospitalization. They are not serious."

Dr. Dykes was accompanied to the Picnic House by a registered nurse. While he was treating the boy, Caroline and Sidney were playing outside. Occasionally young John could be heard crying during the medical treatment.

There was no indication that the Kennedy party would return to the island of Hawaii. They had been there for a week at the Parker Ranch, one of the largest cattle ranches in the United States. The ranch is owned by Richard Smart.

The cookout was on a beach belonging to the nearby Mauna Kea Hotel, which was recently opened by Mr. Rockefeller. The party canceled a planned visit to the northernmost Hawaiian island of Kauai because of the accident.

The accident was the second mishap to befall the Kennedys since they arrived in Honolulu June 5. On June 9, Caroline stepped on a jagged piece of coral while swimming near their Honolulu vacation home. She had five stitches taken and was on crutches for several days.

July 2, 1966

Kennedy Poll a Joke? It Was in This Case

Is Senator Robert F. Kennedy a good father to his nine children?

The question seemingly was settled in the Senator's favor in his September newsletter to his constituents, but now it is wide open again.

The newsletter quotes a letter the Senator got from a 7-year-old Farmingdale, L. I., boy asking: "Do you take good care of your children?" The Senator's reply was: "I asked my children and they voted yes by 4 to 3 with 2 abstentions."

But when a reporter asked about the poll, an aide to Mr. Kennedy admitted that the vote never had been taken and that the item was meant to be a joke.

The aide said he thought at first of making the vote 5 to 4, like a Supreme Court decision, but decided the 4-3-2 vote was funnier. He said the Senator agreed.

September 3, 1966

HOOVER ASSERTS ROBERT KENNEDY AIDED BUGGINGS

F.B.I. Chief Says in a Letter That Ex-Attorney General 'Was Briefed Frequently'

By FRED P. GRAHAM

WASHINGTON, Dec. 10

J. Edgar Hoover has asserted that all wiretapping and electronic eavesdropping carried out by the Federal Bureau of Investigation while Robert F. Kennedy was Attorney General was done with the approval of Mr. Kennedy.

In a letter from the director of the F.B.I. to Representative H. R. Gross, Republican of Iowa, Mr. Hoover broke his long silence over the bureau's eavesdropping and laid the responsibility directly to Mr. Kennedy, a Democrat who is now the junior Senator from New York.

Mr. Kennedy was at P.S. 305 in the Bedford-Stuyvesant section of Brooklyn when the news of Mr. Hoover's letter became known, attending a meeting on redeveloping the area.

Asked for a comment, he replied:

"You can get a statement from my Washington office. I have nothing to say now."

The Senator's office then issued a statement accusing Mr. Hoover of being "misinformed."

Attached to the Kennedy statement was a letter from Courtney A. Evans, the assistant director of the F.B.I., who acted as liaison between the bureau and Mr. Kennedy when he was Attorney General.

Mr. Evans said in the letter that Mr. Kennedy had not been told of electronic bugging because the bureau director had general authority to install hidden microphones without specific authorization.

However, Mr. Evans said, individual requests "in these serious national security cases for wiretap authorization" were sent to Mr. Kennedy by the F.B.I. for approval.

Mr. Hoover's letter to Representative Gross contradicted this statement.

"Mr. Kennedy, during his term of office [as Attorney General], exhibited great interest in pursuing such matters, and, while in different metropolitan areas, not only listened to the results of microphone surveillances, but raised questions relative to obtaining better equipment," Mr. Hoover wrote Mr. Gross.

"He was briefed frequently by an F.B.I. official regarding such matters," Mr. Hoover said.

Mr. Hoover attached a document signed by Mr. Kennedy, in which the former Attorney General discussed the use of leased telephone lines in the operation of hidden microphones "in security and major criminal cases."

In a televised interview on the American Broadcasting Company's "Issues and Answers" last June 26, Mr. Kennedy was asked, "Did you authorize the F.B.I. wiretaps of gamblers' telephones in Las Vegas in '62 and '63?"

"No, I did not," Mr. Kennedy replied.

He said he had never authorized any wiretaps except in national security cases.

Mr. Hoover has been placed in an increasingly awkward position in recent weeks as a series of events have disclosed numerous instances of electronic surveillance by the F.B.I. in organized crime investigations over the last few years.

One such disclosure came to light on May 24 when the Justice Department disclosed in a memorandum to the Supreme Court that Fred B. Black Jr., a Washington public relations man, had been the subject of F.B.I. bugging between Feb. 7 and April 25, 1963, in a hotel suite here.

The Court demanded to know who had authorized the eavesdropping. In a supplemental memorandum signed by Solicitor General Thurgood Marshall, the Justice Department said, "The director [Mr. Hoover] approved installation of the device involved in the instant case."

Asked at that time to comment about the Black bugging, Mr. Kennedy said that he had been given no information about it when he was Attorney General.

The memorandum said that Mr. Hoover had not been required by the then existing Justice Department policy to obtain the Attorney General's permission before authorizing the use of a hidden microphone, or bug.

Wiretaps, which involve the interception of telephone calls, are not used by Federal agents without the express consent of the Attorney General, and then only in national security cases, the Marshall memorandum explained.

Last Monday, Mr. Gross wrote Mr. Hoover observing that Mr. Kennedy had implied in statements that he had not authorized some of the bugging in organized crime investigations. Mr. Gross asked if the F.B.I. had documents to show that Mr. Kennedy had approved the use of bugging, as well as wiretapping.

Mr. Hoover's response, dated Dec. 7, was released by Representative Gross in Jackson, Miss., where he was visiting his brother, E. L. Gross.

To the letter Mr. Hoover attached a document described as a "communication" signed by Mr. Kennedy, which appears to be a letter with the name of the addressee and part of the text deleted.

Dated Aug. 17, 1961, the letter appears to be a request for cooperation in leasing telephone lines in New York City for use in electronic surveillance.

In recent disclosures of electronic bugging by the F.B.I. in Las Vegas, Miami and Kansas City, Mo., leased telephone lines were used to carry the sounds picked up on hidden microphones to monitoring rooms in offices of the F.B.I.

Mr. Hoover also attached a letter from Herbert J. Miller Jr., who was the Assistant Attorney General in charge of the Criminal Division under Mr. Kennedy. In the letter to Senator Sam J. Ervin Jr., dated May 25, 1961, Mr. Miller answered the North Carolina Democrat's questions about the extent of electronic eavesdropping.

Mr. Miller said he had checked with the F.B.I. and had been told that at that time the bureau had 67 bugs in operation, both in internal security and organized crime investigations.

Mr. Hoover added in his letter to Representative Gross that he had discussed electronic surveillance with former Attorney General Nicholas de B. Katzenbach on Aug. 30, 1965, in which he outlined the same eavesdropping policy that he had discussed with other Attorneys General in the past.

Mr. Katzenbach, who is now Under Secretary of State, was in his office this afternoon but declined to comment.

December 11, 1966

MRS. KENNEDY SUES TO HOLD UP BOOK ON ASSASSINATION

By JOHN CORRY

Mrs. John F. Kennedy asked a justice of the State Supreme Court yesterday to block the publication of "Death of a President," a book she said she once had authorized in the interest of "accuracy, good taste and dignity."

Saul S. Streit, the ranking justice of the court, said he would hold a hearing Dec. 27 on her contention that William Manchester had violated her rights with his plans to have published the unapproved manuscript of his book about the assassination of her husband.

Justice Streit said he would "decide the matter shortly" after the hearing.

He ordered Mr. Manchester; Harper & Row, Publishers, Inc., and Cowles Communications, Inc., the publisher of Look magazine, to appear before him to show cause why an injunction against the book should not be granted. All are defendants in Mrs. Kennedy's suit.

At stake are the following:

¶A four-part series of 80,000 words from the book in Look magazine scheduled to begin in the issue on sale Jan. 10.

¶The 300,000 - word book, scheduled to be published in March or April by Harper & Row.

¶Plans for publication of the work abroad in book and serial form.

A spokesman for Look said that, if Mrs. Kennedy was upheld, a substitute issue would not be published. He said there was not enough time to prepare one.

Neither Mrs. Kennedy nor her brother-in-law, Senator Robert F. Kennedy, Democrat of New York, appeared in court here.

The suit joins together in a court fight celebrated names in politics and publishing. It involves old friends from both sides, substantial amounts of money, and, indirectly, political tensions between Senator Kennedy and President Johnson.

Sees 'Irreparable Injury'

It is being fought, Mrs. Kennedy's complaint said, because the publication of "Death of a President" would cause her "great and irreparable injury" and "result in precisely the sensationalism and commercialism which we—Robert F. Kennedy and I—have sought so strenuously to avoid."

"The threatened publication is in total disregard of my rights and, if it goes forward, will utterly destroy them," she said.

Mr. Manchester had two lengthy interviews with Mrs. Kennedy when he gathered material for the book. Her friends say that Mrs. Kennedy "made no attempt at self-censorship" in the interviews and that she had revealed her deepest thoughts.

"I am shocked that Mr. Manchester would exploit the emotional state in which I recounted my recollections to him early in 1964."

This, she had said, is her foremost objection to the book.

The most important issue is whether the defendants had permission from the Kennedys to publish. Mrs. Kennedy and the Senator said they did not.

Three clauses in an 11-point memorandum signed by Mr. Manchester and the Senator on March 26, 1964, are involved.

The first says that Mrs. Kennedy and the Senator must approve the text of the book. The second says that Mr. Manchester may not dispose of subsidiary rights without their approval, and the third that the book may not be published before Nov. 22, 1968, exactly five years after the assassination of President Kennedy.

Harper & Row has said that Senator Kennedy told Mr. Man-

chester in a telegram last July that "members of the Kennedy family will place no obstacle in the way of publication of his book."

However, in a five-page affidavit in support of Mrs. Kennedy, the Senator said that the "telegram makes no statement approving either text, or time, or mode of publication."

The telegram said:

"Should any inquiries arise re the manuscript of your book I would like to state the following:

"While I have not read William Manchester's account of the death of President Kennedy, I know of the President's respect for Mr. Manchester as an historian and a reporter. I understand others have plans to publish books regarding the events of Nov. 22, 1963. As this is going to be the subject matter of a book and since Mr. Manchester in his research had access to more information and sources than any other writer, members of the Kennedy family will place no obstacle in the way of publication of his work.

"However, if Mr. Manchester's account is published in segments or excerpts, I would expect that incidents would not be taken out of context or summarized in any way which might distort facts of or the events relating to President Kennedy's death."

Sent at 'Urging'

Mr. Kennedy said the telegram had been sent at the "urging of defendants Manchester and Harper."

"I was told by Harper's representatives," he said, "that Manchester was becoming ill from an obsession with the thought that the book might never be published."

He sent the telegram, the Senator said, "after repeated requests to send a message which would allay his fear..."

Mr. Kennedy said that before and after the telegram was sent Evan Thomas, the editorial vice president of Harper & Row, and Mr. Manchester "assured me and others associated with me that nothing would be published without the approval of Mrs. Kennedy and myself."

The Senator said that on July 29, the day after he sent the telegram, he spoke with Mr. Manchester and that he had been "specifically and emphatically assured" that the original contract would be followed scrupulously.

Meet With Editors

On Aug. 4, the Senator said, he received the following telegram from Mr. Manchester and Mr. Thomas:

"Homer Bigart of Times is on to book and serial story and has gathered many facts including price of sale. We have been evasive in our replies regarding money. Under existing terms we expect book to be larges [sic] single contributor to library and are delighted with that prospect. In the absence of any further discussion we must assume that original signed agree-

ment prevails."

Senator Kennedy said he had answered Mr. Manchester and Mr. Thomas with the following reply:

"Re telegram where you say quote in absence of any instructions signed agreement prevails unquote. Agree, and that provides that Mrs. Kennedy and I must give permission for publication of book and that has not yet been given."

Throughout the summer, representatives of the Kennedys, notably Richard Goodwin, a former assistant to President Kennedy; John Siegenthaler, the editor of The Nashville Tennessean, and Edwin O. Guthman, the national news editor of The Los Angeles Times, met with editors of either Harper & Row or Look and suggested revisions in "Death of a President."

The defendants are expected to assert that these meetings indicated that the Kennedys were willing to accept both the serialization of the book and the subsequent publication in the spring.

Spokesmen for the Kennedys have said, moreover, that they detected some feeling in the family that the dates specified in the contract might have been waived if material that was considered objectionable was removed.

However, in his affidavit, Senator Kennedy said it was incorrect to infer that because "certain of Mrs. Kennedy's friends and my friends read portions of the manuscript and made suggestions as to its text, Mrs. Kennedy and I have somehow approved the manuscript."

The Senator said that he had never read "Death of a President" and that "no one who read the manuscript had authority to approve it on behalf of Mrs. Kennedy or me."

In her 11-page affidavit, Mrs. Kennedy said:

"I have never seen Manchester's manuscript. I have not approved it, nor have I authorized anyone else to approve it for me.

"I cannot be said to have approved what I have never seen, and yet, because it is widely known that I personally (and the Kennedy family) extended so much help to defendant Manchester, it will only be natural for the public to believe that the manuscript is published with my approval."

Earlier this week, Mrs. Kennedy issued one of her infrequent public statements in which she said that the book contained "inaccurate and unfair references to other individuals."

She did not identify the other individuals, but those who have read the original manuscript insist that it presents President Johnson unfavorably, that it speaks of Mrs. Kennedy and her friends as being infuriated by his behavior after the assassination in Dallas, and that it contains gratuitous insults to Mr. Johnson.

Senator Kennedy and his colleagues are said to have believed

that these characterizations of Mr. Johnson and references to Mrs. Kennedy's annoyance with him would strain future Johnson-Kennedy political alliances.

It was reported yesterday that in October, Mr. Goodwin and Mr. Siegenthaler, as well as Theodore C. Sorensen, Pierre Salinger, Arthur Schlesinger Jr., Burke Marshall, James Greenfield and John Douglas, all of whom were involved in President Kennedy's Administration, met in the Senator's apartment here and suggested that agreement be sought with the publishers.

Other sources have indicated that Senator Kennedy had favored this course, too, and that Mrs. Kennedy was instrumental in pressing the suit. The Senator has been described as being provoked and irritated by the book, but reluctant to sue.

In her complaint, Mrs. Kennedy asked the court for five forms of relief.

She asked first that Mr. Manchester, Harper & Row and Cowles Communications be enjoined permanently from publishing the manuscript and from letting others publish the manuscript until she approved both the text and the date of publication. She also asked that they be barred from giving anyone a copy of the text without her approval.

Secondly, she asked that the three defendants be permanently barred from publishing or using any of the letters from herself and from her daughter, Caroline, to the President, that might be in the possession of Mr. Manchester.

She asked also that the letters and any copies of them that might have been made be returned to her.

The third request Mrs. Kennedy made was that the defendants be barred permanently from using the tape-recorded interviews she gave to Mr. Manchester, and she asked that the tapes and all copies be returned.

Mrs. Kennedy said that Look magazine had used her name in advertisements and promotion circulars. She said the use of her name without permission had violated her rights under Sections 50 and 51 of the New York State Civil Rights Act.

These sections protect the right of privacy and say that the use, without written consent, of anyone's name, portrait or picture for advertising purposes is a misdemeanor.

Mrs. Kennedy asked that Cowles Communications be permanently enjoined from using her name in its advertisements.

Her final request was that her rights be embodied in a declaration and that she be granted both compensatory and punitive damages for the defendant's actions, together with the costs of the suit.

The papers were filed by Martin Gold, a lawyer with Paul, Weiss, Rifkind, Wharton & Garrison, the law firm that will represent Mrs. Kennedy.

December 17, 1966

ACCORD REACHED ON KENNEDY BOOK; SUIT WITHDRAWN

Publisher and Author Agree to Changes in Passages Offensive to Widow

By DOUGLAS ROBINSON

The legal battle by Mrs. John F. Kennedy to prevent publication of the book "The Death of a President" ended yesterday when she withdrew her lawsuit in State Supreme Court.

The settlement of one of the most bitter fights of recent publishing history came when the publisher, Harper & Row, and the author, William Manchester, agreed to delete or modify some of the passages Mrs. Kennedy considered objectionable.

The dispute touched on the lives of President Kennedy and President Johnson and possibly also on the Presidential ambitions of Senator Robert F. Kennedy. It also joined together in legal conflict prominent persons who were friends of long standing.

Signs Consent Decree

Material in the original Manchester manuscript, which deals with the assassination of President Kennedy, brought Mrs. Kennedy to tears during the early stages of the argument. The pressure may also have affected Mr. Manchester's health.

The end of the legal action came shortly before 4 P.M. when State Supreme Court Justice Saul S. Streit signed a consent decree, clearing the way for publication of the modified book.

"The lawsuit has been amicably settled," the white-haired jurist told newsmen in his chambers. "All the parties have consented to a judgment and decree, which the court has signed and approved."

A few minutes later, former Federal Judge Simon H. Rifkind, who represented Mrs. Kennedy in the dispute, was asked if the agreement was a victory for the Kennedy family.

Satisfaction Is Voiced

"I never like to speak in terms of victory or defeat in a law case," Mr. Rifkind said with a smile. "I'll just say we are satisfied."

Later, a close friend of Mr. Manchester noted that neither Mr. Rifkind nor anyone else connected with the Kennedys had claimed a victory.

"That's unlike Judge Rifkind," he said. "We were right, and we knew we were right. The agreement reflects that."

Mrs. Kennedy's objections to some passages in the book were that they contained personal material that would cause her "great and irreparable injury" and that her rights had been violated by Mr. Manchester's plans to have the unapproved manuscript of his book published.

Within a few hours of the settlement in Justice Streit's chambers, both Mr. Manchester and representatives of the Kennedy family held press conferences in which they outlined their versions of the dispute.

A third statement was issued by Cass Canfield, chairman of the executive committee of Harper & Row.

All three parties to the conflict, however, issued a joint statement in the State Supreme Court Building in Foley Square. It read:

"Mrs. John F. Kennedy, Harper & Row and William Manchester have resolved the differences which led to legal action. Certain passages of concern to Mrs. Kennedy have been deleted or modified by mutual agreement of all the parties. Therefore, Mrs. Kennedy terminated her lawsuit. All parties agree that the historical record has not been censored in any way.

"While the settlement regarding the book is satisfactory to all concerned, the parties regret that the questions in dispute could not have been earlier settled. A number of problems arising over a period of several months had to be resolved.

"Harper & Row will, in April, publish William Manchester's book, 'The Death of a President,' in accordance with arrangements made at the outset."

Details of the modification were not made public. But Mr. Canfield, in his statement, said the "changes that have been made, involving a cumulative total of some seven pages in a book of 654 pages of text, have affected neither its historical interest nor its narrative power."

For his part, Mr. Manchester read a prepared statement at the Overseas Press Club, 54 West 40th Street, in which he said that "out-of-court settlements are often called 'compromises.'"

"In this case," he said, "a more accurate description would be 'a resolution of misunderstandings.'"

The author, who wore a bright PT-109 tie clip of the sort made famous by President Kennedy, declined to answer questions after reading his prepared statement. He left almost immediately after completing his remarks, describing himself as a "very sick man" who was under "doctor's orders."

He spent two weeks in a hospital in Connecticut during the negotiations, suffering from pneumonia.

Mr. Manchester, in his statement, took exception to a statement issued by Mrs. Kennedy's office last month that described portions of the book as "tasteless and distorted."

That judgment, the author said, "was based on isolated fragments which had been read to her by associates of the family.

Representatives of the Kennedy family, at a press briefing at Mr. Rifkind's office at 575 Madison Avenue, issued a history of how the book had been born and told of the decision to allow Mr. Manchester to be the sole author to interview Mrs. Kennedy about the tragedy in Dallas.

Attending the briefing on behalf of Mrs. Kennedy were Richard N. Goodwin, a former assistant to President Kennedy; John Seigenthaler, editor of The Nashville Tennessean, and Edwin O. Guthman, national news editor of The Los Angeles Times.

All three men had read the original manuscript on behalf of Mrs. Kennedy.

Although the three discussed the nature of the controversy, they asked not to be quoted by name.

One of the spokesmen said that "in retrospect, the whole agreement to have this book was a mistake."

"In 1964, however, it seemed like a good idea," he said.

The spokesman also declined to alter Mrs. Kennedy's statements on the matter of whether the book was "tasteless" and said the family would have no further comment on the subject.

Earnings Estimated

One Kennedy spokesman said that Mr. Manchester might make $2.75-million from publication of the work. He broke this down into $1.5-million from paperback rights; $650,000 from Look magazine, which is serializing the book; $250,000 from the Book-of-the-Month Club; $150,000 from hardcover sales, and $200,000 from foreign rights.

Under the agreement, all copies of the original manuscript will be destroyed within 45 days, with the exception of one copy each to be kept by Harper & Row and Mrs. Kennedy and two copies to be kept by Mr. Manchester.

In addition, Mr. Manchester agreed to safeguard all source material gathered during preparation of the book and to return to Mrs. Kennedy all letters of a personal nature.

The 10 hours of taped conversation collected by the author from Mrs. Kennedy will be returned to her to be placed under seal at the Kennedy Memorial Library in Cambridge, Mass.

Much of the material objected to by Mrs. Kennedy was contained in these recorded interviews.

A close acquaintance of Mr. Manchester said the author had originally intended to turn the tapes and all the supporting documents over to the Federal Archives in Washington. It was said he also had intended to present the original manuscript to the Government.

The decree resolving the dispute continues "in full force and effect until the expiration of 100 years" from the time of signing.

The judgment also said that

Harper & Row had licensed the Book-of-the-Month Club to distribute the book under its imprint at about the same time that Harper & Row issued its edition.

The agreement was not made public. However, it was understood that each book printed would contain a publisher's note stating:

"Harper & Row wishes to make it clear that neither Mrs. Kennedy nor Senator Robert F. Kennedy has in any way approved or endorsed the material appearing in this book. The author, William Manchester, and the publishers assume complete and sole responsibility."

Another point in the agreement would prohibit the publication of letters from President Johnson to Mrs. Kennedy or her children, Caroline and John, without the express consent of the President.

The agreement affects the publishing of a hard cover edition under the Harper & Row imprint and a paperback edition to be published at least a year later.

It was also understood that the agreement specified that Senator Kennedy waived his rights in a memorandum signed by him and Mr. Manchester on March 26, 1964. The memorandum prohibited publication of the book until Nov. 22, 1968, five years after the assassination.

The memorandum also said that Mrs. Kennedy and the Senator must approve the text of the book, and that Mr. Manchester could not dispose of subsidiary rights without the approval of the Kennedys.

The decree signed by Justice Streit bars all American news media from publishing the excised parts of the original manuscript without the consent of Mrs. Kennedy. Mr. Rifkind said copies of the decree would be sent to newspapers and magazines across the country.

Later, however, a spokesman for the Kennedys said that no member of the family was contemplating suing if the deletions were published in other books, newspapers or magazines.

In reading his prepared statement, Mr. Manchester, who had a thin ribbon of perspiration on his upper lip, said that Mrs. Kennedy had relied on friends to read the manuscript because those close to her "had hoped to spare her the ordeal of a full reading."

"In retrospect, it seems obvious that had she done so then—had her authority not been delegated to designated representatives of the family—we all would have forgone much anguish," he said.

Mr. Manchester said he had made "certain alterations" at Mrs. Kennedy's request, and that her suggestions covered "less than 1 per cent of the manuscript—that is, less than seven pages out of a 700-page book."

He added that during the discussions with Mrs. Kennedy, additional historical matter had been added.

He stressed that none of the deletions "are political in character" and that the modifications were of a personal nature.

"Like Jacqueline Kennedy, I am distressed by flagrant publicity," he said. "Like her, I cherish my privacy and regret the painful notoriety of the past several weeks, and I am aware that on occasion it has unjustly stung the President of the United States, who has been the victim of unauthorized, false and malicious versions of the manuscript's contents."

Mrs. Kennedy brought suit against Mr. Manchester, Harper & Row and Look magazine, published by Cowles Communications, Inc., last Dec. 16.

Five days later, after intensive talks with representatives of Look, that part of the dispute was resolved after the magazine had agreed to remove or modify passages relating to the personal life of Mrs. Kennedy and her children.

The Look serialization, which will run to some 60,000 words,

began in the issue of Jan. 9. The second installment is scheduled to appear next Tuesday.

During the long dispute, Mr. Manchester defended his book by saying that President Kennedy, as a historian, "would have wanted his countrymen to know the truth of those terrible days."

"John Kennedy was my President," he said a few weeks ago. "To suggest that I would dishonor his memory or my association with him is both cruel and unjust."

Mr. Manchester is the author of another book about President Kennedy entitled "Portrait of a President," a work that a review in The New York Times said "can only be described as adoring."

The relationships between some major participants in the conflict have been close and of long duration.

Evan Thomas, the vice president of Harper & Row, edited "Profiles in Courage," for which President Kennedy won a Pulitzer Prize. Mr. Canfield of Harper & Row has said repeatedly that he was "distressed" that Mrs. Kennedy was upset by the book.

Mr. Canfield, furthermore, was once the father-in-law of Mrs. Kennedy's sister, who is now Mrs. Stanislas Radziwill.

Although the legal action in this country has been ended, a lawsuit may be filed against the West German magazine Stern, which bought serialization rights from Look for $72,500. The German weekly has refused to delete any of the material that Look agreed to delete.

Yesterday, Mr. Rifkind said that attorneys for the Kennedy family and Look were studying ways to initiate a lawsuit in West German courts against Stern.

The publication of the excised material, he said, "is incompatible with any taste or dignity."

January 17, 1967

FAIRFAX, Va., Jan. 10 — A jury cleared Mrs. Robert F. Kennedy today of a charge that she had misappropriated a neighbor's horse.

Mrs. Kennedy called her husband, the Democratic Senator from New York, on a telephone in an office behind the courtroom. A few minutes later she stood in front of the picturesque red brick Fairfax County Courthouse and reported what he had told her.

"He said, 'You're not going to be let out again without your keeper'," Mrs. Kennedy said with a twinkle.

The case was considered an important one by animal welfare groups, both because of the issues and because of the attention attracted by the fact

that Mrs. Kennedy was the defendant.

"I just hope it helps the humane societies," she said after the verdict.

Would she do the same thing again — go to the aid of an animal she felt was mistreated — in the knowledge that it could cause such a lawsuit?

"Well, I don't think I could live with myself if I didn't," Mrs. Kennedy said.

The seven-member jury began deliberating at 1:30 P.M., sent a question out to Circuit Judge Albert V. Bryan Jr. at 3:15, then filed in with the verdict at 3:55.

While Mrs. Kennedy and the plaintiff, Nicholas N. Zemo, a horse breeder, leaned forward, Edward E. Young, court clerk,

asked the foreman, William O. Moncure, if they had reached a verdict.

"We have," said Mr. Moncure. "Is it unanimous?"

"It is."

And then Mr. Young read from a slip of paper that the foreman had handed him: "We find in favor of the defendant."

The incident that led to the two-day trial occurred in October, 1963, when Mrs. Kennedy's husband was Attorney General. She and one of her children went horseback riding near their estate at McLean, Va., when they saw Mr. Zemo's horse, Pande, in what they said was a chicken coop.

Mrs. Kennedy rode home and told her groom, Richard Mayberry, to bring the horse

Ethel Kennedy Wins 'Horse Theft' Case After a 2-Day Trial

By MAURICE CARROLL

to the Kennedy property for care. Five days later it died. Two years later, Mr. Zemo sued for $30,000 damages.

Mr. Mayberry testified today that he had found the horse "in bad shape." He added, "You could count the ribs. I mean, he was almost dead."

Mr. Zemo, who had testified at length yesterday, was called back to the stand briefly.

His lawyer, Martin E. Morris, asked him what had happened to his horse.

"He disappeared. Somebody took him away," Mr. Zemo said.

"Had you mistreated the animal?"

"No, sir," Mr. Zemo said.

A prosecution witness, Norman L. Haymaker, guessed that Pande might be worth between $10,000 and $15,000. But a defense witness, Milton J. Dance Jr., who is a horse auctioneer, testified that the horse was not worth more than $1,000.

January 11, 1967

Kennedy Falls Out of Kayak Shooting Hudson Rapids

By JAMES F. CLARITY

THIRTEENTH LAKE, N.Y., May 6 — Senator Robert F. Kennedy fell out of a kayak and was swept through a half-mile of boulder-strewn rapids today on the upper reaches of the Hudson River near here. Although there were about three minutes of moderate anxiety on the shore, where members of the Senator's family and guests on his two-day boating party watched, he was not injured and got back into the 12-foot one-man kayak to continue six hours of "white water" sport. Mr. Kennedy, wearing a black rubber "wet-suit," orange life-jacket and white plastic helmet, fell out of the small craft at least three times during the day. He said later that he did not count his falls, commenting only, "I've been in the water a lot." Accompanying the Senator on the 14-mile run through the rapids were his wife, Ethel; seven of their 10 children; Secretary of the Interior Stewart L. Udall and his wife; James Whitaker, the first American to climb to the top of Mount Everest, and Caroline Kennedy, the daughter of President John F. Kennedy.

They rode the rapids in inflated rubber rafts (for the children and cautious adults), closed canoes (for Mr. Whitaker, Mr. Udall and a few other guests) and kayaks (for the Senator and a few expert boatmen).

Mr. Kennedy arranged for 30 experienced boat handlers, many of them from the Pittsburgh area, where the sport is popular, to guide the rafts and canoes through the icy waters of the river.

The imported experts said they were unpaid volunteers accepting the invitation for the challenge of new waters.

The experts made trial runs on the river yesterday and advised the Senator that it would be safe enough for his party today, despite the warnings of local residents that shooting the rapids was "madness." One of the experienced boatmen described the waters as "moderately challenging."

"We found out," said John Strassner of Greensburg, Pa., "that the locals told tales about the river for hours without catching their breath, but they never went near it except to fish."

A few local residents of this area, near North River, about 40 miles north of Glens Falls, sat on boulders along the river's edge and stared silently in apparent disapproval as the bright yellow rafts and shiny white canoes and kayaks surged past them. In all, the small flotilla included 15 rafts, 10 canoes and six kayaks, which were filled with a total of about 60 people.

The Senator's half-mile trip through the rapids without benefit of boat began about two hours after he put into the water at a private hunting lodge on a splendidly sunny day that seemed to enhance the beauty of the tall pines standing along the river, with the massive Adirondack Mountains in the near background.

In the midst of a span of turbulence, which one boatman said was a "class three" rapids —that is, mildly dangerous— Mr. Kennedy lost control of his kayak and was thrown out head first.

A half-mile downstream, Mr. and Mrs. Udall, several of the Kennedy children and other Kennedy guests were standing on boulders, resting and waiting for the Senator to come into sight around a curve in the river.

"Here he comes!" someone shouted. "He's in the water!"

Around the bend, through the rapids, came Mr. Kennedy, with only his head, shoulders and the top of his lifejacket visible above the water. There was an unsuccessful attempt to throw him a line. He was swept within five or six feet of several boulders before the rapids gave way to calmer water.

He swam eight or ten strokes to the shore, recovered the kayak, dumped water out of it and resumed his ride.

The Senator had spent about three minutes in the 40-degree water. An hour later, when the party went ashore for lunch, he shivered severely until he had drunk a cup of hot chocolate.

Members of the party joked about his fall.

"How do you like it?" Mr. Kennedy asked Mr. Whitaker, who had taken several lesser falls from a canoe.

"It's easier than mountains," Mr. Whitaker said. "Here you just let the scenery flow by. You don't have to put one foot in front of the other."

May 7, 1967

A relieved Bobby greets Ethel who had followed him down the freezing Hudson River in her kayak.

A pathologist from Kansas has concluded that President Kennedy had Addison's disease, although vigorous attempts were made by his physicians, family and friends—apparently for political reasons—not to describe his illness by that name.

Writing in the current issue of The Journal of the American Medical Association, the pathologist, Dr. John Nichols of the University of Kansas Medical Center, said he based his conclusion on a technical article that appeared in the November, 1955, issue of The Archives of Surgery.

The 1955 article described a 37-year-old man with Addison's disease who underwent spinal surgery on Oct. 21, 1954, at the Hospital for Special Surgery in Manhattan to alleviate severe pain caused by a back injury.

The leading author of the 1955 article, Dr. James A. Nicholas of New York, declined to comment yesterday when asked if the patient described was Mr. Kennedy.

Dr. Nicholas, who is an associate in orthopedic surgery at the Hospital for Special Surgery, cited ethical reasons for his refusal.

However, Mr. Kennedy, then Senator from Massachusetts, had disclosed on Oct. 10, 1954, that he would enter the Hospital for Special Surgery for a spinal operation to correct a condition caused by an injury received in World War II. It was later announced that surgery was scheduled for Oct. 21.

No mention was made at the time that the operation would be complicated by Addison's disease.

Addison's disease is a chronic insufficiency of hormone production from the outer layer, or cortex, of the adrenal glands. In about 70 per cent of the cases, the cause of this insufficiency is not known. Since the advent of cortisone in the late nineteen-forties, the disease has become relatively simple to manage and has an excellent prognosis.

A rumor that Mr. Kennedy suffered from Addison's disease was circulated during the summer of 1960, before his nomination as the Democratic candidate for the Presidency.

Supporters of then Senator Lyndon B. Johnson, Mr. Kennedy's closest rival for the nomination, were nettled by references to Mr. Johnson's 1955 heart attack and came back with a statement that Senator Kennedy had Addison's disease.

The Senator's brother Robert emphatically denied the rumor, stating that "Senator Kennedy does not now nor has he ever had an ailment described classically as Addison's disease, which is a tuberculose destruction of the adrenal glands."

He acknowledged that the Senator "had, in the postwar period, some adrenal insufficiency," but emphasized that "this is not in any way a dangerous condition and it is possible that even this might have been corrected over the years."

In addition, Robert Kennedy released a medical report signed by Drs. Eugene J. Cohen and Janet Travell both of New York, that stated:

"With respect to the old problem of adrenal insufficiency, as late as December, 1958, when you had a general checkup with a specific test of adrenal function, the results showed that your adrenal glands do function."

However, medical sources who had been close to the late President said in interviews that Mr. Kennedy had taken regular oral doses of synthetic cortical hormones until his death.

James McGregor Burns, in his book "John F. Kennedy— A Political Profile," published in 1960, said that "while Senator Kennedy's general insufficiency might well be diagnosed by some doctors as a mild case of Addison's disease, it was not diagnosed as the classic type of Addison's disease, which is due to tuberculosis."

Mr. Kennedy's condition, Mr. Burns said, "can be fully controlled by medication taken by mouth and requires a routine endocrinologic checkup as part of regular physical examinations once or twice a year."

The subject was treated in still another book—"A Thousand Days," written by Arthur M. Schlesinger Jr. and published in 1965. Mr. Schlesinger said Mr. Kennedy's adrenal insufficiency "presented no serious problem."

"During these years [the late 1940's and early 1950's], except when his back stopped him, he lived, between politics and athletics, a life of marked and exuberant physical activity," he said.

However, Dr. Nicholas, author of The Archives of Surgery article, said in an interview that in the mid-1950's surgery performed on a person with Addison's disease presented a tremendous risk.

"Surgery requires maximum efficiency of the adrenal gland," he explained, to prevent what he called an "Addisonian crisis" —a condition of shock, massive lowering of the blood pressure, and tremendous loss of salt and water that could lead to death because the patient would have insufficient adrenal hormones to cope with the stress of surgery.

Although cortisone was in use in the mid-1950's, doctors had very little experience with replacing the large amounts of adrenal hormones needed to withstand the trauma of surgery. Today, however, experience in advanced replacement therapy has greatly reduced the risk of surgery in persons with Addison's disease.

In his description of spinal surgery on the 37-year-old man with Addison's disease (presumably, Mr. Kennedy), Dr. Nicholas said he and his colleagues had prepared for an "Addisonian crisis" that did not develop.

He pointed out that "because of the severe degree of trauma involved in these operations and because of the patient's adrenocortical insufficiency due to Addison's disease, it was deemed dangerous to proceed with these operations."

"However, since this young man would become incapacitated without surgical intervention it was decided reluctantly to perform the operation," the doctor said.

"Though the magnitude of his surgery was great, and though complications ensued postoperatively, this patient had a smooth postoperative course insofar as no Addisonian crisis ever developed."

Following his spinal surgery in 1954, Mr. Kennedy is known to have suffered from a severe staphylococcus infection — so serious that last rites were given.

According to Dr. Nicholas, infection is another hazard of surgery in a victim of Addison's disease because both adrenal insufficiency and treatment with cortisone tend to reduce a person's ability to fight infections.

In linking Dr. Nicholas's patient with Mr. Kennedy, Dr. Nichols deplored the fact that no mention was made of President Kennedy's adrenal condition in the autopsy report.

"The diagnosis of Addison's disease could have been firmly established at autopsy and perhaps etiology [cause] determined," Dr. Nichols wrote. "However, the autopsy protocol is curiously silent on this point. The silence . . . may be due to (a) accidental or intentional failure to search and observe, or (b) suppression of autopsy findings and existing clinical records by relatives or Federal officials or both."

According to a spokesman for the American Medical Association, Dr. Nichols's article was reviewed by The Journal's board of editors, all of whom are physicians, as welll as by an outside consultant familiar with the late President's medical history. All passed it as worthy of publication, the spokesman said.

Senator Robert F. Kennedy, Democrat of New York, and Senator Edward M. Kennedy, Democrat of Massachusetts, the late President's two surviving brothers, declined to comment on the article.

July 11, 1967

Mrs. Kennedy Denies A Report She Plans To Be Wed to Briton

Mrs. John F. Kennedy's secretary denied a report yesterday that Mrs. Kennedy would soon announce her engagement to Lord Harlech, the former David Ormsby-Gore.

Earlier, Women's Wear Daily had carried a report that Mrs. Kennedy was about to announce her engagement to Lord Harlech, a former Ambassador to the United States who was a confidant of President Kennedy.

Before this was denied by Nancy Tuckerman, Mrs. Kennedy's secretary, the article was quoted by WCBS-TV on its 6 P.M. news show. However, just after the program went off the air, Miss Tuckerman released a statement saying she was authorized by the President's widow to say that there was absolutely no truth in the report.

Earlier in the day The United Press International reported that Mrs. Kennedy "has, by all indications, a serious suitor for her hand in the person of one of the late President's closest friends, Britain's Lord Harlech." The article cited "sources close to the former First Lady."

The news agency later reported that Lord Harlech was questioned about the report in Norfolk, Va., where he was addressing the Norfolk Forum "I have no comment whatsoever," he told newsmen.

Lord Harlech, who became the fifth Baron Harlech on the death of his father nearly five years ago, left his post in Washington on Jan. 3, 1965. Lord Harlech has five children. His wife was killed in a car crash earlier this year.

Mrs. Kennedy returned to the city Sunday from a visit to Montreal.

October 11, 1967

Kennedy's Mother Remembers

By JACK GOULD

MRS. JOSEPH P. KENNEDY spoke articulately and warmly of the early family life of the late President Kennedy in a half-hour conversation last night with Harry Reasoner on the Columbia Broadcasting System. She easily belied her 70-odd years with her precision of memory.

The interview took place at 83 Beals Street, Brookline, Mass., the President's birthplace, which next year is to be opened to the public as a national historic shrine. Mr. Reasoner did not attempt a program of political consequence, but merely solicited a mother's and grandmother's remembrances of her family.

Mrs. Kennedy said her offspring came so quickly after her marriage that she had to establish a card file listing their names, birth dates, inoculations and other vital statistics. She recalled that the British once described such a move as "American efficiency." Actually, she said, the pioneering effort at data control was only a symptom of "Kennedy despair."

The late President's mother said that her son had been admonished to show up promptly at meal times, but that if he were late he always charmed the cook into satisfying his hunger. She spoke of Senator Robert F. Kennedy, Democrat of New York, as a stern self-disciplinarian. Senator Edward M. Kennedy, Democrat of Massachusetts, she said, radiated more joie de vivre.

The half-hour, produced by Harry Morgan, was a pleasant one.

November 1, 1967

Mrs. Kennedy Visits Ancient Ruins in Cambodia

By TILLMAN DURDIN

SIEMREAP, Cambodia, Nov. 3 —Mrs. John F. Kennedy today began a three-day tour of the relics of the ancient Khmer Empire whose kings ruled much of the Indochina peninsula from 800 to 1400 and built stone temples and palaces that remain marvels of Asia.

She was realizing a childhood ambition as she started a leisurely inspection of a vast area of ruins at Angkor, some overgrown by jungle, some restored to their original state and others simply cleared of roots and trees to show the ravages of time.

The gray stone bas-reliefs on colonnaded walls illustrate charging warriors, the pageantry of kingly processions and peasants fishing, cultivating the fields and engaging in everyday life at home. Statues depict immutable gods, great rulers, priests, ministers, elephants and the sacred naga, or snake, with its fan-shaped hood.

Architectural Gem

The central attraction of the Angkor ruins, for which the little west Cambodian town of Siemreap, 140 miles northwest of Pnomnh, is the point of departure, is the massive Temple of Angkor, or Angkor Wat. This great sandstone structure, with its huge central tower dedicated to the god Vishnu, its long pillared galleries intricately carved with bas-reliefs, and its vast courtyards, is regarded as the finest example of Khmer architecture.

Mrs. Kennedy flew to Angkor on the second day of a six-day stay in Cambodia. She used the private plane of Cambodia's Chief of State, Prince Norodem Sihanouk, and was accompanied by Lord Harlech, former British Ambassador in Washington, Charles Bartlett, a Washington newspaperman, and his wife, and Michael Forrestal, son of the late Secretary of Defense, James V. Forrestal. Reporters were permitted 45 minutes with the Kennedy party as the visitors began their Angkor tour by looking over the Bayon, a many-towered temple complex at the the heart of Angkor Thom, one of the last Khmer capitals.

Television and still cameramen at times blocked progress as Mrs Kennedy said "wonderful, marvelous," to the explanations of Bernard Groslier, French curator of the Angkor ruins and her guide for sight-seeing in Angkor.

Mrs. Kennedy was smiling and relaxed and appeared not to mind the press jumble. She was dressed for sightseeing—trousers and an open-necked shirt.

As the party reached the inner tower of the Bayon temple, beyond which newsmen were told that they could not go, Mrs. Kennedy interceded in a controversy among cameramen as to what she should do by saying:

"Well, you agree among yourselves about what I should do and I will do it."

It was the consensus of photographers that Mrs. Kennedy should walk along an upper parapet and lean against a pillar gazing out over the lower platforms of the Bayon. She did as asked and then entered the structure with Mr. Groslier and her party.

After completing the tour of the temple, unique because of its more than 100 towers, each with carved Buddha heads facing four directions, Mrs. Kennedy and her party lunched at tables set out under giant banyan trees.

Later they went to another ruin, Sras Srang, and after some more sightseeing had tea while watching a troupe perform folk dances. Afterward they visited Angkor Wat, which was floodlit for the occasion.

Mrs. Kennedy's two additional days in the Angkor area will permit her to visit a number of outlying ruins. One is the little temple of Bantay Serai, rated by experts as the most exquisite of the Khmer temples.

The earlier Hindu religious and architectural orientation of the Khmers, received from India, changed in the later centuries into acceptance of the passive religious influence of Buddhism. That influence and the drain in erecting so many buildings are believed to have contributed to the downfall of the Khmer Empire and its conquest from the east by the Chams and from the west by the Thais.

The ruins were discovered in 1860.

November 4, 1967

Senator Says Only New Leaders Can Change Divisive Policies

By TOM WICKER

WASHINGTON, March 16—Senator Robert F. Kennedy of New York said today that he would seek the Democratic Presidential nomination because the nation's "disastrous, divisive policies" in Vietnam and at home could be changed "only by changing the men who are now making them."

With this severe attack on President Johnson, the brother of President Kennedy opened what may become the most serious challenge to the renomination of an incumbent President since Theodore Roosevelt failed to oust William H. Taft in 1912.

Not since James G. Blaine won the Republican nomination from President Chester A. Arthur in 1884 has an incumbent President who sought renomination failed to win it. Mr. Johnson is generally considered a candidate this year.

Will Support McCarthy

Senator Kennedy said he would actively support Senator Eugene J. McCarthy of Minnesota, another candidate against Mr. Johnson, because "it is important now that he achieve the largest possible majority next month in Wisconsin, in Pennsylvania and in the Massachusetts primaries." It is too late for Mr. Kennedy to enter any of those primaries.

He said he would enter his name in the California primary. Officials in Oregon have put his name on the ballot there and the Nebraska Secretary of State placed his name on the ballot today. Mr. McCarthy already has announced his candidacy in all three.

Thus, there will be a three-way contest in each of them for delegates to the Democratic National Convention in Chicago next August. Mr. Kennedy left open the possibility that he might also enter the Indiana primary, where Mr. McCarthy is a candidate.

Since Indiana will vote on May 7, three weeks before the Oregon primary on May 28 and a month before the California primary on June 4, the possibility that Mr. Kennedy might compete in Indiana with Mr. McCarthy could be used as a powerful argument to win the cooperation of the latter.

Mr. Kennedy refused to pledge support to President Johnson, in the event that he was renominated at Chicago. He said he would make up his mind on that point when he had to.

He personally communicated word of his decision to run to one of the President's assistants, he said, and sent his brother, Senator Edward M. Kennedy of Massachusetts, to Wisconsin to inform Mr. McCarthy of the decision.

Fight Just Beginning

Mr. Kennedy said today that, for his part, he would "take any step that is necessary to cooperate and work with Senator McCarthy." But he made it plain that he was in the race for the nomination because "the fight is just beginning and I believe that I can win."

"I made clear to Senator McCarthy," Mr. Kennedy said, "that my candidacy would not be in opposition to his, but in harmony."

In Green Bay, Wis., where he was campaigning today, Mr. McCarthy said he would not turn down Mr. Kennedy's help in Wisconsin, but that he was "not prepared to deal with anyone."

"An Irishman who announces the day before St. Patrick's Day that he's going to run against another Irishman shouldn't say it's going to be a peaceful relationship," Mr. McCarthy said.

He is committed to the race, he said, and considers himself "the best potential candidate in the field."

Thus, an anti-Johnson, anti-Vietnam war faction in the Democratic party will be at least temporarily split between Mr. Kennedy and Mr. McCarthy —a fact that President Johnson may have had in mind when he responded jokingly to the Kennedy announcement.

"These are days when we have to take chances," Mr. Johnson said at a businessman's conference in Washington. "Some speculate in gold — a primary metal — and others just speculate in primaries."

Not in Laughing Mood

The President's campaign lieutenants were not in a laughing mood, however. James Rowe, the Washington lawyer who is chairman of the Citizens for Johnson-Humphrey organization, said pointedly:

"I'm going to watch with fascination Bobby's efforts to convince those former young supporters of his who are now supporting Gene McCarthy that he's neither ruthless nor a political opportunist."

Mr. Rowe also said there was a widespread fear among other Democrats that Mr. Kennedy's entry into the race might "destroy the Democratic party for a generation."

Mr. Kennedy, making his announcement and then answering questions in the Caucus Room of the Senate Office Building, showed himself well aware of charges that he was capitalizing on Mr. McCarthy's strong showing against the President in the New Hampshire primary this week.

The McCarthy vote, he said, has demonstrated that the party was deeply divided over President Johnson's policies; therefore, he added, the New Hampshire primary results have made it possible for him to run without being charged with the responsibility of having split the party because of personal ambition or personal animosity to Mr. Johnson.

"My desire is not to divide the strength of those forces seeking a change" in present policies, he said, "but rather to increase it."

"In no state will my efforts be directed against Senator McCarthy," he said.

'Valiant Campaign'

Praising the latter's "valiant campaign" in New Hampshire, Mr. Kennedy said that "he has strength and I have individual strength."

"I don't think that just supporting an individual delivers that . . . I know that Senator McCarthy has suggestions as to what we should do. But I also have some ideas. And I don't think that the Democratic party or the people of the United States lose at all by considering those.

"I can't believe that anybody thinks that this is a pleasant struggle from now on, or that I'm asking for a free ride. I've got five months ahead of me as far as the convention is concerned. I'm going to go into primaries. I'm going to present my case to the American people. I'm going to go all across this country.

"I'm not asking anybody to hand anything to me. I'm not asking anybody to give anything to me. I'm going to go to the people and I'm going to make an effort and I think it's worthwhile."

Mr. Kennedy conceded that he had no arrangement or agreement with Mr. McCarthy for the kind of cooperation he called for in his statement today.

One example of the emotions aroused by Mr. Kennedy's sudden decision to enter the race after Mr. McCarthy's strong showing in New Hampshire came when Mary McGrory of The Washington Evening Star asked Mr. Kennedy if he would stay out of Wisconsin if Mr. McCarthy asked him to.

"Certainly," Mr. Kennedy replied.

"So he could have the victory for himself," Miss McGrory said, audibly.

Many of Mr. McCarthy's supporters are known to feel that Mr. Kennedy took over the headlines before Mr. McCarthy had a chance to enjoy his success in New Hampshire.

Echoes of President

There were echoes of President Kennedy's prose in his brother's announcement this morning, and Theodore C. Sorensen, the late President's special counsel and speech writer,

was at the New York Senator's side when he entered the crowded Caucus room.

Mr. Kennedy spoke frequently in the present tense, as his brother used to do ("I run because I am convinced, etc,") and at one point he reverted to the theme of John Kennedy's 1960 Presidential campaign, and of Edward Kennedy's 1962 campaign for the Senate in Massachusetts.

"I think we can do better," he said.

Mr. Kennedy emphasized the war in Vietnam—although, in a jab at Richard M. Nixon, considered the leading Republican candidate, he said he could not promise to end it. Mr. Nixon has "pledged" to do so.

Mr. Kennedy said, rather, that he would stop the bombing of North Vietnam, require a greater war effort by South Vietnam, and negotiate with with the National Liberation Front, which he said would have to have a place in the future "political process" of South Vietnam.

As Mr McCarthy has tried to do, however, Mr. Kennedy sought to avoid being tabbed as a peace candidate only.

He seeks new policies, he said, "to end the bloodshed in Vietnam and in our cities, policies to close the gap that now exists between black and white, between rich and poor, between young and old in this country and around the rest of the world."

The most immediate need in domestic policy, he said, is providing new jobs not only in the uneasy cities but also in the rural areas.

Mr. Kennedy spoke of the loyalty with which Mr. Johnson once served John F. Kennedy, and of the kindness the President had shown him after the assassination in November, 1963. Moreover, Mr. Kennedy said of the President:

"I have often commended his efforts in health, in education and in many other areas and I have the deepest sympathy for the burden that he carries today."

So the issue is not personal, he insisted, but "our profound differences over where we are heading and what we want to accomplish."

March 17, 1968

KENNEDY APPEALS FOR NONVIOLENCE

Bids Negroes in Indianapolis Follow Dr. King Example

By R. W. APPLE Jr.

INDIANAPOLIS, April 4— Senator Robert F. Kennedy, moved almost to tears by the death of the Rev. Dr. Martin Luther King Jr., told a street corner rally of Negroes tonight that they must strive for love, wisdom, understanding and compassion toward all men.

The New York Senator stood still in the glare of searchlights, hunched against the cold in a black overcoat, and begged those in his audience not to meet violence with violence.

Because the murderers were apparently white men, Mr. Kennedy said:

"Those of you who are black can be filled with bitterness, with hatred and a desire for revenge. We can move in that direction as a country, in great polarization—black people amongst black, white people amongst white, filled with hatred toward one another.

"Or we can make an effort, as Martin Luther King did, to understand and to comprehend, and to replace that violence with an effort to understand, with compassion and with love."

Senator Kennedy said to the 500 to 600 Negroes that he could feel "in my own heart" what many of them must be feeling.

"I had a member of my family killed," the Senator said, his voice trembling with emotion. "He was killed by a white man. But we have to make an effort in the United States—an

effort to understand."

Mr. Kennedy learned of the assassination of the civil rights leader as he landed in Indianapolis at the end of his first day's campaigning in Indiana.

Stepping to the bottom of the plane board ramp, the Senator, his face drawn and his eyes downcast, read the following statement:

"Dr. King dedicated himself to justice and love between his fellow human beings. He gave his life for that principle, and it's up to those of us who are here—his fellow citizens and public officials, those of us in government—to carry out that dream, to try and end the divisions that exist so deeply within our country and to remove the stain of bloodshed from our land."

Mr. Kennedy went directly from the airport to a street rally in a predominantly Negro neighborhood. He told the audience, which had been waiting an hour and a half, that Dr. King was dead. He waited for the screams of the women and the gasps of the men to subside and then talked earnestly and movingly for about six minutes.

He said that his favorite poet was Aeschylus and that his favorite lines were these:

"Even in our sleep, pain which cannot forget falls drop by drop upon the heart until in our own despair, against our will, comes wisdom through the awful grace of God."

Finally, Mr. Kennedy made one more plea for nonviolence.

"I ask you now to return home," he said, "to say a prayer for the family of Martin Luther King, that's true, but more important to say a prayer for our country, which all of us love, and to say a prayer for understanding and the compassion of which I spoke."

Mr. Kennedy worked with Dr. King during Mr. Kennedy's term as Attorney General from 1961 to 1964, when the Atlanta clergyman was leading protest movements in Birmingham, Ala., and elsewhere in the Deep South.

After returning to his hotel, the Senator telephoned Mrs. King in Atlanta to offer his condolences. At her request he chartered an airplane to take her and members of her family to Memphis tomorrow morning and to return them and the coffin to Atlanta later tomorrow.

Mr. Kennedy also cancelled rallies and motorcades in Ohio and Louisiana scheduled for tomorrow. He will make a scheduled appearance before the City Club in Cleveland at noon and plans to discuss the assassination.

A decision about the remainder of his planned seven-day campaign swing through seven states will be made tomorrow after Mr. Kennedy talks again with Mrs. King, aides said. The Senator will attend the funeral.

April 5, 1968

Mrs. Kennedy Visits Mrs. King And 4 Children Before Funeral

ATLANTA, April 9 (AP)—Two widows, both of whom lost famous husbands by an assassin's bullets, clasped hands and shared words of comfort today.

Mrs. John F. Kennedy, who could perhaps understand the grief of Mrs. Martin Luther King Jr. better than any other, flew to Mrs. King's home today for a brief visit.

The two attractive widows, both clad in black silk suits, spent about five minutes together in private talk in Mrs. King's bedroom, shortly before the funeral.

Mrs. Kennedy, who wore black mesh hose, first signed the guest book when she entered the Kings' simple red-brick home with a friend, Rachel Mellon.

The former First Lady then moved slowly down the long hall to the King bedroom, smiling and speaking softly to friends and relatives of the Kings.

At the end of the hallway, she paused briefly to speak to the four King children, who were dressed up for the funeral.

Twelve-year-old Yolanda, who wore a white lace dress, said Mrs. Kennedy had told her, "I'm mighty glad to be here."

Shortly after their talk, Mrs. Kennedy and Mrs. King left for the funeral in separate limousines.

Before Mrs. Kennedy's arrival, Mrs. King, who had again been up until the early morning hours making final funeral arrangements, remained in seclusion.

April 10, 1968

Kennedy Loses Shoe to an Admirer

KALAMAZOO, Mich., April 12 (AP) — A 27-year-old mother of five proudly showed off a Presidential campaign souvenir to neighbors and newspaper photographers today. It was not a button. It was Senator Robert F. Kennedy's right shoe.

Mrs. Phyllis Jenkins snatched off the shoe on a Kennedy campaign swing into Michigan yesterday.

The New York Democrat had just finished a speech in Kalamazoo and had out-sprinted a group of enthusiastic admirers to a waiting convertible.

Admirers swarmed about as Mr. Kennedy stood in the back seat reaching and shaking hands, many of them reluctant to let go as the car moved slowly forward down Michigan Avenue toward the Kalamazoo airport.

Bent on obtaining a souvenir of "my favorite," Mrs. Jenkins said she quickly snatched off her own shoes to give chase to the convertible. When she reached it, she said she hoisted herself on the back, "but couldn't get a hanky or anything, so I just took his shoe." It came off still tied, but Mr. Kennedy managed to keep his backseat stance.

"He couldn't have kept her from getting it unless he'd kicked her, and he didn't want to do that, obviously," an onlooker recalled.

The shoe turned out to be an 8½, with an arch support, and "London, England," inscribed inside.

April 13, 1968

In Ethel Kennedy Country, Home and Children Come First

By MYRA MacPHERSON

McLEAN, VA., April 19 — Hickory Hill is quite obviously Ethel country. Senator Robert F. Kennedy's wife has decorated it in large bursts of color—yellows, blues, greens and particularly pink. She probably is one of the few people to have a pink and white dining room.

She is here in the six-acre compound most of the time—with her 10 children, the Senator when he's home, her staff, enough animals to stock a small zoo and enough friends to fill a small hotel.

But this year she will be leaving home more than she wants because she is campaigning for her husband, who is trying to become President of the United States. In Indiana this week, in her first days out on her own, she has shown she is one of the Senator's best campaign assets.

She would shake hands, smile and stand there in her white point d'esprit hosiery, slim, hard-lined Ungaro and Courrèges-style dresses three inches above the knees, low-heeled shoes, and tasteful but obviously expensive gold and diamond earrings.

The women of industrial towns in Indiana, in nondescript dresses, or sometimes in slacks, would stare but there was no animosity or disapproval. They would nudge each other and say "Isn't she just darling?" or "She's so cute" or "She sure don't look like she's had no 10 children."

Mrs. Kennedy, who was 40 on April 12, said she considered lowering her hems for the campaign but decided not to, and she's been getting away with it. A woman in Marion said, "People like to look at chic people, even if they're not chic themselves."

At first, Mrs. Kennedy flatly refused to give speeches or interviews.

But on the last day in Indiana this week, she finally wrote out a speech in a car on an envelope and delivered it, haltingly of course.

"In 1960 they sent me to Indiana, Kentucky, Colorado, Utah, Montana, California, Virginia—and we lost every one," she said. "You know what trouble we feel we're in here, if they let me out again."

But no matter how much or how hard she campaigns this year, her home and children come first. When she gets off motorcades with her husband, she dashes to the nearest phone booth to call home. She held up this trip until the last minute because the governess was sick and she wouldn't leave the children.

Finally, the Senator's private secretary and family friend, Angie Novello, came to stay until the governess got well.

Mrs. Kennedy says, "I try not to be away more than three or four days at a time from the gang—I want to see if the house is still there."

Although her basic interests are as wife and mother, what saves her from being an icky 1968 version of a 1940's June Allyson movie is her irreverent and self-effacing sense of humor.

When her luggage was lost for one

night in Indiana she said it wasn't doing without the nightgown that she minded, it was the cold cream. When she was praised for the crowd she drew, she said, "It looked sort of one deep to me."

And, someone told her how everyone said she looked so young she replied, "Well, after one woman shook my hand and said 'I think your son's doing a fine job,' I thought it was time I got off the campaign trail."

In a motel room in Kokomo, sitting on a bed with her shoes kicked off, watching her husband on television saying "South Americer and Africer," she laughed and added "and Indianer."

She pores through newspapers and reads a wide collection of books from current best sellers to religious ones, but she is no intellectual and doesn't pretend to be one.

The sixth of millionaire George Skakel's seven children (he owned the Great Lakes Carbon Corporation), Mrs. Kennedy attended the best Catholic schools, majored in philosophy and English at Manhattanville College of the Sacred Heart, but never gave a thought to a career. She was married in 1950, the year she graduated.

She apparently is not introspective and hates to talk about herself or how she manages her brood. But she did say: "I believe in discipline and when I say 'don't do something,' the kids know I mean it. But they also must have the freedom to make up their own minds. For the first five years it is so important to give them love—after that everything sort of falls into place."

Any moods or sorrows she has are masked, even to friends. Close friends say her religion is her strength.

One place where religion doesn't seem to help her is in an airplane. Both her parents and one brother were killed in private plane crashes, and she is terrified of flying. On takeoffs and landings her hands grip the seats. She refused to take a small private plane hop to Kokomo from Indianapolis and went by car.

Whether campaigning or not, she has an appalling amount of energy. She relaxes by playing tennis, swimming or skiing.

She has the scrubbed look of a coed, even though the laugh lines on her tanned face are deep. She wears false eyelashes and eyeliner at night but doesn't bother with any other make-up except pale lipstick.

Mrs. Kennedy is not an authority on antiques, although her house contains some, nor is she very fashion-conscious. She always asks her friends' opinions of what she buys.

One day recently she tried on a frilly dress and her friends collapsed laughing. She said, "Well, I guess that's a loser." Her lean, 5-foot-5½-inch, somewhat coltish build was not meant for romantic lace and she says she can't get used to the midi-length either. She worries about being hippy and jokes that she wears a 6 in coats, an 8 in dresses "and a 16 in slacks."

She is, of course, free from the daily drudgery of housework. The Kennedys have a governess and a nurse for the baby (Douglas Harriman, one year old in March), two cooks, several maids and secretaries. But Mrs. Kennedy oversees it all, plans the parties and menus. She is desperately looking for a yard man and ended up the other day moving the patio furniture herself.

The help serves to free her not from her children but for them. She changes the baby's diapers, gives him baths, buys all the children's clothes, drives some of the children to school, and reads to the younger ones.

"I think it's important to get them started in the habit of loving books while young," she said.

She rarely goes to women's luncheons or teas, and most of the parties she attends are her own. Her friends have learned to go to Hickory Hill.

This, of course, is not exactly a hardship. The house, built in 1810, looks both expensive and tastefully decorated but also comfortable. Although she works with a New York

decorator, the effect seems to be all Ethel Kennedy.

On either side of the center hall are two matching sitting rooms—small and shuttered in white. The one on the right is in vivid blues and greens. The other is in pinks and yellows with a lime green carpet crossed with diagonal white lines to make a diamond pattern.

The sofas are covered in quilted cottons in vivid floral patterns, and they zip off to wash. Off the left-hand sitting room is the large living room, an addition to the house in 1963. The master bedroom suite is directly above.

There are gleaming dark parquet floors and an Aubusson carpet in front of the living-room fireplace. The room is a blend of French period pieces and modern paintings in the French impressionist style. Two modern sofas in pale yellow flank the fireplace. In a corner is a pale green silk sofa that supposedly belonged to Emperor Franz Joseph.

The other day, a bottle of baby lotion and a child's pull toy were on a Louis XV sofa with a poufy satin seat. There are wicker baskets filled with azaleas, bud vases and countless other vases of flowers around the house.

Beyond the living room picture window is the sloping lawn with its tree houses and swings, the swimming pool, the wading pond, the cabana with its jukebox, and the barn with the ponies and horses.

There are family pictures everywhere—12 on the television set, more on the piano. Many are of John F. Kennedy. A corner is devoted to a full-length American flag.

Every room, including the pool cabana, has two phones—one with five buttons and countless extensions. Most of the older children have their own phones.

April 20, 1968

Indiana Seeing a New Kennedy With Shorter Hair, Calm Manner and Pleas for Local Rule

By JOHN HERBERS

SOUTH BEND, Ind., May 2 —In his six weeks of campaigning for the Presidency, Senator Robert F. Kennedy has gradually developed a new style and a new approach to the issues.

With rare exception, the New York Democrat no longer invokes the memory of his brother. The Senator speaks instead of his own record and frequently he goes so far as to repudiate some of the policies of the Kennedy Administration, saying the changed conditions have demanded new departures.

In his speeches, he is no longer the aggressive candidate whipping up his audiences with emotional rhetoric. His approach is calm and reasoned, almost soft. If he answers charges hurled at him in the Indiana primary campaign at all he does so obliquely with

humor.

The "Sock it to 'em Bobby" signs that appeared in abundance in the early stages of the campaign no longer seem appropriate and, in fact, are rarely seen in Indiana.

Senator Kennedy's personal appearance, too, is more conservative. His hair, though still full, has been clipped progressively shorter.

The finely tailored suit jackets that he wore before entering the race have been replaced by models with less shape. The gray suit he wore with brown shoes on his farm tour yesterday looked as if it had come off the rack of a small-town haberdasher.

In the crowds that turn out to see him, there frequently are women remarking to one another that the 42-year-old candidate has

gray in his auburn hair, and he looks older than they had imagined.

The campaign that Senator Kennedy is conducting in Indiana has the flavor of Main Street America. Musical groups like Simon and Garfunkel, which appeal to the young, have been appearing in the state with Senator Eugene J. McCarthy, also a candidate in the primary. This kind of entertainment is available to Senator Kennedy but has not been used.

The Senator's new style and approach are designed to overcome some of the difficulties facing him in Indiana and other states where the outlook of voters is more conservative than on East and West Coasts.

Studies made by the Kennedy organization had shown

that a number of voters pictured the Senator as a too-aggressive opportunist running on John Kennedy's reputation with too much of an appeal to the very young and immature.

For several years, Senator Kennedy's political speeches had made direct reference to his brother's Administration and policies. Frequently, when making a point he would preface it with a John Kennedy quotation.

He also did this in his first campaign speeches after announcing his candidacy for President on March 16. Appearing on college campuses he spoke with raised voice, "Give me your help, give me your hand and we will build a new America." He smote the air with his fist for emphasis.

He spoke then of American boys dying in swamps of Southeast Asia and of the Johnson Administration appealing to "the darker impulse" of the American spirit. When he spoke of domestic violence he stressed the need to attack the causes of deprivation over the need for law and order.

The change to the new posture began even before President Johnson announced on March 31 that he would not seek re-election and would reduce the bombing of North Vietnam. In the Indiana campaign, the change has become pronounced.

Senator Kennedy's stand on the issues is not without continuity. It is still based largely on his Senate record. His appeal is still to restore a sense of destiny to the country through a new Kennedy Administration and to give hope to the alienated in the process. The change in posture is in emphasis rather than substance.

The Senator still chides the Administration for its Vietnam policy but his remarks are more balanced and more restrained. He still talks of the responsibility of the advantaged groups to help the disadvantaged and the rich to bear a greater share of the tax burden, but he talks more of strict law enforcement and reminds his audiences that for more than three years he was the nation's chief law enforcement officer, the Attorney General.

Senator Kennedy seldom raises his voice now. Most of his speeches are delivered in a much more passive manner. At Purdue University a student asked, "If your name was anything other than Kennedy could you justify your candidacy as being based on anything but opportunism?" The Senator answered with one word, "yes."

He now cites his own proposals almost exclusively over those of his brother's Administration. Asked how he would cut Government expenses, he says there should be reductions in both the space program and development of the supersonic transport, both of which were initiated by the Kennedy Administration.

He says there should be local control of Federal grants for most social programs—a policy that fits perfectly with that advocated by Republican leaders in the House of Representatives.

The Kennedy strategists, however, describe this as a happy meeting of the old conservatism and the new liberalism, which holds that for citizens to become more involved in the government there should be a dismantling of much of the Federal bureaucracy.

In Indiana, Robert Kennedy is preaching this to both the young and the old.

May 3, 1968

KENNEDY SON SEIZED FOR THROWING ROCKS

McLEAN, Va., May 2 (AP)—The 12-year-old son of Senator Robert F. Kennedy was apprehended by the police last week after a stone-throwing incident on a state highway near the Kennedy home in this Washington suburb, the police said today.

David Kennedy and another boy were taken to a police substation after a motorist complained that they were throwing stones at his car, Fairfax County Police Chief William L. Durrer said.

No charges were placed against the boys and they were taken home—David by a governess and the other boy by his parents, Chief Durrer said.

Senator Kennedy, campaigning in Indiana for the Democratic Presidential nomination, issued a statement through his Washington office saying:

"I regret to say that one of my sons in the company of another boy got into trouble last Saturday while my wife and I were away from home.

"He feels very badly about what he has done and has apologized to all concerned.

"He is a good boy who has always been a source of joy and pride to all our family and never has been involved in any trouble whatsoever prior to this incident."

May 3, 1968

MRS. KENNEDY'S TRIP ASCRIBED TO U.S. BID

McCall's says that Mrs. John F. Kennedy was on a secret mission for the United States Government when she visited Cambodia last fall.

The article in the June issue of the magazine, published yesterday, said the idea for the mission came from Robert McNamara, then Secretary of Defense, and was arranged by Ambassador at large W. Averell Harriman. He is now in Paris meeting with the North Vietnamese.

The article was written by Marvin Kalb, diplomatic correspondent of the Columbia Broadcasting System, and his brother, Bernard, who works for the network in the Far East. Bernard Kalb accompanied Mrs. Kennedy on her trip.

A C.B.S. spokesman said that the material had already been presented on the network. Mrs. Kennedy was not immediately available for comment.

The Kalbs said that Mrs. Kennedy's trip "stands revealed as an uncommon adventure in high -level diplomacy."

They said the trip was "a subtle probing mission designed to avoid headlines and to pave the way for further diplomatic exchanges between the two countries."

May 21, 1968

KENNEDY IS SHOT BY YOUTH ON COAST

CONDITION 'STABLE'

Aide Reports Senator Is 'Breathing Well'— Last Rites Given

By WARREN WEAVER Jr.

LOS ANGELES, Wednesday, June 5—Senator Robert F. Kennedy was shot and critically wounded by an unidentified gunman this morning just after he made his victory speech in the California primary election.

Moments after the shots were fired, the New York Senator lay on the cement floor of a kitchen corridor outside the ballroom of the Ambassador Hotel while crowds of screaming and wailing supporters crowded around him.

On his arrival at Good Samaritan Hospital a spokesman described Senator Kennedy's condition as "stable." He was described as breathing but not apparently conscious.

Frank Mankiewicz, Senator Kennedy's press aide, was quoted as saying, at 4:15 A.M.: "He is breathing well and has good heart. I would not expect he is conscious."

Shot Twice In Head

Mr. Mankiewicz said the Senator had been shot twice in the head—once in the forehead and once near the right ear. He was transferred to Good Samaritan Hospital after a brief stop at General Receiving Hospital.

The Rev. Thomas Peacha said he had administered the last rites of the Roman Catholic Church in the hospital's emergency room. This is normal procedure when a Catholic has been possibly seriously injured.

The suspected assailant, a short, dark-haired youth wearing blue denims, was immediately seized by a group of Kennedy supporters, including the huge Negro professional football player Roosevelt Grier. They pinned the assailant's arms to a stainless steel counter, the gun still in his hand.

Wife by his Side

Senator Kennedy lay on the floor, blood running from his back. His right eye was open but the other was partly closed as his wife, Ethel, kneeled at his side. His shirt was pulled open, and a rosary could be seen on his chest.

Richard Tuck, a Kennedy aide who was at his side at the time of the shooting, said the Senator's condition was "very bad." Within minutes he was rushed to a hospital.

Some witnesses reported that he had been shot in the back of the head or neck. Others indicated that at least one bullet had entered his torso.

A physician who gave Senator Kennedy emergency treatment before he was removed from the hotel said that his pulse was 130 but "fu" and bounding" and that the heart beat was good. The Senator was not conscious. He was given oxygen and intravenous plasma.

Dr. George Lambert, a physician with American Airlines, was in the hotel and responded to the call for a doctor. Several doctors responded. Dr. Lambert said that he had not treated Senator Kennedy but that he had treated two others who had been shot. He said one was a man shot in the left side and the other a man shot in the leg, both apparently bystanders. He said they were not seriously wounded and were taken to the same hospital as the Senator.

Senator Kennedy's brother, President John F. Kennedy, was killed by Lee Harvey Oswald in Dallas on Nov. 22, 1963.

It was only moments after the Senator had concluded a brief victory statement to several hundred cheering supporters when the incident occurred. He was being escorted out a back door of the ballroom, behind the rostrum, and through the kitchen corridor to an adjoining dining room that was serving temporarily as a working press room.

Mr. Kennedy had been scheduled to hold a post-election news conference there.

Stood By Table

When four or five shots rang out, reporters and photographers rushed from the press room while other persons from the ballroom audience crowded in from the other side of the hall.

Karl Uecker, assistant maitre d'hôtel at the Ambassador, said he was walking in front of Senator and Mrs. Kennedy when the gunman began shooting.

"I'm right in front of him," Mr. Uecker said 15 minutes after the shooting. "There were three shots, one after the other.

"I recognized the danger and I grabbed him by the neck."

He was describing his capture of the gunman.

Mr. Uecker said the gunman had been standing by the corner of a work table in the kitchen passageway and that "he looked like a houseman."

Mr. Uecker said he was aware that Senator Kennedy had collapsed to the floor behind him.

"The first or second shot hit him," Mr. Uecker said.

The suspect said nothing when the maitre d' grappled with him.

"I wrestled with the gunman," Mr. Uecker said.

He looked over the heads of the reporters interviewing him and said: "I thought it was a joke or something. It sounded like Chinese firecrackers or something. I had my hand on Kennedy, I was leading him, and his wife was on my other hand."

The Senator's assailant was a youthful man with an olive complexion. He had a stocky build and dark curly hair.

Held on Counter

Moments after the shooting he was lifted by Mr. Grier and other persons to the serving counter top and held prone.

All the while frenzied adherents of Mr. Kennedy were screaming oaths at the gunman.

"You bastard, you'll fry for this," one slight, dark man shouted as he jumped up and down on the serving counter.

When the police arrived, they carried the gunman horizontally, four or five of them holding his arms and legs, through the press room and out into the hotel lobby.

Among those who seized the man was William Barry, a bank vice president from New York who has been serving as Senator Kennedy's chief security aide during his primary campaigns.

A half hour after the shooting, the Los Angeles police reported that two suspects had been arrested and that the Ambassador had been surrounded by police. The latter report indicated a suspicion that other men might have been involved in the shooting.

Just after the Senator fell wounded and bleeding, Mrs. Kennedy rose from his side to warn away photographers, reporters and others in the horrified crowd who were pushing in.

"Get back, get back," she shouted, her tanned face drawn. Then, as space opened in the corridor, she returned to kneel beside her husband, who was breathing deeply.

Amid the curses, a voice from the crowd shouted: "Someone pray!" At that, Mr. Kennedy took his rosary beads and tightened his hand about them.

The ambulance carried the Senator to Central Receiving Hospital. Then he was taken to Good Samaritan Hospital in an ambulance with Mrs. Kennedy. His head was bandaged and there appeared to be a plasma bottle in use.

Pierre Salinger, Mr. Kennedy's aide, said at Central Receiving Hospital that the wounds were serious. Mr. Salinger said Mr. Kennedy had been shot in the

BEFORE THE SHOOTING: Senator Robert F. Kennedy at Ambassador Hotel in Los Angeles minutes before he was wounded by gunman.

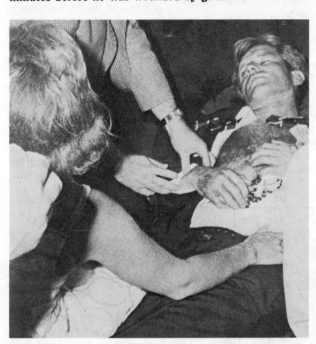

WOUNDED BY A GUNMAN: Senator Robert F. Kennedy lying on floor of anteroom in the Ambassador Hotel in Los Angeles minutes after he was shot early this morning.

head and in the body.

Earl Williman, a Kennedy supporter who had been standing near the Senator at the time of the gunfire, said Mr. Kennedy had been shot near the ear.

"All I could see," Mr. Williman said, "was the man here in the kitchen. He stepped up and shot the Senator right near the ear. I didn't see any more. I hit the man and several of us held him."

Mr. Kennedy had just won a major victory in his campaign for the Democratic Presidential nomination. His short victory speech, full of quiet jokes about his dog and his family, closed with these words: "On to Chicago and let's win there."

June 5, 1968

KENNEDY IS DEAD, VICTIM OF ASSASSIN

Revolver Traced to Suspect —Senator, 42, Failed to Regain Consciousness

By GLADWIN HILL

ROBERT F. KENNEDY

LOS ANGELES, Thursday, June 6—Senator Robert F. Kennedy, the brother of a murdered President, died at 1:44 A.M. today of an assassin's shots.

The New York Senator was wounded more than 20 hours earlier, moments after he had made his victory statement in the California primary.

At his side when he died today in Good Samaritan Hospital were his wife, Ethel; his sisters, Mrs. Stephen Smith and Mrs. Patricia Lawford; his brother-in-law, Stephen Smith; and his sister-in-law, Mrs. John F. Kennedy, whose husband was assassinated 4½ years ago in Dallas.

In Washington, President Johnson issued a statement calling the death a tragedy. He proclaimed next Sunday a national day of mourning.

The Final Report

Hopes had risen slightly when more than eight hours went by without a new medical bulletin on the stricken Senator, but the grimness of the final announcement was signaled when Frank Mankiewicz, Mr. Kennedy's press secretary, walked slowly down the street in front of the hospital toward the littered gymnasium that served as press headquarters.

Mr. Mankiewicz bit his lip. His shoulders slumped.

He stepped to a lectern in front of a green-tinted chalkboard and bowed his head for a moment while the television lights snapped on.

Then, at one minute before 2 A.M., he told of the death of Mr. Kennedy.

Following is the text of the statement from Mr. Mankiewicz:

"I have a short announcement to read which I will read at this time. Senator Robert Francis Kennedy died at 1:44 A.M. today, June 6, 1968. With Senator Kennedy at the time of his death was his wife, Ethel; his sisters, Mrs. Patricia Lawford and Mrs. Stephen Smith; his brother-in-law, Stephen Smith, and his sister-in-law, Mrs. John F. Kennedy.

"He was 42 years old."

Senator Kennedy's body will be taken to New York this morning and then to Washington.

The man accused of shooting Mr. Kennedy early yesterday in a pantry of the Ambassador Hotel was identified as Sirhan Bishara Sirhan, 24 years old, who was born in Palestinian Jerusalem of Arab parentage and had lived in the Los Angeles area since 1957. Sirhan had been a clerk.

$250,000 Bail

Yesterday, he was hurried through an early-morning court arraignment and held in lieu of $250,000 bail.

Sirhan was charged with six counts of assault with intent to murder, an offense involving a prison term of 1 to 14 years.

Five other persons in addition to the 42-year-old Senator were wounded by the eight bullets from a .22-caliber revolver fired at almost point-blank range into a throng of Democratic rally celebrants surging between ballrooms in the hotel. The shots came moments after Senator Kennedy had made a speech celebrating his victory in yesterday's Democratic Presidential primary in California.

The defendant, seized moments after the shooting, refused to give the police any information about himself. He was arraigned as "John Doe."

Three hours later, Mayor Samuel W. Yorty announced at a news conference at police headquarters that the defendant had been identified as Sirhan. He said the identity had been confirmed by Sirhan's brother and a second individual.

Senator Kennedy, accompanied by his wife, Ethel, was wheeled into the Good Samaritan Hospital shortly after 1 A.M. yesterday after a brief stop at the Central Receiving Hospital. A score of the Senator's campaign aides swarmed around the scene.

Grim Reminder

Less than five years back many of them had experienced the similar tragedy that ended the life of President John F. Kennedy.

At 2:22 A.M., Senator Kennedy's campaign press secretary, Frank Mankiewicz, came out of the hospital into a throng of hundreds of news people to announce that the Senator would be taken into surgery "in five or ten minutes" for an operation of "45 minutes or an hour."

One bullet had gone into the Senator's brain past the mastoid bone back of the right ear, with some fragments going near the brain stem. Another bullet lodged in the back of the neck. A third and minor wound was an abrasion on the forehead.

It was after 7 A.M. when Mr. Mankiewicz reported that more than three hours of surgery had been completed, and all but one fragment of the upper bullet had been removed. The neck bullet was not removed but "is not regarded as a major problem," Mr. Mankiewicz said.

He also reported that the Senator's vital signs remained about as they had been, except that he was now breathing on his own, which he had not been doing before the surgery. Then Mr. Mankiewicz said:

"There may have been an impairment of the blood supply to the mid-brain, which the doctors explained as governing certain of the vital signs—heart, eye track, level of consciousness—although not directly the thinking process."

Senator Kennedy was taken from surgery to an intensive-care unit

At 2:15 P.M. Mr. Mankiewicz announced that Senator Kennedy had not regained consciousness and that a series of medical tests had been "inconclusive and don't show measurable improvement in Senator Kennedy's condition."

"His condition as of 1:30 P.M. remains extremely critical," the spokesman continued. "His life forces — pulse, temperature, blood pressure and heart—remain good, and he continues to show the ability to breathe on his own, although he is being assisted by a resuscitator."

The tests included X-rays and electroencephalograms.

Mrs. Kennedy remained at the hospital.

Mrs. John F. Kennedy arrived at the hospital at 7:30 P.M. yesterday, after a chartered plane flight from New York.

A team of surgeons treating Senator Kennedy included Dr James Poppen, head of neuro-surgery at the Lahey Clinic in Boston. He was rushed to Los Angeles in an Air Force plane on instructions from Vice President Humphrey

Mr. Humphrey and Senator Eugene J. McCarthy of Minnesota have been Senator Kennedy's rivals in the Democratic Presidential competition.

Mayor Yorty said the defendant's identification had come through a brother, Adel Sirhan, after the police had traced the ownership of the .22-caliber revolver involved in the shooting to a third brother, Munir Bishari Salameh Sirhan, also known as Joe Sirhan.

The weapon was traced through three owners, one in suburban Alhambra, the next in Marin County, adjacent to San Francisco, and back to an 18-year-old youth in suburban Pasadena. The youth said he had sold it to "a bushy-haired guy named Joe" whom he knew only as an employe of a Pasadena department store.

Detectives identified the bushy haired man as Munir Sirhan. From him, the trail led to the two other brothers, who have been living together in Pasadena.

The snubnosed .22-caliber Iver Johnson Cadet model revolver seized after the shooting was described as having been picked out of a list of 2.5 million weapons registered in California in "just seconds" after the disclosure of its serial number. This was done by a new computer used by the State Bureau of Criminal Investigation and Identification in Sacramento, according to State Attorney General Thomas Lynch.

The defendant was arraigned at 7 A.M., unusually early, before Municipal Judge Joan Dempsey Klein, on a complaint issued by District Attorney Evelle Younger after all-night consultation with the police.

Deputy District Attorney William Ritzi said the case would be presented to the county grand jury on Friday.

The other victims of the shooting were Paul Schrade, 43 years old, a regional director of the United Automobile and Aerospace Workers Union, a prominent Kennedy campaigner; William Weisel, 30, a unit manager for the American Broadcasting Company; Ira Goldstein, 19, an employe of Continental News Service at nearby Sherman Oaks; Mrs. Elizabeth Evans, 43, of Sangus, in Los Angeles County, and Irwin Stroll, 17.

Mr. Schrade, the most seriously wounded of the five, underwent an apparently successful operation at the Kaiser Foundation Hospital today to remove a bullet from his skull.

Mr. Weisel was reported in good condition after removal of a bullet from his abdomen.

The court complaint against Sirhan charged that "on or about the fifth day of June, 1968, at and in the county of Los Angeles a felony was committed by John Doe, who at the time and place aforesaid, did willfully, unlawfully and feloniously commit an assault with a deadly weapon upon Robert Francis Kennedy, a human being, with the intent then and there wilfully, unlawfully, feloniously and with malice aforethought to kill and murder the said Robert Francis Kennedy."

Sirhan was represented at the arraignment by the chief public defender, Richard S. Buckley. He asked Mr. Buckley to get in touch with the American Civil Liberties Union about getting private counsel for him.

Special to The New York Times
WASHINGTON, Thursday, June 6—President Johnson issued the following statement:

"This is a time of tragedy and loss. Senator Robert F. Kennedy is dead.

"Robert Kennedy affirmed this country—affirmed the essential decency of its people, their longing for peace, their desire to improve conditions of life for all.

"During his life, he knew far more than his share of personal tragedy. Yet he never abandoned his faith in America. He never lost his confidence in the spiritual strength of ordinary men and women.

"He believed in the capacity of the young for excellence and in the right of the old and poor to a life of dignity.

"Our public life is diminished by his loss.

"Mrs. Johnson and I extend our deepest sympathy to Mrs. Kennedy and his family.

"I have issued a proclamation calling upon our nation to observe a day of mourning for Robert Kennedy."

June 6, 1968

Mrs. Robert F. Kennedy tried to prevent hospital attendants from administering emergency aid to her wounded husband, the Columbia Broadcasting System reported yesterday.

The report was by Jim Brown, a correspondent for television station KNXT, the C.B.S.-owned outlet in Los Angeles. In his report, carried by both the C.B.S. television and radio networks, Mr. Brown said that Mrs. Kennedy's behavior "undoubtedly was due to the fact that [she] was distraught and upset at this time."

The report quoted Max Behrman, the ambulance attendant who arrived at the Ambassador Hotel shortly after the shooting. He drove with the wounded Senator and his wife to the Central Receiving Hospital in Los Angeles.

"Max Behrman told me that when they reached the second floor of the Ambassador Hotel and prepared to lift Senator Kennedy onto the stretcher, the Senator said to him, 'Don't life me, don't lift me,'" Mr. Brown reported. "Those were the only words that he recalled hearing from the Senator in the entire time, from the time they arrived at the Ambassador through the trip to Central Receiving."

Mr. Behrman also said, according to Mr. Brown, that Mrs. Kennedy had indicated she did not want any assistance and that she had tried to prevent hospital attendants from administering aid of some kind to the Senator.

"This continued even in the ambulance en route to Central Receiving," Mr. Brown reported, "Mrs. Kennedy still, according to Behrman, physically tried to prevent this administering of aid to Senator Kennedy."

Despite Mrs. Kennedy's objections, Mr. Brown reported, ambulance attendants were able to place a pack under Senator Kennedy's head.

The C.B.S. report said that, upon arrival at Central Receiving, Dr. Vasilius Bazilauskas, the attending physician, thought at first glance that the Senator was dead.

"However, as he began his examination and medical treatment," Mr. Brown reported, "he said he realized that there was still life, that he slapped the Senator several times in the face saying, 'Bob, Bob, Bob,' as he did so.

"He did determine," Mr. Brown went on, "there was a heartbeat, and when he did find a heartbeat of Senator

Ambulance Aide Tells of Drive To Hospital After Shooting

By GEORGE GENT

Kennedy, he took the stethescope and put it to Mrs. Kennedy's ear—she was in the room at the time—so that she could hear the heartbeat."

Following the heart massage and other emergency treatment, the report concluded, Senator Kennedy was taken to Good Samaritan Hospital.

June 6, 1968

Kennedy Children Come Home While Staff and Friends Rally

By MYRA MacPHERSON

McLEAN, Va., June 5—Today was almost like any other day at Hickory Hill, the McLean home of Senator Robert F. Kennedy. Fourteen-year-old Bobby Jr. played with friends and members of the Senator's staff rallied around the children at the six-acre compound.

There was, ironically, an air of pastoral peace around the tree-covered estate 10 miles from Washington. Dogs and horses loped slowly around the grounds and there were boisterous shouts from adults and children playing football in 80-degree sunshine.

Routines seemed uninterrupted. Power mowers cut sloping lawns, housemen swept porch steps and yard men cleaned around the pool. Delivery trucks with food and household items arrived and left.

But there were differences. A battery of Fairfax County policemen, along with United States marshals and Secret Service men, blocked all entrances.

Gawkers Come to Stare

An unending stream of gawkers, in open convertibles, buses, trucks, motorcycles and on foot, slowed down and stared.

Friends and relatives came and went all day. Among them was Mrs. Robert S. McNamara, wife of the former Secretary of Defense.

Shortly after 2 P.M., the oldest of the 10 Kennedy children, 16-year-old Kathleen, and her brother, Joseph, 15, arrived from boarding schools, lugging suitcases up the front stairs. Kathleen attends the Putney School in Putney, Vt., and Joe is at Milton Academy in Milton, Mass.

Bobby Jr., shirttails out, was with them. He and 14-month-old Douglas were the only two children at home when Senator Kennedy was shot in California.

The children, at least the older ones, apparently knew that their father had been wounded. Earlier in the day, Bobby Jr. had walked silently around the grounds with a Roman Catholic priest, the Rev. Richard McSorley, professor of theology at Georgetown University.

Await Other Children

Inside the home, with its airy, cheerful rooms friends and members of the household staff waited for the other six children to arrive from Los Angeles on an Air Force jet provided by Vice President Humphrey.

At 7:15 P.M., the six children, accompanied by the Senator's dog Freckles and John H. Glenn Jr., the former astronaut, arrived at Andrews Air Force Base. A Kennedy press aid said they were going home to Hickory Hill. The six were David Anthony, 12; Mary Courtney, 11; Michael Lemoyne, 10; Mary Kerry, 6; Christopher George, 4, and Matthew Maxwell Taylor, 3.

Moments later, at the airfield, the three oldest children—Kathleen, Joseph and Robert Jr.—left for California to be with their mother.

An attempt was made to keep everything as normal as possible at the home. During the football games, played in bathing suits, an unidentified friend of the family came down to the wall surrounding the estate, where photographers were taking pictures, and asked them to stop. He said that the photographers were a constant reminder to the children of the tragedy.

Inside the home, Mrs. Rowland Evans, the wife of the columnist, who has been described as "like an aunt to the children," and Mrs. George Stevens Jr., the wife of the director of the American Film Institute who is a close friend of Mrs. Kennedy's, busied themselves with the baby and waited.

June 6, 1968

Mrs. John Kennedy Arrives

LOS ANGELES, June 5—Mrs. John F. Kennedy arrived at Good Samaritan Hospital here tonight to join other members of the family at Senator Kennedy's bedside after a chartered plane flight from New York.

Mrs. Kennedy, her face set in a sad, impassive smile, had left her Manhattan apartment this afternoon for the flight.

Half a dozen Secret Service men had to force a wedge through a crowd of about 70 onlookers and a score of reporters and television cameramen who blocked the entrance of Mrs. Kennedy's home at 1040 Fifth Avenue, near 86th Street.

Wearing a dark tan coat, the widow of President Kennedy was escorted out of the building at 2:20 P.M. by Roswell L. Gilpatric, an old friend of the Kennedy family and a former Deputy Secretary of Defense. They were almost pushed into a waiting black limousine as the Secret Service agents tried to hold back the surging crowd.

The limousine sped to Kennedy International Airport where a twin-engine jet owned by the International Business Machines Corporation had been made ready for Mrs. Kennedy's departure. As she stepped from the car at the airport, she was greeted by Burke Marshall, I.B.M. vice president and a former Assistant Attorney General in the Kennedy Administration.

Radziwill Arrives

Mr. Marshall clasped Mrs. Kennedy's hand as they waited on the airport apron for the arrival of a commercial airliner from London carrying Prince Stanislas Radziwill, the husband of Mrs. Kennedy's younger sister, Lee. Mrs. Kennedy ran up the boarding ramp to meet her brother-in-law and embraced him in tears.

Princess Radziwill will remain in London for the time being.

Accompanied by Mr. Marshall, they then boarded the I.B.M. jet, which took off at 3:45 P.M., a little more than 12 hours after Senator Kennedy was wounded.

Prince Radziwill's wife, the former Lee Bouvier, telephoned her sister at 3:30 A.M. yesterday from London and told her the news about the Senator's being shot. Mrs. Kennedy had gone to bed a few hours earlier, after having followed the returns of the California election at Kennedy campaign headquarters here.

Early in the morning reporters and others began to assemble around the canopied entrance of the building where Mrs. Kennedy lives. They paid scant attention to angry neighbors who pleaded that she be allowed some privacy.

Building Gates Closed

The iron gates of the building were kept locked and only residents were permitted entry. As Mrs. Kennedy's impending journey was reported on news broadcasts, the crowd outside the building began to grow.

By noon about 40 persons were standing idly around the building. Some had portable radios, ice-cream cones and containers of coffee. Two young women sat on a low railing by the entrance holding soda bottles.

June 7, 1968

Risk, Kennedy Said, Is 'Part of Man's Life'

During "The Next President," a political special seen last Sunday night on Channel 5, Senator Kennedy was asked by David Frost, the moderator, if he enjoyed "physical risk."

Mr. Kennedy replied that it was "part of a man's life."

He recalled a quotation from an Edith Hamilton essay on Aeschylus: "Men are not made for safe havens."

June 6, 1968

French Writer Recalls Kennedy Premonition

PARIS, June 6 (AP)—Romain Gary, the French writer, said today that Senator Robert F. Kennedy told him about two weeks ago that "sooner or later" he would be the victim of an assassination attempt.

Writing in Le Figaro, Mr. Gary recalled a conversation with Mr. Kennedy near Los Angeles. He quoted Mr. Kennedy as having said, in answer to a question about precautions against a possible attack:

"There is no way to protect a candidate during the electoral campaign. You must give yourself to the crowd and from then on you must take your chances. In any case you must have luck to be elected President of the United States. You have it or you don't.

"I know that there will be an attempt on my life sooner or later. Not so much for political reasons, but through contagion, through emulation."

June 7, 1968

Elder Kennedy Accepts News of Death Bravely

HYANNISPORT, Mass., June 6—Although rumors of his own death reached the family summer compound today, Joseph P. Kennedy was reported by a spokesman to have accepted bravely the news of the death of Senator Robert F. Kennedy.

Richard Cardinal Cushing, an old family friend, who made the two-hour drive from Boston yesterday to see Mr. and Mrs. Kennedy, returned to lunch with the ailing elder Kennedy.

While the two old friends were eating, Seantor Edward M. Kennedy, the only surviving son, telephoned his father with the news that Robert Kennedy had died in Los Angeles.

June 7, 1968

McLEAN, Va., June 6 (UPI) —John H. Glenn Jr., the former astronaut, attempted to cheer up the seven youngest children of Robert F. Kennedy today by playing touch football and taking a dip in the swimming pool at Hickory Hill, the Senator's estate in this suburb of Washington.

The three oldest children— Kathleen, 17 years old, Joseph, 15, and Robert Jr., 15— flew to Los Angeles last night to be with their mother when Mr. Kennedy died. They were aboard the plane bearing their father's coffin to New York this evening.

With the seven-acre Hickory Hill closely guarded by the police, most of the younger children were packed up in a station wagon with their pet monkey for a midmorning visit with neighbors.

While they were gone, Mr. Glenn played touch football with David, 12 years old, and Michael 10. Watching from a baby carriage was the youngest, Douglas, 14 months.

When the other children returned about noon, Mr. Glenn joined them in the swimming pool.

After lunch, the boys played stickball while three horses grazed on the estate's broad lawns and three of the Kennedys' dogs mingled with the children.

The estate was sealed off by the police under the direction of James J. P. McShane, chief United States marshal, and two friends of Kerry Kennedy, 8, were unable to deliver personally a small bouquet of home-grown roses and hand-written sympathy notes.

June 7, 1968

Glenn Attempts to Cheer Up Kennedy Children

MOOD ON FLIGHT DESCRIBED ON TV

Vanocur Tells of Family's Emotional Return to City

A close friend of the Kennedy family who was on the plane that brought Robert F. Kennedy to New York last night told in a television interview of the emotion, confusion and bitterness on that flight.

Sander Vanocur, a National Broadcasting Company commentator, said in an interview on the network that Charles Evers, the Mississippi Negro leader and brother of the slain Medgar Evers, burst into sobs as he boarded the Presidential jet in Los Angeles.

He said that Mrs. John F. Kennedy was apprehensive when she thought the plane was the same one that had carried her husband's coffin from Dallas, but that she was reassured when she was told it was not.

Mr. Vanocur reported that members of the Kennedy entourage were upset by the prospect of having Mayor Samuel Yorty of Los Angeles come to the plane. Mr. Yorty, a Democrat, refused to back John F. Kennedy in the 1960 campaign and had an acrimonious exchange with Senator Robert Kennedy during a hearing on urban problems.

The television newsman said that before the plane took off for New York someone "went up to Frank Mankiewicz, the slain Senator's press secretary, and said, 'If you let Yorty near the plane I'll never speak to you again.'"

During the entire four-and-a-half-hour flight, Mr. Vanocur said Senator Edward M. Kennedy sat next to the coffin, talking with David Hacket, a classmate of Robert Kennedy.

He described the Senator's mood as "mad." "He's mad at what happens in this country. He does not know whether it is the act of a single person, or whether this is the act of a conspiracy. His brother [John] was killed by a rather faceless man whom we suspect, though we don't know for sure, was Lee Harvey Oswald.

"His brother was killed by a man they booked and arraigned as John Doe, suspect. The man who killed Dr. Martin Luther King, they do not know of. The man who killed Medgar Evers was freed, acquitted after a trial in Mississippi.

"He's mad. That's the only word I can put. Mad and sad at the same time."

In an interview after the show, Mr. Vanocur said that his appraisal of the mood on the flight was based on conversations he had had on the plane with members of the family. He refused to describe them further.

The commentator reported that about an hour away from New York the wife of the murdered Senator took a seat next to his coffin, lay her head against the purple cover and fell asleep. Jim Whitaker, a mountaineer from Washington, placed a pillow beneath her head and her rosary next to her.

June 7, 1968

Widow Gives Comfort to Strangers and Friends

She Attends Mass, Telling 2 Sons to Serve as Altar Boys, Then Joins Others

By CHARLOTTE CURTIS

Mrs. Robert F. Kennedy, the widow of the slain Senator, spent yesterday comforting strangers, her family and her friends.

"She doesn't cry," said a close friend who was with her in the family's apartment overlooking the United Nations. "She's made it better for all of us."

And so she had. Starting before 9 A.M., when friends began streaming through her doors, Ethel Skakel Kennedy was ministering to others, reaching out a hand to touch those who looked as if they needed assistance.

Those early hours were especially trying for her. Joseph P. Kennedy 3d, her eldest son, had finally given way to tears after serving as an honor guard in St. Patrick's Cathedral.

The 15-year-old boy, wearing a navy blue jacket, gray trousers that he was beginning to outgrow, and loafers, had taken his place beside his father's coffin at 8 A.M.

Stands Silently

For a half hour, he had stood silently, moving his fingers over the coffin's shiny mahogany surface. Now and then he would lean against the coffin, feeling its sides with his hands.

At 8:30, when he was relieved, the boy went to the communion rail and walked on, his head high, his hands in his pockets. His eyes were filled with tears. When he was alone in the ambulatory, he put his hands over his face and wept.

There were other tears back at the apartment, although friends said the two other Kennedy children, Robert F. Kennedy Jr. and Kathleen Kennedy, were very brave. And yet Mrs. Kennedy had a smile for all her visitors, and hot coffee and breakfast rolls for anyone who wanted them.

She kept to what apparently was a well-planned if hectic schedule. At 11 A.M., she appeared on the sidewalk in front of her building, at 870 United Nations Plaza, ready for the private mass at Holy Family Church around the corner. Pope Paul worshipped at Holy Family during his visit here in 1965.

Dressed in Black

She wore a black silk dress, black shoes, black stockings and a simple black ribbon in the back of her freshly combed blond hair, and she carried a black handbag. Her sons were on either side of her. They were joined by about 15 other relatives and friends.

It was a short walk along almost deserted streets on a very hot day, and she moved briskly until four Army sergeants approached her and asked to join the group. Typically, Mrs. Kennedy went to them immediately, embracing and being embraced by Sgt. Maj. Francis Ruddy, who placed the wreath on President Kennedy's grave in November, 1963.

Inside the church on 47th Street between First and Second Avenues, Mrs. Kennedy appointed her two sons as altar boys for the low requiem mass, which was attended by most of the Kennedy family. Msgr. Timothy J. Flynn, pastor of the church, was impressed by her composure.

He said later that when the matter of the altar boys came up, "she just pointed at two of the youngsters and told them to serve."

Go to St. Patrick's

After the service, Mrs. Kennedy and her children were driven to St. Patrick's Cathedral, where they joined with the thousands of mourners who had come to pay final respects to the dead Senator. She led her children into pew seats beside the bier.

Mrs. Kennedy crossed herself, then sat, as if transfixed, her eyes staring at the closed coffin. She and the children bowed their heads for a few moments and rose to stand beside the coffin.

Still staring at the coffin, her face impassive, she reached out her hand, touched the shiny mahogany gently and was gone.

Mrs. Kennedy's afternoon was equally demanding. From the cathedral, she and other members of the Kennedy family went to Mr. and Mrs. C. Douglas Dillon's uptown apartment for lunch. Mr. Dillon was Secretary of the Treasury during President John F. Kennedy's Administration.

"It has been this way all along," said a friend who had traveled with Mrs. Kennedy on the plane from Los Angeles. "She was never worried about herself. She kept walking up and down the aisle, making sure everyone had blankets or pillows. She said they'd been up all night and they needed to rest."

The widow, her oldest son, Joseph, and three daughters returned to the cathedral at 8:30 P.M. and stayed nine minutes.

Mrs. Kennedy knelt as the Most Rev. Terence J. Cooke, Archbishop of New York, prayed by the altar. Then, on leaving, she touched the flag covering the coffin, held the cloth in her fingers for a second and went quietly out.

Some women in the cathedral sobbed as they watched her.

June 8, 1968

BOSTON, June 7 (UPI)—Robert F. Kennedy was legally and medically dead at 6:30 P.M., Wednesday, seven hours before he was officially declared dead, a prominent neurosurgeon said today.

Dr. James L. Poppen of the Lahey Clinic and New England Deaconess Hospital, said he saw Senator Kennedy at about 10 A.M. Wednesday and knew "immediately" that he would not survive.

Dr. Poppen added at a news conference at Lahey Clinic that if medical science had been able to save the Senator's life he would have led a "grave and devastating existence."

Senator Kennedy died officially at 1:44 A.M. Thursday in Los Angeles.

Dr. Poppen said if Mr. Kennedy had lived "he would not have been the same man—not the individual who his family knew."

He said the slain Senator would have been paralyzed on his right side, would not have been able to see on the left and would have suffered a "Parkinson's disease-type" of facial expression.

The 65-year-old surgeon said he saw the Senator about 10 A.M. Wednesday and knew "immediately" that the Senator would not live.

"Everything was done that was possible," the heavy-set neurosurgeon told a news conference at Lahey Clinic. "Nothing could have been done that was not."

Dr. Poppen said Mr. Kennedy's "intellectual faculties would not have survived. There wouldn't have been any recognition. I knew personally that he could not survive. He would have led a very grave and devastating existence."

The neurosurgeon said Senator Kennedy's electrical brain waves stopped at 6:30 P.M. Wednesday, about 18 hours after the shooting, and never started again, although his heart still beat. He said the Senator was legally and medically dead when the brain waves ceased.

He said he had known the Kennedys since the nineteen-forties. He said he was called about 4 A.M. Wednesday by Pierre Salinger, a Kennedy aide, and asked, "Can you come? Can you get ready immediately? The Kennedy family needs you."

Dr. Poppen also said that he received telephone calls immediately afterward from the White House and from Vice President Humphrey, who arranged his transportation.

Dr. Poppen acted as a consultant to the operating surgeons and as a liaison between them and the Kennedy family.

He said that Ethel Kennedy, the Senator's wife, told him that while her husband was lying on the floor at the Ambassador Hotel he requested a glass of water and asked: "How bad is it?"

The surgeon also said Senator Kennedy was a "dead man" from the moment he was hit. He soon lapsed into a coma and never recovered. But, Dr. Poppen said, "destruction was not complete from the moment of impact."

The physician said that Mr. Kennedy still had reflexes in both eyes, arms and legs, but he added, "The eye pupils were wide and did not react to light, which is pretty serious business."

A native of Denthe, Mich., Dr. Poppen treated President Kennedy and administered to Senator Edward M. Kennedy, Democrat of Massachusetts, when he was near death from a 1964 plane crash in which he suffered a broken back.

The neurosurgeon joined the staff of Lahey Clinic in 1933, three years after graduating from Rush Medical School in Chicago. He was named chief of neurosurgery in 1957 and retired from the post in 1964.

June 8, 1968

New York bade a solemn but strangely joyful farewell yesterday to Robert Francis Kennedy, who in death had come to symbolize many people's hopes for a fresh breath of life.

A pontifical requiem mass celebrated in the new spirit of the Ecumenical Council by Archbishop Terence J. Cooke of New York, combined anguished moments of grief with the bright Christian expectations of rebirth.

Then the body of the Senator was put aboard a train to Washington for burial in Arlington National Cemetery near the grave of President John F. Kennedy

More than 2,300 people attending the mass, including President Johnson, heard Richard Cardinal Cushing of Boston cry in his South Boston twang, "Christ have mercy," reminding many of his somber eulogy at the funeral of the Senator's brother five years ago.

'A Good And Decent Man'

But they also heard a white-robed choir high in the loft raise their voices in the exultant "Hallelujah, Hallelujah, Hallelujah" of the chorus from Handel's "Messiah."

And they also heard Senator Edward M. Kennedy of Massachusetts, Robert Kennedy's brother, declare from the white marble sanctuary, just above the African mahogany coffin:

"My brother need not be idealized or enlarged in death beyond what he was in life. He should be remembered simply as a good and decent man, who saw wrong and tried to right it, saw suffering and tried to heal it, saw war and tried to stop it.

"Those of us who loved him and who take him to his rest today pray that what he was to us, and what he wished for others will someday come to pass for all the world.

"As he said many times, in many parts of this nation, to those he touched and who sought to touch him:

"'Some men see things as they are and say why.

"'I dream things that never were and say, why not.'"

But even as he quoted George Bernard Shaw's hopeful words, Edward Kennedy's voice was choked with a grief so deep he clearly had difficulty keeping back the tears.

Edward Kennedy is the sole surviving Kennedy brother, following the assassination of John F. Kennedy, in Dallas, in 1963, and the shooting of Robert early last Wednesday, in Los Angeles.

After the 1-hour 40-minute mass, the coffin, draped with an American flag, was carried out through the cathedral's great bronze doors and placed

THOUSANDS IN LAST SERVICE

JOHNSON AT RITES

Edward Kennedy Eulogizes Brother—Many Faiths at Cathedral Ceremony

By J. ANTHONY LUKAS

The End of An Era

161

in the back of a gray hearse.

More than 50,000 people watched the 75-vehicle cavalcade as it moved at a funeral pace down Fifth avenue and across 34th Street. As the cortege passed the broad white steps of the New York Public Library at 42d Street, several young women in black dresses tossed red carnations onto the avenue.

In the front seat of the hearse, Mrs. Robert F. Kennedy, in a black short-sleeved dress and a shoulder-length black veil, stared blankly at the huge crowds. With her was Edward Kennedy.

The throngs massed along the avenue were silent. Spectators who had been listening to transistor radios turned them down as the hearse passed. The only noise was the click and the whirr of cameras.

Coffin Put on Train

After a 15-minute ride, the cavalcade reached Pennsylvania Station where the coffin was loaded onto a 21-car train for Washington. The train, which also bore nearly 1,000 of the Senator's friends and associates, other dignitaries and newsmen,

left the station at 1:01 P.M. for Washington.

Although the formal ceremonies for the Senator were limited to a small section of midtown Manhattan, the entire city marked the day, which had been declared an official day of mourning by Mayor Lindsay.

Most big department stores and hundreds of neighborhood shops were closed. Many stores put Mr. Kennedy's picture in their windows, often draped with black or accompanied by flowers.

At 359 Sixth Avenue, a sign on the door of McBell's Bar read, "Closed in memoriam Senator Robert Kennedy. We will open today at 4.00 P.M. —The staff."

Many taxicabs and private cars turned on their headlights in the traditional mark of the funeral procession.

From the open windows of crumbling brownstones and sleek apartment towers, the sounds of the mass as broadcast by television and radio drifted onto the sidewalks and merged so they seemed to hang in the air with no definable source.

In a linoleum-paneled bar at 125th Street and Broadway, with a picture of the late Rev. Dr. Martin Luther King Jr. behind the counter, Lee Murray watched the service on television. Mr. Murray, dressed in a sports shirt and soiled cotton pants, said:

"I feel real bad about it. I voted for him for Senator and would have voted for him for President. He's for the working man, for civil rights."

Streets Seem Empty

In most of the city, the streets seemed emptier than normal on a warm spring Saturday morning, perhaps because so many persons were watching the mass on television. A few women with their hair in curlers for the Saturday night out carried grocery bags to market and young men in T-shirts carried laundry bags to the coin laundries.

But it was a very different scene around St. Patrick's in midtown Manhattan.

All day yesterday and up until 5 o'clock yesterday morning, long lines of mourners had passed through the cathedral to see the bier, often to touch it or kiss it. The police estimated yesterday morning that 151,000 persons had filed past the bier in the 23½ hours the cathedral had been open to the public.

When the doors closed at 5 A.M. to permit preparations for the mass, Mrs. Ethel Kennedy, the Senator's widow, was kneeling at the head of the coffin. She bowed her head and prayed silently for a few moments.

While Secret Service men, city detectives and an Army

bomb squad thoroughly searched the huge Gothic structure in preparation for President Johnson's arrival, thousands of persons had already gathered behind gray police barriers on Fifth Avenue.

The day dawned golden and cooler than the last two sweltering days — the temperature was in the low 70's most of the morning.

Fifth Avenue was a forest of flags, flying at half staff from the stately shops and departments stores. Dozens of American flags rippling in the gentle breeze were set off by others: the blue, white and red French flag in front of the Air France Building; the blue and white Greek flag in front of Olympic Airways; the black, gold and red Belgian flag in front of Sabena Airlines; the green, red and white banner of Italy over the Rizzoli Bookstore and—on a side street—the green, white and orange flag of Ireland.

The police closed off all crosstown streets between 47th and 53d Streets more than an hour before the mass as limousines began drawing up to the front steps of the cathedral and discharging hundreds of celebrities.

On Fifth Avenue near the cathedral, the crowd—which appeared to number more than 10,000—gasped, sighed, pointed and jumped for a look at some of the personalities as they entered.

These included four major Presidential candidates: Vice President Humphrey, Senator Eugene J. McCarthy of Minnesota, Governor Rockefeller and former Vice President Richard M. Nixon.

Invitations are Checked

But there were also others like Secretary General Thant of the United Nations; John Kenneth Galbraith, professor of economics at Harvard and former Ambassador to India; W. Averell Harriman, the chief United States negotiator at the Paris peace talks; Walter Reuther, president of the United Auto Workers; Robert Lowell, the poet; Harry Belafonte, Lauren Bacall, Sidney Poitier, Jack Paar and Cary Grant.

As the dignitaries walked up the steps, their invitations were checked carefully by plainclothes men. Mrs. Martin Luther King had her card carefully scrutinized; even Pierre Salinger, President Kennedy's press secretary, had brief trouble getting in.

As the cathedral began filling, the six vigil-keepers who stood beside six tall amber candles around the coffin were changed rapidly to give many eminent persons at least a moment by the bier.

Senator J. W. Fulbright of Arkansas, chairman of the Senate Foreign Relations Commit-

A grieving Ethel Kennedy at the funeral mass for her husband.

THE KENNEDYS: A NEW YORK TIMES PROFILE

tee, stood for a time next to Robert Kennedy's second oldest son, Robert Jr. Others who shifted quickly back and forth around the coffin were Roosevelt Grier, a Los Angeles Ram tackle; Rafer Johnson, former Olympic decathlon champion; James Whittaker, the mountain climber who scaled Mount Kennedy with Robert Kennedy several years ago; Lord Harlech, former British ambassador to the United States; Andy Williams, the singer, and John McCone, former head of the Central Intelligence Agency.

Family Enters Last

When Senator McCarthy entered the cathedral he was seated next to former Senator Barry Goldwater, the 1964 Republican candidate for President.

At 9:42, President Johnson, accompanied by his wife and escorted by several Secret Service men, was ushered up the central aisle by the Most Rev. John Maguire, coadjutor Archbishop of New York. The President was seated in a front pew just to the left of the coffin, where he knelt in prayer for a few minutes.

Mr. Johnson had flown by Presidential jet from Washington to Floyd Bennett Field in Brooklyn this morning and then by helicopter to the Sheep Meadow in Central Park. He was driven directly to the cathedral in a black limousine preceded by a police escort.

The last to enter the cathedral were the Kennedy family—Mrs. Joseph P. Kennedy, the Senator's mother; Mr. and Mrs. Steven Smith; Ambassador to France Sargent Shriver and his wife; Edward Kennedy's wife, Joan; Mrs. John F. Kennedy; her sister, Mrs. Stanislas Radziwill, and several others.

Finally, Mrs. Robert Kennedy entered from the right of the sanctuary. Looking grave, she leaned on the arm of Edward Kennedy. With them came three of her children: Kathleen, 17 years old; Joseph 3d, 15, and Robert Jr., 14. Mrs. Kennedy and her children were seated in the right front pew, directly across the aisle from President Johnson.

At 9:55 A. M. the mass began as the clerical procession moved up the 400-foot central aisle. It was led by a crucifer carrying a tall golden cross. He was followed by white-clad seminarians, monks in brown habits; military chaplains, purple-vested monsignori; bishops in long violet robes and archbishops in purple and cardinals in bright scarlet.

Many Faiths Represented

Among those in the procession were several non-Roman Catholic clergymen. Among them were the Right Rev. J. Stuart Wetmore, Suffragan Bishop of the Episcopal Diocese of New York; the Rev.

Dan M. Potter, executive director of the Protestant Council of the City of New York, and Archbishop Iakovos, Greek Orthodox primate of North and South America.

As the procession moved up the aisle, the choir in the loft sang "All hail, adored Trinity; All hail eternal unity."

When the clerical figures were seated in the elaborately carved wooden seats in the sanctuary, Msgr. Eugene V. Clarke, secretary to Archbishop Cooke, led Edward Kennedy to a wooden lectern set up at the edge of the sanctuary steps.

Dressed in a dark blue suit, Mr. Kennedy read from a set of white cards on the lectern. When he finished, the mass itself began.

The mass was presided over by Cardinal Cushing and Angelo Cardinal Dell'Acqua, Vicar General of Pope Paul VI for the City and District of Rome, who attended as the official representative of the Pope.

The principal concelebrant was Archibishop Cooke and the other concelebrants were Msgr. William McCormack, director of the Archdiocese Office or the Propagation of the Faith; Father John J. Cavanaugh, former president of Notre Dame University; Father Fitzgerald and the Rev. Richard McSorley, a Jesuit and a close friend of the Kennedy family.

After a reading of meditations by a black-clad priest to which the huge throng responded, another priest read from St. Paul's First Epistle to the Thessalonians: "the Lord himself, when the order is given, at the sound of the archangel's voice and of God's trumpet, will come down from heaven and the dead in Christ will first rise."

After a reading of the Gospel, Archbishop Cooke mounted to the ornate pulpit to the right of the sanctuary and, with his hands clasped over his purple robes, delivered the eulogy.

The Archbishop praised the Senator for "his youthfulness, so eager and vibrant that young people yearn to follow him; his sense of mission that impelled him to be his brother's keeper; his faith in God that kept him close to the religion of his childhood." But he urged his listeners not to be the assassin act "demoralize and incapacitate 200 hundred million others."

Children Present Hosts

A high point of the mass was the offertory procession by eight Kennedy children who marched in two's up the sanctuary behind two candle bearers to present the hosts and the wine used in the consecration of the mass.

Another unusual feature was the playing of the slow movement from Gustav Mahler's "Fifth Symphony" by 30 members of the New York Philharmonic Orchestra under the di-

Pallbearers carry the coffin from St. Patrick's after the requiem mass.

rection of Leonard Bernstein. Mr. Bernstein's role in the mass was specifically requested by the Kennedy family, with whom he has been friendly for several years.

The mass ended with Cardinal Cushing performing the blessing of the body and the commendation of the soul. Dressed in a deep purple robe and with a white mitre over his scarlet cap, the 72-year-old prelate, accompanied by several concelebrants, approached the coffin and recited a short prayer.

"May the angels take you into paradise. May the martyrs come to welcome you on your way and lead you into the holy city, Jerusalem. May the choir of angels welcome you and with Lazarus who once was poor may you have everlasting rest."

The Cardinal circled the coffin, sprinkling it with holy water—an ancient rite calling down God's purifying mercy. Then he circled it again swinging a thurible, a metal container on chains filled with burning charcoal and incense—a ceremony symbolic of the prayers of the faithful rising to God.

The ceremony ended with Mr. Williams singing "The Battle

Hymn of the Republic," the choir's Hallalujah chorus and the traditional funeral hymn "For All the Saints."

The coffin, still covered by the flag, was carried out of the cathedral by 13 pallbearers, Edward Kennedy; Joseph Kennedy 3d; C. Douglas Dillon, former Secretary of the Treasury; John Glenn, the astronaut; Lemoyne Billings, a close family friend; David Hackett, a family friend; Mr. Harriman; Robert S. McNamara, former Secretary of Defense; Lord Harlech; John Seigenthaler, a former aide to Mr. Kennedy and now editor of The Nashville Tennessean; Mr. Smith; Mr. Whittaker and Gen. Maxwell D. Taylor (ret.), former chairman of the Joint Chiefs of Staffs.

There was an unexplained delay in forming the cavalcade outside. For what seemed like five minutes, Mrs. John F. Kennedy stood in the bright sunlight on the top step, holding tight to the hand of her son, John Jr. She stared rigidly across the avenue, but John looked around with interest, once gazing up to watch a plane pass overhead in the deep blue sky.

June 9, 1968

The End of An Era

CITY-BOUND TRAIN KILLS 2 MOURNERS

5 Others Hurt in Jersey as Crowds Press In to Catch Glimpse of Kennedys

By EDWARD C. BURKS

A man and a woman were killed yesterday as they stood in a crowd watching the Kennedy funeral train pass the Elizabeth, N. J., railroad station. They were cut down by a New York-bound express moving in the opposite direction.

The 21-car funeral train was passing the packed platforms about 1:25 P.M. when the northbound express rounded a curve at high speed, its whistle blasting. It plowed into the edge of the crowd that had overflowed onto one of the four tracks.

The deaths were part of a string of mishaps that plagued the Kennedy train on its 226-mile trip from New York to Washington. Six other persons were injured. The Penn Central Railroad ordered all northbound trains stopped along the route to prevent further harm to spectators. Delays up to 5 hours resulted.

In large cities, in small towns and even in rural sections saddened Americans thronged the right of way, waiting for the delayed train. Some waved small American flags. Some held up campaign pictures of Senator Kennedy edged in black. At Torresdale, in northeast Philadelphia, spectators scattered roses in the path of the train. At Baltimore, they sang.

All along the route, crowds pressed dangerously close to the right of way and in many cases spectators went boldly out onto the tracks. Police had difficulty holding them back. At some points the people cheered the slowly moving train. A crowd of 25,000 people jammed the North Philadelphia station.

After the accident at Elizabeth, in which at least five other persons were injured, the funeral train was slowed down from its original schedule of nearly 60 miles an hour. There was a further delay because of a brake-shoe difficulty on the last coach, which carried the Kennedy family and the coffin of Senator Robert F. Kennedy.

An 18-year-old boy, Joseph Fausti, was critically burned at Trenton when he stood on a boxcar on a side track and touched a live wire while trying to get a better view of the Kennedy train.

The mechanical difficulty was corrected at Philadelphia, and the train reached Baltimore, four hours late, at 7:30 P.M.

The victims at Elizabeth were identified as Mrs. Antoinette Severini, a widow, and John Curia, a widower, both 56 years old and both Elizabeth residents.

Of the five persons who were injured in the crush, none was hurt critically, according to hospital reports. One of the injured was 3-year-old Debra Ann Kwiatek, granddaughter of Mrs. Severini. The child suffered cuts on her back and bruises.

An eyewitness, Edward Bowers, 37, a machine operator, told the police that about 15 persons were on the tracks at Elizabeth before the accident. He said that he tried to pull Mrs. Severini to safety, "but she slipped, and the train tugged her out of my hands."

According to Mr. Bowers, the little girl was left "spinning like a top" from the rush of the New York-bound train, which does not stop at Elizabeth.

The little girl was reported "doing nicely" at Elizabeth General Hospital last night. Her parents, Mr. and Mrs. Adam Kwiatek of Linden, N. J., who were with her at the time of the accident, were unhurt.

Rail officials said that the engineer of the city-bound express—The Admiral—was unable to stop his train in time.

A few minutes before the tragedy, Mayor Thomas G. Dunn of Elizabeth, who was waiting on the southbound platform, saw as many as 40 people on both northbound tracks and shouted warnings to them. He later said that it "was absurd" for the railroad "to send a train at such speed" in such a situation.

The deaths, the pressing crowds and a mechanical difficulty caused rail officials to cut the Kennedy train's speed by half.

Through many of the stations along the way the black-draped Kennedy train slowed to a near crawl. At some stations, notably New Brunswick, N. J., and Wilmington, Del., there were bands. A bugler sounded taps at the New Brunswick station.

From inside the train Mrs. Robert F. Kennedy and her sister-in-law, Mrs. John F. Kennedy, waved back to the fervent, sometimes cheering crowds.

At Baltimore, someone started singing "The Battle Hymn of the Republic" and others picked it up until nearly the whole crowd was sweetly singing in slow cadence as the funeral train slid slowly by.

The crowd at North Philadelphia, not far from the city's Negro districts, consisted mostly of Negroes. Some carried hand-drawn signs and held them up: "GOODBY BOBBY" "GOD BLESS YOU, BOB," they read.

The Kennedy train began its somber journey from the depths of New York's cavernous Pennsylvania Station without any ceremony. It left at 1:02 P.M., 32 minutes late.

There were no bands, no ritual on the concrete station platform two levels below the main concourse—just the expeditious boarding into the stainless steel and red coaches, and then the "all aboard" call.

There was tight security at Pennsylvania Station, where hushed crowds behind ropes in the black-draped, recently remodeled concourse watched the rapid passage of the nearly 1,000 friends, guests, dignitaries and newsmen through the station to the train waiting below on Track 12.

The Kennedy family did not pass through the station. At about 12:15 P.M., a quarter-hour before scheduled departure of the train, the gray hearse arrived from St. Patrick's Cathedral bearing the Senator's coffin, his widow, his eldest son, Joseph, and his brother, Senator Edward M. Kennedy.

The hearse was driven directly into a truck entrance of the station, and the coffin was then lowered to the station platform on a red cap's baggage elevator that was also draped with black bunting.

The flag-draped coffin was put aboard the last car of the train through a window that had been temporarily removed. It was placed on a foot-high platform covered with red velvet.

Most of the coaches of the funeral train were freshly washed, regular day coaches of the Penn Central, but the last two cars were luxurious private cars known as "business cars."

The last coach, occupied by the Kennedy family, was dark-red, outfitted with bedrooms, lounge, kitchen and dining accommodations and an old-fashioned open observation platform with railing.

As the train moved smoothly out of the station, two Secret Service men were standing at attention on the open rear plaform.

The problem of handling the large number of passengers under maixmum security conditions in the underground corridors and on the stairways apparently accounted for the 32-minute delay in starting. The general public was not allowed anywhere near the stairway to the train platform and newsmen were not permitted to approach the Kennedy private car.

Even those with credentials to board the train found themselves passing one human "blockade" of security men after another as they were taken in groups of 25 or more through the corridors.

As part of the security the cars were numbered in reverse order, with car No. 21 at the head of the train.

At Newark, 15 minutes from New York, where the train slowed for the first time a crowd of more than 6,000 was on the station platform. The widow acknowledged their waves, and then as her car passed the crowd cheered.

For part of the long journey Senator Edward Kennedy rode on the open rear platform, waving back to the crowds.

June 9, 1968

On Train, Kennedy Elan and Courage

By CHARLOTTE CURTIS

WASHINGTON, June 8 — Joseph P. Kennedy 3d was the first of the Kennedys to leave the railroad car that bore his father's coffin, and after him along the aisles came his sister Courtney, his cousin Caroline and his mother, Mrs. Robert F. Kennedy. But Joe, the eldest son, was the first.

Down the swaying train he went, putting out his hand in 19 of the other 20 cars, saying "I'm Joe Kennedy," while outside in the early afternoon sun, the old men of Linden, N. J., stood silently in their undershirts and the women held handkerchiefs to their faces.

"I'm Joe Kennedy," he said to strangers, his pin-stripe black suit not yet a shambles from the failing air-conditioning, his PT boat tie clip neatly in place. "Thanks for coming, thanks for coming."

Joe's sister and cousin had no such responsibilities. The little blonde girls popped in and out among the campaigners and friends with

The Kennedy family leaves the gravesite at the conclusion of the rites.

The End of An Era

what appeared to be a spirit of adventure.

"We'll go that far," Caroline said once, pointing to the front of the dining car, where a lucky few were eating sandwiches and drinking soft drinks.

"O.K.," said Courtney, who was surrounded by women in black dresses and men in black suits,

And then, on the outskirts of Trenton, where a brass band of teen-agers in brightly colored shorts and shirts had gathered in a grassy field beside the tracks to sound taps, there was Mrs. Kennedy, all in black.

She had pushed her chiffon veil away from her face and it streamed down from the back of her silk crown. She was with Roosevelt Grier, the football player, and William Barry, an aide to the Senator, who have hardly left her side since Los Angeles, and LeMoyne K. Billings, a family friend.

"Hello," she said warmly, as awed passengers stumbled to their feet surprised, or, "Nice to see you."

"There they are," she cried out when she recognized members of the Green Berets, who

had been with her at the family's private mass in Holy Family Church in New York. "You thought you could hide from me. Well, you can't."

"Hi Pat, nice to see you," she called to Daniel P. Moynihan, the Harvard expert on urban affairs, and then introduced Mr. Moynihan and his wife to Mr. Billings.

Laughing and smiling, Mrs. Kennedy called to one remembered face after another, always reaching to shake a hand, touch a shoulder, pat a back gently, kiss a cheek, or hug a whole person.

But behind her, where those she was speaking to could not see, her left arm would shoot out nervously, clutching at Mr. Billings's suit, and then drop again to her side. And there were times when her hands shook.

Mrs. Kennedy spoke to nearly all of the 1,100 passengers, and in the last car on her walk, the car that was just behind the locomotive, she paused for a moment and took a vacant seat beneath a New York Telephone Company poster. The train was in North Philadelphia.

Onlookers Surprised

"Have you ever been to Disneyland?" she asked after a few minutes, apparently trying to keep some kind of cheerful conversation going among her aides.

"Disneyland is green and big and there's a mountain."

An assistant gave her a paper cup of Coca-Cola, which she shared with Mr. Barry. She pulled at the black stockings that had wriggled down around her ankles. And she turned to look out of the window.

She smiled and waved a tanned right hand to North Philadelphia and, in turn, the people of North Philadelphia, startled to find her familiar face available to them, smiled and waved and called to her by name.

Like most of the other thousands who had gathered along the 226 miles of railroad tracks that join New York and Washington, the North Philadelphians were looking to the last car draped in bunting for a glimpse of their people— the car with the coffin draped in an American flag and propped up on four chairs so everybody could see it through the windows. Mrs. Kennedy had obviously surprised them.

"If it keeps going like this, we'll never get there," Mrs. Kennedy jokingly told aides. They reassured her. "But what about another train catching up with us?" she asked.

The aides explained that the railroad tracks had been cleared, that the track was safe. They did not tell her that two

persons had been killed trying to view the train and that others had been injured.

After perhaps 10 minutes, Mrs. Kennedy made her way back through the train to the last car. She paused when she reached a stuffy hot car jammed with people.

"You gotta be kidding," she said, looking around at the crowd. "There are lots of other cooler cars, front and back."

No one answered.

"Why are you here?" she demanded, looking at Frank Mankiewicz, Senator Kennedy's press secretary.

Mr. Mankiewicz, in shirt sleeves with perspiration beading on his forehead, told Mrs. Kennedy he had called a briefign session for the press.

"Something's happened," Mrs. Kennedy said.

Mr. Mankiewicz told her he was discussing what he called "arrangements." He had previously told the newsmen that the family did not know about the track-side accident.

Aside from Mrs. Sargent Shriver, who appeared in the car nearest the family car, and Senator Edward M. Kennedy, who passed throught the entire train near Baltimore, the other members of the family remained in the back with the coffin.

June 9, 1968

Kennedys Thank Nation for 'Strength and Hope'

HYANNIS PORT, Mass., June 15—The brother and mother of Senator Robert F. Kennedy thanked the nation today for its sympathy and pledged to "carry on the principles for which Bobby stood." In a statement taped for television on the front lawn of the home of former Ambassador Joseph P. Kennedy, Senator Edward M. Kennedy said his brother's campaign colleagues "will have to decide in a private way" what to do in the future. "I know we'll choose wisely," he said. The Senator, who spoke first, said he hoped the "countless thousands" who had sent ex-

Senator Edward M. Kennedy with his parents, Mr. and Mrs. Joseph P. Kennedy, at their home in Hyannis Port

THE KENNEDYS: A NEW YORK TIMES PROFILE

pressions of sympathy "could realize the strength and the hope that they have given to the members of the family during these last several days." The Senator wore a dark blue suit and a black tie. Mrs. Joseph P. Kennedy wore black. They sat on white wicker chairs with the 79-year-old former Ambassador to the Court of St. James's. The elder Kennedy sat in a wheelchair beside his wife, 77, and only surviving son, 36. He wore a gray suit and black tie. Joseph Kennedy, who suffered a stroke six and a half years ago, was visibly moved as his wife and son read their statements. Mrs. Kennedy, whose voice quivered several times in the bright sunshine, said in her statement, "We have courage for the future, and we shall carry on the principles for which Bobby stood."

Watching the taping out of camera range were several relatives, including Mrs. John F. Kennedy. No newsmen were permitted to watch the taping. One pool press photographer accompanied the television crew.

June 16, 1968

The Heirs

Kennedy Bars Race, Saying That Reason Is 'Purely Personal'

By TOM WICKER

WASHINGTON, July 26—Senator Edward M. Kennedy announced in Boston today that it would be "impossible" for him to run for Vice President this year.

His decision, he said, has been made for "purely personal" reasons and is "final, firm, and not subject to further consideration."

The Massachusetts Senator, who was sailing this afternoon off Cape Cod, issued the statement through a spokesman. He could not be reached for further comment.

In political circles here Mr. Kennedy's refusal to consider the Vice-Presidency this year was considered about as conclusive as he could have made it. Nevertheless, it was expected that there might still be an effort to draft him at the Democratic National Convention in Chicago next month, particularly if the Presidential nominee is Vice President Humphrey.

The brief Kennedy statement, also made available here, was as follows:

"Over the last few weeks, many prominent Democrats have raised the possibility of my running for Vice President on the Democratic ticket this fall. I deeply appreciate their confidence. Under normal circumstances such a possibility would be a high honor and a challenge to further public service. But for me, this year, it is impossible.

"My reasons are purely personal. They arise from the change in my personal situation and responsibilities as a result of the events of last month. I know that the members of the Democratic party will understand these reasons without further elaboration.

"I have informed the Democratic candidates for the Presidency and the chairman of the convention that I will not be able to accept the Vice-Presidential nomination if offered, and that my decision is final, firm, and not subject to further consideration.

"I believe, however, that there are certain vital foreign and domestic policies our party must pursue if it is to be successful in the coming election and is to solve our nation's problems. I will be speaking out on these issues in my capacity as United States Senator in the future."

Spreading Movement

Mr. Kennedy issued this statement in response to a rapidly spreading movement within the Democratic party to make him Mr. Humphrey's running mate.

Democratic professionals and office-holders widely assume that Mr. Humphrey will be nominated for President, although Senator Eugene J. McCarthy of Minnesota and his supporters insist that the Vice President by no means has the nomination "locked up."

July 27, 1968

Kennedy Death Seen By Son, Doctor Writes

David Kennedy, the 13-year-old son of Senator Robert F. Kennedy, witnessed the detailed live television coverage of the assassination of his father early on June 5, a psychiatrist has reported.

Theodore White, the writer and historian, found the boy "devastated at the sight he had just seen," Dr. Gerald Caplan wrote in an article entitled "Lessons in Bravery" published in the September issue of McCall's.

Dr. Caplan said the three eldest children, Kathleen, 17 years old, Joseph, 15, and Robert J., 14, were in boarding schools in the East and were awakened by members of the staffs, told of the accident and flown to Los Angeles.

The six younger children, ranging in age from 3 to 13, were in a suite of rooms at the Ambassador Hotel, believed to be asleep. But Mr. White, Dr. Caplan reported, immediately went to make sure.

Mr. White, Dr. Caplan wrote, "did not arrive in time to prevent David from learning the news in the worst possible way, but he was able to immediately cushion the blow."

August 22, 1968

KENNEDY QUASHES DRAFT MOVEMENT

He Unequivocally Says No, Hours Before Nominations

By R. W. APPLE Jr.

CHICAGO, Aug. 28—Senator Edward M. Kennedy unequivocally took himself out of the 1968 Presidential competition today, only 12 hours before the Democratic National Convention was to choose its nominee. The draft-Ted movement evaporated almost immediately.

In a statement issued from his Washington office, the 36-year-old Massachusetts legislator asked his supporters "to cease all activity on my behalf so that the convention can choose its nominee from among the capable and dedicated candidates already in contention."

The reasons, Senator Kennedy added, were the same that prompted him a month ago to state his nonavailability for the Vice-Presidential nomination: "personal and family reasons."

But within the small circle of friends and relatives who had hoped against hope that the convention could somehow be swung behind the last of the four Kennedy brothers, another explanation was offered: The votes simply weren't there.

The Kennedy boom probably reached its height early last evening, when Stephen E. Smith, who is married to the Senator's sister Jean, conferred with Senator Eugene J. McCarthy in the McCarthy suite at the Conrad Hilton Hotel.

Senator McCarthy confirmed today that he had offered to swing his support to Senator Kennedy before the first ballot.

He said he had made the offer because he knew he himself could not win, because he thought Senator Kennedy might draw 200 or more votes away from Vice President Humphrey and because he was absolutely convinced, after hearing Mr. Humphrey at the California caucus yesterday, that Mr. Humphrey would never swerve from support of the Johnson Administration on Vietnam.

From the start, Mr. Smith and other Kennedy intimates had thought there was very little chance of a Kennedy victory.

But they had been willing to wait to see whether a genuine draft—"something that almost never happens," as one of them conceded three days ago—would develop out of the convention's sense of frustration and defeatism.

Mr. Smith set up a listening post at the Standard Club in the Loop, six miles north of the International Amphitheatre. He was aided in assessing the situation by John Siegenthaler, editor of The Nashville Tennessean and a former aide to Robert Kennedy; David Hackett, a family friend; Jerry Bruno, a New York delegate who ran Robert Kennedy's office in Syracuse, and Senator Abraham A. Ribicoff of Connecticut, who was nominally backing Senator George S. McGovern for the nomination.

Jesse M. Unruh, the leader of the 174-vote California delegation, was a prime mover in promoting the draft plan.

Informal polls were taken in several delegations on Monday evening and all day yesterday. The results showed Kennedy strength in Massachusetts, Missouri, Ohio, New Jersey, California, New York, Nebraska, Kansas, Pennsylvania, even

Georgia and Alabamba.

But it was hard to provide Senator Kennedy with anything approaching a precise count—something he felt he had to have before plunging into a fight.

Moreover, a substantial part of the Kennedy strength, which may at one point have been in the neighborhood of 900 or 950 votes, was coming from supporters of Mr. McCarthy and Mr. McGovern or from delegates who were still truly uncommitted.

According to the men who were counting, relatively few delegates were being taken from Mr. Humphrey, and hence it became difficult to see how he could be stopped on the first ballot.

Attention then began to focus on Mayor Richard J. Daley of Chicago, in the hope that he would declare for Senator Kennedy, thus providing the signal demanded by the others.

The final word from Mr. Daley came yesterday afternoon. Before abandoning the draft idea altogether, Mr. Smith called on Senator McCarthy, Mr. Unruh held a series of meetings, and other figures made a final reappraisal of the situation.

Later Senator Kennedy called Mr. Unruh (he did not inform Mr. Humphrey and Mr. McGovern of his decision until this morning). When Mr. Unruh emerged after midnight last night from the Standard Club, he knew that the game was up, and he looked tired and crestfallen.

With an ambiguity that may have been intentional, he told a waiting reporter, "It's too late for me to comment."

August 29, 1968

Joan Kennedy on the Campaign Trail: Tears and Wolf Whistles

By NAN ROBERTSON

INDIANAPOLIS, Oct. 3 — Leaving a trail of damp hankies and wolf whistles behind her, Joan Kennedy campaigned across Indiana yesterday for a man to whom she owes an unpayable debt.

He was Senator Birch Bayh, who crashed in a light plane four years ago with Mrs. Kennedy's husband. Although badly injured, he pulled Senator Edward M. Kennedy from the wreckage, probably saving his friend's life while risking his own.

Mrs. Kennedy told the tale at every one of five stops in the state the natives call "Hoosierland." She reduced some listeners in her audience to sniffles and all of them to fascinated silence.

A True Beauty

The enthusiastic whistles came from teen-aged boys at Fort Wayne and elsewhere, for 32-year-old Mrs. Kennedy is a true knockout—the only beauty in the Kennedy family to rival her sister-in-law, Jacqueline.

With her blond lion's mane, dazzling blue-green eyes, clunky pilgrim shoes and mustard tights to match a shift that stopped four inches above her kneecaps, she looked as exotic as a butterfly beside the ladies in blue permanents and sparkly harlequin glasses.

"She's gorgeous—what a doll!" gasped one woman at the Gary airport after she had grabbed Mrs. Kennedy's hand. Another, in Hammond, said: "I didn't realize she had such a mop of hair." Then she added, a touch cattily, "And it's a little dark at the roots, too."

Mrs. Kennedy has probably campaigned more on her own than any other woman in the clan. In 1964, she spoke all alone in her husband's race for the Senate while he lay hospitalized for months after the plane crash with a broken back.

Last spring she campaigned alone across Indiana in the primary won by Senator Robert F. Kennedy. And last month, she stumped in Massachusetts to help another friend, Representative Edward P. Boland.

Yet she is hardly a polished performer. Yesterday, she nervously studied her speech cards while waiting on the platform. At the podium, she is a wedding-band twiddler and hand-clencher, and the voice is a bit trembly as she begins.

"She kind of stammered and stuttered and looked at her speech cards too much," said Mary Woodke, a student at St. Mary's College in South Bend. But Kim Helland thought "She looked like a great friend—I mean someone you'd really like to know."

And Ginger Birskovich, another St. Mary's girl, said: "She was just so natural, giggling and all."

Mrs. Kennedy made her Catholic audience at St. Mary's giggle, too.

"You know," she confided, "when I was in school, the sisters made us go to hear outside speakers. I used to sneak out."

She forgot to introduce the Rev. John Cavanaugh, the former president of Notre Dame and close friend of the Kennedy family, sat down, then clapped a hand over her mouth and ran back to the rostrum.

She then confided that Father Cavanaugh "was the first one to know our secret" in 1958 that she and Ted were engaged.

"Ted and I wanted him to marry us, but then Cardinal Spellman said that he should be the one to do it. And so . . . anyway, that was that," Mrs. Kennedy said. The two were married in Bronxville, N. Y., her home town, that November.

Natural and Unaffected

Mrs. Kennedy is a natural and unaffected woman on stage and off. In the plane, while munching some "fingerlickin' good" fried chicken, and at one speaking stop where she could wiggle her toes behind the podium, she kicked off her buckled patent-leather shoes.

She was introduced at all five stops by Marvella Bayh, the Senator's wife and a socko speaker by any stand-

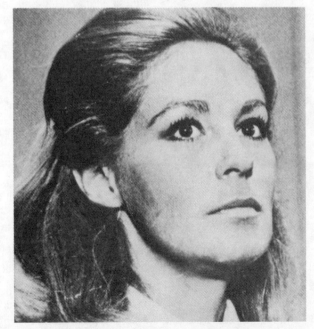

Mrs. Edward M. Kennedy

ards. The Bayhs met at a national extemporaneous speech contest in Chicago in 1951. She placed first; he was the runner-up. They were married eight months later.

Mrs. Bayh quoted Toynbee, H. G. Wells and Adlai Stevenson in her eloquent pitches for her husband. Mrs. Kennedy quoted Teddy.

"My Ted and Birch," she would say. She put the weight of the Kennedy name again and again behind Mr. Bayh. She spoke of how highly President Kennedy and Senator Robert Kennedy thought

of him, and "now my husband Teddy."

Mrs. Kennedy was able to speak of the dead President with apparent equanimity. But on several occasions, she brought out the name of Robert Kennedy, assassinated only four months ago, with obvious difficulty.

"It must be terribly hard for her to come out of deep mourning and campaign like that," commented a nun at Central Catholic High School, where Mrs. Kennedy was greeted with thunderous applause and a storm of whistles. "Most of us would have

sat back and forgotten the world."

Mrs. Kennedy began her 14-hour day with an apology. It came in Hammond at what she called her "first official press conference."

"You'll have to bear with me," she said. "I'm a bit nervous, but I think my heart's in the right place."

The news conference, in which she had to face a thicket of microphones and hot television lights, proved to be the hardest event of her day.

"I'm used to girly chats over coffee with a couple of

reporters," she confessed.

Throughout the day, microphones proved a problem, too. She either had to bend over to speak into them or wait until someone adjusted them for her. Five-feet 7-inches tall, with coltish legs, she mentioned her height just once. That was at Fort Wayne, after someone had fiddled with the microphone.

"I don't guess there are many of you out there who are 12 years old," she remarked, "but I was this tall when I was 12, and it wasn't fun then, either."

October 4, 1968

Mrs. Kennedy to Wed Onassis

WEDDING PLANNED FOR NEXT WEEK

President's Widow Flies to Greece With Her Children and Sisters-in-Law

By MARYLIN BENDER

Mrs. John F. Kennedy, 39-year-old widow of the 35th President of the United States, will marry Aristotle Socrates Onassis, the 62-year-old divorced multimillionaire shipowner of Greek ancestry and Argentine citizenship.

Shortly after an announcement yesterday of her plans, capping years of speculation and gossip and a day of intense rumor and reports, Mrs. Kennedy emerged from her Fifth Avenue apartment with her two children, Caroline, 10, and John, 7. She made her way, with the aid of Secret Service men, through a dense throng of the curious, and left by limousine for Kennedy Airport.

After 90 passengers had been shifted to another aircraft, Mrs. Kennedy boarded a jet belonging to Olympic Airways, one of

Mr. Onassis' enterprises, to begin an eight-and-a-half-hour flight to Greece.

In the party aboard the Boeing 707, in addition to Mrs. Kennedy and her children, were two of the late President's sisters, Mrs. Patricia Lawford and Mrs. Stephen Smith, and Mrs. Kennedy's stepfather, Hugh D. Auchincloss of Washington, and her mother, Mrs. Auchincloss, who announced the impending marriage yesterday afternoon.

Late last night, reports circulated at the airfield that Mr. Onassis was also aboard the plane. But Michael J. Trittas, director of ground operations for Olympic Airways at the airport, flatly denied this.

At 3:30 P.M., amid deepening speculation, insistent reports and swiftly circulating rumor, Nancy Tuckerman, Mrs. Ken-

nedy's secretary in New York, relayed a statement from Mrs. Auchincloss. Miss Tuckerman said:

"Mrs. Hugh D. Auchincloss has asked me to tell you that her daughter, Mrs. John F. Kennedy, is planning to marry Mr. Aristotle Onassis sometime next week."

Miss Tuckerman added that "no place or date has been set for the moment," but sources close to Mr. Onassis in Athens said that the wedding would take place on Skorpios, an island he owns in the Ionian Sea off the west coast of Greece.

The jetliner carrying Mrs. Kennedy and her family was scheduled to land at 10:30 A.M. today (4:30 A.M. New York time) at Andravida Airport, in the Peloponnesian peninsula of Greece, about 45 miles from Athens.

Because Mrs. Kennedy is a Roman Catholic and Mr. Onassis, a member of the Greek Orthodox Church, is divorced, questions were raised about recognition by Mrs. Kennedy's church of the planned marriage. The Catholic church forbids its members to enter into marriages with divorced persons.

Yesterday, the Archdiocese of New York declined to answer the question of church sanction. "It depends on the circumstances," said Msgr. Thomas McGovern, director of information for the archdiocese. "Many things are possible."

Mr. Onassis' marriage to the former Athina Mary Livanos, a member of another wealthy shipping family, was terminated in 1960 by an uncontested divorce in Alabama on the ground of mental cruelty. Two children of that marriage, Alexander, 20, and Christina, 18, are citizens of the United States.

The first Mrs. Onassis married the Marquess of Blanford in Paris on Oct. 23, 1961.

The first indication of Mrs. Kennedy's impending marriage came from a story in The Bos-

Mrs. John F. Kennedy

Associated Press

Aristotle Socrates Onassis

ton Herald-Traveler yesterday that predicted the wedding would take place before the end of the month.

The report gained substance when Richard Cardinal Cushing, an intimate of the Kennedy family and the cleric who had married the former Jacqueline Lee Bouvier to the then Senator John F. Kennedy in Newport, R. I., on Sept. 12, 1953, indicated that he knew what was about to be announced.

Cardinal Silent

Cardinal Cushing said in Sioux Falls, S. D., where he had gone for the consecration of Bishop-elect Paul Anderson: "No comment. My lips are sealed. No comment at all."

But he prophesied that an official announcement of the marriage "may be coming up tonight — tonight or tomorrow."

Richard Drayne, press aide to Senator Edward M. Kennedy, Mrs. Kennedy's brother-in-law, said in Washington that the Senator was in Boston, and issued this statement for him:

"I talked to Jackie several days ago, and she told me of her plans. I gave her my very best wishes for their happiness."

Mrs. Joseph P. Kennedy's secretary said yesterday in Hyannis Port, Mass., that the mother of the slain President would not comment in any way on her daughter-in-law's wedding plans. Mrs. Robert F. Kennedy, widow of the late Senator from New York, also declined comment.

Reports Had Circulated

Reports of the romance between Mrs. Kennedy and Mr. Onassis had been circulating in recent weeks, at variance with earlier stories of an impending marriage between Mrs. Kennedy and Lord Harlech, a widower and longtime friend of the late President.

When she released Mrs. Auchincloss's statement, Miss Tuckerman fended off additional questions from reporters by pleading, "I didn't even know until a half-hour ago."

At 6 P.M. Mrs. Kennedy left the building where she has lived in an apartment on the 15th-floor overlooking Central Park since September, 1964. She moved there from Washington, seeking the privacy and shelter from curious tourists that has escaped her since her husband was elected President in 1960.

Smiling and clutching her children, Mrs. Kennedy advanced past about 200 people and a welter of television cameramen and reporters toward a waiting car.

She was wearing a gray wool dress, black shoes and matching handbag, and was preceded by four Secret Service men carrying four small pieces of luggage.

A spokesman for the Secret Service said last night that Mrs. Kennedy would continue to have its protection until next March. The children will have the protection of the agents until they are 16, he said.

While Mrs. Kennedy left through the front door, about six trunks and suitcases were being taken through a side entrance. Some of the spectators, drawn by the crowd, did not know what was happening.

Others who had heard the news on the radio or by word of mouth rejoiced and lamented the decision of Mrs. Kennedy to marry a man more than 23 years her senior.

But Mrs. Kennedy heard none of the remarks nor did she respond to questions flung at her by newsmen. She entered a car, the driver of which had been gunning the motor and edging the vehicle forward.

The car arrived at Kennedy Airport at 6:45 P.M. in a motorcade and drove to the American Airlines terminal. Olympic Airlines uses the terminal for departures.

She bypassed the boarding ticket counter and went straight to the ramp where the jetliner, regularly due to leave as flight 412 at 8:30 P.M., was waiting. The 90 passengers, who had been booked to leave for Athens on it, left on another flight an hour and 15 minutes later.

Mrs. Kennedy waited at the ramp, hatless and coatless, for a few minutes before walking up the steps into the plane. At 7:20 P.M. her sisters-in-law arrived in another car.

They boarded the plane 10 minutes later. Mrs. Lawford was accompanied by one of her daughters. A total of 11 passengers was aboard.

The plane taxied away from the ramp and took off at 8:02 P.M. It was bound for Andravida Airport, a military airfield near Pyrgos, about 145 miles from Athens and about 60 miles from Skorpios. Olympic Airlines runs a helicopter service that could transport the party to either destination.

Mrs. Kennedy and Mr. Onassis have known each other about 18 years, Pamela Turnure Timmins, Mrs. Kennedy's former press secretary, said yesterday.

Mrs. Timmins could not remember the circumstances of the meeting. "I do recall that they [Mrs. Kennedy and her husband] visited on his yacht shortly after they were married," she said. "That's where they first met Winston Churchill. So that must be about 14 years ago."

In recent years, Mrs. Kennedy's sister, Mrs. Lee Radziwill, and her husband, Prince Stanislas Radziwill, a London businessman, have been close friends of Mr. Onassis. Mrs. Radziwill was reported to be on vacation in Tunisia.

Mr. Onassis has been a constant companion of Maria Callas, the opera star, for many years. Miss Callas was in New York last month to attend the opening of the Metropolitan Opera. She complained bitterly to friends here about the break-up of her friendship with Mr. Onassis.

Last night, in Paris, where she is now living, Miss Callas refused to comment on the announcement of the marriage.

The reports of a romance between Mrs. Kennedy and Mr. Onassis began in August, when she flew to Skorpios, accompanied by Senator Kennedy, to join him for a cruise on the Onassis yacht, the Christina.

In July, Mrs. Kennedy and Mr. Onassis were seen together at Bailey's Beach in Newport, R. I., where the Auchinclosses have a summer estate. Last May, Mrs. Kennedy, accompanied by a Secret Service man, flew to the Caribbean to board the yacht for a two-week cruise.

At least twice during the last month, Mr. Onassis has visited at the Kennedy compound in Hyannis Port, Mass. On one occasion, he dispatched an aide in New York to buy Lucite yo-yos as gifts for Mrs. Kennedy's children.

As recently as last week, Mrs. Kennedy attended a performance of "The Boys in the Band," with Lord Harlech, who was British Ambassador to the United States during the Kennedy Administration.

Last October, Mrs. Kennedy toured the ruins of Angkor Wat in Cambodia with Lord Harlech and Michael Forrestal, a New York lawyer.

Scores of reporters and photographers dogged their footsteps and fueled the gossip about what many of Mrs. Kennedy's and Lord Harlech's friends considered would be an ideal marriage.

Some of these friends, were surprised by the announcement of the impending wedding to Mr. Onassis. One was Roswell L. Gilpatric, a former Deputy Secretary of Defense, and a partner in Cravath, Swaine & Moore, a law firm here.

"No, I didn't know about it," he said. "I wish her every happiness."

Mr. Gilpatric, who had accompanied the former First Lady to Palm Beach, Fla., and Mexico earlier this year, was with her the night before her brother-in-law Senator Robert F. Kennedy was assassinated and took her to the plane when word came of his death.

"She once told me," Mr. Gilpatric said, "that she felt she could count on him [Onassis]. It was an attribute she looked for in all her friends. One of the things she is looking for for herself and her children is a private life—not being in the public eye all the time—and he can afford to give her that privacy and protection."

October 18, 1968

Public reaction here to Mrs. John F. Kennedy's engagement to Aristotle Onassis, the Greek shipping magnate, was generally a combination of anger, shock and dismay with the emphasis on dismay.

Very few of those questioned in Times Square, Rockefeller Center, Central Park and on Fifth Avenue seemed to think that Mrs. Kennedy's engagement was her own business.

Miss Ann Farber, 70 years old, of the Bronx, a retired bookkeeper who was watching the skaters in Rockefeller Center, said:

"I'm terribly disappointed. She could have done better. To us she was royalty, a princess, and I think she should have married a prince. Or at least someone who looked like a prince."

Peter Moraites, 45, manager of the Pantheon, a Greek restaurant at 689 Eighth Avenue, was one of the few who seemed overjoyed at the news.

"As far as I'm concerned, this is the greatest thing that ever happened," he said. "everyone in the Greek community is enthused. Onassis ate here in 1952, and I think he's a great man. As far as religion is concerned, this is a step in combining Catholicism with the Greek Orthodox religion."

Rubin Gralla, 55, of Brooklyn, who has been a cab driver for 33 years, said:

"There's an image about Jackie. I think of her as a lady, a lady. You know what I mean, somebody who's above the other people. Now that she's marrying this fellow, I think: she's going to lose some

The Reaction Here Is Anger, Shock and Dismay

By JUDY KLEMESRUD

of the shine. She's no longer on her pedestal. You wouldn't have had this uproar if she had married Lord Harlech. But I think this Aristotle is going to be a good husband. He has the maturity. He'll count to 100 before he loses his temper."

"Everyone in my office is shocked," Miss Gloria Saunders, a 38-year-old secretary from Brooklyn, said as she came out of Saks Fifth Avenue. "That's all we talked about today. She should have married an American businessman or someone connected with the arts. She certainly doesn't need the money."

Capt. Charles Brown, 32, of New Orleans, an Air Force pilot who was vacationing in New York, said he had another man in mind for Mrs. Kennedy.

"I was pulling for the Prime Minister of Canada [Pierre Elliott Trudeau]," he said. "He's single, and it would have given her the chance to be a First Lady again."

Several long-haired teen-agers sitting around the Bethesda Fountain in Central Park indicated favor of the marriage.

"It's Jackie's life, and she should do what she wants to with it," said Lorelle Heacock, 16, of Manhattan.

Another, Amel Rush, 17, of Dobbs Ferry, N.Y., didn't say much. He just played "The Wedding March" on his harmonica.

October 19, 1968

Many in Europe Shocked

LONDON, Oct. 18—The dominant reaction in Europe to Mrs. John F. Kennedy's plan for remarriage was put bluntly in a headline this afternoon in "Jackie—How Can You?"

Everywhere on the Continent there was intense public interest in the news, with heavy press and broadcast coverage. And there was a widespread sense of shock and disappointment at Mrs. Kennedy's choice of Aristotle Onassis on her second husband.

Only in the Soviet Union did the news go unreported.

The reaction was perhaps strongest in France, where a correspondent said the news had hit the people like a national tragedy.

In Paris, groups, mostly women, stood around newsstands in a way they had not since the Arab-Israel war of June, 1967. Early this morning, in a St. Germain-des-Pres brasserie, every table buzzed with comment, all of it critical.

Le Monde, France's leading serious newspaper, published a negative comment by its distinguished foreign editor, André Fontaine. He said Mr. Onassis was "the antithesis" of President Kennedy's dream of "a less cruel world."

Onassis Is Disparaged

Mr. Onassis "is concerned more with dominating this world than with reforming it," Le Monde said. "Is it this appetite for power, with all that it reveals of a quasi-animal energy, that charmed the widow of John Kennedy?"

"Her decision, and the motives of that decision, are nobody's business but hers. But it is to be feared that the second Mrs. Aristotle Onassis will cause to be forgotten the radiant Snow White who contributed so much to the popularity of her husband."

If Le Monde saw Mrs. Kennedy as a fairy-tale character, the West German Bild-Zeitung treated her image as holy. The banner headline in the four-million-circulation tabloid read: "America Has Lost a Saint."

There was disappointment in Mrs. Kennedy's choice. A student, Annemarie Kusten, said:

"I first thought it was a cheap joke, the goddess of American multimillionaire. I think this will be shattering news for idealists the world over."

On the other hand, there were some in West Germany— and elsewhere—who thought Mrs. Kennedy was entitled to remake her life as she saw fit after all the tragedies through which she has lived.

'The World Is Indignant'

"All the world is indignant," a Bild-Zeitung editorial said, "but Jackie is not a national monument that has to remain immaculate until her death. Let Jackie become happy with Ari on that expensive island."

Then Bild-Zeitung, leaving nothing unsaid, ran a second editorial on the opposite side, criticizing the decision.

The story continued to get heavy play in British newspapers and was the major item all day on British Broadcasting Corporation news programs.

The evening newspaper placards said, "Jackie: Why Onassis?" But the papers contained only speculation by way of answer.

In a barbershop in Twickenham, a genteel London suburb, horse racing and even the olympic games were displaced as topics of conversation by Mrs. Kennedy.

One customer, a man edging past 50, drew sympathetic laughter when he remarked, "This gives hope to all us old buggers."

Most Italian newspapers displayed the story prominently, with a hint of reproach. Giornale d'Italia, for example, said in a comment, "She is no longer the widow of a myth."

The Vatican newspaper, L'Osservatore Romano, was one of the few that did not carry the news.

In Switzerland, person after person began his conversation by saying something such as, "Of course, she is free to do whatever she pleases."

Characteristically, this was followed by an expression of surprise and disappointment.

In Ireland, which felt especially close to President Kennedy and which is 90 per cent Roman Catholic, observers reported a sense of national bewilderment at Mrs. Kennedy's decision to marry Mr. Onassis.

October 19, 1968

'Very Happy' Mrs. Kennedy and Onassis Married

By ALVIN SHUSTER

ATHENS, Oct. 20 — Jacqueline Kennedy became Mrs. Aristotle Socrates Onassis today in a candle-lit wedding ceremony in a tiny chapel among the cypress trees on the island of Skorpios.

The 39-year-old widow of President Kennedy, two inches taller than her new husband, stood beside the 62-year-old multimillionaire during a 30-minute ceremony and gazed intently at the officiating Greek Orthodox prelate.

Her two children, Caroline, 10, and John, 7, flanked the couple, holding two slim white candles.

Rain was falling outside— Greeks believe this brings good luck on a wedding day — as the couple walked around the altar three times in the Dance of Isaiah, the traditional closing rite of the Greek Orthodox service.

The bride had a bouffant hairstyle with a single braid falling from the back. She wore a beige chiffon and lace two-piece dress with long laced sleeves and a pleated, knee-length skirt. In her hair was a ribbon of the same color. The bride, who is 5 feet 7 inches tall, wore low-heeled shoes that also matched her dress. It was designed by Valentino, the Roman couturier who makes many of her costumes.

As she came to the church, she appeared bright-faced in the rain. "We are very happy," she said.

Mr. Onassis wore a double-

MR. AND MRS. ARISTOTLE SOCRATES ONASSIS leaving chapel on island of Skorpios after ceremony yesterday.

breasted blue suit and a red tie.

"Do Thou now, Master; send down Thine hand from Thy holy dwelling place and unite Thy servants, Aristotle and Jacqueline, for by Thee woman is united to man," said the 32-year-old prelate, the Right Rev. Polycarpos Athanassiou of the Church of Kapnikarea in downtown Athens. The church is the chapel of Athens University.

The priest, who has a black beard and wore a gold robe, told reporters that he first met Mr. Onassis in 1964 while he was serving as deacon under Archbishop Iakovos, the Greek Orthodox Primate of North and South America.

Twenty-one persons—relatives and friends only—crowded into the tiny, white-washed chapel, which was decorated with small gardenia trees. Some guests had to stand along the walls of the 75-year-old Chapel of the Little Virgin.

Among the guests were Mr. and Mrs. Hugh D. Auchincloss, the bride's stepfather and mother; Prince and Princess Stanislas Radziwill, her brother-in-law and sister, and their two children, and two sisters of President Kennedy, Mrs. Stephen Smith and Mrs. Patricia Lawford.

Also there were Mr. Onassis' two children by his first wife —Alexander, 20 years old, and Christina, 18. His sister, Mrs. Artemis Garofalides, served as the sponsor, the equivalent of attendant.

The couple exchanged rings during the ceremony, which was conducted mostly in Greek. Then came the crowning of the couple with white wreaths connected by a white ribbon. Mrs. Garofalides exchanged the wreaths three times over their heads. The couple then drank from a cup of red wine, a symbolic declaration of their "oneness."

After the ceremony, the couple emerged in a driving rain with Mrs. Onassis smiling and Mr. Onassis saying to a reporter, "I feel very well, my boy."

Caroline With Couple

They climbed into a small yellow golf cart. With Mr. Onassis behind the wheel and with Caroline sitting on her mother's knee, they drove off for the Onassis yacht, the Christina. John Jr. came along later.

At the yacht, on which the couple will take their wedding trip, champagne began to flow in the ship's big dining room and bar, which is equipped with stools covered with whaleskin.

The couple were intent on keeping the ceremony as private as possible. Motorboats of the Greek Coast Guard patrolled the Ionian Sea and Mr. Onassis own security men covered the island.

Press coverage was limited to a small group of cameramen and reporters, who were kept outside the church. They briefed their colleagues on their return to Athens tonight, under a pool arrangement. The films were also shared.

The reporters on the island were kept outside the chapel by a United States Secret Service agent, who wore a "PT 109" tiepin, one of those that President Kennedy often gave to friends and associates.

Even after the Orthodox ceremony, the question of Mrs. Onassis' future relations with the Roman Catholic Church remains unanswered.

Contacts Reported

Rumors circulated in Athens

The Heirs

today of contacts between Mrs. Onassis and the hierarchy of the Roman Catholic Church, which forbids its members to marry divorced persons. Under extraordinary circumstances, the Roman Rota, the church's supreme marriage court, can grant an annulment, declaring that there never was a valid marriage. Such a decision, for example, was granted to Mrs. Onassis' sister. Her earlier marriage, to Michael Canfield, was annulled.

Mr. Onassis was divorced by Athina Mary Livanos, a member of another wealthy Greek family and now the Marchioness of Blandford, in Alabama in 1960. The divorce was subsequently approved by an ecclesiastical court of the Orthodox Church in New York.

A church spokesman here said the only condition attached to the marriage today was a

pledge that any future children would be raised in the Orthodox faith.

Mr. Onassis, a stocky, gray-haired man who likes to wear sunglasses, is a legend in Greece because of his rise from poverty to his position as one of the world's richest men, his flare for grand living, his publicized romances, and his ability to befriend famous people. He also draws attention because of his occasional flings in Athens night clubs, where he is known to have smashed pottery to the music of the bouzouki.

Mystery About His Age

He was born in Smyrna, now Izmir, the son of a well-to-do Greek tobacco merchant. He and his family fled the city in Asia Minor after the Turks captured it in 1922 and went to Greece. The young Onassis left Europe at the age of 16 and went to Argentina, arriving

there with about $100.

It was at this time that the mystery of Mr. Onassis' age developed. He later said that he had added six years to his rightful age in order to qualify for a job he wanted in Argentina. While he gives his age now as 62, those who have seen his passport say it lists him as 68.

After working as a telephone operator and at other minor jobs, he went into the export-import business. By the time he was in his mid-twenties, he had raised enough money to buy some freighters. He built his first tanker before World War II, and at its end, he decided to go into the tanker business in a big way.

He married his first wife in New York immediately after the war. She is a daughter of the late Stavros Livanos, then the richest Greek in shipping. She was 17 years old, more than 20 years his junior.

Mr. Onassis ran into difficulties with the United States authorities when he purchased some surplus naval vessels from the Government in 1954. Only American corporations were eligible to buy the ship, and the United States moved against him because he had provided the financing for an American corporation. He was arrested, indicted and released on bail.

Finally, after years of negotiations, he settled the case with the Government and paid $7-million.

His personal wealth, meanwhile, was rising by the day. While all Greeks might not like the way he does business, they agree that he has the nerve and gambling spirit characteristic of tycoons. The estimates vary, but his total wealth, which includes control of some 30 companies, is said to be somewhere around $500-million. He owns a merchant fleet larger than that of most countries.

It was the beginning of a new life for the former Jacqueline Lee Bouvier, whose first husband, President John F. Kennedy, was assassinated in Dallas on Nov. 22, 1963. They had been married 10 years.

That new life will provide her with opportunities for complete seclusion on an island or a yacht far from New York City. It will also involve the hectic pace of a busy hostess, entertaining travelers and industrialists, members of royalty and leaders of the arts, and those who belong to that vague community known as international society.

Her husband, who rose from rags to tankers, is known not only for his far-reaching busi-

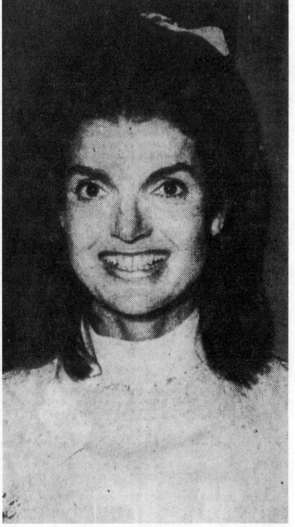

Associated Press

DURING RECEPTION: Mrs. Onassis aboard the yacht Christina following wedding ceremony on Skorpios Island.

THE KENNEDYS: A NEW YORK TIMES PROFILE

ness interests but also for the company he has kept and the hospitality he has afforded to notables, ranging from Winston Churchill to members of the jet set.

For her travels, she will now have at her disposal Mr. Onassis' transportation network—ships, helicopters, amphibious planes and the Boeing jets of Olympic Airways, which he owns.

Mr. Onassis met his wife and her first husband when Mr. Kennedy was still a Senator from Massachusetts. Mr. Onassis made his yacht available to them for brief cruises. After the assassination, he was among the first to call and offer condolences.

His bride was aboard the yacht and the island this summer, and he has recently visited her in New York, Rhode Island and Hyannisport, Mass. Even so, the word of the engagement, announced by the bride's mother, last Thursday, came as a complete surprise.

The wedding marked the end of the Secret Service protection that has surrounded the former First Lady since assassination, although by law the children may still be kept under guard at her option.

The engagement ended speculation in the world press about whom Mrs. Kennedy would turn to. She had told friends occasionally that she. wanted to remarry but could not find a man of the equal of John Kennedy. Lord Harlech, a widower and the British Ambassador in Washington when the Kennedys were in the White House, was most frequently mentioned. But she was often seen with others in New York.

Although Mrs. Onassis is planning to return to New York, where her children have been in school, she undoubtedly will be traveling considerably. Apart from his yacht and island, Mr. Onassis owns a villa in Monte Carlo, a penthouse in Paris, a hacienda at Montevideo, Uruguay, and a mansion outside Athens. The couple have said they would retain the bride's cooperative apartment in New York at 1040 Fifth Avenue. Mr. Onassis has maintained a suite at the Hotel Pierre.

October 21, 1968

ROME, Nov. 6—The authoritative Vatican weekly, L'Osservatore della Domenica, without mentioning the name of Mrs. Aristotle S. Onassis, made it clear today that a Roman Catholic in her present marital state is barred from the sacraments and is in "a state of spiritual degradation...a public sinner."

The church paper gave the most detailed and specific analysis of canonical issues raised by the marriage of the widow of President Kennedy to the divorced Greek multimillionaire on Oct. 20. The analysis was published in answer to a hypothetical question as to whether "a noted wordly event" involved formal excommunication of "the Catholic party."

The answer to this was negative. But the analysis went on to observe that the effect was almost the same for one who infringed church law by marrying a divorced partner —exclusion from the Eucharist and penance and church burial unless there was manifested sincere repentance prior to death.

"The contraction of matrimony with a divorced person already bound by the preceding matrimonial tie implies for the Catholic partner the assumption of an attitude of practical renunciation of his own faith and of finding himself automatically in a state of spiritual degradation by which the ecclesiastical community feels itself mortified," the article said.

"The contracters [of such a matrimony] put themselves automatically in a state of irregularity for which the existing ecclesiastical legislation does not hesitate to qualify them as public sinners and to warn of the penalties which, if they do not reach the gravity of excommunication, carry with them just the same the deprivation of certain acts held by the church to be a sign of vital and absolute adherence to its doctrine and its laws."

The purpose of these penalties, the article continued, was to warn against infraction of divine law and to stimulate violators to find the way of repentance and redemption.

The article did not specify the paths of repentance that would be required of a Roman Catholic in such a situation. However, it is a standard rule of the church that the repentant sinner must give up the sin. Therefore, the L'Osservatore della Domenica seemed to imply that forgiveness and full reacceptance into the church could be accomplished only when the sin was no longer being committed.

Presumably, this would mean that a couple in an irregular situation would have to be separated by choice or by death.

November 7, 1968

Vatican Newspaper Describes Mrs. Onassis as Public Sinner

By ROBERT C. DOTY

WASHINGTON, Dec. 12 (UPI)—Mrs. Ethel Kennedy, widow of Senator Robert F. Kennedy, gave birth early today to their 11th child, an 8-pound 4-ounce girl described by a friend as "a real pretty baby with light brown hair."

The infant was delivered by Caesarean section at 8:40 A.M. at Georgetown University Hospital. The late Senator's brother, Senator Edward M. Kennedy of Massachusetts, was in the delivery room. A family spokesman said that mother and child were in "excellent condition."

The birth came six months and a week after the Democratic Senator from New York died of an assassin's bullet in Los Angeles, where he had just won the California Presidential primary June 4.

Mrs. Kennedy now has seven sons and four daughters.

It was the fifth Caesarean for Mrs. Kennedy, a 40-year-old vivacious and athletic woman who likes to play tennis and touch football. Few women have more than three such operations.

Mrs. Kennedy will probably remain in the hospital for a week or 10 days, the spokesman said.

Dr. John W. Walsh. clinical professor of obstetrics and gynecology at Georgetown University, delivered the child. He has delivered several other Kennedy children, including John F. Kennedy Jr. in the same hospital.

Mrs. Kennedy entered the hospital last night with her brother-in-law, the Senator, and two close family friends, Frederick G. Dutton and Rafer Johnson, the 1960 Olympic decathlon champion.

Also along was Mrs. Louella Hennessy, the nurse who has attended the birth of every grandchild of Joseph P. Kennedy Sr. except for one of Mrs. Patricia Lawford's children.

December 13, 1968

Ethel Kennedy Has 11th Child, a Girl

KENNEDY CHOSEN AS SENATE WHIP

By JOHN W. FINNEY

WASHINGTON, Jan. 3 — Senator Edward M. Kennedy moved into the position of a Congressional spokesman today—and perhaps laid a stepping stone to the Presidency—by capturing the post of Democratic whip, or assistant leader, of the Senate.

In a coup against the Southern-dominated Senate establishment, the 36-year-old Massachusetts Senator, heir to the Kennedy political organization, unseated Senator Russell B. Long of Louisiana as the 91st Congress convened.

On the Republican side, too, the liberals made surprising inroads on the Senate leadership. Senator Hugh Scott, a liberal from Pennsylvania, upset the once dominant conservatives by winning the post of Republican whip over Roman L. Hruska of Nebraska.

McCormack Is Retained

The House, however, remained under the control of an Old Guard coalition of New Deal liberals and Southern conservatives. Voting along strictly party lines, the House gave another term as Speaker to 77-year-old John W. McCormack, Democrat of Massachusetts.

Yesterday Mr. McCormack, with the aid of Southern conservatives, put down a palace revolt among a small band of liberals in a House Democratic caucus that endorsed him for the post.

On the opening day of what is expected to be a middle-of-the-road Congress inclined to cooperate with the new Republican Administration, the House and Senate were preoccupied with their own organizational problems. Not until Richard M. Nixon is inaugurated as President on Jan. 20 is it expected to settle down to legislative business.

The Senate girded for another battle next week on whether to modify the anti-filibuster rule requiring a two-thirds vote to cut off debate.

The House became bogged down in a quarrel over Adam Clayton Powell, Democrat of Manhattan. Tonight, after five hours of wrangling, it voted to seat him and to punish him with a $25,000 fine for alleged misuse of House funds while he was chairman of the House Education and Labor Committee. He also loses his 22 years of House seniority.

'Winds of Change'

In a secret ballot in the Senate Democratic caucus today, Senator Kennedy won the whip post by a surprising 31-26 margin. Faced with opposition from the entrenched Southern conservatives, the Massachusetts Senator had been given only a narrow chance of winning. His victory was all the more impressive to his Senate colleagues for the way he had been able, in a week of campaigning, to round up a decisive lead.

Senator Kennedy attributed his victory to the "winds of change" blowing through the Senate. Rather than a personal victory, he said, his election reflected a demand throughout the country that the Senate "should be a creative, positive and aggressive forum," presenting a constructive, positive legislative program.

Senator Long, Democratic whip for the last four years, attributed his defeat to the nationwide political organization built up by the Kennedy family.

"I had him outgunned in the Senate," the 50-year-old Louisianian told reporters, "but he had me outgunned in the nation."

Noting that he had "used all of my resources" in his effort to obtain reelection, Senator Long said, "I do not think I could have been beaten by anyone else in the United States Senate."

This assessment was one generally concurred in by other Senators.

To his political embarassment now, Senator Edmund S. Muskie of Maine, the Democratic Vice-Presidential nominee, had weighed making the race for whip and decided he could not unseat Senator Long, one of the most powerful members of the Senate establishment.

As chairman of the tax-writing Senate Finance Committee, Senator Long has considerable influence, particularly in arranging for campaign contributions, such as from the oil industry, for his colleagues. There was every indication that he attempted to use his influence in a personal way in his bid for a job that in the past has carried more prestige than power.

For example, on one day this week, it was learned, Senator Fred R. Harris of Oklahoma received phone calls from six oil company executives urging him to vote for Senator Long, who has protected the oil industry's tax interests in the Senate. Although he represents an oil-producing state, Senator Harris voted for Senator Kennedy.

Against this Senate power of Senator Long, Senator Kennedy had three assets at his command in his personally managed campaign for the whip job.

He had, first, the political magnetism of the Kennedy name, with its ability to draw contributors to fund-raising dinners and voters to the polls. He had the recognition among many Democrats of the need for new blood in the Democratic leadership to offset the increasingly younger, more aggressive Republican minority.

And he was aided, finally, by a widespread personal dissatis-

Mike Mansfield of Montana, Democratic leader in Senate, with Edward M. Kennedy of Massachusetts, chosen as whip.

faction with Senator Long because of his flamboyant manner and frequent disregard of the party leadership of Senator Mike Mansfield, the Democratic leader.

In the showdown, Senator Kennedy drew his support primarily from Northern and Western Senators. But he made some critical inroads in the otherwise solid Southern front by picking up the votes of William B. Spong Jr., a Virginia moderate, and Ralph W. Yarborough of Texas, who is up for re-election in 1970 and was under some political obligation for past campaign assistance from Senator Long.

Senator Long, nominated for the post by Clinton P. Anderson of New Mexico, a former leader of the liberals, got the votes of most of the Southern and Southwestern Senators.

But in return for political favors or because of his power as Finance Committee chairman, he was supported also by some Northern and Western Senators, such as Thomas J. Dodd of Connecticut, whom he defended against censure; Vance Hartke of Indiana, a member of the Finance Committee; Gale W. McGee, who comes from the oil-producing state of Wyoming, and Gaylord P. Nelson, whom he permitted to become chairman of the Senate's Select Committee on Small Business by withdrawing himself.

The Long vote that was causing the most gossip in the Senate cloakrooms was that of Eugene J. McCarthy of Minnesota, the candidate of many Democratic liberals for the Democratic Presidential nomination.

Senator McCarthy had been under considerable pressure from his former liberal supporters, such as the Americans for Democratic Action, to support Senator Kennedy. But earlier this week Senator McCarthy told Senator Kennedy he would vote for Senator Long because a Kennedy election would result in the illusion rather than reality of leadership reform and thus tend to retard actual reform.

Sitting in a Capitol Hill restaurant after the vote, Senator McCarthy was twitted on his vote by a Democratic campaign aide. Alluding to the fact that during the Democratic convention Senator McCarthy at one point had said he would be willing to support Senator Kennedy for the Presidential nomination, the aide asked:

"How is it that you can vote for him as Pope but not as pastor?"

To this gibe from a fellow Roman Catholic, Senator McCarthy smilingly replied:

"I can think of a lot of people I would like to see as Pope but would not like to see as my pastor."

Speculation on Vote

Senator McCarthy fended off all reporters' requests for explanation of his vote. But the widespread speculation was that in voting for Senator Long, Senator McCarthy, a member of the Finance Committee, was reflecting obligations to his committee chairman as well as his differences with the Kennedy family, dating to 1960 when he nominated Adlai E. Stevenson against John F. Kennedy for the Presidential nomination.

Three members of the Finance Committee broke with their chairman and thus risked political retaliation — Senator Harris, Albert Gore of Tennessee and Abraham A. Ribicoff of Connecticut.

Senator Kennedy promptly moved from his back row seat, where he has played mostly a silent role, to a front row seat only one removed from the Democratic leader's chair. In terms of his political future, the move was symbolic.

January 4, 1969

WASHINGTON—"The thing about being a Kennedy," Edward M. Kennedy was saying, "is that you come to know there's a time for Kennedys, and it's hard to know when that time is, or if it will ever come again."

It was after midnight in the cozy twin-engine six-seater plane whirring eastward from Kentucky on a recent long flight to Cape Cod.

There were storm warnings. The night was black. The throb of the engines added to the cocoonlike atmosphere in the tiny cabin.

It was not a time for paperwork from the ever-present briefcase. The week's work was done. It was time for a drink, for a scrawny sweet filipino cigar, for easy conversation.

It also was one of those rare moments when a Kennedy—the last of the Kennedy brothers—will talk about himself. Swirling the drink in its plastic tumbler, he gazed out into the blackness, and mused on the problem of being a Kennedy, and what that means for his future.

"I mean, is the country going to be receptive? Will it be the time? And if it is, is it really the best thing for me to do And how much of a contribution could I make, even if . . .?"

The question, of course, was whether he will do in 1972 what everyone seems to expect: become the third Kennedy brother to seek the Presidency of the United States.

If that is inevitable, Senator Kennedy insisted he did not know it yet. Now, a year after the slaying of his brother Robert, he said it was up to fate and that at the moment, he would gladly let it pass.

"I'm really very unresolved right now," he said, twisting in his seat to remove his coat and find a comfortable position for the aching, tightly braced backbone. He lapsed into the familiar Kennedy speech pattern of half-sentences left dangling, completed with a shrug, a wave of the hand, a grin.

"Maybe over the summer . . . some sailing . . . the family . . . I think perhaps by fall I'll be settled, have some idea . . ."

This is Edward Moore Kennedy, senior Senator from Massachusetts and assistant majority leader of the United States Senate at the tender political age of 37; a nationally known figure, tempered by unspeakable tragedy, beset by scores of public and private pressures, buoyed, yet weighted down, by a magic name, earnestly trying to come to terms with himself.

He is eye-deep in politics, moving at a dead run, spreading himself thin. The Kennedy brothers, after all, were teethed on politics and Government service.

But he muttered that the fun had gone out of what was once, for him, a joyous profession. The assassinations of two brothers in Presidential politics, one at the pinnacle, the other reaching, have seen to that.

'What's It All For?'

"Good crowd tonight," someone said of the shouting, clutching rally of Kentucky Democrats in white Kennedy straw skimmers he had just left.

"I guess so," he said automatically.

And then: "You know, those kinds of things pretty much turn me off now. When I first came on into this in 1962 it was really good, easy. But the kicks aren't . . . I mean, meeting Molly Somebody and hearing all about her being Miss Something.

"What's it all for? I used to love it. But the fun began to go out of it after 1963, and then after the thing with Bobby, well . . ."

His thoughts returned to the Presidency. He dwelled briefly and candidly on the personal risk. He was aware of it — had to be — and he thought foremost about the family: his wife Joan, his three children, Robert's 11, John F. Kennedy's two, and in Hyannis Port, his stricken, fading father.

"So, even if the time is right," Senator Kennedy went on, "why should I?"

He said: "You talk about the family obligation, the public service. Is running for this the best way to meet that? When my father — I mean, then I'll really be it, and that's a lot.

"Just so many responsibilities. I worry about the kids, never feel I'm giving enough . . .

"You know, I'd really be delighted to see someone else go for it. Someone like Ed Muskie, someone like that. I mean, I'd be here, on up in the Senate. I could put the blowtorch to him, be effective that way."

True, but if his party calls, could he reject it?

"Damned right I could, in an instant. I honestly don't feel any obligation to pick this on up." The preposition "on" crept regularly into his speech,

Kennedy Reflects on Being a Kennedy... and the Future

By JOSEPH E. MOHBAT

after the action verbs.

"I mean I'm just not sure running around the country, taking on the tough issues and waving the Kennedy flag and running on in everywhere, stirring people up—is that helpful? Bobby did it, I know, spoke right on up on what bothered him, raised all that excitement—and then they can elect someone like . . .

"You just can't tell what the country will be like then," he said.

There also was the question whether the Kennedy name would still be magic in 1972 or 1976.

"I just don't know," Senator Kennedy sighed as the little plane touched down at the deserted Hyannis airport on Cape Cod. "I really think all of these things are predestined."

Gingerly easing himself out of the cramped plane, he quickly dispelled the heavy mood of the conversation in a raucous contest to see who could first spot the North Star. He took the victory, with loud, contagious Irish laughter.

He was home.

June 8, 1969

Ex-Secretary's Article Scores Mrs. Onassis

Former First Lady Held Insensitive To Her Husband

By FRED FERRETTI

The agent who sold a candid account of Mrs. Jacqueline Bouvier Kennedy Onassis' White House years written by her personal secretary said yesterday that when the book is published "it will contain a great many passages of high praise for Mrs. Kennedy . . . some things good and kind."

Very few passages of praise for the former First Lady are contained in the first serialized excerpt from the book, "My Boss, Jackie Kennedy," by Mary Barelli Gallagher.

The article, in Ladies' Home Journal, pictures Mrs. Kennedy as a woman who overspent, then, to compensate, went on economy binges; as a wife who appeared to be rather insensitive to the wishes of her husband; as an employer who was tightfisted about raises, and as a person who desired expensive jewelry with such a passion that she sacrificed personal gifts to get what she wanted, and then economized further by requesting her staff to shop where trading stamps were dispensed.

The book was edited by Frances Spatz Leighton, the collaborating author with Mrs. Lillian Rogers Parks in the 1961 best-seller, "My 30 Years Backstairs at the White House."

That book detailed White House life from the time of President William McKinley, when Mrs. Parks's mother was presidential maid, through the years from Presidents Calvin Coolidge through Dwight D. Eisenhower, when Mrs. Parks was a maid.

The release of the book prompted President and Mrs. Kennedy to exact written pledges of secrecy from all White House staff members. Pierre Salinger, White House press secretary under President Kennedy, disclosed that signed pledges had been received from the staff.

It was not clear then whether all White House staff members had signed the promise not to write about their employers.

Nor was it clear yesterday whether Mrs. Gallagher had signed a pledge in 1961. Her agent, Oscar Collier, of Seligmann & Collier, said that Mrs. Gallagher "does not remember signing such a pledge." He added that even if she had "it really wouldn't mean anything."

It is doubtful if such a pledge would be legally enforceable.

Mrs. Gallagher, who was secretary to Mrs. Onassis' mother, Mrs. Hugh D. Auchincloss, before moving to the White House, writes that the former First Lady ordered her staff to cut down on drinks to White House guests.

"She instructed Anne [Lincoln of the staff] to tell the butlers to refill those glasses that looked relatively unfinished and didn't have lipstick marks on the edge. Jackie said to pass them around again."

On the other hand, Mrs. Gallagher wrote, Mrs. Kennedy spent $21,461.61 more than the $100,000 President Kennedy earned in 1962.

Mrs. Gallagher wrote that Mrs. Kennedy sold off her old and unwanted clothing under Mrs. Gallagher's name and address. As the various items were sold and the checks remitted, she wrote: "I would deposit it in my personal account. At the same time I would write out a check for the same amount to be deposited in Jackie's account."

Of Mrs. Kennedy's relationships with her husband, Mrs. Gallagher says:
"I sometimes thought it would be nice if Jackie would eat breakfast with the Senator —or at least come downstairs to see him off." And:
"I always felt there were two things that John F. Kennedy wanted in his home; a comfortable, familiar, unchanging place to read in peace and quiet— and no money worries. Strangely enough these two things remained elusive."

Mrs. Gallagher recounts her personal attempts to get an increase in salary. There was a 15-month battle, she says, during which Mrs. Kennedy became angry and stamped her foot for emphasis. Mrs. Gallagher eventually received an increase, apparently not as high as the $8,000 or $9,000 she wanted.

Mrs. Gallagher says that once Mrs. Kennedy wanted an antique pin valued at $6,160 and got it by selling an aquamarine given her by the Government of Brazil, a gold and emerald pin she had received while visiting Greece, a diamond clip she had received as a wedding gift and a ruby and diamond pin that had been a Christmas gift from President Kennedy.

The First Lady netted $4,400, Mrs. Gallagher says, and made up the difference herself after being dissuaded from removing diamonds from a sword given her husband by King Saud of Saudi Arabia.

Mrs. Kennedy also discovered trading stamps, Mrs. Gallagher wrote, and instructed her staff to shop at stores that gave the stamps so that with them "we can trade them in for these marvelous gifts."

Mr. Collier would not reveal the proceeds thus far from publication and serial rights, except to say that it was "in six figures."

Serial rights for Britain have been purchased by The London Daily Mirror and sales have already been made in Japan, Sweden, Norway, Denmark, Germany, Italy and France.

Mr. Collier was asked if the material had been offered for sale in Greece, where Mrs. Onassis now lives with her husband, Aristotle Onassis.

"The sale to smaller countries," Mr. Collier said, "is handled by United Press International's international foreign department. I expect that it will be offered to Greece."

Mrs. Gallagher was unavailable to comment on her manuscript. However, through her publisher and agent, she let it be known that she had nothing to add to the published material.

June 28, 1969

The personal bills of Mrs. Aristotle Onassis, which totaled $28,000 during one two-month period when she was President Kennedy's wife, were a source of worry and annoyance to the President, her former personal secretary has written.

In an excerpt from her book, "My Life with Jacqueline Kennedy," which appears in the August issue of the Ladies' Home Journal, Mrs. Mary Barelli Gallagher says there were perennial "budget disputes" in the Kennedy household and she was "always in the middle."

After the President's assassination, Mrs. Kennedy tried to economize by cutting down on staff salaries and could not understand "that her small staff did not like being called on to provide all the services, accommodations, conveniences and comforts that she had grown so used to receiving from a much larger staff during her years at the White House," Mrs. Gallagher says. "Her staff's attitude, as far as I could see, puzzled her," the article continued.

The book has been attacked by a number of Mrs. Onassis's friends and former associates as unfair and a betrayal of trust. But the former First Lady has made no comment or any move to enforce an agreement that Mrs. Gallagher, like other members of the First Lady's staff, signed promising not to publish any inside stories about the household.

Ran 'The Other Way'

Mrs. Gallagher says that a number of times Mr. Kennedy demanded accountings of his wife's expenses, and the secretary wrote that she would have to work late into the night preparing the figures. Finally, Mrs. Gallagher says, she decided to "run the other way or use the waiters' elevator" when she heard the President ring for the regular elevator because she wanted to avoid new confrontations over the budget.

Listing her employer's bills, Mrs. Gallagher says the First Lady spent about $5,000 for clothing, $7,000 for liquor and food, $340 for hairdressing and $1,600 for works of art in the month of January, 1962.

"The totals for January and February, 1963, indicated some improvement over the first two months of 1962," she reported to the President.

"Jackie's personal expenses for the first two months of 1963 had come down by more than $12,000—to a total of about $16,000," the magazine article says.

Mrs. Gallagher says this resulted partly because Mrs. Onassis was pregnant and was not buying many clothes.

Trying to cut down on her expenses, Mrs. Onassis wrote regretfully to "her clothes scout in Paris" in April, 1963, that she could not afford to try a new French designer who "sounded fabulous," Mrs. Gallagher says. But Mrs. Onassis, now the wife of the Greek multimillionaire, suggested that her sister, Princess Lee Radziwill, "buy a suit so Jackie could borrow it anytime."

After the assassination, the former First Lady decided she could not "afford to pay all my help from the $50,000" appropriation from Congress, Mrs. Gallagher wrote.

She says Mrs. Onassis asked her to work part-time rather than pay her the $12,000 a year the secretary considered "a fair annual salary." She says Mrs. Onassis tried to arrange for her maid, Providencia Parades, to work "in Washington as a top maid, free-lancing around for parties and things during the summer" so the First Lady would not have to pay the maid's $100-a-week salary while away. And, the article continues, Mrs. Onassis used the two Navy stewards assigned to cook for her as "butlers and moving men" in addition to their regular duties.

Mrs. Gallagher described a series of misunderstandings that she says led to a "blast" from Mrs. Kennedy and the accusation that "you're throwing your weight around." She says the attack left her so "hurt and humiliated" that she refused to take any telephone calls from her employer for 24 hours.

The secretary was also bitter about the way in which Mrs. Onassis announced she was moving from Washington to New York and would no longer need her services. Mrs. Gallagher says Mrs. Onassis told her this by long distance telephone.

"Actually, moving to New York had been the very least of my desires and expectations, but I had hoped and expected that, when the time would come for Jackie to announce she no longer needed me, it would be in a warm, face-to-face manner. Obviously, I had expected too much," Mrs. Gallagher says.

However, Mrs. Gallagher says her association with Mrs. Onassis ended on a happier note. The former First Lady sent her a gold and turquoise pin and a card signed with "deepest affection always," Mrs. Gallagher says, and she is grateful for the way in which her employer "enriched my life by letting me put one foot in Camelot."

July 22, 1969

Kennedy Gets a Lesson In Student Protesting

WASHINGTON, May 8 — Senator Edward M. Kennedy has received first-hand evidence of the student unrest movement. Otuside his bedroom door the other morning, he found two sheets of primary school work papers inscribed:

"You are not ascing me questungs about the 5 pages. You are not creting [correcting] by home work, it is a free world."

The militant was 7½-year-old Teddy, submitting "non-negotiable demands" after an evening of school review with his father.

"And then," said Senator Kennedy, "I called for the campus police . . ."

May 9, 1969

The Heirs

Woman Passenger Killed, Kennedy Escapes in Crash

Senator Tells the Police He Wandered About in Shock After Car Ran Off Bridge Near Martha's Vineyard

EDGARTOWN, Mass., July 19 —A 28-year-old woman passenger drowned today when a car driven by Senator Edward M. Kennedy plunged 10 feet off a bridge into a pond on Chappaquiddick Island near this community on Martha's Vineyard.

Senator Kennedy was at first believed to have escaped injury, but tonight a family physician, Dr. Robert D. Watt, said in Hyannis Port, Mass., that the Senator had "a slight concussion in the back of the head." He said the Senator had been given a sedative.

The woman was Mary Jo Kopechne of Berkeley Heights, N. J., a former secretary to the Massachusetts Democrat's brother, the late Senator Robert F. Kennedy.

The police here said that Edward Kennedy had told them he wandered around in apparent shock after the accident and did not report it to them for about eight hours.

"I remember walking around for a period of time and then going back to my hotel room,"

Senator Kennedy was quoted by the police as saying. "When I fully realized what had happened this morning, I immediately contacted the police."

In a telephone interview tonight, Police Chief Dominick J. Arena said there was "apparently no criminal negligence involved in the accident itself."

But the Edgartown police said late tonight that a formal charge of leaving the scene of an accident, a misdemeanor, would be filed against Senator Kennedy Monday morning in the Dukes County Courthouse in Edgartown.

The incident was another in a series of violent events that have hounded the Kennedy family ever since it came to prominence in American political life.

Senator Kennedy had come to Martha's Vineyard to join several friends and staff members at the weekend boat races.

The statement by Dr. Watt in Hyannis Port, where the Kennedys have their summer home, said:

"He has a slight concussion in the back of the head. I gave him a sedative for the pain. He has retired and is resting comfortably. I'll see him tomorrow."

According to Kennedy staff members, there was a party on Chappaquiddick Island for David Hackett, a friend of Robert Kennedy.

One spokesman for the Senator said tonight that Miss Kopechne was one of a number of women who had been invited to Martha's Vineyard for a

weekend regatta and "reunion of former campaign workers."

Senator Kennedy went to the party late last night, according to his statement to the police, and then left, driving Miss Kopechne to the ferry to Edgartown.

"On July 18,, at approximately 11:15 P.M." the police quoted Senator Kennedy as saying, "I went over to Chappaquiddick. Later, I was driving my car on Main Street, Chappaquiddick, to get the ferry back to Edgartown. I was unfamiliar with the road and turned right onto Dyke Road instead of bearing hard left on Main Street.

Car Turns Over and Sinks

"After proceeding for approximately half a mile on Dyke Road, I descended a hill and came upon a narrow bridge. The car went off the side of the bridge. There was one passenger with me, one Miss Mary (the Senator did not give the name at this point), a former secretary of my brother, Senator Robert Kennedy.

"The car turned over and sank into the water, and landed with roof resting on the bottom. I attempted to open the door and the window of the car, but had no recollection of how I got out of the car.

"I came to the surface and repeatedly dove down to the car in an attempt to see if the passenger was still in the car. I was unsuccessful in the attempt.

Police Are Notified

"I was exhausted and in a state of shock. I recall walking back to where my friends were eating. There was a car parked in front of the cottage and I climbed into the back seat. I then asked someone to bring me back to Edgartown."

The Senator's statement did not relate how or precisely when he returned to Edgartown, where he was staying at the Shiertown Inn. There are no ferries from Chappaquiddick Island to Martha's Vineyard, a few hundred yards across a channel, from midnight to 7:30 A.M.

The police in Edgartown said that Senator Kennedy appeared at the police station to report the accident about 9 A.M.

According to A. M. Silva, the Edgartown fire chief, the accident apparently occurred about 12:50 A.M. It was first reported to the police shortly after 8 A.M. by the mother of a boy who sighted the overturned car in the pond when he went fishing.

It is understood that the Kennedy party gathered last night at a house rented for eight days on Chappaquiddick by Joseph F. Gargan, a cousin of the Senator.

The house is known as the

Fatal accident involving **Kennedy** car occurred at cross

THE KENNEDYS: A NEW YORK TIMES PROFILE

Sidney K. Lawrence Cottage. It is set on 10 acres of oak woodland in the center of the island, bordering on the Chappaquiddick Highway. The house is small, with two bedrooms and a bath.

Flies to Hyannis

Word of the accident was telephoned to Chief Arena by Mrs. Pierre Malm, who has a summer home near the scene of the crash, about a mile and a half from where the party was held.

Mrs. Malm's son sighted the overturned car, with one wheel out of the water, when he left his home to go fishing.

At about the time Chief Arena was going to the scene of the accident, Senator Kennedy was heading for the police station to report it.

He left the station several hours later, refusing to talk to reporters, and flew to the Kennedy family home in Hyannis, Mass., on the mainland.

Chief Arena said that when Mrs. Malm's call reached him, he went to the scene of the accident "and saw a car in the water upside down."

Scuba Divers Called

"You could just about see one of the tires," he said.

"I borrowed a bathing suit and dove in," the chief continued. "I couldn't see much, because of the strong current. The top of the car was crushed. I couldn't get in, so I sent for a scuba diver."

Scuba divers from the Edgartown Fire Department reached the Kennedy car about 8:25 A.M. and removed the body of Miss Kopechne.

Dr. Donald Mills of Edgartown, the medical examiner, said that Miss Kopechne, a thin freckled blonde about 5 feet 4 inches tall, had died of accidental drowning.

Dr. Mills said he was summoned to the scene of the accident at about 9:30 A.M. and pronounced Miss Kopechne dead. He estimated that she had been dead "six hours or more."

The woman, according to Dr. Mills, was clad in a white blouse and slacks at the time of her death.

John Farrar, one of the divers, said it took 25 minutes to extricate the body from the car, which was submerged in about eight feet of water beneath the bridge.

Mr. Farrar said that the body of Miss Kopechne was found in the car's back with her face upward, toward the floor of the overturned vehicle.

Rescue workers from the Edgartown police and fire departments used chains, cables and power winches to haul the car from the pond.

Workers removed the auto from the water at about 10 A. M. and it was taken to an Edgartown garage, where the registration plates were removed.

Police Chief Arena said a purse belonging to Rosemary Keogh, Senator Kennedy's staff secretary, was found in the car, leading the authorities at first to believe that she was the woman found there.

The police said the window on the driver's side of the car was open, the windshield was smashed, both doors on the right side were severely dented, but the front and rear of the car were intact.

The bridge from which Senator Kennedy's black four-door Oldsmobile sedan plunged is a small wooden structure 10 feet 6 inches wide and 30 feet long. The bridge is known by residents of Edgartown and Chappaquiddick Island residents as the Dyke.

It is between Pocha and Cape Pogue Ponds on Chappaquiddick Island and replaced a dirt dike that once separated incoming ocean tides from the fresh water of the ponds.

The approach to the humpbacked bridge is unmarked and the bridge itself, which is approached by a dirt road, is difficult to see at night.

The dirt road approaching the bridge is narrow, with the entry to the bridge angling off to the left. There is no warning sign on the approach. The Kennedy auto went over the right side of the bridge into the water.

Police Chief Arena said he was convinced that "the accident is strictly accidental."

"As far as the circumstances surrounding it," he said, "there doesn't appear from the principal evidence to be any excessive speed there."

Miss Kopechne was registered at an Edgartown motel, the Dunes, a former naval station on Martha's Vineyard. There were reportedly five other women in her party, including Esther Newberg of Arlington, Va., and Rosemary Keogh of Washington.

An employe of the Dunes said the reservations had been made by John D. Crimmons of South Boston.

Mr. Crimmons is a longtime political aide of the Kennedys.

Chappaquiddick is a five-mile-long island off the eastern tip of Martha's Vineyard, separated from that larger island by a narrow channel.

Mr. Kennedy's wife was reported to be at their summer home in Hyannis Port today.

Senator Kennedy, who is 38 years old, was elected to the United States Senate in 1962 and is currently the majority whip. He is regarded as a possible contender for the Democratic Presidential nomination in 1972.

The Senator narrowly escaped death on June 19, 1964, when he was in a plane crash. He suffered serious back injuries in that accident.

Senator Kennedy's eldest brother, Joseph, was killed on Aug. 12, 1944, while he was a Navy pilot on combat duty in Europe. The Senator's brother, President John F. Kennedy, was assassinated on Nov. 22, 1963, and his brother, Robert, died on June 6, 1968, the day after he was shot by an assassin in Los Angeles. Senator Kennedy's sister, Kathleen, died in a plane crash in 1948 in France.

July 20, 1969

Mary Jo Kopechne in a picture taken in 1962 for the Caldwell College yearbook.

3 Kennedys Attend Funeral for Drowned Secretary

By NAN ROBERTSON

PLYMOUTH, Pa., July 22—Mary Jo Kopechne, whose life and death were intertwined with the Kennedy family, was buried here today on a high green hillside above the slag heaps of this mined-out anthracite town. She would have been been 29 years old next Saturday.

Senator Edward M. Kennedy, his wife Joan and Ethel Kennedy, widow of his assassinated brother Robert, flew from Hyannis Port, Mass., to the funeral of Miss Kopechne, who drowned when a car driven by the Senator plunged off a bridge on Martha's Vineyard Island during the weekend.

She had been a secretary and campaign worker for Senator Robert Kennedy and a friend of the family for years.

Today, Edward Kennedy was wearing a neck brace, presumably as a result of the accident. He looked grim and distracted throughout the requiem mass, as he was engulfed by a curious and excited crowd on the street outside and during the brief service at the grave.

His wife and sister-in-law appeared stunned. Mrs. Joseph Kopechne, the mother, seemed crushed with grief. She wept bitterly during the service for her only child in the Roman Catholic Church of St. Vincent, with its elaborate carvings and paintings, a block from Plymouth's main street.

Her husband helped her to her feet for the responses, clasped her tightly about the waist, murmured to her and once laid his head against hers. They were alone in a pew across the aisle from the Kennedys, and looked neither at them nor at anyone else as the mass was said.

The two families had consoled each other earlier in the front parlor of the adjoining rectory, according to two priests who were there.

A large entourage of friends and associates of both the Kennedys and Miss Kopechne converged here today. They included seven of the 12 persons who, according to Senator Kennedy's aides, were at the cookout party preceding Miss Kopechne's death.

They were Nance Lyons, a legislative aide to Senator Kennedy; her sister, Maryellen, an assistant to State Senator Beryl Cohen of Massachusetts; Rosemary Keough, who works for the Children's Foundation in Washington; Susan Tannenbaum, from the office of Representative Allard K. Lowenstein, Nassau County Democrat; Esther Newburg, of the Urban Institute in Washington;

Joseph Gargan, a cousin of Senator Kennedy, and the Senator himself.

The young women kept to themselves, speaking only with the Kopechne family or Kennedy associates. They frequently burst into tears, both at the church and earlier at the funeral home of John J. Kielty, where they viewed the body of their friend. She lay in an open coffin, clad in a pale blue gown and clasping a crystal rosary.

Aides of Senator Kennedy spoke freely to reporters about the Senator's movements today and also of what they called "repeated" offers by the Kennedys to pay for Miss Kopechne's funeral, which her parents have refused.

They would say nothing about what happened in the nine hours between the accident off Martha's Vineyard and Mr. Kennedy's appearance on Saturday morning at the police station to report it.

Except for those who knew the dead woman, the scene today in Plymouth was not one of sorrow but of curiosity. Her parents moved from Plymouth when Miss Kopechne was only a year old. and live now in Berkeley Heights, N. J., where her father is an insurance man. But the family burial plot is still in the hilltop cemetery of St. Vincent's Church.

This morning, a crowd of 700 people waited outside the funeral home and the church or craned from front porches of little frame houses along the streets. Msgr. William E. Burchill, St. Vincent's pastor, waited nervously at the rectory door with his assistant, the Rev. Charles Smith.

At 9 A.M. the Kennedy plane, a DC-3 belonging to Mrs. Robert Kennedy's family, landed at the Wilkes-Barre-Scranton Airport nearby. Shortly thereafter the Kennedy cars rolled down Church Street to the rectory.

The meeting inside was brief. Present were the two priests, who withdrew after the introductions; the three members of the Kennedy family; the Kopechnes; William J. Vanden Heuvel, a Kennedy friend who is a New York lawyer, and David Burke, the Senator's administrative assistant.

The hushed church across the grassy yard was full, with people stand along the sides and back and in the balcony. Almost all in the congregation were women, with many teenagers.

The funeral party entered by a side door at the front of the high-ceilinged edifice. When the Kennedys appeared, a loud buzz and murmur swept across the congregation. Senator Kennedy, in a dark suit and black tie knotted loosely beneath his neck brace, cast his eyes on the floor.

So did his wife, who was

dressed in white, with a black bow at the back of her blonde curls. Mrs. Robert Kennedy was all in black, with a short lace mantilla over her hair.

With K. LeMoyne Billings, a friend from New York, they moved to the fourth pew behind three empty rows. The two robed priests with their acolytes moved down the center aisle to meet the coffin at the church door.

Eight pallbearers carried the heavy metal coffin, and Monsignor Burchill began the words of "De Profundis":

"Out of the depths I cry to you, O Lord . . . My soul waits for the Lord."

Six of the pallbearers were cousins of Miss Kopechne. The two others were K. Dun Gifford, Senator Kennedy's legislative assistant, and David Hackett, who helped keep the delegate count in a Washington office during Senator Robert Kennedy's Presidential campaign last year. Miss Kopechne and seven other young women worked there.

Today, all but one of these seven women were in the church.

When the coffin was set down between the Kennedy and Kopechne families, Monsignor Burchill began the requiem mass.

Near the end, he said: "Do not hand her over to the powers of the enemy and do not forget her, but command that this soul be taken up by the holy angels and brought home to paradise." Mrs. Kopechne buried her face in her hands.

The ranks of friends in the pews behind the Kennedy family across the aisle contained many who became noted through their association with Robert Kennedy.

They included Frank Mankiewicz, Mr. Kennedy's press secretary and now a columnist, who announced the Senator's death a year ago; Peter Edelman, associate director of the Robert F. Kennedy Memorial, and Adam Walinsky, an adviser.

As the funeral party emerged from the church for the procession to the cemetery, shouts of "There he is!" burst from the camera-clicking crowd. They surged around Mr. Kennedy and the others, pushing for position close by. The Senator and all with him showed deep distress; many of Miss Kopechne's women friends were sobbing as they struggled to reach their cars.

After about 10 minutes, the motorcade was able to move up a long, winding road to the gravesite. the narrow route was jammed with hundreds of cars, their occupants perspiring in the mugginess of the gray day.

The Kopechne family was seated in rows of chairs under

an open-sided tent for the brief ceremony. Senator Kennedy, flanked by his wife and sister-in-law, stood at the back, his head tilted, staring abstractedly until it was over.

The Kennedy party, after accompanying the Kopechne family to a brief gathering at the nearby Kingston House Inn, flew back to the family compound at Hyannis Port on Cape Cod.

July 23, 1969

HYANNIS PORT, Mass., July 25—Edward M. Kennedy described tonight as "indefensible" his failure to report immediately a fatal automobile accident last week and said he was considering whether to resign his Senate seat.

He invited his constituents from Massachusetts "to think this through with me" and help him arrive at the right decision.

Senator Kennedy went on national television to present his account of the accident, in which a young Washington secretary, Mary Jo Kopechne, drowned when his car went off a bridge and overturned in a pond. The Senator spoke 10 hours after he pleaded guilty in a court on Martha's Vineyard to a charge of leaving the scene of the accident.

Sentence Is Suspended

His plea resulted in a suspended sentence of two months in jail, the minimum sentence provided in the law. The presiding judge said of Mr. Kennedy:

"He has already been and will continue to be punished far beyond anything this court can impose."

Mr. Kennedy, who until last week was considered one of the Democratic party's likeliest candidates for the Presidency in 1972, addressed himself early in his television statement to what he called "ugly speculation" linking him romantically with the 28-year-old Miss Kopechne.

"There has never been a private relationship between us of any kind," he declared.

He also denied that he was driving "under the influence of liquor" at the time of the accident.

When his car plunged off the wood bridge on Chappaquiddick Island, the Senator said, water entered his lungs and he "actually felt the sensation of drowning."

Returned to Scene

Later, he went on, he returned to the bridge with two companions, Joseph F. Gargan, a cousin, and Paul Markham, a former United States attorney, and attempted for a second time to dive for Miss Kopechne's body.

His account of a return to the scene after midnight could help resolve a discrepancy over the time of the accident between Mr. Kennedy's original statement and the testimony of a witness.

The witness, Christopher Look Jr., a Dukes County deputy sheriff, thought he saw a car carrying three persons turn down the dirt road to the bridge about 12:40 A.M. Saturday. Mr. Kennedy's original statement, made to the police when he first reported the fatality about 9 A.M. Saturday placed the time of the accident at about 11:15 P.M. Friday.

Conduct Makes 'No Sense'

In his televised statement tonight, Mr. Kennedy said, "My conduct and conversation during the next several hours make no sense to me at all."

He added, "I regard as indefensible the fact that I did not report the accident to the police immediately."

Speaking slowly, the Senator recounted some of the irrational thoughts that he said raced through his mind after the accident. He said he wondered whether "some awful curse" really did hang over the Kennedys, or whether Miss Kopechne might still be alive.

He was, he said, "overcome by a jumble of emotions."

Mr. Kennedy said he had returned to his hotel in Edgartown by swimming the narrow channel that separates Martha's Vineyard from Chappaquiddick Island — a distance of about 150 yards. Earlier it was assumed that he had made the crossing in a private boat.

The 37-year-old Senator said that the accident, the speculation about it and his plea of guilty this morning all could shake the confidence of the people of Massachusetts in his ability to serve them.

He said that they were entitled to a Senator "who inspires their utmost confidence" and that he could understand why some people might feel he should resign.

The Senator, first elected to fill an unexpired term in 1962, would come up for re-election in 1970.

"If at any time," Mr. Kennedy said, the citizens of Massachusetts should lack confidence in their Senator's character or his ability, with or without justification, he could not in my opinion adequately perform his duty and should not continue in office.

Then, in a gesture that will inevitably be compared to that of Richard Nixon's so-called "Checkers speech" in the 1952 campaign, he asked the people to send him their advice.

Mr. Nixon's speech, defending his use of funds raised privately to support his activities, ended with a plea that the voters assure the Republican party of their confidence in him.

At Home of Father

Mr. Kennedy spoke tonight from the residence here of his father, Joseph P. Kennedy, in the compound of Kennedy homes. He did not wear the neck brace he wore Tuesday at the funeral of Miss Kopechne in Plymouth, Pa.

The Senator is the youngest of four Kennedy sons and the only one still living. He said last year that he was picking up the "fallen standard" of his dead brothers—Joseph P. Kennedy Jr., President John F. Kennedy and Senator Robert F. Kennedy.

In heavy fog and rain, Senator Kennedy left Hyannis Port for Martha's Vineyard, and his appearance in court, about 7:30 o'clock this morning aboard a family yacht, the Marlin. He was accompanied on the short trip across a choppy Nantucket Sound by his wife, Joan, and his brother-in-law, Stephen E. Smith.

The yacht docked at the town of Oak Bluffs, where a detachment of state policemen was waiting to accompany the party to the Dukes County Courthouse in Edgartown.

It was 8:35 when the Senator, in a dark blue suit but coatless and hatless in the rain, walked up the courthouse steps with Mrs. Kennedy beside him. She wore a short coatdress in a black-and-white plaid with a matching hairband. The couple looked somber but composed.

The Senator was ushered into the probation office and filled out an identity card for the court, a routine procedure for a defendant.

Moments before the bells in a church across the street chimed 9 o'clock, Mr. Kennedy strode stiffly into the peach colored courtroom beneath portraits of various county clerks and probate judges. He was preceded by his local lawyer, Richard J. McCarron.

Kennedy Sits Alone

The Senator was seated alone in a row of chairs behind the bar. He clasped his hands together and rested his chin upon his fingers and stared at the floor.

The gavel was pounded and the court officer intoned, "The District Court of Dukes County is now in session. God save the Commonwealth of Massachusetts!"

The state's senior Senator stood at rigid attention as District Court Judge James A. Boyle settled himself behind his heavy oak bench. Then the clerk announced the case of the Commonwealth v. Edward M. Kennedy.

The clerk, Thomas A. Taller, asked the Senator to make his plea on the charge of leaving the scene of an accident involving personal injury.

Mr. Kennedy rose, softly uttered the word "Guilty," then swallowed and said it again so the whole courtroom could hear it.

It was the only word he was to say in court.

Calls Statement Improper

The county prosecutor, a lean, seemingly nervous lawyer named Walter Steele who has been on a first-name basis with Mr. Kennedy since they served together as assistant district attorneys in Suffolk County in 1961, then called his first witness, Edgartown's police chief, Dominick J. Arena.

The chief summarized the case from a prepared statement. He noted that Mr. Kennedy had taken more than 10 hours, by his own account, to report the accident in which Miss Kopechne drowned.

"There appears that there were opportunities for the defendant to make himself known to the proper authorities after the accident," he said.

Senator Kennedy sat with bent head and eyes that appeared shut as Chief Arena read his statement. The Senator's wife, seated across the courtroom from him, stared straight ahead, her face expressionless.

Chief Arena said he had found no evidence of negligence in the operation of the car.

"I'd be most interested to know," Judge Boyle asked when the officer was through, "whether at any time a deliberate effort was made to conceal the identity of the defendant."

"Not to my knowledge, your nonor," the burly chief replied.

The judge sat back and Mr. McCarron rose. He started to say that Mr. Kennedy's attorneys had advised him that "legal defenses could be presented in this case."

"Just a minute," Judge Boyle said, leaning forward again. "I don't think that's a proper statement to make."

He asked the lawyer if he meant to change his client's plea. The lawyer said he did not.

"On a plea of guilty — that's a confession — I don't think you should argue there are legal defenses," the judge declared.

Mr. McCarron then said that the Senator had been "adamant" in his wish to plead guilty. He did not explain why.

Because of the guilty plea, Mr. Kennedy was not required to undergo cross-examination on his actions before and after he drove his black 1967 Oldsmobile off the narrow wooden bridge on Chappaquiddick Island late Friday night or early Saturday.

Asks Minimum Sentence

Mr. Kennedy's lawyer concluded his brief statement by arguing against a sentence in jail for his client, whose character, he said, "is well-known to this court and the world."

Next, Mr. Steele wound up the state's case by asking that "this defendant be incarcerated in the house of correction for two months and that execution of the sentence be suspended."

The word "incarceration" seemed to echo through the courtroom, but the prosecutor was merely requesting the minimum sentence allowed by law.

"The ends of justice will best be served," he declared, "by a suspended sentence."

The judge, alluding to the lasting damage that may have been done to Senator Kennedy's reputation and career, agreed.

The clerk then read out the sentence and the court rose.

The whole proceeding had taken a little more than nine minutes.

Senator Kennedy joined his wife and brother-in-law and they were led down a back staircase, then out to the steps of the building, where photographers and television crews came jostling and surging forward.

Mr. Kennedy paused at the head of the steps and announced, in a voice that could hardly be heard over the din of the newsmen, that he had asked the television networks for time in the evening "to make my statement to the people of Massachusetts and the nation."

A moment later the state police cleared a path to the unmarked car in which the Kennedy party had arrived, and the party drove off for the airport and a quick flight back to Hyannis Port.

As the car disappeared down Main Street, the newsmen besieged Chief Arena, who said he regarded his investigation of the case as closed.

Earlier, the Dukes County medical examiner, who examined Miss Kopechne's body when it was removed from the submerged car Saturday morning, issued a statement say he did not have "the slightest inkling" that Senator Kennedy was involved in the accident when he decided at the accident scene that no autopsy would be required.

Had he known the Senator had been the driver of the car, Dr. Donald R. Mills said, he might have ordered an inquest —but only, he said, "to protect his public image against speculation."

July 26, 1969

Mother of the Victim Opposes an Autopsy And Backs Senator

BERKELEY HEIGHTS, N. J., July 25 (UPI)—Mrs. Josephine Kopechne, whose daughter Mary Jo drowned in Senator Edward M. Kennedy's car, said tonight that in the light of his statement, she no longer felt it was necessary to have an autopsy performed on the young woman.

Mrs. Kopechne had said earlier in the day she would authorize such an autopsy if that was the only way to stop the "snide remarks" and "vicious mail" she had been receiving.

About a half-hour after Senator Kennerdy spoke about the case on television and denied having had any immoral relationship with the young woman, Mrs. Kopechne appeared outside the home of a neighbor, where she had spent most of the day, and in a halting voice read a short statement.

"I am satisfied with the Senator's statement and do hope he decides to stay on as Senator," she said.

Mrs. Kopechne refused to answer any questions, but in a telephone interview the neighbors with whom she is staying said she felt the autopsy was "no longer necessary."

Earlier in the day, Mrs. Kopechne said her only interest in the case was the light in which her daughter's "character and background" emerged.

July 26, 1969

Kennedy to Stay in Senate; Implies No '72 Candidacy

By ROY REED

WASHINGTON, July 30 — Senator Edward M. Kennedy will stay in the Senate and keep his post as Democratic whip, or assistant majority leader, but he apparently has taken himself out of the Presidential race in 1972.

A statement made public today by his Boston office said:

"Senator Edward M. Kennedy is returning to Washington to resume his duties as United States Senator and assistant majority leader.

"He is grateful to the people of Massachusetts for their expressions of confidence and expects to submit his record to them as a candidate for re-election in 1970. If re-elected, he will serve out his entire six-year term."

Although that apparently means a decision against seeking the Presidency in 1972,

Mr. Kennedy's aides declined to discuss the matter further.

Richard Drayne, his press aide here, said, "I don't interpret the Senator's statements."

Asked if the statement meant what it seemed to mean, he added, "It seems unambiguous to me."

July 31, 1969

Mrs. Kopechne Is 'Confused' by Daughter's Death

Poses 'Heavy Questions' on Acts of Kennedy Friends at Scene of Drowning

The mother of Mary Jo Kopechne said yesterday that she still had "heavy questions" about the death of her daughter last month in a car driven by Senator Edward M. Kennedy.

"It's confusing," Mrs. Gwendolyn Kopechne said in a telephone interview from her home in Berkeley Heights, N. J. "Reading all the different versions of what happened, it really gets you all confused."

In the telephone conversation, Mrs. Kopechne amplified on an interview that appeared in yesterday's editions of The New York Post.

Mrs. Kopechne said she was particularly puzzled about the inactivity of Paul F. Markham and Joseph F. Gargan, two Kennedy associates, after they returned to the scene of the accident on Chappaquiddick Island, Mass., with the Senator.

Senator's Account

The Senator was driving with Miss Kopechne, a 28-year-old Washington secretary, on the island off Martha's Vineyard on the night of July 18 after a party. Mr. Kennedy's car ran off a narrow wooden bridge on the island and plunged into a tidal pond. Miss Kopechne was found drowned in the car the next morning.

The Senator's account said that he "somehow struggled" out of the submerged car. He said he dove repeatedly in an effort to save Miss Kopechne but had to stop in "utter exhaustion." Then, according to his account, he made his way back to the cottage to get Mr. Gargan, a cousin, and Mr. Markham, a lawyer and family associate.

The Senator said that Mr. Gargan and Mr. Markham re-

turned to the pond and tried to find the car by diving. They were unsuccessful. Not until nine hours later did Senator Kennedy, Mr. Markham or Mr. Gargan tell the police about the accident or attempt to summon aid.

Can't Understand Shock

"There is no sense in denying it," Mrs. Kopechne said. "I wonder what those men were doing."

"Why wasn't help called for my daughter by Gargan and Markham? I can understand shock but I don't see where they went into shock. Gargan and Markham are my puzzle. I mean they're human."

Mrs. Kopechne said she was also puzzled about a possible conflict in the time of the accident. Senator Kennedy said he and Miss Kopechne left the party at 11:15 P.M. and had driven only a mile when the accident occurred. But Christopher Look Jr., a deputy sheriff, said he saw a car closely resembling the Senator's near the scene of the accident at 12:45 A.M.

"There are so many questions about the time," Mrs. Kopechne said.

"I would love to sit down and listen to the whole story," she added. "I'd like to hear it all, everything, good or bad, about how it happened. I'd love to hear all of them [Senator Kennedy and the others involved], all of it pieced together."

Senator Kennedy's press spokesman was unavailable for comment on Mrs. Kopechne's remarks.

Mrs. Kopechne and her husband, Joseph, have steadfastly

resisted an effort by Edmund Dinis, the district attorney for Southeastern Massachusetts, to have their only child's body exhumed for an autopsy. Their daughter is buried in Larksville, Pa., near where she was born.

Mr. Dinis is scheduled to make his formal petition for the exhumation at a hearing in Wilkes-Barre on Aug. 25. The Kopechnes have retained a lawyer to fight the petition. Mrs. Kopechne said yesterday that she and her husband would go to the hearing.

Told There Was No Mark

She said that at the funeral home before her daughter's burial an attendant had told her that there was no mark on the body.

She said that Mr. Kopechne, an insurance salesman, was talking about going to an inquest into the accident beginning before Judge James A. Boyle of Edgartown, Mass., District Court on Sept. 3. "If he goes, I will go with him," she said.

Mrs. Kopechne said she had no hard feelings against the Senator. She said she had not been in communication recently with anyone in the Kennedy family or on the Kennedy staff.

In The New York Post interview, she said:

"I have no hate. Mr. Kopechne and I can form no hate for anyone. There's always something good in a person, no matter what his faults. We look for the good in a person and overlook hate.

"Nothing can help us with our daughter now. Why hate? No one can bring her back or console us."

August 17, 1969

HYANNIS, Mass., Aug. 28 (AP) — Mrs. Edward M. Kennedy, wife of the Massachusetts Democratic Senator, suffered a miscarriage tonight at Cape Cod Hospital, the hospital authorities reported.

She was taken to the hospital shortly before 8 P.M. by her sisters - in - law, Mrs. Stephen Smith and Mrs. Robert F. Kennedy.

Dr. Leonard Smith said that Mrs. Edward Kennedy was resting comfortably. She had been expecting a child in February.

The Kennedys have three children—Kara Anne, 9 years old; Edward M. Jr., 8, and Patrick Joseph, 2. Mrs. Kennedy, 32, had had two previous miscarriages.

Senator Kennedy, who was on an overnight camping trip to Nantucket Island off the Massachusetts coast, flew to Hyannis when notified of the miscarriage.

He was accompanied Representative John C. Culver, Democrat of Iowa, a classmate of

his at Harvard.

A family friend said that Mrs. Kennedy had planned to go on the camping trip but that she didn't feel well when the party left this afternoon.

Others in the overnight camping party, the family friend said, included Mr. Kennedy's cousin, Joseph Gargan, Mrs. John Culver, two of his children, and John F. Kennedy Jr., son of the late President.

August 29, 1969

Third Miscarriage Is Suffered by Wife Of Edward Kennedy

Photographer Says Mrs. Onassis Used Judo on Him

A newspaper photographer said that Mrs. Aristotle Onassis threw him to the sidewalk with a judo flip yesterday after he had taken pictures of her at a movie theater where she had been watching "I am Curious (Yellow)".

The photographer, Mel Finkelstein of The Daily News, said he thought what he called the "Jackie Onassis judo demonstration" resulted from her having "hit the panic button" and "overreacted to the presence of the news media" outside the Cinema 57 Rendezvous, 57th Street between the Avenue of the Americas and Seventh Avenue.

Mr. Finkelstein said that Mrs. Onassis first went up to another News photographer, Anthony Casale, outside the theatre and "grabbed him by the arm." He added, "Tony's pretty big . . ."

Mrs. Onassis then said, "Now wait," and walked over to him, Mr. Finkelstein said.

"I thought she was going to say something," said Mr. Finkelstein, who said he had stayed "a discreet distance... 15 feet" from Mrs. Onassis as he took photographs. Instead, he said, Mrs. Onassis "grabbed my right wrist" with her right hand, grasped his elbow with her other hand, "put her leg out and flipped me over her thigh."

Mrs. Onassis and her husband of slightly less than a year, Aristotle Onassis, had arrived at the theater about 4:15 P.M. Mrs. Onassis, according to the manager, left her seat about halfway through the erotic Swedish film and, on discovering photographers in the lobby, asked if they could be made to leave. They left, Mr. Finkelstein said, and Mrs. Onassis followed them out.

Mr. Finkelstein said he was both shocked and amazed at the incident—shocked that Mrs. Onassis had done such a thing and amazed that she was able to do it. The photographer is 5 feet 10 inches tall and weighs 168 pounds; Mrs. Onassis, 40 years old is two inches shorter.

He said he would not press charges. "This is Jackie Kennedy..." he said.

He said he thought Mrs. Onassis would expect photographers to be waiting outside the Metropolitan Opera if she were there "but not where 'I Am Curious (Yellow)' is playing."

The theater doorman, Bernardo Rojas, disputed Mr. Finkelstein's account, saying that the photographer slipped while trying to take Mrs. Onassis' picture.

Mrs. Onassis, who could not be reached for comment, did not return to the theater, where her husband remained until the film's conclusion at 6 P.M., the manager said.

October 6, 1969

Did Mrs. Onassis Apply Judo? A Witness and a Friend Say No

The story that Mrs. Aristotle Onassis threw a newspaper photographer to the ground with a judo flip here Sunday was denied yesterday by a witness and by a friend of the former First Lady.

Peter Tufo, an assistant to Mayor Lindsay and head of the city's office in Washington, said he was walking with his wife on 57th Street at the time of the incident involving three photographers and Mrs. Onassis, the widow of President John F. Kennedy.

Mr. Tufo said that Mel Finkelstein of The Daily News fell to the ground apparently after being jostled by one of the other photographers or because he slipped.

"Mrs. Onassis didn't touch him with her hands," he added. "She didn't make a move toward him.

"I saw the whole thing. There were three men with cameras and Mrs. Onassis walking very briskly down the street. She was trying to get away. Two of them were jostling, trying to get in front of her. One appeared to push the other, and he fell in front of her. He was laughing and brushed himself off."

Forceful Flip Charged

The incident took place near the Cinema 57 Rendezvous, on 57th Street between the Avenue of the Americas and Seventh Avenue, after Mrs. Onassis emerged from the movie "I Am Curious (Yellow)."

Mr. Finkelstein said that he had been at a "discreet distance," taking pictures of her, but that she came over to him, "grabbed" his right wrist with her hand, his elbow with the other hand, "put her leg out and flipped me over her thigh."

Mr. Tufo summed up his version of the scene: "As a former Marine [1963], I know a judo toss when I see one. She didn't use any judo."

Last night Mr. Finkelstein asserted: "I stick exacly with what I said."

Earlier in the day Mrs. Onassis' former secretary, Nancy Tuckerman denied that the former First Lady had knocked down Mr. Finkelstein. "I congratulated her this morning." Miss Tuckerman said, "told her I thought it was a neat trick, but she said she hadn't done it.

"The story, as told by Mr. Finkelstein is completely untrue," Miss Tuckerman said.

The theater doorman, Bernardo Rojas, also said that the photographer had slipped and fallen, that Mrs. Onassis had not pushed him.

A picture of the aftermath of the incident, showing Mr. Finkelstein on the pavement, was taken by the other photographers there, including John Lent of The Associated Press.

Mr. Lent said that he had seen no evidence of any scuffle between Mrs. Onassis and Mr. Finkelstein. "I can't say I saw her touch him," he said, adding that he was busy at the moment trying to take a picture. Mr. Tufo and his wife could be seen in the background of Mr. Lent's picture.

October 7, 1969

Joseph P. Kennedy Dies at Home at 81

HYANNIS PORT, Mass., Nov. 18 — Joseph P. Kennedy, the patriarch of a political dynasty beset by tragedy, died peacefully today at his summer home at the age of 81.

A family spokesman said that death came at 11:05 A.M. in a second-floor bedroom overlooking Nantucket Sound. Mr. Kennedy had been unconscious since last Saturday when he suffered another in a series of heart attacks.

At his bedside were his wife of 55 years, Mrs. Rose Kennedy, and the last of his four sons, Senator Edward M. Kennedy of Massachusetts.

Also in the room were the widows of two other sons, Mrs. Aristotle Onassis, who was married to President John F. Kennedy, and Mrs. Ethel Kennedy, who was married to Senator Robert F. Kennedy of New York.

President Kennedy was assassinated in 1963 and Robert Kennedy in 1968.

Others present were Mrs. Eunice Kennedy Shriver and her husband, R. Sargent Shriver, Ambassador to France; Mrs. Joan Kennedy, wife of Edward Kennedy; Mrs. Jean Kennedy Smith, and her husband, Stephen Smith, and Mrs. Patricia Kennedy Lawford.

Mr. Kennedy had been in ill health since 1961 when he suffered a stroke in Palm Beach, Fla. His constant companion since then, Ann Gargan, a niece, was also at the bedside.

President Nixon led the nation in expressing sorrow. In a statement, the President said:

"Joseph P. Kennedy leaves a long and distinguished record of service to his country, a genuinely unique record that involved his entire family in the making of American history. He enjoyed with grace the triumphs of his life and he endured its tragedies with great dignity."

Richard Cardinal Cushing, a long-time friend and spiritual adviser to the Kennedys, said:

"His exceptional abilities were generously placed for many years in the service of his country. He instilled a sense of purpose in his family so that all its members extended their increasing maturity into careers of unparalleled public service and achievement. We can truly say of Joseph P. Kennedy that he was a father of the family in our time."

Messages of condolence also were sent by Secretary General Thant of the United Nations and President Eamon DeValera and Prime Minister Jack Lynch of Ireland, homeland of Mr. Kennedy's grandfather.

Funeral services will be simple for the man who served as United States Ambassador to London just before World War II.

A white funeral mass will be celebrated at 9 A.M. Thursday at St. Francis Xavier's Roman Catholic Church in Hyannis, where the family has worshiped, especially during summers, for many years. The mass is called white because the clergy will wear white instead of purple vestments, in accordance with post-Vatican II precepts of accenting the message of resurrection after death rather than mourning.

Cardinal Cushing is expected to preside at the mass. Only the family and a few close friends will attend the service in the church, a white clapboard structure that bears a memorial to Joseph P. Kennedy Jr., a Navy flier who died in action over the English Channel in World War II.

Burial will be in the family plot in Holyhood Cemetery in Brookline. Before the service, Mr. Kennedy's body will remain in his home in the family compound here. There will be no wake.

The official announcement said: "Ambassador Joseph P. Kennedy died peacefully today at his home in Hyannis Port. He was 81 years old. Mr. Kennedy was pronounced dead at 11:05 A.M. by his physician, Dr. Robert D. Watt. With him at the time of his death were his wife and members of his family."

Following his stroke eight years ago, Mr. Kennedy had suffered a brain spasm, several heart attacks and in 1967 a heart "block," for which he was given oxygen. Tonight at 6 o'clock, members of the family attended a special mass at St. Francis Xavier's Church. It was celebrated by the Rev. John J. Cavanaugh, former president of the University of Notre Dame and now chaplain at St. Mary's College in Indiana.

Six of the eldest male grandchildren will serve as honorary pallbearers at the funeral. They are Joseph P. Kennedy 3d; Christopher Lawford, Robert Shriver, Stephen Smith Jr., John F. Kennedy Jr. and Edward M. Kennedy Jr. There are 27 grandchildren in the family.

November 19, 1969

MAGAZINE CRITICIZED BY SENATOR KENNEDY

WASHINGTON, Dec. 8 (UPI) —Senator Edward M. Kennedy, Democrat of Massachusetts, has protested as "unnecessarily cruel" a news magazine's article on the death of his father, Joseph P. Kennedy.

In a letter published in the current edition of Newsweek, Senator Kennedy cited three examples of what he termed unjustified statements in the article.

The first was that the eldest Kennedy son, Joseph Jr., had been "reckless" in the World War II bombing mission that cost him his life.

The second was a statement that the elder Kennedy had been "ashamed" of the fact that a daughter, Rosemary, was mentally retarded.

In the third example, the Senator took issue with the article's implication that his father had "sired" his children and abandoned them "to be raised by my mother."

At another point, the Senator wrote: "I wish you could have devoted at least a line to the generosity, humor and heart my father had in such abundance, but nowhere were these qualities indicated. I could not recognize my father from your portrayal of him."

December 9, 1969

AUTOPSY DENIED IN KOPECHNE CASE

Need Unproved, Judge Rules in Kennedy Accident

By DONALD JANSON

WILKES-BARRE, Pa., Dec. 10 —Judge Bernard C. Brominski denied today a request by Massachusetts authorities for an autopsy on the body of Mary Jo Kopechne.

He said a two-day hearing in the Court of Common Pleas of Luzerne County seven weeks ago had produced no testimony sufficient to indicate that Miss Kopechne's death might have been caused by anything other than drowning.

The 28-year-old secretary, who once worked for the late Senator Robert F. Kennedy, died the night of July 18 when a car driven by Senator Edward M. Kennedy plunged off a bridge and into a tidal pond on Chappaquiddick Island, Mass.

Senator Kennedy reported the accident more than nine hours later, after it had been discovered. In an examination at the scene, Dr. Donald R. Mills, associate medical examiner for Dukes County, Mass., found tht death was due to drowning. Three days later Miss Kopechne was buried in Larksville, a suburb of Wilkes-Barre near her home town of Plymouth, Pa.

Her parents, Mr. and Mrs. Jospeh A. Kopechne, now of Berkeley Heights, N.J., today expressed satisfaction with Judge Brominski's ruling. They had fought the request for exhumation and an autopsy sought by Massachusetts authorities as part of an inquest into the accident.

"This means I will come here often to visit my daughter," Mrs. Kopechne said at a crowded news conference in the Luzerne County Courthouse. "I could never have gone to that cemetery if her grave had been disturbed."

Mr. Kopechne, an insurance salesman, said, "Now we are waiting patiently for the inquest."

It will be conducted before Judge James A. Boyle of the Dukes County District Court in Edgartown, Mass. Judge Boyle said on Nov. 6 that he would wait until Judge Brominski ruled on the autopsy request before setting a date for the inquest.

Joseph F. Flanagan, attorney

for the Kopechnes, said at the news conference that Judge Boyle had denied a request that a representative of the parents be permitted to attend the inquest. The Supreme Judicial Court of Massachusetts, granting a request by Senator Kennedy, has ordered that the inquest be closed to the press and public.

In a 14-page decision today Judge Brominski found that "from the testimony before this court every reasonable probability leads to a conclusion that supports the original finding of . . . death by drowning."

District Attorney Edmund S. Dinis of the Southern District of Massachusetts, said in seeking the autopsy that it was vital to a sound medical determination of the cause of death. He produced expert witnesses who concurred.

The Kopechnes, on the other hand, produced experts who said the time was past for an effective autopsy.

Judge Brominski said the presence of blood on the back of the victim's blouse was explained logically by Dr. Werner Spitz, deputy chief medical examiner for the State of Maryland, as a "froth" from the nose—common in drownings—that could have run down Miss Kopechne's face to the back of the neck and shoulders.

The judge noted that Dr. Mills had found the death "an obvious case of drowning" from water in the chest, with no evidence of foul play or any criminal conduct."

He added that Eugene Frieh, the mortician who prepared the body for burial, testified to finding no bruises or cuts except on a finger.

The judge said that even if an autopsy showed injuries, they could have been caused in the accident and would not necessarily change the finding of death by drowning.

"To consider any other cause of death at this time would give loose rein to speculation unsupported by any medical facts of record," he wrote.

He said in an interview that his words "any other cause" alluded

particularly to suggestions by Armand Fernandes Jr., assistant to Mr. Dinis, that Dr. Mills's external examination had not ruled out the possibility of "manual strangulation."

Mr. and Mrs. Kopechne repeated today that they were satisfied with Senator Kennedy's explanation that their daughter's death following a party was accidental.

The Massachusetts Democrat pleaded guilty to leaving the scene of an accident, was given a suspended two-month jail term and lost his driver's license for a year.

Judge Brominski noted that the hearing brought out minor discrepancies between the report of the accident Senator Kennedy gave the police and the Senator's televised speech about the accident six days later. But the judge said, "These discrepancies do not alter the determination of the cause of death."

Nor, he said, did testimony by Deputy Sheriff Christopher Look Jr. of Dukes County that the accident may have occurred an hour and a half later than the Senator reported.

The judge said the Massachusetts authorities had voluntarily passed up their right to perform an autopsy before burial.

After interment, he said, "the law will not reach into the grave in search of the facts except in the rarest of cases, and not even then unless it is clearly necessary and there is reasonable probability that such a violation of the sepulcher will establish that which is sought."

"The petitioners," he concluded, "have failed to meet their burden of proof . . . that there is a reasonable probability that that which is sought warrants a violation of the sepulcher."

He said it was incumbent upon the court to consider the wishes of the parents. Mr. Kopechne testfied at the hearing that they were "unalterably opposed" to exhumation and autopsy.

"In view of the facts presented to this court," Judge Brominski said, "their objections are well-taken."

December 11, 1969

Joseph Kennedy Jr.'s Death Recalled

The Federal Government kept secret from his family how President Kennedy's older brother was killed in World War II, according to a book published today.

Joseph P. Kennedy Jr., brother of the President and oldest son of the late Ambassador Joseph P. Kennedy, died because of faulty gear aboard a planeload of explosives he was flying to a useless

target, according to the author, Jack Olsen, who served in the Air Force and the Office of Strategic Services during the war.

In "Aphrodite: Desperate Mission" (G. P. Putnam's $6.95), Mr. Olsen said the Kennedy family had been told that their son, a Navy flier, was a hero. But Mr. Olsen said the Kennedys had not been told:

¶That the electrical system aboard his PB4-Y plane was faulty.

¶That a Navy ground officer had tried to get the mission canceled because he knew the system was faulty.

¶That the target, a German rocket site in France, had been abandoned by Hitler's missile men three months earlier.

Mr. Olsen wrote: "The exact details of the death of the 29-year-old 'star of our family,' as his father once described him, were kept secret from the family.

"The Kennedy family comforted itself with a letter from a naval officer who had gone to college with Joe Jr. 'As you no doubt are aware,' the young lieutenant wrote to Jospeh P. Kennedy Sr., 'the mission was an extremely important one of an experimental nature and exceedingly dangerous . . . You may not have heard that he was succesful and through Joe's courage and devotion to what he thought was right, a great many lives have been saved."

March 20, 1970

EDGARTOWN, Mass., April 7 —The Dukes County grand jury voted today to indict no one in the death of Mary Jo Kopechne. District Attorney Edmund Dinis said, "The case is closed."

The jury of 10 men and 10 women, which had met for two days, heard less than 20 minutes of testimony from four witnesses.

Miss Kopechne drowned when a car driven by Senator Edward M. Kennedy plunged from a narrow bridge into a tidal pool on Chappaquiddick Island nine months ago. The Senator, who pleaded guilty last summer to leaving the scene of the accident, received a suspended sentence of two months, and his driver's license was suspended for a year.

But until today he faced the possiblity of an indictement on more serious charges, including manslaughter.

The grand jury, which reconvened yesterday, was told at the outset by Circuit Court Judge Wilfred J. Paquet that he would not release the transcript of the secret January inquest at which Senator Kennedy, under oath, gave his version of the drowning.

Judge Paquet had no power to release the transcripts, for the state's highest court had ruled that inquest testimony could never be admitted into criminal proceedings.

District Attorney Dinis, on emerging today from the 111-year-old red brick courthouse on Main Street, said "There is no proposed prosecution in this case."

His announcement cleared the way for the release of the inquest transcript and of the report and recommendations of District Court Judge James A. Boyle, who presided at the inquest.

The transcript was impounded on orders of the Supreme Judicial Court of Massachusetts, which held that the testimony and Judge Boyle's report could be released only after it had been determined that no further prosecution was planned.

Mr. Dinis, who is seeking reelection on the Democratic ticket with Senator Kennedy next November, was asked: "Is this the end of the Kennedy story?"

TV Address Recalled

He replied, "No comment," then added: "This is the end of this particular investigation into the death of Mary Jo Kopechne. The case is closed."

Senator Kennedy now seems safe from further legal action. Impending, however, is disclosure of the inquest testimony, which, presumably, will contain the Senator's sworn story of why he had failed to notify the police until nine hours after the death of Miss Kopechne.

He admitted to "panic" and "confusion" in his televised statement of the accident. But his report, to many viewers, left some questions unanswered. One question was whether he had spent some of this time trying to find a way to absolve himself of responsiblity.

This was one of the questions that inspired the grand jury's decision to investigate the case. The initiative came not from the District Attorney but from a 29-year-old Vineyard Haven druggist, Leslie H. Leland, the jury foreman.

When the jury assembled yesterday morning, Mr. Leland seemed convinced that the panel could begin a bold, independent investigation even if Judge Paquet refused to let it see the transcript. However, Judge Paquet lectured the jurors on their subservience to the court.

Not one of the jurors, it was learned reliably, called for the appearance of Senator Kennedy. Neither did any of them ask for the two other key witnesses at the inquest: the Senator's cousin, Joseph Gargan, and Paul Markham, Kennedy's friend.

Swam to Edgartown

Both Mr. Gargan and Mr. Markham attended a cook-out with the Senator, Miss Kopechne and other former Kennedy workers on the night of the drowning. It was to them that Senator Kennedy went for help after his car ran off the bridge. He took them back to the bridge, he said, and they dived repeatedly in a vain attempt to extricate Miss Kopechne from the car.

Then, according to his story, he swam the narrow channel to Edgartown and his hotel, leaving them behind.

Neither Mr. Gargan nor Mr. Markham, a former United States Attorney, reported the accident.

None of the four witnesses summoned by the grand jury had appeared at the inquest. And it was reported that nothing they said had helped to fill any gaps in the Chappaquiddick story.

This morning, the jury heard testimony from Benjamin Hall, projectionist at Ye Olde Town House Photoplays, the local movie house, and from Robert J. Carroll, former Democratic Selectman and part owner of the Harbor View Hotel.

Mr. Hall was summoned, apparently, because he lives across the street from the Shiretown Inn, where Mr. Kennedy had registered, and might have observed the Senator's return from the channel swim.

Mr. Carroll said that he had been called because of old rumors that he had flown Senator Kennedy off the island in the early hours of July 19, after the drowning, presumably to Hyannis on Cape Cod, and then back to Martha's Vineyard. The Senator has a summer home at Hyannis Port. Mr. Carroll dismissed the story as "ridiculous."

Yesterday the jury heard from Mrs. Nina L. Trott, who was reservations manager last summer at the Shiretown Inn, and from Stephen Gentle, manager of the Edgartown Airport. Mrs. Trott said that she had quit work at midnight on July 18 and hadn't seen the Senator return from Chappaquiddick.

Mr. Gentle said that he knew of no mysterious flights from his airport on July 19.

Shortly after 10:30 this morning, the jurors voted unanimously to make no presentment. They were excused at 10:56 A.M. with the thanks of Judge Paquet.

April 8, 1970

Kopechne Case 'Closed'; No One Indicted by Jury

By HOMER BIGART

Kennedy Veracity Questioned By Judge in Kopechne Inquest

Report Says Senator May Have Driven Car Negligently

By JOSEPH LELYVELD

BOSTON, April 29—The judge at the inquest into the death of Mary Jo Kopechne reported that he could not accept as the truth key elements of Senator Edward M. Kennedy's sworn testimony at the hearing.

Judge James A. Boyle of the Dukes County District Court found neither "responsible" nor "probable" these assertions by the Senator about the drowning of Miss Kopechne last July:

¶The Senator's testimony that he and Miss Kopechne had left a party at a cottage on Chappaquiddick Island with the intention of catching a ferry back to Martha's Vineyard.

¶His testimony that it was a wrong turn that took him onto a dirt road that led to a narrow, unmarked bridge on Chappaquiddick.

Judge Boyle, who conducted the inquest six months after the Senator's car plunged off the wooden bridge, also took note of testimony showing that both Mr. Kennedy and Miss Kopechne had been driven over the same bridge earlier on the day of the accident.

From this he concluded that there was "probable cause" to believe that the Senator had been driving negligently and that such driving might have contributed to Miss Kopechne's death.

It was a decision by the local authorities not to proceed with prosecution that cleared the way for the release here this afternoon, by the Massachusetts Superior Court, of Judge Boyle's findings and the 763-page transcript of the inquest. No explanations for that decision were available here today.

A spokesman for Robert H. Quinn, the Attorney General of Massachusetts, said that prosecution could have been initiated by Judge Boyle himself, by District Attorney Edmund Dinis of New Bedford, or by Police Chief Dominick Arena of Edgartown on Martha's Vineyard. Since none of these officials acted, the spokesman said, "the matter is at an end as far as the Attorney General is concerned."

Mr. Dinis, at his office in New Bedford, declined comment.

The release of the transcript appeared to constitute the final act of a legal drama that has lasted more than nine months since Miss Kopechne was trapped and drowned in the Senator's overturned Oldsmobile the night of last July 18-19.

When Mr. Kennedy testified at the inquest last Jan. 5, it was the first time that he had submitted to questioning about the accident. His testimony did not appear to contradict his earlier statements.

The judge's "presumptions of fact" as to what really happened on the night of accident were based on testimony that Miss Kopechne left her purse in the cottage when she left with the Senator and that she told none of her friends where she was going. According to the testimony, Mr. Kennedy spoke only to his driver, John B. Crimmins, when he asked for the keys to the car.

Judge Boyle apparently found it strange that Mr. Kennedy did not ask Mr. Crimmins to drive him and Miss Kopechne back to their hotels at Martha's Vineyard. This would have enabled the driver to bring the car back to Chappaquiddick and pick up the other girls who had not been planning to spend the night in the small cottage where the party was held.

Cross-Examination Barred

However, Senator Kennedy was not subjected to aggressive cross-examination during nearly two hours on the stand. The judge held that cross-examination was not appropriate in an inquest.

At no point were Senator Kennedy or any of his companions at the party asked directly whether they had ever considered concealing his involvement in the accident.

Mr. Kennedy testified that he had never been on Chappaquiddick before the day of the accident and that he himself had not been at the wheel of his car when he visited the island earlier in the day.

Asked whether he realized that he was not heading to the ferry after turning onto the dirt road, he replied: "At the moment I went off the bridge, I certainly did."

The next thing he was conscious of, the Senator said, was Miss Kopechne struggling next to him on the front seat of the car as it overturned in the water, then "the rushing of the water, the blackness, the fact that it was impossible even to hold it back."

Mr. Kennedy, who testified that he was "absolutely sober" when the car went off the bridge, told of diving to the point of exhaustion to save Miss Kopechne, after struggling out of the car, then of being swept out into the pond by a strong current.

Denies Seeing Lights

He said he never saw the lights of the houses near the bridge, and returned to the cottage where the party was being held to get help.

Asked why he did not then try to phone the police, Mr. Kennedy said he had intended to do so.

But first, he said, he returned with Joseph Gargan, his cousin; and Paul Markham, a former United States Attorney from Massachusetts, who dived for 45 minutes in an attempt to reach Miss Kopechne.

According to the Senator's testimony, it was past 1 A.M. when Mr. Gargan and Mr. Markham drove him to the ferry slip. On the way, he said, they repeatedly stressed the importance of his phoning the police when he reached Edgartown on Martha's Vineyard.

Mr. Kennedy said he agreed but was more preoccupied by worries about how he would meet his duty to notify Miss Kopechne's parents or his own family. This concern led him to the desperate hope, he said, that what he knew to be fact was only nightmare.

'To See Her Walking'

"I was almost looking out the front window and windows trying to see her walking down that road," he said. "I related this to Gargan and Markham and they said they understood this feeling, but it was necessary to report it."

Before diving impulsively into the channel to swim to Edgartown, he said, he told his companions, "You take care of the girls, I will take care of the accident."

Mr. Gargan said he was not worried by the Senator's sudden dive because he knew his cousin to be a strong swimmer. But Mr. Kennedy testified that the swim nearly cost him his life and left him in an even deeper state of confusion and exhaustion.

Back in his hotel room, the Senator testified, he continued to wrestle with his hope that Mary Jo Kopechne was still alive. "I somehow believed that when the sun came up and it was a new morning that what had happened the night before would not have happened and did not happen," he said.

He could not find, he said, "the strength within me, the moral strength to call Mrs. Kopechne at 2 o'clock in the morning and tell her that her daughter was dead."

Tells of Phone Call

The only reason he returned to Chappaquiddick Island the next morning, he testified, was to make a call in private to Burke Marshall, a family friend and former high Justice Department official under Robert Kennedy. That done, he said, he went directly to the police.

Edmund Dinis, the District Attorney questioning the Senator, noted the discrepancy between this testimony and his original statement that he went "immediately" to the police in the morning. But Judge Boyle would not let him ask Mr. Kennedy to explain it.

When Mr. Markam took the stand at the inquest, he testified that Mr. Kennedy had tried to keep him and Mr. Gargan from becoming implicated in the case. "Look," he quoted the Senator as saying, "I don't want you people in the middle of this thing. . . . As far as you know, you didn't know anything about the accident last night."

Esther Newburgh, one of the five young women who remained behind in the cottage, said that Mr. Gargan collapsed on a couch after returning there. According to the testimony, Mr. Markham, also exhausted from the diving, dropped on a couch too and slumped across a girl's legs.

He testified that the young woman was annoyed—that all the young women were in an irritated mood over having been stranded at the cottage, but apparently unaware still that anything serious had happened.

All the witnesses agreed there had been no heavy drinking at the party. Mr. Crimmins told of taking the leftover vodka and rum back to his cottage in the Kennedy compound in Hyannis Port.

The only corroboration for Senator Kennedy's testimony that Miss Kopechne wanted to leave the party because she was tired came from Mr. Crimmins. "She was bothered by the sun on the beach that day," the driver said.

A series of five affidavits and medical reports were introduced in evidence by Senator Kennedy's lawyers to demonstrate that he suffered a concussion in the accident and that his disoriented frame of mind was not unusual, in the opinion of specialists, for persons in that condition.

Mr. Kennedy did not attempt to resolve a discrepancy over the time of the accident between his testimony and that of Christopher Look Jr., who testified that he was almost certain he had seen the Senator's car some 90 minutes after the accident occurred if the times given by Mr. Kennedy were accepted as correct.

Judge Boyle did not attempt to resolve this discrepancy either. His report put the time of the accident between 11:15 P.M. and 1 A.M.

The only charge ever brought against Senator Kennedy in the case was for leaving the scene of an accident. He pleaded guilty before Judge Boyle on July 25, and thereby was spared cross-examination. The judge gave him a two-month suspended sentence.

The following week the case was reopened by Mr. Dinis, who chose to call for an inquest into Miss Kopechne's death rather than to take the more usual route of bringing it before a grand jury himself.

The closed inquest lasted from Jan. 5 to Jan. 8. A grand jury eventually did study the case but took no action.

April 30, 1970

WASHINGTON, April 29 — Senator Edward M. Kennedy rejected as "not justified" today a Massachusetts judge's report that the Senator may have driven negligently and contributed to the death of Mary Jo Kopechne at Chappaquiddick Island last July.

In a statement issued by his office, Mr. Kennedy said:

"At the inquest I truthfully answered all questions asked of me. In my personal view, the inference and ultimate findings of the judge's report are not justified.

"Even though the legal procedures resulting from last summer's accident have come to a close, the tragedy of that event will never really end—for the Kopechne family, for my family and myself. We must all live with the loss of Mary Jo and the pain that this has inflicted upon us.

"The facts of this incident are now fully public, and eventual judgment and understanding rests where it belongs. I plan no further statement on this tragic matter. Both our families have suffered enough from public utterances and speculations."

A few moments after the public statement was issued, however, reporters found Senator Kennedy on the Capitol steps and he added a few comments. Asked if Miss Kopechne's parents might file a civil action against him, he replied, "I suppose that's always a possibility," but added that he had no such indication.

One reporter asked if Mr. Kennedy believed the transcript of the inquest might be used against him in his re-election campaign. The Senator said he did not know and added: "That really isn't the uppermost thing in my mind."

The imputation of negligence and untruth in Judge James A. Boyle's report came as a surprise to Senator Kennedy's associates. They were aware that the release of the inquest report would produce a revival of public interest in the accident, but they thought its contents would be relatively noncontroversial.

The Senator's aides had been pressing for the release of the report as soon as possible, believing that it would mark the legal close of the Chappaquiddick incident and would clear the political atmosphere in Senator Kennedy's re-election campaign this fall.

G.O.P. Eyes 1972

As a political matter, the report appeared certain to focus even more importance on the Senator's re-election campaign as the first real test of whether the public accepts Mr. Kennedy and his story of the accident.

Before today's events, few people believed that the Senator could exceed his 1964 majority of 1.13 million votes this year. The 1964 campaign involved special circumstances: Mr. Kennedy was in a hospital, recovering from an airplane crash; President Johnson was opposed by Senator Barry Goldwater and the assassination of President Kennedy was still fresh in sympathetic Massachusetts minds.

A number of Democratic politicians expect the Republican party to make a substantial investment in the Massachusetts Senate race, not because they stand much chance of beating Senator Kennedy but because they could weaken his standing as a potential national candidate in 1972 if his majority could be trimmed this year.

The report came at a time when party leaders were increasingly speaking of Senator Kennedy again as not just a Presidential candidate, but as the Presidential candidate. The cloud of scandal seemed to have blown away; his spirits and his Senate activity appeared reinvigorated.

None of the Senator's potential competitors for the Democratic nomination had caught the fancy of the voters, and party leaders were beginning to talk of drafting Senator Kennedy, regardless of whether he was interested in running.

Recording Canceled

There also was evidence that the Massachusetts Senator was prepared to move more freely into the public arena. He had not appeared on a radio or television interview since Senator Robert F. Kennedy's assassination in June, 1968, but he had accepted such an engagement with Metromedia News; the interview was to have been recorded tomorrow morning.

Tonight Mr. Kennedy's office reported the cancellation of that appointment. One aide rescheduled the recording for Friday, but another said he must be in Boston at that time.

If Democratic politicians were uncertain after today's report, Senator Kennedy seems to have been uncertain before it. A visitor to his home last weekend came away with the report that the Senator had talked about what he might do if he left politics altogether—write, teach, travel.

His commitment to the Massachusetts campaign seems firm. But after that campaign, no one—least of all the Senator himself—seemed to know what was ahead on the political track.

April 30, 1970

Kennedy Statement Rejects Findings as 'Not Justified'

By WARREN WEAVER Jr.

Friends of Miss Kopechne Said They Were Told She Was Safe

By JOSEPH LELYVELD

BOSTON, April 30 — Joseph F. Gargan, a cousin of Edward M. Kennedy's who was with him immediately after his July accident on Chappaquiddick Island, told three of Mary Jo Kopechne's friends that night that she had returned to Martha's Vineyard alone in the Senator's Oldsmobile, according to the friends' testimony at the inquest into Miss Kopechne's death.

Mr. Gargan offered this assurance, the testimony indicates, after he and another companion of the Senator's, Paul Markham, had spent 45 minutes diving to rescue her body from the Senator's submerged car.

The car had overturned in a tidal inlet after plunging off a wooden bridge.

The inquest transcripts were released here yesterday along with a report from the presiding judge at the hearing, James A. Boyle. The judge questioned elements of the Senator's testimony and concluded that negligent driving might have been responsible for Miss Kopechne's death.

Mr. Gargan and Mr. Markham testified that, having watched Mr. Kennedy dive into the narrow channel that separates Chappaquiddick from Martha's Vineyard, they drove around the island for more than a half hour discussing whether one of them should attempt to pursue him.

Finally, they decided to follow his instructions and return to the cottage to look after the five remaining young women who had been stranded there with no way to return to their rooms at the Katama Shores Motor Inn on Martha's Vineyard.

Senator Kennedy, in his own testimony, said he had asked Mr. Gargan and Mr. Markham not to "alarm" Miss Kopechne's friends because he feared they would "go to the scene of the accident and dive themselves," with "a good chance that some mishap might have occurred to any one of them."

Swimming the Channel

It was close to 3 A.M. on July 19 when Mr. Gargan told three of these girls—Maryellen Lyons, her sister Ann and Esther Newburgh—that Miss Kopechne had returned to the motel by herself. He said that the Senator had gone back to Martha's Vineyard later by swimming the channel.

District Attorney Edmund Dinis asked Maryellen Lyons whether she found this unusual. "Not at the time," she replied.

Miss Lyons also testified that Mr. Gargan said he and Mr. Markham had dived in after the Senator because they were concerned about his ability to make it across the channel safely. The two men themselves testified that they had remained on the ferry slip because they had confidence in Mr. Kennedy's ability to make the swim.

The next morning Mr. Gargan also told Charles C. Tretter, one of those who had been at the party at the cottage, of diving in after the Senator. According to Mr. Tretter's testimony, Mr. Gargan said Mr. Kennedy had returned to the cottage in a distraught frame of mind and asked to be driven immediately to the ferry slip.

This is essentially what the Senator was saying at about the same time in a statement he was dictating for the police.

Mr. Gargan made no mention of efforts by him and Mr. Markham to rescue Miss Kopechne. Mr. Markham testified that the Senator had told his friends not to implicate themselves in the accident or in his failure to report it.

'Red-Faced and Exhausted'

The only young woman questioned as to whether she noticed anything unusual about the appearance of Mr. Gargan and Mr. Markham on their return to the cottage was Esther Newburgh. She said they looked "red-faced and exhausted."

No one, it appears, realized that they had been swimming. Both men explained in their testimony that "they had taken off their clothes before deving into the ponds."

Four of the five young women said they had noticed Miss Kopechne leave with the Senator soon after 11:15, but none of them was struck by this departure because, they said, those at the party had been walking in and out of the small cottage all evening.

Miss Kopechne told none of her friends where she was going. "Wouldn't it have been surprising to you," Judge Boyle asked Ann Lyons, "if they were leaving the party permanently without saying a word to anybody?"

"Yes, sir," replied Miss Lyons, a member of the Senator's legislative staff.

Miss Kopechne's casual departure, combined with the fact that she left her purse behind in the cottage, was a factor in causing Judge Boyle to doubt Mr. Kennedy's testimony that he was driving her back to her motel because she was tired.

Three of the five women corporated the Senator's account of his return to the cottage at about 12:15, after the accident. Mr. Kennedy had attracted the attention outside of Ray La-Rosa, a sailing companion. Ann Lyons recalled that Mr. La-Rosa then "just came in and said in a rather loud voice, because people were talking, that Mr. Gargan and Mr. Markham, Senator Kennedy would like to see you."

Her sister, Maryellen, testi-

fied that those left behind calmly speculated that the Senator's car might have got stuck in the sand, a not infrequent occurrence in that area. When the second car drove off, leaving them without any transportation, they realized they would probably have to spend the night in the cottage.

It wasn't until the morning, after Senator Kennedy was on his way to the police, that Mr. Gargan told the young women at the cottage about the accident at the bridge 10 hours earlier. But even then, it appears, his account was so sketchy that they did not realize their friend was dead.

'She Was Missing'

"He just said there was an accident and she was missing," Maryellen Lyons recalled. They besieged him with questions—for instance, why hadn't the Coast Guard been called?—but he replied that he did not yet know the details.

They returned to their motel, Ann Lyons said, "really fully expecting to find Miss Kopechne there, but she wasn't and we sat and waited."

"Mr. Gargan said he would call us as soon as he had any details," she testified.

The call finally came with definite word. Then Mr. Gargan drove to the motel to comfort the women and face their questions.

Esther Newburgh recalled, "Mr. Gargan said the Senator dove repeatedly to save her and kept repeating, 'I want you all to know that I believe it and I want you all to know that every single effort possible was made to save her.'"

She was asked what happened then. "And then," she replied, "you have five girls who lost a friend and who can't remember very much at that point."

Familiar With Bridge

The young women were familiar with the bridge where the accident occurred — known as the Dike Bridge — because they had been driven over it that afternoon to go swimming on what is called East Beach. Miss Kopechne—an excellent swimmer, according to Miss Newburgh — had been among them.

While most of them were still on the beach, Senator Kennedy arrived and took a dip. The fact that both he and Miss Kopechne knew the beach made Judge Boyle skeptical of his testimony that they had taken a wrong turn.

Mr. Gargan also understood immediately where the accident had occurred even though, he recalled, Mr. Kennedy said nothing more on his return to the cottage than "There has been an accident. Mary Jo was with me down at the bridge. Let's go."

"Did he say what bridge?" Mr. Dinis asked.

"No," the witness replied.

After their rescue efforts had failed, Mr. Gargan said, the Senator kept repeating, "Can you believe it, Joe, can you believe it, I don't believe it, I don't believe this could happen."

Mr Markham also testified as to the Senator's state of mind at this point. "He was sobbing and almost on the verge of actually breaking down crying, he said, "This couldn't have happened. I don't know how it happened.'"

Both Mr. Markham and Mr. Gargan had been astonished to find the next morning that the Senator still had not gone to the police.

"I just couldn't believe he didn't report it," Mr. Markham said.

May 1, 1970

BOSTON, May 28 (UPI)—A telephone call to Mrs. Aristotle Onassis' Cape Cod home, charged to Senator Edward M. Kennedy's credit card, was made shortly after Mr. Kennedy reported his automobile crash in which Mary Jo Kopechne died, documents showed today.

A New England Telephone Company listing of calls charged to Mr. Kennedy's card showed a 23-minute 54-second call to Mrs. Onassis' home at Hyannis Port at 10:57 A.M. last July 19. Mrs. Onassis was in Europe at the time.

Mr. Kennedy's car plunged off a bridge on Chappaquiddick Island about midnight July 18, and the accident went unreported for about nine hours.

The call to Mrs. Kennedy's former sister-in-law, the widow of President Kennedy, was the first call logged after he reported the mishap. The document does not say who made the call.

The credit card listing was one of several exhibits introduced at a secret four-day inquest last January into Miss Kopechne's death. The exhibits were released today in the office of Superior Court Clerk Edward V. Keating.

Other calls made were to Arlington, Va., where the Senator lives; to Mary Carroll, who lived with Miss Kopechne, in Washington; to Mr. Kennedy's aide David Burke, and to others.

May 29, 1970

KENNEDY PHONE LOG DISCLOSED BY COURT

Mrs. Edward M. Kennedy says she believes "everything Ted said" about the events surrounding the accident on Chappaquiddick Island last summer that involved her husband, Senator Edward M. Kennedy of Massachusetts, and took the life of a young secretary, Mary Jo Kopechne.

Referring to the Senator, Mrs. Kennedy said in an interview in the July issue of Ladies' Home Journal: "I believe in giving him all the support I can. It was very unfortunate . . . a tragic accident."

In reply to a question about whether she believed stories that Miss Kopechne and Senator Kennedy were going for a midnight swim, Mrs. Kennedy said: "No, I'm sure they weren't."

The interview, with Betty Hannah Hoffman, is the first one she has granted since last July, when the accident occurred.

In the interview, which is the first installment of a two-part article, Mrs. Kennedy denied that there was any pressure from the Kennedy family on Senator Kennedy to run for the Presidency.

"What family?" she asked. "What's left of the Kennedys? Besides Ted, only women and children. You don't seriously think we want Ted to be President, do you?"

June 30, 1970

MRS. KENNEDY BACKS HUSBAND'S VERACITY

BARNSTABLE, Mass., Aug. 6 —Robert F. Kennedy, Jr., and Robert Sargent Shriver 3d were, in effect, placed on a year's probation after a private hearing in Juvenile Court here today on charges of possessing marijuana.

Judge Henry L. Murphy, who presided over the hearing, said the cases had "been continued without finding" for one year and that "unless they get into trouble again" the two will be subject to no further legal proceedings.

The 63-year-old judge's action was said to be customary in cases which juveniles were charged with their first offense.

Young Kennedy, second oldest child of the late Senator Robert F. Kennedy, was accompanied to the hearing by his mother, Mrs. Ethel Kennedy, and his uncle, Senator Edward M. Kennedy. Young Shriver appeared before the court with his father, the former U.S. Ambassador to France and mother, the former Eunice Kennedy.

Both boys are 16 years old and legal proceedings against them are, under the law, not open to the press or public.

According to sources here, the basic question put to the youths by the judge was: Is it true or not true that you were delinquent in that on July 10 you were in possession of marijuana?

Both youths reportedly answered: "Not True."

After studying the record, which presumably included affidavits of undercover agents, the judge lectured the two and then continued their cases without finding until Sept. 16, 1971.

Ten other juveniles, some charged with violating drug laws on the same date—July 10 — as the Kennedy and Shriver youths, also appeared before the judge and received similar continuances.

All were charged as the result of a summer-long investigation, involving undercover state police agents, into drug use in this resort area. Yesterday, 24 adults were arraigned on charges ranging from selling heroin to "being present where drugs were used."

Today, drawn by the Kennedy name, nearly 100 newsmen—including 17 sound television cameras and their crews —waited outside the hulking gray Barnstable District Courthouse at 10 A.M. for the arrival of the youths and their parents.

After the hearing, which lasted 23 minutes, the families were crushed in the swarm of television cameras and technicians as they jockeyed for position while trying to move toward the car that awaited the family.

Mr. Shriver paused briefly to say: "Judge Murphy went over all the documents connected with this case. The boys, of course, are in this — they made an appearance in Juvenile Court — for the very first time in their lives. Under the laws of the Commonwealth of Massachusetts all the proceedings in juvenile chambers are confidential. The boys will be returned home with their parents."

Kennedy, Shriver Boys on Probation

By BILL KOVACH

Robert F. Kennedy Jr. arrives for arraignment at courthouse in Barnstable, Mass. He is accompanied by his mother, Mrs. Ethel Kennedy, and uncle, Senator Edward M. Kennedy.

Senator Kennedy, asked to comment, said only, "I think that (Mr. Shriver's statement] about says it."

With the help of local policemen the Kennedys then left, but the Shrivers — parked farther away—were enveloped by newsmen who moved with them down the center of the street for about 100 yards to their car.

Both youths — tall and slender — were dressed in sports jackets and ties and attempted to ignore the hubbub that flowed about them. At one point, young Kennedy — still wearing a cast on his right wrist, which was injured in the spring while he attempted to rescue a pet falcon — spotted a young friend in the crowd and flashed a bried grin of recognition.

The police are still reluctant to discuss these or other drug arrests this summer despite vague suggestions that they might have been an effort to embarrass Senator Kennedy, who is up for re-election this year.

The announcement of the charges came just one day before some 30 fellows of the Robert F. Kennedy Memorial Foundation were scheduled to meet the Sheraton Hotel in Hyannis to evaluate their work.

The foundation, organized to promote the ideals and works of the late Senator, has supported young men and women in all parts of the country working with communities and minority groups to help solve specific local and individual problems.

August 7, 1970

Kennedy an Easy Victor; He May Get 60% of Vote

By BILL KOVACH

BOSTON, Wednesday, Nov. 4 —Senator Edward M. Kennedy won re-election last night and appeared headed for the convincing victory required to retain his position as a national leader of the Democratic party.

His total vote was expected to pass the 60 per cent mark that most observors believed necessary to demonstrate continued stature as a major force in the party.

With 48 per cent of the vote counted, the tally was:

Kennedy 448,116
Spaulding 255,958

Mrs. Louise Day Hicks, the 47-year-old South Boston housewife who gained national attention in 1968 for her support of neighborhood schools, swept to victory in her race against Laurence Curtis and Daniel J. Houston. She will succeed retiring House Speaker John W. McCormack in Congress.

Meanwhile, in the Third Congressional District, a Jesuit priest, Robert F. Drinan, ran slightly ahead in his bid to become the first Roman Catholic priest elected to Congress. His moderate Republican opponent, John McGlennon, was drawing an unexpectedly strong vote in the liberal suburban communities near Boston, whose vote had helped Father Drinan to win in the primary.

The returns showed that Mr. Kennedy's concern that the accident on Chappaquiddick Island last year would result in some kind of a moral blacklash against him was inflated.

Throughout the campaign against Republican Josiah A. Spaulding, Mr. Kennedy sought through personal contact to mimimize any reaction to the accident that took the life of Mary Jo Kopechne in the Senator's car.

The Senator's vote was even more impressive when read against the surprising strength shown by the Republican Governor, Francis W. Sargent, who overwhelmed his Democratic challenger, Kevin H. White, the Mayor of Boston.

Governor Sargent pulled a h e a d
early on the basis of a strong showing in Boston, where he was stealing Mayor White's basic strength in inner city precincts.

Democrats, especially Senator Kennedy and Mayor White, had little trouble making economic conditions the No. 1 campaign issue. Massachusetts ranks today as the state hardest-hit by shifts in the economy. Five of the state's eight labor areas are officially labeled "depressed" areas. More than 160,000 workers, including many engineers and supervisory personnel, are out of work.

This was the issue hammered at by Senator Kennedy in one of the hardest campaigns he has run. Concentrating on personal visits and handshaking tours, the Senator sought to pile up a majority large enogh to overcome damage inflicted on his image by the tragic accident at Chappaquiddick last year. It is the first opportunity voters have had to register their reaction to that incident.

His opponent, Mr. Spaulding, former head of the state Republican party, ignored most is-

sues and tried to overcome a lack of money and national backing by assailing the Senator for his "unswerving assault on the Presidency, which he persists in assuming is his divine right."

Without television or a platform for statewide attention, Mr. Spaulding's campaign was totally ignored by his rival.

Senator Kennedy was also allowed the luxury of freedom from a tough law-and-order opponent. Within the relative safety of such a campaign, the Senator spoke against "bomb throwers and anarchists" without being acccused of shifting his position. At the same time, he accused the Nixon Administration of paying only lip service to the problems of crime.

So comfortable was the campaign for the Senator that he traveled out of state frequently

to aid other Democrats and, when Mayor White was incapacitated by an emergency operation, helped pick up that sagging campaign.

Mayor White's illness, an emergency operation for a perforated ulcer, turned out to be the spark that brought his campaign alive. Until that point, a week and a half before the election, the Democratic party was badly split, and Mayor White had failed to score effectively against the quiet, popular Governor Sargent.

Following his hospital stay, Mr. White forced the Governor into a statewide television debate that began to focus on the issues. Mayor White accused the Governor of inability to respond to economic problems because they were "part of the Republican program" in Washington.

Governor Sargent, on the

other hand, stressed his leadership in reorganizing state government and asked "a chance to finish what I started."

Governor Sargent moved into his job two years ago to complete the term of former Gov. John A. Volpe, who moved to Washington as President Nixon's Secretary of Transportation.

Father Drinan's Congressional race caught fire shortly before his Democratic primary victory over Representative Philip J. Philbin, an incumbent of 28 years.

Running primarily against the Vietnam war and the Nixon Administration "priorities" during the primary, Father Drinan shifted his emphasis to economic problems for the general election.

November 4, 1970

WASHINGTON, Jan. 21 — Senator Edward M. Kennedy, was toppled as assistant majority leader of the Senate today as the Democratic-controlled 92d Congress convened amid infighting in the Democratic ranks.

In a surprise coup that shook the Senate leadership and might affect any Presidential prospects of Senator Kennedy, Senator Robert C. Byrd of West Virginia ousted the Massachusetts Democrat as majority whip by a 31-24 vote in the Senate Democratic caucus.

Senator Kennedy, who had staged his own coup in winning the whip post two years ago, was stunned by his defeat, as were his liberal allies in the Senate. Right up to the vote, Senator Kennedy had been predicting his re-election.

Scott Is Re-elected

The Republican Senate leadership remained intact, with Senator Hugh Scott, the Republican leader, staving off a challenge from his conservative flank.

In the House, Representative Carl Albert of Oklahoma, chosen by the Democratic majority Tuesday to be Speaker, was formally elected by the House and installed.

Awaiting the new Congress was a heavy legislative workload that included many Administration bills left over from the last Congress, dealing with such matters as Social Security, welfare reform, trade quotas, revenue sharing and the supersonic transport plane. To this list President Nixon undoubtedly will add new items when he appears before Congress tomorrow night to present his

State of the Union Message.

In a speech before the Democratic caucus, Senator Mike Mansfield of Montana, the majority leader, predicted that the war in Indochina and the "recession" at home would be "the overriding questions of the 92d Congress." Senator Mansfield used the occasion to criticize what he called the expansion of the war in Cambodia and to raise questions about the feasiblity of the revenue sharing plan that is expected to be one of President Nixon's principal proposals to the new Congress.

With a Presidential election in the offing, the Democratic Congress is expected to assume an increasingly partisan stance toward the White House, thus complicating the Administration's already difficult relations with Congress. On the opening day, however, Congress, as is customary, was engrossed in its own organizational problems.

Senator Scott of Pennsylvania retained his post as Republican leader by fewer votes than he had expected in defeating Howard H. Baker Jr. of Tennessee in the Republican caucus. The vote was 24 to 20.

Senator Mansfield was re-elected majority leader by acclamation by the Democratic caucus. But as his principal aide, Senator Mansfield now has a whip who has been identified with the more conservative wing of the Democratic party in the Senate.

With the new Congress, therefore, the Senate Democratic leadership, which had swung over to the moderate to liberal side with the election of Senator Kennedy as whip two years ago, tended to shift back into the control of the conservative Establishment that had ruled the Senate for decades.

Senator Byrd, who had been secretary of the Democratic Conference — the third-ranking job in the Democratic leadership—has tended to align himself with the Southerners and

the committee chairmen, and it was with their base of support that he built up the votes to unseat Senator Kennedy.

As whip, Senator Byrd will be responsible for making sure that Democratic Senators are present for crucial votes.

Senator Byrd, who has alternated between voting with the conservatives and liberals on issues, pledged that he would work in his new job as a "legislative technician," seeking to expedite the flow of legislation and not to impose any ideological outlook on his colleagues.

But the immediate reaction of his Democratic colleagues was that Senator Mansfield, who has tried to steer a moderate course, would now have to lead alone without a liberal whip running interference for him.

Aside from the potential impact on the Democratic leadership, the defeat of Senator Kennedy contained several personal political ironies such as are seldom seen in the political dramas played on Capitol Hill.

His defeat at the hands of his Senate colleagues came 10 years and one day after John F. Kennedy was inaugurated as President. The defeat undoubtedly diminished the prospects that the late President's brother will become a resident of the White House.

When Senator Kennedy was elected whip two years ago, ousting Senator Russell B. Long of Louisiana, it was the first time in recent history that the ruling Establishment had been thwarted in choosing the Senate leadership. Senator Kennedy lost the post on the same day that Senator Richard B. Russell of Georgia, the patriarchal symbol of the Senate Establishment, died after a long illness.

But if Senator Russell had died four hours earlier, Senator Kennedy might still be whip.

KENNEDY OUSTED AS WHIP

THE SESSION OPENS

Coup by Byrd Dismays the Liberals—Scott Keeps His Post

By JOHN W. FINNEY

Senator Byrd told reporters that he had decided to make the race only after determining at the last minute that Senator Russell, who had given him a proxy vote, was still alive. That meant that Senator Byrd had 28 certain votes, enough to win. Four hours after his victory, Senator Russell died at the Walter Reed Army Hospital.

January 22, 1971

Notes on People

Mrs. Rose Kennedy said she was "never particularly incensed" at the assassins of her two sons, President John F. Kennedy and Senator Robert F. Kennedy. Mrs. Kennedy, who is 80 years old, told David Frost, during a taped television interview, that if the killers had realized what they were doing, "I don't think they'd have done it." Of Robert's death, she said, "I don't think anyone would deliberately destroy the father of 11 children." Of her surviving son, Senator Edward M. Kennedy, and the possibility of his running for President, she said: "Well, he assured me that he is in no hurry. And he assured me that I would still campaign for him, even though I was 90. So I'm in no hurry as far as my plans are concerned."

June 29, 1971

Notes on People
Kennedy's Fears

The "most crushing" consideration in his decision not to seek the 1972 Presidential nomination, said **Senator Edward M. Kennedy**, was the possibility of an assassination attempt.

He said in an interview published in Look magazine that he was aware of the pressures on him to carry on in the tradition of his slain brothers.

"But on the other side are the overriding personal considerations," he said. "My family and I take seriously my responsibility to my brothers' children as well as my own, and the tragedies—my brothers, the plane crash, the death at Chappaquiddick—anybody would be enormously affected by such experiences."

Mr. Kennedy said: "I try not to think about the Presidency. I don't discuss it with my family. We just don't talk about it. That business about promising my mother not to run, well, that's just not true."

But, he added, "even if I were willing to reach out for this opportunity [to run for the Presidency], personal pressures are overriding—subjecting my family to fears over my safety . . . the tensions on my mother . . ."

Another factor, Mr. Kennedy said, is the current mood of the nation as it would apply to a Kennedy candidacy.

"I feel it in my gut that it's the wrong time, that it's too early," he said. "Then too, maybe I would like to do it later on, in a different climate, more on my own."

July 27, 1971

Notes on People

All summer long, Mrs. Rose Kennedy and other inhabitants of the Kennedy compound at Hyannis Port, Mass., had been annoyed by the blaring loudspeakers on boats taking tourists around Hyannis harbor. A lawyer for Mrs. Kennedy last week filed a complaint with the selectmen of Barnstable, who heard testimony from a Secret Service agent, who said that one tour guide went so far as to broadcast vivid descriptions of the assassinations of Mrs. Kennedy's sons, John F. and Robert F. Kennedy. That was enough for the selectmen, who have secured an agreement from the operators of two concerns that conduct the boat tours to turn off their loudspeakers when the boats pass the Kennedy compound.

August 13, 1971

HYANNIS, Mass., Aug. 23 (UPI)—Robert F. Kennedy Jr., 17-year-old son of the late New York Senator, was ordered to pay $50 in court costs on a loitering charge today after he allegedly spat ice cream into a policeman's face. He was arrested last night, about two weeks after his probation ended for a marijuana offense.

The policeman said the youth had been talking to a girl in a parked car that was obstructing traffic on busy West Main Street. He said the youth had refused to move along.

The youth, long-haired and wearing sandals, a blue work shirt and patched dungarees, pleaded nolo contendere (no contest) when arraigned in Barnstable District Court. He did not have the money to pay the fine. Judge Henry L. Murphy gave him one week to pay. The youth appeared alone and without a lawyer in court.

The arrest was his second in just over one year. Last summer, he and his cousin, Sargent Shriver Jr., son of the former Ambassador to France, were arrested on a marijuana charge and placed on probation for one year.

With expiration of the probation Aug. 6, the marijuana charge was placed on file.

About 10:30 P.M., yesterday, Patrolman Frederick Ahern testified, young Kennedy was standing outside the car talking to a girl inside and eating an ice cream cone.

Patrolman Ahern said he had asked young Kennedy to move along because the car was snarling traffic. He said the youth had made no effort to do so.

The policeman said the youth's eyes had been "bloodshot" and so he had asked young Kennedy if he was drunk. The youth replied, "no," the policeman said, and spat ice cream on him.

Young Kennedy was asked by the judge if he had anything to say and replied, "The officer is lying."

However, Judge Murphy said the youth had no right to try to refute the police testimony unless he pleaded innocent or guilty.

August 24, 1971

Onassis Marriage Contract Said to Contain 170 Clauses

LONDON, Oct. 31—According to Christian Kafarakis, former chief steward on Aristotle Onassis's yacht, Christina, the marriage contract between Mr. Onassis and his wife, the former Jacqueline Kennedy, was so complex that it required 170 clauses.

Mr. Kafarakis worked aboard the Christina for 10 years. His story of "the extraordinary marriage contract that was thrashed out between the respective lawyers and signed by the couple in New York three days before the ceremony on the isle of Skorpios" appears today in The People, a popular Sunday newspaper.

Mr. Kafarakis, who is also to publish a book on the subject, did not explain in the copyrighted article how he became privy to the contract. The marriage took place three years ago.

"I am one of the few people who have been privileged to learn the contents of this remarkable document with its 170 clauses, covering down to the smallest detail the married life of this celebrated couple," he wrote.

According to Mr. Kafarakis, the contract stipulated "separate bedrooms" for the couple and lays down the times of the year they spend together. This explains, he said, why "Jackie has her own house on the isle of Skorpios, and why, in New York, she always stays in her flat on Fifth Avenue while her husband rents a suite on the top floor of the Hotel Pierre four hundred yards away."

The financial arrangements, which Mr. Kafarakis claimed to know in detail, show, he said, Mr. Onassis's "greatest generosity."

He said that Mr. Onassis is committed to laying out at least $600,000 for his wife's travel, pleasure, safety and children. This is in addition to his gifts to her and the provisio of a sumptuous manner o living.

So that his wife may b "sheltered from want," th agreement laid down, accordin to Mr. Kafarakis:

"If Onassis should ever parı from Jackie he will have to give her a sum amounting to nearly £4.2-million [$9.6-million] for every year of their marriage.

"If she leaves him, then her payoff will be a lump sum in the neighborhood of £7.5-million [$18 mllion]—which is a highly desirable neighborhood. That is if the parting comes before five years.

"If she sticks it out for longer she will receive, in addition to the £7.5-million, an alimony of £75,000 a year for 10 years.

"If Onassis dies while they are still married she will inherit the staggering sum of £42-million [$100-million]."

November 1, 1971

AIDE OF MRS. ONASSIS DENIES BRIDAL PACT

WASHINGTON, Nov. 1 (UPI)—A spokesman for Mrs. Jacqueline Kennedy Onassis today described as "ridiculous" a report that a marriage contract exists between her and Aristotle Onassis, the Greek shipping magnate, that specifies separate bedrooms and an outlay of $600,000 a year for her travel, pleasure, safety and children.

"That's ridiculous," said Mrs. Onassis' personal secretary, Nancy Tuckerman. "Honestly there's no such thing. It's really quite unfair and unkind. It's so fabricated."

Christian Kafarakis, described as a former chief steward aboard Mr. Onassis' yacht, Christina, told of the alleged marriage contract in an interview that appeared in the London Sunday newspaper The People.

In his article, Mr. Kafarakis wrote that the contract, said to contain 170 clauses, was signed by he couple in New York three days before they were married in 1968 on the Isle of Skorpios.

According to Mr. Kafarakis, Mrs. Onassis stays in her apartment in New York and her husband rents permanently a suite on the top floor of the Pierre Hotel there.

"He doesn't have an apartment at the Pierre," said Miss Tuckerman. "There is no contract."

November 2, 1971

Notes on People

A bill that would preserve the natural state of Chappaquiddick Island and other islands of Nantucket Sound by placing them under a local-Federal trust has been introduced by **Senator Edward M. Kennedy**. Chappaquiddick is the island where a car carrying the Senator and a secretary, Mary Jo Kopechne, plunged off a bridge, resulting in the death of Miss Kopechne. Richard Drayne, a press secretary for the Senator, said Mr. Kennedy was aware that his bill might renew talk of the accident.

"What kind of Senator would he be," Mr. Drayne asked, "if he hesitated to introduce a bill because Chappaquiddick is involved?"

April 14, 1972

Notes on People

"I have been seeing a psychiatrist since January, 1971, because I had lost my self-confidence," **Mrs. Edward M. Kennedy** said in an interview in the June issue of Good Housekeeping magazine. Mrs. Kennedy declared: "It's very easy to feel insecure when you marry into a very famouse, intelligent, exciting family. I certainly don't regret having done it, but it's been very difficult. You start comparing yourself to the other Kennedy women and somehow your confidence in yourself begins to evaporate. "In trying to bolster her self-esteem, the Senator's wife said she tried to imitate her Kennedy sisters-in-law, and that only made matters worse. And, she said, she used attention-getting clothes imprudently, such as appearing at White House functions in micromini outfits and see-through blouses. "Let's just say, I don't need to do that sort of thing anymore," she was quoted. Mrs. Kennedy also said that she no longer opposed the idea of her husband running for President, but she hopes it won't be this year. "Four years from now," she said, "I'll be more able to cope."

May 16, 1972

U.S. Judge Bars Photographer From Going Near Mrs. Onassis

By MAX H. SEIGEL

United States District Court Judge Irving Ben Cooper ruled yesterday that the activities of Ronald E. Galella, the self-styled "paparazzo" photographer, had "relentlessly invaded" the right to privacy of Mrs. Aristotle Onassis and had interfered with the protective duties of the Secret Service.

The judge permanently enjoined the photographer from approaching Mrs. Onassis or her children to take their photographs; from carrying out surveillance of them; from using photographs of Mrs. Onassis for advertising or trade purposes without her consent; or from communicating, or attempting to communicate, with Mrs. Onassis or her children.

At the same time Judge Cooper dismissed a $1.3-million suit filed against Mrs. Onassis by Mr. Galella, who charged that she had interfered with his livelihood as a photographer. Judge Cooper held that the fact that Mrs. Onassis wore sunglasses, or a dark dress, or a veil did not constitute behavior to warrant a suit for damages.

Mr. Galella had charged in addition that Secret Service agents had interfered with his picture-taking activities on several occasions and that he had been pushed by agents more than once. But Judge Cooper ruled that hardly more than a faint glimmer of evidence had been introduced to show that Mrs. Onassis had been in any way responsible.

"Further," the judge's opinion added, "we find that the pushings never happened," with the exception of one incident after a movie screening. In that instance, the ruling held, the act "was justified."

Judge Cooper also granted a permanent injunction authorizing the United States Government to keep Mr. Galella from harassing Mrs. Onassis's children.

Assistant United States Attorney Michael D. Hess, who represented the Government, said afterward:

"The Government feels that this is a significant precedent, in that it is the first injunction granted to the Secret Service to aid it in the performance of its protective duties."

Judge Cooper found that Mr. Galella's behavior, both before and during the trial, constituted civil contempt of court on three counts.

Two counts involved violations of temporary restraining orders issued Oct. 8 and Dec. 2, 1971. The orders were designed to keep the photographer from harassing Mrs. Onassis and her children by approaching them to take photographs. The third count was for "willfully and knowingly failing to produce photographic matter called for in the deposition subpoena."

Judge Cooper declared that the Court would impose a fine for each of the acts of civil contempt but would set the amount after a hearing to be held later.

A special section of the 130-page opinion related to the activities of Mr. Galella's trial counsel, Alfred S. Julien. Judge Cooper said he felt constrained to take Mr. Julien to task for "what we believe was unprofessional conduct throughout the trial, persisted in even after warnings that he desist."

The judge cited repeated charges during the trial by Mr. Julien that the Court was biased; an accusation in open court that the judge was guilty of unprofessional conduct (followed by an apology the following day); false accusations by Mr. Julien that Mrs. Onassis's lawyers were guilty of unprofessional conduct; obstructive tactics in rearguing objections following rulings of the Court, and misleading of the court and witnesses by misquoting and inaccurately summarizing prior evidence.

"Mr. Julien evidenced disrespect of the Court," Judge Cooper said. "He roared, mocked and facially expressed his disdain and derision for the other side and its counsel. When we found ourselves duty-bound to rule against him, his utterances were accompanied by simulated grief."

But Judge Cooper said that while he could hold Mr. Julien in civil contempt, he preferred to refer this matter to the bar association to determine Mr. Julien's "fitness as a member of an honorable profession."

Mr. Julien said outside the

courtroom later:

"A lawyer's job is to stand up for his client as courageously and professionally as he can. I did it. And I believe Judge Cooper is in error in many respects. After reviewing the papers thoroughly, I would expect that the matter will be appealed."

The permanent injunctions granted to Mrs. Onassis and the Government yesterday direct Mr. Galella or any of his agents not to approach within 100 yards of the home of Mrs. Onassis and her children, or within 100 yards of the schools attended by the children. At all other places and times Mr. Galella must stay 75 yards from the children and 50 yards from Mrs. Onassis.

The injunctions will not go into effect until July 17, after they are submitted in detail to Judge Cooper and court orders are signed.

In his 130-page opinion — written after a study of more than 4,700 pages of testimony, hundreds of exhibits and hun-

dreds of pages of post-trial briefs—Judge Cooper reviewed the credibility of the principals on the witness stand.

In discussing Mr. Galella's testimony, Judge Cooper said: "The record is studded with instance after instance where the testimony was clearly perjurious . . . not a single event, episode or incident, out of scores with which the total trial record deals, was established in his favor."

Judge Cooper added that he was convinced Mr. Galella's suit had a double purpose: to get Mrs. Onassis or her husband to pay money to him to end his harassment, or to take advantage of the publicity his action would promote.

As for the testimony of Mrs. Onassis, the judge said it fully met the burden of credibility by a preponderance of proof. He described the cross-examination of her by Mr. Julien as "bitter, repetitious, prolonged and rasping," but remarked that she was candid and careful, frequently searching for the proper word

to be precise.

Judge Cooper described the testimony by the Government's witnesses as convincing and corroborated to a great extent by the evidence of Mrs. Onassis.

In terms of law, the trial had assumed some importance since it represented, among other things, a test of freedom of the press against the right of privacy. In his opinion, Judge Cooper declared: "We see no constitutional violence done by permitting defendant to prevent intrusion on her life which serves no useful purpose."

Taking a generally broad view of privacy, the judge said it was the function of the Court to draw the lines to accommodate both the rights of a free press and the privacy of the individual. He pointed out that privacy was guaranteed by the Constitution.

"The First Amendment," he said, "protects the right of freedom of association. The Fourth Amendment protects the individual from unreasonable searches and seizures. The

Fifth Amendment, and its privilege against self-incrimination, safeguards the individual in a zone of privacy into which the Government may not intrude, and the Ninth Amendment provides that the enumeration in the Constitution of certain rights shall not be construed to deny or disparage others retained by the people."

Against this, the judge said, the First Amendment does not give newsmen unrestricted rights.

"We conclude," he said, "that the First Amendment does not license Galella to trespass inside private buildings, such as the children's schools, lobbies of friends' apartment buildings and restaurants. Nor does that amendment demand that Galella be permitted to romance maids, bribe employes and maintain surveillance in order to monitor defendant's leaving, entering and living inside her own home."

July 6, 1972

MIAMI BEACH, Thursday, July 13—Senator Edward M. Kennedy turned down an offer this morning to run for Vice President on the ticket headed by Senator George McGovern. Mr. McGovern said through a spokesman here that he had made the offer in a telephone conversation with Mr. Kenneddy after receiving the Presidential nomination at the Democratic National Convention.

Later, Mr. Kennedy said in

Hyannis, Mass., that he was "honored and humbled" by the offer but had to decline for "overriding personal considerations." In particular, he cited "personal family responsibilities" to his own family and those of his late brothers, John and Robert.

Won't Be Chairman

Mr. Kennedy added that he would consider taking a prominent role in the campaign but ruled out the possibility that

he would be its national chairman. He said he would talk to Mr. McGovern again today on the matter of other possible running mates for Senator McGovern.

In his statement here, the nominee expressed regret over Mr. Kennedy's refusal but said he "fully understood the Senator's position."

"The Kennedy family has already made great sacrifices to the nation," he added.

July 13, 1972

Kennedy Informs Nominee He Won't Be Running Mate

By DOUGLAS E. KNEELAND

MIAMI BEACH, Friday, July 14 — Senator Edward M. Kennedy of Massachusetts, the man who shunned his party's Presidential nomination this year, electrified the Democratic National Convention this morning with praise for Senator George McGovern and an exhortation to victory in November.

He brought the whistling, clapping, shouting, foot-stomping crowd to its feet time after time as he compared Senator McGovern, the Democratic Presidential nominee, to all the great men of the party's past—Jefferson and Jackson, Wilson and Franklin D. Roosevelt, Hubert H. Humphrey and Lyndon B. Johnson and his own brother, John F. Kennedy.

Mr. Kennedy quoted Woodrow Wilson's maxim to the effect that a great purpose makes a great party and said this convention and this candidate had met it.

And, indirectly, he urged

party unity by admonishing the new elements who have dominated the Miami Beach meeting not to treat with disdain "those who have worked a lifetime in the cause of human dignity."

He might well have been thinking of Mayor Richard J. Daley of Chicago—an old family friend who was denied a seat here—when he said "No one in this hall, no one in this land" had the right to write off the party's old warriors.

Mr. Kennedy scored the Republicans, telling the more than 3,000 delegates that "They had their chance and they failed, and the failure of leadership will be rewarded with failure at the polls in November."

With his wife, Jean, smiling behind him in a powder-blue dress, the Massachusetts Senator said that there was "a new wind rising over the land" — and then introduced the subject of his metaphor in the time-honored way as "the next President of the United States."

The crowd set up the mightiest roar of the night.

Thus a member of the most Illustrious family in the Democratic party's modern era electrified a Democratic National Convention for the fifth time in a period of 16 years.

In 1956, it was the boyish junior Senator from Massachusetts, John F. Kennedy, little known beyond Boston and Georgetown, doing battle for the Vice-Presidential nomination at Chicago with the late Estes Kefauver, who beat him.

In 1960, it was the same man, victor over Hubert H. Humphrey and the fear of Roman Catholic candidates and the suspicions of the old guard, claiming the Presidential nomination in Los Angeles.

Speech by Robert Kennedy

In 1964 at Atlantic City, with John Kennedy dead but a year, it was Robert F. Kennedy standing mute on the podium for 16 minutes while the applause surged up from below, then hushing the crowd, with words from Romeo and Juliet:

KENNEDY EXHORTS PARTY TO VICTORY

Electrifies Convention With Praise for McGovern and Appeal for Unity

---

By R. W. APPLE Jr.

The Heirs

"When he shall die, take him and cut him out in little stars. . . ."

In 1968, Robert Kennedy was assassinated like his brother, and it was Stephen Smith, a brother-in-law, who came to Chicago to wheel and deal in the Standard Club downtown while "draft-Teddy" rumors and plots floated through the chaotic convention hall until they were finally stilled.

Even before he flew to Florida tonight, Edward Kennedy had played a major role in this convention. Many of the anti-McGovern liberals clung to the last to the hope that a deadlock would prompt a draft. Representative Wilbur D. Mills of Arkansas and his agents fanned those embers all through the week.

July 14, 1972

SHRIVER IS CHOSEN BY M'GOVERN TO FILL SECOND SPOT ON TICKET

DECISION HAILED

Successor to Eagleton Called Favorite of Nominee's Staff

By CHRISTOPHER LYDON

WASHINGTON, Aug. 5—Senator George McGovern chose Sargent Shriver as his Vice-Presidential running mate today after Senator Edmund S. Muskie had rejected his invitation to join the Democratic ticket.

Mr. Shriver, the first director of the Peace Corps under his brother-in-law, President Kennedy, and of the antipoverty program under President Johnson, will be put in nomination before an expanded 303-member Democratic National Committee here Tuesday night.

He will succeed Senator Thomas F. Eagleton, who resigned from the race last Monday after disclosing that he had been hospitalized three times in the nineteen-sixties for nervous exhaustion and depression.

Mr. Muskie, the Democratic Vice-Presidential nominee in 1968 and the early front runner for the Presidential nomination this year, cited family considerations in becoming the sixth man to reject Mr. McGovern's offer.

Other Rejections

Earlier this week, Mr. McGovern had been turned down by Senators Edward M. Kennedy of Massachusetts, Hubert H. Humphrey of Minnesota and Abraham A. Ribicoff of Connecticut. In addition, Senator Gaylord Nelson of Wisconsin and Gov. Reubin Askew of Florida were thought to have been given chances to express interest but declined.

Mr. McGovern made his announcement for television cameras, sitting before a wooden desk in front of a false marble fireplace in a small room in the Capitol.

Mr. Shriver, who had sailed this morning off Hyannis Port, Mass., was playing tennis at the Kennedy family compound there when he received Mr. McGovern's firm offer.

Before leaving for Washington from the Barnstable, Mass., airport Mr. Shriver said he was "very happy and very proud" to have been chosen.

Staff Favorite

Mr. Shriver had been the choice of several factions within the McGovern organization at the Democratic National Convention three weeks ago, and was the staff's favorite after Mr. Eagleton's candidacy collapsed.

He has political roots in Chicago, where he once managed the Merchandise Mart, one of the world's largest office buildings, for the late Joseph P. Kennedy, and in Maryland, where he considered running for Governor in 1970. But he has never been a candidate before, a point that his advocates felt confirmed the antipolitics or beyond-politics air that the McGovern campaign began.

Mr. Shriver was recommended to Mr. McGovern at the convention at Miami Beach by the black members of his campaign staff and by Pierre Salinger, the White House press secretary during the Kennedy Administration.

But he was also thought to be an attractive figure in most of the Democratic party—a friend of Mayor Richard J. Daley of Chicago, for example, and warmly endorsed to Mr. McGovern last week by Senator Humphrey.

Last week, his outspoken backers came to include Congressional figures as diverse as Representatives Shirley Chisholm of Brooklyn, Wayne L Hays of Ohio, Sam M. Gibbons of Florida and Lester L. Wolff of Nassau County.

"He is attractive, personable and well-liked by a broad cross-section of groups," Mrs. Chisholm wired Mr. McGovern last week. "He knows the Hill and is an experienced and respected businessman, but he is equally at home with the poor and minority groups whose affection and support he earned during his tenure as head of the Office of Economic Opportunity."

Wife Foe of Abortion

There had been suggestions that the determined views of Mr. Shriver's wife, the former Eunice Kennedy, against abortion would be an obstacle in his selection. Senator McGovern has tried to keep the abortion issue out of the national campaign, saying it was a matter for the states to decide.

It had also been thought that Senator Kennedy, who discouraged Senator Humphrey's interest in Mr. Shriver as a running mate in 1968, might veto his selection this year.

But Mr. Kennedy was reported not to have involved himself in the consideration of Mr. Shriver this year. And on the abortion issue, Mrs. Shriver's strong convictions and her independence were considered to have an appeal even to people who disagreed with her.

August 6, 1972

Joseph Kennedy 3d Injured On Coast in Auto Accident

BERKELEY, Calif., March 25 (AP)—Joseph Kennedy 3d, eldest son of the late Senator Robert F. Kennedy, was reported in satisfactory condition at a hospital here today after suffering chest, skull and neck injuries in an automobile accident.

Mr. Kennedy, 20 years old, was placed in the intensive care ward for observation of a blow to the head he received in the accident, a spokesman at Herrick Memorial Hospital said.

X-rays showed no bone fractures, but Mr. Kennedy was expected to remain in the hospital through tomorrow.

He was injured last night when a car swerved in front of his auto near a busy Berkeley intersection, the police said. The two cars collided and Mr. Kennedy's auto then struck a parked car, the policemen said.

The other driver, a 16-year-old youth, was uninjured, the police said.

March 26, 1973

Notes on People

The nurse who attended the late Joseph P. Kennedy when he was incapacitated after suffering a stroke said that **Mrs. Aristotle Onassis**, then wife of President John F. Kennedy, was the member of the family who "completely accepted" the elder Mr. Kennedy's affliction. The nurse, **Rita Dallas,** related the Kennedy family's attitude toward the elder Kennedy's illness in excerpts from her forthcoming book, "The Kennedy Case," in the May issue of McCall's magazine.

Mrs. Dallas wrote: "One thing I always admired about the First Lady was that she completely accepted Mr. Kennedy's condition.

April 19, 1973

Robert Kennedy's Son Among 6 Injured When Jeep Overturns

NANTUCKET, Mass., Aug. 13 —David Kennedy, the 17-year-old son of the late Senator Robert F. Kennedy, and five other young people were injured this afternoon when a jeep driven by David's brother, Joseph, 21, overturned on a highway six miles east of here.

Joseph escaped injury, but David and three others were admitted at the Cape Cod Hospital in Hyannis, Mass., where they were flown by ambulance plane from this island 25 miles south of the Cape Cod elbow.

David was said by a hospital spokesman to be in "satisfactory" condition with a possible back sprain. He had no broken bones. The spokesman said that Pamela M. Kelley, 19, of Hyannis Port, was in serious condition with a possible spinal fracture. Mary Schlaff, 23, of Grosse Point, Mich., was listed in good condition. Patricia E. Powers, 22, of Spring Lake, N.J., was treated for neck and back injuries and released.

Kim Marie Kelley, 18, of Hyannis Port, was released after treatment of a minor leg injury, and Francesca de Onis, 18, of Centerville, Mass., was treated at the Nantucket Cottage Hospital for cuts and bruises.

The Nantucket police issued a summons to Joseph Kennedy for "operating negligently so that the lives and safety of the public might be endangered." A hearing on the charge was set in Nantucket District Court for next Monday.

The police said Joseph "lost control" of the jeep at 2:30 P.M. on the Polpis Road and all seven young people were thrown out when the vehicle overturned. The vehicle was described as a total wreck. No other vehicle was involved in the accident, the police said.

The Kennedys reside in McLean, Va., and have a summer home at Hyannis Port. Hospital officials at Hyannis said Mrs. Robert F. Kennedy, the Senator's widow, was at David's bedside.

August 14, 1973

Joseph Kennedy Is Found Guilty Of Negligence in Road Mishap

NANTUCKET, Mass., Aug. 20 (UPI)—Joseph P. Kennedy 3d, oldest son of the late Senator Robert F. Kennedy, was convicted today of negligent driving that resulted in an accident that at least temporarily paralyzed a teen-age girl. He was fined $100.

"You had a great father and you have a great mother," District Court Judge George Anastas told Mr. Kennedy, 20 years old. "Use your illustrious name as an asset instead of coming into court like this."

Mr. Kennedy, who pleaded not guilty and did not testify, was accompanied to the crowded court by his mother, Ethel, and his uncle, Senator Edward M. Kennedy, Democrat of Massachusetts.

A jeep-like vehicle driven by Mr. Kennedy and carrying six other persons including his brother, David, 18, overturned a week ago at an intersection on this vacaction island. David and two girl passengers were injured.

Francesca de Onis, 18, another passenger, said that Mr. Kennedy had been driving the Toyota at about 15 miles an hour but had accelerated and swerved at the intersection to avoid an oncoming car operated by Merrill Lindsay.

"I thought we were going to make it when the car driven by Kennedy got back on the pavement, and then it flipped," Miss de Onis said. "I was horrified."

Wayne Holmes, the defence counsel, said that if Mr. Kennedy had not speeded up, the Lindsay car would have "cut them in half."

Mr. Lindsay testified that he had been moving at 35 to 40 miles an hour when he saw the Kennedy vehicle "coming toward me in my lane." He said he braked his car and swerved left as Mr Kennedy swerved to the right and accelerated.

Bill Carlton, the investigating policeman, testified that Mr. Kennedy said "the accident was entirely his fault."

Miss de Onis said there were seats for everyone in the Kennedy vehicle, but Assistant District Attorney Robert Mooney said it had a capacity for only four.

Sandra Peterson, driver of a sightseeing bus, testified that she had seen the Kennedy vehicle before the accident. "People were hanging all over. Some were standing up," she said.

Judge Anastas, a college classmate of Mr. Kennedy's uncle, Joseph Jr., who was killed in World War II, asked Mr. Kennedy whether he believed a jail sentence was a deterrent to highway accidents. Mr. Kennedy said he did not think so. He said a "seriously hurt" person was more of a deterrent to a defendant in highway accident cases.

The prosecutor did not recommend a jail sentence on the charge, a misdemeanor carrying a maximum jail term of up to two years or a 200 fine or both.

The most seriously injured person in the crash was Pamela Kelley, 18, of Centerville. She suffered a back injury that left both her legs paralyzed.

August 21, 1973

Kennedy Son's Leg Amputated Because of Cancerous Growth

WASHINGTON, Nov. 17 (UPI) —The 12-year-old son of Senator Edward M. Kennedy had his right leg amputated today in an operation for cancer.

A hospital spokesman said the condition of Edward Moore Kennedy Jr. was "satisfactory." Four hours after the operation, the hospital said he was "making an uneventful recovery."

The Senator and his wife, Joan, were at Georgetown University Hospital during the operation.

The hospital spokesman said young Kennedy was taken into the operating room at about 8:30 A.M. and was taken out at 10 A.M. The surgery, performed by the hospital's chief of orthopedic surgery, Dr. George Hyatt, took about one hour.

While his wife remained behind, the Senator left the hospital 20 minutes later for Holy Trinity Church in Georgetown, one block from the university campus, for the wedding of Kathleen Kennedy, 22, the oldest of the 11 children of his slain brother, Robert F. Kennedy. The Senator gave the bride away.

He returned to the hospital after the ceremony.

Young Kennedy's right leg was amputated above the knee, although the malignant growth, discovered only last week, was below the knee.

November 18, 1973

Wedding Ceremony Brings Happier Moment to Kennedy Family

By LINDA CHARLTON

WASHINGTON, Nov. 17 — Kathleen Kennedy, the eldest of the late Senator Robert F. Kennedy's children, was married today to David Lee Townsend, a Harvard graduate student, in a ceremony slightly dimmed by yet another family tragedy but ebullient enough to include the singing of "When Irish Eyes Are Smiling."

Miss Kennedy, who is 22 years old, was escorted up the aisle of Holy Trinity Church promptly at 11 A.M. by her uncle, Senator Edward M. Kennedy, who had come to the church directly from Georgetown University Hospital, only a few blocks away. Senator Kennedy's 12-year-old son, Edward M. Kennedy Jr., had his right leg amputated because of bone cancer in an operation that ended an hour before the wedding.

The Senator's wife, Joan Kennedy, remained at the hospital. Mrs. Jacqueline Kennedy Onassis also was absent, but there were still plenty of Kennedys to fill the family pews, which were marked by bouquets of white roses and greenery tied up with green ribbon, matching the altar bouquet.

Well-Known Guests

The official word was that 160 persons had been invited, but the general impression was that considerably more than that were present, including a smattering of such well-known faces as John Glenn, the astronaut Frank Mankiewicz, who served as Senator Robert Kennedy's press secretary; Senator and Mrs. George McGovern, and Art Buchwald, the columnist.

Intensely correct in its externals—the ushers were in cutaways (whose fit was as random as is usual), boutonnieres and grey gloves, the groom and best man equally formal, and all the women in the wedding party in floor-length dresses—the service was comparatively informal. Both Miss Kennedy and her 25-year-old bridegroom had been deeply involved in working out the sort of ceremony they wanted.

The 55-minute wedding service was in English except for two songs, "Ave Maria" and "Panis Angelicus", crooned by Andy Williams, who sang "The Battle Hymn of the Republic" at Senator Robert F. Kennedy's funeral five years ago. The service included readings from the Song of Songs—"My Beloved Is Mine and I Am His"—and readings by the just-married couple of poetry they had chosen.

Mrs. Townsend, who wore a simple, long, white lace dress with a wrist frill, and a wreath of stephanotis and greenery in her abundant brown hair, chose a poem by Anne Bradstreet—a 17th century bluestocking who was the wife of a Massachusetts Bay Colony governor—entitled "To My Dear and Loving Husband." Mr. Townsend, tall, smiling, with reddish hair and Lincolnesque beard, chose "Fast-Anchor'd Eternal O Love!", a short poem by Walt Whitman.

The couple exchanged vows —"I, Kathleen, take you, David, my friend, to be my husband . . ." and with no "obey"—and rings, hand made by Mr. Townsend himself, during the course of the mass.

And then the young Jesuit priest, the Rev. James English, said, "and it is my great happiness to announce that we have a new Mr. and Mrs.

Senator Edward Kennedy escorts his niece, Kathleen Kennedy, daughter of the late Robert Kennedy.

THE KENNEDYS: A NEW YORK TIMES PROFILE

David Townsend, and to share in their great happiness by singing, 'When Irish Eyes Are Smiling.' " The words had, thoughtfully, been provided on a separate sheet of paper inserted into the white-covered order of service, which had the couple's first names on the cover in Gaelic.

There had been some muted strife about whether this went too far even for this church, whose liberalism is so renowned that one parishioner said jestingly that he was surprised they would allow the two songs in Latin.

Then came Mr. Williams, in high-heeled shoes and a flowered shirt, followed by Communion for the wedding party and anyone in the congregation who wished.

There were four Kennedys among the bride's attendants, including Caroline Kennedy and two of Mrs. Townsend's sisters, Courtney, 19, who was maid of honor, and Kerry. Aunt Jean Kennedy Smith, Stephen Smith's wife, was matron of honor.

They were all dressed in long velvet dresses of a green that the bride's mother, Ethel Kennedy, described as "emerald," but which looked a lot more like the darker green called "racing." The bridesmaids had wide, possibly Irish, lace collars and cuffs, with floppy hats to match; the maid and matron of honor, in the same color and material, wore perfectly plain high-necked and long-sleeved dresses. Mrs. Kennedy, smiling, wore an off-white coat with a matching pillbox far back on her head.

Six of the ushers were Kennedys, too, all of them Kathleen's brothers, along with David Hackett, a very old friend and prep school roommate of her father. John F. Kennedy Jr. was one of the altar boys.

Traffic was blocked from the street in front of the Greek Revival-style white church, which John and Jacqueline Kennedy attended when they lived nearby. A crowd of well-wishing sightseers stood in the crisp, sunshiny weather to cheer the bride when she arrived and as she and her new husband emerged just before noon to take off for the reception in the rumble seat of a 1932 car.

The number of other "generally newer" cars parked in the nearby lot reserved for wedding guests promised a traffic jam unusual even for a Saturday in Georgetown, that section of Washington that is perhaps most like New York's Greenwich Village—tawdry, raffish and elegant.

Mr. Townsend is the son of Mr. and Mrs. L. Raymond Townsend of Timonium, Md.. His father is an elementary school principal, and his family, too, is of Irish descent.

Replica of a Raft

The reception at Hickory Hill, the 19-room Georgian mansion in McLean, Va., that is the family home, was planned to be as traditional as the wedding, with a receiving line; a buffet luncheon of what was described as "gourmet-ish" cooking

that has kept the family's chef busy for the past week; champagne for the wine bibbers, and a bar stocked with the harder stuff for those who think the bubbly wine is strictly for christening ships.

Atop the wedding cake was an entirely nontraditional ornament replacing the usual doves, wedding figures or bells: It was a small replica of a raft, made for the occasion by 10-year-old Chris. Kathleen and her new husband didn't actually meet on a raft or anything, but during the summer of 1972 they and three friends constructed. what they thought was the sort of raft Mark Twain wrote about, and floated down the Mississippi River on a 21-day trip.

And there was dancing planned to the music of a band led by Chuck McDermott, an old friend of Kathleen, before the newlyweds took off on a honeymoon to that place almost always referred to as an "undisclosed location."

No one was talking about the wedding presents except for those made by some of the Kennedy children, such as a quilt hand-quilted by 14-year-old Kerry Lawford and 15-year-old Victoria Lawford, her cousins. Her small brothers and sisters have contributed the furnishings of the Cambridge, Mass., apartment that Mr. and Mrs. Townsend will live in, making such small indispensables as pillows and wastebaskets.

The Townsends met about two years ago when the then-

Miss Kennedy, an American history major who plans to go on to law school after she graduates from Radcliffe next spring, was studying Southern writers. Mr. Townsend was her tutor; he is a doctoral candidate in English at Harvard and a cofounder of a fledgling publishing house called Ministrel Books that is planned to specialize in modern literature and poetry.

Although "the family"—a term that for the Kennedys embraces what sociologists call the "extended family" rather than the "nuclear" one — was well represented among the participants in the wedding ceremonials, there was still plenty of room for others, what with more than 20 attendants.

Six Nonfamily Bridesmaids

So there were six nonfamily bridesmaids, all described as friends of the bride. They were Melinda Ludtke, Sophie Spurr, Mary Fullman, Barbie Grant, Margery Morton and Anne Coffey.

The ushers, aside from Mr. Hackett and four Kennedy boys—Joe, Robert F. Jr., David and Michael—included the bridegroom's brother, Larry Townsend, and friends Charles Seluzicki, William Johnson, Kenneth Howard, David Bownan and Fred Greenberg. And two of the small Kennedys, of course—Christopher and 8-year-old Max—were junior ushers; two more, 5-year-old Rory and 6½-year-old Doug, were the ring-bearers.

November 18, 1973

Marilyn Monroe had been having a romance with President John F. Kennedy for almost a year when she died, and among her last words were, "Say good-by to the President," Earl Wilson, a syndicated columnist, reports in a new book.

Mr. Wilson said he had carried on a three-year investigation to establish the fact of a "dalliance" between Miss Monroe and the President but had withheld the story for years. He said he had decided "to set the record straight" because of Norman Mailer's book on Miss Monroe, which dwelled on her friendship with Attorney General Robert F. Kennedy.

Mr. Wilson's book, "Show Business Laid Bare," scheduled to be published Jan. 28, said Miss Monroe had been trying to arrange another rendezvous with President Kennedy through a mutual friend, Henry Rosenfeld, a New York textile manufacturer, the week she died on Aug. 5, 1962 at the age of 36. She was anxious to go to Washington for the opening

of the play "Mr. President," using Mr. Rosenfeld as a cover date to get together with Mr. Kennedy, according to Mr. Wilson.

"And she was so proud to be the girl having an affair with the President of the United States, because that was important," Mr. Wilson quotes Mr. Rosenfeld as saying: "She wouldn't always mention his name. She would sometimes say to me, 'You know who!' "

However, Miss Monroe died of an overdose of sleeping pills before she could make the trip to the capital. Mr. Wilson said that Peter Lawford, a Kennedy in-law, believed he was speaking with Miss Monroe on the phone when she lost consciousness. He told the columnist her last words were:

"Say goodbye to Pat [Pat Kennedy Lawford], say goodbye to the President, and say goodbye to yourself, because you're a nice guy."

December 14, 1973

A New Book Links President Kennedy To Marilyn Monroe

Notes on People

President Kennedy and his wife, Jacqueline, now **Mrs. Aristotle Onassis**, "had one of the most loving, understanding and devoted relationships that I can imagine," says **Mrs. Rose Kennedy** in another excerpt from her autobiography appearing in the March issue of Woman's Day. "He loved her and was proud of her and appreciated her," said the mother of Mr. Kennedy. "And it would be hard to imagine a better wife for him. She brought out in him so many things that helped fulfill his character. She developed his interests in art, music and poetry—he learned to delight in poetry because she took such pelasure from it."

Of her own relationship with Mrs. Onassis, Mrs. Kennedy has this to say: "Jackie and I have been through a chain of life's events together and I still feel the bonds of understanding and love between Naomi and her daughter-in-law, Ruth."

February 19, 1974

Joan Kennedy Enters A Clinic in California

WASHINGTON, Sept 12 (AP) —Joan Kennedy, wife of Senator Edward M. Kennedy, Democrat of Massachusetts, has entered a private clinic in California for a rest, a spokesman for the Kennedy family said today.

Mrs. Kennedy made two visits earlier this summer to a New Canaan, Conn., sanitarium for treatment of what was described as fatigue and mental strain caused by the illness of her oldest son, Edward Jr., who lost a leg because of bone cancer.

She has been spending the summer at the family compound on Cape Cod, Mass. Mrs. Kennedy, 37 years old, flew to California last weekend, the spokesman said. He said he could not disclose the location of the clinic or give details of her condition or the planned length of her stay.

September 13, 1974

Kennedy Rules Out '76 Presidential Race

Bars Even a Draft, Citing His Family Responsibilities

By R. W. APPLE Jr.

BOSTON, Sept. 23—Senator Edward M. Kennedy, the heir to one of the great family traditions in American politics, removed himself without qualification today from the 1976 Presidential contest.

At a tumultuous news conference in the Parker House hotel, just below Beacon Hill, Mr. Kennedy said he was forswearing a campaign for national office because "I simply cannot do that to my wife and children and the other members of my family."

Until he spoke, the 42-year-old Massachusetts Democrat had been considered by the leaders of his party the favorite for its Presidential nomination two years from now, despite growing misgivings about his chances of defeating President Ford.

Mr. Kennedy's eyes were bloodshot but he appeared calm and resolute as he described his attitude. His language left little room for doubt that his decision was definitive.

"This decision," he said, "is firm, final and unconditional. There is absolutely no circumstance or event that will alter the decision. I will not accept the nomination. I will not accept a draft. I will oppose any effort to place my name in nomination in any state or at the national convention.

"And I will oppose any effort to promote my candidacy in any other way."

The decision of Mr. Kennedy, brother of an assassinated President and of an assassinated Presidential candidate, threw the 1972 Democratic Presidential competition into chaos.

Senators Walter F. Mondale of Minnesota, Lloyd Bentsen Jr. of Texas and Henry M. Jackson of Washington have already started their campaigns. So has Representative Morris K. Udall of Arizona. Govs. George C. Wallace of Alabama, John J. Gilligan of Ohio and Reubin Askew of Florida, among others, have been waiting in the wings.

None has been able to make much headway so far; it was hard to raise money or line up support while Mr. Kennedy's candidacy was still being bruited. His absence from the field, together with the prospect of at least 25 primary elections, now points toward an open nominating convention.

Senator Kennedy, dressed in a blue suit, a striped shirt and a blue-and-red tie, explained his decision solely in terms of his family responsibilities. He said he would be "unable to make a full commitment to a campaign for the Presidency."

His Third Removal

"Therefore, in 1976, I will not be a candidate for President or Vice President of the United States," the Senator said. For the third straight time — he also did so in 1968 and 1972 — Mr. Kennedy thus removed himself from consideration for high national office.

Although he said earlier that he would not make a decision until mid-1975, and later advanced the deadline to "late this year," Mr. Kennedy in fact made up his mind more than a month ago, according to intimates. He informed his family and his staff about 10 days ago.

"I have chosen to announce the decision now," he said, "in order to ease the apprehensions within my family about the possibility of my candidacy, as well as to clarify the situation within my party."

Mr. Kennedy did not specify the nature of the personal responsibilities that led to his statement today. But they are widely known, both to the public and to Democratic insiders.

As the last surviving Kennedy brother, he is father to three children and surrogate father to the offspring of his brothers;

his wife, with whom his relationship has sometimes been difficult, has been undergoing psychiatric care, and his son, Edward Jr., had a leg amputated last year in the hope of arresting a rare form of bone cancer.

The Senator's wife, Joan, clad in a white dress with red and blue stripes, sat behind him as he made his announcement. She appeared composed but drawn. She has been under treatment in a California hospital and, according to a member of the Kennedy staff, is expected to return there shortly.

Mr. Kennedy's son was reported, both by aides and by informed members of the Boston medical community, to be in no imminent danger. However, doctors familiar with the rigorousness of the treatment to which he is subjected every month said it was "punishing" and produced both physical and emotional side effects difficult for him and his parents to cope with.

Although Mr. Kennedy said this morning that it was not a major factor, his auto accident at Chappaquiddick Island five years ago almost certainly played some part in the Senator's decision. At a time when "morality" and "candor" have become watchwords in American politics, the accident itself —in which Mary Jo Kopechne, a passenger, drowned—and Mr. Kennedy's subsequent explanations were counted as political liabilities.

"I can live with my testimony," the Senator told the crowded news conference. "It is a deep, personal tragedy, and although I regret the incident, I believe that I could have focused the attention of the country on other issues."

He said that he believed that if he had run he would have been elected.

Despite the vigor of his own language, Mr. Kennedy was asked whether he would be willing to adopt the words of Gen. William Tecumseh Sherman, who said, apropos of efforts in 1884 to draft him for the Republican Presidential nomination, "I will not accept if nominated, and will not serve if elected."

"I think he's gotten too much publicity, anyway," said Mr. Kennedy with a smile.

A long-time associate of the Massachusetts Senator said that Mr. Kennedy was resigned to the probability that some diehards would not accept his statement. But the associate insisted that "there were no loopholes left and none intended."

Sources close to Mr. Kennedy who plans to seek re-election to the Senate in 1976, said they doubted that he would even attend the 1976 national convention, if only because his presence there would inevitably promote rumors.

Asked about subsequent years, Mr. Kennedy said he expected the 1976 Democratic nominee to win and then to be re-elected, thus foreclosing h own ambitions at least unt 1984. Thus, he said, his decisio holds "for any forseeable f

ture."

But by 1984—presuming th his forecast is accurate—M Kennedy will be only 52 yea old, reasonably young in term of the White House. So h chances for the Presiden were being written off by fe political professionals.

The Senator said that neith the party leadership nor h potential rivals for the Pre idential nomination ha brought pressure on him to d cide early. However, significar elements in the Democratic pa ty have made it clear—indirec ly but unmistakably—that the considered a declaration h Mr. Kennedy essential to th task of developing a candidat with any reasonable chance defeating President Ford i 1976.

In the process of selectin that candidate, Mr. Kenned said, he will try to avoid choos ing up sides because "th people tend to resent pr nouncements by elected off cials."

September 24, 1974

BOSTON, Oct. 26 (UPI) — Senator Edward M. Kennedy said in an copyrighted interview in The Boston Globe's Sunday issue that his conduct immediately after the 1969 incident at Chappaquidick Island in which a woman companion drowned was "irrational and indefensible and inexcusable and inexplicable."

However, in the interview, the first that Senator Kennedy has given to the press about the incident of July 18, 1969, he denied that either he or his companion had been under the influence of alcohol. The Senator also denied that he really was driving to the beach with her instead of to the ferry back to the mainland.

The woman, Mary Jo Kopechne, died when the car that Senator Kennedy was driving went off a narrow bridge and plunged into the water. The accident came after a party that the Senator and several aides attended.

The Senator, a Massachusetts Democrat, recently withdrew from consideration for President in 1976, saying as he did so that the Chappaquiddick incident had no bearing on his decision. He later acknowledged, however, that Miss Kopechne's death would undoubtedly have become a point of sharp questioning had he chosen to run for the Presidency.

In the interview with The Globe, Senator Kennedy acknowledged that he had been wrong when, in reporting the accident to police, he failed to inform them that two of his friends had tried to rescue Miss Kopechne but failed.

However, he said that an inquest judge was "erroneous and mistaken" in characterizing his driving of the car as probably "criminal."

The Senator gave to The Globe a copy of a study made for him in 1969 by the Arthur D. Little Company, which concluded that "braking only" would not have prevented a car going 20 miles per hour from going off the bridge, and that Senator Kennedy's headlights could have illuminated the bridge no sooner than three seconds prior to the accident.

Senator Kennedy also denied in the interview reports that he had asked a cousin who was at the party, Joseph Gargan, to take the blame for the accident. And he denied that he left the party at a later our than he has testified and that the rescue efforts of Mr. Gargan and another companion, Paul Markham, were made the following morning rather than moments after the accident.

Senator Kennedy, who did not report the accident to police until the following morning, said Mr. Gargan and Mr. Markham should not be faulted for not having reported it because he had told them he would do it.

However, he told The Globe, he almost drowned while swimming across the 500-foot channel from Chappaquiddick Island to Edgartown and was "absolutely exhausted" when he reached the other shore.

Senator Kennedy also repeated earlier denials that the party of Kennedy workers had been a "married man's night out." He said that his wife, Joan, had intended to be present at the party but "because of illness related to her pregnancy, she was unable to be there, really at the last moment."

October 27, 1974

Kennedy Labels as 'Indefensible' His Conduct at Chappaquiddick

---

BOSTON, Oct. 29 (AP)—Senator Edward M. Kennedy's cousin, Joseph Gargan, almost accepted responsibility for the Chappaquiddick auto accident that killed Mary Jo Kopechne in 1969, The Boston Globe quotes a "highly knowledgeable source" as saying.

In a copyrighted article in today's editions, The Globe reported what it termed "contradictions" between Mr. Kennedy's testimony and public statements about the accident and the statements of other persons involved.

The newspaper said that its unidentified source had said a plan to have Mr. Gargan take the responsibility was abandoned shortly before Mr. Kennedy reported the mishap to the police. Mr. Kennedy has said the report was made almost 10

COUSIN OF KENNEDY SUBJECT OF REPORT

hours after the accident.

The Globe quoted its source as saying that its conclusion was based on more than speculation and testimonial inconsistencies, and that Mr. Kennedy abandoned the plan because he "decided the alibi either couldn't work, or he couldn't live with it."

The Globe said that it found in a two-month investigation nearly 100 discrepancies in the testimony and statements of several persons.

October 30, 1974

$140,923 Insurance Said to Be the Total Paid to Kopechnes

BOSTON, Oct 30 (AP)—Auto insurance held by Senator Edward M. Kennedy paid $140,923 to Mary Jo Kopechne's parents after she died in a 1969 crash in the Senator's car at Chappaquiddick.

In a copyrighted story appearing today, The Boston Globe quoted Joseph F. Flanagan, the Kopechne's lawyer, as saying, "That was the total they received either directly or indirectly from the Senator."

Mr. Flanagan said he had disclosed the figure to end speculation about the amount of the settlement, which was paid by the General Accident Group of Philadelphia. Some published reports have placed the settlement as high as $500,000.

The lawyer said that Senator Kennedy, Democrat of Massachusetts, had made no payment out of his own pocket to the Kopechnes.

The amount paid was based on an actuarial estimate of Miss Kopechne's lifetime earning potential, Mr. Flanagan said.

According to The Globe article, all but one of the men and women who had attended a party with Miss Kopechne and Senator Kennedy before the accident would not consent to be interviewed. The women were characterized as "stoic, sad and silent," and the men as having "nothing left to say," beyond the record of an official inquest held on Miss Kopechne's death.

Raymond LaRosa was the sole party-goer who spoke to The Globe. He said that he had seen a dark car at the same time a deputy sheriff observed it, 90 minutes after Mr. Kennedy had said the accident occurred.

Mr. LaRosa said "I just don't recall," according to The Globe, but went on to say, "It could clear Kennedy once and for all if I told you it wasn't his Oldsmobile. But I really can't say."

October 31, 1974

KENNEDY CRITICIZES SERIES ON ACCIDENT

BOSTON, Nov 4 (AP)—Senator Edward M. Kennedy says that some articles published in The Boston Globe last week about his Chappaquiddick auto accident in 1969 contained charges that were "ugly, untrue and grossly unfair."

The Globe series included a tape-recorded interview with the Massachusetts Democrat about the accident in which Mary Jo Kopechne, a passenger in Mr. Kennedy's car, drowned.

In a letter published in the Globe yesterday, Mr. Kennedy disputed an allegation that he had intended to take Miss Kopechne for a walk on the beach, not to her motel as he had contended. They had been guests at a party for Kennedy aides.

"It is regrettable in the atmosphere of doubt and suspicion which enshrouds us as a people that the truth cannot compete with the unnamed sources, the groundless suggestions and the speculation which is nurtured by articles of sensationalism," he wrote.

The Globe editor, Thomas Winship, said the newspaper did not rely on just a single source in a two-month investigation of the Chappaquiddick incident. He said the writing team "carefully considered the integrity and knowledgeability of its sources before publishing any information provided by them."

November 5, 1974

Notes on People

Joan Kennedy was fined $200 and her driver's license suspended for six months yesterday after she pleaded guilty to charges of driving under the influence of alcohol. The wife of Senator Edward M. Kennedy, Democrat of Massachusetts, was to have appeared today in court in Fairfax, Va., for a hearing on the charge which was entered Oct. 9 after her car bumped into the rear of another stopped at a red light.

Instead, her lawyer yesterday entred a guilty plea for her in absentia and said "Mrs. Kennedy wants to accept her responsiblity in the matter." There were no injuries in the accident, her lawyer noted, although total damages were estimated at $1,400. The car Mrs. Kennedy hit crashed into another automobile.

November 7, 1974

PARIS, March 15—Aristotle Onassis, the Greek shipping magnate, died today at the American Hospital in nearby Neuilly-sur-Seine.

Mr. Onassis was taken to the hospital by special plane from Athens last Feb. 7 and underwent an operation to remove his gall bladder two days later. Although the operation was successful, he was also suffering from myasthenia gravis, a debilitating neurological disease, which had affected his heart.

Dr. Maurice Mercadier, one of his physicians, said death was due to bronchial pneumonia, which "resisted all antibiotics." Mr. Onassis had been receiving cortisone treatment, which, the doctor said, lowered his resistance to infection and made the pneumonia "uncontrollable."

Mrs. Onassis, the former Jacqueline Kennedy, was in New York today, but left for here by air in the evening. Mr. Onassis had not left the hospital since he arrived five weeks ago, and his wife had taken to commuting between Paris and New York.

Christina Onassis, the shipowner's daughter by his first marriage, was at the hospital with her father today.

His son, Alexander, died in an airplane crash in Greece two years ago.

Burial on Skorpios

ATHENS, March 15—Aristotle Onassis will be buried on his private island of Skorpios next to his son, Alexander, family friends said today.

Prof. Ioanis Georgakis, a close associate and legal adviser to the multimillionaire, had already left here for the island to make the arrangements, the sources said.

They said that details of the funeral would be announced tomorrow.

Skorpios is a 350-acre, pine-covered island off the west coast of Greece in the Ionian Sea.

Shrewd and Adventurous
By ALBIN KREBS

A shrewd and adventurous businessman who amassed a fortune estimated at more than $500-million, Aristotle Socrates Onassis knew the uses of money and the power that came with it.

He was said to have used these, often, to move quietly and with secrecy into positions of influence in the international shipping and petroleum industries and in high finance. He also knew how to use his influence with political leaders in his native Greece.

Known to both admirers and detractors as "the Golden Greek," the oil-tanker magnate professed to despise publicity, but loved spending lavishly at nightclubs and for many years carried on an internationally headlined romance with Maria Callas, the soprano.

Despite his oft-repeated protestations against press attention, he attracted it more than ever after 1968, when he married one of the most famous women of her time, Jacqueline Bouvier Kennedy, widow of President Kennedy.

Mrs. Kennedy's surprise choice of Mr. Onassis for a husband took his name off the shipping, financial and society pages of newspapers around the world and put it on Page One.

Gave Varying Birthdates

At the time of their marriage on Oct. 20, 1968, Mr. Onassis was, depending on which of his birthdates he gave at various times, 29 or 23 years older than his 39-year-old bride. He maintained that he was 62, but an Argentine passport issued to him in 1927 gave his birthdate as Sept. 21, 1900, and World War II draft board reports indicated that at one time he had sworn he was born in 1900. But he later said the year was 1906, contending that he had had to falsify his age because Argentina would take in no immigrants below the age of 22.

He was born in Smyrna, now Izmir, a Turkish city on the Aegean with a large Greek colony, to Greek parents, Socrates Onassis, a tobacco merchant, and Penelope Dologlu Onassis. Greece won the city for its part in World War I, but it was recaptured in 1922 by Kemal Ataturk's troops, who herded Greek males between the ages of 16 and 40 into concentration camps.

Mr. Onassis said that one of his uncles had been lynched before his eyes, but that he himself managed to flee with the rest of the family to Greece. In 1923 he boarded a freighter at Piraeus bound for Argentina. He arrived there with about $60 in his pocket.

Working for 25 cents an hour, Mr. Onassis served as a lineman and operator for the United River Plate Telephone Company in Buenos Aires. He listened in on overseas calls to learn several languages.

Gradually, Mr. Onassis worked himself into the tobacco import business, taking advantage of an Argentine fondness for Turkish and Bulgarian tobaccos, which had recently been introduced there. In two years he had made more than $100,000, and by 1930 was a millionaire.

For a time during the nineteen-twenties, Mr. Onassis, who held Greek and Argentine passports, served as Greek consul in Buenos Aires. It was a job that required his dealing with many Greek freighter captains, and it was during this period that he became interested in ships.

Bought Ships for $20,000

In London, in 1930, Mr. Onassis learned that the Depression had forced the laying up of ships around the world. "You could pick up a ship for the same price as a Rolls-Royce," he later recalled.

At $20,000 each, Mr. Onassis bought six freighters — which had cost $2-million each to build in 1920 — from the Canadian National Railway. In the decade that followed, he added more freighters and tankers to his fleet, and when World War II came, he owned many of the precious tankers in Allied waters.

The war, followed by the Marshall Plan, the Korean war, the Indochina war, the Suez crises and the Vietnam war, gave the shipping industry its golden age of growth and profits. By 1968, Mr. Onassis, using shipping as a base but dabbling in other interests, had amassed an estimated total of $500-million.

As the controlling figure in about 100 companies in a dozen countries, Mr. Onassis operated a fleet of about five million tons displacement under "flags of convenience." His holdings included hotels (a quarter interest in the Pierre in New York, for example), banks, pier facilities and real estate, as well as Olympic Airways, the Greek national airline, for which he obtained from the Greek Government a concession set for expiration in the year 2006.

Aristotle Onassis Is Dead Of Pneumonia in France

Amassed a $500-Million Fortune in Shipping— Wed Mrs. Kennedy

Aristotle Onassis

But by late last year, the airline's fortunes had declined, and Mr. Onassis canceled his contract. The Greek Government then began proceedings to take over the airline.

By that time, too, his multi-million-dollar Olympic Towers, a New York building planned to include offices as well as condominium apartments, was nearing completion at Fifth Avenue and 50th Street.

The yacht he had ordered, in 1970, as a 41st-birthday present for Jacqueline Onassis, was still being built late last year and the couple were still using the yacht Christina, which had been Mr. Onassis's floating home for years.

Mr. Onassis also owned a house in Athens, a villa in Monte Carlo, a hacienda near Montevideo, Uruguay; a Paris penthouse filled with 18th-century paneling and Louis XV furniture, and the island of Skorpios in the Ionian Sea. He and Mrs. Kennedy were married in the island's chapel in Greek Orthodox ceremonies.

Increased Tanker Size

Before Mr. Onassis got into the oil-tanker business, the largest tankers built were about 12,000 tons. "It doesn't take a genius to realize that the bigger the vehicle the lower the cost of transportation," he said, and acting on that premise, he built a 20,000-ton tanker.

In the middle nineteen-fifties he ordered five 28,500-ton tankers at a cost of $35-million. A decade later he and other shipowners were building 250,000-tonners.

Mr. Onassis had been told that such supertankers would never make money, as they could not negotiate the Suez Canal. The closing of the canal in 1956 by President Gamal Abdel Nasser of the United Arab Republic was a stroke of luck for Mr. Onassis, who made millions with his speedy supertanker hauls around the Cape of Good Hope. And when the 1967 Arab-Israeli war again closed the canal, the freight rate on oil soared from $5 to $18 a ton. By 1974, with the advent of the oil crisis, the price had almost doubled.

The international nature of Mr. Onassis's operations was reflected in the history of the Tina Onassis, a 45,000-ton tanker. The ship was built in Germany, mortgaged in the United States, insured in London, financially controlled from Monaco and manned by Greeks. It flew the flag of Liberia.

"My favorite country," Mr. Onassis once said, "is the one that grants maximum immunity from taxes, trade restrictions and unreasonable regulations."

Indicted in U. S.

Mr. Onassis's wheelings and dealings got him into trouble with several countries, notably the United States, which in-dicted him on civil and criminal conspiracy charges under the Shipping Act of 1916.

Mr. Onassis had bought 20 surplus Liberty ships after World War II, at cut-rate prices, with the understanding that they would be operated by American-controlled companies. But the Government charged that he controlled the companies in fact, if not in name. Ultimately, the criminal charges were dropped and the civil suit was settled for $7-million.

When he first met with Justice Department officials to arrange the civil settlement, Mr. Onassis grinned and asked one of them, "Well, what is the ransom?" Later, at a Congressional hearing, he was asked what he meant by the remark. "Ransom means recapture of your freedom," he answered smoothly. "It used to happen among the best people. Kings used to take kings and pay ransom."

In 1954, just after some of Mr. Onassis's tankers were seized by the Federal Government as a down payment on the settlement, the rest of his tanker fleet was boycotted by the big oil companies when it was revealed that he had made a deal to monopolize the oil-carrying market of Saudi Arabia. Mr. Onassis knuckled under to the oil producers, and the Saudi Arabian deal was called off.

He also took a loss in his dealings with Prince Rainier of Monaco. In 1952, wanting to rent office space in Monte Carlo, he approached the Société des Bains de Mer, the corporation that controls the gambling concession and the major hotels and clubs in the principality. His suggestion that he be rented space in the unused Winter Sporting Club was ignored.

Secretly, Mr. Onassis, through the 49 Panamanian companies he then controlled, started buying the Monaco corporation's shares on the Paris stock market, at about $5 a share.

He soon gained a majority interest and became known as "the man who didn't break, but bought, the bank at Monte Carlo."

For some time afterward, Mr. Onassis got along well with Prince Rainier, who appreciated the fact that when it became known the shipowner was injecting capital into the Monaco corporation, its shares doubled in value. The tourist business started booming, too.

Rift With Rainier

But Mr. Onassis had a basic dislike for gambling, Monaco's chief attraction for tourists. When he pushed the idea of tearing down tourist hotels and clubs and building office buildings in their place, he and Prince Rainier reached a parting of the ways.

In 1967, Mr. Onassis finally bowed to the Prince and sold his shares back to the corporation for $10-million. He said the shares were worth "six or seven times what they paid me." Despite the break, Mr. Onassis continued to operate several of his corporations from Monaco, taking advantage of the principality's tax laws.

In running his vast complex of business enterprises, the peripatetic Mr. Onassis caromed from one major city to another, usually carrying only a small briefcase. He maintained duplicate wardrobes in his various homes and in leased hotel suites in a dozen countries, and thus seldom needed luggage.

Mr. Onassis's social headquarters for many years was the Christina, formerly the Canadian frigate Stormont, which he bought in 1954. He spent $2.5-million converting it into a floating palace with vast staterooms, baths of Siena marble with gold fixtures, lapis lazuli fireplaces, a mosaic dance floor that drops to become a swimming pool, and its own amphibian plane.

A 50-man crew tended the Christina, whether she was anchored in the harbor at Monte Carlo or on one of the many cruises of the Mediterranean, Aegean and Caribbean on which Mr. Onassis took his friends.

End of First Marriage

It was during one such cruise, in 1959, that Mr. Onassis and his first wife decided to end their marriage, and another cruise, in 1963, that he met his second wife, Mrs. John F. Kennedy.

In 1946 Mr. Onassis had married Athina Livanos, daughter of Stavros Livanos, an even wealthier Greek - born shipping magnate than Mr. Onassis or Stavros Niarchos, also a shipping multimillionaire, who married another Livanos daughter, Eugenie. Tina Onassis and her husband had two children, Alexander, born in 1948, and Christina — for whom the yacht was named— born in 1950.

On the Christina's summer cruise in 1959 were, among others, Sir Winston Churchill and his wife and daughter Diana; Battista Meneghini, a Milan industrialist, and Mr. Meneghini's wife, the soprano Maria Callas. Mr. Onassis had met Miss Callas in 1956, and despite his evident dislike for opera—he was known, later, to be subject to snoring in his box during a Callas performance — they became extremely close. By the time the 1959 cruise began, gossip columns had begun linking them romantically. By the time it ended, it was evident the Onassis and Meneghini marriages would also end.

The Onassises were divorced in 1960, the same year the Meneghinis were legally separated. Mr. Onassis and Miss Callas remained close until 1968, although they never married.

She maintained apartments in the same hotels he did in Paris and Monte Carlo. In 1968, Mr. Onassis told his semiofficial biographer, Willi Frischauer: "There was an affinity between us. No more than a friendship. . . ."

Meeting Mrs. Kennedy

Mr. Onassis met his second wife in the fall of 1963, when Mrs. Kennedy was on holiday in Greece after the birth and death of her second son, Patrick Bouvier Kennedy. With her was her sister, Princess Lee Radziwill, an old Onassis friend. Mr. Onassis brought them aboard the Christina for one of his standard tours of the Aegean, which included a stopover on Skorpios. After President Kennedy's assassination later that year, Mr. Onassis often visited the Kennedy family in Hyannis Port, Mass.

But there were few, if any, rumors of a romance developing between the shipowner and the President's widow and so, when it was announced that they would be married in October, 1968, the news created shocked—and sometimes incredulous — headlines in the United States and abroad. "Jackie, How Could You?" was the headline in Expressen, of Stockholm.

The furor was probably a result of the fact that at home, the much admired, elegant widow of a President had been put on a pedestal, while abroad she had virtually been enthroned. And she was marrying a much older man, a self-made, mostly unschooled, tough, high-living businessman and playboy.

At the time of his second marriage, Mr. Onassis had thick, silvery hair that contrasted sharply with his black eyes. He clothed his rather squarish 5-foot, 5-inch physique in expensive, though often baggy, suits.

Although he had little formal education, Ari, as some of his friends called him—to others he was Telis — was fluent in Greek, English, Turkish, Spanish, French, German and Italian, and he was well read in Greek and English history. His taste in art ran toward the old masters, and among the dozens of paintings he owned was a $200,000 "Madonna and Child" by El Greco. It hung in the Christina's salon.

In 1973 it became apparent that Mr. Onassis was in deteriorating health. He was suffering from myasthenia gravis. Last fall, he spent a week in a New York hospital, after he had been photographed with his eyelids taped up to keep them from drooping.

Mr. Onassis was also said to be still in grief over the death, in the crash of a private plane in 1973, of his only son, Alexander. And in recent months he had gone through an exhausting, unsuccessful campaign to convince residents of a New Hampshire town that they should allow him to build a $600-million refinery there.

Rivalry With Niarchos

Mr. Onassis's enmity toward his business rival and onetime brother-in-law, Stavros Niarchos, which was evidently returned, was epic in its proportions. When Mr. Niarchos divorced his wife some years ago and married Charlotte Ford, 32 years his junior, Mr. Onassis is said to have commented, "Poor fellow, he's going through a change of life." In 1968, when Mr. Onassis married a woman much younger than himself, Mr. Niarchos was able to reply in kind.

In 1971 Mr. Onassis's first wife, Tina, was married to Mr. Niarchos. She died in October, 1974.

For years the two men engaged in a heated game of one-upmanship. When Mr. Niarchos built a 106,000-ton supertanker, it was reported to have been because Mr. Onassis's biggest tanker at the time was 105,000 tons. Mr. Niarchos bought the 700-ton schooner Creole; Mr. Onassis came up with the 1,600-ton Christina. The acquisition by Mr. Onassis of Skorpios for $84,000 came after Mr. Niarchos had purchased a smaller, cheaper Greek island.

His feud and rivalry with Mr. Niarchos reached a climax in early 1969, when they fought over a lucrative Greek oil refinery concession. Mr. Onassis had offered the Greek Government an investment "package" worth $400-million in order to obtain the concession and thwart an attempt by Mr. Niarchos to undercut him with a $500-million investment offer.

Mr. Onassis finally won the concession with a $600-million investment offer, but the contract was later canceled with the Government's consent.

Often Mr. Onassis confided to his friends that he couldn't understand why people looked upon him as a mystery man and, too often, regarded him with suspicion. He believed he had an unfavorable image, he said, because "they think I'm a Greek with too much money."

He agreed with those who said he "always seemed to be at war with someone," whether it was the United States Government, or world oil interests. "Taking up these challenges has been most strenuous, dangerous and expensive," Mr. Onassis said, "but I thank God that I have been able to afford it and that I have a strong stomach."

March 16, 1975

Miss Onassis Denies Her Father Planned Divorce

PARIS, April 17 (AP)—Christina Onassis, daughter of the late Aristotle Onassis and principal heir to his shipping fortune, denied today that her father had planned to divorce Jacqueline Kennedy Onassis.

"These stories are totally untrue," she said.

In a statement issued here, through the offices of Olympic Airways, Miss Onassis, 24 years old, also said her relations with her stepmother, described by many intimates as strained, were based on friendship and respect.

"There are no financial or other disputes separating" her father's widow and herself, Miss Onassis said.

The statement followed reports from New York that Mr. Onassis had asked a lawyer last December to consider being his attorney in divorce proceedings. There were also reports of disputes between Miss Onassis and her stepmother concerning the inheritance.

[Meanwhile, Miss Onassis filed a lawsuit in Athens seeking the annulment of the marriage of her dead mother, Tina, to Stavros Niarchos, the shipping tycoon, Reuters reported.

[Miss Onassis's suit contended that her mother's marriage to Mr. Niarchos—who is Christina's uncle—was not valid because she was his fifth wife and a close relative. Greek law allows a Greek Orthodox to marry up to three time and forbids wedlock between close relatives.]

The New York Times reported last Saturday that, on Dec. 3 of last year, an associate of Mr. Onassis called Roy M. Cohn, the lawyer, and asked him if he would represent Mr. Onassis in a divorce action against Mrs. Onassis.

Reached by telephone yesterday, Mr. Cohn said that The Times article was correct.

"It was true, exactly as printed," he said.

Mr. Cohn, who was not the source of the original Times article, declined to comment further.

However, it has been learned that the conversation on Dec. 3 between Mr. Onassis's associate, John Meyer, and Mr. Cohn was not their first, and that Mr. Cohn had been consulted several times before that about an Onassis divorce.

It was also learned that Mr. Onassis had made inquiries about hiring a private investigator to gather evidence he could use in a divorce proceeding.

April 18, 1975

Robert Kennedy's Son, 20, Is Held on Speeding Charge

WOODSTOCK, Va. July 13 (AP)—David Kennedy, 20 years old, son of the late Senator Robert F. Kennedy, was arrested and accused of driving 92 miles an hour down Interstate 81 near here last night.

Mr. Kennedy of McLean, a suburb of Washington, was charged with reckless driving and failing to have a driver's license and auto registration in his possession. He was arrested near New Market after his car was clocked by radar at 92 miles an hour in a 55-mile-an-hour zone, the state police said.

County Magistrate David Scott said Mr. Kennedy had been held briefly in Shenandoah County jail here until the state police verified with the police in McLean that he had a driver's license and that the 1974 Toyota he was driving was registered properly. Mr. Kennedy was then issued a summons and released. He is scheduled to appear in general district court here July 25.

July 14, 1975

Will Gives Mrs. Onassis $250,000 a Year

ATHENS, June 7—Aristotle Onassis left the bulk of his estate to his daughter Christina, but provided for an annual allowance of $250,000 to his widow, Jacqueline Kennedy Onassis, according to his will published here today.

Mr. Onassis stated in his will that half of his estate should be used to finance a foundation, to be known as the Alexander Onassis foundation, to carry out welfare activities, for the most part in Greece. The foundation is dedicated to Mr. Onassis' only son, who died following a plane crash in 1973.

The bequest to Mrs. Onassis breaks down to $100,000 a year from tax-free bonds, plus an additional $100,000 a year in personal income for herself and $50,000 a year for her children.

The foundation, to be set up in Vaduz, Liechtenstein, will be financed through two new companies, Alpha and Beta, in which Miss Onassis, who is 24 years old, will hold a substantial number of shares.

Miss Onassis and her stepmother will also be on the board of directors of the foundation.

Miss Onassis, like her stepmother, will also receive an annual allowance of $250,000. If she marries, her husband will receive $50,000 a year for life.

Mr. Onassis died in a Paris clinic in March at the age of 69 after a long illness.

According to the handwritten will, drafted by Mr. Onassis on Jan. 3, 1974, on his private jet on a trip from Acapulco, Mexico, to New York, Mrs. Onassis signed a document in New York, in which she gave up all rights to her husband's estate.

In exchange, she receives the allowance, which includes $25,000 for each of her two children, John and Caroline Kennedy. After they are 21 the entire allowance will be paid to their mother.

Earlier reports said that Mrs. Onassis would receive bequests ranging from $3-million to $200-million.

Mrs. Onassis also inherits a fourth of the family's private island of Skorpios, in the Ionian Sea, and a like share of the yacht Christina. Miss Onassis inherits the remaining three-quarters of the island, and the yacht.

Mr. Onassis said in the will that if the women are unable to maintain the island and yacht, the island should go to the Greek state and the yacht to the head of the Greek state.

Miss Onassis, the daughter of the late Tina Livanos Onassis, also inherits all the shares of the Victory Carriers Company, which is believed to control all the Onassis business enterprises.

She also inherits 50 shares of the Beta Company and 450 of the shares of the Alpha Company as well as 61 per cent of the 90 per cent of her father's shares in Olympic Airways, the Greek national airline. She will be a member of the committee set up to carry out Mr. Onassis's will.

The bequests will be paid to Mrs. Onassis through the new foundation, which will be set up in Liechtenstein, with the allowance being readjusted annually to comply with the present value of the dollar.

Others who shared in the will include Mr. Onassis's three sisters, a cousin and a number of associates, servants and friends.

Mr. Onassis said in the will that if Mrs. Onassis resorted to the courts over the estate, despite the contractual agreement, a committee should oppose the action.

The will, which begins "To my dear daughter," stipulates that Miss Onassis is responsible for carrying out her father's wishes. The will was made public two days after an Onassis legal adviser in Athens read a statement here on behalf of Miss Onassis, disclosing that half of her father's estate would be given away through the nonprofit foundation.

Will Tells of a 'Resignation'

ATHENS, June 7 (UPI)—In his will published today Aristotle Onassis wrote: "I have received from my wife her resignation from any claims of inheritance through a notarized agreement in the United States."

"If my wife raises any inheritance claims," he went on, "then she will not be given her annuity of my estate. If she wins a final ruling from a court that cannot be appealed, then she will receive one-eighth of the estate of Christina."

Stelios Papadimitriou, Mr. Onassis's legal adviser and an executor of his will, refused to disclose whether Mrs. Onassis had accepted the will or intended to contest it.

June 8, 1975

KOPECHNES VOICE DOUBT ON MISHAP

They Seem to Be Unsatisfied by Report of Kennedy

WASHINGTON, Aug. 24 (AP)—The parents of Mary Jo Kopechne indicate in an article published by New Times magazine that they are not satisfied with Senator Edward M. Kennedy's account of the auto mishap that took their daughter's life.

In the interview, the Kopechnes say they believe Miss Kopechne was sleeping in the back seat of Mr. Kennedy's car when it plunged off a bridge on Chappaquiddick Island six years ago.

Her mother, Gwen Kopechne, is quoted further as saying that she believes Mr. Kennedy a Massachusetts Democrat, "was still confused" about the mishap when he made his first statements and also "had poor advice, right from the time it happened." "I think the got so involved in this lousy advice and then couldn't back out and tell the truth. He got deeper and deeper into it," Mrs. Kopechne is quoted as saying in the magazine article scheduled to be published tomorrow.

Miss Kopechne was a 28-year-old former campaign worker for Mr. Kennedy's brother, Robert, and attended a party with a group of other persons on the small island adjoining the island of Martha's Vineyard on the night of July 18, 1969.

Mr. Kennedy's sworn statement is that he was returning to his hotel and taking Miss Kopechne back to hers when he made a wrong turn and accidentally drove off the bridge. He said he had managed to escape from the submerged car but had been unable to rescue the young woman.

"What hurts most," Joseph Kopechne is quoted as saying, "is to think that my daughter had to be left there all night. At least his [Mr. Kennedy's] two buddies [Joseph Gargan and Paul Markham] could have telephoned. There was an outside possibility my kid could have been saved."

Mr. Kopechne also said, according to the magazine, that he and his wife had rejected an autopsy of their daughter because "we were made to believe that the autopsy was primarily to find out if my daughter was pregnant."

August 25, 1975

Jacqueline Kennedy Onassis has been retained as a consulting editor at Viking Press, Thomas H. Guinzburg, president of the New York-based publishing house, announced yesterday.

The widow of President Kennedy and of Aristotle Onassis, the shipping industrialist, will report for work next Monday, Mr. Guinzburg said, but although she will maintain an office at Viking she will not work set hours and her retainer fee, the amount of which he would not disclose, would be modest.

Mr. Guinzburg noted that Mrs. Onassis moves in "a wide circle of social, political and international contacts," and he suggested that her role at Viking would be that of a scout for possible Viking manuscripts. "As far as I know, she has no present plan to write a book herself," he said.

Her editorial suggestions will be available to all areas of the company, Mr. Guinzburg said, including adult trade and children's books and the paperback division. He said that her decision to associate herself with Viking was a logical one, as "we have been friends since our college days."

September 17, 1975

Jacqueline Onassis Is Editor at Viking

LONDON, Oct. 23—A bomb exploded this morning under a car parked outside the home of a Member of Parliament who is serving as host to Caroline Kennedy, 17-year-old daughter of the late President. The blast killed one of Britain's leading cancer specialists.

Miss Kennedy, who is studying in London, was in the house of the M.P., Hugh Fraser, at the time and preparing to depart in the car that was bombed. She was described by Mr. Fraser as "very shaken" and was quickly taken to a neighbor's house.

Later in the day Miss Kennedy briefly left home in Campden Hill Square, in the Kensington section, with several friends. "I am fine," she said. "I am sure this has nothing to do with me."

October 24, 1975

Bomb Kills a Doctor Near London Home Of Caroline Kennedy

By BERNARD WEINRAUB

SAN DIEGO, Dec. 17—Judith Campbell Exner maintained today that, although she had had a close personal relationship with President Kennedy while she was dating two leaders of a Chicago crime syndicate, she had never acted as an intermediary between the Mafia and the White House.

At a news conference here called to dispel what she termed "wild-eyed speculation," Mrs. Exner, who is about 41 years old, said she had never discussed with Mr. Kennedy her relationships with the late Sam Giancana, then head of the Chicago syndicate, or John Rosselli, an associate of Mr. Giancana.

Nor, she said, had she ever been aware during the time she was seeing President Kennedy and the two crime figures that Mr. Giancana and Mr. Rosselli, were helping the Central Intelligence Agency to recruit agents in an unsuccessful plot to assassinate Prime Minister Fidel Castro of Cuba.

Mr. Castro's name, the woman said, was never mentioned in the numerous telephone conversations she had with Mr. Kennedy, beginning in March 1961, or during what she said were a number of private White House lunches in the President's office.

Mrs. Exner, whose tanned face was partly hidden behind saucer-shaped sunglasses, said that all of her discussions with the President, whom she said she had also seen on some occasions while he was traveling outside of Washington, were entirely "of a personal nature."

Mrs. Exner declined to comment on a report that she had spent some time with Mr. Kennedy in Palm Beach, Fla., but she said that she had paid for whatever trips she had taken to meet Mr. Kennedy when he was traveling around the country.

She added that, although she had not worked during the two years that she was close to Mr. Kennedy, she "was always financially able to take care of

Kennedy Friend Denies Plot Role

Judith Campbell Exner at news conference in San Diego

Judith Campbell Exner in 1960, the year she said she met Mr. Kennedy.

myself." She said she got her money from her family.

She repeatedly declined to elaborate on her relationship with any of the three men, and replied with a "no comment" when asked whether she had also known the late Robert F. Kennedy, the President's brother, who served as Attorney General in the Kennedy Administration.

A Government source said, however, that Mrs. Exner was known to have attended "a party or two" with Robert Kennedy when he was the Attorney General.

In a prepared statement read before reporters and cameramen crowded into a suite at the downtown Westgate Hotel, Mrs. Exner, who was accompanied by her attorney, Brian Monaghan, and her husband of eight months, Daniel Exner, said that she hoped to "set the record straight" about her relationships with the Mafia, which have been the subject of leaks to newsmen from the Senate Select Committee on Intelligence, and about what she called "distortions" concerning her friendship with "Jack Kennedy" by former White House aides.

The first account of Mr. Kennedy's relationship with the woman, then known as Judith Katherine Campbell, was published in The Washington Post on Nov. 16. The Post article reported that Senate investigators had been intrigued by, but had later discounted, the possibility that Miss Campbell might have learned of anti-Castro plots from one of the Mafia leaders and passed on her knowledge of them to President Kennedy.

The Senate committee's report on the C.I.A. assassination plots, released four days later, concluded that there was no evidence to show that Mr. Kennedy or any of his aides had been made aware of the plots while they were under consideration between 1960 and 1962.

Mentioned Briefly

The report mentioned the Campbell relationship briefly, but did not give her name or sex or identify her as other than a "close friend" of Mr. Kennedy who had also known Mr. Giancana and Mr. Rosselli. The committee said, however, that it had no reason to believe the friend had had any knowledge of the involvement of her friends in a plan to kill Mr. Castro.

Mrs. Exner said today that subsequent reports by the Scripps-Howard news organization, The Chicago Daily News, The New York Times "and other papers" had implied "that I was a go-between for the Mafia," and that leaks of her secret testimony before the committee had been "distorted so as to implicate me in these

bizarre assassination conspiracies."

All the news accounts of the matter have noted, however, that the Senate committee concluded that Miss Campbell did not know of the conspiracies. But she insisted today that her sole motive for summoning reporters was nonetheless to clear her name. She said she had no wish to sell the rest of her story to book publishers or to the news media.

Safire's Accusation

William Safire, a columnist for The Times, accused the Senate commitee in an article published Monday of having sought to cover up the details of the Kennedy-Campbell relationship on partisan grounds, but the committee's chairman, Senator Frank Church, Democrat of Idaho, said the decision to include only the barest information about the matter in the assassination report was approved by all the members of the committee—Republicans as well as Democrats—after it was established that the matter was not relevant to the topic of assassinations.

Senator John G. Tower, Republican of Texas, the panel's vice chairman, said last night that Senator Church had "bent over backwards to avoid the appearance of a coverup," and that he did not believe the committee had been used by Mr. Church or anyone else for "political purposes."

Mrs. Exner said in answer to questions regarding her relationship with Mr. Kennedy and the circumstances surrounding her introduction to him and to Mr. Giancana that she would "clarify" such details at a later time and under unspecified conditions.

She said she met Mr. Kennedy through a "mutual friend" in Las Vegas, Nev., in February 1960, when Mr. Kennedy, then a Democratic Senator from Massachusetts, was beginning his successful campaign for the Presidency.

There has been some speculation that that relationship might have been initiated by Mr. Giancana in the Mafia's interest, but Mrs. Exner said today that she had not met Mr. Giancana until March 1960, while attending a party in Miami Beach.

Mr. Giancana, who she said subsequently introduced her to Mr. Rosselli, ran his end of the Castro assassination plot from a suite in the Fontainebleau Hotel in Miami Beach. According to the Senate report, however, that plot was not conceived within the C.I.A. until the following August.

Mrs. Exner declined today to name the friend who introduced her to Mr. Kennedy and then to Mr. Giancana, but Senate sources identified him as Frank Sinatra, the singer.

Lawyers for Mr. Sinatra, whom Mrs. Exner described as a "friend," had no immediate comment on his alleged involvement.

Asked whether she had been aware at the time that Mr. Giancana and Mr. Rosselli were important figures in the Mafia, Mrs. Exner said at first that she "didn't really know," but conceded later that she "probably knew they were members of the underworld."

Although she said that, to her knowledge, Mr. Kennedy had not know that she was also seeing the two Mafia figures, Mrs. Exner added that she thought Mr. Giancana was aware of her relationship with the President, although she said she never told him of it or discussed it with the Chicago crime leader. Mr. Giancana was slain last June 20 at his home in Oak Park, Ill.

Mrs. Exner emphatically denied reports that she had called Mr. Kennedy at the White House from a telephone in Mr. Giancana's home. One source familiar with the records obtained by the Senate committee said they showed at least one such call from Oak Park, although not necessarily from the Giancana residence.

Asked whether she had ever called Mr. Kennedy from her own home in Los Angeles or anywhere else, Mrs. Exner, who seemed nervous during most of her 45-minute appearance, quickly answered, "Oh, yes."

According to Justice Department sources, the Federal Bureau of Investigation became aware of Miss Campbell not through her relationship with Mr. Kennedy, but in the course of an investigation of Mr. Giancana's activities in the crime syndicate.

One such source said today that the F.B.I. subsequently discovered that Miss Campbell had placed two calls to the White House switchboard from her home in Los Angeles, and that the apparent relationship between her and the President was eventually brought to the attention of Robert Kennedy and Kenneth O'Donnell, a special assistant to the President, in a memorandum from the late J. Edgar Hoover, then director of the F.B.I., dated Feb. 27, 1962.

The Senate committee reportedly obtained from the John F. Kennedy Presidential Library copies of the telephone logs kept by Evelyn Lincoln, the President's private secretary, which showed 70 telephone calls to the White House from Miss Campbell between March 29, 1961, and March 22, 1962.

Telephone Log

William Moss, the chief archivist at the Kennedy Library, said in a telephone interview today that Mrs. Lincoln's logs only showed calls made to the President's office in the

White House, and not any calls he might have made to Miss Campbell or anyone else.

Some of the 70 calls, Mr. Moss said, were placed from Palm Springs, Calif., and Los Angeles, as well as other places around the country.

Mr. Moss added that there were no records at the library of any calls to or from Mr. Kennedy during periods in which he was away from the White House, and he said that, although none of the library's records of visitors to the Oval Office bore Miss Campbell's name, those records were not as inclusive as the ones kept by the Secret Service.

Jack Warner, a spokesman for the Secret Service in Washington, declined today to say whether his organization had any record that Mrs. Exner had ever been cleared for admission to the White House or to the President's office.

Mr. O'Donnell was traveling and could not be reached for comment. Mrs. Lincoln, according to the Senate report, told the committee that she had received a copy of Mr. Hoover's Feb. 27 memorandum describing Mrs. Exner's Mafia associations and "believed she would have shown it to the President."

Angie Novello, who was Robert Kennedy's secretary when he was Attorney General, said in a telephone interview today that, while she did not recall seeing the memorandum, it might have been delivered directly to the Attorney General by the F.B.I agent who then acted as the bureau's liaison with the Justice Department.

Mrs. Lincoln reportedly told the Senate panel that she recalled Mrs. Exner only as a worker in the President's California primary campaign in 1960, and did not believe the woman had ever seen Mr. Kennedy at the White House or anywhere else after his election in November 1960. Mr. O'Donnell reportedly endorsed this recollection.

Mrs. Exner expressed irritation today at what she characterized as efforts by Mrs. Lincoln and Mr. O'Donnell to sully or distort my personal relationship with Jack Kennedy."

"To me he was Jack Kennedy and not the President," Mrs. Exner said.

Mrs. Lincoln's friends said she was traveling in Europe and could not be reached for comment.

Mrs. Exner said that, whenever she called the White House, she would "always talk to Eve-

lyn Lincoln first," and would then be put through to the President immediately, "if that was my purpose for calling."

Pressed by reporters to say what other reason she might have had for calling the White House, Mrs. Exner said she could think of none.

The Senate committee reported that the F.B.I. briefed Mr. Hoover on Miss Campbell's associations with the Mafia a second time, just before a March 22, 1962, luncheon meeting between Mr. Hoover and the President.

The committee said there was no record of whether that subject was discussed during the hour-long meeting, although another participant, who has asked not to be identified, said it never came up while he was present.

The committee report noted, however, that the last telephone call between Mr. Kennedy and Miss Campbell shown in Mrs. Lincoln's log took place a few hours after the Hoover luncheon.

Mrs. Exner said today she could not recall that conversation with Mr. Kennedy or ever having discussed Mr. Hoover or the Mafia with the President. "I know nothing about that meeting other than what I've read," she said.

One source familiar with the evidence said there was "some indication" that Miss Campbell attempted to call the President after March 22, 1962, but that she was rebuffed.

Mrs. Exner said today, however, that "Jack Kennedy and I last talked in late 1962," about a year before the President was assassinated in Dallas on Nov. 22, 1963.

She said she last spoke to Mr. Giancana toward the end of 1964, and had not talked to Mr. Rosselli for "five or six years."

Mrs. Exner said that the Senate committee staff had read portions of the file compiled on her by the F.B.I. in the course of her testimony, and that what she heard seemed "prying, insidious and sounded more like a scandal sheet than a governmental investigation."

She and Mr. Monaghan, her attorney, said they intended to seek the contents of that file under the Freedom of Information Act.

An F.B.I. spokesman in Washington categorically denied that the bureau had used "illegal techniques" against Mrs. Exner in its investigation, or had "harassed" her, as she contended today.

December 18, 1975

Kennedy's Mother Recalls Pledge He Wouldn't Run

WASHINGTON, Jan. 4—Rose Kennedy has said in a published interview that she extracted a promise from her last surviving son, Senator Edward M. Kennedy of Massachusetts, that he would not run for President this year.

But she was quoted as saying, "I feel Teddy may be pressured into running for President this year. I don't want him to, but the pressures may force him."

Senator Kennedy has filed formal affidavits required to keep him off the primary ballot in some states, asserting that there were "no circumstances" that could make him a Presidential candidate in 1976.

Informed of his mother's interview today while he was campaigning in Massachusetts for re-election to the Senate, Mr. Kennedy insisted, "Nothing has changed, and nothing will change."

His mother's remarks appeared in a Palm Beach interview in The National Enquirer with Charles Van Rensselaer, an acquaintance of the Kennedy family who used to write for the Hearst newspapers under the name Cholly Knickerbocker.

'He Promised Me'

In the interview, the 85-year-

old Mrs. Kennedy said that the assassinations of two of her sons—President Kennedy and Senator Robert F. Kennedy—had prompted her to appeal to Edward Kennedy not to run for the Presidency.

"He promised me, he promised me faithfully that he would not run," she said. "I told him I did not want to see him die, too, that I could not stand another tragedy like the deaths of his brothers, John and Bobby.

"I have made Ted promise me repeatedly that he would not run for the Presidency. I told him that his family needs him too much, that John's children and Bobby's children need him as the father they no longer have.

"But even though he has given me his promise that he will not run, I realize there are considerations that could make him change his mind. He may feel it is something he has to do, or the party may feel he must. And if that is his decision, I would support him. I'll campaign for him, anywhere he wants me to. You know, I'm quite a campaigner."

'He Shouldn't Run'

But she quickly added: "He shouldn't run, though. Oh, no. No. We've had so many trag-

edies already. I have prayed so much about this and I have asked God that Teddy will be led to the right decision. But in the end I have put it all in God's hands and I will follow His will, no matter what it is."

By the admission that she would not hold her son to his promise, Mrs. Kennedy seemed to open a crack in a political door that Senator Kennedy has repeatedly and insistently slammed shut. His firm comment today seemed intended to squelch any expectations that his mother's published comments might arouse.

Among some voters and a few old Kennedy hands an ember of hope still glows about a deadlocked convention and unforseen political conditions that could overwhelm all those disclaimers. But in the polls and in political circles, Senator Kennedy has convinced more and more people that he means exactly what he says.

January 5, 1976

Mrs. Exner Plans a Book On Kennedy Friendship

By JOHN M. CREWDSON

Judith Campbell Exner, who has described herself as President Kennedy's "close friend," has decided to tell what she says that she knows about Mr. Kennedy and other prominent personalities in return for what her literary agent, Scott Meredith, said yesterday would be a sum of money "substantially into six figures."

Mr. Meredith announced at a news conference here that he was accepting bids for Mrs. Exner's memoirs from "appropriate American publishers," and that the National Enquirer had purchased serialization rights to the as yet unwritten book for $150,000.

Mrs. Exner, whose relationships with the late President and a Mafia leader, Sam Giancana, who was slain last year, were first disclosed by the Senate Select Committee on Intelligence, maintained at a news conference in San Diego last month that she had no wish to profit from her purported friendship with the two men.

She left a number of questions unanswered on that occasion, saying that she was speaking out only to clear herself of any involvement in plots by the Central Intelligence Agency to assassinate Prime Minister Fidel Castro of Cuba, and that details of her personal life would be made public at a more appropriate time.

The Senate panel said that although Mrs. Exner had been close to Mr. Kennedy and Mr. Giancana in the early 1960's, when the organized crime figure was helping the C.I.A. in its unsuccessful assassination attempt, it had found no evidence that she had known of the plot or acted as a liaison between the Mafia and the Kennedy White House.

Mr. Meredith said yesterday that hundreds of requests from the news media for details of Mrs. Exner's life and sizable offers of money for her story, had led to her decision to answer the remaining questions in a book.

"It just seems the best way to do it," he told reporters assembled in the Savoy Room of the Plaza Hotel. He said "everything is going to be revealed" in the memoirs when they are published next summer.

Mrs. Exner, he said, was unable to attend the news conference because "she has no money." He said that she was living in a mobile home near San Diego.

A hint of the book's contents was contained in a 10-page outline being circulated to prospective publishers and released yesterday by Mr. Meredith. Asked how his agency could be sure that Mrs. Exner's story, which none of Mr. Kennedy's former aides have corroborated, was truthful, Mr. Meredith replied that he was "satisfied" that her assertions were ac-

curate.

"We know that when this book comes out, everybody will be satisfied," he said. He added that Mrs. Exner had "a fairly substantial collection of photographs" of herself with the figures about whom she would write, including Mr. Kennedy and Mr. Giancana.

Mr. Meredith said that the Senate committee, and not his client, first disclosed details of her relations with the President. "She didn't break this story," he said.

According to the book outline, which Mr. Meredith said had been prepared by his office and approved by Mrs. Exner and her lawyer over the telephone, Mrs. Exner already knew Mr. Kennedy's sister Patricia and her husband, Peter Lawford, the actor, when she met John Kennedy, then a Senator.

That introduction, she said, took place at a dinner party at the Sands Hotel in Las Vegas on Feb. 7, 1960, at a time when Mr. Kennedy and his youngest brother, Edward, who is now a Democratic Senator from Massachusetts, were involved in the 1960 Presidential primary campaign.

The mutual friend who arranged for her to attend the dinner was Frank Sinatra, the singer, whom she had been dating for several months. Mrs. Exner said in the outline that she and the singer had by that time discovered a divergence in their sexual preferences, but "remained good friends."

Mrs. Exner described the evening that followed as an early morning "round of gambling" with Edward Kennedy, who she said attempted to take her with him to Denver later that day and who became "childishly temperamental" when she insisted on keeping a luncheon date with his older brother.

John Kennedy, she said, later told her that he shared her opinion of "Ted's tendency to childishness" and expressed doubts that "Ted would act responsibly enough" to ever become President.

A spokesman for Mr. Sinatra said he had no comment on Mrs. Exner's assertions, and an aide to Senator Kennedy said that the Senator could not remember ever having met her.

The picture that Mrs. Exner painted of what she said was her affair with John Kennedy was one of a sexual and emotional relationship that began in earnest during a four-day assignation at the Plaza Hotel here in March, 1960. She said that the relationships extended over the next two years to Palm Beach, Los Angeles, Chicago and Washington, where, she said, she saw Mr. Kennedy first at his Georgetown home and later at the White House.

In mid-1961, she said, she met with the President at the White House about 20 times. At one point, she said, Mr. Kennedy told her that his marriage had been "in poor shape" and that his wife, Jacqueline, had made known her intention to divorce him.

The Kennedy family managed to hold the marriage together, Mrs. Exner said, by telling Mrs. Kennedy that "a divorced Catholic from Boston stood small chance" of gaining the Democratic Presidential nomination or winning the general election.

Mrs. Exner said that Mr. Kennedy had promised to take her on "a two or three-months cruise" if he did not win the nomination.

She said that she remembered the President as "a warm, extraordinarily energetic and inquisitive man" who "was fascinated by Hollywood gossip and [by] who was sleeping with whom among the stars."

Her relationship with the President, the 41-year-old Mrs. Exner said, ended in the fall of 1962, about a year before his assassination in Dallas, not out of bitterness, but because the difficulty in maintaining their clandestine relations produced too many "frustrations."

During nearly all that time, she said, she was also seeing Mr. Giancana, to whom she was introduced by Mr. Sinatra about a month after she first met Mr. Kennedy. She said that she had turned down a proposal of marriage from Mr. Giancana.

Mr. Sinatra, she said, "seemed aware" of her relationship with Mr. Kennedy when he introduced her to Mr. Giancana at a party in Miami Beach.

She said that she and Mr. Giancana never discussed the C.I.A. assassination plot or Mr. Giancana's other business, although Mr. Giancana "joked" with her about her relationship with the President.

Mr. Giancana, who was murdered in his suburban Chicago home last June, once bragged to Mrs. Exner, she said, that he "had thrown his weight behind" Mr. Kennedy in the close Presidential election in 1960.

Mr. Kennedy's victory in Illinois was a crucial factor in his defeat of Richard M. Nixon that year, and Illinois' electoral votes were pushed into the Democratic column by Mr. Kennedy's margin in Cook County, which includes Chicago, where Mr. Giancana's influence was strongest.

The outline of Mr. Exner's book also said that she, John and Jacqueline Kennedy were all treated by Dr. Max Jacobson, a Manhattan practitioner who specialized in providing his patients with injections of amphetamines, and whose relationship with the late President has been rumored but never established.

January 15, 1976

The Kennedy fortune, estimated at $300 million to $500 million, has advanced the political careers of a United States President and two Senators from one of the nation's best-known families.

And it almost certainly will smooth the path for a new generation of office-seeking Kennedys—such as 24-year-old Joseph P. Kennedy 3d, who was in New York recently seeking a quick education on the intricacies of state and municipal financing. The visit was a possible prelude to his running for State Treasurer of Massachusetts.

Typically, Mr. Kennedy (the eldest son of the late Senator Robert F. Kennedy) was not in Manhattan to immerse himself in the details and management of the family fortune. Indeed, partly because the Kennedys have traditionally avoided such involvement, the Kennedy millions and the men who oversee this wealth remain obscure to a degree almost unknown among other great American fortunes.

The dimensions and details of the Kennedy family holdings—amassed by the late Joseph P. Kennedy, who was a deft entrepreneur and master speculator in real estate and stocks—are known only to a small group of accountants and tax experts retained by the family.

Aided by an I.B.M. System 3 computer, they manage the fortune from a flamboyantly decorated suite of offices on the 30th floor of the Pan Am Building in New York.

Contributing to the air of mystery surrounding the family's affairs are the silver-lettered inscriptions at the entrance to their offices—a sanctum where outsiders seldom intrude.

On the left-hand side of a double door is printed: "Joseph P. Kennedy Enterprises." No such company exists.

Only slightly more revealing is the adjacent inscription: "Park Agency Inc." This is the family's real estate holding company, which is named after the avenue in New York where it has been situated for almost three decades.

Despite all the secrecy, valuable clues to both the fortune and the men who oversee it can be gleaned from tax returns, court documents and other sources of financial information plus interviews with businessmen and financiers associated with the Kennedys.

Accumulated by the family patriarch in the 1920's, 30's and 40's, the Kennedy riches today are heavily invested in real estate, to a lesser degree in a variety of stocks, bonds and tax-exempt securities and to some extent in oil and gas enterprises.

These investments are deployed in a series of trust funds, foundations and privately held companies designed to preserve the family's capital. The chief overseer is Stephen E. Smith, 49 years old. He is the husband of Jean Kennedy, youngest of Joseph P. Kennedy's daughters.

Mr. Smith, described as bright, brash and sometimes abrasive, is a native of Brooklyn and comes from a wealthy family. His grandfather made a fortune operating a tugboat company called Cleary Brothers Inc., now defunct.

Working alongside Mr. Smith in handling the Kennedy finances is Thomas J. Walsh, a lively, 60-year-old certified public accountant. He says family affairs are kept so secret that John F. Kennedy once asked him during a visit to the White House who was

richer—the President or his youngest brother, Edward. Mr. Walsh says he wouldn't tell.

Acting as "Mister Inside" to Mr. Smith's "Mister Outside," Mr. Walsh handles the day-to-day operations of the Kennedy family enterprises and carries the title of president or treasurer of a number of the individual companies and foundations.

Under the supervision of Mr. Smith and Mr. Walsh, a dozen employees—eight of them accountants and two of them former agents for the Internal Revenue Service—manage the family holdings.

Simultaneously, Gertrude Ball, an office secretary, plays "mother hen" to the Kennedy grandchildren. The other day, for example, a daughter of Patricia Kennedy Lawford popped into the office for help in arranging a cross-country auto trip.

The operations of the staff lie in three major areas:

¶Overseeing the assets of trust funds set up in 1926, 1936, 1949 and 1959. The trusts serve as repositories for a total of about $100 million and provide taxable income of about $500,000 a year for each of Joseph Kennedy's five surviving children and for his widow, Rose.

¶Managing such companies as the Park Agency, which operates the gigantic Merchandise Mart and the new Apparel Center, both in Chicago. Other family enterprises include the Kenoil Corporation, the Mokeen Oil Company and various other real estate, oil and mineral holdings that produce income for the Kennedys and their trusts.

¶Operating charitable and memorial activities, including the Joseph P. Kennedy Jr. Foundation and such affiliated operations as the John F. Kennedy Library, the Robert F. Kennedy Memorial, the Park Foundation and the Special Olympics Inc.

As in many wealthy families, the central staff not only manages the Kennedys' investment portfolios and enterprises but also prepares family members' tax returns, coordinates their charitable contributions, handles a variety of individual requests and pays the salaries of domestic help.

The vivid décor of the Kennedy offices in the Pan Am Building provides a startling contrast to the subdued appearance of typical financial offices. A visitor who walks into the reception foyer of "Joseph P. Kennedy Enterprises" might think he is entering a discotheque:

The carpet is a bright red plaid. The wall facing the door is covered with bold zigzag stripes of red, yellow and blue. The furniture is plastic modern. The only sobering touch is an enormously framed photograph of the Merchandise Mart.

The suite contains a dozen individual offices, situated off a corridor that begins at the left rear of the reception room and ends with two corner offices—occupied by Mr. Smith and Mr. Walsh—that offer a spectacular view of midtown Manhattan.

Much of the work that goes on in these offices revolves around the series of trusts set up from 1926 to 1959 by Joseph and Rose Kennedy.

The trusts provide income for their five surviving children—Senator Edward M. Kennedy, Eunice Kennedy Shriver, Jean Kennedy Smith, Rosemary Kennedy and Patricia Kennedy Lawford—as well as for Rose Kennedy herself. Joseph Kennedy died in 1969.

The trusts also provide income for the heirs of the late President Kennedy and the late Senator Robert Kennedy. Two of Joseph Kennedy's children—Joseph P. Kennedy Jr., and Kathleen Kennedy Hartington—died without leaving either spouses or children, so the income from their trusts is distributed to other members of the family.

The two largest sets of trusts were established in 1926 and 1936 by Joseph Kennedy. A third and lesser set of trusts was established in 1949 by Rose Kennedy. The fourth set of trusts, still smaller, was set up in 1959 on behalf of Joseph Kennedy's grandchildren.

The details of the trusts are closely guarded, but their basic size and profitability can be deduced from examining Senator Edward Kennedy's income tax returns—which he has made available to newspapers in Boston for several years.

His 1975 return, for example, lists taxable income of $192,299 from the 1926 trust and $115,409 from the 1936 trust. In addition, he received $39,587 from the 1926 trust as a distribution from his sister Kathleen's share, and $38,700 as a distribution from his brother Joe's share.

Altogether, Senator Kennedy's taxable trust income in 1975, including dividends, totaled $417,542. It is not possible to determine from his tax return whether he received additional tax-exempt income as well.

Persons close to the family say the major trust funds are allocated in roughly $10 million segments for each of the 10 recipients or their estates.

Some of the control of the principal from the trusts has already passed into the hands of Joseph Kennedy's heirs. He stipulated that at certain intervals (such as his children's 40th and 45th birthdays) control of the principal would begin to move from the trustees to the male beneficiaries.

The trustees who watch over the funds are close friends or spouses of the Kennedys. Serving as trustees for both the 1926 trusts and the 1949 trusts are R. Sargent Shriver Jr., Eunice's husband, and K. LeMoyne Billings, 62, who went to school with John Kennedy.

Mr. Shriver, now 61, ran the Merchandise Mart in the 1940's and 1950's. In 1953 he married Eunice, and later he worked in John Kennedy's Presidential campaign. Mr. Shriver was the Democratic nominee for Vice President in 1972. He is a partner in the Washington law firm of Fried, Frank, Harris, Shriver & Kampelman, which handles some of the Kennedy family's legal affairs.

Other firms that do legal work for the Kennedys are Ropes & Gray of Boston and Lawrence Krieger of New York.

Mr. Billings sometimes works in his shirtsleeves at a desk in the Pan Am Building suite. He is not, however, a paid employee of the Kennedy organization.

The trustees of the 1936 trusts are John T. Fallon, president of the Boston real estate firm of R. M. Bradley & Company, and Stephen Smith. Mr. Billings oversees the 1959 trusts.

Over the years, the trustees have changed occasionally. As recently as 1970, one of the trustees of the 1926 trusts was Andre Meyer, senior partner of the investment banking firm of Lazard Frères & Company and long-time friend and financial adviser to the Kennedys. The other trustee was Thomas J. Watson Jr., former chairman of the International Business Machines Corporation.

The main reason for setting up trusts is to avoid a heavy burden of death taxes, and Joseph Kennedy succeeded in doing this. Despite the vast fortune he accumulated, taxes of only $134,330.90 were levied on his estate when he died.

While the trusts have kept the family capital intact and have given Kennedys the financial independence to pursue political careers, it is the family enterprises that have really made the dollars roll in.

The primary enterprise is Park

Agency Inc., established in 1949 and now headed by Mr. Smith. Its crown jewel is the Merchandise Mart, the huge Chicago building that contains offices and wholesale showrooms. It was built in 1930 and was bought by Joseph Kennedy in 1945 with a cash outlay of about $1 million. Real estate experts estimate that it is worth $150 million today.

With about 1,000 tenants, the 24-story Merchandise Mart brings in annual rentals totaling $20 million or so. Perhaps one-third of this amount remains as pre-tax profit after expenses, the experts suggest.

The Kennedys' experience with the Merchandise Mart has been so successful over the years that additional money, partly from the sale of other family real estate, has been invested in the new Apparel Center next door. It is said to have cost more than $50 million, and it is expected to rival New York's Seventh Avenue with its collection of clothing manufacturers' showrooms. Experts say rentals at the Apparel Center could top $10 million a year.

Although the purchase of the Merchandise Mart was considered Joseph Kennedy's greatest coup, his business career, which began in Boston, was extremely diverse.

At the age of 25 he was being called the youngest bank president in the nation (at the tiny Columbia Trust Company of East Boston). Soon he was active on Wall Street, participating in stock pools.

In the mid-1920's, he became interested in movies with the purchase of a theater chain in New England. This led to ownership of a movie production company called F.B.O. He also became chairman of Keith-Albee and Pathé Exchange, and he engineered a merger that involved many of his movie interests and resulted in Radio-Keith-Orpheum.

Liquidating most of his holdings in 1928, shortly before the stock market crashed, Mr. Kennedy made large prof-

its in the aftermath by selling stocks short. Later, through a company called Somerset Importers, he became a major importer of Scotch and gin. After World War II he began investing heavily in real estate.

One of the techniques used with great success by Mr. Kennedy in buying and holding real estate was leverage—the maximum use of somebody else's money.

Over the years, for example, the Merchandise Mart has been heavily mortgaged. The first such loan, a $12.5 million mortgage from the Equitable Life Assurance Society, dates back to 1945.

A $30 million mortgage on the building is currently held by the Prudential Insurance Company of America. At various times in recent years the Kennedys' own financial entities have held smaller mortgages on the building—partly for tax purposes, partly to provide cash for other ventures. Financial reports for the Joseph P. Kennedy Jr. Foundation for 1975, for example, show a mortgage loan of $16.7 million, which a family spokesman says was written on the Merchandise Mart and has since been retired.

Joseph Kennedy's will also disclosed a loan of $4 million from the family's 1926 trusts to him at 7 percent interest. Collateral for the loan was Mr. Kennedy's one-eighth outright interest in the Merchandise Mart.

Although Mr. Kennedy was a heavy speculator in Manhattan real estate during the 1940's, the family has sold most such holdings. Its real estate today is more likely to be in Texas and Florida. In addition to commercial real estate and undeveloped land, family members own valuable residences in New York, New England and Florida.

Mr. Kennedy's will listed real estate holdings in Aransas County, Texas (valued at $116,000) as well as non-producing oil royalties and mineral interests (valued at $100,000) in Alabama, Florida, Illinois, Kansas, Mississippi, Oklahoma and Texas. As for per-

THE KENNEDYS: A NEW YORK TIMES PROFILE

sonal property, the appraised value of the Joseph Kennedy home in Palm Beach, Fla., was $250,000.

Overall, financial reports on the Park Agency indicate holdings of six primary pieces of real estate, but Mr. Smith says the number has risen at times to 20. Sources close to the family say its real estate holdings are worth about $300 million altogether (including the Merchandise Mart and the Apparel Center).

In addition to real estate, there is a family portfolio of securities, including New York City bonds and the so-called MAC bonds issued by the Municipal Assistance Corporation.

Mr. Walsh says the portfolio is diversified and conservative, containing such blue chips as I.B.M., Eastman Kodak and Exxon. He says the family does not favor any particular Wall Street brokerage house for its transactions but has used at various times such firms as Hallgarten & Company; White, Weld & Company; and Howard, Weil, Labouisse & Friedrichs, which is based in New Orleans.

Among the family's other enterprises are several small oil companies that specialize in exploration, development, drilling and production.

Serving as an umbrella for the Kennedy oil interests—which are worth a total of about $15 million by one estimate—is the Kenoil Corporation, headed by Mr. Walsh. Started in 1960, it coordinates the family's oil holdings in Texas, Louisiana, Mississippi and California.

A related oil enterprise is the Mokeen Oil Company of Corpus Christi, Texas, also headed by Mr. Walsh and managed by Armand H. (Lucky) Jones, a Texas oil man. Mokeen oversees the family's oil and gas interests in Texas.

The Kennedy family also has a relationship with the Sutton Producing Corporation of San Antonio, Tex., a company formed in 1966 to manage

oil properties. In addition, Senator Edward Kennedy has reported income from the Forest Oil Corporation of Bradford, Pa., an exploration and production company.

Besides managing joint family enterprises, Mr. Smith, Mr. Walsh and their associates also keep an eye on the personal investments of such family members as Ethel Skakel Kennedy, Robert's widow, who is a shareholder in the Skakel family business—the Great Lakes Carbon Corporation, one of the largest privately owned corporations in the country.

In addition, they serve as the central managers of the family's charitable and memorial activities, principally the Joseph P. Kennedy Jr. Foundation, which was established after World War II to honor Joseph Kennedy's oldest son, who was killed in a plane crash in Europe in 1944.

According to the tax return the foundation filed last year, it had a net worth of $21.8 million—$16.7 million of it in the mortgage on the Merchandise Mart. An additional $2.7 million was in Government securities as well as $2.2 million in non-Government bonds, $190,000 in cash, $128,000 in land and $127,000 in corporate stocks.

When the mortgage was liquidated, the $16.7 million was invested mainly in high grade corporate and utility bonds, according to a family spokesman.

The foundation made $3.3 million in grants and distributions in 1975—chiefly $1 million for the John F. Kennedy Library and $945,000 for the Special Olympics, the family's athletic program for retarded children.

One of the most useful foundations for family members is the Park Foundation, which in 1975 handed out $93,513 in gifts. The money for the Park Foundation comes from the Joseph P. Kennedy Jr. Foundation, and it is funneled into various church, school and medical groups favored by family members.

In 1975, for example, the Park Foundations's two largest gifts were $10,000 to the Archbishop of Boston and $7,800 to the Pawling Central School in Pawling, N.Y., where the Stephen Smiths have a weekend estate.

A gift of $5,000 was made to the Collegiate School in New York, which a number of the Kennedy children have attended. And $1,000 went to Manhattanville College, alma mater for some of the Kennedy women.

For larger donations, the family turns to the Joseph P. Kennedy Jr. Foundation. In 1975 the foundation gave $282,996 to Georgetown University, Mr. Smith's alma mater, and $191,785 to Harvard University, attended by Joseph Kennedy, his sons and some of his grandchildren.

In general, there seems to be a feeling among Wall Streeters that the Kennedy family fortune is handled conservatively, more as a holding action than as a fund to be aggressively manipulated.

Discussions with insiders reinforce that view. "We're very conservative," said one Kennedy financial expert. "I wouldn't exactly say we go in for dollar averaging, but we're not too far from it."

It's an approach that the patriarch would probably have agreed with. Although Joseph Kennedy was a restless adventurer in his own financial operations, he sometimes talked disparagingly of the business world. And he often boasted that his success in that world had given his sons the freedom to seek their life work elsewhere.

The seeds were well sown: Notwithstanding one summer of employment at the Merchandise Mart by Joseph P. Kennedy 3d, none of the Kennedy heirs has shown the slightest interest in a business career or in trying to pyramid the family millions into an even more massive fortune.

June 12, 1977

Mrs. Onassis Said to Get 20 Million In a Pact With Christina Onassis

By NICHOLAS GAGE

ATHENS, Sept. 19—Jacqueline Onassis has negotiated what her friends here call "an astounding settlement" with her late husband's daughter under which the shipowner's widow will receive $20 million in return for abandoning all further claims to his estate.

This represents more than double what she would have received under the terms of Aristotle Onassis's will and almost seven times what she would have received if he had lived to complete the divorce proceedings that his friends say he had planned.

In his will, Mr. Onassis left the bulk of his assets to his daughter, Christina, now 26 years old, and to a foundation in memory of his late son, Alexander. He limited his bequest to Mrs. Onassis to $250,000 a year, of which $50,000 was to be set aside for her two children, Caroline Kennedy and John F. Kennedy Jr.

Under those terms Mrs. Onassis, 45 years old when Mr. Onassis died in 1975, could have ultimately received about $10 million if she lived into her 80's.

Miss Onassis's friends here said she had agreed to such a generous settlement for her stepmother because she was eager

to cut all ties to her and because she had been advised that Mrs. Onassis would not consider anything less than $20 million without pressing her claims in court. [Neither Christina Onassis nor her stepmother could be reached for comment.]

"Although she was raised in America, Christina is exceedingly Greek," said Stelios Papadimitriou, her principal attorney here and an executor of her father's estate. "She is strong-willed, emotional and impulsive."

Mr. Papadimitriou, who represented Miss Onassis in the negotiations with her stepmother, would not discuss the settlement, but he indirectly confirmed that one had been reached. Although Mr. Onassis's will left his widow a quarter interest in his private island of Skorpios and a quarter share of his yacht, the

Christina, Mr. Papadimitriou said when questioned about the settlement:

"I can't even tell you there was an agreement, but, no, Mrs. Onassis no longer has any involvement with any part of the Onassis estate."

Mr. Papadimitriou has represented the Onassis family since 1954, when he was 24 years old.

Although initial reports after Mr. Onassis's death had contained speculation that his widow would receive as much as $200 million from the estate, when his will was finally made public in June 1975 it revealed that he had left her only $100,000 a year from tax-free bonds and $100,000 a year in other income for herself plus the $50,000 for her children. The bequest was to have been paid through a foundation in Lichtenstein.

In addition, Mr. Onassis, her second husband, had stipulated that any attempts by his widow to resort to court action over terms of the estate should be opposed.

The handwritten will, drafted by Mr. Onassis on Jan. 3, 1974, indicated that Mrs. Onassis had signed a document in New York in which she gave up all rights to his estate. But, according to other friends of her stepdaughter's, Mrs. Onassis and her brother-in-law, Senator Edward M. Kennedy, began pressing the young heiress soon after the shipping magnate's death to improve the bequest to Mrs. Onassis.

Formal negotiations were begun later between lawyers representing Mrs. Onassis and Mr. Papadimitrious, representing the stepdaughter. The negotiations continued for 18 months, and Mrs. Onassis refused to lower her demand below $20 million, according to her stepdaughter's friends. Mr. Papadimitriou then was reported to have advised Miss Onassis that he thought they could not avoid a court battle unless she agreed to the $20 million.

In his will, Mr. Onassis wrote: "I have received from my wife her resignation from any claims of inheritance through a notarized agreement in the United States. If my wife presses any inheritance claims, then she will not be given her annuity of my estate. If she wins a final ruling from a court that cannot be appealed, then she will receive one-eighth of the estate of Christina."

Mr. Onassis divided the bulk of his estate between his daughter, who has been married and divorced twice, and a foundation set up in memory of his son, who died after an airplane crash in 1973 at the age of 25.

Miss Onassis's half of the estate has been estimated at more than $250 million, and on this basis if her stepmother had gone to court and won all her claims, she could have received at least $10 million more than she is said to have received in the settlement.

This may have been a factor in Miss Onassis's decision to settle out of court, although her friends feel she was motivated more by the fact that a long court battle would have kept her and her stepmother financially linked to each other for years.

The friends said Christina Onassis opposed her father's marriage in 1968 to the widow of President John F. Kennedy and was never able to become close to her stepmother. The relationship was said to have become even more strained after Mr. Onassis's death, although his daughter made a public statement to the contrary and denied that her father had planned to divorce his wife.

Close friends of Mr. Onassis said here, however, that he had told them he intended to divorce his wife and that he had an agreement with her limiting the divorce settlement to $3 million.

September 20, 1977

Mrs. Onassis Resigns Editing Post

By DEIRDRE CARMODY

Jacqueline Kennedy Onassis has resigned as a consulting editor at the Viking Press because of its publication of a novel that depicts Senator Edward M. Kennedy, her brother-in-law, as the target of an assassination attempt.

Several months ago, Mrs. Onassis was informed by her long-time friend, Thomas Guinzburg, the president of Viking, that the publishing house planned to sign a contract to publish the novel "Shall We Tell the President?" by a British author and former member of Parliament, Jeffrey Archer.

At the time, Mrs. Onassis reportedly did not attempt to dissuade Mr. Guinzburg from acquiring the book. However, she apprently became "extremely upset" this week when an article in The Boston Globe and the review of the book in The New York Times seemed to suggest that she was connected with publication of the book.

"Last spring, when told of the book, I tried to separate my lives as a Viking employee and a Kennedy relative," Mrs. Onassis was quoted by Nancy Tuckerman, her spokesman, as having said.

"But this fall, when it was suggested that I had had something to do with acquiring the book and that I was not distressed by its publication, I felt I had to resign," Mrs. Onassis said, according to Miss Tuckerman.

Late Thursday afternoon, Mrs. Onassis sent a hand-written letter of resignation to Mr. Guinzberg. Neither Miss Tuckerman nor spokesmen at Viking would divulge the exact contents.

"After being friends for more than half our lives, I more than ever deeply regret Mrs. Onassis's decision to resign from the Viking Press without a personal discussion of the incident which resulted in her decision."

"My own affecton for the Kennedy family and the extremely effective and valued contribution which Mrs. Onassis has made to Viking over the past two years would obviously have been an overriding factor in the final decision to publish any particular book which might cause her further anguish," the Guinzburg statement said in part.

"Indeed, it is precisely because of the generous and understanding response of Mrs. Onassis at the time we discussed this book and before the contract was signed which gave me confidence to proceed with the novel's publication."

The subject of a Presidential assassination is an unusually delicate one for Mrs. Onassis who has worked at Viking for two years. She was sitting next to her husband, former President John F. Kennedy, when he was assassinated in a motorcade in Dallas on Nov. 22, 1963. Five years later, another brother-in-law, Robert F. Kennedy was assassinated while seeking the Democratic presidential nomination.

The passage in Wednesday's Boston Globe article that apparently most upset Mrs. Onassis was a quotation from Mr. Guinzburg saying that she "didn't indicate any distress or anger when I told her we bought the book in England several months ago."

"She," he continued, "has a feeling of resignation that people will go on using this bleak material."

Point of Reference

According to Miss Tuckerman, Mrs. Onassis had been upset when Mr. Guinzburg told her about the book, but did not feel she should interfere with its publication. Mr. Guinzburg apparently advised Mrs. Onassis at the time not to read the book because he felt it would distress her.

The passage in The New York Times's book review last Monday by John Leonard that distressed Mrs. Onassis was the last paragraph, which said:

"There is a word for such a book. That word is trash. Anybody associated with its publication should be ashamed of herself."

Although her name was not mentioned in the review, Mrs. Onassis apparently felt that the reference was clearly to her. She felt it suggested unfairly that she had been involved in the editing of the book, which she had not.

Mr. Leonard said yesterday that he had indeed meant to refer to Mrs. Onassis.

"Of course I was partially referring to her," he said. "She should have objected [to the publication of the book]. She could have stopped its publication if she wanted to."

Mr. Leonard said that the reference could also be read by those knowledgeable with the book as meaning Deborah Schabert Owen. Mrs. Owen is an American literary agent who is married to the British Foreign Minister, David Owen. It was she who negotiated the contract with Viking. She also sold the paperback rights to Fawcett Publications for $500,000 and the movie rights to David Niven Jr., the film producer, for $250,000.

In his statement, Mr. Guinzburg referred to "the grossly unfair imputation in The New York Times connecting Mrs. Onassis with the publication of 'Shall We Tell the President?' which precipitated this unfortunate affair."

Mr. Leonard said in his review that the book, which takes place in a White House occupied in 1983 by Edward Moore Kennedy, was a "bad thriller" that exploited a terrible fantasy. Other assessments of the book in reviews have rated it from good to dreadful.

Mr. Guinzburg sent the book to Stephen Smith, who is married to Senator Kennedy's sister Jean. Mr. Smith later told Mr. Guinzburg, according to The Boston Globe's account, that "we would all be better off in no one published the book."

A spokesman for Senator Kennedy said that the Senator had "flipped through the book," but that he did not want to comment on it.

October 15, 1977

220

Notes on People

A lawyer for **Caroline Kennedy** is expected to have her plead guilty today to a reduced traffic violation charge and, under a plea-bargaining arrangement, she will be permitted to keep her driver's license. The 20-year-old Miss Kennedy, a student at Radcliffe College in Boston, will not have to appear in Suffolk County Court in Hauppauge, L.I. She was given a speeding ticket last July 4 for driving 86 miles an hour on the Long Island Expressway, near Yaphank, in a 55-mile-an-hour zone. Her lawyer, **Thomas McVann Jr.**, said that the District Attorney's office would allow her to plead guilty to driving at 70 miles per hour, thus avoiding the rule that requires revocation of a driver's license when an offender is found guilty of driving more than 25 miles an hour over the limit. Mr. McVann said that Miss Kennedy ticket was for a first offense, and a spokesman for the District Attorney's office said that she "was not given any preferential treatment." She does face a fine of $100.

March 17, 1978

Notes on People

It's been a year now since **Joan Kennedy** has had a drink, she told an interviewer recently, and she's now ready to speak openly about her alcoholism. Mrs. Kennedy, now living in Boston, where she is a full-time music student at Lesley College of Fine Arts, said that she and her husband, **Senator Edward M. Kennedy**, had recently approved for publication an article in which she details her problem. The article will appear in the August issue of McCall's magazine. "In Alcoholics Anonymous they say it's good to talk about it after you've been sober for a year, and I have," said Mrs. Kennedy. "I've talked about it with my friends until they're bored silly, but I've never talked about it publicly before. Ted is so pleased that I've found myself and am so happy." She added that she spends weekends with her husband and children at their home in Virginia or the Kennedy family compound in Hyannis Port, Mass.

July 11, 1978

Kennedy Presses for Health Plan

By WARREN WEAVER Jr.

MEMPHIS, Dec. 9—Senator Edward M. Kennedy issued a ringing challenge to the Carter Administration and Congress today to enact a comprehensive national health insurance program that would "make health care a right for all our people now."

In a shouting, lectern-pounding speech that brought repeated cheers from an audience of 2,500 fellow Democrats, the Massachusetts Senator attacked the theory, implied if not stated by President Carter, that inflation and Federal budgetary strictures stand in the way of providing health insurance in the immediate future.

"There could be few more divisive issues for America and for our party than a Democratic policy of drastic slashes in the Federal budget at the expense of the elderly, the poor, the black, the sick, the cities and the unemployed," Mr. Kennedy told a workshop at the Democratic party's midterm conference here.

The conference is scheduled to choose tomorrow between a resolution reaffirming the 1976 national Democratic platform's support for national health insurance and an alternative that repeats the same language but adds that "this is the year" to enact the legislation.

Possibility of Compromise

The first resolution has the support of the Carter Administration and the Democratic national chairman, John C. White. Before Senator Kennedy spoke, a White House official doubted the possibility of a

compromise, but a spokesman for Senator Kennedy said later that compromise language was possible.

The Senator, regarded by some Democrats as a potential challenger to President Carter for renomination in 1980, was scheduled to fly back to Washington this afternoon. He is not a conference delegate and could not participate in tomorrow's debate without special permission.

The workshop Mr. Kennedy addressed drew the largest attendance of any of the 24 held today. Its audience voiced strong support of his position with applause, cheers and two standing ovations, a more visibly supportive response than President Carter received when he addressed the full conference last night.

While an accurate nose count was not practical, it was entirely possible that a majority of the 1,633 delegates to the conference were in the Kennedy audience this afternoon.

Califano Offers Analysis

Two Administration spokesmen shared the platform with Senator Kennedy. Joseph A. Califano Jr., Secretary of Health, Education and Welfare, spoke before Mr. Kennedy and confined himself largely to an analysis of the health care crisis in the

nation.

Mr. Califano said his department would have ready "early next year" tentative legislation based on proposals outlined by the President last July. That bill will go back to the White House, and then a final recommendation will be sent to Congress, he said.

A major problem, the Secretary observed, would be "how to phase it in," strongly indicating that the Administration did not want to proceed as rapidly and comprehensively as Senator Kennedy.

Eizenstat Cites 'Phased Steps'

Stuart E. Eizenstat, the President's chief domestic adviser, warned that enactment of national health insurance legislation "may take a little longer" than hoped. Any plan, he said, would be adopted "in adjustable and prudently phased steps."

Noting that the Democratic Party has officially supported health insurance for more than 25 years without any Congressional action, the White House official asked: "Why are the cheers we hear tonight not translated into legislation? Have we sought too much too soon?"

December 10, 1978

The Heirs

CARTER SAYS PARTY HAS NOT BEEN SPLIT BY KENNEDY'S VIEWS

DIFFERENCES TERMED 'MINOR'

President Finds Democrats Back His Plan to Curb Spending — Senator Standing Firm

---

By MARTIN TOLCHIN

WASHINGTON, Dec. 12—President Carter asserted today that his differences with Senator Edward M. Kennedy did not signal a widening "schism" within the Democratic Party and told a news conference that his belt-tightening fiscal policies had the support of a majority of Democrats.

In a low-key appraoch, the President said that his difference with the Massachusetts Democrat were "minor." But Senator Kennedy was not so sanguine. Minutes after the news conference, the Senator said in a telephone interview that his differences with the President on na-

tional health care were "unchanged and fundamental and rather basic."

At the 41st news conference since he took office, the President dealt not only with his political differences with Senator Kennedy and the health of the Democratic Party but also spoke at length about the Middle East and the Shah of Iran.

In the 30-minute session, he also rebuffed Alfred E. Kahn, his new anti-inflation chief, by declaring his opposition to organized consumer boycotts of companies that do not comply with wage-price guidelines.

Relationship With Kennedy

In his discussion of relations with Mr. Kennedy, the President's manner contrasted with the Senator's outspoken attack on Mr. Carter's policies at the Democratic Party's midterm convention last weekend. But Mr. Carter's outwardly conciliatory tone nevertheless suggested irritation with Mr. Kennedy.

The President rejected a questioner's suggestion that the Democratic Party was being torn between supporters of his proposal to curtail social welfare programs in the fight against inflation, on the one hand, and those, including Senator Kennedy, who have called for a rededication to the party's traditional commitment to help the poor, minorities, unemployed and disinherited.

"First of all, I don't consider there is a schism, a growing schism, in the Democratic Party at all," the President said.

"And as a general principle, and almost entirely," Mr. Carter continued,

"Senator Kennedy and I communicate well. We have a good relationship; we espouse the same ultimate goals. We have some differences, which are expected, on exactly how to achieve those goals.

"I have a unique perspective in this country as President. I can look at a much broader range of issues than does Senator Kennedy. He is extremely interested, for instance, in the comprehensive health program, having devoted several years of his legislative life to that position."

The President's emphasis on party harmony was not without statements that could be interpreted as an oblique attack on the Massachusetts Democrat, who emerged last weekend as the President's major critic within the Democratic Party.

Kennedy Family Cited

Some political observers saw a cutting edge in the President's statement that Senator Kennedy represents a family within the Democratic Party that "is revered because of his two brothers and the contribution of his family to our party."

At a lunch on Capitol Hill today, a leading Democrat suggested that, perhaps unintentionally, the President seemed to be asking whether the newsmen would be paying as much attention to the Massachusetts Democrat if his name were not Kennedy.

The Democrat also said that the President's statement invited a comparison of his own political origins and those of Mr. Kennedy, who had considerable help from his family.

December 13, 1978

Kennedy Says He Informed Carter Of Likely Support for Nomination

---

By ADAM CLYMER

WASHINGTON, June 13—Senator Edward M. Kennedy said today that he told President Carter more than two months ago that he expected to support him for the Democratic nomination next year instead of running against him.

Mr. Kennedy said in an interview that on March 21, after a White House meeting on health care, he met privately with Mr. Carter and "indicated my tentative support of him." He said their conversation on that subject consumed only "10 or 15 seconds" of a meeting that lasted an hour.

Many Democrats Skeptical

Previously, Senator Kennedy's standard comment on the 1980 Presidential race had emphasized that he expected Mr. Carter to be renominated and that he expected to support the President in the general election. Today he made known his position on a Carter nomination after reports arose that the President had predicted he would "whip" Mr. Kennedy if the Senator opposed him for the nomination.

Mr. Carter's comment, made to sev-

eral Democratic Representatives at a White House dinner, was disclosed yesterday, with some White House encouragement to Congressmen to confirm it. But Mr. Carter's emphatic language was greeted here today with surprise and skepticism by many Democrats who do not share the President's expectation that he would win such a contest.

In the interview today, Mr. Kennedy shrugged his shoulders and declined to discuss the President's remark. Earlier in the day he said jokingly: "I'm sure the President must have been misquoted. I think what he meant to say was that he was going to whip inflation." But he also said, in another appearance, "If I were to run, which I don't intend to, I would hope to win."

Discussing Mr. Carter's political situation, Mr. Kennedy said today: "I would think he'd have a good chance of winning. A lot depends on the state of the economy." About his most serious current dispute with Mr. Carter, the issue of national health insurance, the Senator said, "I haven't doubted his belief in trying to

achieve it."

He said that he had not had Mr. Carter in mind yesterday when he said of the program, "One of the principal reasons we've been unable to enact it is we didn't have a President who was strongly committed to it." He said that he had meant former Presidents Richard M. Nixon and Gerald R. Ford, who "were strongly opposed to it."

Asked if that comment did not imply that he would have to seek the Presidency to get the program enacted, Mr. Kennedy shook his head and said, "I'm thinking of the here and now and the foreseeable future."

The here and now of Mr. Carter's situation has been reported in a variety of polls, which showed his standing at its lowest point yet, and reflected by moves to get another Democratic candidate. Evan S. Dobelle, head of the Carter reelection committee, conceded today that there were significant problems but said, "We don't need a poll to know what's wrong."

The Congressmen who met with Mr. Carter thought that frustration over the polls was behind the President's remark to them. Representative Thomas J. Downey of Suffolk County and Anthony Toby Moffett of Connecticut had been talking about the relation of heating oil shortages and costs to the New England primaries next year, and Mr. Downey said that he had remarked that those problems would be even more severe if Mr. Kennedy ran.

Mr. Carter then said, according to Mr. Downey and Representative William M. Brodhead of Michigan, that he was not worried about 1980 and "if Kennedy runs, I'm going to whip his ———."

Mr. Brodhead said that he had not heard the comment clearly and was startled by it and asked Mr. Carter to repeat it. He said that Mr. Moffett said that perhaps the President should not, but Mr. Carter did, explaining that in 1976 he was prepared to run against and defeat Mr. Kennedy and was still ready.

White House Approves Release

Mr. Brodhead, who said today that the President's emphatic tone and repetition of the statement were a clear indication that he wanted his views made public, told The Detroit Free Press of the remark, and news agencies sought to confirm it from others present.

Some of the Representatives avoided the question on the ground that the dinner had been a private meeting. But then Frank Moore, assistant to the President for Congressional liaison, called some of them, including Mr. Downey, and said that it was all right to go ahead and confirm it.

Mr. Kennedy, who said as the interview began that he had been delayed by a meeting of the Human Resources Com-

mittee called to vote approval of Mr. Carter's legislation on the containment of hospital costs, sought to convey the impression that he was unconcerned by Mr. Carter's comment.

And his tone when he spoke about Mr. Carter's health legislation indicated disappointment. He contended that his measure had been altered to meet Mr. Carter's earlier objections to its cost and lack of a role for the private sector. "I thought we would have been together on the issue" after those changes were made, he said.

June 14, 1979

BOSTON, Nov. 7 — Senator Edward M. Kennedy, who had declined entreaties to run for President in the last three campaigns, formally declared his candidacy for election in 1980 today with a pledge to provide a "forceful, effective Presidency" that would get the nation "on the march again."

To an ardently partisan crowd of three generations of the Kennedy family and political allies such as Mayor Jane M. Byrne of Chicago, Gov. Joseph E. Brennan of Maine and Senator John A. Durkin of New Hampshire, as well as to 5,000 Bostonians, he declared in Faneuil Hall that he felt "compelled by events and my commitment to public life" to oppose President Carter. And he contended that the contest would strengthen rather than divide the Democratic Party.

Here and in later campaign appearances today, the 47-year-old Massachusetts Democrat charged that President Carter had "taken the single most inflationary step" by lifting price controls from domestic crude oil last spring, and he attacked the President for saying that the American people were suffering a crisis of spirit.

'Malaise' of Leadership

"I say it is not the American people who are in a malaise," he told a crowd of several hundred supporters in nearby Manchester, N.H. "It's the political leadership that's in a malaise."

Mr. Kennedy issued his 1978 tax return, as well as a medical report saying he was in "excellent health." [Page A17.] The White House response to the announcement was muted, but a memorandum has begun circulating among senior officials with advice on rebutting the Senator's challenge. [Page A17.]

Mr. Kennedy also accused Mr. Carter of letting bureaucrats and subordinates — such as Robert S. Strauss, his longtime adviser; Alfred E. Kahn, head of the Council on Wage and Price Stability, and Paul A. Volcker, the new chairman of the Federal Reserve Board — lead the Administration's fight against inflation, rather than taking personal charge of that battle.

"But they weren't elected President," he told a pep rally in Portland, Me., tonight. "Jimmy Carter was."

"I question no man's intentions," Mr. Kennedy declared in his announcement

Kennedy Declares His Candidacy, Vowing New Leadership for Nation

By HEDRICK SMITH

address, "but I have a different view of the highest offfice in the land — a view of a forceful, effective Presidency, in the thick of the action, at the center of all the great concerns our people share.

"I believe in the hope and daring that have made this country great," he said to rousing cheers. "The only thing that paralyzes us today is the myth we cannot move."

Immediately after his announcement, Senator Kennedy flew to Manchester, Portland and Chicago to begin a fast-paced, four-day campaign swing through New England, the Middle West and such Southern cities as Miami, Charleston, S.C., and Nashville, Tenn., to show that he intends to press his challenge into President Carter's home base of support in the South.

The Senator came to Boston for his announcement to strike a contrast with his brothers, President John F. Kennedy and Sentor Robert F. Kennedy, who made their Presidential announcements in 1960 and 1968 in the caucus room of the Senate.

But evoking history and family tradition in a 17-minute speech to which Richard Goodwin, one of John Kennedy's speechwriters, had contributed, he echoed a number of his brothers' campaign themes, notably John Kennedy's assertion in 1960 that he wanted to "get the country moving again" and Robert Kennedy's concern for the poor and minorities. In his travels today, he carried a pair of cufflinks that had belonged to his brother John.

In recent weeks there has been a crescendo of attacks by Mr. Kennedy against Mr. Carter's Administration, and although he made few new specific charges today, his tone was sharper and more explicit.

One of the warmest and most emotional rounds of applause came in a question period for his wife, Joan, who appeared on stage with the Senator and their three children. Mr. Kennedy had been asked about his wife's role in the campaign, given her living in Boston while he lives in Washington.

Squeezing his arm as she approached the microphone and speaking in a shaky voice, she said she was "looking forward

very, very enthusiastically" to campaigning for him and to his election "as the next President."

Family Members Present

Also on hand were his mother, Rose; his sisters-in-law, Jacqueline Kennedy Onassis and Ethel Kennedy, and their children; and other members of his family, including Stephen and Jean Smith, Patricia Kennedy Lawford, and Sargent and Eunice Shriver.

Conspicuously absent, however, were Mayor Kevin H. White, who won election to a fourth term yesterday, and Gov. Edward J. King of Massachusetts, both of whom have feuded with Senator Kennedy in the past, and House Speaker Thomas P. O'Neill Jr. Mr. O'Neill is expected eventually to back Senator Kennedy, but has remained publicly neutral thus far. Mr. O'Neill's son, Lieut. Gov. Thomas P. O'Neill 3d, who has been named New England coordinator for Mr. Kennedy's campaign, was on hand.

It was a moment Kennedy partisans had awaited since the assassinations of John F. Kennedy in 1963 and Robert F. Kennedy in 1968. Three times — in 1968, 1972 and 1976 — other Democrats had urged Mr. Kennedy to run but, citing family responsibilities, he refused.

A huge crowd was on hand, although only about 350 invited guests and 500 journalists made it into Faneuil Hall.

Crowds Outside the Hall

Outside the hall, construction workers paused in their labors to sit down on the scaffolding to hear him speak. Children climbed atop trucks or perched on fences, and a crowd jammed the Quincy Market area adjacent to the hall, waiting for him to emerge and give them a pep talk.

The Senator, dressed in a blue suit, blue shirt and blue tie, deplored the Carter Administration's "stark failures" in the economy, which he said were pressing workers to take second jobs and forcing the poorest 10 percent of the population to "go without" essentials because of skyrocketing inflation.

"For many months, we have been sinking into crisis," he declared in his announcement speech. "Yet we hear no clear summons from the center of power.

Aims are not set; the means of realizing them are neglected. Conflicts in direction confuse our purpose. Government falters. Fears spread that our leaders have resigned themselves to retreat."

And then, drawing his first strong burst of applause, he declared:

"This country is not prepared to sound retreat. It is ready to advance. It is willing to make a stand. And so am I."

He accused the President of inconsistency, recalling that in the 1976 campaign, Mr. Carter had told the people "that Americans were honest, loving, good, decent, and compassionate."

"Now, the people are blamed for every national ill and scolded as greedy, wasteful, and mired in malaise," he said, alluding to a number of President Carter's speeches since taking office.

"Which is it? Did we change so much in the these three years? Or is it because our present leadership does not understand that we are willing, even anxious, to be on the march again."

As if in response to some supporters who have worried that he might move toward more moderate positions on economic and social issues, he affirmed that he would steadfastly retain the principles of the Democratic Party and "convictions rooted in the life of my family and in my own career."

November 8, 1979

Senator Edward M. Kennedy at Faneuil Hall in Boston.

Kennedy Seems Pleased
By Question About Wife

By B. DRUMMOND AYRES Jr.

BOSTON, Nov. 7 — There were boos and hisses this morning from the supporters and friends in Faneuil Hall when a reporter asked Senator Edward M. Kennedy what role his wife Joan might play in the coming campaign.

For the Kennedy partisans attending his formal announcment that he was a candidate for the Presidency, questions about his personal life appeared to be either in bad taste or provocative, especially because the Senator was already volunteering statements concerning his health and personal finances.

But almost in recognition that the press and the public have unquenchable curiosity about the private side of all the Kennedys, the Senator, in the first mo-

ments of his new candidacy, seemed to welcome the question about Mrs. Kennedy, as though he wanted to confront all the most sensitive issues right from the start.

Rare Public Appearance by Wife

Motioning with his arms to dampen the protests of his supporters, he turned to his wife, who was making one of her rare public appearances with him since they separated in early 1978 to live apart, and said, almost gleefully:

"Well, Joan, why don't you . . . "

Mrs. Kennedy was out of her chair before he could finish and took the microphone.

"I look forward to campaigning for him," she said firmly. "And not only that, I look forward very, very enthusiastically to my husband being a candidate

Senator Edward M. Kennedy and his wife, Joan, in Boston.

and to his being the next President of the United States. Soon I will be talking to the press.''

The crowd jumped to its feet and roared its approval. Mrs. Kennedy flashed a smile and returned to her seat next to her three children, Patrick, who lives with the Senator, and Kara and Edward Jr., both college students.

Spent Night at Wife's Home

Thomas Southwick, the Senator's press secretary, said later that Mr. Kennedy spent the night at Mrs. Kennedy's apartment before the day's announcement. "He always spends the night there when he's in Boston,'' Mr. Southwick added.

The scene, as played out today, will not dispel all the gossip and speculation about the Senator's private life, particularly about the events that took place at Chappaquiddick in 1969, when a young woman passenger in his car died in an accident.

Mr. Kennedy was not asked directly today about the Chappaquiddick incident, though it has been the subject in the past few days of a number of articles, editori-

als and television programs.

The press itself is debating the ethics of how far to carry the inquiry into the Senator's personal behavior. Just recently, The New Republic magazine rejected a 3,000-word article that reportedly discussed his relationships with other women.

Reports on two topics normally personal, taxes and health, were issued by the Senator before his announcement this morning.

The health report, based on a physical examination last week at Georgetown University Hospital in Washington, said that doctors had found him to be "excellent condition.'' However, he was reported to suffer "minor residual effects'' from extensive back injuries suffered in a 1964 plane crash, and it was disclosed that early last summer he underwent a "routine'' operation in which a skin cancer was removed from his chest.

"The laboratory report showed it be a skin cancer of the basal cell type,'' the Senator's health summary said. "It was fully excised. Basal cell cancers are the

commonest form of skin cancers, are thought to be due primarily to sun exposure, and almost never metastasize, In this routine case, the entire lesion was removed. There are no other comparable lesions.''

The summary went on to report that the Senator, 47 years old and a sports enthusiast, turned in an "excellent performance'' in a physical stress test. The summary put his weight at 211 pounds and said that his pulse, while he was resting, was 56 and "regular'' and and that his blood pressure was 115/70.

Mr. Kennedy's report on his taxes consisted of a reproduction of his 1978 Federal tax return. It showed that he had a total income that year of $702,697, on which he paid $315,508 in taxes after taking $200,104 in deductions.

The majority of his income, $419,794, came from a trust set up for him by his late father, Joseph P. Kennedy, a self-made millionaire. The majority of his deductions came from state and local taxes, from home mortgage payments and from business expenses.

November 8, 1979

CHICAGO, March 15 — Senator Edward M. Kennedy has begun a series of unusually personal television advertisements that cite the deaths of his brothers, the Chappaquiddick accident and the loss of his son's leg to cancer as evidence of tragedies that have strengthened him and made him "a more mature man.''

The Kennedy television ads, part of a $175,000 media effort in the final days before the Illinois Presidential primary Tuesday, contrast somewhat with President Carter's.

The President's heavy advertising

campaign includes an appeal to Jewish voters, a discussion of Mr. Carter's commitment to a strong national defense and an emphasis on Mr. Carter's "character'' and family life.

'Husband, Father, President'

In one advertisement, as Mr. Carter sits at a table with his daughter, Amy, and wife, Rosalynn, the President's voice is heard: "I don't think there's any way you can separate the responsibilities of a husband and father and a basic human

KENNEDY ADS STRESS TRAGEDIES IN FAMILY

By BERNARD WEINRAUB
Special to The New York Times

being from that of the President. What I do in the White House is to maintain a good family life which I consider to be crucial to being a good President."

An announcer says: "Husband. Father. President. He's done these three jobs with distinction."

Several other Carter ads, which were made by Gerald Rafshoon, the media consultant, mention the President's "character." In one ad, for example, as Mr. Carter addresses a town meeting, an announcer says: "You may not always agree with President Carter, but you'll never find yourself wondering if he's telling you the truth. It's hard to think of a more useful quality in any person who becomes President than telling you the simple truth."

Character Called Key Issue

Moments later, the announcer says: "President Carter. For the truth."

Charles Guggenheim, an Academy-Award-winning filmmaker who is Mr. Kennedy's media consultant, said that the issue of "character" was now crucial in the campaign, making it necessary to create advertisements for Illinois and the New York primary, on March 25, that deal with Mr. Kennedy's personality.

"We really would have preferred to have focused on inflation and foreign policy," said Mr. Guggenheim. "But the polls show the voters feel, 2 to 1, that Carter is doing a poor job, yet they're voting, 2 to 1, for him. I don't think there's any other conclusion that you can make, but that character is the issue."

One ad shows Mr. Kennedy working in the Senate, and then the setting shifts to an assortment of scenes: Mr. Kennedy listening to some wounded Vietnam

veterans, talking to an elderly woman about her difficulties, visiting sick children and walking on the beach with his wife, Joan, and their family.

Survivor of 4 Brothers

"He was the survivor of four brothers, and tragedy had shadowed him much of his life," an announcer says. "It has been his companion when his plane fell from the sky, leaving him near death and with a broken back. It has been his companion at Chappaquiddick and twice at the cemetery in Arlington. And it has been his companion when his eldest son had lost his leg to cancer."

In keeping with the personal tone of the ads, Ethel Kennedy is seen on a tennis court talking about her brother-in-law's "wonderful quality" with children. Joan Kennedy is also scheduled to make a commercial for her husband.

Mr. Carter's television and radio ads, while emphasizing the President's "character," lean heavily on film footage of the Camp David conference and agreement. Prime Minister Menachem Begin of Israel is shown, at one point, seated beside Mr. Carter and President Anwar el-Sadat of Egypt, saying: "The Camp David conference should be renamed. It was the Jimmy Carter conference."

The ads were made before the controversy over Mr. Carter's disavowal of the United States vote for a United Nations Security Council resolution rebuking Israel for establishing Jewish settlements in lands that have been occupied by Israel since the 1967 Middle East war settlements. The vote upset Israel and some Jewish leaders in this country.

March 18, 1980

On the Issues: Edward Kennedy

By B. DRUMMOND AYRES Jr.

Ask the average Democrat who is the party's leading liberal and the answer that comes back is very likely to be Senator Edward M. Kennedy of Massachusetts.

There may be more ideologically pure Democratic liberals. But in the minds of a great many party members, probably a great majority, the name Senator Kennedy is a definition of Democratic liberalism. He is seen as the ultimate champion of the party's hard-core constituency of blue-collar workers, minorities, the poor and the aged.

As the Senator has discovered in a series of caucuses and primaries, that perception does not automatically translate into overwhelming support from members of his party. Other perceptions of Mr. Kennedy, particularly doubts about his character, appear to have cost him dearly at the polls.

Activist for Underprivileged

Nevertheless, the record of the Senator's speeches and 8,500 roll-call votes, cast in 17 years on Capitol Hill, fully support the perception that he is well on his party's ideological left, a politician who is convinced that it is the function of Government to intervene in order to protect the underprivileged

from the money and power of the privileged, especially big business.

The Senator has been a leading advocate or strong supporter of many traditional liberal causes — civil rights, tax and labor law reform, health and jobs programs, antitrust legislation, disarmament, détente and withholding aid from dictatorships.

Two avowedly liberal groups, Americans for Democratic Action and the Committee on Political Education of the American Federation of Labor and Congress of Industrial Organizations, report that Mr. Kennedy has supported their positions on key issues more than 90 percent of the time. By contrast, two conservative groups, Americans for Constitutional Action and the American Conservative Union, say he has voted with them less than 3 percent of the time.

A Shift Perceived

When he decided last fall to challenge President Carter for the 1980 Democratic nomination, Mr. Kennedy made several speeches in which he seemed to move toward the political center. For example, in an address to New York businessmen, he declared:

"We are making a clean break with the New Deal and even the 1960's. We reject the idea that government knows best across the board, that public planning is inherently superior or more effective than private action. There is now a growing consensus, which I share, that government intervention in the economy should come as only a last resort."

The Senator was far ahead of Mr. Carter in the polls when he spoke in New York and apparently was thinking more about running against a Republican in the November general election than against a fellow Democrat in the spring and summer caucuses and primaries. When the President, who already occupied a good part of the middle ground, later moved ahead in the polls and swept the crucial Iowa caucuses, Mr. Kennedy quickly moved back to the left.

There he has remained, opposing budget cuts, demanding a wage-price freeze and asserting at every opportunity that he is a pure Democrat, whereas Mr. Carter is a closet Republican.

Following are the Senator's record and positions on some major domestic and foreign issues:

Economics

Mr. Kennedy believes that inflation is the country's foremost problem and advocates an immediate six-month freeze on wages, prices, profits, dividends, interest rates and rents. He would follow the freeze with selective controls and concentrated efforts to spur productivity, investment and more foreign trade.

Until a few weeks ago, the Senator favored voluntary compliance with wage-price controls. But President Carter, he contends, failed to put pressure on companies to hold down prices voluntarily, thereby necessitating mandatory controls.

Conservatives consider the Senator a "big spender," and he has voted many times for social programs that ultimately required deficit financing. But over the last several years, he has joined with other legislators in expressing concern about unbalanced budgets.

Nevertheless, he does not favor balancing the budget and slowing inflation by slashing expenditures for social programs that provide the needy with jobs, food and special education programs, as President Carter's new anti-inflation policy provides.

The Senator contends that the impact on inflation of cuts in such areas would be minimal. He suggests, instead, that a better way to balance the Federal budget would be to close tax "loopholes" available to big corporations and wealthy individuals, a step he has advocated repeatedly since first showing up on Capitol Hill.

Energy

Although the Kennedy family has extensive petroleum interests and profits considerably from the tax advantages they offer, the Senator has often spoken out and voted against big oil. He opposed decontrol of domestic oil prices and has argued since that the proposed "windfall" profits tax should be increased to hold down corporate profits.

Rather than permit oil prices to rise to encourage conservation, Mr. Kennedy would offer incentives to homeowners and businessmen to install energy-saving devices. He also would place greater reliance on coal, solar and hydroelectric power, but would go slow on developing synthetic fuel until it looks more promising. Finally, and most controversially, he would begin to phase out nuclear power and would immediately institute gas rationing.

As for gasoline rationing, Mr. Kennedy argues that it is inevitable. In fact, he says, there already is rationing by price, which he contends is unfair to the poor.

Business

Never considered a very good friend of big business, the Senator not only has tried repeatedly to close what he considers corporate tax "loopholes" but also has backed legislation that would slow corporate mergers, particularly in the energy industry. He has supported moves that would make it easier for consumers to sue corporations and has pushed for deregulation of the airline and trucking industries, steps that he maintains are consistent with his liberalism because they would result in more competition and therefore lower consumer costs.

As the nation's economy has worsened, he has become more friendly toward business, however, and has advocated steps to help American industry modernize and compete, including programs to encourage capital formation and retooling.

Labor

Big labor considers the Senator a good friend. He has backed higher minimum wages and has called often for reforms that would make unionizing less difficult.

Health Care

Few senators have pushed harder for health measures than has Mr. Kennedy. He has spent much of the last decade fighting to enact a medical cost-containment program and a national health insurance system. He also has supported programs to set up neighborhood health centers in the slums, has backed larger grants for research and the training of health personnel and has advocated preventive care programs.

The Senator's health insurance proposal is one of the most controversial issues on Capitol Hill and is bitterly opposed by much of the powerful medical lobby. Initially, he sought to have the Federal Government pick up a large part of the cost. But as opposition built to that proposal, he proposed a system that would involve the mandatory purchase of insurance from private companies. Passage of the measure remains in doubt but Mr. Kennedy has vowed to continue the fight.

Abortion

The Senator favors Federal financing for abortions for poor women with serious medical problems. He maintains that his position is consistent with his advocacy of federally financed health care of all types for the underprivileged.

Welfare

Over the years he has supported public service jobs programs, rent supports, housing grants, an expanded food stamp program and special nutrition and legal assistance programs for the elderly. He has proposed a reformed welfare act that would set minimum payments at 65 percent of the poverty level, with the Federal Government providing much of the money, and that would enourage families to remain together.

Civil Rights

Mr. Kennedy has been one of the Senate's leading civil rights advocates. He has supported open housing, full Congressional representation for the predominantly black population of the District of Columbia, speedier desegregation of public schools, in the North as well as the South, equal rights for Hispanic Americans and Indians and passage of the equal rights amendment for women.

Crime

Another of the Senator's legislative efforts has been the rewriting of the entire United States criminal code. He says he seeks only to simplify it by reducing duplication and contradictions in its hundreds of sections. The result, he argues, will be speedier and more equitable justice. But some of his liberal allies counter that the rewriting, in some instances, is too favorable to the police.

Gun Control

Since the assassinations of his brothers John and Robert, Mr. Kennedy has been a strong advocate of gun control. Initially he sought widespread registration and controls. But in the face of strong opposition from the gun lobby, he now seeks only to register handguns and to outlaw so-called Saturday night specials.

Military Spending

Mr. Kennedy has long been classified as one of the Senate's doves. He was not in the vanguard of those who opposed the war in Vietnam, but once against it, he worked hard to bring it to an end.

At various times in the last decade, he has voted against a number of major weapons systems, including the B-1 bomber and the antiballistic missile system. He opposes deployment, though not development, of the MX mobile intercontinental ballistic missile system.

Lately, as pressure has increased for greater military expenditures, Mr. Kennedy has become somewhat less dovish. He says he still opposes "goldplated" military systems and warns against too much involvement in Southwest Asia.

But he now favors the Carter Administration's proposal to increase military expenditures by 3 percent, after allowing for inflation, and he has called for improving conventional forces and favors acquiring rights to use bases in other countries in times of tension.

The Senator opposed establishing an all-volunteer armed force during the Vietnam War, arguing that it would draw mainly from the poor and would therefore result in unequal distribution of the military service burden. But after the war, he backed the concept. He opposes President Carter's proposal to reinstitute registration. Should registration be resumed, however, he thinks both men and women should be required to sign up. And should the draft be resumed, he favors inducting women.

The Senator favors approval of the strategic arms limitation treaty recently negotiated with the Soviet Union. But he agrees with President Carter's decision to table it pending settlement of the Afghanistan issue.

Foreign Affairs

The Senator has not been as concerned with foreign issues as with national issues. But he has traveled abroad periodically and has taken an interest in major overseas matters, particularly relations with the Soviet Union and China and, more lately, United States involvement in the Middle East and Southwest Asia.

He was among the earliest legislators to advocate resumption of diplomatic and economic ties with China. His view of the Soviet Union is that it will alternately test and cooperate with the United States and that this country should not be surprised at either action but instead should be prepared to go in either direction.

As for the Middle East, he is one of Israel's staunchest supporters on Capitol Hill. He contends that the Carter Administration has exhibited too much willingness to deal with the Palestine Liberation Organization and should not have sold sophisticated jets to Arab nations. He has voiced serious doubts about the conduct of American foreign policy in its handling of the recent vote in the United Nations, later repudiated, on Israeli settlements policy. His own position is that Egypt and Israel should be left alone to work out the settlement question.

The Hostages in Iran

Mr. Kennedy thinks the hostage situation in Iran could probably have been avoided, had the United States refused to admit the deposed Shah Mohammed Riza Pahlevi for medical treatment. Though he has been criticized for calling the Shah a repressive, greedy dictator, he stands by the characterization.

He believes the United States encouraged the Soviet Union to invade Afghanistan by not maintaining a hard stance on the presence of Soviet troops in Cuba and by not speaking out as Soviet troops massed near Afghanistan. But he also believes that President Carter overreacted to the incursion and exaggerated the danger to United States interests in the region.

The Senator is a strong advocate of withholding United States aid and recognition from countries that abuse human rights. He has spoken out often about alleged violations in Chile, South Korea and Iran. He also opposes aid for Turkey because of that country's actions in Cyprus.

March 20, 1980

Kennedy's Mood: Despite Losses, He Stays Calm

By B. DRUMMOND AYRES Jr.

With a dismal string of primary and caucus defeats behind him and prospects not very bright for future successes, Senator Edward M. Kennedy of Massachusetts might well be a discouraged, unhappy, even embittered politician. Instead, he gives the opposite impression.

News Analysis At times there is a joy in his quest for the Democratic nomination that, to some, evokes memories of the late Hubert H. Humphrey of Minnesota. Week after week, loss after loss, he has bounced back with a smile, a bit of graceful depreciation and a vow to try harder the next Tuesday.

Commuters who shook hands with him at the Forest Hills subway station in Queens last Wednesday morning met a hearty backslapper who was full of banter and chuckles, not a dispirited politician who had just absorbed another 2-to-1 beating at the hands of President Carter.

What is even more striking to many who have watched the Senator closely in the last five months is the inner peace and self-confidence that he appears to have acquired in adversity.

He will not discuss this development himself, although it would seem to militate against some of the criticism about his character; but the impression he leaves is of a man who is thoroughly satisfied with the merit of his cause and the effort he has made to persuade others to join it. How else to explain his continued willingness to submit, with almost no complaints, to overwhelming defeats and intense scrutiny by the communications media?

Determined to Stay the Course

The Senator's cause is undiluted Democratic liberalism. Voters have rejected it thus far in 1980 — or at least they have rejected the man who is espousing it — but Mr. Kennedy seems undeterred. In fact, he has begun saying lately that he will remain in the race all the way to the party's August convention, if only to keep the flame of Democratic liberalism burning. More and more he seems to see his challenge to President Carter as a crusade.

"The New York primary will be a referendum on the direction of the Democratic Party," he said Tuesday night as he shrugged off his loss to Mr. Carter in Illinois and pointed determinedly toward the test next Tuesday. On Wednesday, in Rochester, he added, "I'm in this race for the course because I believe that the issues that I'm raising are important"

Yesterday, he continued hammering those themes as he campaigned throughout New York City.

The Kennedy crusade is increasingly lonely and wearing, made ever more difficult by a shortage of campaign funds and an inability to shake voter doubts about the Kennedy character.

Many of the Senator's long-time liberal allies and close friends, especially fellow legislators and big-city mayors, have sided with the President or have remained neutral. Some were in the vanguard of those who initially urged Mr. Kennedy to run. But then they detected a conservative tide spreading across the country, or began to perceive the Senator as a loser, or became fearful of the power of an incumbent President.

The Senator has refrained from criticizing the defectors and the uncommitted. Aides say privately that he is hurt by the absence of support. Yet he doggedly continues clambering on to stages to be introduced by obscure city councilmen and maverick legislators, often having to glance at cue cards to get their names right.

Strains Begin to Show

The Senator has also been uncomplaining about the steady deterioration in creature comforts in his campaign. The Kennedy campaign began with a 90-seat chartered jet and aides making up to $50,000 annually. Lately, however, as campaign funds have become scarce, the Senator has been flying tourist class on scheduled commercial flights and has been spending nights in hotels that have seen better days.

Inevitably, the strain of defeat and five months of hard campaigning is beginning to tell. First, the wardrobe of blue suits began to stretch at the seams and shine in the seat and around the elbows. Next, the eyes grew tired and the furrows below them deepened. Finally, the Senator's back began to give trouble after too many bumpy plane rides and too many 18-hour days.

Mr. Kennedy injured his back in a plane crash in the 1960's and has since worn a brace. In the early days of the campaign, the problem did not seem to bother him. Now, however, he is frequently in pain, walking with a distinct tilt and occasionally smarting so badly that he grimaces in public.

Off and on in the campaign there has been speculation that Senator Kennedy did not really have his heart in the contest but has been running to satisfy those who have been clamoring for his candidacy since the death of his brothers John and Robert.

Whatever the answer to the speculation, he has plunged into the contest wholeheartedly, in terms of time and energy, and has maintained that pace even as his problems have grown. Now he says he will continue the effort, even if his list of problems grows longer, and he says furthermore that he is broadening his goals to include not only winning the Democratic nomination but also preserving the liberal purity of the Democratic Party.

March 26, 1980

Senator Edward M. Kennedy decisively defeated President Carter in the New York and Connecticut Presidential primaries yesterday, giving his campaign for the Democratic nomination a breath of new life.

With inflation and Israel major issues in the contests, the Massachusetts Democrat won the New York primary largely on the basis of a landslide victory in New York City. He won more narrowly in Connecticut by capturing the Democratic cities of Hartford, New Haven, Bridgeport, Waterbury and New Britain.

The Vote Tally

With 99 percent of the 14,042 election districts reporting, the Democratic vote in New York was:

Kennedy 573,708 (59%)
Carter 399,405 (41%)

In Connecticut, with all 707 districts reporting, the Democratic vote was:

Kennedy 98,096 (47%)
Carter 86,447 (41%)
Uncommitted 12,899 (6%)
Lyndon LaRouche 5,646 (3%)
Edmund G. Brown Jr. ... 5,316 (3%)

The delegate count in the two states generally reflected the popular vote. Senator Kennedy won 161 delegates in New York and 29 in Connecticut, while the President captured 121 in New York and 25 in Connecticut.

At the White House, the President's press secretary, Jody Powell, told reporters: "I'm sure this is a welcome victory for Senator Kennedy and his people. He deserves the congratulations."

Senator Kennedy needed a victory in the two primaries to slow a Carter rush to renomination. The Senator still faces difficulties because of delegates the President has already won and unfriendly primary territory still ahead.

Until yesterday, the President had won 17 primaries and caucuses with Senator Kennedy winning only two, Massachusetts and Alaska. The cumulative delegate count had been 692 for Mr. Carter to 218 for Mr. Kennedy.

The Kennedy victories were apparently fashioned from discontent with the President's economic and foreign policies that had shown up consistently in voter surveys and were finally reflected at the voting booth yesterday.

At the same time, the Senator picked up the support of voting groups that had once been part of the natural Kennedy constituency but had not rallied to him in early primaries except in his home state.

March 27, 1980

KENNEDY WINS UPSET IN NEW YORK, ALSO TOPS CARTER IN CONNECTICUT

By FRANK LYNN

The Heirs

Suggested Reading

Bradlee, Benjamin C. *Conversations with Kennedy.* New York: Norton, 1975.

Burns, James M. *Edward Kennedy and the Camelot Legacy.* New York: Norton, 1976.

Exner, Judith. *My Story.* New York: Grove Press, 1977.

Halberstam, David. *The Unfinished Odyssey of Robert Kennedy.* New York: Random House, 1969.

Kelley, Kitty. *Jackie Oh!* New York: Lyle Stuart, 1978.

Kennedy, John F. *Profiles in Courage.* New York: Harper and Row, 1956.

Kennedy, Rose F. *Times to Remember.* New York: Doubleday, 1974.

Manchester, William. *Death of a President: November Twentieth to November Twenty-Fifth, Nineteen Sixty-Three.* New York: Harper and Row, 1967.

O'Donnell, Kenneth P. & Powers, David. *Johnny, We Hardly Knew Ye.* Boston: Little, Brown, 1965.

Schlesinger, Arthur M., Jr. *A Thousand Days.* Boston: Houghton Mifflin, 1978.

_____ *Robert Kennedy and His Time.* Boston: Houghton Mifflin, 1978.

Sherrill, Robert. *The Last Kennedy: Edward M. Kennedy of Massachusetts, Before and After Chappaquidick.* New York: Dial Press, 1976.

Sorenson, Theodore. *Kennedy.* New York: Harper and Row, 1965.

Whalen, Richard J. *The Founding Father: The Story of Joseph P. Kennedy.* New York: New American Library, 1964.

Wicker, Tom. *Kennedy Without Tears: The Man Beneath the Myth.* New York: Morrow, 1964.

Index

Kalb, Marvin, 153-54
Katzenbach, Nicholas deB., 98, 142
Kazan, Elia, 78, 79
Keating, Kenneth, 133, 135-37
Kefauver, Estes, 24-25, 87
Keith-Albee-Orpheum Circuit, 2, 218
Kennedy, Caroline, 36; birth of, 26; and birth of John, Jr., 56; bombing near home of, 213; and death of J.F.K., 117, 120-21, 123-24; diplomatic passport of, 91; interruption of news conference by, 59; and Jacqueline's marriage to Onassis, 172-74; at Kathleen's wedding, 205; life of, at White House, 67, 92-94, 139; in magazines, 103; nursery class for, 65; in Onassis will, 219; on sleigh ride, 84; speeding ticket for, 221
Kennedy, David, 153, 170, 203, 211
Kennedy, Edward M.: African trip of, 57; as assistant D.A., 75; at birth of R.F.K.'s 11th child, 177; and Carter, 222-24; and Chappaquiddick incident, 182-87, 190-95, 200, 207-8, 212, 225; cheating by, 85-86; criticism of Newsweek by, 189; at Democratic National Convention (1972), 201-2; and Edward, Jr., 181, 204; first public post of, 64-65; health plan of, 221; and Jacqueline's marriage to Onassis, 173; at J.F.K. funeral, 120, 122-23; Joan's support of, 224-25; and Judith Campbell Exner, 216; marriage of, 27; at marriage of Kathleen, 204-5; and Onassis will, 220; in plane crash, 130, 161; political plans of, 179-80, 193, 198, 215; and presidential candidacy, 170-71, 186-87, 206-7, 223-25; and R.F.K. assassination, 160-63, 165; and R.F.K. Mount Kennedy climb, 138; Rose as campaigner for, 93-94; and Senate whip position, 178-179, 197-98, in senatorial campaign, 85, 134; senatorial victories, 97, 136-37, 196-97; and Shall We Tell the President?, 220; speeding ticket for, 26; televised thanks to nation of, 166-67; and vice presidential slot, 170, 201; and Warren Report, 129; wealth of, 217-19
Kennedy, Edward M. Jr., 181, 204
Kennedy, Ethel: birth of 11th child of, 177; and Chappaquiddick incident, 184; fall into pool of, 91; in horse show, 75; horse theft case of, 145-46; and Jacqueline's marriage to Onassis, 172; and R.F.K. assassination, 154-57, 160-62, 165-66; and R.F.K. presidential campaign, 151-52; and R.F.K. senatorial campaign, 133-34, 136-37; and Robert, Jr., 195-96
Kennedy, Eunice. See Shriver, Eunice
Kennedy, Jacqueline: ankle injury of, 23; and birth of John, Jr., 55; Cambodian visit by, 148-49, 153-54; campaigning of, 34; and Chappaquiddick incident, 195; and Coretta King, 151; cruise on Onassis yacht of, 108; and culture, 78-80; and Death of a President, 142-45; and death of Onassis, 209-12; and death of Patrick Bouvier, 107; and family privacy, 139; and fashion, 42-43, 46; as First Lady, 55, 77-80, 82-83, 92-93; foreign language broadcasts by, 47-48; and J.F.K. assassination, 112-14, 117, 120-24, 126, 128; at J.F.K. inauguration, 63-64; and J.F.K. presidential nomination, 39; and Joseph, Sr.'s stroke, 203; and Khrushchev, 72; magazine stories about, 102-3; marriage of, to J.F.K., 20-21, 206, 216; marriage of, to Onassis, 172-77, 199; marriage rumors about, 148; and memories of J.F.K., 125-26; miscarriage of, 26; move of, to New York, 131; and My Boss, Jackie Kennedy, 180-81; and Onassis inheritance, 219-20; in Paris, 71-72; and photographers, 188, 200-201; portrait of, 54-55; and R.F.K. assassination, 156-59, 163; and Roman Catholic Church, 172, 177; ski trip of, 140; sleigh ride of, 84; spending of, 180-81; and sympathy letters, 126-27; and Viking Press, 213, 220; White House tour by, 82-83
Kennedy, Jean Ann. See Smith, Jean Ann
Kennedy, Joan: alcoholism of, 221; campaigning of, for Bayh, 171-172; and Chappaquiddick incident, 184-86, 195; drunk driving of, 208; marriage of, 27; miscarriage of, 187; psychiatric care of, 200, 206-7; and son's leg amputation, 204; and Ted's plane crash, 130; and Ted's presiden-

tial campaign, 224-25
Kennedy, John F.: assassination of, 112-24, 126-29, 156, 198; and blacks, 26, 97-98; as Boy Scout, 61; and business interests, 90; Cabinet appointments of, 58-59; and Camelot, 125-26; and Caroline, 56; and communism in Cuba, 69-70; and Cuban missile crisis, 98-101; and culture, 78-80; death of son of, 107; and defense, 70-71, 73-74; and desegregation in Mississippi, 97-98; and domestic staff, 65; donation of salary to charity by, 102; on draft rolls, 11; emergency phone of, 75; escalator mishap of, 39; and fashion, 33, 47, 106; first term of, 109; fortune of, 44-45; at golf, 69; Harriman appointment by, 59; hate mail to, 61, 84; health problems of, 17, 19, 22, 73, 147; as host to children, 74; inauguration of, 62-64; and Jacqueline's spending, 180-81; J.F.K. initials in press, 60; job of, at embassies, 8; and Judith Campbell Exner, 213-16; and Khrushchev, 72, 74; and labor, 27-29; and Latin American aid, 67-68; and Marilyn Monroe, 205; marriage of, to Jacqueline, 20-21, 206, 216; as model for Vatican angel, 92; and national budget, 70-71; newspaper reading by, 91; New York visit of, 76; and nuclear test ban treaty, 106-7; parodies of, 103, 125; as presidential candidate, 32-34, 36-51; as presidential contender, 26; presidential victory, 52-53; private plane of, 49; as PT boat hero, 13, 15; religion of, as issue, 45-46; and Representative race, 16, 19; rocking chair of, 68; secret marriage rumor about, 95-96; space program of, 70-71; speech therapy for, 44; and steel industry, 86-89; and Stevenson, 24; television debate vs Nixon, 49-50; and U.S. world position, 22; and vice presidential nomination, 24-25; and Vietnam, 83; in West Berlin, 105-6; in West Virginia primary, 34-35; in White House, 77-80
Kennedy, John F., Jr.: birth of, 55; burn injury of, 141; and death of J.F.K., 117, 120-21, 123-24; and Jacqueline's marriage to Onassis, 172-74; at Kathleen's wedding, 205; life of, in White House, 92-93, 139; in Onassis will, 219; at R.F.K. funeral, 163; on sleigh ride, 84
Kennedy, Joseph P., Jr., 4, 7-8, 11-12, 15-16, 189-91
Kennedy, Joseph P., Sr.: as Ambassador to Great Britain, 5-7, 12; anti-Semitism of, 60; death of, 189; and Democratic primary (1940), 11; family of, 9-10; and fascists, 7; fortune of, 217-219; and Germany in WWII, 18; hospitalization of, 139; isolationism of, 10, 12; and J.F.K. campaign, 60; and Joseph, Jr.'s injury, 4; and Pope Pius XII, 8; and R.F.K., 26, 159; rise of, 2; SEC post of, 3-4, 6; stroke of, 76-77, 203; televised thanks to nation by, 166-67; and World War II, 10, 12, 18
Kennedy, Joseph, III, 158-60, 165, 170, 202-3, 219
Kennedy, Kathleen (daughter of Joseph, Sr.). See Hartington, Kathleen
Kennedy, Kathleen (daughter of Robert), 158-160, 170, 204
Kennedy, Patricia. See Lawford, Patricia
Kennedy, Patrick Bouvier, 107, 124-25, 210
Kennedy, Robert F.: assassination of, 154-67, 198; as Attorney General, 58-59, 129; and blacks, 97-98, 104, 150; children of, 141; and Death of a President, 143, 145; and death of Patrick B. Kennedy, 107; at Democratic Convention (1964), 201-2; and desegregation, 97-98, 104; dog of, 94; donation of salary to charity by, 102; as father of the year, 36; and football, 66; frugality of, 26; goodwill trip of, 81-82; hair of, 152; and Hoffa, 29; at J.F.K. funeral, 120-24; and J.F.K.'s health, 147; and J.F.K.'s presidency, 81-82; and J.F.K.'s presidential campaign, 53; and Judith Campbell Exner, 214; kayak accident of, 146; and King assassination, 150; and labor unions, 28-29; and McCarthy hearings, 19, 22; Mount Kennedy climb of, 137-38; as presidential candidate, 149-53; as seaman, 16; seminars at home of, 76; and Senate Committee on Labor and Management, 28, 29; and senatorial race (1964), 133-37; and steel industry, 87-89; swim of, 139; and vice presidential nomination, 131-32; and wiretaps, 142; and WWII plane, 141